CW01023880

A Portrait of the Artist as a Political Dissident

A Portrait of the Artist as a Political Dissident: The Life and Work of Aleksandar Petrović

Vlastimir Sudar

Arts & Humanities
Research Council

First published in the UK in 2013 by
Intellect, The Mill, Parnall Road, Fishponds, Bristol, BS16 3JG, UK

First published in the USA in 2013 by
Intellect, The University of Chicago Press, 1427 E. 60th Street,
Chicago, IL 60637, USA

Copyright © 2013 Vlastimir Sudar

Portraits of young Aleksandar Petrović on the front cover by Bogoljub
Boba Jovanović, used by kind permission of the artist.

All rights reserved. No part of this publication may be reproduced,
stored in a retrieval system, or transmitted, in any form or by
any means, electronic, mechanical, photocopying, recording, or
otherwise, without written permission.

A catalogue record for this book is available from the
British Library.

Cover images: Bogoljub Boba Jovanović
Cover designer: Holly Rose
Production manager: Jelena Stanovnik
Copy-editor: Michael Eckhardt
Typesetting: Planman Technologies

ISBN 978-1-84150-545-9

Printer Bell & Bain, UK

With thanks to Carlsberg
Srbija

MIX
Paper from
responsible sources
FSC
www.fsc.org   FSC® C007785

to my mother and father, in memory of a time and place that we have lost…

Figures

Acknowledgements

The research for this project was initially part of a postgraduate programme leading to a doctoral dissertation, which was completed in the summer of 2007. Subsequently, it took a significant amount of time to expand this work in order to turn it into a book. Throughout this period, I have been able to rely on the consistent support and unfaltering understanding of my mother and father. Without their selfless, tireless and constant assistance, I would not have been able to finish this work and my gratitude goes to them first.

I also owe much gratitude to the late Branislava Branka Petrović, who has made numerous valuable documents and photographs available for my research. Her kindness, fairness and immense commitment to her late husband's work will never be forgotten, and I hope that they will also continue to live on in this work now in front of you.

As this book is based on my doctoral dissertation of the same title, which ended up being the first doctorate in the then newly formed Department of Film Studies at the oldest Scottish university – St Andrews – my thanks go to Dina Iordanova for forming this department. I would also like to thank Dina for initiating the Balkan Film Project and winning the AHRC grant to finance it. The current work, in this form, was only possible thanks to the AHRC's assistance, to whom I am also grateful. I also owe much to a number of academics, particularly those who served as my supervisors during work on the dissertation, and firstly to Graham Petrie, whose serenity, knowledge and immense experience have helped this work significantly. In St Andrews, I am also very grateful for the patience and support of Helen Chambers, Peter Clark, Nigel Denis and Elisabetta Girelli. Zoran Milutinović of the School of Slavonic and East European Studies in London, and Dejan Jović of the University of Stirling have helped with research materials and invaluable advice on Yugoslav history. I would like to thank Pamela Church Gibson and Andrew Hill for their support and interest in my work, and John Caughie for his priceless advice on the auteur theory. In Serbia, I would like to thank Nevena Daković and Radoslav Lazić of the University of Arts in Belgrade for information and advice on research materials. Without the academic backing of these individuals, this work would never have been completed.

Finally, I thank all those scholars whose work has informed and preceded mine.

I owe much gratitude to numerous friends and colleagues who have helped with my work on the dissertation and subsequently the book. I am especially grateful to Canan Balan and David Fleming in St Andrews, who red earlier drafts and were generous with precious criticism, as well as helping as friends in times of crisis. I'd also like to thank Carmen Cvetković and Colin Guillemet, Corine Wiesenbach, Jan Grill, Kasia Molga and Mohira Suyarkulova, for helping me translate research materials from French, German, Czech, Polish and Russian respectively. Marin Tošković and Nikola Marjanović supplied me with computers and patient IT assistance, and they certainly count as more than friends. I should like to thank Vinod Mahindru and Oliver Tringham for their kind support and advice – particularly in matters of grammar and writing. I thank my brother Vladimir, and Tamara, for putting up with me – especially when I worked in their house.

I also wish to thank all the people I interviewed, along with everyone else who helped with the project. These include Bora and Dragana of the library of Jugoslovenska Kinoteka, the staff of the National Library in Belgrade, the staff of the British Film Institute library, and the staff of the British Library in London: they have all been most helpful in my research. At the Department of Film Studies at the University of St Andrews, I would like to thank Karen Drysdale for her kindness and assistance. I would also like to thank Melanie, Jelena and everyone at Intellect Books in Bristol, as well as Michael Eckhardt for his patient copy-editing.

Special thanks go to Maja Vučićević and the Carlsberg Serbia, without whose understanding and support, completion of this book would have been impossible. I am also grateful to Božo Vukoje for digitising – sometimes very old – photographs and for making them presentable. And, I owe many thanks to the painter Bogoljub Boba Jovanović for allowing me to use his exceptional portraits of the young Aleksandar Petrović on the cover of this book.

Through writing this work, I have learnt the value of help that is generously and selflessly given: it is an asset that makes anything possible. Although books, as opposed to films, are mainly perceived as individual rather than collective work, I have learned that this is not the case, as without the collective help of those I have and have not mentioned, this work would never have materialised. I'd therefore like to express my gratitude to all those who have, in one way or another, helped me acquire this additional understanding. Still, regardless of the generous support and comprehension I have received, I bear full responsibility for the content and ideas expressed in this work, and this responsibility remains solely mine.

Notes on Language

The fact that the Socialist Federal Republic of Yugoslavia does not exist as a country anymore created several issues in my research, which are best addressed prior to and outside the arguments that are to unfold. As Aleksandar Petrović made most of his films (all but one, which was produced in Germany and France) in Socialist Yugoslavia, I talk about these films as Yugoslav, and about himself as a Yugoslav filmmaker. This appears to be common practice in film studies, as these films, at the time of their release, were archived as Yugoslav films. Similarly, it is also common, for example, still to talk about Soviet filmmakers and Soviet films. At the same time, and by also taking the Soviet example into account, I had no desire to divorce Petrović and his work from the context to which they currently belong. As Petrović lived in Belgrade, was of Serbian origins, and ultimately filmed most of the material for his films in Serbia, which were then post-produced in Serbian film studios, I have also referred to him as a Serbian filmmaker. Today, he is studied and perceived as belonging to Serbian cultural heritage, in the same way, I suppose, as Andrei Tarkovsky is discussed as a Soviet and as a Russian filmmaker. Consequently, I have tried, where possible, to talk about Petrović as equally Yugoslav and Serbian, while understanding that the two are not synonymous, and also bearing in mind that this context was amorphous even in the period I am describing. Yugoslav filmmakers were perceived as Yugoslavs in an international context, but within Yugoslavia they were perceived as Serbian, Croatian, Slovenian, etc. This fact is particularly relevant in Chapters 4 and 5.

The break-up of the country not only created a confusion about cultural heritage: it also left a still unresolved debate over the issue of what used to be a common language. This issue also affected my research slightly, although I believe not significantly. As the films were made in Yugoslavia, and I perceived them to be Yugoslav, I have followed the spelling rules as they were accepted in Yugoslavia at the time, and predominantly, I call this language Serbo-Croat. However, as with the issue of heritage, and particularly considering those Petrović's films which are set in rural environments, where the characters in the films refer to the language they speak as Serbian, I also often use this name for the language. In no way have I wanted to contribute to, or participate, in the agonising debates over what used to be called Serbo-Croat, and which has now separated into four languages (Bosnian, Croatian, Montenegrin and Serbian), with the potential for yet more. As the land has been divided amongst the successor states, so was the language and culture.

I have also decided to follow the Latin version of Serbo-Croat's original alphabet when transliterating Yugoslav names and titles. Consequently, I talk about Petrović, and not Petrovich, Petrovitch, or even Petrovic. The Roman-Latin alphabet was used in former Yugoslavia equally, alongside the Cyrillic alphabet. Considering that Petrović was from Serbia, where the Cyrillic alphabet is still more commonly used, I could have justifiably spelled his name Александар Петровић. However, for the sake of clarity and accessibility, and as both alphabets are used equally in Serbia today, I have opted for the Roman-Latin version. I have also decided not to use the special orthographic character Đ (or lower case đ), and have replaced this with 'Dj' (or lower case 'dj'), as in the name Djordje, since this was (and is) also considered acceptable and correct in Serbo-Croat. I have elsewhere used Serbo-Croat characters consistently.

I have tried to respect the original transliteration of various other non-English names that are mentioned in the text, these being most commonly French, German, Czech, Slovak and Russian. It is only with Russian names that again, for the sake of clarity, I have transliterated them to the Roman-Latin alphabet, rather than keeping them in Cyrillic. Consequently, the name of the Soviet film critic mentioned in Chapter 3 is not spelled as Зеленко, but as Zelenko. Apart from Russian, I have been loyal to the original spellings of the respective languages.

It is also important to point out that all the translations from the original Serbo-Croat texts, whose translations otherwise were not available in English, are my own. All the translations from other languages where it was impossible to locate existing translations in English were made specifically for this work. The translations from French were made with the help of Carmen Cvetković and Collin Guillemet; from German the translator was Corine Wiesenbach; from Czech, Jan Grill; from Polish, Kasia Molga; and from Russian, Mohira Suyarkulova. I would like to use this opportunity again to thank these individuals for their selfless help with this project. As far as the translations are concerned, every effort has been made to keep them as close as possible to the originals.

Introduction

There are more interesting things here than my personal story. This, our cinema, and the events that surrounded it – through them you could tell the whole history of our society. Our cinema was like a seismograph, which recorded tremors, and it reflected some other "tectonic shifts" below the surface of the ice cap. It would be interesting to write such a history of Yugoslav cinema, which would constantly correspond to the history of our society.

Aleksandar Petrović, September 1987[1]

Aleksandar Saša Petrović (1929–1994) was one of the most significant filmmakers to come out of Socialist Yugoslavia.[2] He was by far the most awarded director on a national level, winning three Golden Arenas at the Yugoslav Film Festival in Pula, as well as receiving all the highest state awards. He was also acclaimed internationally, and the first Yugoslav director to win prizes at the Cannes Film Festival, in 1967, as well as Oscar nominations in 1967 and 1968. His film, *I Even Met Happy Gypsies* (1967), was seen by 200,000 people in Paris alone, and was extensively distributed worldwide. It was the first film ever to be made in the Romany language spoken by the Roma community in Yugoslavia. Its popularity started the trend – the genre even – of the subsequently ever more popular "Gypsy films". Petrović's later films were made as international co-productions involving European stars including Isabelle Huppert, Romy Schneider, Annie Girardot, Alain Cuny and Erland Josephson. Yet now, almost two decades after his death, Petrović's work is not easy to see. Although he is usually mentioned in general books on cinema and given appropriate attention in histories of Yugoslav cinema, there are no scholarly monographs dedicated to him or his work, nor has he merited the attention that, at least according to this brief introduction, he certainly deserves.[3]

What is perhaps one of the key reasons for this neglect is the fact that he was a Yugoslav filmmaker, who died on an operating table in France in 1994 as his country was disintegrating in a brutal conflict between its constituent federal units.[4] Furthermore, his last film, *Migrations*, which was supposed to open the Cannes Film Festival in 1989, failed to do so as a result of legal disputes among its French producers. This combination of extraordinary bad luck – legal complications and then war – was germane to the disappearance of Petrović's work from view. Finally, the conflict in what had once been Yugoslavia, which continued throughout the century's final decade, allowed a thick patina to occlude the once sparkling cinematic culture of that country.

The cruel nature of the Yugoslav conflicts has been well documented by the media and press in this age of modern communications and technology. The images of the wars have travelled fast and surprised many. They have influenced the popular view of the country and its people, even changing the view of those who, up to that point, had known the country. The fact that the political system – socialism – on which the country was based, had collapsed across Europe, clearly hinted that there was more than a single thing "rotten in the state" of Yugoslavia. In the media's attempts to understand what was happening, the focus was predominantly on the outcomes of the conflicts, rather than their causes. Similarly, the larger picture of the fall of socialism in Eastern Europe focussed initially only on the downsides of the system, and expectedly so, scrutinising numerous cases of political repression that had aimed to silence any dissenting – or diverse – political thought. The belief that socialism was rigidly uniformed might have prevailed had it not been already well known that socialist countries in general, and Yugoslavia in particular, produced intriguingly elaborate reflections on their politics, specifically through their culture and arts. Perhaps, after the collapse of this political edifice, the thick cloud of ideological dust needed to settle first, before its remains could be seen clearly again.

At one point, it seemed as if all the intriguing achievements of this system, particularly in the arts, would remain well hidden behind the thick layer of dust, and be forgotten for some time. This appeared to be the case in most of the former socialist countries, which were seeking to swiftly embrace the new political system – of liberal democracy – and perhaps create new cultures distinctly different from the ones before. This was particularly the case in Yugoslavia, as the newly formed independent states had more reason to distance themselves not only from their ideological past, but also the country they had left behind. The way the break-up and conflict were reported in the media seems to have portrayed Yugoslavia and its socialist system as one of intolerance, discrimination and brutal repression – for which there was no option but to end violently. As a consequence of the country breaking apart along its ethnic seams, it also appeared that Yugoslavia's interethnic relations had been under pressure for decades. Yet one of Petrović's most popular films dealt precisely with the position of a significant ethnic minority in Yugoslavia, as mentioned earlier. Furthermore, the film's characters spoke in their own language, whereas today the Roma – or Gypsies as they are still better known – are the largest ethnic minority in the European Union without their own nation state. This film then, points towards a different vision of the country and its political system from the one that prevailed throughout the media of 1990s. Indeed, I argue in this study that much can be learned about political life and discourse under socialism as a system, and Yugoslavia as a country, by looking at the films of this – mainstream – filmmaker. The resulting understanding seems to provide a nuanced and detailed picture of the many political problems the country and its political system faced throughout their development. It has felt as if the time were overripe for re-evaluation of both Petrović and the Yugoslav socialism in which he lived and worked. However, the layer of soot covering the subjects of this study has left shapes of its own, which further obscure the process of re-evaluation.

At a brief – and somewhat facetious – glance, it could be said that most phenomena could be perceived through the prism of pop trends. They are at first popular, and thus almost ubiquitous to the point of not being able to escape them. They then lapse from popular circuit, and eventually become scorned and are regarded with embarrassing disdain. And then they slowly are missed and, through a nostalgic haze, brought back into discourse: with some of the old values rehabilitated and some entirely new ones – more reflective of the new atmosphere – attached. This analysis has been written less than 25 years after the fall of the Berlin Wall, and the above process could be seen to apply to the so-called real-socialist states of Eastern Europe,[5] as they were referred to before they became "New Europe".[6] Throughout the 1990s, as the socialist systems of these countries were retrospectively scrutinised for their common inconsistencies, they were even often likened to fascism. In the first decade of the twenty-first century, however, for many reasons,[7] the first blooms of nostalgia, even regret, proudly came into the open. This is perhaps most evident in the case of the former Democratic Republic of Germany, or simply East Germany. As this is a film study, the two films could be used to encapsulate the best of the tensions mentioned earlier. *Goodbye Lenin!* (2003) portrayed life in the once communist East Berlin as one deprived of the corrupting thrust of western consumerism: the inhabitants lived serene, if naïve, lives filled with comradeship and compassion for others.[8] A sharp riposte quickly followed in the shape of *The Lives of Others* (2006), which showed how this innocent naivety was brutally enforced by the covert Stasi (secret police), acting illegally and not flinching from medieval tortures in dark, hidden chambers.[9] Interestingly enough, neither of the two films was made by directors from the former East Germany, but both authors had been born, brought up and trained in the former West.[10] What was once the communist East has become a battleground of projections and desires more reflective of those who pursued them than of the realities that actually existed.

It can be easily established that this is also very much the case with what is now called *former* Yugoslavia, if not even more so. As Yugoslav socialism was independent of the Soviet one, the feelings of nostalgia can elevate that past to almost mythical proportions. As the state's breakdown was spectacularly cruel, the dismissals of its accomplishments, for some, can be close to absolute. This study has tried hard to distance itself from both these positions, and has attempted to construct – as much as possible – some kind of objective scrutiny of the achievements and failures of Yugoslav socialism in relation to its film industry. This has been done by bearing in mind two continuing contradictory facts: on the one hand, it is difficult to find any evidence against the premise that there was any film industry in Yugoslavia outside socialism; and on the other, that the political system had the most devastating demise of all those in Eastern Europe. In between these two radical extremes, this study has sought to trace the achievements as well as the setbacks, and attempts to not allow one to prejudice the other.

However, the heaviest deposit of soot covering the picture of this time and space, and the well-known filmmaker within, remains to be the conflict that tore Yugoslavia apart. As mentioned earlier, in the spirit of this age, the images promulgated by the media have "authorised" an image of Yugoslavia and the states that inherited it. As Edward Said famously warned in relation to the notion of Orientalism, it is constructed and authorised by those who need such an image of the "Orient", rather than being a reflection of what the real picture of the space may be. He constructed an apt warning that is applicable to the former Yugoslavia of the 1990s.[11] I genuinely have no intention of criticising the global media and press for their portrayal of that war, as they have done what they always do for, to them, very significant reasons: essentially, accentuated sensation at the expense of illuminating the context and its subtleties. However, in order to conduct this study properly, it was important to distance it from the established views on the situation – and the country – and rebuild the context from scratch in order to understand and be able to take a new look at the films of Aleksandar Petrović. An attempt has thus been made to "excavate" Petrović and his films from the shadows of time, as well as from the "mediated" soot that has, as the fallout from hostilities, further covered and obscured his work's existence. In this process of excavation, it became clear that the layers of ideology and politics played an important part in both enabling the production of Petrović's work, as well as in the circumstances that led to its coming to an end: it thus became important to focus on the representation of politics in these films. The aim of the study became to unravel the political picture of the time and place, as it can be deciphered from viewing Petrović's films.

Although this study intended to reconstruct a political and historical picture, its main subject – and its real focus – was a group of films. These were a group of films by one author, and an author who belonged to that famous generation of filmmakers that inaugurated New Waves across Europe in the 1950s and 1960s. As will be shown in this study, Aleksandar Petrović admired André Bazin's *Cahiers du Cinéma*, and not only was he a follower, but also that the other editor of this famous magazine, Jacques Doniol-Valcroze, co-scripted Petrović's final film. This period, at least as far as film studies are concerned, is most significant for introducing the idea of a "romantic artist" into cinema, one with a single authorial vision, the idea that was later elaborated as the auteur theory. With an awareness of how the theory developed, including its complete disqualification, and recent "non-dominant" resuscitation, it seemed appropriate to use it in this study, which after all, deals with the work of a director who himself contributed to the development of the theory in the 1960s. Early in his career, Petrović accepted assessments by several Yugoslav film critics that the themes, which define his "authorial signature", are the themes of love and death. In this study, I have accepted this view, even though a very different set of themes have subsequently been identified: themes, storylines and dialogues which reflect on the political situation of the period under scrutiny. And although the auteur theory has its limitations, the theory's emphasis on pursuing repetitions in "semantic structure" continues to be of interest. To look for consistent themes in the films of Aleksandar Petrović that comment on the political reality around him became the operating mode for this study. As a result, I have defined four themes that have, particularly in Petrović's mature work, consistently provided a sharp and thorough commentary on political life and its contradictions. Petrović regularly investigated:

- interethnic relationships, and/or the position of ethnic minorities
- the position of religion in society (or societies)
- the relationships between political establishments and non-privileged (or marginal) groups in society (or societies)
- the dogmatic nature of ideologies and/or religions.

As Petrović scrutinised these themes, he introduced a specific anti-dogmatic position of his own, which permeates his later films. This position became a significant element of his authorial signature – if one admits a continuing concern for notions of authorship.

While searching for these specific political themes, it became necessary to introduce a thorough historical background in order to assess their authenticity – a background to the political history,[12] as well as to the history of cinema.[13] By juxtaposing Petrović's view with a historical (and political) perspective, it became possible to outline these "political" themes. The themes that are not results of his own "personal" interests (such as love and death), but were perhaps "imposed" on him by the gravity of the political situation in which he lived and worked.[14] Through defining these themes, this study contributes to an understanding of Petrović not only as an auteur, but also as a political auteur. As the auteur theory further instructs, and is worth emphasising here, the auteur should be conceived of as a structure – a structure constructed from the films the auteur produced. I am thus predominantly speaking not of Aleksandar Petrović, but of "Aleksandar Petrović" – the structure produced on the basis of his films. Aleksandar Petrović still remains a subject for a detailed biography – which this study is not, as its primary focus was his films. Considering the current context of this work, and having no desire to undermine the theory mentioned earlier, it is nevertheless clear that this approach has needed to be somewhat "negotiated", rather than adhered to rigidly, or – dare I say – dogmatically. As this is, so far, the only study committed to Petrović's work outside his own country, it would have been frustrating and limiting, and perhaps counter-productive to omit a host of relevant biographical details. These details are therefore introduced and, where appropriate, integrated into the main argument of the text. In places, however, this has inevitably led to the primary "authorial" approach being offset by this opposing – biographical – one, which has hence forced a retreat from an utterly rigorous adherence to one approach. I have thus taken liberty in conflating the authorial approach with a biographical account, breaking the strict delineation between them where this was necessary to advance the argument towards the ultimate aim of this work. This thus leads to the main caveat in relation to the study: neither could the authorial approach be sufficient to fulfil the tasks of this study, nor could its modifications of this kind provide for an exhaustive study of a cinematic work.[15] Again, as this is a preliminary study, it was necessary to first involve these initial methods, which are already frequently applied elsewhere. Due to such approach, the focus shifted from Petrović to "Petrović" and back again. To combine auteurism and biography as a way of studying an artist by scrutinising the political context in which she or he worked was nevertheless – at least in current circumstances – the most appropriate approach to take.

The aim of this work was to learn about the history and politics of Socialist Yugoslavia by looking at the films of one of its most distinguished directors. In the process, this director – Aleksandar Petrović – was examined as an author, with the intention of unearthing his work and restoring him to his rightful place of authority within film studies. Petrović is placed in a global context that includes Dostoyevsky's literature, Buñuelian surrealism, the French New Wave, as well as the aesthetics of Bertolt Brecht, amongst much else. In addition, throughout this process, careful attention has been given to the political and historical context in which Petrović worked. What Andrew Horton said of Theo Angelopoulos applies equally to Petrović: "some filmmakers, artists, and writers need to be understood in the context of their cultures if their works are to be appreciated on a more than superficial level."[16] In this process, I promised to not dismiss the productive legacy of the socialist system, and to not fall into the trap of nostalgia. It is, of course, easy to make such promises, but the success of navigating between the various sources of information – all of which are, by their very nature, biased (not forgetting the biases of the author himself) – is still open to question. One can perhaps find comfort in Jacques Derrida's bold admission that "we should no longer waste our energy in affirming or denying subjectivity", as this is inherently given.[17] Nevertheless, I do not believe my choice of Petrović's work as the case study for this research implies that his work is any better or more conducive to providing better answers than that of other Yugoslav directors. To return to Derrida again, a multiplicity of truths exists, even in one given text, and more importantly "no one truth can claim precedence over any other: a hierarchy of truth-value cannot be etched in stone."[18]

This study cannot claim that it provides the only accurate view of any of the phenomena in question, but it does want to contribute to making their overall image sharper and clearer, and to help move the general focus of attention from the political consequences to the artistic analysis of its causes. It is thus worth pointing out that even "the political dissident" from the title of the book should not be taken too literally. Political historians are strict in bestowing such a qualification. Someone like Milovan Djilas in Socialist Yugoslavia, who was part of the political establishment and then knowingly dissented from it, has earned this title. Aleksandar Petrović does not qualify, although the argument here shows how the sympathy he had for one political idea developed over time on an abstract level, only to collide with the mainstream implementations of this same idea in political practice. This gave birth to Petrović's anti-dogmatism – where dogmatism in itself is defined and understood on its basic level – as an undisputed assertion of principles and doctrines without allowing them to be questioned. This is identified as the key to Petrović's artistic analysis of the political context in which he worked, and which ultimately led to its collapse.

In order for the story of Petrović's artistic development to unfold, from a young leftist in Socialist Yugoslavia to a disillusioned anti-dogmatist, I have first provided in Chapter 1, a brief historical background of the country and its film industry. This starts with the early pioneers in the Kingdom of Serbia, to the real establishment of a film industry with the communist takeover after War World II. Petrović's biographical background is also provided, focusing on his teenage years as a Partisan volunteer during the war, when he first encountered the detrimental effects of political dogmatism. Petrović spent his post-war years as a young cinephile, and went to study film directing in Prague, Czechoslovakia. After mapping the context, Chapter 2 continues tracing his early career, and focuses on the short documentary films he co-directed with Vicko Raspor once he had returned from Prague. His first two feature-length films, *Two* (1961) and *Days* (1963) are also scrutinised, specifically the latter, as it caused Petrović's first problems with the authorities. With Chapter 3, a standard pattern for analysis is introduced. The political background in the country is provided first, followed by an introduction to the film being analysed, and a brief synopsis of its plot. Chapter 3 focuses on the war drama, *Three* (1965), and Chapter 4 on the most successful of Petrović's films, *I Even Met Happy Gypsies* (1967). Chapter 5 examines *It Rains in My Village* (1968) as well as the Yugoslav Black Wave movement. Chapter 6 examines his first major literary adaptation, *The Master and Margarita* (1972), as well as the so-called *Plastic Jesus* incident after which Petrović had to go into exile. Chapter 7 focuses on *Group Portrait with Lady* (1977), the only film he made outside Yugoslavia. Chapter 8 explores his last and troubled production, *Migrations* (1989), in the context of Yugoslavia's rapid decline. Throughout the chapters, the development of his four political themes is explored, as well as his anti-dogmatic stance.

This study, of course, does not exhaust all the interpretative possibilities, nor does it want to reduce these possibilities to this specific method. The critical method applied here appeared as the most appropriate, allowing the focus to be on the films and equally enabling the scrutiny of the political context exposed by these films. Therefore, it also appeared to be the most relevant method, but only at present time. This approach is not exclusive, and in time, new perspectives on Petrović's work should arise – they will be more than welcome. Only then a broadly diverse view of Petrović's work could inform us fully about its various aspects. Here perhaps, the work of another famous Petrović could be invoked – that of the Romantic poet and ruler of Montenegro. Petar II Petrović Njegoš stated that "posterity will judge our deeds", and this applies and will continue to be applicable to the poet, Petrović's films, and this and other works on both of them. I have thus been as careful as possible to make sure that all the facts in this book are accurate, but I should not wish to hide that this may have not been achieved. Still, I could not abandon this study due to the inevitability of such numerous limitations, but was somewhat guided by those famous verses of that very modernist writer and poet, Samuel Beckett: "Ever tried. Ever failed. No matter. Try again. Fail again. Fail better."[19]

Notes

1   An interview with Aleksandar Petrović; see Jovo Paripović, "Aleksandar Petrović: Sakupljač za *Seobe*", *Studio*, 18 September 1987, p. 12.

2   The full name of the country was the Socialist Federal Republic of Yugoslavia. For the sake of brevity, I will refer to it as Socialist Yugoslavia hereafter in the text, in order to differentiate it from the earlier Kingdom of Yugoslavia, and the subsequent – but not long-lasting – Federal Republic of Yugoslavia.

3   The only monograph on Petrović is by Petar Volk, although this is available only in Serbian; see *Let nad močvarom: Aleksandar Petrović svojim životom, delom i filmovima* (Beograd: Institut za film; Novi Sad: Prometej, 1999). Petrović's work is discussed at length in Daniel Goulding's seminal work on Yugoslav cinema; see Daniel Goulding, *Liberated Cinema: The Yugoslav Experience* (Bloomington: Indiana University Press, 1985). As far as general books on cinema are concerned, Petrović usually merits a mention; see for example Kristin Thompson and David Bordwell, *Film History: An Introduction* (New York: McGraw Hill, 2003), p. 464.

4   Socialist Yugoslavia was a federation of six republics (Bosnia and Herzegovina, Croatia, Macedonia, Montenegro, Slovenia and Serbia).

5   As a term, "real socialism" was coined in a similar vein to *realpolitik*. It refers to socialism put into political practice, as it once was in the countries of Eastern Europe, as opposed to socialism as political theory, for example.

6   The term "New Europe" was coined to refer to the majority of these East European countries that joined the European Union in 2004 and 2007.

7   The main reason perhaps is the rabidly biting qualities of the quick transition to capitalism and the free market, for which the economies of most of these countries were more than ill-prepared, physically and culturally – it could be said.

8   See *Goodbye Lenin!* (dir. Wolfgang Becker, Germany, 2003).

9   See *The Lives of Others* (dir. Florian Henckel von Donnersmarck, Germany, 2006).

10   It is interesting that both films were nominated for Oscars, and while the one that criticised the socialist past won, the film with a more affirmative view did not. How tempting it is to discern draughts of the Cold War still breezing through the American Film Academy.

11   In Edward Said's words: "Orientalism is […] a Western style for dominating, restructuring and having authority over the Orient"; see his classic Edward W. Said, *Orientalism* (New York: Vintage Books, 1978).

12   The historical framework relied primarily on four scholarly histories, representing different authors and approaches. Misha Glenny's work observes the history of Yugoslavia in the context of the Balkans, whereas John Lampe's focuses specifically on the history of Yugoslavia, the country. Dejan Jović's work was simultaneously published in Serbia and Croatia in 2003, and represents the first "post-Yugoslav" history of Yugoslavia, focusing on Tito's Yugoslavia – the period that was of most significance for this study. Finally, Jasna Dragović-Soso's history of the political intelligentsia and dissent in Socialist Yugoslavia, concentrating on events in Serbia, was also relevant. Apart from Glenny, the three other books are available in both Serbian and English. (See Misha Glenny, *The Balkans 1804–1999: Nationalism, War and the Great Powers* [London: Granta Books, 1999]; John R. Lampe, *Yugoslavia as History: Twice There Was a Country* [Cambridge: Cambridge University Press, 1996]; Dejan Jović, *Jugoslavija – Država koja je odumrla: Uspon, kriza i pad Četvrte Jugoslavije* [Beograd: Samizdat B92; Zagreb: Prometej, 2003]; Jasna Dragović-Soso, *'Saviours*

of the Nation': Serbia's Intellectual Opposition and the Revival of Nationalism [London: Hurst & Company, 2002].)

13 Four key works have been exceptionally useful for this study. Apart from Goulding's history of Yugoslav cinema, mentioned earlier, Mira and Antonín Liehm's history of East European cinema, also originally published in the United States, was a valuable source. From Yugoslavia, Petar Volk's seminal history of Yugoslav cinema was invaluable, as well as a more recent history by Ranko Munitić, entitled *Goodbye Yugo Film*. (See Mira Liehm and Antonín J. Liehm, *The Most Important Art: Soviet and Eastern European Film after 1945* [Berkeley and Los Angeles: University of California Press, 1977]; Petar Volk, *Istorija jugoslovenskog filma* [Beograd: Institut za Film, Partizanska knjiga 1986]; Ranko Munitić, *Adio, Jugo-film!* [Beograd: Centar film, Srpski kulturni klub; Kragujevac: Prizma, 2005].)

14 This distinction is, perhaps a little subtle, as the themes that were "imposed" by social and political circumstances were also "personal". Equally, it could be said that the themes dealing with personal issues, such as "love and death", also relate to external nature and experience. However, this distinction has been pertinent to this study – the delineation of themes that were more the result of his personal interests and experiences, from those connected to the socio-political context in which Petrović worked.

15 It has to be added here that a more complete authorial study would expect this work to provide a detailed stylistic analysis of Petrović's feature length films, along the lines of the analysis of his short documentary films. Instead, I have focused on a detailed narrative analysis of Petrović's feature films, as that was more pertinent to the main aim of this investigation. This is in contrast to the more stylistic analysis of the shorts. A more thorough stylistic analysis of the features would explore auteur theory further in relation to Petrović's films, and this just proves that studies of Petrović's work are at the beginning, and that further studies would be more than welcome.

16 See Andrew Horton, *The Films of Theo Angelopoulos: A Cinema of Contemplation* (New Jersey: Princeton University Press, 1997), p. 25.

17 For this quote and interpretation of Derrida's work, see an introduction to his essays: "Jacques Derrida" in *Knowledge and Postmodernism in Historical Perspective*, ed. by Joyce Appleby et al. (London, New York: Routledge, 1996), p. 435.

18 "Jacques Derrida", p. 436.

19 The quote is from *Worstward Ho*; see Samuel Beckett, *Company, Ill Seen Ill Said, Worstward Ho, Stirring Still*, ed. by Dirk van Hulle (London: Faber and Faber, 2009), p. 81; *Worstward Ho* is pp. 79–103.

Chapter 1

Beginnings

1. 1. The State

1. 1. 1. Early Cinema in Serbia and Yugoslavia

After the Lumiére brothers had their first film screening in December 1895, it did not take long before this invention toured Europe like any other technological novelty of the time. The brothers' employees, André Carre and Jules Giren, organised the first film screening in Belgrade,[1] then in the Kingdom of Serbia, on 6 June 1896,[2] barely six months after its first screening in Paris. "The cinematograph" was very popular with local people; hence this travelling cinema stayed until the end of the month,[3] and returned in February 1897 of the Julian calendar,[4] or rather in March 1897 of the currently accepted Gregorian calendar.[5]

As was the custom in the early days of cinema for the shows to travel like circuses, André Carre, a photographer himself, decided to film scenes of Belgrade life once he was back in the city.[6] He did so following the style of his employers, the Lumière brothers, and first filmed a short newsreel – *Workers Leaving a Tobacco Factory*. He then shot numerous other episodes, including trams leaving the station and people greeting the king as he returned from his travels. These newsreels are the earliest films made in the Balkans.[7]

Although these films from early 1897 are now lost, they made an enormous impact at the time. They seduced many local entrepreneurs and young adventurers into starting their own film businesses, hence the development of this new industry unfolded with steady progression in a "romantic" spirit of modernism. The first projection equipment was acquired by a local entrepreneur in 1900,[8] and today the oldest surviving film is an hour-long documentary footage of the crowning of King Peter Karadjordjević in 1904.[9]

The most ambitious new film entrepreneur was Svetozar Botorić, who opened the first regular cinema in Belgrade in December of 1908.[10] Before this, all the cinemas had been only travelling attractions whether from foreign or local individuals or their companies. Botorić was a hotelier who "took a note of great interest amongst the public, and the good proceeds travelling cinemas were gaining" and decided to open the first true film company.[11] Botorić initially signed a contract with the French firm Pathé Frères, and was their representative for Serbia and Bulgaria, exclusively premiering their films and newsreels in his cinema.[12] He also regularly produced local newsreels, with Pathé's assistance, who provided equipment as well as their experienced cameraman, or cinematographer, Louis de Beéry.[13]

Botorić's interest in production would grow and was particularly inspired after he had seen the French film *The Assassination of the Duke of Guise* (*L'Assassinat du Duc de Guise*, 1908) directed by Charles Le Bargy and André Calmette. Botorić was quite impressed by this film, which is today referred to as an early example of narrative cinema, as its authors essentially filmed a theatre performance. Noël Burch discusses *The Assassination of the Duke of Guise* and its approach as one of the key elements that helped shape the culture of cinema as it is known today, a film culture based on narrative structures involving specific modes of representations.[14]

It was Botorić's idea to make a film on Karadjordje, the leader of the first Serbian uprising against the Ottoman Empire, which historian Misha Glenny described as "the rebellion [that] marked the beginning of modern history on the Balkan peninsula."[15] Botorić's intention evidently was to (re-)represent history in the new medium, recreating old myths in a way that was to characterise cinema's first century, a way that Burch criticises in his seminal work *Life to Those Shadows*.[16]

As a pioneer of early cinema, Botorić faced numerous obstacles. In Serbia at the time, according to film historians Mira and Antonín Liehm, as in most countries, cinema was criticised as being mindless entertainment lacking any cultural value.[17] In order to address this criticism, a film based on a famous historical event, dedicated to a forefather of the then Serbian royal family, appeared to be a project with great historical and cultural significance. To grant further cultural credibility to the project, and following the French example, Botorić employed actors from the National Theatre in Belgrade to play roles in the film. Furthermore, it was to be directed by the veteran actor Ilija Stanojević, with whom Botorić had already made a few short fiction films. With De Beéry as cameraman, a large-scale production of this "historical drama" was completed and shown in 1911 under the title *Life and Deeds of the Immortal Leader Karadjordje* (*Život i dela besmrtnog vožda Karadjordja*), and was distributed and known simply as *Karadjordje*.[18]

Botorić's idea of making cinema as art and part of "high culture", regardless of Burch's later criticisms of the modes of representation such practices initiated, may now be perceived as noble and advanced for its time.[19]

According to the Yugoslav film historians Petar Volk and Dejan Kosanović, *Karadjordje* was commercially very successful in Serbia. This was perhaps due to the fact that the Karadjordjević family took over the throne not long before the film was released, and was welcomed as a way of re-establishing the myth of Karadjordje, the dynasty's founder, and the great leader and liberator. Botorić, encouraged by its success, immediately started another large "historical" production with the same crew and recipe, although the film *Ulrih Celjski and Vladislav Hunjadi* (1911) subsequently flopped. In itself, this would not have been such a problem had the previous film secured international distribution. Although successful at home, Pathé refused to buy it for foreign markets, and only the domestic profits could not cover the expenses. Both films also failed to receive any support from the king's government, even though their subjects were popularising what appeared to be nationally important historical figures and events. Botorić, who by this time had invested considerable amounts of his own money into these projects, flinched and decided to stop producing fiction films as they proved to be very costly. Ilija Stanojević, his director, went back to theatre and stayed there until the end of his career, whereas Louis de Beéry went back to filming newsreels, documenting everyday life in Serbia.[20] The last copies of *Karadjordje* were lost sometime in the early 1920s.[21]

After World War I and the creation of the Kingdom of Serbs, Croats and Slovenes (renamed as the Kingdom of Yugoslavia in October 1929),[22] the situation in the local film industry did not improve, but worsened. The new country Yugoslavia was conspicuously larger and economically stronger than Serbia had been, but still could not sustain a film industry based on the concept of market economy. Although attempts were made to introduce laws that would help protect the local industry – the most significant of which was passed in 1931[23] – the large American and German distributors, through their influence in the government, managed to disable the law within a few years.[24] The country entered a period of what Nina Hibbin describes as "the sporadic nature of film production."[25] In reality, the national film industry only came into being after the communist takeover and the industry's nationalisation in 1945.

Some film historians, such as the American Michael Stoil, express the view that "communist film historians" were intentionally ignorant of their national film production prior to the socialist revolutions.[26] In his book, *Balkan Cinema*, written in the late 1970s, and in a tone somewhat reminiscent of the Cold War inspired ideological quarrels, he praises *Karadjordje* as an example of a Balkan history film,[27] even though at that point the film had not been seen for decades. Other American scholars did not share Stoil's enthusiasm for *Karadjordje*, and Mira and Antonín Liehm[28] therefore claim "the virtual non-existence of film" in the pre-socialist period in Yugoslavia.[29] Daniel Goulding in his authoritative history of Yugoslav film reiterates this view, and further quotes the Liehms and their assessment that "motion pictures in Yugoslavia before World War Two were purely commercial and of no cultural interest, and were also outside the framework of national traditions."[30] Such dismissive views of the early industry became prevalent and accepted in scholarly writing.[31] Petar Volk, the renowned Yugoslav film scholar, defied such views, contrary to Stoil's assessment of what he called the "communist scholars". Volk had to admit that early cinema in Yugoslavia was meagre and not often of high quality, but claimed it was still worthy of scholarly attention,[32] which indeed he pursued.[33]

The established scholarly views on early Yugoslav cinema quoted earlier were all written before 16 July 2003, when – it could be said miraculously – an integral version of Botorić and Stanojević's 1911 film *Karadjordje* was found in Vienna, in the Austrian Film Archive.[34] Once the film had been restored and screened, it was evident that it was advanced for its time. It was a large-scale epic on a historical event of almost mythical proportions. This ambitious project was unrepeated in "the golden age"[35] of later Yugoslav film production, although Aleksandar Petrović himself wanted to direct a film on the same subject and even under the same title. Unfortunately, finances and sufficient interest were not forthcoming.[36]

It is thus clear that early Serbian and Yugoslav cinema consists of work that has merit and certainly deserves more scholarly attention and respect than it has had in the past. However, these early works were rare and the result of great enthusiasm and love for cinema, rather than of organised production. The argument on "when does the national cinema actually start in Serbia and Yugoslavia?" could be concluded with the words of Aleksandar Petrović, taken from a speech delivered in March 1971 addressing the Union of Film Workers of Yugoslavia, as their president:

> The Yugoslav cinema industry was created as one of the results of the revolutionary changes instigated in Yugoslavia in the period between 1941 and 1945. Emphasising this fact, I have no intention of negating any of the pioneering attempts in the widest field of film work and artistry. However, I would like to draw attention to the date when the cinema industry emerged as an organised activity in society with established historical continuity, rather than an activity which only depended on the enthusiasm of a few individuals in particular circumstances.[37]

Michael Stoil also, perhaps reluctantly, concludes that the "nationalization of the film industry under the socialist regimes can be viewed as a necessary step for the survival of national film industries rather than a mere act of political repression."[38]

1. 1. 2. Socialist Yugoslavia and the Creation of a National Film Industry

Vladimir Ilich Lenin's well-known dictum on film as "the most important art" is generally accepted as the explanation for all the young socialist states investing vast amounts of their scarce resources and energy in hurriedly building up their film industries. Some historians, such as Mira and Antonín Liehm, have attempted to challenge this belief speculating that if Lenin had made a similar statement 50 years later, he would have identified television rather than film.[39] I would be tempted to add that if Lenin said something of the sort 90 years after he spoke of film, he would probably talk about the Internet. However, I believe that such speculations are of little value. As the Liehms also point out, once these words were spoken they had an enormous impact on the countries later to become communist.[40] The Liehms also claim that Lenin's nationalisation law of the industry was the second such law, as Hungary introduced an earlier nationalisation law after the communist revolution there led by Béla Kun in 1919.[41] As this revolution failed within a very brief period of time, I would nevertheless identify Lenin's law on nationalisation of the film industry as the first and most important. It was the one that bore results and made a global impact, even beyond the realm of socialism. Lenin's doctrine led socialist countries across the world to build their own film industries even where previously they had been practically non-existent (as in Cuba[42] or Albania[43]) or where they needed to be completely rebuilt (as in Poland[44] after World War II).[45]

With the introduction of socialism to Yugoslavia during World War II, the film production swiftly followed. However, Josip Broz Tito and his Partisan fighters were not simply heeding Lenin's dictums as filmmaking had another perhaps more pressing purpose in their political struggle. Tito's Partisans were at first unrecognised on the international political stage as a resistance movement to Nazism. It was thus essential to convince, principally the leaders of the Allied countries, that the Partisans were at the heart of the resistance, rather than the Royalist Chetniks of Draža Mihajlović who had initially been accepted and supported by the British government.[46] Tito's Partisans therefore documented, as much as they could, their efforts against the German army in order to show the scale and ferocity of the struggle. Most of this filmed documentary material was destroyed in 1943 when the aeroplane carrying the young Partisan diplomat Ivo Lola Ribar, travelling to Italy to negotiate with the Allies, was shot down.[47]

The importance of film for Tito and his Partisans was evident without the need of Lenin's dictum to remind them, and policies on cinema were introduced while the war was still raging. After forming the Partisan Film Section in 1943,[48] Tito's cabinet formed the State Film Enterprise in November and a film section as part of the Agitprop Department in December 1944.[49] The two sections were amalgamated into the Film Enterprise of the People's Republic of Yugoslavia[50] in the summer of 1945. This was in turn disbanded in the summer of 1946 when the Committee for Cinema was formed and headed by the pre-war surrealist writer, Aleksandar Vučo.[51] From 1945, cinema was under the Ministry of Education, which was also a radical change in practice from pre-war Yugoslavia, in which cinema had been under the jurisdiction of the Ministry of Commerce.[52] Therefore, the active attempt to create a cinema industry, which, in Volk's words, would treat "film as an art and agent of social force, of the widest influence and importance",[53] commenced as soon as the communist Partisans began implementing their policies in the country.

Although the Yugoslav film industry surfaced to meet the needs of the Partisans, its development took place with the help of the Soviet Union, which in the words of Michael Stoil "supplied extensive assistance".[54] As in the other emerging socialist states, the lack of trained personnel and equipment was resolved by Soviet donations, while Soviet filmmakers went to these countries to produce films that could serve as training opportunities for local filmmakers. One such film made in Yugoslavia was Abram Room's *In the Mountains of Yugoslavia* (*V gorakh Yugoslavii/U planinama Jugoslavije*) co-produced by the two countries in 1946. Among the Yugoslav filmmakers trained on this project was Vjekoslav Afrić, who worked as one of Room's assistants and who directed the first Yugoslav post-war film, *Slavica* (1947), the following year.

Technical expertise was not the only knowledge Yugoslav filmmakers acquired from the Soviets. The more noteworthy realisation was, as the Yugoslav historian Petar Volk emphasised, the fact that Soviet "socialist realism" was inadequate for representing the complexities of the Yugoslav situation and its history.[55] It is worth noting that socialist realism was never really accepted in Yugoslavia, even in literature. The cultural historian Andrew Wachtel claims that "the Yugoslav version of socialist realism as such, was only imposed between 1945 and 1952, and it was never imposed with as much uniformity as it had been in the Soviet Union", and continues to conclude that in the work of some writers "was practically absent".[56] In the same vein, many film historians agree that socialist realism never played an oppressive or even restrictive role in Yugoslav cinema.[57] Daniel Goulding elaborates that in the Yugoslav case it was replaced by a sort of "national" or "nationalist realism", particularly after Tito took the country out of the Eastern Bloc in 1948.[58] The view that Yugoslavia had its own variant of the infamous artistic doctrine is accepted in scholarly work.[59] However, Mira and Antonín Liehm described it as more moderate, although substantially containing some of the same attributes as the Soviet variety, these being "artistic *dogmatism* and *intolerance*".[60]

By 1949, Yugoslavia had formed a national film industry in the same context as the other socialist countries by accepting Soviet help and doctrines. Due to its political development and the split with Stalin in 1948, avenues opened up for more independent and authentic development. Furthermore, as early as 1946, the Committee for Cinema had started a process of decentralisation of the film industry by opening regional committees in all the Yugoslav republics, as well as two film studios, one in Belgrade and one in Zagreb.[61] John Lampe characterised this early development of the film industry immediately after the war as the result of an "inconsistent cultural policy".[62] However, lacking the strict constraints of socialist realism, and with the industry becoming increasingly decentralised, the cinema must have appeared as one of the most attractive activities to join in 1949, when the young Aleksandar Petrović did so.

1. 2. The Artist

1. 2. 1. Early Years

Aleksandar Petrović was born into a wealthy, upper-class, Serbian family. His father's family originally came from Montenegro, via Bosnia and Herzegovina, and finally settled in Banja Koviljača, western Serbia.[63] The town eventually became a popular tourist resort with a spa, and Petrović's grandfather, whose wife Leposava was a schoolteacher[64] (and a chain smoker),[65] was the owner of its "best hotel".[66] As the place turned into one of the most famous tourist spots in late-nineteenth-century Serbia, Petrović's grandfather became increasingly wealthy, and after World War I moved to Marseille, France, with his family. He was treated there for wounds suffered during that war and died.[67] Petrović's mother was from a well-known Belgrade family of Hristić,[68] and her relative, Filip Hristić, was a famous governor of the National Bank of the Kingdom of Serbia.[69] Aleksandar's mother's maternal grandfather Svetozar Vasiljević, originally from Kruševo in central Serbia,[70] was also a banker.[71] Petrović's father Dragomir[72] studied technology in Paris,[73] and his mother Anka[74] was a chemical engineer,[75] also schooled in France.[76] In Petrović's words, his strictly bourgeois background had "cost him a lot".[77]

Aleksandar Petrović was born in Paris on the 14 January 1929. His older brother Petar and younger brother Milan were born in Paris as well. Only the youngest sister Radmila was born in Belgrade,[78] then the capital city of the Kingdom of Yugoslavia, after the family moved back there in 1931.[79] After one year of lodging, the family settled in their own place in the Vračar area, inhabited by the professional artisans and middle-classes.[80] This popular neighbourhood was, and still is, known by the church of Saint Sava in its centre. The family lived there until their home was destroyed in air raids during World War II. They also suffered two more tragedies: Petrović's younger brother Milan died at the age of four before the war,[81] whereas his older brother Petar died at the end of World War II, both of illness. Aleksandar Petrović was thus only outlived by his younger sister.[82]

In 1935, Petrović started school in Belgrade,[83] and in his autobiography *All of My Loves/The Blind Periscopes* (*Sve moje ljubavi/Slepi periskopi*, 1995) he claimed that even though he was born in Paris, he felt like a Belgradian.[84] In an interview given to Radoslav Lazić, Petrović also stated: "going to the cinema was the most important entertainment in my childhood. I was brought up in cinemas, watching films."[85] However, in his autobiography, Petrović highlights another childhood activity that later influenced his adulthood. He explains that the strongest memory he maintained through his life about the pre-war years in Belgrade was a peculiar popularity and widespread culture of gambling.[86] He believed that Belgrade was the Monte Carlo of the Balkans and remembers games that children used to play while gambling for small change, emulating the grown-ups. This affinity for hazard, an insecurity that can at anytime result in loss, was the driving force that helped him deal mentally with the forthcoming war. Atrocities that the young Petrović was to witness during World War II would affect him for life, making him understand existence as something extremely fragile and volatile.

> I stopped playing poker for good, but I haven't stopped gambling. I'll be gambling as long as I'm alive, because life is one big gamble, and I am still alive […].[87]

1. 2. 2. The Years of War

Aleksandar Petrović predominantly commits his autobiography *All of My Loves* to his memories of World War II, describing lessons he learned from its diverse but overwhelmingly traumatic events. The war for him was undoubtedly a formative experience out of which it is important to outline several incidents, which could help understand his films and his motives for making them.

Petrović spent most of World War II between Belgrade (where his family kept on moving as their house was destroyed in air raids) and a nearby village. It was common for many city dwellers to move, or rather evacuate themselves, to the country during the war and occupation, as the control of Nazi Gestapo was not as notoriously assiduous in the countryside as in the cities.[88]

He remembered the increased politicisation of youth during and just before the war. Although from a wealthy family and still at a fairly young age, he considered himself to be politically a "lefty", the only one in the family.[89] He described how his young friends from the neighbourhood divided themselves politically and argued amongst each other. In 1942, most of them had sympathies towards the communists – including Petrović – as opposed to being sympathetic towards the monarchist Chetniks.[90] The fact that these were mainly children from rich, bourgeois families was not an oddity in Belgrade. After the war, many senior officials of the Yugoslav Communist Party were young men and women from upper- and middle-class families.[91] Serbian writer Miloš Crnjanski, a Yugoslav diplomat before the war, wrote a controversial article entitled "Rich Kids are Playacting Communists" in 1935.[92] This was certainly partly accurate, although Petrović would later adapt Crnjanski's famous novel *Migrations* (*Seobe*) for the screen as his final project.[93]

The Kingdom of Yugoslavia entered the war against Nazi Germany later than the other European countries. The fragile state, which was governed by a so-called bipolar government, created in an attempt to represent Serbs and Croats equally, with the prime minister and his deputy drawn from each of the ethnic groups, signed an alliance pact with Nazi Germany in March 1941.[94] The government of Cvetković and Maček, terrified by the swift victories of the German army in Poland and France that had forced the British troops to retreat back across the Channel, decided to try and save the country by keeping it out of the conflict and cooperating with Adolf Hitler.[95]

This was, however, not what the majority of the population wanted, particularly in Serbia. Within days of the treaty being signed, spontaneous demonstrations occurred in cities across Serbia where anti-German sentiment had been strong since World War I.[96] Additionally, Germany was to use Yugoslavia as a springboard to launch its attack on Greece, which successfully defended itself from the Italian fascists.[97] As Serbian sympathies were with Greece, and as there were many anti-fascist political groups in general in Serbia,[98] the public unequivocally aligned itself against the treaty. In such an atmosphere, on the morning of 27 March 1941, a military coup took place in Belgrade, which overthrew the government that had signed the pact with Hitler, and installed a new government backed by the young Crown Prince Peter Karadjordjević, at that time still a minor.[99] Hitler was infuriated by these developments and he postponed his attack on the Soviet Union in order to deal with Yugoslavia and Greece first. He especially ordered for Belgrade to be punished for its recalcitrance: the town was heavily bombed on the 6 April taking as its toll, amongst other places, the National Library, where numerous invaluable books and old manuscripts were destroyed.[100]

Immediately after the occupation, Serbia found itself in the most difficult position.[101] As Croats often felt under pressure in Yugoslavia, they tended to welcome the Germans as liberators.[102] Hitler in return allowed them to form an independent state loyal to the Axis powers. The Independent State of Croatia became infamous for its support of Nazi policies at home and abroad.[103] Bosnia was annexed to the new Croat state; Montenegro was occupied by Italy as was part of Slovenia, whereas the rest of Slovenia was taken by Germany; Macedonia was carved up between Albania and Bulgaria, both of which were led by pro-fascist regimes. Serbia was also divided and occupied by neighbouring countries loyal to the Axis powers – Albania, Bulgaria, Hungary and Romania, whereas the heartland of Serbia around Belgrade was under strict German control.[104] However, holding such a tight rein quickly backfired, and an uprising started on 7 July 1941, barely three months after the occupation had begun.[105]

The German occupying forces were severely brutal in their efforts to curb the dissent. Belgrade and Serbia were littered with corpses of resistance members and patriots. Aleksandar Petrović remembered the Gestapo bus driving around Belgrade, arresting on the spot suspected patriots, communists, Jews, Gypsies and anyone else who might allegedly be dangerous to the system. These buses were brought from Germany and had a little gas chamber at the back where a suspect could be executed immediately, and their body thrown on the road.[106] The Gestapo was happy that the Serbs knew what was going on in the buses, expecting that this intimidation would discourage them from rebelling.[107]

In his autobiography, Petrović described the river Sava covered with corpses of Serbs, Jews, Gypsies, communists of all nationalities, murdered in the Independent State of Croatia[108] and intentionally thrown in to float downriver, often with little boards around their necks "explaining" the reasons for their execution.[109] Petrović's resolve that one has to fight for freedom rose as he listened to the stories and rumours from young volunteers in the Partisan army, who joined the fight against the fascist occupiers. Some of these boys were from his neighbourhood, and he knew them personally.[110]

In 1944, Petrović encountered the first combined units of the Yugoslav Partisans and the Soviet Red Army fighting their way towards Belgrade. Although only 15 at the time, he decided to join the Partisans. Disregarding his father's disapproval (he had once already dissuaded him from joining),[111] Aleksandar spent the last six months of the war as a young soldier fighting the retreating Germans and their collaborators.[112]

Petrović clearly felt vindicated by the arrival of the triumphant Red Army and justified in his decision to join the Yugoslav Partisans and contribute to the defeat of fascism. His idea of war would soon change, however, and his original romantic fervour would evaporate, as the teenager was about to witness several senseless and traumatic brutalities, this time committed by the "good guys". As at that point the war was coming to an end, Aleksandar did not get the chance to participate in any "glorious battles", as they had all already been fought. Instead, he was there to see the cruel treatment of prisoners of war and the vicious settling of political scores between the rival groups aspiring to take power once the war was over. The communist Partisans that Petrović had just joined were popular across Yugoslavia and were supported by Stalin and the Soviet Union. The monarchists Chetniks were less popular, particularly as the young King Peter II had escaped to London at the beginning of the war. Although the king, then still a crown prince, left to avoid being captured by the German army and coerced into collaborating, many people took his departure as treason. The Chetniks' policies were often perceived as fickle, and they were accused of collaboration with the occupiers by the Partisans. However, the British government supported the Chetniks and hoped to reinstall the monarchy in Yugoslavia after the war.[113]

The two groups fought against each other from 1942. As the war came to an end, these conflicts grew in cruelty. They affected the civilian population and were to become the subject matter of many Yugoslav films in the following years. Petrović's contemporary and colleague Živojin Pavlović directed *The Ambush* (*Zaseda*) in 1969, a Black Wave film par excellence dealing with the subject, whereas another Black Wave director, Mića Popović, directed the first film to deal with the Chetniks' morality in 1964, *The Man from the Oak Wood* (*Čovek iz hrastove šume*).[114]

Petrović was in a unit stationed near the border with Austria where the Anglo-American troops had taken over. The Partisan unit were guarding the border when they arrested a large group of Chetniks from Montenegro who were probably trying to get through to obtain protection from the British army. The Chetniks were initially offered the chance to switch sides and join the Partisans, but this decision was revoked a few hours later with the arrival of a Partisan intelligence officer. He ordered the execution of all the Chetniks from this unit. The unit numbered around 400 people who were then all executed in groups of five within a couple of hours. As some of the Chetniks attempted to run away, Petrović's 16-year-old comrade hit one of them with the handle of his unlocked rifle and, in this tragically bizarre accident, shot himself in the stomach. Petrović rushed to take his wounded friend to hospital, but the boy died before they arrived. It is this uncanny and disturbing incident that Petrović indicated in his autobiography to be one of his strongest memories of the war, an afterimage of relentless brutality and senseless carnage.[115]

Petrović wrote about those days with mixed feelings. In his autobiography, *All of My Loves*, he is clear that the defeat of Nazism was necessary and he understood and sympathised with the Red Army that "walked from Stalingrad to Belgrade" generating an unforgiving stance towards the fascists.[116] This unforgiving stance, which Petrović describes, had accumulated so much by 1945 that it made the anti-fascist block merciless towards its enemy, almost as merciless as the enemy initially was.

Petrović somehow managed to develop a more humane outlook on how post-war problems should have been dealt with, and this marked the final and, it could be said, most important experience he drew from World War II. From his autobiography, it is unmistakably clear that he was an anti-fascist and that he held a left wing political position. In late October of 1944, Petrović thus joined the Union of Young Communists of Yugoslavia – SKOJ – and remained a member for more than a year.[117] Once back from the frontline, and after some time in Belgrade, he was supposed to move to another branch of the party where he was to hand in his letter of recommendation. Databases not being so perfect in those days, Petrović was able to change his mind and throw the letter away; he never rejoined the party. The recommendation also contained a critique of his party loyalty, stating that he was sometimes a "hesitant" member.[118] This hesitation was evidently not the result of his beliefs, as he even described communism as his "first love".[119] Considering Petrović's experience on the frontline, and the fact that he had witnessed other unjustifiable brutalities committed in the name of communism, it could be concluded that his hesitance was not to do with communist ideas, but with their implementation. Petrović was aligned

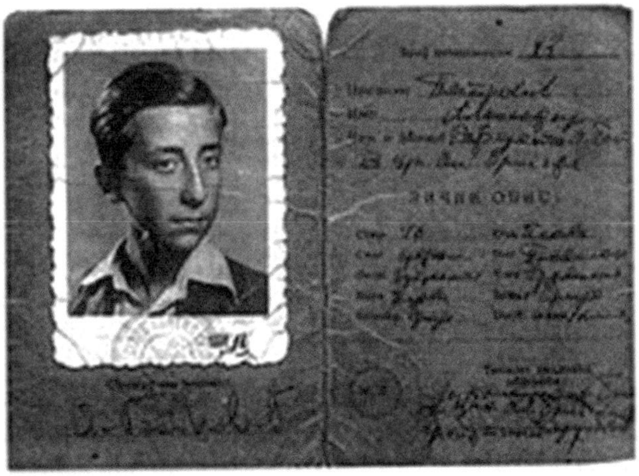

Figure 1.1: Aleksandar Petrović's ID card as a teenage volunteer of a Partisan youth brigade.

with communist ideology but baulked at its recklessly dogmatic and pitiless enforcement at the end of the war. His doubts were not about the ideology (or ideologies), but more about the groups or individuals who imposed them dogmatically by disregarding common sense and even basic notions of what is good and what is not. These doubts were born at this point in his life as the ambiguities of what is a just struggle and all the complexities of war unrolled in front of him. These doubts subsequently emerged to become the focus of his intellectual inquiries, and finally, they were to become significant themes represented in his films. The seeds of his anti-dogmatism were planted at the end of the war.

1. 2. 3. The Young Filmmaker

After the war ended and Aleksandar Petrović's early political aspirations faded, he went back to school in Belgrade. In 1947, he graduated at the age of 18. He found out about a new faculty that had opened in Prague, Czechoslovakia, in which film could be studied, and decided to apply.[120] Years later, when as an acclaimed filmmaker, he was asked to explain how and why he went to Prague, he could not answer precisely:

> I was only 18 years old! I wanted to do something to do with films, somehow generally. The decision to become a director I made somewhere on my train journey between Budapest and Prague.[121]

The Prague film school, or FAMU, was formed in 1947 as part of the Academy of Music and Dramatic Arts and was one of the first national film schools in the world.[122] After its opening, it attracted a large number of candidates, mainly from the Eastern Bloc countries, as it was probably geographically closer and more accessible than the VGIK film school in Moscow.[123] Petrović was one of many young hopefuls from the new-born socialist states who went to apply, knowing that the recently established industries would have a need for skilled film personnel. The one thing he fondly described about his entry exam and interview was that, at a certain point, he was asked to sing a song. Inexplicably, he sang a very old Serbian folk song (as sung by the peasants): "You Are a Pretty Girl, Yana" ("*Ubava si Jano*").[124] This anecdote amused him decades later as he thought of himself – very much a city child – gaining a place at a prestigious school by singing an archaic folk song. Thirty other hopefuls from Yugoslavia had to go back, however, with the exception of a young man called Nenad Jovičić,[125] who enrolled for a film photography course.[126]

Before arriving in Prague, Petrović later claimed, he had been influenced by only a few films. He was enchanted by Marcel Carné's *Les Enfants du Paradis* (France, 1945), a French poetic realist classic, and a Czech film, which Petrović then only remembered by its title – *The Violin and the Dream* (*Housle a sen*) – made in 1947.[127] It is interesting that this film was directed by Václav Krška, who another – internationally better known – Czech director Jan Němec described as "a champion of film as an independent art", and "a forerunner of Antonioni".[128] As Petrović's career took off internationally in the early 1960s, the Italian director Michelangelo Antonioni was becoming one of the most celebrated European directors, and Petrović was frequently accused of copying him, or being his epigone, much to the former's disapproval and frustration.[129] This disapproval may not be unfounded, if his style or sensibility perhaps came under the subconscious influence of the Czech director Václav Krška. Later in his career, Petrović would also mention films by Georges Lampin, a French director who made an acclaimed adaptation of Dostoyevsky's *The Idiot* (as *L'Idiot*) in 1946.[130]

In 1947, when Petrović became a film student, his influences already indicated certain distinctive features of his later, mature work. His love for French poetic realism showed a propensity towards portraying characters and events on the margins of society, or even outside the society, which were often to be the focus of his films. His understanding of film as an independent art form (pre-Antonioni), combined with his passion for Russian classical literature, would all later be very characteristic of his films. All of these features appeared present before his studies commenced.

Petrović later reminisced with great fondness on his first year of study at FAMU in Prague.[131] He often stressed that he was taught by Béla Balázs, whom András Kovács described as "one of the first important theorists of cinema, proclaiming its independence as an art form."[132] In Prague just after World War II, FAMU was a school based on the socialist doctrines. Balázs himself had spent the war in Moscow and had "communist allegiances"[133] and his seminars were influenced by the theories of the Hungarian Marxist aesthetician György Lukács.[134] The ideological framework in which Petrović studied was thus clearly a communist one. Balázs's seminars also had a vital impact on him, so he published an article *Style and Audacity*, once back in Yugoslavia, in which he summarised key ideas he had learned from Béla Balázs.[135]

In the summer of 1948 after completing his first year of study at FAMU, Petrović had to return to Belgrade. The leader of the Yugoslav Communist Party, Josip Broz Tito, and the General Secretary of the Soviet Communists, Josef Stalin, had made their disagreements public in June 1948, and Tito decided to take Yugoslavia out of the alliance of socialist countries.[136] This brought the two countries, or rather one country and one bloc, to the brink of war. All Yugoslav citizens residing, working or studying in the other socialist countries were ordered to return to Yugoslavia, which included students such as Petrović. As Misha Glenny explains, regardless of its break with Stalin "in domestic affairs the KPJ [Yugoslav Communist Party] remained true to its Stalinist practices."[137] Yugoslavia left the Eastern Bloc never to return and subsequently built its own version of socialism, different from the Soviet model. Aleksandar Petrović had to leave his studies, and never went back to graduate.[138] This incident was thus the first time that politics interfered, albeit indirectly but nonetheless significantly, in his film career.

Upon his return to Belgrade, Petrović and other film students, including the ones returning from Moscow, were eagerly awaited by the management staff of the recently opened Zvezda Film Studio in Belgrade. Although he had studied for only one year and was just 19 years old, the new Yugoslav film industry was in such a need of trained workforce that Petrović and all the other returnees were immediately employed by the studio.[139] Shortly after, Petrović was assigned as an assistant director to Vladimir Pogačić on his feature-length fiction film *The Factory Story* (*Priča o fabrici*, 1949),[140] which could be understood as a stroke of luck for Petrović.

Out of the first generation of post-war Yugoslav directors, all of whom had trained on the Soviet production *In the Mountains of Yugoslavia*, the film critic and historian Ranko Munitić identifies Pogačić as the most significant.[141] He was the first director who, in the words of Vida Johnson, describing another East European filmmaker (but whose description perfectly fits Pogačić), was "avoiding schematic socialist realist plots and characters and presented genuine human conflicts and rich characterizations."[142] Munitić adds that Pogačić's characters "were deprived of heroic and exemplary traits but were vulnerable and full of dilemmas" and "without faith in the pathetic ideological concepts of the 'new world' and the 'new man.'"[143] The fact that socialist realism never found its place in Yugoslav cinema requires no better illustration than the films of Vladimir Pogačić. *The Factory Story* received a state award upon its opening, while Pogačić became the first Yugoslav auteur, and a true predecessor of the New Film which was to emerge in the early 1960s.[144]

Pogačić afterwards edited the important film magazine *Film danas* (*Film Today*) in 1958 and 1959, and was a long serving president of the Yugoslav Film Archive (Jugoslovenska Kinoteka).[145] Petrović certainly learned from him and accrued important experiences while working on his films, although he also remembered one thing that made him dislike Pogačić. When, at one point, Pogačić was asked by the heads of Zvezda Film to recommend a young filmmaker to be given a chance to direct, Pogačić answered that there was no one worth recommending. When he told this story to his assistants, including Petrović,[146] the latter felt personally offended. However, there was someone else at the studio who noticed Petrović's enthusiasm, and who would later be very important for his career. This was Zvezda Film's artistic director, Vicko Raspor.[147]

Vicko Raspor was born in Boka Kotorska on the Adriatic coast in 1918 and spent his youth during the pre-war years in Zagreb. There, he became an active member of the Communist Party, and also developed a proclivity for a "bohemian lifestyle".[148] Raspor fought during the war as a member of the resistance and had an impeccable communist record. After the war, he wanted to work in the field of culture, and according to Munitić, Raspor was an author of the first post-war film review.[149] Raspor later became one of the sharpest film critics, who without hesitation delivered harsh critical blows even to the film directors favoured by the party.[150] Raspor was a committed communist, but one that believed in the avant-garde rather than any conservative approach to art, and after Yugoslavia had broken with Stalin, Raspor criticised the political conservatism of the Soviet Communists.[151]

In his articles, he called for new Yugoslav films to be "bold in their choice of content, and audacious in their treatment of the form."[152] In 1950, Raspor published an article on creative film criticism,[153] and Munitić concludes that Raspor was one of the most important early film critics, who, through his writings, influenced the character of the Yugoslav cinema that was to emerge in the 1960s.[154] Raspor became Petrović's first collaborator once their filmmaking careers took off in the mid-1950s, together with another young man Petrović met at Zvezda Film – Nikola Majdak. Majdak was a camera assistant on Pogačić's films, and friends with Petrović as they both enrolled for a degree course in History of Art at the Belgrade University parallel to working at the studio.[155] Petrović's friendship with Raspor and Majdak lasted for many years, after the three of them had worked on their first project. However, this first project did not happen at Zvezda Film. More political changes were about to disturb the temporary refuge the three new colleagues had found at the studio.

1. 3. The State and the Artist

After securing power in Yugoslavia after World War II, the communists led by Josip Broz Tito wanted to rapidly develop socialism, and wanted to achieve this, as John Lampe explains, by "replicating the Soviet advances in heavy industry and armaments of the 1930s".[156] Tito intended to double the levels of pre-war national income by 1951, and in order to accomplish this, a full-scale five-year plan for 1947–51 was announced.[157] This Five Year Plan was in Lampe's assessment "wildly ambitious"[158] including its planned giant increase in production for the film industry, stipulating that Belgrade's Zvezda Film should produce some 20 films by 1951.[159] It is for this reason that the young film trainees such as Aleksandar Petrović were so easily recruited, as the studio expected to instigate production on a large scale immediately. However, in 1949, only two films were produced, and the gap between the plan and the possible seemed unbridgeable.[160] As a result, in 1950, changes in the organisation of production ensued, and Petrović and the other young filmmakers, who had been so easily employed the previous year, lost their jobs. Still, fortunately for them, workers were not just "laid off" under socialism, but a new arrangement was conceived.

In April 1950, all film workers joined the Union of Film Workers of Yugoslavia (Savez Filmskih Radnika Jugoslavije, with the acronym SFRJ, the same as that for the full name of the state).[161] Consequently, many of them then changed their status from being employed by the studio to being "free artists".[162] The status of "free artist" essentially meant that they were "freelancers", but with rights to all the social benefits and protection.[163] Although they would only be paid when they were actually working, their status was otherwise unchanged. When Pogačić started filming his next feature project, *The Last Day* (*Poslednji dan*, 1951), both Petrović as an assistant director and Nikola Majdak as a camera assistant were on the production team.

The reason for Zvezda Film being unable to achieve its high production target was very simple: the lack of money. This financial deficit did not affect only the film industry, for after Tito severed relations with Stalin and the rest of the socialist world in 1948, Yugoslavia found itself on the brink of economic collapse. Misha Glenny explains that "the Soviet Union and people's democracies supplied Yugoslavia with most of its raw materials, including almost all its oil."[164] Additionally, John Lampe claims that chief among the wide spectrum of reasons for Tito's and Stalin's disagreement was the economic development of Yugoslavia and its ambitious Five Year Plan, which would "impose" a drain "on Soviet resources."[165] Tito was saved, but only just, by American President Truman who decided to keep him "'afloat', as a potential ally in the global war against Soviet communism."[166] This did not mean that Yugoslavia was about to give up socialism. On the contrary, Yugoslav ideologues, primarily two of Tito's closest advisors – Milovan Djilas and Edvard Kardelj – started working on the development of the distinctly Yugoslav version of socialism.[167] In 1950, however, the overall situation was extremely difficult for the country. Its independence from Stalin was achieved at great cost to the economy, and the career of Aleksandar Petrović was affected in two ways.

Firstly, he lost his regular job at the studio, but the second impact was perhaps indirectly positive. Due to its break with the Soviet Union (which made Yugoslavia re-establish its relations with the West), there was an increased distancing from the constraining practices of socialist realism and a further liberalisation and decentralisation of the arts and culture. This liberalisation had continued well into the 1960s, and benefited filmmakers such as Aleksandar Petrović.

1. 3. 1. The Belgrade Circle of Critics

As Aleksandar Petrović found himself out of work in 1950, his passion for film manifested itself in writing and publishing articles about it. These articles demonstrate a keen interest in the theory of cinema, as exemplified by *Style and Audacity* from 1951, mentioned earlier. Petrović wrote a great number of film reviews too.[168] One of them on *Legends of Anika* (*Anikina vremena* by Vladimir Pogačić, 1954) was highlighted by a Belgrade scholar, Svetlana Bezdanov Gostimir (who wrote a critical history of Yugoslav film criticism in 1993), as "the most complete analysis of this film". Petrović "seeks to develop his critical text as a new form of creative writing" and "the film is used as the pretext for a new creative act, reformulating a work from another domain of art."[169] However, this "new creative act" did not stop Petrović from thoroughly analysing the film, showing a genuine commitment to its subject as well as a fondness for film in general.[170]

Apart from his theoretical contemplations and reviews, Petrović's most telling texts are the ones in which he speculates on what a "new" or "contemporary" Yugoslav or international film should be. Most of these essays were published in the magazine aptly and simply titled *Film*, which was the first magazine fully committed to cinema in post-war Yugoslavia.[171] Its editor was Petrović's friend and colleague from Zvezda Film, Vicko Raspor. Their friendship continued around this periodical, and, thanks to articles published therein, it is easy to map out a few important features of Petrović's ideas on cinema.

In one of his very early items, published in *Film*, Petrović debates the use of literary texts as the bases for film scripts. He explains:

> However paradoxical it may appear, the necessary pre-condition for the adaptation of poetic literary material would be the complete elimination of literary structures. The literary basis only needs to be an impulse [inspiration] for achieving a completely new *filmic* quality.[172]

Further on in this essay, Petrović reiterates that cinema is "image and sound"[173] confirming his belief in the need for cinema to reaffirm its own language based purely on cinematic means. In this respect, this article, published in 1951, demonstrates that Petrović's thinking on cinema was very close to what was then of interest in film theory worldwide, specifically to the ideas then being pursued by André Bazin, the editor of *Cahiers du Cinéma*.

Petrović was also concerned with the notion of a national Yugoslav cinema. He contemplated what would be its specific contribution to world cinema, and what its characteristic language would be. Writing in the Belgrade daily newspaper, *Borba*, Petrović emphasised that Yugoslav cinema should develop its:

> [...] new language! While other traditional art forms – with already developed forms of expression – are looking for authenticity in the domain of content, in cinema such a step should be reflected in the synchronised development of form and content.[174]

Later in the same year, in the Belgrade daily *Politika*, Petrović clarified what national cinema should not do:

Yugoslav film is giving us some romantic folklore type characters, usually appropriated from nineteenth-century literature. The imperative should be to show the characters of our everyday life; without this, our cinema will not be able to find its own identity.[175]

Clearly, in these paragraphs printed in 1953, Petrović was asking for contemporary life to be critically scrutinised as opposed to representing the past in the style of "banal nationalism". Another important trait of his comments is also a commitment to the author's film, if not yet the auteur theory.

There is no doubt that film directors, those who have the intention of creating *serious artworks*, need to find their own themes, if not to write their own scripts. Ultimately, they have to be passionate about their themes; these themes have to be part of them, a part of their world that they want to express with film. Thus it is natural they need to find the themes themselves.[176]

This extract, from an article published in 1958, adds a final important contour to Petrović's theoretical thinking prior to him embarking on his filmmaking career. To conclude, he believed that cinema has its own inherent language that needs to be developed and explored; he believed that this could be done in a way that could also be a distinctly Yugoslav cultural contribution; and finally, an author with his or her own individual style and approach should be behind such a project. These views were not only his and Vicko Raspor's at the time: there was a whole generation of filmmakers waiting for their chance to display their knowledge of film by writing about it.

1. 3. 2. The First Love – Communism

Obsessive writing about film was so widespread amongst these young enthusiasts in the late 1950s that Ranko Munitić identifies them as a movement, calling them the Belgrade Circle of Critics.[177] Munitić favours the publication *Film Danas* (*Film Today*) as the most interesting one, although it had only 13 issues during 1958 and 1959.[178] He compares this magazine, edited by film director Vladimir Pogačić, to the French *Cahiers du Cinéma*. During these two years, those who contributed would later become the most important directors of the Yugoslav New Wave, or Black Wave as it was also known from the late 1960s onwards. Munitić includes Aleksandar Petrović in this group, as well as Dušan Makavejev and Živojin Pavlović.[179] These three directors – Aleksandar Petrović, Dušan Makavejev and Živojin Pavlović – were the most prominent authors of the Yugoslav New Wave and Black Wave.[180] Makavejev and Pavlović wrote extensively about film, and were also young communists, even more so than Petrović.[181] Pavlović was a party member until 1956 when the Soviets invaded Hungary.[182] Makavejev never left the party: he was expelled in 1973, following the scandal with his film *WR: Mysteries of the Organism* (*W.R. – Misterije organizma*, 1971).[183] During the 1950s, their articles were very much conceived from a Marxist perspective, but as with Raspor and Petrović, they assumed a role of the left intellectual as a critic and not an appeaser or propagator of party policies. Moreover, Pavlović and Makavejev, in the spirit of Marxism, also wrote about the need to educate the young, especially children, about the new medium of film.[184] The aim was to help develop their critical faculties, particularly towards the "Hollywood rhino"[185] mass-producing "kitsch, melodrama, silly sentimentalism and mythologised history."[186] Such blunt statements do not mean that Pavlović was brashly didactic in his suggestions for film education. In his essay, *Film in Primary Schools* (*Film u školskim klupama*, 1954–57) he explains:

> How should one watch a film? There is no single rule. Still, some parameters could be traced. Schools should examine them and make steps forward. Not to dictate, but to help.[187]

Together with Pavlović's essay, Dušan Makavejev published a book titled *24 Little Pictures Per Second* (*24 sličice u sekundi*) intended for school children, with the aim of educating them in film culture. These texts, planned for the youngest members of society, nevertheless remained evocative of their own views on cinema, similar to Petrović's and Raspor's, and their belief in the exploration of cinema language through the expression of the authentic styles of individual authors. Like Petrović, Pavlović would exclaim, anticipating their own films: "Give us finally a true film document about ourselves!"[188]

Makavejev and Pavlović did not only write for children, and some of their remarks were substantially more polemical. As Ranko Munitić notes, from 1958 onwards, Pavlović took over from Vicko Raspor as the "harshest" critic.[189] What distinguishes these two filmmakers from Petrović is that although the latter became a professional early on, Makavejev and Pavlović were amateurs congregating around Belgrade's amateur film club, Kino Klub Beograd.[190] Together, they produced a considerable number of short films shown at various amateur festivals and events. One of these events was critically reproached by Otto Deneš, a Slovenian film director and committed party member. Deneš attacked the young amateurs for portraying Yugoslav contemporary socialist reality as dark and pessimistic, which he believed was inaccurate. He pleaded with the filmmakers to show what he thought was "the real picture" of society. Pavlović famously attacked Deneš for this "paternalism" in his essay *Discrimination towards the Spirit of Amateurism* (*O diskriminaciji duha amaterizma*) in 1959.[191] Pavlović's argument was based on the idea that "the spirit of amateurism is the spirit of art"[192] and that amateurs shall not make "banal propaganda",[193] and thus he disclosed a discrepancy in the understandings of Marxism within one party. Both Deneš and Pavlović appear to argue what a young socialist filmmaker is to do from a Marxist point of view. This discrepancy in viewpoint widened over the years, causing major conflict between the filmmakers and the party in the early 1970s. The debate, between the party and the filmmakers, on the role of the filmmaker in the new society, was won by the party; as were most other debates the party had with various segments of the society.

1. 3. 3. New Wave

The ardent writing about cinema in which Yugoslav directors-to-be were engaged in the 1950s and 1960s – that orbited around several film journals – was clearly similar to a better known phenomenon, happening more or less simultaneously in France. French film directors such as Jean-Luc Godard, François Truffaut, Agnés Varda, Claude Chabrol and others, who brought "a breath of fresh air" by producing "innovative films" known as the *nouvelle vague*,[194] also prepared themselves for filmmaking by first writing reviews for the now historic *Cahiers du Cinéma* edited by André Bazin.

As these French cineastes produced their films two or three years before the Yugoslavs, there is an assumption that the Yugoslav New Wave – as well as the New Waves of other countries – was nothing but an imitation of the French one. At the time, when Yugoslav films started appearing at film festivals, they were often judged in comparison with their French counterparts, which usually caused great annoyance to the Yugoslav filmmakers, particularly to Aleksandar Petrović.[195] Undoubtedly, the French New Wavers released their feature films first, and they certainly produced a significant body of work, but as Yugoslav film historian Ranko Munitić argues, New Wave should not be seen strictly as a French phenomenon that was then replicated elsewhere. Reminding us that the Yugoslav filmmakers made their short films and published their own articles clearly identifying what their films were going to be like *at the same time* as the French cineastes, Munitić argues that the New Wave was a global phenomenon having expression in many different countries.[196]

In the same vein, other film historians defended other New Wave movements.[197] According to Peter Hames, Czechoslovakian directors, including Miloš Forman, Ivan Passer, Jiří Menzel and others, formed a movement that developed autonomously and ought to be understood as such, although comparisons with the French *nouvelle vague* were sometimes counterproductive.[198] Paul Coates notes that Roman Polański's debut *Knife in the Water* (*Nóż w wodzie*, Poland, 1962) was also compared to the *nouvelle vague*, although it is clear that the film primarily sprang out of the director's obsessions already evident in his previous short films, released before the explosion of French films.[199] It is this global, or at least pan-European, New Wave movement that peaked in the late 1960s, to which Dušan Makavejev, Živojin Pavlović and Aleksandar Petrović belonged as a generation and "in spirit".[200] Petrović's career and work have often been perceived and judged as part of this movement, which in Yugoslavia and internationally was also known as the Black Wave.

Notes

1   Petar Volk, *Istorija jugoslovenskog filma* (Beograd: Institut za Film, Partizanska knjiga, 1986), pp. 1–2.

2   This was actually on 25 May 1896, because the "old" Julian calendar was then in use in Serbia (as in Tsarist Russia), and according to that calendar it was on 6 June, see: Dejan

Kosanović, "Sto godina filma u Srbiji", in *Filma Vek 1895–1995*, ed. by Dejan Kosanović (Beograd: Jugoslovenska Kinoteka, SANU, 1995), p. 156.

3 Radoslav Zelenović, "Vek filma", in *Filma Vek 1895–1995*, ed. by Dejan Kosanović, pp. 16–17.

4 Petar Volk, *Istorija jugoslovenskog filma*, p. 2.

5 Radoslav Zelenović, "Vek filma", p. 17.

6 As "the cinematograph" was used as a projector as well as a camera, Lumière brothers' employees, who travelled the world with this invention, often filmed short films wherever they went.

7 Dejan Kosanović, "Sto godina filma u Srbiji", p. 156; and Petar Volk, *Istorija jugoslovenskog filma*, p. 15.

8 Dejan Kosanović, "Sto godina filma u Srbiji", p. 157.

9 Dejan Kosanović, "Sto godina filma u Srbiji", p. 158; and Petar Volk, *Istorija jugoslovenskog filma*, p. 16.

10 Petar Volk, *Istorija jugoslovenskog filma*, p. 4; although Kosanović claims that this was in 1909, this may be due to the temporal difference of two weeks between the calendars; see Dejan Kosanović, "Sto godina filma u Srbiji", p. 159.

11 Dejan Kosanović, "Sto godina filma u Srbiji", p. 159.

12 Dejan Kosanović, "Sto godina filma u Srbiji", p. 159; and Petar Volk, *Istorija jugoslovenskog filma*, p. 24.

13 Dejan Kosanović, "Sto godina filma u Srbiji", p. 160.

14 Noël Burch, *Life to Those Shadows* (Berkeley: University of California Press, 1990), pp. 56–57, 156, 189, 236.

15 Misha Glenny, *The Balkans 1804–1999: Nationalism, War and the Great Powers* (London: Granta Books, 1999), p. 2.

16 See Noël Burch's *Life to Those Shadows*.

17 Mira and Antonín Liehm, *The Most Important Art: Soviet and Eastern European Film after 1945* (Berkeley: University of California Press, 1977), p. 12.

18 Petar Volk, *Istorija jugoslovenskog filma*, pp. 37–38; and Dejan Kosanović, "Sto godina filma u Srbiji", p. 161.

19 Burch rightly criticises films such as *The Assassination of the Duke of Guise* (*L'Assassinat du Duc de Guise*, 1908) as early films that have helped reduce cinema culture to what it is today. Understanding that a "film" is something that will last for approximately two hours, telling us a fiction story interpreted by actors as in the theatre, was only a very narrow way that films could be made, distributed and received in the early days of cinema. However, it is the way that has prevailed, eliminating all others, and thereby reducing film culture to this sole "mode of representation", for which Burch criticises efforts such as Botorić's. Still, Botorić could not have conceived what might be the overall outcome of such filmmaking, and was himself excited about cinema being understood as art and culture.

20 Petar Volk, *Istorija jugoslovenskog filma*, pp. 37–39; and Dejan Kosanović, "Sto godina filma u Srbiji", p. 161.

21 Petar Volk, *Istorija jugoslovenskog filma*, p. 38.

22 John R. Lampe, *Yugoslavia as History: Twice There Was a Country* (Cambridge: Cambridge University Press, 1996), p. 162.

23 Petar Volk, *Istorija jugoslovenskog filma*, pp. 86–87.

24 Petar Volk, *Istorija jugoslovenskog filma*, p. 103.

25 Nina Hibbin, *Eastern Europe: An Illustrated Guide*, Screen Series (London: A. Zwemmer Ltd; New York: A. S. Barnes & Co., 1969), p. 172.

26 Michael J. Stoil, *Balkan Cinema: Evolution after the Revolution* (Ann Arbor, MI: UMI Research Press, 1979), p. 9.

27 Michael J. Stoil, *Balkan Cinema*, p. 60.

28 Mira and Antonín Liehm were actually born in Czechoslovakia, although it was only after they moved to the United States that they published their work on the history of East European cinema. I thus consider their perspective to be American, as this was where their work was published.

29 Mira and Antonín Liehm, *The Most Important Art*, p. 19.

30 Daniel J. Goulding, *Liberated Cinema: The Yugoslav Experience* (Bloomington: Indiana University Press, 1985), p. 1; see this quote also in Mira and Antonín Liehm, *The Most Important Art*, p. 20.

31 See for example Ilja Gregory, "Fragments of Nationhood: 'Novi Film' as Seen from the 1990s: Revisioning Yugoslav Social and Political Reality (1947–1972)" (unpublished master's thesis, London: British Film Institute, Birkbeck College, 1995/96), p. 7.

32 Petar Volk, *Savremeni jugoslovenski film* (Beograd: Univerzitet Umetnosti, Institut za Film, 1983), pp. 6–7.

33 On the early Yugoslav cinema, see Petar Volk, *Istorija jugoslovenskog filma* (Beograd: Institut za Film, 1986); or Petar Volk, *Svedočenje: Hronika jugoslovenskog filma 1896–1945*, vol. 1 (Beograd: Slobodan Mašić, Petar Volk, 1973).

34 See, for example, Petar Blečić, 'Za filmom o Karadjordju Kinoteka tragala više od šest decenija', *Blic Online*, 31 July 2011, available at: http://www.blic.rs/Vesti/Reportaza/268857/Za-filmom-o-Karadjordju-Kinoteka-tragala-vise-od-sest-decenija [last accessed 3 September 2012].

35 This is generally accepted to be the period between 1961 and 1973 (during which Aleksandar Petrović produced most of his work), see Mira and Antonín Liehm, *The Most Important Art*, p. 413; and Daniel J. Goulding, *Liberated Cinema*, p. 61.

36 See Petrović's interview in: Predić, Z., "Biće skoro propast filma!", *Radio revija*, 13 November 1970, pp. 22–23.

37 Aleksandar Petrović, *Novi Film, crni film 1965–1970* (Beograd: Naučna Knjiga, 1988), p. 320.

38 Michael J. Stoil, *Balkan Cinema*, p. 20.

39 Mira and Antonín Liehm, *The Most Important Art*, p. 35.

40 ibid.

41 Mira and Antonín Liehm, *The Most Important Art*, p. 34.

42 Paul A. Schroeder, *Tomas Gutierrez Alea: The Dialectics of a Filmmaker* (London, New York: Routledge, 2002), pp. 1–2.

43 *The BFI Companion to East European and Russian Cinema*, ed. by Richard Taylor et al. (London: British Film Institute, 2000), p. 12.

44 *The Cinema of Central Europe*, ed. by Peter Hames (London, New York: Wallflower Press, 2004), p. 8.

45 I wish to make a brief disclaimer here, and emphasise that I have no intention of equating ideologies with cinema industries, or with the political systems inspired by these ideologies, which subsequently helped create those industries. Hungary, for example, had the best year in film production to this day in 1943, during the Nazi regime (see *The Cinema of Central Europe*, ed. by Peter Hames, p. 8; and *The BFI Companion to East European and Russian Cinema*, p. 104). Although there are various historical reasons for this, such as Germany moving its film studios to Hungary to avoid the Allied bombings, such cinematic achievements could not justify Nazism as an ideology – quite the opposite! With this example, I am also *not* trying to equate socialism and Nazism in any way, as I am aware that some historians do. This subject is in any case outside the scope of this book. I would just add that comparing Nazism to the socialist societies, such as the ones that existed in Eastern Europe, would – if we were to compare primarily the content and artistic merits of the films produced – indicate that socialism was an incomparably healthier society in which to live, regardless of the aberrations that ultimately led to its downfall.

46 On Allied policies towards Tito's Partisans, see John R. Lampe, *Yugoslavia as History*, pp. 213–17; and also on the Allied recognition of the Chetniks as opposed to the Partisans in 1941, see Misha Glenny, *The Balkans*, p. 493.

47 Petar Volk, *Istorija jugoslovenskog filma*, p. 123.

48 ibid.

49 Petar Volk, *Istorija jugoslovenskog filma*, pp. 124–25; and Daniel J. Goulding, *Liberated Cinema*, p. 3.

50 Renamed the Federal Peoples Republic of Yugoslavia in 1946.

51 Petar Volk, *Istorija jugoslovenskog filma*, p. 130; and Daniel J. Goulding, *Liberated Cinema*, pp. 3–4; and Mira and Antonín Liehm, *The Most Important Art*, p. 20.

52 Petar Volk, *Istorija jugoslovenskog filma*, p. 127.

53 ibid.

54 Michael J. Stoil, *Balkan Cinema*, p. 45.

55 Petar Volk, *Istorija jugoslovenskog filma*, pp. 137–38.

56 Andrew B. Wachtel, *Making a Nation, Breaking a Nation: Literature and Cultural Politics in Yugoslavia* (Stanford: Stanford University Press, 1998), p. 273 (note 67).

57 See Michael J. Stoil, *Balkan Cinema*, pp. 2, 34–39; Mira and Antonín Liehm, *The Most Important Art*, pp. 127–28.

58 Daniel J. Goulding, *Liberated Cinema*, p. 11.

59 See for example Ilja Gregory, "Fragments of Nationhood", p. 7.

60 The emphasis in the quotation is mine; see Mira and Antonín Liehm, *The Most Important Art*, p. 128.

61 Daniel J. Goulding, *Liberated Cinema*, p. 4.

62 John R. Lampe, *Yugoslavia as History*, pp. 233–34.

63 An interview with Aleksandar Petrović; see Savković, D., "Dan kada je letelo perje", *Auto svet*, October 1982, p. 43.

64 ibid.

65 Aleksandar Petrović, *Sve Moje Ljubavi/Slepi periskopi* (Novi Sad: Prometej, Tajanstvena Tačka, 1995), p. 156.

66 An interview with Aleksandar Petrović, quoted from Ranko Munitić [ed. by Radoslav Lazić], "Smisao filma kao umetnosti: Poslednji razgovor sa Aleksandrom Sašom Petrovićem", in *Prizor*, no 2, ed. by Snežana Nešković-Simić (Loznica: Centar za kulturu 'Vuk Karadžić', 2003), p. 101.

67 Savković, D., "Dan kada je letelo perje", p. 44.

68 ibid.

69 Ranko Munitić, "Smisao filma kao umetnosti", p. 101.

70 Savković, D., "Dan kada je letelo perje", p. 44.

71 Aleksandar Petrović, *Sve moje ljubavi*, p. 122.

72 Aleksandar Petrović, *Skupljači perja* (Beograd: Jugoslovenska Kinoteka; Novi Sad: Prometej, 1993), p. 147.

73 Savković, D., "Dan kada je letelo perje", p. 44.

74 Aleksandar Petrović, *Skupljači perja*, p. 147.

75 Aleksandar Petrović, *Sve moje ljubavi*, p. 143.

76 Savković, D., "Dan kada je letelo perje", p. 44.

77 Ranko Munitić, "Smisao filma kao umetnosti", p. 101. Other East European directors felt the same during socialism, like Czechoslovakian Jiří Menzl, for example, who received an Oscar in 1968 for *Closely Observed Trains*, the same year that Petrović was a contender with his *I Even Met Happy Gypsies*.

78 Personal interview with Branka Petrović (11 September 2005).

79 Aleksandar Petrović, *Sve moje ljubavi*, p. 101.

80 ibid.

81 Aleksandar Petrović, *Sve moje ljubavi*, p. 102.

82 Personal interview with Branka Petrović (11 September 2005).

83 Aleksandar Petrović, *Sve moje ljubavi*, p. 105.

84 Aleksandar Petrović, *Sve moje ljubavi*, p. 146.

85 Radoslav Lazić, *Traktat o filmskoj režiji: U traganju za estetikom režije od Aleksandra Petrovića do Emira Kusturice* (Beograd: Institut za Film, 1989), p. 43.

86 Aleksandar Petrović, *Sve moje ljubavi*, p. 106.

87 Filmmaking, of course, could be understood as gambling; see Aleksandar Petrović, *Sve moje ljubavi*, p. 108.

88 Aleksandar Petrović, *Sve moje ljubavi*, pp. 101–93.

89 Ranko Munitić, "Smisao filma kao umetnosti", p. 101.

90 Aleksandar Petrović, *Sve moje ljubavi*, p. 133. The word "chetnik" has its root in the Serbian word *četa* – which translates as a small army unit. Chetniks were the special forces of the pre-World War II Kingdom of Yugoslavia's army. Their task was to organise guerrilla warfare against the Nazis, in case the organised military defence of the country collapsed and Yugoslavia ended up being occupied. As this collapse happened very quickly, the

Chetniks were supposed to start a resistance movement, but the Communist Partisans – although "uninvited" – took over that role, it could be said in considerably more effective fashion, than the Chetniks. Chetniks remain a much debated historical topic, especially as Tito's communist regime dismissed them after the war as traitors. They will be further discussed in this, and following chapters.

91 For example, already mentioned Ivo Lola Ribar, then Koča Popović, Olga Humo, Vladimir Velebit and many others.

92 See the biography of Miloš Crnjanski: Radovan Popović, *Život Miloša Crnjanskog* (Beograd: Prosveta, 1980), p. 167.

93 To be discussed in Chapter 8.

94 Glenny claims that the treaty signed by Regent Prince Paul, the sovereign of the state as Crown Prince Peter was still a minor, was incredibly advantageous for the Yugoslavs. The latter had no obligations towards the Axis powers other than to allow their troops transit through the country. As Hitler was already in a hurry to attack the Soviet Union, he gave Yugoslavs a very good deal. See Misha Glenny, *The Balkans*, p. 474.

95 On the extremely complex political and ethnic relationships, particularly between Serbs and Croats, in the Kingdom of Yugoslavia on the eve of World War II, see John R. Lampe, *Yugoslavia as History*, pp. 190–96; and Misha Glenny, *The Balkans*, pp. 471–77.

96 Winston Churchill's famous comment was "now Yugoslavia has found its soul"; see John R. Lampe, *Yugoslavia as History*, p. 198; and Misha Glenny, *The Balkans*, p. 471.

97 "The Italian advance quickly bogged down and turned into retreat" – is how John Lampe describes the Italian invasion of Greece in October 1940. See John R. Lampe, *Yugoslavia as History*, p. 195.

98 Although illegal, the Communist Party was strong, and it was known to have sent a considerable number of its members to fight in the Spanish Civil War against the fascists.

99 Lovett Edwards, a BBC journalist in Belgrade in 1941, described the event in the following words: "There are few events in history which can be said in all truth to have occurred because of the spontaneous, lively and popular enthusiasm. The Yugoslav *coup d'état* was one such event" – quoted from Misha Glenny, *The Balkans*, p. 475.

100 According to Lampe, Hitler was eager "to settle accounts with the 'Serbian renegades' he blamed for starting the First World War" – see John R. Lampe, *Yugoslavia as History*, p. 198. The bombing of Belgrade in 1941 was a subject of many films: Slobodan Šijan's *Who's Singing over There* (*Ko to tamo peva*, SFR Yugoslavia 1980) probably provides the best picture of Yugoslavia on the eve of World War II.

101 Lampe describes this situation as follows: "In the first days of the occupation, the Germans made sure that there was no interruption in the terror administered to Belgrade and then to all of Serbia" – John R. Lampe, *Yugoslavia as History*, p. 200.

102 The archive film footage of Slovenes and Croats welcoming the German troops, while the streets of Serbian towns were all empty with shops and windows shut, was most famously exploited in Emir Kusturica's acclaimed film *Underground* (France, FR Yugoslavia, Germany, Hungary, 1995).

103 See *The Decline of the Century: Testament L.Z.* (*Zalazak stoljeća: Testament L.Z.*), directed by Lordan Zafranović (Austria, Croatia, Czech Republic, France, 1994).

104 Lampe adds: "The partition of the first Yugoslavia that followed is too complex to comprehend without looking at a map" – John R. Lampe, *Yugoslavia as History*, p. 199.

105 This day was celebrated as a national day in Socialist Serbia, as on that day a member of the Communist Party opened fire at the police, thus starting an uprising against the occupying forces.

106 Aleksandar Petrović, *Sve moje ljubavi*, p. 108.

107 These buses, or trucks, are also mentioned in history books; see Misha Glenny, *The Balkans*, pp. 504–05.

108 The infamous Ustaša movement that took over Croatia in 1941 "was a fascist movement from the start" according to Lampe. See John R. Lampe, *Yugoslavia as History*, p. 172. Misha Glenny describes the movement and its leader, Ante Pavelić, as a "small gang of fascist thugs" and concludes that: "The installation of Pavelić's brutal fascist regime resulted in the single most disastrous episode in Yugoslav history, whose consequences were still being felt in the 1990s" – see Misha Glenny, *The Balkans*, p. 476.

109 Aleksandar Petrović, *Sve moje ljubavi*, p. 132.

110 Aleksandar Petrović, *Sve moje ljubavi*, p. 134.

111 Aleksandar Petrović, *Sve moje ljubavi*, p. 174.

112 Aleksandar Petrović, *Sve moje ljubavi*, p. 211.

113 The Chetniks fought against the Nazis at the beginning of the war, often together with the communist Partisans, but they reduced their activity in the face of the German reprisals against the civilian population – which were often incredibly brutal. Subsequently, the Chetniks often went along with the Germans rather than siding with the communists, and some of the Chetnik commanders certainly collaborated with the Nazis. Still, the largest rescue operation of American pilots whose planes were shot down over Nazi controlled territory was conducted by the Chetniks in 1944. On the fickleness of their policies and the changes in British relations with them (British support for the Chetniks dwindled by 1943), see John R. Lampe, *Yugoslavia as History*, pp. 214–15; and Misha Glenny, *The Balkans*, pp. 493–495.

114 The Black Wave will be discussed later in this chapter, and in Chapter 5.

115 This event is described in Aleksandar Petrović, *Sve moje ljubavi*, pp. 211–214.

116 Aleksandar Petrović, *Sve moje ljubavi*, p. 185.

117 Aleksandar Petrović, *Sve moje ljubavi*, p. 178.

118 Aleksandar Petrović, *Sve moje ljubavi*, p. 179.

119 Aleksandar Petrović, *Sve moje ljubavi*, p. 178.

120 Pavel Branko, "Rozhovor s Aleksandrem Petrovićem", *Film A Doba*, February 1966, pp. 66–78.

121 Savković, D., "Dan kada je letelo perje", p. 43.

122 *The BFI Companion to East European and Russian Cinema*, p. 72.

123 On VGIK, see *The BFI Companion to East European and Russian Cinema*, p. 256.

124 Pavel Branko, "Rozhovor s Aleksandrem Petrovićem", p. 66.

125 Jovičić later became a well-respected cinematographer in Yugoslavia, and he filmed the first Yugoslav colour film. See Milutin Čolić, *Filmski portreti: Od Manakija do Makavejeva* (Beograd: Prosveta, 2007), pp. 353–56.

126 Ranko Munitić, "Smisao filma kao umetnosti", p. 106.

127 Pavel Branko, "Rozhovor s Aleksandrem Petrovićem", p. 66.

128 Quoted in Peter Hames, "O slavnosti a hostech, The Party and the Guests", in *The Cinema of Central Europe*, ed. by Peter Hames, p. 140.

129 An amusing example of this is an interview with Petrović in *Cahiers du Cinéma*, after he had released his first film in colour (two years after Antonioni had released *his* first colour film). As soon as Petrović was asked about the use of colour, without Antonioni being mentioned, Petrović asserted that he did not use colour because of Antonioni, but for other reasons. Evidently, as this was happening in the mid-1960s, when colour film was replacing black and white globally, perhaps there is no need to look for further explanation. See Bontemps, J. and Yamada, K. "Entretien avec Aleksandar Petrovic: J'ai même rencontré des Tziganes heureux", *Cahiers du Cinéma*, no. 191., June 1967, pp. 42–43.

130 Savković, D., "Dan kada je letelo perje", p. 44.

131 Pavel Branko, "Rozhovor s Aleksandrem Petrovićem", p. 66.

132 *The BFI Companion to East European and Russian Cinema*, p. 26.

133 ibid.

134 Petar Volk, *Let nad močvarom: Aleksandar Petrović svojim životom, delom i filmovima* (Beograd: Institut za film; Novi Sad: Prometej, 1999), p. 28.

135 Aleksandar Petrović, *Novi Film, crni film*, p. 18.

136 On Tito's split with Stalin, see Misha Glenny, *The Balkans*, pp. 532–36; and John R. Lampe, *Yugoslavia as History*, pp. 241–47.

137 Misha Glenny, *The Balkans*, p. 536.

138 Ranko Munitić, "Smisao filma kao umetnosti", p. 106.

139 Petar Volk, *Let nad močvarom*, p. 29.

140 Petar Volk, *Let nad močvarom*, p. 30.

141 Ranko Munitić, *Adio, Jugo-film!* (Beograd: Centar film, Srpski kulturni klub; Kragujevac: Prizma, 2005), p. 29.

142 Vida T. Johnson, "The Films of Andrei Konchalovsky", in *Before the Wall Came Down: Soviet and East European Filmmakers Working in the West*, ed. by Graham Petrie and Ruth Dwyer (Lanham, MD: University Press of America, 1990), p. 37.

143 Ranko Munitić, *Adio, Jugo-film!*, p. 26.

144 ibid (New Film was the Yugoslav version of the New Wave).

145 Ranko Munitić, *Adio, Jugo-film!*, pp. 29–30.

146 Pavel Branko, "Rozhovor s Aleksandrem Petrovićem", p. 68.

147 Petar Volk, *Let nad močvarom*, p. 29.

148 Ante Peterlić (ed.), *Filmska enciklopedija 2 (L–Ž)* (Zagreb: Jugoslavenski Leksikografski Zavod 'Miroslav Krleža', 1990), pp. 404–05.

149 Ranko Munitić, *Adio, Jugo-film!*, p. 284.

150 Ranko Munitić, *Adio, Jugo-film!*, p. 115.

151 Daniel J. Goulding, *Liberated Cinema*, p. 10.

152 Ranko Munitić, *Adio, Jugo-film!*, p. 97.

153 Ranko Munitić, *Adio, Jugo-film!*, p. 47.

154 Ranko Munitić, *Adio, Jugo-film!*, p. 61.

155   Personal interview with Nikola Majdak (30 April 2006).

156   John R. Lampe, *Yugoslavia as History*, p. 238.

157   ibid.

158   Tito was warned about this by his own economists, but he replaced them with more "agreeable" ones. See John R. Lampe, *Yugoslavia as History*, p. 238.

159   Petar Volk, *Let nad močvarom*, p. 30.

160   ibid.

161   The full name of the state was Socijalistička Federativna Republika Jugoslavija – the Socialist Federal Republic of Yugoslavia. The Union was formed on 5 April 1950, and the inaugural speech was given by Vicko Raspor. See Petar Volk, *Let nad močvarom*, p. 33.

162   Nikola Majdak claims that all the bureaucrats kept their jobs whereas it was the actual film workers who "got the boot". Personal interview (30 April 2006).

163   Personal interview with Nikola Majdak (30 April 2006).

164   Misha Glenny, *The Balkans*, p. 536.

165   John R. Lampe, *Yugoslavia as History*, p. 242.

166   Misha Glenny, *The Balkans*, p. 536.

167   Misha Glenny, *The Balkans*, p. 575.

168   The bibliography of Petrović's writings compiled by Ivana Carić lists eight reviews of Yugoslav films and 42 reviews of foreign films, all published in various Belgrade media; see Petar Volk, *Let nad močvarom*, pp. 370–71.

169   Svetlana Bezdanov Gostimir, *Filmom do kritike & vice versa* (Beograd: Institut za film, 1993), p. 99.

170   Svetlana Bezdanov Gostimir, *Filmom do kritike & vice versa*, pp. 99–100.

171   *Film* magazine was founded and edited by Radoš Novaković between 1946 and 1949; see Ranko Munitić, *Adio, Jugo-film!*, p. 30. The magazine was then revived by Aleksandar Vučo and Vicko Raspor between 1950 and 1952, although in its later stages it was edited only by Raspor; see Ranko Munitić, *Adio, Jugo-film!*, p. 30, and specifically p. 49.

172   The emphasis in the quotation is mine. See Aleksandar Petrović, *Novi film 1950–1965* (Beograd: Institut za Film, 1971), p. 13.

173   Aleksandar Petrović, *Novi film 1950–1965*, p. 16.

174   Aleksandar Petrović, *Novi film 1950–1965*, p. 19.

175   Aleksandar Petrović, *Novi film 1950–1965*, p. 21.

176   The emphasis in the quotation is mine; see Aleksandar Petrović, *Novi film 1950–1965*, p. 40.

177   Ranko Munitić, *Adio, Jugo-film!*, p. 50.

178   Ranko Munitić, *Adio, Jugo-film!*, p. 183; while Daniel Goulding states that "*Film danas* involved itself in an eclectic, progressive, and free examination of new film trends in international cinema, a lively discussion of film aesthetics and theory, and stimulating critiques and reviews of domestically produced films." See Daniel J. Goulding, *Liberated Cinema*, p. 42.

179   Ranko Munitić, *Adio, Jugo-film!*, p. 183; and see p. 50.

180   See, for example, a general film history book such as *The Oxford History of World Cinema* – Marek Hendrykowski, "Changing States in East Central Europe" in *The*

Oxford History of World Cinema, ed. by Geoffrey Nowell-Smith (Oxford: Oxford University Press, 1996), p. 637; or a scholarly work that specifically deals with the history of Yugoslav cinema such as Daniel J. Goulding, *Liberated Cinema*, p. 73.

181 Živojin Pavlović, *Planeta filma* (Beograd: Zepter Book World, 2002), p. 13.

182 Živojin Pavlović, *Planeta filma*, p. 24.

183 Daniel J. Goulding, *Liberated Cinema*, p. 79.

184 This was in a way a voluntary reaction to a speech of one of the highest officials of the Yugoslav Communist Party – Edvard Kardelj – who called for film education in schools, see Živojin Pavlović, *Davne Godine (1954–1963)* (Beograd: Institut za Film; Novi Sad: Prometej, 1997), pp. 21–22.

185 Pavlović borrows this phrase from Miroslav Krleža; see Živojin Pavlović, *Davne Godine*, p. 21.

186 Živojin Pavlović, *Davne Godine*, p. 94.

187 This whole essay is reprinted in Živojin Pavlović, *Davne Godine*, pp. 9–54, and for this quote, see p. 13.

188 Živojin Pavlović, *Davne Godine*, p. 158.

189 Ranko Munitić, *Adio, Jugo-film!*, pp. 115–16.

190 On this important film institution, see Ranko Munitić, *Kino klub Beograd: Trojanski konj jugoslovenskog modernog filma* (Beograd: Centar Film; Kragujevac: Prizma, 2003).

191 Živojin Pavlović, *Davne Godine*, pp. 90–94.

192 Živojin Pavlović, *Davne Godine*, p. 93.

193 Živojin Pavlović, *Davne Godine*, p. 92.

194 Ginette Vincendeau, "The Popular Art of French Cinema", in *The Oxford History of World Cinema*, ed. by Geoffrey Nowell-Smith, p. 352.

195 An interesting interview with Aleksandar Petrović where he comments frequently on the relationship of various New Waves is in Adamović, D., "Borba za novi filmski izraz i za jeftin film", *NIN*, 11 November 1962, p. 12.

196 Munitić calls it an "all European New Wave"; see his very interesting comparative analysis of a large group of Italian, French and Yugoslav films produced in that period, Ranko Munitić, *Adio, Jugo-film!*, pp. 171–72.

197 Film historian Dudley Andrew detailed this argument in his talk delivered at the University of St Andrews' conference *Cinema at the Periphery*: "Many New Waves, one Sea!", 16 June 2006.

198 Peter Hames, "O slavnosti a hostech, The Party and the Guest", in *The Cinema of Central Europe*, ed. by Peter Hames, p. 139.

199 Paul Coates, "Nóż w wodzie, Knife in the Water", in *The Cinema of Central Europe*, ed. by Peter Hames, p. 82.

200 Ranko Munitić, *Adio, Jugo-film!*, pp. 165–80.

Chapter 2

Shoulder to Shoulder

Tito's break with Stalin in 1948 became one of the key political events in Europe immediately after War World II, demonstrating for the first time that more than one vision of socialism and communism existed, and that Moscow did not have a monopoly on this vision. According to Misha Glenny, the fact that Tito managed to prevail transformed him "from being a 'little Stalin' into a figure of genuine historical significance",[1] setting a precedent for future fragmentation of the global communist alliance. Although Tito initially tried to downplay the conflict, explaining it as a "temporary misunderstanding",[2] Stalin was known to be unwilling to tolerate any form of dissent.[3] The rift between the two socialist countries widened and two of Tito's closest allies from his "inner circle"[4] seized the opportunity to convince him that Yugoslavia needed to develop its own variant of socialism, thus giving the conflict a distinct ideological flavour. The Montenegrin Milovan Djilas and the Slovene Edvard Kardelj, two members of the Central Committee trusted by Tito on questions of ideology, persuaded him that Yugoslavia needed to abandon its centrally-planned Soviet-style state run economy, in order to relegate power "to autonomous but presumably Communist-led workers' councils" and thereby to "start creating [Karl] Marx's free association of producers."[5] According to Dejan Jović, Tito's conflict with Stalin therefore became "primarily ideological" resting on the key problem of what should come first – socialism or the state – creating a possibility of different "interpretations of Marxism" in real politic.[6] Tito accepted Djilas and Kardelj's proposal and they subsequently created the concept of "self-management",[7] which redefined Yugoslav socialism as clearly distinct from Soviet, and according to Glenny generated "Yugoslavia's unique contribution to socialist theory."[8]

Although Glenny describes self-management simply as "the devolution of economic decision-making away from the political centre to the shop floor",[9] he adds that this "did not turn Tito into a democrat".[10] John Lampe corroborates the view that self-management presupposed liberalisation, at least in comparison with other Eastern Bloc countries, and he also states that "Tito and his inner circle debated the issue of how to decentralize without losing political control".[11] Despite the situation in which, as it seems, Tito was liberalising with one hand but holding back the process with the other, the overall atmosphere was one of appearing to encourage debates and diverse – not to say pluralist – thinking on various social, political and cultural issues. It was precisely in this atmosphere that Aleksandar Petrović, and other young filmmakers-to-be, wrote on film and culture as described in the previous chapter. The incident that perhaps is most illustrative of this controversial liberalising process was the ousting and expulsion from the Central Committee of Milovan Djilas, one of the architects of self-management no less. Djilas, a pre-war communist and Tito's "brother in arms", developed a friendship with Aneurin Bevan of the Labour Party and became "impressed with the gradual progress toward socialism in Britain under a multi-party system" in 1951.[12] According to Jasna Dragović-Soso "Djilas continued to press for a greater democratisation of Yugoslavia's system, pushing out the boundaries of public discourse and, finally, directly challenging the legitimacy of the regime to which he himself belonged."[13] During 1953, Djilas published numerous articles in which he inveighed against the system he had also helped to create, claiming that many of his comrades were becoming a "new class" thirsty for power and commodities, and careerists far removed from the true spirit of communism.[14] He proposed the formation of other political parties – albeit all on a socialist platform – and free democratic elections as a solution. This was seen as true heresy by his comrades, and in January 1954 at the Fourth Plenum of the Central Committee – in the words of Dragović-Soso – "he was slandered and accused of being a traitor in the service of hostile Western forces" and promptly expelled from the party.[15] As a result, Milovan Djilas became the first "true" dissident in Tito's Socialist Yugoslavia.

Although Djilas's case reveals the scope of intellectual debate on political issues in the country, another aspect of life was also facing liberalisation on a significant scale: an aspect that would have a direct impact on the film industry and future career of Aleksandar Petrović. Tito's break with Stalin brought the economy to near collapse in 1949, as a result of which Petrović was practically jobless in 1950.[16] In the hope of having Yugoslavia as an ally in a potential war against the Soviet Union, the West decided to help Tito. This western aid, predominantly from the United States, injected life back into the Yugoslav economy in 1951, peaking in 1953.[17] After this period, Tito was practically compelled to introduce "a more competitive and export oriented"[18] – or, simply, more market – economy. This in return guaranteed further economic loans and continuing relations with the West. After Stalin's death in 1953, a discreet reconciliation with the Soviet Union began, although Glenny claims that Djilas was "forfeited" to appease the Soviets.[19] In 1955, Yugoslavia "normalised" its relations with the Soviet Union and "enjoyed such warm relations with the West while being acknowledged as a full, yet independent member of 'the socialist camp'."[20] This meant that the economy recovered from its earlier shock, and also that some financial surpluses began to flow into film production, as is evident from the increase in the number of films produced.[21] Along with the healthier economic situation, the laws on the decentralisation of production, which had previously made Petrović jobless, turning filmmakers into "free artists", finally seemed as if they were not actually introduced to cover up for the reductions in film funding but perhaps as a genuine attempt to better the industry. Aleksandar Petrović got his first opportunity to direct a film in 1955, at the age of 26.

2. 1. An Invitation from Vicko Raspor

As finances streamed back into the film industry, the law on the "free associations of workers" introduced on 27 June 1950, establishing the notion of "workers self-management",[22] heralded a new sensibility in film production. The law enabled freer and more modern tendencies to hit the Yugoslav film screens, both in form and in content. As described earlier, throughout the 1950s, there were many aspiring filmmakers, who spent their time writing passionately on film in various publications, with an intention to define precisely what these new films should look like. Aleksandar Petrović subsequently remembered this period of the early 1950s as being spent mainly in Belgrade's café bar Mažestik. Here, Vicko Raspor, then editor of the magazine *Film*, would have his drinks, while young aspiring film critics and filmmakers congregated around him.[23] Petrović called Raspor the "*spiritus movens*" of this group, which strongly pledged itself to the avant-garde tendencies in cinema.[24] Raspor, whom Petrović also praises as the best film critic of them all,[25] actively sought ways to put these ideas into practice. As a former art director of Zvezda Film where he had met the young Petrović,[26] Raspor was more familiar with the situation in the industry and had foreseen ways of capitalising on the improved financial situation once opportunities arose. Since the introduction of laws on decentralisation in 1951, when Zvezda Film had been incorporated into Avala Film, thereby becoming Serbia's major film studio,[27] Raspor had tried to develop the potential for increased independent production through UFUS (Udruženje Filmskih Umetnika Srbije – The Association of the Film Artists of Serbia), and had also participated in establishing the smaller film studio, Slavija Film.[28] All these production activities – major and minor – were funded by the republic;[29] thus it was only when the economy started to improve that the possibility emerged to activate these "non-central" film organisations.

2. 1. 1. *Shoulder to Shoulder*

Vicko Raspor had written a short documentary film with another journalist, Nusret Seferović. Seferović already had some minor scriptwriting experience, although at that time, any such experience could be considered significant. Together, they wrote a script entitled *Shoulder to Shoulder* (*Uz druga je drug*, literally *Comrade along a Comrade*), which was to be read as voice-over throughout the duration of the film.[30] The script, and hence the film, essentially retells the history of the International Workers' Movement, which at one point seamlessly segues into the history of the workers movement on the territory of what was to become Yugoslavia. Petar Volk, the Yugoslav film historian, assesses the film as showing how revolutionary activity in "various European cities affected the change in the workers' consciousness" in the lands that would become Yugoslavia.[31] However, when the narrative is placed in its political context, it is clear that the film attempts to show a more straightforward point that fitted with the official doctrines of the time.

The film opens with a citation from Karl Marx, which is then linked to the introduction of self-management in Yugoslavia, claiming that the act of handing factories over to workers' management is the correct realisation of Marx's aims. Indirectly, this meant that the Yugoslav path to communism (and, in 1955, the factories were handed to the self-managed workers' councils – as shown in this film), is the right path and true to Marxism, as opposed to the Soviet model, which believed in the interference of the state in running its enterprises. After such an opening, and in order to make this point even clearer, the narrative moves back in time to retell the history of the Viennese revolution, the Paris Commune, the life of Karl Marx and Friedrich Engels, and finally the history of the workers movements in Yugoslavia. In the Yugoslav part of the story, the emphasis is on Svetozar Marković, a "pre-socialist" who coined the term "self-management", and on Dimitrije Tucović, a leader of the pre-World War I Serbian social democrats, who voted against the war. The fact that Raspor and Seferović charted the history of the workers movement by identifying a direct link between Karl Marx and Yugoslav self-management, while carefully avoiding mention of the Soviet revolution, yet at the same time not excluding Lenin, shows that they followed the official line of the Yugoslav communists. This line sought to portray Yugoslav socialism as loyal to Karl Marx, and not to Stalin. Historian Dejan Jović claims that the change of the party's name from the "Communist Party of Yugoslavia" to the "League of Communists of Yugoslavia" in 1952 was done with precisely this ideological reason in mind,[32] to show that the state is not important but the idea is.[33] This is exactly what the script, and the film *Shoulder to Shoulder*, does: explains self-management as the embodiment of Marxist ideas. Consequently, the content of the first film Petrović co-directed unambiguously lionised the party doctrine. However, Petrović had not worked on the script.

Raspor was known as a film critic who believed that documentary films should be "strongly socially engaged",[34] which is certainly what *Shoulder to Shoulder* was. He also believed that stories should be told with "unconventional and modern film language",[35] and in order to achieve this for his script, he invited young Aleksandar Petrović to co-direct the film. He knew Petrović as a young assistant director and perhaps more significantly as a writer of film articles advocating "new cinema".[36] It may have been for these reasons that Raspor believed Petrović was the right person to help him with the film. Petrović invited Nikola Majdak to be the cameraman,[37] as the latter had also worked for Zvezda Film.[38] According to Nikola Majdak, who was a camera assistant on several films on which Petrović assisted the director, the two spent considerable time together discussing their future projects. Additionally, they both graduated on the same day in 1955, in History of Art at the Faculty of Philosophy, the University of Belgrade.[39] They shared alike sensibilities, which they brought to Raspor's project. While writing the script, Raspor had in mind a large archive in Belgrade that kept many documents, still photographs, prints, posters and other similar material from the history of International Workers Movement. It is out of this material, all still, that most of the 38-minute-long film was made. Raspor, according to Majdak, left Petrović and Majdak to film the material in a way that would suit the story and perhaps be "unconventional and modern". Nikola Majdak adds that Raspor had a more advisory role while he and Petrović started work on "illustrating" the script.

Funding was scarce and they used a very old camera for its time – a *Le Debrie*, model *Parvo L* from the 1920s – which nevertheless allowed them certain additional possibilities: they were able to wind the film back in the magazine, thereby creating in camera double exposures, fades and other basic film tricks. As there was no funding to create such effects in post-production, they had to be filmed in this way – in camera – so this was quite opportune. Majdak also notes that they improvised their film – or rather an animation – studio in a kitchen. They filmed all the material they had accumulated there, while Petrović and Majdak did their best to "liven it up". As Majdak was already familiar with animation techniques, he tried to add visual elements to the photographs, making them more cinematic. In a scene of the execution of Viennese students, he made the little hats on their heads fly away to simulate movement. Petrović added single flash frames in editing to simulate gunshots and explosions, which worked well with the soundtrack. Even with the photographs that were sometimes only the size of a matchbox, the two filmmakers always filmed them by starting with the image as a whole, and then moved the camera towards a detail in the picture, then towards another detail, and then back to the total, or the other way around. This was arduous work, particularly technically considering the equipment they had, but it proved fruitful in the end.[40]

As director, Petrović also looked for certain details in the photographs that had significance beyond the ostensible subject matter, but which could perhaps be linked with other material on a different plane. He settled for close-ups of hands, usually a worker's hands, which almost came to serve as a visual motif for the film. Such lyrical detail – a close-up of hands taken out of a larger image, which is not necessarily as gentle as the close-up may suggest – is a stylistic element that Petrović would develop in his later work; its embryo can be found in this very first project. During editing, he also added a brief newsreel sequence at the beginning of the film, containing "live action" footage, although the rest of the film remains an animation. With an intense and grandiose musical score by Aleksandar Obradović, *Shoulder to Shoulder* turned out to be quite a dynamic film with an unrelenting tempo. Were it not for its washed out black-and-white picture quality and crackly mono soundtrack, the film would look contemporary even today. Petrović later stated that he was proud of the work, explaining how difficult it had been to make a film using purely static material.[41] *Shoulder to Shoulder* was completed in late 1955, credited with co-direction by Vicko Raspor and Aleksandar Petrović. According to Petar Volk's study of the published reviews of the film,[42] and Nikola Majdak's memories,[43] it was as successful as a short documentary film could be at the time. The most significant indication of its success was that relatively soon afterwards, Petrović found opportunities to make more films, and his career moved swiftly on.

2. 1. 2. *Flight over the Swamp*

As *Shoulder to Shoulder* had been well received and Aleksandar Petrović had proved himself a capable and promising young director, his script for another short documentary film, *Flight over the Swamp* (*Let nad močvarom*), was accepted for production in 1956.[44] The atmosphere in Slavija Film was evidently favourable, so he quickly got another chance, although the studio only had the capacity to produce short documentaries. This time, the script was entirely Petrović's, and thus closer to the sensibility of the then 27-year-old filmmaker, in contrast to the previous film, which had handled rather complex historical and ideological issues that were clearly of more interest to the old revolutionary, Vicko Raspor. The script describes the wild life in the swamps of Pančevački Rit and Savska Močvara, not far from Belgrade.[45] Both places were quite well suited for photographing and filming, due to their natural beauty. Petrović's script is a love story of two ducks that are disturbed by a poacher. The scenes with the poacher were of course fictionalised, slightly disrupting the genuine documentary aspect of the film. However, such "reconstructions" of events were common in documentaries, as they still are today, particularly in television. In this film, the scenes with the poacher enabled Petrović to work with an actor, and make the film more dramatic and suspenseful. It also helped Petrović to have a wholesome storyline, which shows how a male wild duck flies back to help when a hunter shoots its mate, even though it means certain death for the surviving lover. The documentary thus revolved around this tragic love story of the wild birds.

Once the script was accepted by the studio, Petrović went on to direct the film on his own. He turned to Vicko Raspor for help, who wrote the text that would be read out as voice-over.[46] During the filming, Raspor came on sets occasionally,[47] but *Flight over the Swamp* became Aleksandar Petrović's truly first film. It is possible only to speculate on Raspor's lack of interest in the project, although it may be worth exploring some of these avenues. Nikola Majdak claims that Raspor was less interested in directing or making films, than in encouraging filmmaking and writing about cinema in general.[48] His later career tends to confirm this, because after he became the first artistic director and then director of Dunav Film, some of the most significant documentaries were made in Serbia during the 1960s and 1970s under his creative directorship.[49] Raspor could perhaps be considered a Bazinian figure in the history of Yugoslav New Film. In the case of this particular example, he was also probably not very inspired by Petrović's script, as it made no social or political comment. The film, which Ranko Munitić described as a "lyrical poem–metaphor on the love and death of two wild birds in a large swamp",[50] gives no insight into any of the social or political issues of the period, unlike his previous film. Consequently, it could be said that it lacks any input into understanding the political reality of the country at the time, and that its analysis would not contribute noticeably to the main theme of this book.

It is still important, however, to emphasise several other points. In a very positive review of the film published in the Belgrade daily newspaper, *Politika*, and signed only with the initials M. M., the reviewer notes that Petrović celebrates the beauty of nature, disturbed and spoilt by human intervention.[51] It would be perhaps too much to extrapolate Petrović's views on life and society from this possibly unintentional critique of human nature and behaviour. Regardless, it is worth noting that an aspect of general pessimism towards the human condition would persist throughout his later work and would become increasingly critical of society. To draw such a conclusion could not be argued for certain or suggested as deliberate on the filmmaker's part, but the primary significance of *Flight over the Swamp* is in the presence of Petrović's other motifs. As Munitić explained earlier, the film is about "love and death", and Petar Volk also emphasises that these two motifs are distinctly recognisable in this early work by Petrović.[52] Petrović himself accepted the motifs of love and death as part of his own "authorial persona", and one of the themes permeating his oeuvre.[53] He stated that it was the journalist Žika Bogdanović who had first defined these motifs as the crux of his authorial signature: they were afterwards widely accepted, as Petrović's work continued to revolve around them. These themes are clearly visible in this film, which is hence the first to be identified as Petrović's from an auteur theory point of view. Other major motifs developed with Petrović's later, more mature work. However, *Flight over the Swamp*, which Petrović completed in January 1957, had another significance.

In *Flight over the Swamp* Petrović, for the first time, worked with "live action" material rather than still images that needed to be animated. He showed great skill here, and stylistically made further progress in relation to his previous work. This time he worked with Jovan Jovanović as cameraman, as Nikola Majdak was doing his national service, although he joined the crew later.[54] While capturing the life of wild birds, Petrović resorted to frequent use of telephoto lenses and, consequently, often used close-ups. Following on from the previous film, he again chose to use details in order to convey atmosphere, as he continued to do in his later work. Particularly dramatic were the scenes with the poacher, an actor who was appropriately cast for the role. Close-ups of his sinister expression peering out from under his hunter's hat, with close-ups of his fingers cocking the gun, his eyes prying on the two birds in love, is closer to Hitchcock – and as Dušan Makavejev noted – certainly far away from "Flaherty or Disney".[55] This dramatic development indicates that Petrović really wanted to make fiction narratives, although his only opportunity was to film this documentary, into which he introduced drama and suspense. In this way, under the umbrella of the documentary genre, he subverted it creatively to his needs.

This 14-minute-long film, a short in the traditional sense so that it could fit onto one reel, demonstrated that Petrović had elaborate skills, and it was shown at the Cannes Film Festival in the same year. The film had a not insignificant budget for a short film and included a scene from a helicopter, as well as a brief underwater scene. Nevertheless, Petrović had to again be resourceful, particularly in the scenes where the camera appears as if gliding on water. These scenes were shot from a boat that could not use a motor, so as not to disturb the surface of the water. Petrović himself pushed the boat through a rather muddy and unpleasant swamp, earning his reputation as a doggedly committed filmmaker.[56] The scenes were thus again made attractive by any means possible, and were again rhythmically edited to the music, this time to Beethoven's *Pastoral*, securing the film favourable reactions in Cannes.[57] This early work certainly proved that Petrović had talent, and the *Politika* reviewer concluded:

> Aleksandar Petrović has mastered all the craft of contemporary cinematic expression. All the richness and complexity of the subject chosen for his film, he simplified to the classic sense of taste and measure.[58]

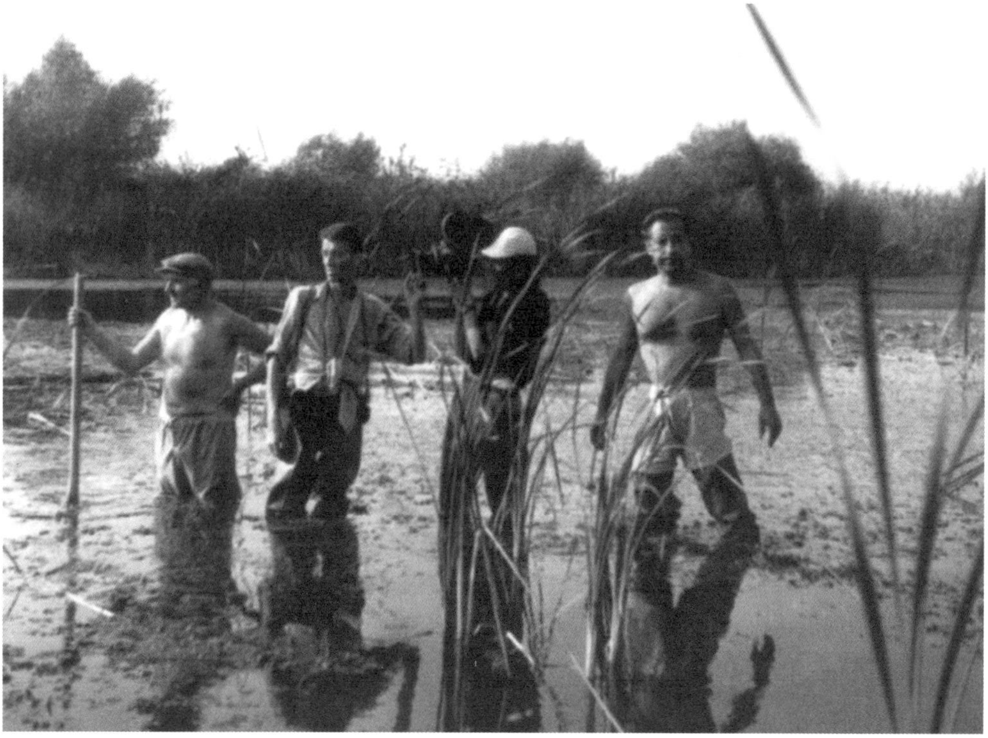

Figure 2.1: On the set of *Flight over the Swamp*: Aleksandar Petrović is first on the right.

2. 2. Raspor and Petrović: Rise and Fall

Vicko Raspor was older than Aleksandar Petrović and unquestionably better connected within the Yugoslav cultural and political establishment of the time. This was primarily due to the fact that he was a pre-war communist with an impeccable record as a resistance fighter,[59] someone who could have risen considerably higher within the post-war Yugoslav political establishment had he sought to. Instead, Raspor joined the film industry, in which his political record was certainly neither ignored nor forgotten. How were individuals entering the industry after the war to initiate and direct their own projects? This remains a mystery, but a good communist background certainly helped.[60] Nikola Majdak explained that he and Petrović used to send their ideas to the film studios in the early 1950s but none of these were ever accepted. He added that this might have been due to the fact that they were not only young and inexperienced, but also not members of the Communist Party.[61] Their entry into the industry hence came through Vicko Raspor, who was a communist, and who invited them to work on a film. After they had made *Shoulder to Shoulder*, Petrović then received an opportunity to direct on his own and make *Flight over the Swamp*. Although this appears as logical, it would be difficult to prove that one had to be a communist in order to make films. The next project Petrović and Majdak worked on came again purely through Raspor's connections, friends and his good will to have them on board.[62]

Vicko Raspor was a close friend of Miroslav Krleža, one of the most influential intellectuals in post-war Yugoslavia. Krleža was a writer and one of the first card-carrying communists in the Kingdom of Yugoslavia.[63] He was a somewhat controversial persona, staying in Zagreb during the war where he continued working, although he was not associated with Ante Pavelić's fascist regime. The fact that after the war the communists never questioned whether he collaborated or not explains what his intellectual authority meant in the country.[64] Sometime in the 1950s, Krleža entertained himself with the idea of writing a film script having published in probably all literary forms.[65] The script was to be for a short documentary film on his friend Petar Dobrović, a Belgrade painter who died tragically in a lift shaft just before the war in 1941. Dobrović, an unquestionable artistic talent, also had a colourful biography, which included his participation in the Béla Kun's communist revolution in Hungary just after World War I.[66] Krleža had been Dobrović's friend, and he now wanted to honour his life and work with a short film. Raspor managed to convince Krleža that Petrović and he should direct this project. The film was produced by Zagreb Film, a smaller studio for documentaries and animation, based in Croatia, and Nikola Majdak and Jovan Jovanović (who had filmed *Flight over the Swamp*), were to be cameramen on the project.

2. 2. 1. *Petar Dobrović*

Miroslav Krleža's script was not really a screenplay, but a text to be read out as voice-over during the film. As with *Shoulder to Shoulder*, it was now up to the filmmakers to illustrate the narration, again with considerable freedom. Krleža's text charted the main biographical details of Dobrović's life, placing a heavy accent on his painterly style. As Petrović and Majdak had recently graduated in History of Art, they were undeniably suitable for the job. This film similarly provided no social comment on Yugoslavia, and is thus not directly relevant to the subject of this investigation. Nevertheless, Petrović's stylistic development during the production is worthy of a brief analysis. While the project was already in production, in September 1957, Petrović got married.[67] He spent his honeymoon in Dubrovnik where several scenes for the film were to be shot. His wife Branislava – Branka – helped out during the production, and at one point, carried one of the camera batteries,[68] which further contributed to her husband's reputation as a stubbornly committed filmmaker. This anecdote is not the only one to indicate the level of commitment the filmmakers had for the project. Nikola Majdak, for example, brought back stones and pressed leaves and flowers from Dalmatia, in order to be able to show them to the film laboratory technicians so that the colours could be meticulously matched to the real objects they had filmed.[69] This was their first film to be shot in colour.

Like *Shoulder to Shoulder*, there was no live action in the film and its images mainly consisted of the painter's studio, the paintings themselves and frequent images of Dalmatia, the landscapes of which had been an inspiration and model for Dobrović's work. Dalmatian colours and light were, according to the script, Dobrović's ultimate stimulation, and he dropped the influences of classical and modernist painters alike for the natural glow of this part of the Balkans. It is this authentic light and colour that the film manages to capture. Further emphasising Dobrović's obsession with colour, the filmmakers included a scene with revolving primary colours, produced as a cinematic optical effect but edited to correspond to several of Dobrović's motifs. The work they had done on *Shoulder to Shoulder* helped them bring "the stillness" of the paintings to life. One of the more memorable images is of a slow camera pan over one of the details from the paintings. A small boat with a sail, floating in the sea, is scanned by the camera from left to right several times, suggesting the illusion of movement but, at the same time, (self-) awareness of this manipulation. The filmmakers thus deftly simulated movement, but playfully revealed this simple cinematic trick. As in their previous film, the editing is restless, even vivacious, not allowing viewers time for respite. In terms of stylistic elements, the film again discloses a propensity for detail, where a telephoto lens was used to enable the details to convey the atmosphere. These elements were to become a part of all of Petrović's future work, in addition to the music that defined the rhythm of editing, which also features in *Petar Dobrović*. The space to visually abscond from the paintings and landscapes arises when the only salient biographical detail enters the narrative – the fact that Dobrović died in a lift. At that moment, Petrović and Raspor come closest to an ordinary documentary by filming the lift shaft, and Dobrović's self-portrait descending into the darkness, literally illustrating this tragic event.

The film *Petar Dobrović* was under 14 minutes in duration and was completed at the very end of 1957.[70] With the images of paintings and Dalmatia in the sunshine, the film was visually very seductive and was highly praised in an early review by the film journalist, Stevo Ostojić. Writing in *Politika*, he called the film "a significant film debut by Miroslav Krleža",[71] ascribing the film's qualities to its famous "scriptwriter". This review demonstrates how difficult it was for the young filmmakers to make a name for themselves. In the opening credits for the film, Krleža's name appears first, thus Ostojić perhaps should not be criticised for seeing the film as Krleža's, who was in his life to write only one more script, for another short documentary.[72] Ostojić also praises all the four filmmakers (both directors: Petrović and Raspor; and the cameramen: Majdak and Jovanović) adding that it is commendable that "the circle of filmmakers is getting wider" and that it is positive that new names and talent have emerged in the Yugoslav film industry.[73] The film was screened later in 1958 at the Yugoslav National Film Festival at Pula, but Raspor and Petrović's talent was actually noticed slightly earlier when they got an opportunity to make their first full-length feature film.

2. 2. 2. *The Only Exit*

Zastava Film was a film studio belonging to the Yugoslav People's Army, whose primary purpose was to produce educational films and newsreels. Its role was also to maintain the image of the glorious War for Liberation against the Nazis, the war that was, according to Dejan Jović, "turned into one of the main constitutive myths of Socialist Yugoslavia."[74] The studio hence produced its share of Partisan films, the genre Andrew Horton defines as "an instructive example of filmmakers generating national identity and 'history'",[75] further explaining that in a country as culturally diverse as Yugoslavia, "cinema emerged as the perfect unifying medium."[76] The war or Partisan film was thus an important representation of this identity and production of this "genre" never faltered, from the very first film *Slavica* in 1947 to the last winner of the Yugoslav Pula Film Festival in 1990 – *Silent Gunpowder* (*Gluvi barut*) – also a Partisan film.[77] According to the film historian Daniel Goulding, the early 1950s saw a "re-examination of war experience and its aftermath".[78] In particular, films on the war by Žika Mitrović, who made them as action thrillers, were very popular.[79] It was perhaps with this in mind that, in early 1958, Zastava Film acquired a script by Antonije Isaković, a war veteran and emerging writer who was joined by the scriptwriter, Stjepan Zaninović, to dramatise a real event of Partisan action against the Nazis during the war. The script – *The Only Exit* – was then entrusted to Vicko Raspor and Aleksandar Petrović, supposedly with the hope that they would be capable of illustrating it as they had their documentaries, in a new and original way. However, this did not happen. According to Petar Volk, Raspor and Petrović did not like the script, but at the same time they would not give up an opportunity to direct a feature film.[80] Upon the film's release, the script was criticised for being full of clichés, characters that suffer from lack of motivation and for its plot being predictable and revealing in its title.[81] Frustrated by the script on the shoot, both directors nevertheless continued making their first feature-length fiction film with actors. Raspor, as Petrović's senior colleague, perhaps anticipated that he would be under pressure should the film fail. He thus decided to take greater control of the project. As a consequence, Raspor and Petrović ended up arguing and disagreeing consistently.[82] The film was completed in the summer of 1958,[83] and shown at the Pula Film Festival to an exceptionally bad reception. It is interesting to note that the forthright attacks on the film were most often directed at Raspor because, according to Ranko Munitić, Raspor had himself always been a very harsh critic. Now that he had made a film that happened to be vulnerable to criticism, the assaults were so severe that Raspor gave up filmmaking completely and almost ceased his film criticism.[84] He worked afterwards in Dunav Film, a smaller-scale studio, as an art director,[85] where he helped Petrović with later projects.[86] Evidently, Raspor and Petrović remained friends, while their decision to accept the offer from Zastava Film to direct *The Only Exit* with hindsight seems opportunist and naïve. However, it was a decision that had a lasting and mainly jarring effect on their careers.

As *The Only Exit* was neither initiated nor scripted by Petrović, and only co-directed by him, it is difficult to extract with certainty from it any of his personal views, either on the political or social state of the country, or on art and life in general. Further analysis of the film would be unlikely to unearth anything constructive concerning either the author or the time and space in which he worked. However, it may still be worth exploring what the film meant for his career, and speculating on one narrative motif that would emerge in his later intellectual inquiries. Firstly, working on a feature-length fiction film in that capacity for the first time was undoubtedly a useful experience for young Petrović. Although the acting might appear somewhat stilted and unconvincing, for first-time directors this is not uncommon. However, Petrović subsequently employed Mija Aleksić – who has a part in the film – in three of his later films.[87] To cast Aleksić though was an unfortunate choice, as by that point he had already become a popular comedian on Serbian television. As a consequence, regardless of his admirable acting skills, audiences frequently laughed as soon as he appeared on screen.[88] This was not what his role entailed, and Raspor and Petrović were admonished for their work with actors.[89] If their work with the cast was not commended, their visual artistry certainly was. The film was neatly photographed by Jovan Jovanović in colour; no small achievement considering the stock and equipment available, in conjunction with the fact that most of the film was set in a cave without natural light and with only limited scope for manoeuvring studio lights.[90] The two directors were more successful on this level, staging spectacular explosions and battle scenes in the famous grotto of the Postojnska Jama.[91] Again, a sense of detail fed the story: for example, close-ups of cigarette butts revealed the number of Partisans involved in the depicted action. Milutin Čolić stated in his review that the directors "provided viewers with a nice collection of images", which are "dramatically dysfunctional."[92] Regardless, producing the film was inevitably a significant training for Petrović, and finally, there was an aspect of the film that could be perceived as a foreboding.

The story observes a small group of Partisan Special Forces who destroy German facilities deep behind their lines. The drama revolves around the arrival of a new commander just before they are about to go into action. One member of the group distrusts the new commander, whereas another does so hesitantly and with tragic consequences. Although the "rebel" in the group learns that commanders ought to be trusted, the narrative explores the notion of questioning authority. The fact that authority is reasserted in the end, and subsequently portrayed as benevolent, enables an interpretation of the film as affirmative of the politics and ideology that produced it. However, the existence of this theme – the questioning of authority – is something that would continue in Petrović's mature work, and would lead him towards his criticism of dogmatism. To pursue this line of investigation further with this particular film would be highly speculative considering the level of Petrović's involvement, the context in which the film was produced (the army's film studio) and the reception the film had. Milica Zdražilová assessed the film in a later article as being "in terms of its form and content completely within the framework of Yugoslav production of the time with limited perspectives of genre and expression."[93] Petrović never renounced the film, although he held it in low esteem,[94] and 20 years later commented: "We tried to make an entertaining, slightly adventurous film, whilst we should have made a serious film, which would also have been entertaining."[95] As opposed to Raspor's, his filmmaking career was far from over.

2. 3. Reclaiming the Experience

2. 3. 1. *The Roads*

Both films, *The Only Exit* and *Petar Dobrović*, were shown at the Pula Film Festival in the summer of 1958. As outlined earlier, the documentary was well received, the feature fiction was not. Nevertheless, Aleksandar Petrović was undeterred. He wanted to capitalise on his collaboration with Vicko Raspor that had been valued, and in the same vein wrote a script on his favourite painter – Sava Šumanović. The project was to be another short documentary similar to *Petar Dobrović*, as there could presumably be no doubt that he could produce another accomplished film on a painter and his work. The script was submitted to Avala Film, the major film studio in Serbia, and accepted. Petrović therefore embarked on the second project to be scripted and directed by himself, after *Flight over the Swamp*. The short documentary on the Serbian painter Sava Šumanović was filmed in the autumn of 1958, and completed in colour at the very end of that year.[96] As the first screenings of the film took place in 1959, this is often taken as the year of the film's production. It was released under the title *The Roads* (*Putevi*) and became a much celebrated short film. It brought Petrović his first significant awards: firstly, an award for artistic achievements to commemorate the Serbian National Day in July 1959;[97] and secondly, a prestigious award at the Pula Film Festival in August of the same year.[98] Petrović had invited his old friend and collaborator Nikola Majdak to be cameraman, and he too received awards for his work on this, and other short films he photographed that year.[99] An indication of *The Roads'* acclaim was not only in the awards that it did or did not receive,[100] but also in the fact that it was much loved and admired by Petrović's contemporaries and two well-known filmmakers-to-be – Živojin Pavlović[101] and Dušan Makavejev.[102] The film, lasting just under 18 minutes, managed to provide biographical details of Sava Šumanović in a political and historical context, while at the same time focusing on an analysis of his paintings. The script could also be perceived as skilfully accomplished, as it was slightly shorter than Miroslav Krleža's on *Petar Dobrović*,[103] providing the same relevant information. As the latter was considerably shorter in duration, it is evident that Petrović in *The Roads* manages to say more with images than in the voice-over. Like *Petar Dobrović*, *The Roads* is an artist's biography and an essay in style, which perhaps hints at the growing political liberalisation in the country at the end of the decade. The film neither engages in social issues nor is redolent with the party lingo as *Shoulder to Shoulder* is. Nevertheless, the film verifies Petrović's initial evolution as a filmmaker, particularly in his cinematic style and his ability to develop content. It is therefore worthwhile to survey and briefly explore some characteristics of this film, specifically his rather mature contemplation on the nature of art and the destiny of artists from "marginal" cultures.

The film is an essay on Sava Šumanović, a prodigal son of Yugoslav painting, who was arrested as an ethnic Serb and executed by the Croatian fascists in 1942. Petrović starts his film with a brief interview with the painter's mother, an old lady who remembers the morning when the police of the NDH[104] came to arrest her son, and take him away down his favourite road, which he had painted relentlessly, thus inspiring the title of the film – *The Roads*. Petrović's script then quickly moves back in time to observe the young and talented Šumanović in Paris for the first time, where he went to try his luck in the world capital of painting. After several exhibitions and shows, Šumanović's health deteriorated due to his bohemian lifestyle. He was known to be mentally sensitive and was thus soon back in Yugoslavia for rehabilitation, where he kept on painting while cherishing memories of his Parisian experience.

Petrović proceeds to explore Šumanović's thoughts on art, particularly the ones that were relevant to the filmmaker. Šumanović was obsessed with the issue of originality in art and, in being original himself. He sought to create his own artistic world, which would be his contribution to art – both formally and ethically. The film shows how Šumanović went back to Paris for the second time in the 1930s as a stronger artist and painter, but sadly no more mentally stout. After shows that attracted attention in a vigorously competitive atmosphere,

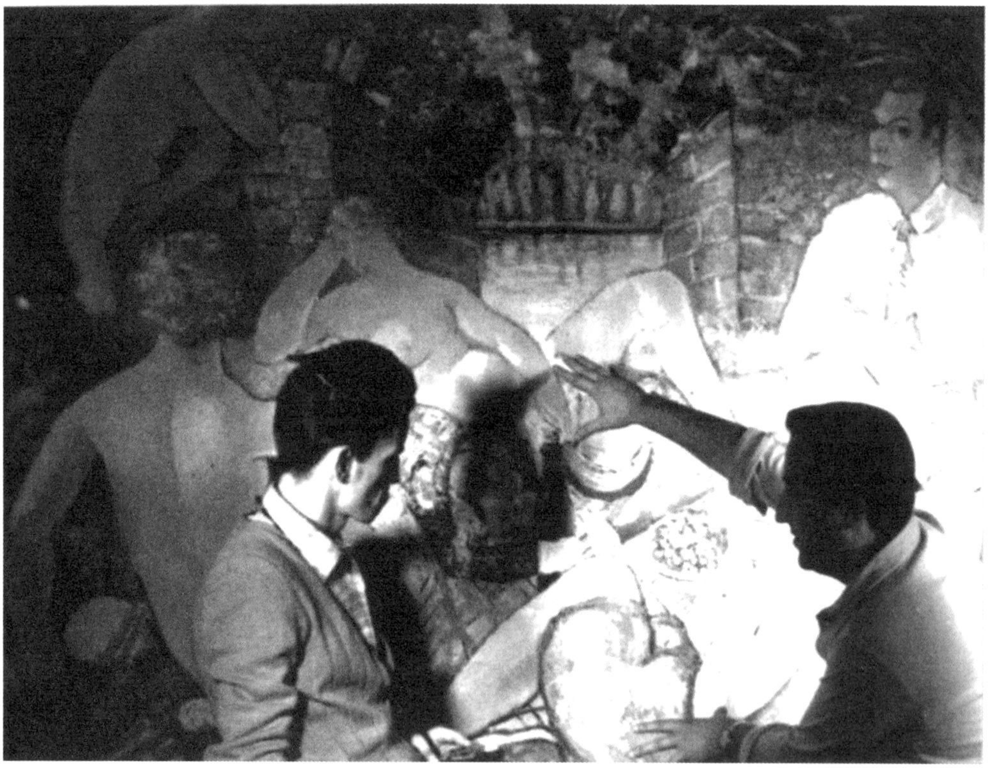

Figure 2.2: In front of a large-scale canvas by Sava Šumanović: cameraman Nikola Majdak (left) and Aleksandar Petrović (right).

Šumanović exhibited one of his early masterpieces, *The Drunken Boat* (*Pijani brod*), an interesting amalgamation of cubism and fauvism combined with his own sensibility. The painting depicted a debauched party on a little vessel, which caused uproar and mixed reactions. Even though it was beneficial for the young painter that the Paris scene was debating his painting, his fragile state of mind was not capable of coping, and Šumanović had a nervous breakdown. He returned to Yugoslavia again and started recovering slowly in his village where he was in peace. Once he started painting again he developed a new technique, which brought him even closer to his ideal of true art. Petrović summarised this in his script, explaining that Šumanović almost completely dropped brushes and started painting with a painters' knife. At the outbreak of World War II, Šumanović stopped signing his paintings as a sign of internal protest.

Although he had clues that in his town of Šid in Serbia, which is very close to the border with Croatia, Croatian fascists had begun persecuting Serbs, Šumanović refused to leave. This was a tragic mistake, and Petrović's script supports the assumption that he was still so mentally disturbed that he did not understand how precarious the real situation was. He was arrested and shot dead with hundreds of other Serbs, and then thrown in a mass grave. When the grave was opened after the war and his body identified, experts believed that he had still been alive when buried and his eyes were wide open, full of limestone thrown in the grave by the executioners.

Petrović ended his film with this tragic story but emphasised that art lives on. Stylistically, Petrović is closer in this film to more traditional ideas of documentary. The camera often follows the script when the paintings are filmed, and in Petrović's now usual manner, focuses on details rather than choosing objects more obvious due to their visual attractiveness. Petrović introduces negative film stock in a scene depicting Šumanović's breakdown, as well as various animation techniques when searching for cinematic equivalents to Šumanović's paintings.[105] This experimentation was again under firm control, and was employed to invigorate the narrative rather than as an aim in itself. Petrović's formal innovation was carefully integrated into the more traditional documentary form, making the film very dynamic and at the same time coherent in its content. For his economic but frequent exploitation of cinematic means to pursue his narrative, Petrović was assessed by Dušan Makavejev as the filmmaker who "perfectly knows not only the laws of film poetry, but also the laws of film technology."[106] Due to this measured interplay of form and content, both his short films on painting are praised by the film critic Slobodan Novaković:

> *The Roads* and *Petar Dobrović* are not only films on painting, which manage to inform us in a subtle way on the creative opuses of Šumanović and Dobrović, but are films on the intimate human drama of the artists themselves.[107]

Petrović raised another interesting subject in his script, based on Šumanović's experience. The young painter arrived in Paris from a "small" nation inhabiting a poor country. To what extent was his work to influence the global culture, or culture in general? Whether this is irrelevant, or whether artists from "smaller" cultures have to produce proportionately larger and more significant work in comparison with their peers from wealthier nations in order to be noticed and affect the bigger market, remains the question posed by Šumanović's case and is underlined by Petrović in this film. Here there is a significant parallel between Šumanović's and Petrović's later career, whereas the filmmaker's focus on this aspect of the painter's experience proved prophetic for him. In his years in exile, decades after this short film, the issue of an artist from a "small" country was to re-emerge again in Petrović's life.[108]

2. 3. 2. *The War on War*

The awards and critical triumph of *The Roads* during 1959 solidified the relations of Aleksandar Petrović and Avala Film in Belgrade, which produced the film. Petrović could at that point boast that he had directed two short films, co-directed another two shorts, co-directed a feature and also had experience as an assistant director. Added to this one year of studying filmmaking and a set of published magazine articles, Petrović confidently submitted a script for his first feature film to the studio with him as director in 1959.[109] Avala Film expressed a genuine interest in the script, but before they were able to produce it, another short documentary came into being. Aleksandar Petrović directed *The War on War* (*Rat ratu*) for them, and this 19-minute film was completed at the end of 1960.[110]

If *The Roads* was Petrović's attempt to rework and reclaim his experience of *Petar Dobrović*, then it appears even more evident that *The War on War* was a reworking of his other, or rather first collaboration with Vicko Raspor, *Shoulder to Shoulder*. Nusret Seferović, who co-scripted the latter with Vicko Raspor, was back to write the script on his own for the new project.[111] As *Shoulder to Shoulder* told the story of the national and international workers' movements, including brief histories of revolutions and key figures in these events, it can be assessed as somewhat overambitious in scope for its 38 minutes. Seferović hence dropped such a historical scale for *The War on War* to focus on a single figure that the previous project had merely reflected on in passing – that of Dimitrije Tucović. As the film teaches us, he was the first editor of a Marxist newspaper in the Balkans, a leader of various workers groups and demonstrations, and finally, from 1908, the leader of the Social Democrat Party of the Kingdom of Serbia. Tucović was also curiously born on 1 May 1881.[112] As the film focuses on only one protagonist from the socialist movement, the film manages to be a detailed and well paced biography of Dimitrije Tucović, and it could be perceived as having a better structured and more coherent narrative than the overwhelmingly broad *Shoulder to Shoulder*. It astutely emphasises the idea that many European social democrats prior to World War I abandoned their internationalist principles by trying to reconcile nationalism and socialism. This opened a path for the possibility of the first Great War. Tucović was one of those rare social democrats who fervently opposed the idea that the working classes of different nations should be killing each other, and he embraced the motto of another social democrat who also opposed the war.

This was the Russian, Vladimir Ilich Lenin, who famously proclaimed "the war on war", an idea Tucović accepted and supported, even when mobilised at the beginning of the war. This anti-war slogan plainly inspired the title of the film. Petrović directed the story, making certain parameters explicitly clear, and Tucović and his pacifist socialists are portrayed as good, whereas the forces of international capital supported by the imperialist policies of the Great Powers are exposed as reckless culprits for the first great tragedy of the twentieth century. It is therefore easy to conclude that with this work, Petrović, as with *Shoulder to Shoulder*, accepted the view of history framed by the socialist ideology in power at the time, and also unambiguously propagates this view in the film.

Stylistically, as well as in its content, *The War on War* is not much different from *Shoulder to Shoulder*. The only major disparity is that *The War on War* was filmed in colour and Petrović uses this in a daringly interesting way. The use of colour film is somewhat surprising as again most of the material for this film came from old photographs and black-and-white documents, so filming them in colour was simply futile. Petrović, evidently aware of this, downplays colour almost completely – which was rather courageous for 1960, when colour film was still very precious – making his film look more sepia, thus in tune with the archival material he was filming. However, he brings the density of colour back on two occasions only, in order to clarify certain points. The first time is when he shows the Serbian national three-coloured flag, as the narrative explains Serbian nationalism was a liberation movement from Imperialist supremacy. The story moves on to describe how Tucović soon thought that nationalism had to be abandoned for internationalism – representing true philanthropy and humanism. Tucović believed in this as a Marxist, who also promoted socialism as the system in which exploitation and discrimination would disappear. Thus, after showing the Serbian flag in full colour, towards the end of the film Petrović also shows the international red flag with the yellow hammer and sickle in deeply saturated colours. Serbian nationalism thus needed to be replaced with the humanist proletarian internationalism. This of course fitted into the official doctrine in Yugoslavia, so that Petar Volk criticises the film as an evident piece of agitprop of its time, a rare example of Petrović not demonstrating his critical wit. Volk also speculates that Petrović had probably been obliged to accept this project.[113] However, in an interview, Petrović's widow Branka stated that her husband never felt compelled to take on any film project. He had genuinely found Tucović an admirable historical person, and a worthy subject for a film.[114] Considering that Dimitrije Tucović represents the most humane and philanthropic understanding of Marxism, coupled with his tragic death in the war he opposed,[115] it would be difficult not to agree with her point of view. Petrović made this film voluntarily, out of his own beliefs, as they corresponded with Tucović's idealistic views on socialism as a society that could be truly egalitarian and nonviolent. Although both Volk's and Branka Petrović's view on the filmmaker's motives are speculative, it is clear from the films that Petrović made in the late 1950s that he was very sympathetic to the ideology Yugoslavia had embraced, and towards the system Socialist Yugoslavia was creating. However, how this would develop in the early 1960s is the subject of the rest of this chapter.

2. 4. First Films, First Problems

The reception of *The War on War* was not as enthusiastic as for *The Roads*, and the film neither received awards nor was specifically singled out at festivals. This may be indicative that 1960 was a breakthrough year for Yugoslavia, a year in which it became clear that the country was on the path of liberalisation. Films that appeared to regurgitate the party's doctrine were thus no longer as popular or attractive. Furthermore, the fact that *The Roads*, a biography of a troubled painter, did well, whereas *The War on War*, a biography of a politician, did not, suggested an intellectual atmosphere in 1960. Petrović remembered this mood at Avala Film, where its new director Ratko Dražević felt that the studio had to start with something fresh, and abandon the simplistic political propaganda of the post-war years.[116] Dražević was a truly controversial character, a pre-war communist who had fought in the war and become a high-ranking officer of the notorious State Security Service (OZNA, later SDB). However, he eventually ended up in the film export company Jugoslavija Film, and then became general director of Avala Film.[117] According to Petrović, Dražević brought about important and very constructive changes very quickly, employing Borislav Mihajlović Mihiz as his advisor.[118] Mihiz was, according to Jasna Dragović-Soso, "a prominent literary critic and a well-known intellectual nonconformist" who often fell foul of the authorities.[119] Dražević's choice may therefore appear somewhat curious. According to Petrović, these two new helmsmen of the studio (one an ex-policeman, the other a dissident)[120] pledged themselves to regenerate the cadre of film directors.[121] As Yugoslavia received a major economic credit from the USA in 1960 that visibly refreshed the economy,[122] 1961 became one of the best years for the film industry, with 32 films released.[123] Following Dražević and Mihiz's pledge, which was in the spirit of the rest of the country, many of these films were by first-time directors. According to Daniel Goulding, the most significant films out of these 32 belonged to such debutants, namely Boštjan Hladnik with his *A Dance in the Rain* (*Ples v dežju*) and Aleksandar Petrović with *Two* (*Dvoje*).[124]

2. 4. 1. *Two*

As early as 1952, Aleksandar Petrović defined what he fervidly believed an aesthetic of New Film should be: it should consist of "material for specific arguments – arguments to be written with the camera."[125] Petrović had an almost romantic commitment to the ideas yearning for a more cinematic language in films, and wrote extensively on this subject during the 1950s.[126] It was perhaps to be expected that when he got a chance to direct his first full-length feature on his own, this film would be a little manifesto or pamphlet of the New Film language, as Petrović often declared his first film *Two* to be.[127] Petrović explained his stylistic concerns and struggle for the New Film language as being against the hegemony of the narrative. In a later interview given to Ivo Pondělíček of Prague's film magazine, *Film A Doba*, Petrović articulated his main ideas by claiming that he abandons "the dramaturgy of the 'I'm telling you a story' type", further explaining:

I am not dramatising stories, but so much as the inner poetic content of the work. I am not explaining ideas; I try to dramatise psychological and emotional states, rather than actions. That which is usually understood as the story serves, in my films, only as a necessary requisite of "reality", as a certain kind of life façade, behind which "the real" things are happening – the internal life.[128]

Although this interview was given eight years after *Two* was made,[129] the statement articulates perfectly and concisely Petrović's artistic intentions for all his films, which were clearly apparent in his first. The first film – *Two* – thus became an exercise in formal exhibitionism, a catalogue of purely "cinematic" means of telling a story. Petrović already used these elements in his short documentaries. Therefore, in *Two*, he uses negative film in one scene, animates still photographs for another, uses frame-within-a-frame techniques, and makes the camera as mobile as possible, even filming from a merry-go-round. He also resorts to certain "associative" scenes, as when a lover is waiting for another, he shows children playing hide-and-seek. Similarly, an abandoned lover observes empty benches and spaces – hence creating visual associations, which Petrović called "open metaphors". In the opening scene, he took the camera to the streets of Belgrade to capture "real" passers-by, and the film's protagonists amongst them. After its first screening at the Pula Film Festival in the summer of 1961, the film found supporters amongst many young filmmakers-to-be. Živojin Pavlović, who very much loved the opening scene and mentioned it in his own written manifestos,[130] found the film to be "a complete work" in which "Petrović transformed sheer banality into pure film poetry."[131] For the young Pavlović, it was certainly commendable and recognisable that "Petrović completely abandoned narration, choosing metaphor instead as the basis for his film language."[132] Daniel Goulding states that the film clearly triggered mixed reactions, with more conservative critics vehemently disparaging it, mainly for the lack of characterisation and the superficial storyline.[133] It is probably true that Petrović in his attempt to create his own artistic language, as had his hero painter Sava Šumanović, had sacrificed the narrative, making it somewhat secondary.

The story itself was very plain. A young architect Mirko (Miha Baloh) meets a student of music Jovana (Beba Lončar) and falls for her. They start a relationship, which lasts for a year, but he then realises that he is not in love anymore and breaks the relationship off. This very simple narrative, the characters of which are painted with the widest strokes possible, with few supporting characters, reasonably disappointed viewers and critics who had no sympathy for formal developments. Petrović's characters are also very middle-class – an architect and a student of music – and their meetings at classical concerts and in theatres demonstrated the existence of such a class in socialist Belgrade. That this was an intended issue Petrović wanted to raise with this film would be difficult to argue, even though Petrović was known to point out that such a bourgeois class existed in Yugoslavia and had the "same problems" as their counterparts anywhere else.[134] However, as this was not shown with any intention of social criticism in mind (and it would be difficult to extract any from this film on two lacklustre lovers), it could

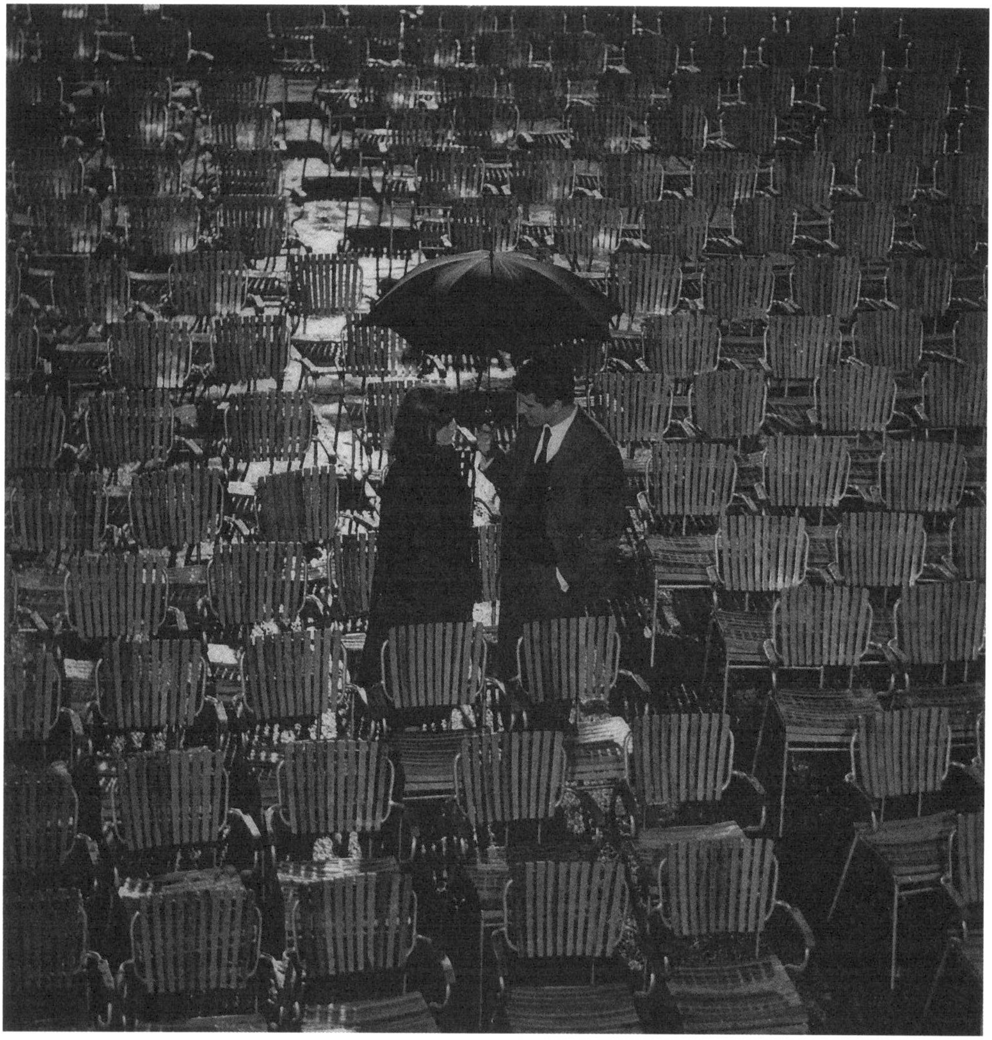

Figure 2.3: *Two*: lovers in an empty outdoor cinema.

be concluded that Petrović's first film lacks any social criticism or observation. Although it shows the streets of Belgrade incessantly, it was also deprived of any real context as well. This love story for Petrović had a different kind of political significance. For him, the film was intended to belong to a group of films he called "intimate films".[135] *Two* could be understood as one of the first of the intimate films where Petrović's radicalism existed in the fact that he deliberately rejected the tradition of socialist filmmaking of the time.[136] He did so by depriving the film of any celebration of social progress and settling for what Goulding calls an exploration of a "failed love relationship, played out in an alienated urban environment."[137] The focus on love stories often meant that a post-Stalinist thaw had started in the films of the Soviet Union and some of its other satellite countries.[138] In Yugoslavia this was not strictly the case, and a love story in itself was not necessarily a groundbreaking factor.

After the Pula Film Festival, the film was invited to Cannes, where it represented Yugoslavia in 1962.[139] In Yugoslavia, Petrović received an October Prize for the film, a major award from the city of Belgrade.[140] It could be said that overall, *Two* was successful in Yugoslavia, and it enabled Petrović to continue working, even though the film's international reactions were as mixed as the ones in Yugoslavia. The French critic Gilbert Guez praised the fact that "the film continuously invents its own language" and thus "innovates" discreetly.[141] The English critic John Francis Lane in his report from Cannes, obviously unimpressed with the formal innovations, assessed the film as "a modest love story with no particular merits."[142] It could be said that with time, *Two*'s formal innovations, which have now become common in cinematic language, are no longer as interesting, so that watching the film with this temporal distance makes its feeble storyline stand out, hence is overall not as interesting as upon its release. However, the real value of *Two* is historical, as it not only truly started Aleksandar Petrović's career, but also "open[ed] up new paths of development in Yugoslav feature films", as Daniel Goulding assessed it.[143] Petrović's first film, with Hladnik's *A Dance in the Rain*, spearheaded the Yugoslav New Film, a new wave in national filmmaking.

There is one subtle trait, however, which could be extrapolated from Petrović's slender narrative, a trait that would significantly develop in his later work. *Two* takes as its main motif the impermanence of human relationships and the fragile nature of love. What becomes the main existential problem for its protagonist Mirko is his understanding that he is unable to form a lasting relationship, and that he falls out of love as easily as he falls in love. Petrović's accomplishment here is that he is not concerned with explaining this, or exploiting it for melodramatic purposes, but he needs this situation so that his character can face his own shortcomings. This problem reappeared in most of his films where the drama revolved around his characters having to face themselves and realise their own mistakes and misgivings. This then becomes the real drama of his film, whereas plots and subplots are only the means to reach a point where the characters have to get to know themselves, however awkward that might be. Mirko, visibly upset with himself, asks his best friend, before the end of the film, why he has failed again. Petrović is not judgemental at this point – quite the contrary. He may even want us, arguably, to empathise with his character. He shows human beings as obviously not perfect, and that as this imperfection is deep in human nature, it cannot be held against us. This struggle to face oneself would become particularly interesting as it acquired a social dimension. A similar idea would pervade his next film; only in that instance such thinking was understood as political defeatism, perhaps because the new socialist state could not become what it had set out to be, with individuals wallowing in their imperfections, just like the characters of Petrović's films.

2. 4. 2. *Days* – the Premise

In the autumn of 1962, Aleksandar Petrović had already commenced filming his next feature *Days* (*Dani*),[144] which was completed in the spring of 1963.[145] Petrović's arrangement with Avala Film was pretty much the same as with his first film. He directed the film on one-third of the average budget, thus he had to work, in his own words, "very economically."[146] Regardless, the low budget evidently meant no tampering with the project from the studio, so Petrović expressed no remorse about the scarcity of funds.[147] It appears that the most

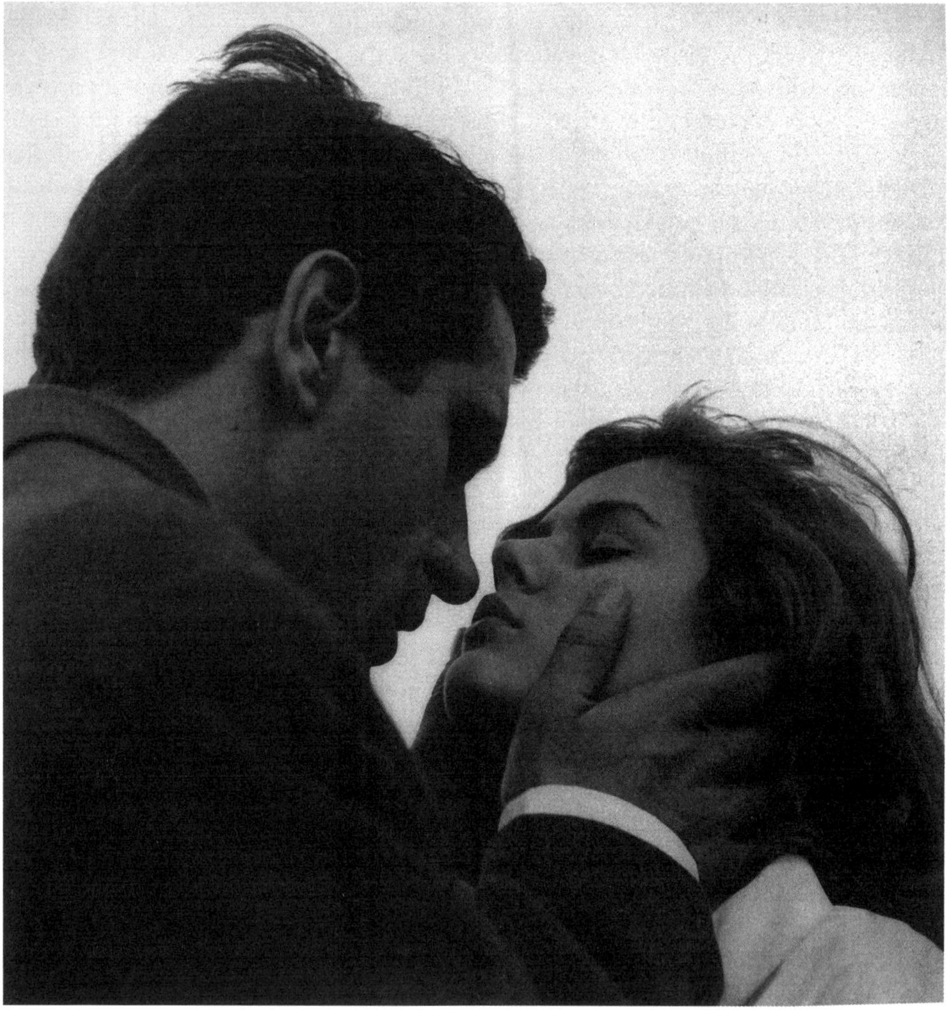

Figure 2.4: *Two*: Miha Baloh as Mirko and Beba Lončar as Jovana.

important thing for him was to continue working. The second film *Days* is, in many respects, quite similar to *Two*, which partly may have something to do with the similar conditions of production. Stylistically, Petrović sacrificed some of the visual flamboyance of the first film to open up space for a more complex narrative. In comparison, *Days* was thus subjected to considerably less cataloguing and demonstration of cinematic language. This does not mean that Petrović abandoned his project of creating moods at the expense of showing action. On the contrary, *Days* is also very much a film of moods and emotions just like its predecessor, but the main difference lies in the fact that the visual elements were

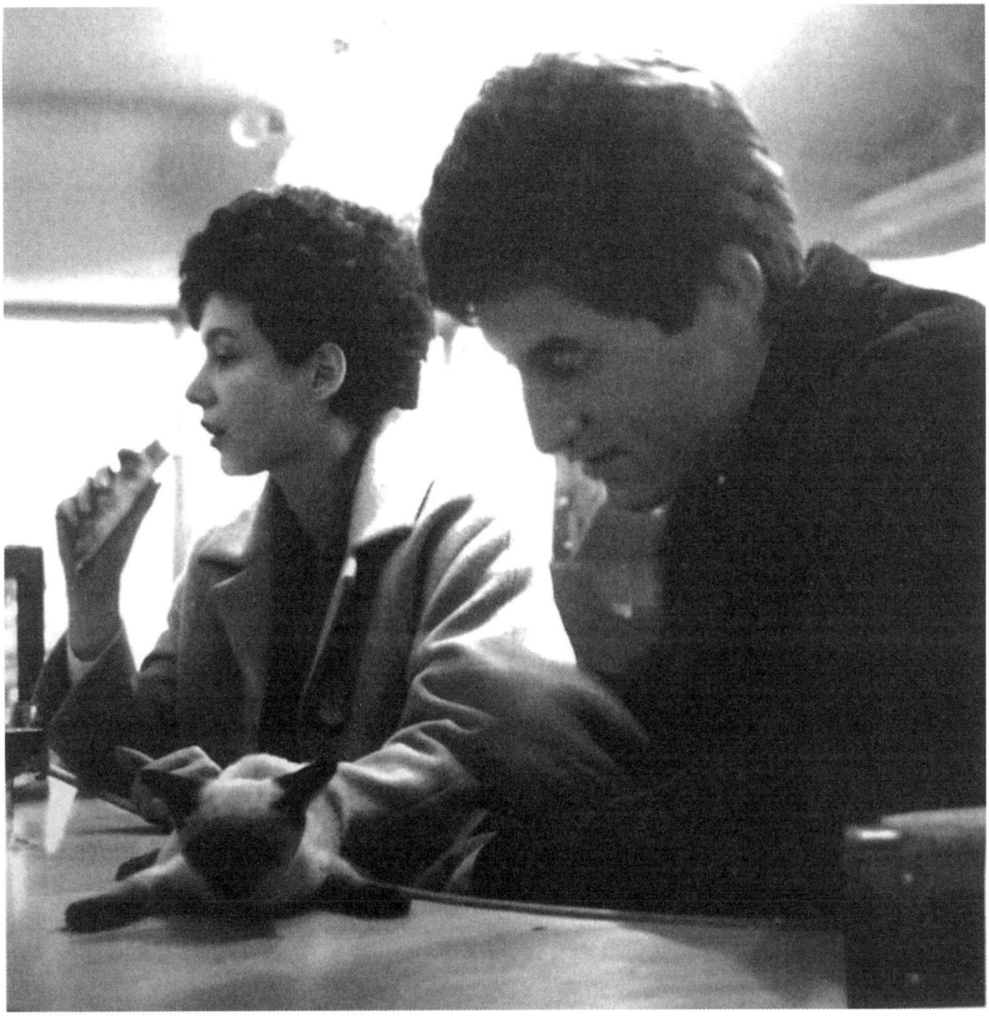

Figure 2.5: *Days*: Olga Vujadinović as Nina and Ljubiša Samardžić as Dragan.

made to work for and with the narrative, rather than the other way around, where the narrative appeared to exist because of the visual language. The key progress Petrović made was in learning how to balance the story and the visual elements, and *Days* provided a more detailed story of the time and space in which it was made. In his work on the script, Petrović enlisted the help of his senior friend and recognised poet, Dušan Matić, and writer, Bora Ćosić. Inevitably, their participation contributed to crucial improvements in the content of this work.

As in *Two*, *Days* is also about a doomed love affair played out in an urban environment, only this time vividly portrayed as alienating. As opposed to the previous film, the main character is a young married woman, Nina (Olga Vujadinović), who engages in a careless one-day relationship with a younger man, Dragan (Ljubiša Samardžić), leaving him at the end to go back to her monotonous life. Her dull existence is underlined in the opening scene as the camera searches for her at the window of a new suburban high-rise, a geometric monster that initially appears to deny the possibility of any human presence. Nina insipidly observes the roundabout in front of her building, a common feature of the hurriedly developed post-war suburbs, and a hapless figure running to catch a bus at the station. As the lonely individual is about to reach the bus, it sets off, leaving the person alone on a wide new boulevard. This lays down the mood of the story to unfold. Nina is alone in her flat. Her husband is away on business and stepson is with his mother on that day, the ex-wife who dislikes Nina. To ease her loneliness, Nina goes downtown where she meets a younger man, Dragan, and more or less unintentionally spends time with him; this culminates in an affair in the evening. At the end, Nina admits she is married and leaves Dragan in the city crowd to go back to her suburban flat and loneliness. Before Nina's Belgrade adventure with Dragan starts, she realises that her watch had stopped working, only to notice the time at the end of their affair. Petrović makes his protagonist enter some kind of a time warp, a Lewis Carroll-type space in which she is allowed to experience a different life, but also an "other" Belgrade.

The suburban backdrop in the story becomes an imposing difference to the previous film, entirely set in the old (and then well-kept) part of Belgrade, which looked as though it could have been almost anywhere in Europe. *Days* starts in the suburbs, suggesting a marginality that would then develop further in the film, creating a context that the first film lacked. Petrović again creates this context visually, rather than through literal means and dialogue, remaining loyal to his principles on the purity of cinematic language. In the first film, the couple was shown against the backdrop of a classical concert, a theatre and a modern looking café, whereas the lovers in this new film, before they find sanctuary on a derelict airport, come across a group of diverse marginal characters. In a bar, a group of idle youths entertain themselves dancing to the jukebox; on the street, another group of idle youths antagonise Dragan, almost ending in a fight, which is prevented by a policeman. In their aimless *flâneuring* through the back streets of Belgrade, Nina and Dragan come across an old and incoherent homeless guy, whose relentless ranting amuses them at first. He then starts describing himself as religious and thus marginalised and ridiculed by communism, whereupon the smiles disappear from the protagonists' faces. It is as if his appearance had reminded them that their society has created new inequalities and marginalised groups. The Belgrade of *Days* could be seen as a sleepy and stagnant town, becoming decayed and demented like Nina's auntie whom she goes to visit. The few scenes that Petrović does have in the film, showing the town as vibrant and changing, could not alleviate the general feeling of loneliness, alienation and desperation overall, with Dragan every now and then on the phone with his terminally ill father. What Petrović manages to capture is a rather bleak image of the society and the complete aimlessness of certain segments. It would be extremely difficult to substantiate the claim that this representation of Belgrade was made with an intentional social critique in mind. It would be equally possible to think that this was a product of Petrović's youthful artistic and intellectual curiosity, perhaps subconsciously influenced by Italian neorealism, Buñuel, or perhaps even Dostoyevsky. Petrović even pokes fun at himself: in one scene when Nina and Dragan ridicule the posters of his previous film *Two* as they pass them on the street. However, Petrović's unearthing of images and strata in a society of which the socialist state was not proud (and were certainly not inclined to show in official bulletins) caused reactions which alarmed Petrović. These reactions sent him a message to take a more conscious approach to the issues his films revealed.

2. 4. 3. *Days* – the Conflict

According to John Lampe, due to the liberalising economic reforms started in the early 1950s, "Yugoslavia's economy grew at a faster pace from 1953 until 1961 than most others in the world, including those of the Soviet block."[148] This economic growth inevitably improved standards of living and enabled an increase in film production. The rapidly expanding economy also resulted in certain phenomena not representative of socialist countries. Most notably, by 1961, unemployment in the social sector had risen by 6 per cent,[149] and discrepancies in income between the developed and undeveloped regions almost doubled.[150] In an attempt to address these emerging problems, Tito's government introduced the new Five Year Plan for 1961–65, a plan that inadvertently caused a dramatic decline in the country's enviable industrial development and production, so it was scrapped within a year-and-a-half.[151] I would therefore assume that in mid-1962, Yugoslav communists faced a momentary "crisis of identity",[152] which could be felt in Tito's speech in Split, May 1962, where he emphasised "the need for the party to take the lead in integrating the economy".[153] In his speeches throughout the year, Tito vented his anger and frustration in assorted ways as economic growth implied social inequalities that the society could not endorse. Most importantly for the film industry, in his address at the Seventh Youth Congress, and later in his New Year's message of 1963, "Tito himself attacked various foreign, antisocialist influences in the cultural and artistic life of Yugoslavia."[154] Tito inveighed against "decadent phenomena" that "negates all the results of our development" and had "a negative influence on our people – above all on the young."[155] There is no evidence to suggest that organised and systematic political repression followed as a result of Tito's speeches. They were just words, but words that came from the president of the Federation and the leader of the League of Communists, thus words that sent tremors through the ranks of the party (the league, that is) with tangible consequences. Party meetings were organised to debate the issues raised by Tito. One such meeting was held in June 1963 at Avala Film, where its general director, Ratko Draževič, admitted that one of these decadent films had been produced by his studio, and that this film was Aleksandar Petrović's *Days*.[156] As a consequence, *Days*, as well as Petrović's Slovenian counterpart in the struggle for New Film – Boštjan Hladnik – and his new film, *Sand Castle* (*Peščeni grad*, 1962), did not compete at that year's Pula Film Festival.[157] When *Days* was afterwards invited to the Melbourne Film Festival, Jugoslavija Film decided to decline the offer. On Petrović's request for an explanation he was "unofficially" told, "*Days* cannot represent Yugoslavia [abroad], as our public assessed it as an ideologically wrong film", which would, to "the international audiences, create an inaccurate picture about us."[158] The fact that the film was held back from international screenings for several years[159] prompted Petrović to later talk about *Days* as his first banned film, even if the ban only applied to screenings outside Yugoslavia.[160] In addition, *Days* was not the only film to be ostracised. At the Pula Film Festival, *The City* (*Grad*, 1963), a feature-length multi-episode film directed by Živojin Pavlović, Kokan Rakonjac and Marko Babac was screened, only to be banned by a court order in Sarajevo, as the production company that made it was registered there.[161] At this point, the filmmakers raised voices in their defence, Petrović himself amongst them, passionately defending *The City* as well as his own work.[162] At various meetings and forums, Petrović confidently rebuffed all accusations against his work and that of the other young filmmakers, rejecting allegations that they were decadent and derivative of corrupting western-capitalist influences.[163] Considering the sincerity of these speeches, they corroborate the view expressed before that, with *Days*, Petrović had no intention of creating a subversive or demeaning critique of the system. This could also be confirmed by the reaction of the party officials who accepted these pleas as genuine, as there were no repercussions against Petrović or any of the other filmmakers. The party's reaction was verbally sharp, but overall could be understood as benign. Daniel Goulding also emphasises that the speech by Veljko Vlahović, then the president of the Ideological Commission of the Central Committee of the Communist Party in Serbia, delivered to a meeting of Communist Party film workers and *aktivs* in December 1963, was given with "the primary purpose" to "provoke discussion and debate".[164] Consequently, it is clear that this first conflict between the party and the filmmakers, which unfolded in an atmosphere of dialogue rather than harsh repression or intimidation, could be identified as a "misunderstanding" rather than a conflict. It was a misunderstanding that came at the moment when the liberalising processes in Yugoslavia, which had begun in 1950, had faltered for the only time before this process was stopped altogether in the early 1970s. One of the victims of this "faltering" was Petrović's film *Days*.

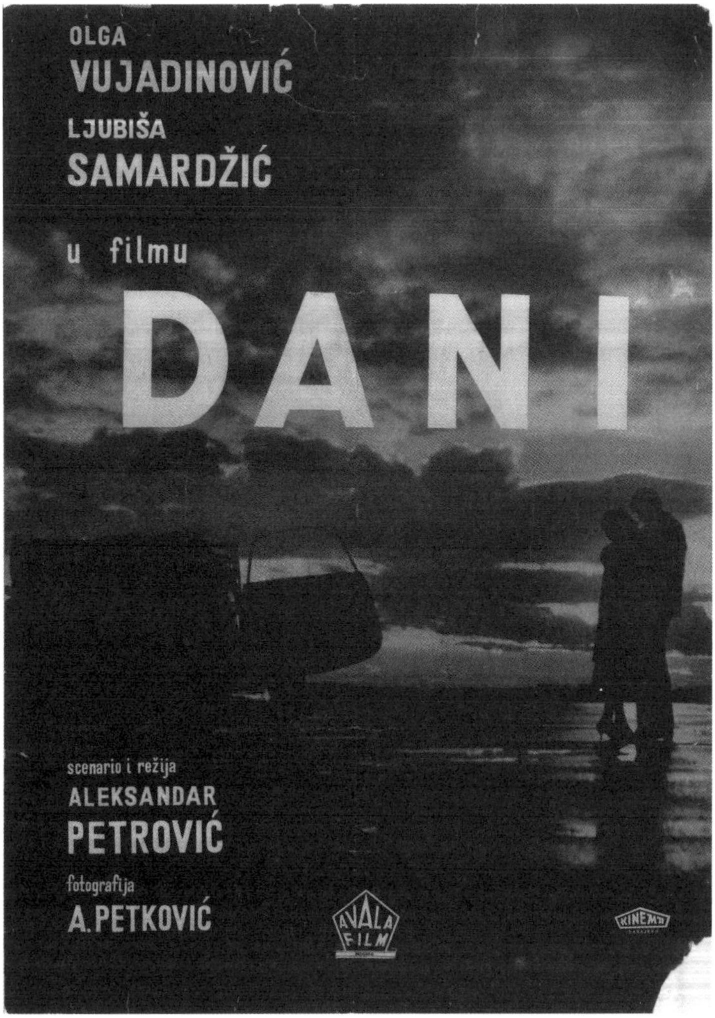

Figure 2.6: Poster for *Days*: the lovers at an abandoned airport.

Notes

1 Misha Glenny, *The Balkans 1804–1999: Nationalism, War and the Great Powers* (London: Granta Books, 1999), p. 573.
2 John R. Lampe, *Yugoslavia as History: Twice There Was a Country* (Cambridge: Cambridge University Press, 1996), p. 246.
3 Stalin allegedly said that he only needed to "shake [his] finger" and Tito and his Yugoslavia would be on their knees. See John Lampe, *Yugoslavia as History*, p. 245; and Misha Glenny, *The Balkans*, p. 536.

4   On Tito's "inner circle" see Misha Glenny *The Balkans*, p. 573.

5   John Lampe, *Yugoslavia as History*, p. 250.

6   Dejan Jović, *Jugoslavija – Država koja je odumrla: Uspon, kriza i pad Četvrte Jugoslavije* (Beograd: Samizdat B92; Zagreb: Prometej, 2003), p. 127.

7   This term was actually coined and theorised by Svetozar Marković, a Serbian "pre-socialist" of the nineteenth century, who, it could be argued, was given a similar role of a national hero in Socialist Serbia and Yugoslavia to the one Jose Marte had in Socialist Cuba.

8   Misha Glenny, *The Balkans*, p. 575.

9   ibid.

10 Misha Glenny, *The Balkans*, p. 574.

11 John Lampe, *Yugoslavia as History*, p. 253.

12 John Lampe, *Yugoslavia as History*, pp. 258–59.

13 Jasna Dragović-Soso, *'Saviours of the Nation': Serbia's Intellectual Opposition and the Revival of Nationalism* (London: Hurst & Company, 2002), p. 17.

14 On Djilas's "fall from grace", see Jasna Dragović-Soso, *'Saviours of the Nation'*, pp. 17–21; John Lampe, *Yugoslavia as History*, pp. 258–59; and Misha Glenny, *The Balkans*, pp. 577–78.

15 Jasna Dragović-Soso, *'Saviours of the Nation'*, p. 18.

16 See the introduction to section 1.3. in the previous chapter.

17 John Lampe, *Yugoslavia as History*, p. 250; on the western aid also see pp. 253–56.

18 John Lampe, *Yugoslavia as History*, p. 256.

19 Misha Glenny, *The Balkans*, p. 578.

20 Misha Glenny, *The Balkans*, p. 570.

21 A total of four feature films and 33 documentaries in 1950 increased to 12 features and 82 documentaries in 1955. See Nina Hibbin, *Eastern Europe: An Illustrated Guide*, Screen Series (London: A. Zwemmer Ltd; New York: A. S. Barnes & Co., 1969), p. 171; *The Filmography of Yugoslav Cinema* also states that there were four feature films made in 1950 but puts the total of feature films in 1955 at 14. These data emphasise greater spending within the film industry; see *Filmografija jugoslovenskog igranog filma 1945–1980*, ed. by Branislav Obradović (Beograd: Institut za Film, Časopis Filmograf, 1981) – see the table at the end of the book.

22 John Lampe, *Yugoslavia as History*, p. 252.

23 Aleksandar Petrović, "Razmišljanja o avangardnom u našem filmu, naročito o Predigri", in *Prizor* (annual magazine no 2.), ed. by Snežana Nešković-Simić [articles on Aleksandar Petrović ed. by Radoslav Lazić], (Loznica: Centar za kulturu 'Vuk Karadžić', 2003), p. 15.

24 ibid.

25 ibid.

26 See the previous chapter (section 1.2.3).

27 See more on this in Petar Volk, *Istorija jugoslovenskog filma* (Beograd: Institut za Film, Partizanska knjiga, 1986), p. 167.

28 Petar Volk, *Let nad močvarom: Aleksandar Petrović svojim životom delom i filmovima* (Beograd: Institut za film; Novi Sad: Prometej, 1999), p. 37.

29 Petar Volk, *Istorija jugoslovenskog filma*, p. 167.
30 On technical data and crew, see *Filmografija jugoslovenskog filma 1945–1965*, ed. by Momčilo Ilić (Beograd: Institut za Film, 1970), p. 98; see Filmography.
31 Petar Volk, *Let nad močvarom*, p. 37.
32 The idea was that the name of the party does not sound as CPSU (the Communist Party of the Soviet Union), but differently; see Dejan Jović, *Jugoslavija – Država koja je odumrla*, p. 129.
33 This view is also corroborated by John Lampe in: *Yugoslavia as History*, p. 258.
34 Ranko Munitić, *Adio, Jugo-film!* (Beograd: Centar film, Srpski kulturni klub; Kragujevac: Prizma, 2005), p. 142.
35 ibid.
36 See the previous chapter (section 1.3.1).
37 Personal interview with Nikola Majdak (30 April 2006).
38 See the previous chapter (see the final paragraph of section 1.2.3).
39 Personal interview with Nikola Majdak (30 April 2006).
40 ibid.
41 Pavel Branko, "Rozhovor s Aleksandrem Petrovićem", *Film A Doba*, February 1966, p. 68.
42 Petar Volk, *Let nad močvarom*, pp. 41–42.
43 Personal interview with Nikola Majdak (30 April 2006).
44 For technical data and crew, see *Filmografija jugoslovenskog filma 1945–1965*, p. 114; see Filmography.
45 Nikola Majdak verified these specific locations in a personal interview (30 April 2006).
46 Vicko Raspor is credited for this in the closing titles of the film, and in *Filmografija jugoslovenskog filma 1945–1965*, p. 114.
47 Personal interview with Nikola Majdak (30 April 2006).
48 ibid.
49 Ranko Munitić, *Adio, Jugo-film!*, p. 106.
50 Ranko Munitić, *Adio, Jugo-film!*, p. 72.
51 M. M. "'Let nad močvarom' odličan domaći dokumentarni film", *Politika*, 28 January 1957, p. 10.
52 Petar Volk, *Let nad močvarom*, p. 46.
53 Pavel Branko, "Rozhovor s Aleksandrem Petrovićem", p. 72.
54 Personal interview with Nikola Majdak (30 April 2006).
55 Quoted in Petar Volk, *Let nad močvarom*, p. 49.
56 Personal interview with Nikola Majdak (30 April 2006).
57 Dušan Adamović, "Festivalsko pismo iz Kana, Ko od četvorice?", *NIN*, 17 May 1957, p. 18.
58 M. M. "'Let nad močvarom' odličan domaći dokumentarni film", p. 10.
59 See the previous chapter (section 1.2.3).
60 Radoš Novaković and Vjekoslav Afrić, the first two post-war directors, had both been pre-war communists as well as Partisans during the war. However, Vladimir Pogačić, the director Aleksandar Petrović assisted in the late 1940s and early 1950s, once famously

explained: "I was told by Aleksandar Vučo [head of the State Film Enterprise after the war – see the previous chapter] that I am going to be sent to direct a film. If I make a good one, then I am a director, and if I make a bad one, no film school would ever help me to become one." See Ranko Munitić, *Adio, Jugo-film!*, p. 24.

61 Personal interview with Nikola Majdak (30 April 2006).

62 ibid.

63 Krleža was actually the first member of one of the worker's parties that was later to be renamed as the Communist Party.

64 Miroslav Krleža's intellectual influence was without equal in the second half of the twentieth century in Yugoslavia, and Aleksandar Petrović designates him as the most important intellectual in the country in his autobiography; see Aleksandar Petrović, *Sve moje ljubavi/ Slepi periskopi* (Novi Sad: Prometej, Tajanstvena Tačka, 1995), pp. 227–29. However, his literary work in particular has not aged as well as that of his contemporaries, and with the collapse of communism, his intellectual influence has largely diminished in the countries that have inherited Yugoslavia.

65 Krleža was known for his theatre plays, novels, poetry, essays, etc.

66 On what were the most interesting parts of Petar Dobrović's biography for Miroslav Krleža as a scriptwriter, see his notes for this script in: Miroslav Krleža "Prvi koncept o Petru iz 1938. godine (na temelju razgovora sa Petrom Dobrovićem)", and Miroslav Krleža, "AD o Petru Dobroviću, motivi", in *Prizor* (annual magazine no 3.), ed. by Snežana Nešković-Simić [articles on Aleksandar Petrović ed. by Radoslav Lazić], (Loznica: Centar za kulturu "Vuk Karadžić", 2004), pp. 115–21.

67 See an interview with Branka Petrović in Dajana Djedović, "O reditelju Saši Petroviću i njegovim filmovima: Razgovor sa Brankom Petrović", in *Prizor* (annual magazine no 2.), p. 88.

68 This story is corroborated in two different interviews, one with Branka Petrović (11 September 2005), the other with Nikola Majdak (30 April 2006).

69 Personal interview with Nikola Majdak (30 April 2006).

70 See *Filmografija jugoslovenskog filma 1945–1965*, p. 132.

71 Stevo Ostojić, "Krug se proširio", *Politika*, 18 February 1958, p. 8.

72 This other short documentary was made a few years later, when Krleža contributed a script on another Yugoslav painter, Krsto Hegedušić, whose name was again used as the title of the film. For the best reference to Krleža's "film biography" see *Filmska Enciklopedija 1 (A–K)*, ed. by Ante Peterlić (Zagreb: Jugoslavenski Leksikografski Zavod "Miroslav Krleža", 1986), p. 728.

73 Stevo Ostojić, "Krug se proširio", p. 8.

74 Dejan Jović, *Jugoslavija – Država koja je odumrla*, p. 119.

75 Andrew Horton, "The Rise and Fall of the Yugoslav Partisan Film: Cinematic Perceptions of a National Identity", *Film Criticism*, 12: 2 (Winter 1987–88), p. 18.

76 Andrew Horton, "The Rise and Fall of the Yugoslav Partisan Film", p. 19.

77 *Gluvi Barut* (dir. Bata Čengić, 1990). Čengić was Petrović's assistant for his second feature film *Days* filmed in 1962.

78 Daniel Goulding, *Liberated Cinema: The Yugoslav Experience* (Bloomington: Indiana University Press, 1985), p. 47.

79 Daniel Goulding, *Liberated Cinema*, p. 46.

80 Petar Volk, *Let nad močvarom*, p. 68.

81 See the following detailed review: Milutin Čolić, "Filmovi koje gledamo, 'Jedini izlaz'", *Politika*, 16 April 1959, p. 10.

82 Personal interview with Branka Petrović (11 September 2005).

83 See *Filmografija jugoslovenskog igranog filma 1945–1980*, pp. 14–15.

84 See a detailed account on this in Ranko Munitić, *Adio, Jugo-film!*, p. 115; Raspor's surname in Serbo-Croat literally means "to tear apart" and could be translated as "The Ripper". After the film *The Only Exit*, other journalists made jokes about "ripping apart the Ripper's bad film". Munitić adds that Raspor, following his moral principles, withdrew from film criticism, as he was known to "rip apart" other peoples' films. This withdrawal was not entirely permanent, although the number of his reviews dramatically decreased.

85 Ranko Munitić, *Adio, Jugo-film!*, p. 106.

86 These projects will be discussed in Chapters 3 and 6.

87 These are: *I Even Met Happy Gypsies* (1967), *It Rains in My Village* (1968) and *Group Portrait with a Lady* (1977). Aleksić also respected Petrović very much, which is clear from the obituary he wrote when Petrović died, calling him an "actors' director", see Aleksić, M., "Zaštitnik glumaca", *Večernje novosti*, 22 August 1994 (the clipping file).

88 Milutin Čolić, "Filmovi koje gledamo, 'Jedini izlaz'", p. 10.

89 Petar Volk, *Let nad močvarom*, pp. 68–70.

90 Nikola Majdak, a colleague of cameraman Jovanović, drew my attention to these limitations. Majdak explained that they used Ferrania film stock, which, as with many film stocks of the time, was very slow, or rather not very sensitive to light. Consequently, he considered lighting the scenes in a cave for that type of stock to be quite an achievement (personal interview with Nikola Majdak, 30 April 2006).

91 Postojnska Jama is a famous cave in Slovenia, a popular tourist spot even before World War II, where the event depicted in the film actually took place, and where the film was actually shot.

92 Milutin Čolić, "Filmovi koje gledamo, 'Jedini izlaz'", p. 10.

93 Milica Zdražilová, "Gladiátor z arény zvané jugoslávská kinematografie", *Film A Doba*, January 1989, p. 48.

94 Dajana Djedović, "O reditelju Saši Petroviću i njegovim filmovima", p. 88.

95 Milomir Marić, "Vreme relaksacije", *Duga*, 6 January 1979, p. 21.

96 See *Filmografija jugoslovenskog filma 1945–1965*, p. 154.

97 Petrović received 100,000 dinars; see unsigned article "Nagrade za ostvarenja našeg kulturnog stvaralaštva", *Politika*, 3 July 1959, p. 8.

98 Amongst others, a later famous writer, Meša Selimović, and the already well-known film critic Milutin Čolić were on the jury. Petrović received another 150,000 dinars; see unsigned article "Prva nagrada za režiju kratkometražnog filma pripala je Aleksandru Petroviću", *Politika*, 7 August 1959b, p. 8.

99   The other two films were *Jugo* and *Kamera 300*; Nikola Majdak's work was honoured with a special mention by the Pula Film Festival jury. See an unsigned article "Nagradu za režiju dobio Jože Babič za film tri četvrtine sunca", *Borba*, 7 August 1959a, p. 6.

100 After the Pula Film Festival, the film was shown at the Italian film festival in Bergamo, where it did not receive any award. Stevo Ostojić wrote a bitter article attacking the judges for not recognising the film's qualities; see Stevo Ostojić, "Drugi 'Gran Premio Bergamo', uspeh bez pogovora", *Politika*, 14 September 1959, p. 7.

101 Živojin Pavlović praises the film in his autobiography; see Živojin Pavlović, *Planeta Filma* (Beograd: Zepter Book World, 2002), p. 222. It is also interesting that Pavlović made his first short documentary film in 1958, although as an amateur production, but on a painter as well – *Ljuba Popović*; see Ranko Munitić, "Sivo sa ružičastim odbleskom: Onirički lavirint Živojina Pavlovića" in *Živojin Pavlović*, ed. by Borislav Radović et al. (Beograd: Centar Film, RTS; Kragujevac: Prizma, [supported by the 38th International Thessaloniki Film Festival] 1997), p. 13. According to the *Filmografija jugoslovenskog filma 1945–1965*, short documentaries on painting and painters were quite popular at the time.

102 Makavejev wrote an article full of praise for *The Roads* and *Petar Dobrović* in 1959 under the title "A Happy Walk"; see Dušan Makavejev, "Srećna šetnja", *Politika*, 22 March 1959, p. 18.

103 For the text read out in *The Roads*, see Aleksandar Petrović, "Tekst za kratkometražni film 'Putevi'", in *Prizor* (annual magazine no 2.), ed. by Snežana Nešković-Simić, pp. 11–13; and for the text of *Petar Dobrović* see Miroslav Krleža, "O Petru Dobroviću", in *Prizor* (annual magazine no 3.), pp. 121–23.

104 NDH stands for Nezavisna Država Hrvatska – Independent State of Croatia – the fascist state formed during World War II and supported by Adolf Hitler; see the previous chapter (section 1.2.2).

105 Nikola Majdak remembers this film as particularly arduous, with many effects created in camera, which required meticulous planning and patience in execution; personal interview (30 April 2006).

106 Dušan Makavejev, "Srećna šetnja", p. 18.

107 Slobodan Novaković, *Vreme otvaranja: Ogledi i zapisi o 'Novom Filmu'* (Novi Sad: Kulturni centar, 1970), p. 107.

108 Šumanović was friends with the Serbian writer Miloš Crnjanski, whom Petrović also admired (and adapted his novel *Migrations* into a film; see Chapter 8), and who also ended up in exile, pondering a role of an artist inhabiting another culture.

109 Petrović submitted the script in late 1959. He was subsequently asked to make certain improvements and corrections, mainly to do with the dialogue. See his interview in Dragoslav Adamović, "Borba za novi filmski izraz i za jeftin film", *NIN*, 11 November 1962, p. 12.

110 *Filmografija jugoslovenskog filma 1945–1965*, p. 195; see Filmography.

111 Aleksandar Obradović, who made the music for *Shoulder to Shoulder*, also worked on this project. Only Nikola Majdak did not work as a cameraman, although his and Petrović's other collaborator, Jovan Jovanović, did.

112 Curiously, as 1 May is (obviously) the International Workers Day.

113   Petar Volk, *Let nad močvarom*, pp. 65–66.

114   Personal interview with Branka Petrović (11 September 2005).

115   Tucović was said to be one of those pacifist soldiers who fired their rifles in the air rather than at the trenches opposite them. The film shows Tucović refusing to shoot at Bulgarians, objecting consistently to war, but ending up being shot at directly in the heart in 1914.

116   This is from an unpublished interview with Aleksandar Petrović on 5 March 1987. The interviewer was another director, Boro Drašković, who wanted to publish these interviews as a book – *Roman reditelja* – but this has not happened yet. These statements by Petrović are on page 35 of my manuscript copy.

117   Not much has been written about this apparently colourful character. My main source of information is Živojin Pavlović's autobiography; see Živojin Pavlović, *Planeta Filma*, pp. 49–52; Dražević's photo is on p. 267. Also see actress Olivera Katarina's autobiography: Olivera Katarina *Aristokratsko stopalo* (Beograd: Prosveta, 2006).

118   Boro Drašković, *Roman reditelja*, p. 35; see note 116.

119   Jasna Dragović-Soso, '*Saviours of the Nation*', p. 14.

120   There is not much written evidence on how these two got along, but obviously, considering the work they produced, they did. However, Olivera Katarina mentions that Mihiz was of course wary of Dražević, not only as he was an ex-State Security officer, but also because it was known that he executed people at the end of the war; see Olivera Katarina *Aristokratsko stopalo*, p. 138.

121   Boro Drašković, *Roman reditelja*, p. 36.

122   John Lampe, *Yugoslavia as History*, p. 270.

123   This figure was later never surpassed, thus this year is generally accepted as one of the best for the industry – at least in terms of quantity. See Daniel Goulding, *Liberated Cinema*, pp. 63–64; and Mira and Antonín Liehm, *The Most Important Art: Soviet and Eastern European Film after 1945* (Berkeley: University of California Press, 1977), p. 412.

124   Daniel Goulding, *Liberated Cinema*, p. 67; this view is shared by Mira and Antonín Liehm, *The Most Important Art*, p. 414.

125   Quoted from Ranko Munitić, *Adio, Jugo-film!*, p. 168.

126   See the previous chapter (section 1.3.1).

127   Branka Petrović reiterated this in an interview given in January 2003; see Dajana Djedović, "O reditelju Saši Petroviću i njegovim filmovima", p. 88.

128   Ivo Pondělíček, "Aleksandar Petrovič dokončil svůj nový film", *Film A Doba*, January 1969, p. 43.

129   See basic data on the film in *Filmografija jugoslovenskog igranog filma 1945–1980*, p. 21; see Filmography.

130   Živojin Pavlović, *Djavolji film: Ogledi i razgovori*, 2nd edn (Beograd: Jugoslovenska Kinoteka; Novi Sad: Prometej, 1996), p. 175.

131   Živojin Pavlović, *Davne godine (1954–1963)* (Beograd: Institut za Film; Novi Sad: Prometej, 1997), pp. 146–47.

132   Živojin Pavlović, *Davne godine*, p. 146.

133   Daniel Goulding, *Liberated Cinema*, p. 68.

134 See Petrović's speech delivered at the Cinematheque Française in 1965, in Aleksandar Petrović, *Novi film, crni film 1965–1970* (Beograd: Naučna Knjiga, 1988), p. 40.

135 On Yugoslav "intimate film", see a chapter committed to these films in Daniel Goulding, *Liberated Cinema*, pp. 112–125.

136 See Petrović's brief quote and on "intimate film" in Mira and Antonín Liehm, *The Most Important Art*, p. 414.

137 Daniel Goulding, *Liberated Cinema*, p. 67.

138 On how a film which focused on a love story meant a break with Stalinist dogma in Bulgaria, see an article on the 1964 film *Peach Thief* – Alexander Grozev, "Kradetsat na praskovi, The Peach Thief", in *The Cinema of The Balkans*, ed. by Dina Iordanova, (London, New York: Wallflower Press, 2006), p. 24.

139 Dragoslav Adamović, "Borba za novi filmski izraz i za jeftin film", p. 12.

140 ibid.

141 Gilbert Guez, "Post-scriptum Yougoslave", *Cinéma 64*, June 1964, p. 29.

142 John Francis Lane, "Cannes", *Films and Filming*, July 1962, p. 46; Francis Lane could be taken as a rather strict critic; for example, on page 17 of the same article, he calls Tony Richardson, director of the UK entry *A Taste of Honey*, a "wannabe Antonioni". He is however positive about some films.

143 Daniel Goulding, *Liberated Cinema*, p. 69.

144 Dragoslav Adamović, "Borba za novi filmski izraz i za jeftin film", p. 12.

145 See basic data on the film in *Filmografija jugoslovenskog igranog filma 1945–1980*, p. 25; see Filmography.

146 Dragoslav Adamović, "Borba za novi filmski izraz i za jeftin film", p. 12.

147 ibid.

148 John Lampe, *Yugoslavia as History*, p. 272.

149 John Lampe, *Yugoslavia as History*, p. 273.

150 John Lampe states: "At the opposite ends of the spectrum, Slovenia's per capita income was three times that of Kosovo in 1950 and five times by 1960." See John Lampe, *Yugoslavia as History*, p. 276.

151 John Lampe, *Yugoslavia as History*, p. 278.

152 See more on this "crisis of identity" in Chapter 3.

153 John Lampe, *Yugoslavia as History*, p. 278.

154 Daniel Goulding, *Liberated Cinema*, p. 70.

155 ibid.

156 Dražević said: "When Tito spoke about film and when this whole analysis of failures in cinema started, we understood that there were four problematic films, one of which was ours [referring to *Days*]." Parts of the minutes of this meeting held in the presence of journalists are reprinted in Aleksandar Petrović, *Novi film 1950–1965*, (Beograd: Institut za Film, 1971), pp. 130–32.

157 Mira and Antonín Liehm, *The Most Important Art*, pp. 415–16.

158 Aleksandar Petrović, *Novi film 1950–1965*, p. 138.

159 Further liberalisation of the country within a few years enabled the "lifting" of this unofficial ban (or precaution, perhaps), so the film was belatedly shown at the Porretta Terme festival

in 1966. See Laurent, "IVe Festival international de cinéma libre de Porretta Terme (24–29 juin 1966)", *Cinema International*, 12, 1966, p. 523.

160   Miodrag Milojević, "Intervju – Saša Petrović", *Pogledi*, 6 December 1990, p. 33.

161   Mira and Antonín Liehm, *The Most Important Art*, p. 416.

162   On *The City* Petrović said: "As a result of a lack of comprehension and understanding, one of the best films Yugoslavia has produced was tossed into the wastebasket." See Mira and Antonín Liehm, *The Most Important Art*, p. 416. Also on Petrović's defiance, see Daniel Goulding, *Liberated Cinema*, pp. 70–72.

163   Daniel Goulding, *Liberated Cinema*, p. 72.

164   On Vlahović's arguments see Daniel Goulding, *Liberated Cinema*, pp. 71–72.

Chapter 3

Art as an Inquiry

Yugoslavia's close economic ties with the West – particularly with the United States[1] – brought this socialist country to a contradictory situation. Throughout the 1950s, the financial systems kept on being liberalised, which, by 1960, raised overall living standards. However, they also produced economic "side effects" such as unemployment, and within Yugoslavia's complex structure – more agonisingly – the deepening of regional differences.[2] Rising unemployment and increasing rich-poor divide were precisely the sort of things a socialist society should stand against, thus Tito decided to put an end to these developments. When the new Five Year Plan, introduced in 1961 (with the precise aim of addressing these problems), collapsed in mid-1962, the country, and more significantly the party, found itself on the threshold of open divisions.[3] Historian John Lampe explains that: "The period from 1963 to 1966 witnessed the most intensive political debate over economic reform in the history of second Yugoslavia."[4] Tito had two old comrades remaining in his "inner circle".[5] One was the Slovene Edvard Kardelj, an ideologue of "self-management";[6] the other was the Serbian Aleksandar Ranković, head of the State Security Service. Perhaps because Slovenia was benefiting most from the economy's liberalisation, Kardelj was one of the top party officials who supported further liberalisation. Ranković had Kosovo under his jurisdiction, where the economy was suffering due to the liberalisation, thus making its complex and volatile ethnic fabric even more dangerously sensitive.[7] Ranković therefore resolutely opposed further "marketisation" of the country. Tito initially supported centralisation and a return to sterner, if not more genuine, socialist values, signalled by his speech in Split in 1962.[8] He was thus closer to Ranković at this time. By the end of 1964, Tito had changed his mind, and aligned himself more closely with Kardelj and the market reformers, which opened the path for completely new policies from late 1965 onwards.[9] What happened in 1966 and thereafter will be the subject of the following chapter, whereas the focus of this chapter will be the period between 1963 and 1965, when debate was raging and Tito was changing his mind. This short period of indecisiveness, doubt and confusion, which is already described as a temporary "identity crisis" of the communists, was to have a distinct effect on the film industry and Aleksandar Petrović.

The "identity crisis" and polarisation of the party also had its ideological background. Dejan Jović explains Ranković's position as the "more realist concept" wanting to "maintain the state apparatus and order", whereas Kardelj's concept was "more utopian – and more Marxist – insisting on the withering away of the state, the development of self-management, and fulfilment of national aims in socialism."[10] Consequently, the Yugoslav concept of self-management found itself threatened, from "the right – in the form of liberal democracy [capitalism], or the left – in the form of Soviet style state socialism."[11] In 1962, Tito was trying to decide the best way to go for the country, where economic progress seemed to have come at the cost of compromise with some of his socialist values. As noted earlier, Tito eased his angst by publicly lambasting intellectuals, and, somewhat curiously, filmmakers.[12] It is open to speculation why filmmakers were receiving reprimands from Tito at this time of uncertainty, but what is certain is that other socialist leaders behaved in the same way during similar crises. Nicolae Ceaușescu in 1971, after he had brought Romania to a crossroads due to his disagreements with the Soviets in 1968, "delivered a speech that was severely critical of the intelligentsia, claiming that they did not show enough support in building the ideal communist state."[13] Film historians Mira and Antonín Liehm confirm that when Ceaușescu talked about the intelligentsia, it was the filmmakers who suffered.[14] It is not my aim here to investigate Tito's motives for blaming filmmakers, but it is certainly of interest to scrutinise the consequences of Tito's address. Perhaps the primary consequence was that Ratko Dražević, then general director of the largest film studio in Serbia – Avala Film – who had pledged a few years prior to bring new authors into the industry with the aim of creating new, different and more interesting films, had to reconsider his plans.[15] These plans had guided Avala Film to produce Petrović's second film, *Days*, which was, according to Ranko Munitić, for ideological reasons thrown out of the Pula Film Festival's competition with an "imposingly scolding campaign".[16] In addition, Avala Film managed to release another film in 1963 that was to exacerbate the party's resentment towards the studio. According to Petrović's account, he was told by Borislav Mihajlović Mihiz, an advisor of Dražević, that they intended to commission the painter Mića Popović to direct a film.[17] This film, *Man from the Oak Forest* (*Čovek iz hrastove šume*, 1963), "was twice banned before being released in a reedited version in 1963", according to Daniel Goulding.[18] Goulding further explains:

> The film was criticised from its inception to its eventual release for providing ideological variations from accepted dogma about the War of Liberation. Criticism from official party sources was quite intense and focused mainly on the heresy of making a Chetnik the principal protagonist of the film and providing him with a psychologically compelling and interesting characterization.[19]

The Chetniks were of course a contentious historical issue, specifically for the communists, who feared that the Chetniks might have enabled the monarchy to come back to Yugoslavia after the war.[20] The communists therefore led a campaign to discredit them as German collaborators, which lasted until the late 1980s, even though it was also widely known that the Chetniks and Partisans had fought together against the Nazis, at least until mid-1942. Popović's film was thus essentially unacceptable. Even though his protagonist was portrayed as a "bad Chetnik", problems arose from the numerous subplots, such as the one about the repressed sexual tensions between the Chetnik and a Partisan woman – scenes that were ultimately removed from the film.[21] After the official reactions to this film, and Petrović's

Days, Draževič and his creative team at Avala Film had to put the brakes on their "daring" projects and exercise great restraint in 1964. As this happened across the country, according to Munitić, the 1964 Yugoslav Film Festival in Pula reflected this "cautiousness in production" in its programme.[22] Nevertheless, Munitić adds that young filmmakers and critics expressed their indignation at this situation,[23] but to no avail. No studio in the country was willing to aggravate the situation further and take risks with challenging projects. As Petrović's *Days* was one of the contested films, it was clear that he would not get to work on another project of his own for an unknown period of time. The temporary "crisis of identity" amongst the political establishment in the country meant a temporary delay in the career of Aleksandar Petrović.

3. 1. Two New Documentaries

Prior to his experiences with *Days* in 1963, Aleksandar Petrović started teaching film direction at Belgrade's Academy for Theatre, Film, Radio and Television in 1962.[24] In the academic year of 1962–63, a new course was started where film directing could be studied as a vocation, and the first generation of students enrolled. Petrović was involved with teaching and creating the academic curriculum.[25] As *Days* encountered a hostile reception in 1963, Petrović knew that it would be difficult to begin another project with Avala Film. However, he was working at the academy, and found solace and understanding amongst his old collaborators. Vicko Raspor, with whom he had directed his first short films, was at that time a creative director of a small Belgrade studio, Dunav Film, which was predominantly engaged in the production of short documentary films.[26] As it was only a small-scale studio, Dunav Film was not under close scrutiny from the party, and anyway, Raspor himself was an old communist. He also wanted to produce new and innovative films, and thus was happy to give Petrović an opportunity to work. Raspor, evidently, was not too concerned about the reception of Petrović's *Days*. In late 1963, an arrangement was made between Petrović and the studio, as a result of which he would direct a series of short documentaries for them.[27]

3. 1. 1. Exposing the "Invisible"

In 1964 and 1965, Aleksandar Petrović directed and scripted two short documentary films for Dunav Film. The two films marked a significant stylistic and intellectual development in Petrović's work, leaving a distinct legacy for his following projects, as they initiated the pattern of introducing political themes into the work. The first film was entitled *The Record No 1* (*Zapisnik br 1*), although the title could also be translated as *The Report No 1*. I will refer to it simply as *Record*, as its Serbian title – *Zapisnik* – is often referred to without the number that follows. The reason was that Petrović was supposed to make a series of these *Records* (or *Reports*) that were to be identified with numerals. As this never materialised, the number from the title was often dropped.[28] *Record* was completed in late 1964,[29] although Petrović gives hints in his autobiography that the second part was never made due to censorship and more pressure from the party.[30] There is no evidence to substantiate this claim, although *Record* was an almost belligerently contentious and critical film. Nevertheless, Petrović was to make another documentary after this one for the same studio, and to work on another feature film. Therefore, it may be that Petrović simply lost interest in the concept. This concept may be indicative, however, of how he felt after the reception of *Days*. As *Days* was essentially a love story, the main line of its narrative was probably not what had upset the party. The context in which it was set, described in brief episodes as the lovers wander through Belgrade, exposed characters that the party's ideological minders thought unrepresentative or perhaps even non-existent in a socialist society.[31] From Petrović's reaction to the attacks on the film, it seems likely that this background was not there to provoke, but because Petrović genuinely believed it to be intrinsic to the story. The dialogues he had with party officials regarding this issue were not yet over for him, and so with this short documentary it seems that he wanted to make his point and show things that the party would rather not see.

In those days before television, people went to the cinema to watch the so-called journals before the main features, these journals resembling TV news today. Petrović explains in his autobiography that these journals or newsreels, rather, in the socialist period almost by default portrayed only achievements and positive developments in the society, often even more embellished for the screen. Petrović decided to make a "critical journal" and reveal precisely the things that the official journals usually failed to show.[32] This somewhat spiteful intellectual insolence was to enable Petrović to see and portray his country in a new light.

3. 1. 2. The *Record* on the "Invisible"

Record demonstrated further improvements in Petrović's formal approach and his handling of content. The film opens with images of a road from a moving car. As the road markings pass, we see, in the rear-view mirror, the film crew inside the car. This "self-referential" image, one that puts filmmakers and their objects of inquiry together, reappears throughout the film, and becomes a link between different events. So as the images of the road are seen in the film frame, and an auto-portrait of the film crew is seen within this frame, a voice-over instigates the narrative. The voice-over gives statistics on how many kilometres of roads have been laid in Yugoslavia since the war, and the figures seem impressive, with tens of thousands of kilometres of new tracks around the country. Petrović then inserts a sequence from an official film journal made some 15 years before his film. The footage shows the construction of an enormous bridge over the river Sava near Belgrade, involving heavy machinery and a complex work process. The tone of the voice-over in that piece of inserted "found footage" reflects on the country and its development in the most affirmative and optimistic language, the kind of language often associated with socialist agitation-propaganda. Petrović then edits his own footage of the same bridge shot some 15 years after the inserted film footage. The tone of the voice-over accompanying Petrović's material is immediately different from the one heard in the inserted clip. Instead of exuding confidence and assertiveness, it is more inquisitive and perhaps sceptical, whereas the images show the bridge years later as almost finished but completely deserted. The narrator explains that the bridge was completed but the building of the road it was supposed to cater for was abandoned. The voice-over then interprets this as a case of appalling planning causing a scandalous waste of public funds. Some five minutes into his film, Petrović thus confronts a piece of state-produced film footage with his own footage, showing the reality as exactly the opposite from the one officially represented. He could have not been more openly critical, and his message to the critics of *Days* any less unequivocal – the reality is not what you say or think it is. His personal argument with the Yugoslav powers-that-be vehemently continues in this film.

As we see the car on the road again, the voice-over praises the opening of all types of sports associations for young people. It then focuses on a string of provincial boxing clubs at whose tournaments there had been a strikingly high number of deaths. In 18 years there were 13 deaths, making this the most terrible record in comparison to any other boxing federation. Petrović's crew films a man who had killed another boxer in a fight. He was released in court as the victim had been ill-trained and unprepared for the match. Petrović reconstructs the court case with the help of still images from the court, proficiently using animation techniques from his early shorts. As the voice of the boxer who committed the "crime" is heard, explaining that he was never going to go to a boxing match again and certainly would not want to fight any more due to his bad conscience, Petrović films him in his daily routine, working in his garden. The voice-over asks, if it wasn't the pugilist's fault, who is responsible? The film then ascertains that the problem is in allowing untrained boxers to fight at competitions without adequate preparation. As in the previous story, Petrović shows a well-intentioned social initiative – sports clubs for young people – which, due to being poorly thought through, probably caused more damage than benefits. In his autobiography Petrović adds that it was widely known that behind these mushrooming boxing clubs were people from the State Security, aiming to keep youngsters, particularly potentially problematic ones, off the streets.[33] Whether this was a fact or not, does not affect the conclusion that with this story Petrović again criticises and questions ideas and commitments of the party in power.

The third story continues in the same manner. Petrović records interviews with illiterate people in Belgrade, who formed an embarrassingly high percentage (16 per cent) of the population. Petrović's film admits that although the introduction of socialism had reduced this number dramatically, it had evidently not been enough. The voice-over gives another statistic explaining that the number of students in Belgrade was very high in comparison to other countries, and if each student were to make one of these illiterate people literate, the problem would be solved. While filming the interviews with the unlettered, Petrović does not show them, evading the complex issue of the exploitation of subjects in documentary cinema. However, he cunningly shows public boards in front of state institutions that could perhaps address the problem. On these boards, titles such as the Institute for Comparative Law, the Institute of Linguistics, and alike can be read, with Petrović unambiguously pointing towards palpable problems and the society's institutional lack of resolve. Finally, Petrović films a Gypsy orchestra playing in a bar full of drunk and cheerful people. The voice-over explains that an average Yugoslav spends almost three times as much money drinking in bars than the state spends per capita on culture. Although the statement sounds critical of the behaviour the images disclose, it is important to note that the images do not come across as accusatory. However, as in his previous film, the camera searches for details, and stops at a young and attractive (although seemingly very drunk) woman, enjoying the music while saving a flower pot on the table from falling and breaking, by passing it to a waiter. The orchestra also seems happy, playing a Gypsy song *"Djelem, djelem"*, which Petrović was to use in his two following feature films. He evidently sympathises with these people, and the criticism on culture spending is addressed elsewhere. Veljko Vlahović, a member of the Central Committee, who criticised Petrović's *Days* and other similar films in 1963, suggested that the filmmakers' behaviour bordered on the criminal by squandering scarce public resources on these films with such "ideological and aesthetical straying".[34] It is evident that Petrović took these words to heart, and was prepared to show who was really plundering state funds by showing their futile investments in useless public resources, and through creating institutions incapable of taking care of the people.

With his film *Record*, which curiously was only just over 15 minutes in duration, Petrović stages an open and brusque critique of the system in which he lived, but not without a certain empathy and appreciation for what the system had managed to achieve. Petrović was a critic, but as Herbert Eagle explains, "citing Marx's call for 'the merciless critique of all existing conditions'", any true Marxist intellectual is a critic.[35] Petrović, with his empathy and acknowledgement of the progress society had achieved, could thus be understood at that point to be this "true" Marxist intellectual, whose role it was to criticise, in order to improve. This is the overall tone of his film *Record*, which thus became the first film of his that was, in Herbert Eagle's words, "emblematic of the central conflict in present-day Eastern European socialist societies between Marxist humanist praxis and repressive regimented institutions".[36] These words were originally written about the work of Petrović's peer, Dušan Makavejev, in the 1980s, when the socialist institutions had become incredibly rigid and regimented, and hence dogmatic. However, at the time Petrović made his film *Record*, almost 20 years earlier, it was evident that he believed films like his were needed, and that intellectuals' criticism should be listened to in socialist society. To conclude then, by creating this "critical" dialogue with society, Petrović deliberately produced an embryo of one of the four political themes, which were to permeate all of his later films: a theme that revolves around the need to investigate (and confront) dogmatic and rigid understandings of (in this case socialist) ideology.

How this investigation was to develop in his next documentary will be examined after the discussion on an evident influence Petrović drew from an eminent filmmaker.

3. 1. 3. The Legacy of Luis Buñuel

With *Record*, Aleksandar Petrović exposed phenomena in society that are often "invisible" in the official representations of the country. As argued earlier, this was predominantly motivated by a certain sense of intellectual responsibility, the responsibility specifically suited to a Marxist intellectual. However, in conjunction with this and other motives described of Petrović's enthusiastic flair for social criticism, there is another significant influence that requires attention. In various interviews Petrović elaborated on the acclaimed international filmmakers that he admitted had influenced him, mainly authors of modernist tendencies.[37] It is, however, important to note that there was one filmmaker who had a perennial artistic, cinematic and intellectual influence not only on Petrović and his peers – most notably Živojin Pavlović and Dušan Makavejev – but also on a much broader swathe of Yugoslav filmmakers. When Vladimir Pogačić, a post-war director of the first generation, whom Petrović assisted when he joined the film industry, was asked at a later stage in his career whether there was anyone he would single out as a major influence, he answered – Luis Buñuel.[38] Buñuel was a Spanish-born filmmaker who made his first films in France, and then had a long and tumultuous career in the United States, Mexico, France and Spain. He was at first known for his association with the surrealist movement in 1930s Paris, and his friendship with the painter Salvador Dalí. However, as Paul Hammond explains in his study on Buñuel, this association with the surrealists was short-lived due to the political and ideological realities of 1930s Europe.[39] Hammond explains that the surrealist group had broken apart by early 1932, revolving around disagreements of the liberal André Breton and the pro-Soviet communist Louis Aragon, both of whom were surrealist poets. Buñuel was in the minority of surrealists who followed Aragon and joined the Communist Party, defining themselves as pro-Soviet and pro-Stalin.[40] The "pro-Stalin" affinity certainly may sound improbable today, as Buñuel was well known for his "unfailing belief in the pursuit of freedom and the overthrow of political and religious oppression,"[41] but this allegiance should be understood in its historical context. In the early 1930s, the realities of the Soviet Gulag were still unknown, and it was the threat of Hitler that attracted young intellectuals to the official Moscow viewpoint. As a result, as Hammond explains, Buñuel stopped perceiving surrealism as a way to criticise bourgeois society, and in 1932 embraced realism, whose doctrines Aragon had just brought as a directive from Moscow.[42] Buñuel's shift from the highly surrealist films – *Un chien andalou* (*An Andalusian Dog*, 1929) and *L'Âge d'or* (*The Golden Age*, 1930) – to the harsh realism of *Tierra sin pan* (also known as *Las Hurdes, Land Without Bread*, 1933), demonstrates clearly that these aesthetic changes in Buñuel's work were informed by the developing

Marxist thought.[43] It is precisely this Buñuel, of harsh realism as represented in *Land Without Bread*, and even more so in his later and acclaimed *The Forgotten Ones* (*Los olvidados*, 1950), that had a major influence on the Yugoslavs. Živojin Pavlović, who in 1967 claimed that Buñuel "was and is the artist with whose obsessions I correspond with most intensely",[44] further explained in 1968:

> I more appreciate those films of Buñuel's in which he employed the elements of surrealism in more complex ambitions (*Él, Nazarín, Los olvidados*). It was a stroke of luck that after *An Andalusian Dog* and *The Golden Age* he parted with Salvador Dalí. While a much stronger film, although less known, was his following one – *Land Without Bread*, which had elements of his aesthetics, but without the surrealist capriciousness and artificiality. Turning towards life, he completely found himself.[45]

Aleksandar Petrović, as a young aspiring filmmaker in Paris in February 1955, arranged an interview with Luis Buñuel.[46] From the introduction it was apparent that the young Yugoslav was in awe of the great filmmaker. Petrović was further charmed when Buñuel turned out to be accessible and convivial.[47] Buñuel did not hide his communist allegiances and sympathies while talking about the Spanish Republic,[48] sympathies the 26-year-old Petrović shared. Petrović's questions were mature and exact, and some of Buñuel's answers seem to inform the direction that Petrović's work was to take subsequently. Buñuel asserts:

> I am interested in the content and moral aspect of a problem. I am not a surrealist although I was influenced by surrealist poetry. Certain elements of surrealism I accept as a form of revolt against the outside reality. My outlook on the world is dialectical materialism. The nonconformist attitude of surrealists is certainly close to me, but I dislike their tactics. I am a lot closer to [dialectical] materialist tactics. I am always trying to be humane. Humanism is the base and aim of my work. I don't think my films lead to desperation. We need to show the world is bad, so that we can make it better.[49]

Additionally, Buñuel clarified the last point in two more sentences he relayed to Petrović, sentences that anticipate Petrović's later films. Buñuel said: "There is still a lot more tragedy and horror in this world. We cannot close our eyes to it, because if we do, we become complicit."[50]

3. 1. 4. "The Invisibles" Assembling

In late 1964, Aleksandar Petrović was to continue his work for Dunav Film, and start work on another short documentary – *Assemblies* – which was completed in March, 1965.[51] The original title of the film – *Sabori* – could also be translated as *Fairs*, but as the meaning of "*sabori*" in this context is somewhat idiosyncratic, I will use the translation *Assemblies*, which appears more in the spirit of other translations of Petrović's work.[52] *Sabori* were medieval fairs or assemblies of people around churches, or monasteries, on the day of a particular saint. These meetings certainly preceded the contemporary idea of a holiday: people gathered to go first to a church mass, then to eat, drink, play, dance, socialise and trade amongst each other for the rest of the day. This custom was common in the Serbian medieval state, prior to its conquest by the Ottomans. The custom subsequently continued although in a somewhat clandestine atmosphere, as the Ottomans tried to introduce a different religion. The custom of *sabori* was proudly revived after Serbia liberated itself from the Ottomans, and was valued as something that had helped maintain the national identity under the "colonial yoke". With time the custom was inevitably slipping into desuetude, but after the communists took power these assemblies were again put in a somewhat uncomfortable position. The communists in Yugoslavia robustly and quickly secularised the society after taking power. In theory, the church as an institution was not persecuted, but it was aggressively marginalised. There certainly were no individuals in the Communist Party – hence anyone in power – who was publicly religious. Religion was banned in schools, and overall, after the war, the number of religious people severely declined. Nonetheless, there still were a small but significant number of people who practised their faith. These people were most often from the remote, rural and poor areas, but a portion of the pre-war bourgeoisie in the cities also continued to observe religious traditions. One occasion where adherence to the church, and perhaps the old regime of the king, could still be seen was during these "assemblies". These events were of course not advertised in the official press or media. They had the form of a self-organised, or perhaps even an alternative event, but one that was certainly not promoted by the state, quite the opposite. Petrović's decision to film these events thus continues his search for phenomena in society that appeared "invisible" to the official media. His uncovering of this peculiar marginal group, one that appears to acknowledge that they might not be cut out for the socialist system, continues his inquiry into the true breadth of Yugoslav society (as in his previous film, *Record*), as opposed to the one accepted and proselytised by the state. Petrović is here on the same wavelength as Buñuel with his *Land Without Bread*, where Mercè Ibarz explains that Buñuel "did not set out on a search for the Other/Different, as did the makers of travelogues or documentaries in the style of *Nanook* [*of the North*] (1922). Buñuel went in search of the Other/Same."[53] Ibarz then continues to explain the significance of this by adding that this was:

> [...] not the Other/Same of the kind sought in two other key documentary themes of the time: the cities of Vertov, Ruttmann or Vigo, or the labour of working classes of Ivens, Grierson or Strand. He went in search of an Other/Same excluded from progress.[54]

Just as Buñuel uncovered Spain's neglected and excluded, Petrović exposed the marginalised segments existing, or rather coexisting, in Serbia as the Other/Same. In the process, Petrović reinforced one crucial thematic development that he had introduced in *Record*, and made another stylistic development.

Assemblies was only just over 11 minutes in duration, and conceptually very simple. The images of the people at these fairs, following the church rites, and the subsequent eating, dancing and trading outside, are juxtaposed with the same kind of images painted on the church frescoes. The camera often settles for details, which by this point has become a trait of Petrović's, such as a priest eating from a plate, or a musician plucking his instrument. Edited into these details were images from the frescoes, portraying people doing the same thing, in the same location, only some seven centuries previously. The film revolves around these juxtapositions, and its brief synopsis in the Yugoslav filmography book states the following:

> The motives of church assemblies were used by the fresco painters in the Serbian monasteries during the middle ages. The film compares the scenes from frescoes with the scenes of contemporary assemblies, held at the churches' courtyards.[55]

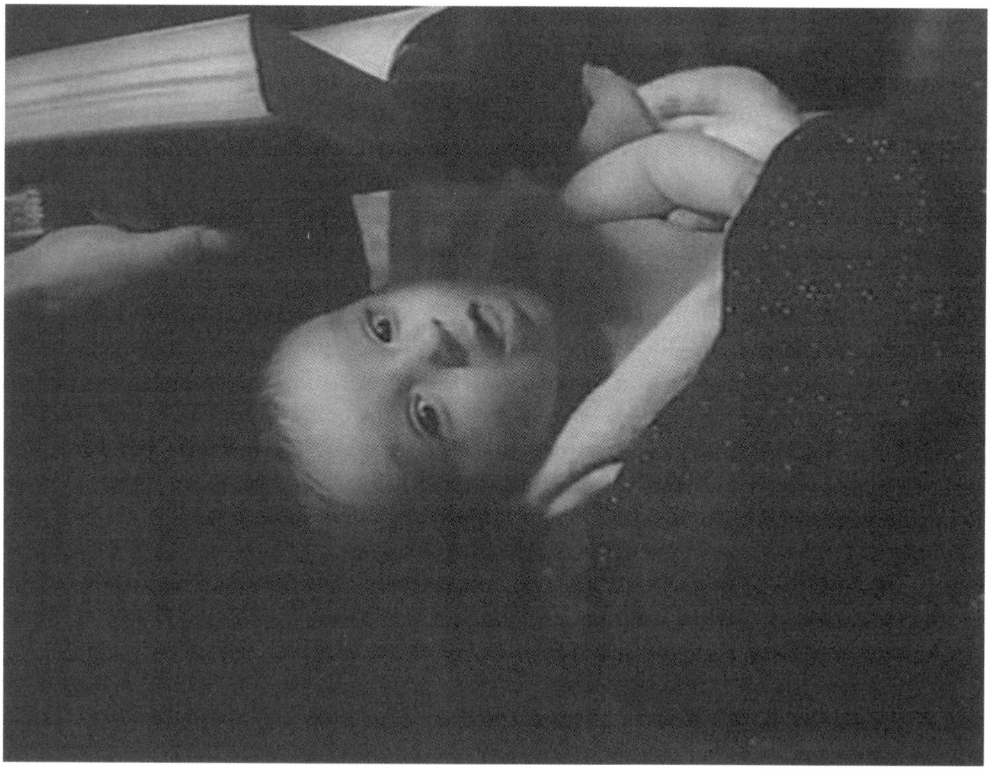

Figure 3.1: Juxtaposing representations in *Assemblies*: baptising in front of the camera…

The dynamic of the film thus entirely rests on the juxtaposition between "the represented" and "the real". As at the beginning of *Record* where the news footage of bridge building is juxtaposed with Petrović's own footage and interpretation of its construction, in *Assemblies* also Petrović examines an institutional representation of life. Although this time the institution is the Church, rather than the state, he questions it with his own images of the same subject. The investigation, or inquiry into the representation of life asserted by institutions, the institutions that often represented the so-called grand narratives (ideologies or religions), would, from this point on, become an important trait of Petrović's work. This trait of his is inseparable from the thematic concerns with which his films were to be preoccupied, and thus became an element of his authorial signature. How this was to develop with the later work will be the subject of the following chapters, although an interesting aspect of *Assemblies* is that he maintained an undetermined attitude. Whereas evidently identifying a discrepancy between the mediated (the thirteenth-century frescoes), in contrast to "the present day" in 1965 (the people at the fair), Petrović does not seem to take a critical tone, certainly not the

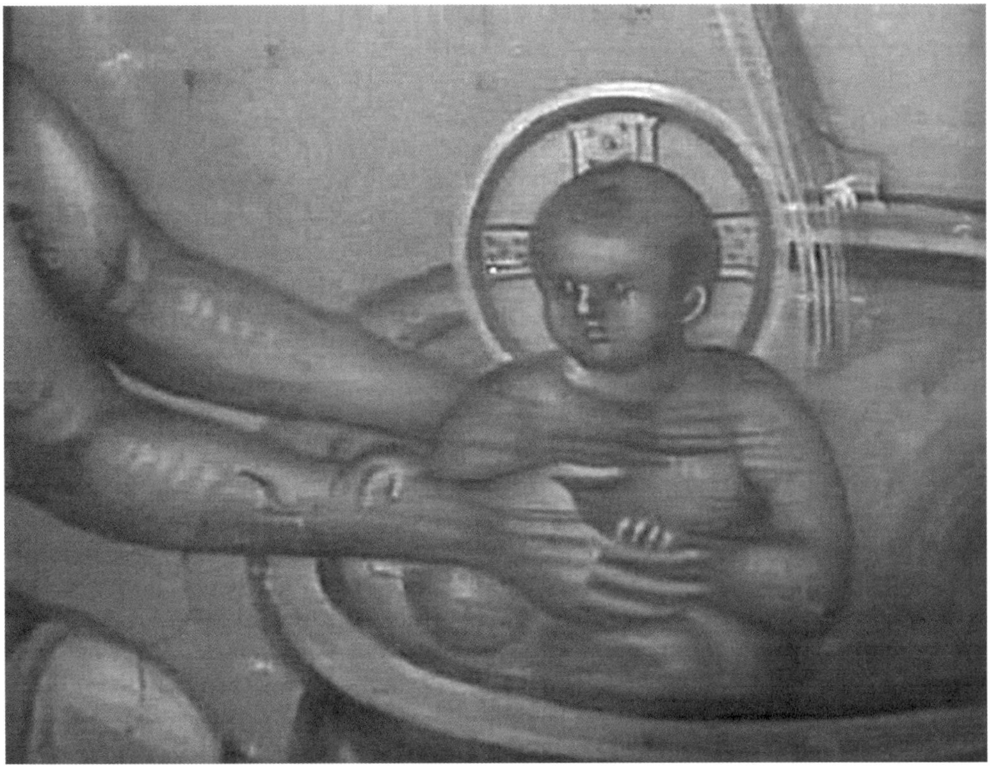

Figure 3.2: … and baptising in the fresco.

one he used in *Record*. As we look at the sequences of the people present, regularly alternated with the sequences of the people as painted on frescoes, there seems to be a lack of accusation, and conversely an approval, or even a glorifying tone of these events. This is best supported by the fact that Petrović, in this film, completely eliminated the voice-over, which would usually guide viewers through the film. He opts for the sounds and music recorded on location, juxtaposing the church singing inside and the popular folk songs outside. Again, there is no judgement offered by the filmmaker – this is left to viewers. By eliminating the voice-over, Petrović eliminates didacticism, achieving an interesting stylistic improvement in comparison to the previous work, which made him state in a later interview that *Assemblies* was probably his best documentary film. Petrović's famous assertion that he abandons "the dramaturgy of the type 'I'm telling you a story'" in order to make films reveal "the internal life",[56] and thus focus on ideas rather than on action, is well illustrated with this elimination of didacticism. He also managed to expose this phenomenon of assemblies without judging it – thereby maintaining human empathy. So this elimination of judgement was a result of his abstaining from a determined attitude, either against – which would place his film within the framework of accepted state policies – or for, which would make him support this particular (and then politically oppositional) group. Any judgements are left to the viewers. *Assemblies* therefore becomes a truly significant film, which also anticipated his future work, in which Petrović restrained himself from didacticism, and thus also his own dogmatism.

The filming of *Assemblies* was in itself a somewhat undetermined affair. The clergy was very wary at the time, and the priests gave permission to film only after Nikola Majdak, who filmed this project, and Aleksandar Petrović introduced themselves as art history graduates.[57] It is significant to note that with this film, Petrović, very much a child of the city, found himself immersed in an "alien", rural environment. This is perhaps why one of the images in the film is a close-up of a woman's feet in bright city shoes with heels, dancing to traditional folk music in the mud. The motif of urban intervention in a bucolic setting was to become a recurrent motif, or rather theme, in the three feature films he was about to make. With *Assemblies*, Petrović, a middle-class urbanite with basic left-wing convictions (re-) discovers the "other" side of Serbia: rural, religious, superstitious, obsessed with folk music and culture, marginalised by the communists at the time. He finds himself in the world that official politics of the time would have preferred not to exist. However, for Petrović, this discovery becomes a key to his artistic development. Inevitably, he falls in love with this "invisible'" life in the country. As Pavlović noted, that Buñuel "found himself" once he had abandoned the "capriciousness and superficiality" of surrealism, Petrović also seems to have "found himself" once he discovered the countryside, for which he abandoned the "capriciousness" of formal experimentation of his film *Two*. With *Assemblies*, Petrović, like his "teacher" Buñuel, in *Land Without Bread*, had found life.[58]

Both *Record* and *Assemblies* premiered at the 12th Film Festival of Documentary and Short Film, Belgrade in March 1965. At the time, short documentary films on fresco paintings and old Serbian churches were not uncommon, as were various ethnographic films observing diverse rural groups.[59] Nevertheless, there was nothing such as *Assemblies*, dispensing with commentary, and focused on the difference between myth and reality. *Assemblies* was not selected for the official competition, a decision criticised by Dragoslav Adamović, who assessed *Record* and *Assemblies* as just "one step away" from being "true art" in his exhaustive report on the festival in the Belgrade weekly *NIN*.[60] An unsigned report in the daily *Politika* confirmed that *Record* received special mention from the jury for its "original idea".[61] Furthermore, *Record* and *Assemblies* should also be considered in their context. Yugoslav film historian Ranko Munitić explains that Vicko Raspor, as creative director of Dunav Film, fought hard for short film production,[62] and that he gathered together an interesting group of directors to make films in this studio, thereby creating a Belgrade School of Documentary Film.[63] These films were all daring in their own right, and in his critical article, Adamović admits that contemporary Yugoslav documentary had "penetrated contemporary themes", while finding "many aspects of life that were considered as not photogenic before", and finally praised the fact that the filmmakers hadn't turned their backs on reality, but pointed "their lenses" towards reality.[64] However, Munitić explains that these films were not fully appreciated in Yugoslavia at the time, and their full recognition happened abroad. Individual awards were given to some of these films at the Oberhausen Film Festival in Germany, and collectively they were admired at the Porretta Terme Film Festival in Italy in June 1966.[65] Their collective success was so prominent that a retrospective of these short documentaries was organised at the Museum of Modern Art, New York, in 1967.[66] Raspor talked about, amongst others, Milenko Štrbac, Žika Čukulić, Krsto Škanata – and Dušan Makavejev and Aleksandar Petrović as the most important representatives of the school.[67] Film historians Mira and Antonín Liehm also emphasise that the directors of these documentaries moved on to make feature films, once the production "suddenly jumped in volume".[68] Daniel Goulding also identifies the Dunav Film productions and staff as an element that was to "anticipate" and help the explosion of the Yugoslav New Film in the second half of the 1960s.[69] Before this explosion could happen, Yugoslavia was to go through more significant political changes. In the meantime, Aleksandar Petrović was fortunate enough to receive another opportunity to make a full-length fiction film.

3. 2. *Three*: Things "Invisible" in the War

3. 2. 1. The Atmosphere at Avala Film

The general director of Avala Film, Ratko Dražević, who took over the company in the early 1960s, had done so with the aim, according to Aleksandar Petrović, of producing more modern and daring films.[70] In order to achieve this, Dražević was to fill the studio's creative board with the intellectuals capable of helping him bring the right projects to production.[71] His first advisor was Borislav Mihajlović Mihiz and, according to Petar Volk, by 1964 the board had gathered an interesting group of like-minded intellectuals who claimed that it was "necessary to openly support authorial initiatives".[72] They hence made an "appeal for more liberal understanding in the contemporary cultural moment", concluding that they were prepared to "ignore ideological attacks on artistic freedom".[73] Amongst others, Dušan Stojanović was a member of the board, who was to become, in Nevena Daković's assessment, "the greatest Yugoslav film theorist",[74] and writer Slobodan Selenić, who was to become, in Jasna Dragović-Soso's words, one of "Serbia's foremost intellectuals".[75] However, Lazar Stojanović, Petrović's most famous student,[76] unambiguously disputed Volk's assessment about the board ignoring the ideological pressures.[77] For example, Stojanović neither disputed Selenić's literary talent, nor his intellectualism and cosmopolitanism, but claimed that Selenić was a proud card-carrying communist who put his ideology before his writing or intellectualism. That Stojanović's claim may not be correct could be deduced from Dragović-Soso's account of Selenić's 1968 novel entitled *Memoirs of Pera the Cripple* (*Memoari Pere bogalja*), which "broached several taboo subjects", amongst them a very sensitive one about the inhumane treatment of imprisoned pro-Stalinist communists in 1948 Yugoslavia.[78] Nevertheless, the fact that corroborates Stojanović's view is that Selenić stopped production of the first feature film by Živojin Pavlović *The Return* (*Povratak*) in 1963 for ideological reasons. The film was completed and released in 1966,[79] after Yugoslavia had gone through further liberalising processes. However, Pavlović explained in 1988 that Selenić had had to either ban his film or resign, as the injunction really came from "above", or more precisely from Slobodan Penezić, a high official of the State Security Service, who deemed the film unacceptable.[80] If Slobodan Selenić is to be taken as an example of the board he was chairing, it could be concluded that Ratko Dražević and everyone at Avala Film (including Selenić) was genuinely willing to start producing films of daring aesthetic and thematic quality, but were to start production cautiously and within the limits of the permissible.[81] Concurrently with the fact that in 1963 Yugoslav communists entered a period of an "identity crisis", exemplified by internal ideological disagreements that caused the liberalisation process started in the early 1950s, if not to stop, then to enter a temporary limbo, the Avala Film executives were careful not to be too audacious in broadening the scope of their production. As Michael Stoil explains, East European regimes were "frequently tinkering with the content of mass-media, sometimes allowing greater freedom and sometimes re-imposing control."[82] The period of 1963–65 became, after almost a decade of increasing freedoms, a period of re-imposed control, anticipating similar incidents in the future. During that period, the creative board of Avala Film maintained their intention of refreshing the industry, but to do this without disturbing the – by then highly sensitive – party. They came with an interesting proposal. Aleksandar Petrović was known as the director whose film *Two* had instigated the new tendencies, but whose thematic concerns in his following film *Days* had caused problems in 1963.[83] Avala Film was to offer him another project, but to be based on the short stories of Antonije Isaković. Isaković was a communist Partisan fighter during the war, and his literature described those experiences. By making Petrović base his new film on the subject of the war, Avala perhaps wanted a modern film, but one that would not enable Petrović to tamper with sensitive contemporary issues. Mira and Antonín Liehm claim that in Eastern Europe, the themes of "the occupation and the war were used as a package to smuggle in contemporary themes" thus the "films about the recent past became a disguise for contemporary commitments."[84] It is also possible that Avala wanted to enable Petrović to do precisely that: to use a "safe theme" in order to transform it into a contemporary work. In any case, Aleksandar Petrović directed his third, aptly-titled, feature film *Three (Tri)* in 1965,[85] which according to Petar Volk, was that year's flagship project for Avala Film.[86]

3. 2. 2. The War Themes and the Prose of Antonije Isaković

In the words of Ronald Holloway "nothing is more sacred than the Partisan film in Socialist countries".[87] This statement may appear presumptuous, but statistics show that it was probably correct, certainly in Socialist Yugoslavia. Munitić states: "Between 1947 and 1990, there were 890 feature length films, out of which 250 were on the theme of the National War of Liberation."[88] Stoil adds that prior to 1956, the percentage of what he calls "antifascist films" was even higher, standing at 80 per cent, and it was only later that the thematic scope widened.[89] This obsession with the Partisan struggle against the Nazi occupiers during World War II is not surprising if judged against its context. It is widely accepted that "the official version of the 'common struggle against the occupier and domestic traitors' [the National War of Liberation]" was the most important "of all the legitimising myths of the Yugoslav regime," in the words of Dragović-Soso.[90] It should also be taken into account that Milan Ranković reasserted in 1970 that in Yugoslavia, film "has a relatively special position amongst other arts",[91] and, as Andrew Horton also pointed out, due to Yugoslavia's diverse cultural mosaic, "cinema emerged as the perfect unifying medium."[92] It was thus inevitable that the most important art was to represent the most important social and political myth.

As early as 1947, Aleksandar Vučo, the director of the Federal Committee for Cinema, gave four points of directive for future filmmakers, and in the second one he states that films should:

> [...] serve heuristic and propagandistic purposes aimed at inspiring viewers with a deeper understanding of the revolutionary struggle which the country as a whole, as well as its various nations and nationalities, had just passed through, and they should forge a deep collective bond in meeting the challenges of creating a new socialist state.[93]

Consequently, the first Yugoslav film, *Slavica*, directed by Vjekoslav Afrić in 1947, was a Partisan film. After *Slavica*, a whole line of Partisan films followed, but according to the Liehms, these films "were marked with clumsiness, naïveté and exaggerated pathos".[94] Stoil adds that "the primary focus in antifascist film content has been to romanticize and simplify the Partisan campaigns"[95] making the war look "as Tito's Partisans might have wished it to be".[96] This did create mediocre work, and Stoil points out that by 1953 the repetition of this formula had worn out, and with the increase of foreign imported films, the interest in the genre needed rejuvenating.[97]

Consequently it is not strange that by 1964 the creative board of Avala Film was impatient to enable the production of more modern and daring films. As they had to confine themselves to Partisan film, their choice of collaborators is telling. The decision to take Aleksandar Petrović as director was undoubtedly indicative of their desire to continue experimenting with modern films. Additionally, their choice of basing the script on the stories of Antonije Isaković further proves the point that if they were to make a Partisan film, it would be a modern one. Isaković had joined the Partisans at the beginning of the war at the age of 18, and started writing stories about his experiences in the early 1950s. According to the literary critic Petar Džadžić, his writing was noticed, as in that period socialist realism was completely abandoned in literature and replaced with more daring and modern tendencies, of which he was one representative.[98] Isaković's prose was imbued "with smouldering moral and psychological drama",[99] and was thus far removed from the simplified representation of the war Stoil had talked about. Most notably, Isaković adapted some of his short stories into a script in 1960, which resulted in the film *Partisan Stories* (*Partizanske priče*), directed by another war veteran, Stole Janković.[100] In Goulding's words, Janković "deplored films which idealised the war experience and obscured its human costs with shallow heroics" and thus made "one of the most realistic and affecting Partisan films of the period".[101] Subsequently, Petrović and Isaković were to make one of the most audacious Partisan films ever, thereby rising above their unsuccessful experience of *The Only Exit* in 1958, which Petrović had co-directed and Isaković co-scripted.

3. 2. 3. Adapting Isaković

The atrocities Aleksandar Petrović witnessed as a young boy during the war left a deep psychological scar, and much of his autobiography describes these traumatic events.[102] It was thus to be expected that the war was to be addressed in his work at some point. An anticipation of the war emerging as a subject could be found in his second film, *Days*. In this, the male protagonist Dragan asks his female counterpart Nina, while they wander near the military museum, whether she remembers the war or not. He suggests that for him it has almost faded from view. She contradicts him, claiming that she is older and that she still has a vivid image of it. Petrović, who wrote these lines, was about to confront his own war memories in his next film *Three*, introducing his own war experience into the script.

Petrović and Isaković wrote the script for the film together. All the material came from Isaković's collection of stories, then recently published as a book, entitled *The Fern and the Fire* (*Paprat i vatra*). They chose four stories and made them into three, adding one new character. The new character was partly invented and partly an amalgamation of the existing characters. As Isaković's writing was very much embedded in his language, following the "stream of consciousness" of his protagonists, the new character helped translate these internal dramas into action suitable for a film. The new character connected the three unrelated stories into one continuous experience, making the whole as important as the individual parts – which had not been the case with the book – and turning the script into a protagonist-driven narrative. The script was still fairly loyal to the original, and whole parts of the stories were almost literally transcribed for the screen, including the dialogues.

The two scriptwriters' choice of stories was important in creating a new meaning for the film as a whole.[103] The fact that they opened the film with a story, which deals with the beginning of the war and followed it by a story set during the height of World War II, and finally, ended the film with a story dealing with the very end of the war – when the power relations had fully shifted – added a new dimension: the film became a film about the war itself, rather than a film dealing with incidents that took place in the war. The new character they created (the protagonist) became a vehicle to portray the effects war has on the human psyche. As all three stories depicted the protagonist's encounters with death, the film charted the dehumanising process war has on all its participants.

The influence Petrović had in the adaptation is evident from his autobiography. His memories were clearly strong and relieved of any mythical or simplified ideas of warfare. The deaths he witnessed were most often cold-blooded murders rather than deaths in combat. Such experiences defined Petrović's participation in the process, so the three deaths depicted in the film are also cold-blooded executions, rather than heroic deeds of the participants. Petrović's message was unambiguously an anti-war one:

> An experience gained through history taught us that war is the most horrifying way to resolve human relations, so seen from this perspective, the film *Three* demonstrates an anti-war attitude, and could be seen as a warning.[104]

Isaković's stories of well-portrayed characters with fine psychological nuances under pressure during wartime, coupled with Petrović's own dramatic wartime experiences, were accurately transformed into an effective film script. The film became the first acclaimed scrutiny of the war in Yugoslav cinema, mature and uncompromising, hence abandoning the need to rewrite history. Instead it faced it head-on, thus Petar Volk concludes in his book: "It is not difficult to say that *Three* convinces us that the war and revolution were a lot harder and more oppressive on humans, than we had tried to show so far in our films."[105]

3. 2. 4. The Film *Three*

The film is structured in three chapters, featuring the protagonist Miloš Bojanić in three different episodes of World War II. In the first story, we meet him as a young student from Belgrade, as he arrives at a provincial train station to try and board a train that can evacuate him from the frontline and the advancing German army. He finds a large group of refugees there on the verge of panic and rebellion, as a policeman brutally tries to maintain order. The policeman stops everyone from getting on the next train, as it is full of the retreating soldiers of the Kingdom of Yugoslavia. As it is evident to the crowd that the country is falling apart, they advance to ransack a wagon full of supplies. They are interrupted by an army patrol, which fires in the air and begins a random check of identification cards. In that inopportune moment, a stranger who happens to have a camera and an odd accent,[106] but no documents, approaches the station. The crowd starts to cheer believing the spy has been caught, and the soldiers proceed to execute him. Only Bojanić raises his voice against such rushed and dramatic action, but to no avail. Shortly after, a woman with a child approaches the crowd inquiring about her husband. It transpires that the executed man was not a spy, but was telling the truth about himself.

In the second story, Bojanić is a Partisan in ragged clothes, running through the woods from a group of German soldiers. As he manages to escape temporarily, he meets another lonely Partisan who is also trying to save his life. They proceed together and become friends. The Partisan admits to Bojanić that he was afraid. As they are trying to get through a marsh to the liberated territory, they realise that they are surrounded by a German unit. The Partisan suggests they split up, as it would be easier to hide and break through the circle. The Partisan is then captured by the Germans and brutally executed, whereas his capture enables Bojanić to survive. Bojanić, though, remains aghast at his comrade's savage murder.

In the final story, Bojanić is a Partisan commander stationed in a large country house at the end of the war. In the yard below, a group of Germans and local collaborators are assembled, amongst them a beautiful young woman. Although Bojanić exchanges glances

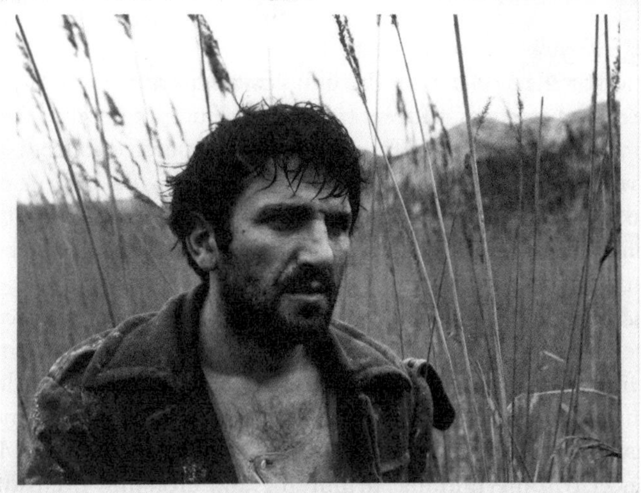

Figure 3.3: Escaping certain death in *Three*: Velimir Bata Živojinović as the hunted Partisan Miloš Bojanić.

with her, and a local peasant woman pleads for her life, Bojanić reluctantly remains adamant that she will be executed. As the woman tries to run away, she is apprehended by a group of Partisans, and taken for her execution. Bojanić walks anxiously down to the yard, but his attention is diverted by a wedding party that is approaching on the other side of the road. We see his tired and weary face, at the end of the film.

3. 2. 5. Personal History Against the Official Myth

With his third feature film, and the last one shot in black-and-white, Aleksandar Petrović managed to use his experiences gained from the previous projects, and demonstrate it in a way unseen up to that point. His proclivity for formal experimentation struck the right balance with the need to convey the story. Thus with *Three*, all his favourite cinematic audio-visual elements support the narrative, whereas the narrative itself seems to be waiting for precisely this type of formal approach. Perhaps proof of the film's well-balanced formal and thematic aspects is the fact that it opened to great critical acclaim, and is widely accepted today as the work that marked Petrović's national and international "real breakthrough".[107]

Petrović opens the film with a strong title sequence, forcefully anticipating the story to unfold. The sequence is strong as it is an animation of still documentary photographs taken by the advancing German army when they were occupying Yugoslavia in April 1941, with titles superimposed over the pictures. The images of destruction and the army's might, with a few images of hanged patriots – over which Petrović superimposed the credit title with his name as director – are accompanied by the sound of a loud siren warning against air raids. This literally loud and strong opening, formally based on Petrović's audio-visual austerity experimented with in his documentaries, makes this scene operate like a little film in itself, clearly delineating the story to come.[108]

The introduction to the first part of the film proves appropriate, as at the beginning of the first story we meet a group of refugees trying to evacuate themselves from the relentless advance of Nazi might and brutality. These civilians are huddled in front of the provincial railway station, where they hope to board a train that would take them further from the frontline and the oncoming Germans. Stylistically, the scene looks as if it is based on the previous short film *Assemblies*, which served as a rehearsal or sketch to direct this type of crowd scene (until then unseen in Petrović's narrative work). Petrović repeats the strategy used in *Assemblies* by establishing shots taken from the air in order to place the crowd and its segments in relation to each other. He then edits back into close-ups and details, which help create the intended atmosphere. The link with the previous two documentaries is evident in one important detail: while filming *Assemblies*, Petrović had come across a group of Roma Gypsies, who attended these fairs with a bear. The bear (somewhat unwillingly) performed a dance to some minimal drumming and crooning from the Gypsies. This minimal and abrasive soundtrack formed an unsettling audio leitmotif, which reappears throughout the film in moments of heightened moral tension and psychological ambiguity or anxiety.[109] Therefore, recycled from the previous documentary where it was shown purely in the context of the fair, the scene, and particularly the sound, has found here a dramatic purpose in *Three*. By visually linking the dancing bear and its Gypsy owner from the first story to this sound, it was also explained diegetically. The Gypsies are also shown at the station, waiting for the train, which, as in a Beckett play and in the spirit of modernism, may not even arrive. There, they use the bear to entertain the units of the retreating army of the Kingdom of Yugoslavia, who occupy the first train that passes – the one that the civilians were not allowed to board. Petrović adds another *"cinema verité* group" found and filmed while he was working on *Record*. The orchestra of Mikajlo Lakatoš, who played their song *"Djelem, djelem"* in that short documentary, was again cast in this film. Petrović introduces and shows prominently this group of Roma Gypsies as representing a segment of Yugoslav and Serbian society of the time. The group of refugees gathered at the station embodies a microcosm of this society. His following feature film was to take Roma as its focus, whereas the initial interest in them as a social group is evident in the opening of *Three*. This also represents a direct link to his previous two documentaries, where he observed Gypsies as part of a larger picture of society.

In the first story, which runs for approximately 25 minutes, thus in itself operating like a short film, Petrović shows a society that is falling apart and, most importantly, the general moral erosion that comes out as a result. This moral erosion, which is and was rarely depicted not only in Yugoslav, but also in international cinema in general, describes a rather troubling image of war, revealing the mental frailty of humans as individuals and in groups. Andrew Horton described the film as a "generalised existential study of men and women under pressure."[110]

In order to depict this moral decline under oncoming calamity, Petrović creates a microcosm of the society gathered at the station, trying to run away from being occupied by the Nazis. Although this may imply a group that nobly refuses to yield to Nazi power, the reality of the situation would reveal the group's dramatically increasing vulnerability. Apart from the group of Roma Gypsies already mentioned, Petrović introduces a group of young recruits wanting to join the army, then a collection of peasants, pensioners, various social classes and ultimately various representatives of the state that is falling apart: most notably a brutal policeman perhaps hiding his insecurity below the surface of assertiveness, as well as the lenient station manager who cannot say whether there will be more trains or not. Additionally, a religious zealot with a crucifix also shows up, and is ridiculed by the crowd, while observing the religious phenomena in society becomes a regular feature, or rather a theme, of Petrović's work. As noted already, by placing Roma Gypsies as a part of this microcosm of society, Petrović reminds us of its varied ethnic and social fabric, which is another politically conscious theme (together with the investigation of religion and society) that will become a constant feature in his successive work. In the first story of *Three*, the two themes are only indicated, but were to be further examined and expanded upon in the films to follow. As part of the group waiting for the train there is also the protagonist of the film, Miloš Bojanić, a young student from Belgrade.

As already noted, Petrović moves from wide shots of the crowd, where they are identified as a group, and their actions are perceived as such, to numerous close-ups where we get to know some of the participants individually. This enables Petrović to show the collective moral breakdown tragically, without any beautification, in wide shots. He also creates empathy with the individual characters in the process, through close-ups, as he opens up the process of increasing anxiety to intense scrutiny, which soon leads the group to its terrible misjudgements. Firstly, the individuals inflame each other's fears through their dialogue, consequently making them all, as a group, commit their first mistake, which is when they decide to ransack a wagon full of supplies. This decision causes chaos: the goods in the wagon are mainly destroyed and fuel is spilled, rather than anyone managing to capitalise on the process. The commotion is stopped by an army patrol that tries to reintroduce order through intimidation. By randomly selecting individuals in order to check their documents, they attempt to bring order to the crowd. When at that inopportune moment, a stranger appears with a photo camera and no identification papers, the group is quick to assume that he is a spy. Petrović's protagonist – student Bojanić – is used as a moral parameter, the only individual who does not succumb to a whirlpool of paranoia that is becoming progressively deeper. He objects to this rushed and unsought accusation, yet the tragedy is already inevitable. His voice of reason is not only rejected, but he is threatened with more paranoid assumptions, with some in the crowd suspecting that he himself might be a spy too. Bojanić thus restrains himself, realising that the situation has deteriorated beyond salvation. The stranger is executed, and the group, faced with the consequence of their behaviour, realises that this might have been a mistake. When shortly afterwards, the victim's wife turns up with their little child, Petrović makes his characters face their brutal misjudgement and moral failure. They all quietly board the last train.

With this story Petrović describes the moral erosion instigated by extreme social conditions – war in this instance – elucidating a phenomenon not commonly portrayed in cinema in general, and war films in particular. As Jan Svoboda pointed out, the film "touches the sensitive places of national consciousness at full risk",[111] implying that the films on World War II in general portrayed groups trying to heroically reassert moral values, be it resistance groups or allied forces. Petrović, however, decided to portray precisely this unpleasant reality: that human morals and social values easily melt under pressure. Such a representation of war is certainly far removed from what Michael Stoil assessed as the almost obligatory focus on the "romanticisation and simplification" of war,[112] but is a result of the traumatic personal experience and view of history, especially given Petrović's later autobiographical accounts.

The narrative appears to segue seamlessly into the second story, but it is soon evident that there is a difference between the second and first part. The difference is not only emphasised by the progression of the narrative, as Bojanić is now unshaven and in ragged clothes running away from a German army unit, but it is also eventually evident that Petrović in effect changes the genre with this story. Whereas in the first section he resorts to a drama played out by a large group of characters, the second part follows Bojanić's escape over a barren landscape, making the story rely on physical action rather than dialogue. In the final story, Petrović was to switch genres again, moving back from the action of the second story, and the group psychology of the first. Set in the interior of a country house bedroom, he allows his protagonist the possibility of quiet introspection and confrontation with himself. Petrović explained that "the stylistic representation of each story was conditioned by the nature of action and ambience",[113] confirming the earlier argument that the film manages to reconcile its form with its content. It is also important to emphasise here that Petrović's demanding genre shifting within one film relied very much on the actor who played the protagonist Bojanić – Velimir Bata Živojinović. Živojinović managed to combine three characters in one, following the character's mental decline and responding to the various demands the role required. Petrović later cast Živojinović in almost all his films, and the actor became one of the most wanted in Yugoslavia, specifically for the roles of Partisan fighters.[114]

In the second story, Petrović continues to distance himself from the official myths of the war. As the first story portrayed the frailty of human morals under pressure, the second moved to show the further dehumanisation of the main protagonist, up to this point almost morally untainted. The investigation into Partisan emotions and fears becomes the main focus of the second part, while Petrović also slightly but significantly alters the representation of the German army, that "most vile" of enemies, particularly in cinema. A German army unit well equipped and in camouflage uniforms chases Bojanić through cold weather and desolate landscape for the duration of this part. Bojanić initially does not speak much and is struggling to survive, overpowering a German soldier with his own hands, and taking his rifle to defend himself while the bullets last. In the frugal economy of Petrović's style, this scene refers to the historical fact that the Partisans acquired most of their weapons and ammunition by seizing them from the occupiers in battle. Bojanić then encounters another Partisan and strikes up a brief but close friendship with him. The unnamed Partisan starts a conversation with Bojanić, and another myth is revealed that surrounded most of the resistance movements – fear and fearlessness.[115] The Partisan, who was hidden in a graveyard under a tombstone for days, listening to the Germans looking for him, can suppress his fear no longer now that he has someone in whom he can finally confide. Although the Partisan myth rested on the legend of fearlessness, Petrović here creates an episode in which precisely this myth is questioned. Again, he does this with empathy, as it is difficult to understand how this character would not be frightened, suffering such long periods of isolation, with his life hanging on a thread. Confirming that such feelings are only human, Bojanić promises the Partisan that he would not reveal his secret to anyone, and that he too had been alone for days, hunted by a German unit like "an animal". Hence, he understands and sympathises with his fellow comrade. Therefore, Petrović's Partisans are not heroes, but human beings. As the two Partisans are walking through a marsh towards the liberated territory, they are discovered by a German reconnaissance plane. As they realise that they are then surrounded by a unit of German soldiers, the Partisan suggests that they split up. Believing that it would be easier for them to break through individually, he reassures Bojanić not to worry, as he is not afraid anymore. Bojanić hides safely in the tall grass remaining unnoticed, but the Partisan is captured by the Germans. As he refuses not to look at the firing squad during his execution, he is forced into a little shepherd's hut and burnt alive. After this brutal execution, the Germans leave and Bojanić comes out of hiding in shock and disbelief.

While his character screams in despair, Petrović managed to stage another complex examination of the realities of war. As in the first story, Bojanić is again faced with a brutal execution that he cannot affect. Petrović was careful in constructing empathy with his character, as it was clear in both cases that an intervention would have been futile and would only have led to Bojanić's own death. The motive is even more tragic in the second story, as the capture of his comrade meant the German unit would stop their pursuit: the death of his friend ensured his own survival. Bojanić is completely broken mentally, acutely frustrated by his inability to intervene. Insofar as his restraint saved his life in the second story, his frustration is only larger and more painful, as shown by his reaction. Petrović exposes the cruel laws of war, while, in the assessment of Daniel Goulding, gently "moving the viewer through troubling and ambiguous moral landscapes, where 'right' and 'truth' were not easily discerned."[116]

In the second story, Petrović brings his protagonist into this difficult and morally ambivalent situation, from which his character cannot leave unscathed. The overall impact is that Petrović, in the words of the Czechoslovak film critic Jan Svoboda, "destroys a myth, illusion and taboo in which war happenings are veiled", thus Petrović "offers a demystification of reality".[117] This demystification of reality in the second story concerned not only the representation of the Partisans, but also European post-war film's archenemy – the Germans. As Miloš Bojanić is chased by the group of German soldiers, he manages to get hold of an automatic rifle from a Nazi soldier whom he physically overpowers. Bojanić fires back at his pursuers, and in a close-up shot, we see the wound his bullet has inflicted on the arm of one of his enemies. The camera pans up to reveal the agonised painful expression of a German soldier, thereby giving him, regardless of his negative role, a human face. Elsewhere in the film Petrović represents the German army in mainly stereotypical fashion – as a tireless occupying force, prepared to chase a single Partisan over an awkward barren landscape with unremitting vigour and tenacity. Helped by the reconnaissance plane above, they are able to track his movements. The Germans, as in most of the war films, are well equipped, committed, efficient and brutal. But in this short shot of a wounded German soldier, Petrović reminds us that behind the Third Reich army's tireless killing machine, there was also a human face, a face that suffered, felt and was mortal. This detail is not an ornament within the overall narrative, as Petrović is a truly frugal filmmaker for whom each detail has significance. This is confirmed shortly afterwards, for, when the unit is reassembled to continue their chase, the camera dwells on the face of this same soldier who was earlier wounded. It then proceeds to pan down and shows the close-up of his hand, now wrapped in a bandage. While showing the Germans as indefatigable in their pursuit, it is also clear that Petrović feels for human pain regardless of whom it belongs to, and thereby making his anti-war message and "warning" very clear. Andrew Horton correctly concludes: "Clearly

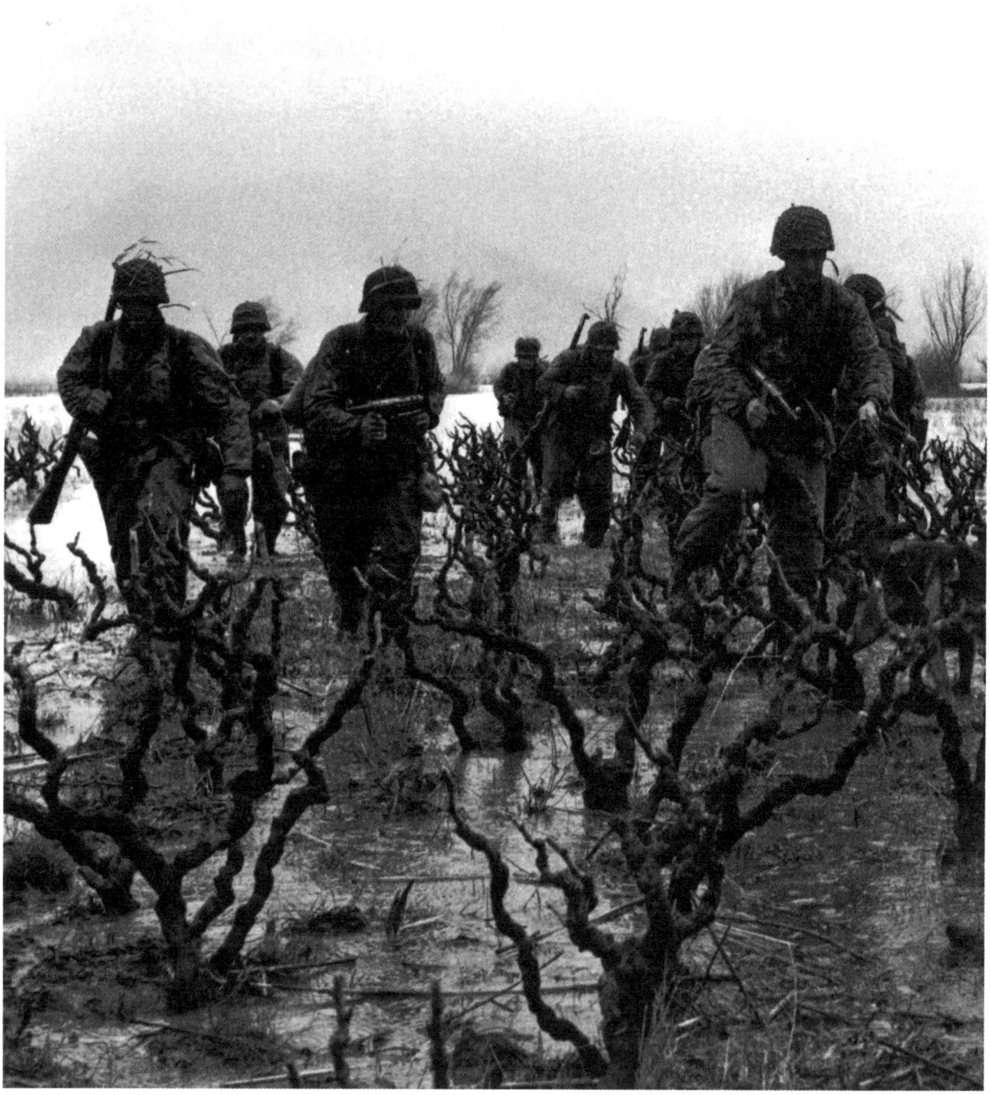

Figure 3.4: The death race in *Three*: German soldiers as the hunters…

with such a film we have left patriotism, idealism, and the simple representation of history far behind."[118]

After showing moral erosion in the first, and forced dehumanisation in the second, Petrović stages the final warning in his third story: one that questions man's ability to regain humanness after the experience of war. Bojanić is seen as a Partisan commander, as in the beginning clean-shaven and well-groomed, but in uniform. He is stationed in the top room

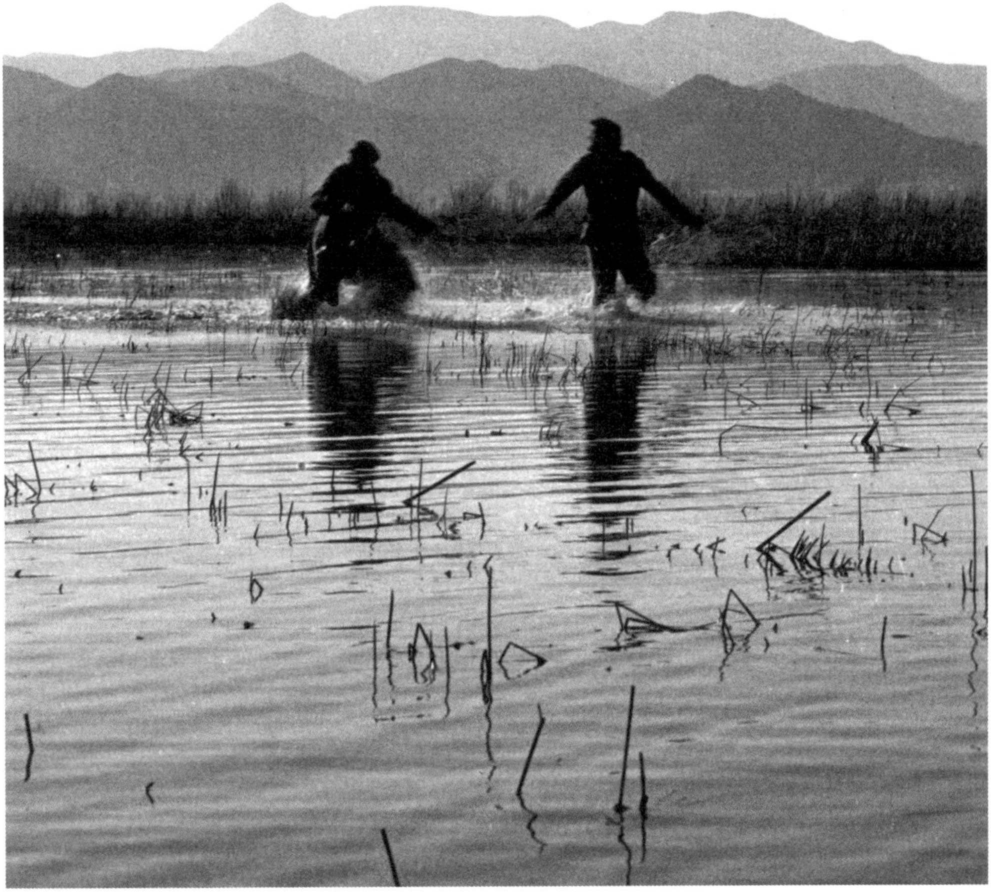

Figure 3.5: …and the Partisans as the hunted.

of a country house. As he is struggling to write a report on the movements of his units, a group of German soldiers and local collaborators are brought into the yard, among them a beautiful young woman. Everything indicates to Bojanić that the war is nearing its end, and that everyone is expecting a "return to normality", including the cold intelligence officer who informs him that everyone in the yard will be executed by that evening, even the young woman, who was courted by a Gestapo officer. This news startles Bojanić, as a streak of infatuation with the woman is noticed when their eyes meet across the yard. Bojanić paces around in the room, where he sees his reflection in the portraits of married members of the house's family on the wall. A local peasant woman comes in and pleads for the young woman's life, but Bojanić has become a hardened and withdrawn individual. He refuses to interfere once he has heard about her involvement with the Gestapo officer. The young woman in the yard senses her fate and tries to run away, but is easily captured and taken to her death. Bojanić anxiously walks down to the courtyard, but his attention is captured by a wedding party on the other side of the road. The last image in the film is of his tired and concerned face.[119] With the final story, the process of dehumanisation is complete as Bojanić is finally in a position to influence the imminent execution, but is no longer able or willing to react. Although Petrović shows him struggling to decide whether to save the girl's life or not, ultimately it seems that the war has taken the better part out of his character, and Bojanić once again accepts the ruthless lunacy and inhumanness of war's brutal laws. Through this inability to forgive at the end, Petrović questions one more myth in the official Partisan representation: that of their nobility and generosity.[120] Bojanić, in this very complex story that Petrović has built, acts like a human being, by being inhumane. What else can one expect from a man who has witnessed such cruelty? How can he forgive someone who he knows was part of the mechanism inflicting that cruelty? In a position of power, he is now as removed from the woman in the yard as the soldiers of the king's army were from the alleged spy in the first, and the German unit from the Partisan in the second story. Petrović in these instances introduces his third politically conscious theme, one aware of the distance between the people in power and the ones that are not. In the film, this distance results in death for the ones who happen to be disenfranchised. By showing these, in Goulding's words, "three tragic and ethically troubling deaths",[121] Petrović created a deeply complex representation of the war, far removed from the one usually found in Yugoslav Partisan films.

By creating such a complex representation of the war, Petrović through his three stories gradually deconstructs its official myths, the ones that were characterised in cinema by "excessive idealisation and demagogic simplification".[122] Petrović deconstructs the myths, and builds his own view of history to oppose the official, Socialist Yugoslav one. As in his two previous documentaries, where in one he juxtaposed footage from an official journal with his own footage, and in the other a medieval representation of an assembly with a contemporary one, in *Three* he creates his own vision of the War of Liberation – one extrapolated from his own experience of it. His vision becomes far removed from the accepted one, based on "the official ideological recipe of glorious Partisan representation",[123] thus allowing for two important conclusions. Firstly, by making this – in Andrew Horton's assessment – "critical war film",[124] Petrović managed to make a modern film, which also, in the assessment of Milan Ranković, although set in the past during the War of Liberation, develops a "specific echo of social–critical orientation".[125] This social criticism is epitomised by the fact that Petrović reconfigures, or replaces, the official view of history with his own; thus with *Three* he palpably started to develop an anti-dogmatic attitude, based on developing the confrontation between given representations and his own. It should be added here that, as a second conclusion, Petrović also did this out of a certain intellectual responsibility as, in the words of his friend Draško Redjep, "history was for Aleksandar Petrović in essence unfinished, and an inconsistently told story".[126] From *Three* onwards, this tendency to question established narratives and dogma would become a regular trait and thematic concern of Petrović's films, thus becoming a constituent element of his "authorial persona" – as will be demonstrated in the following chapters.

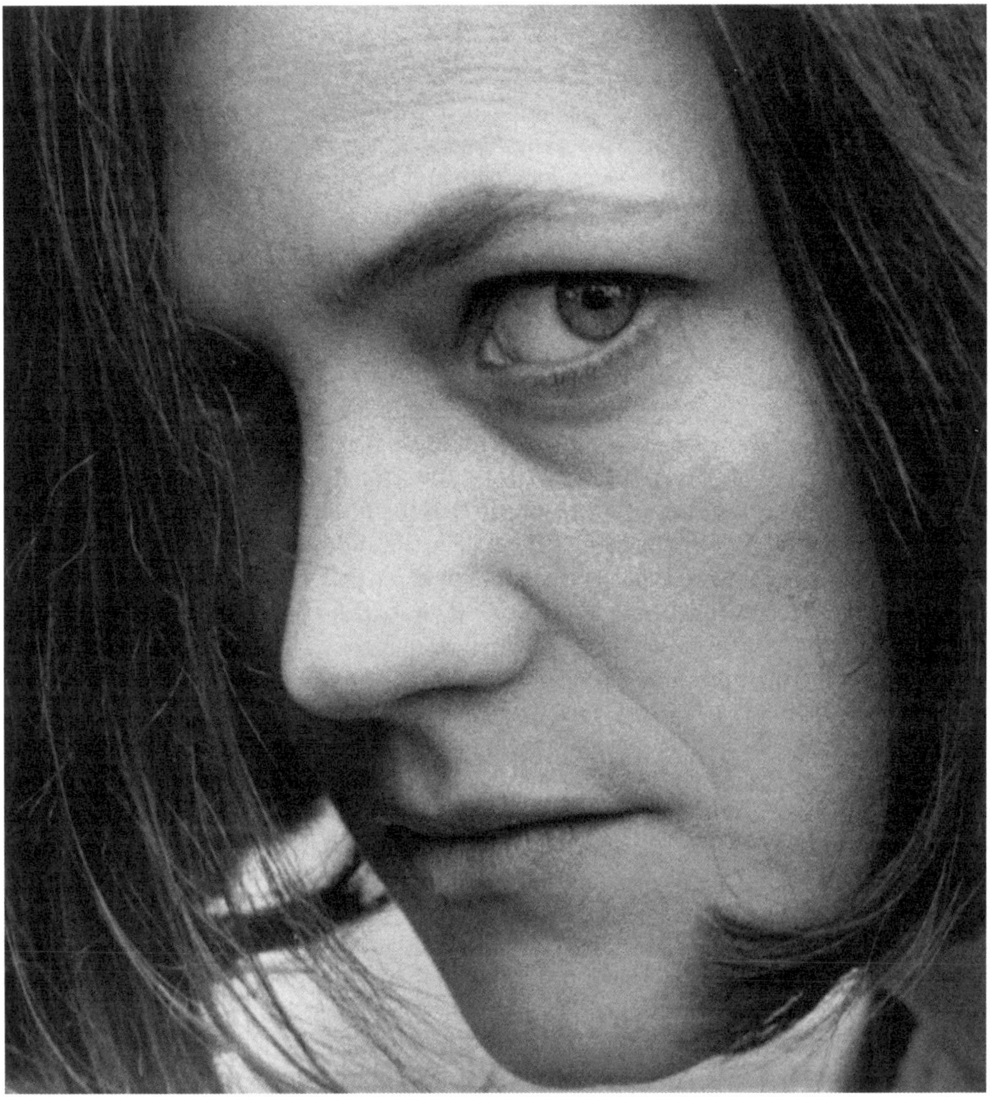

Figure 3.6: Facing certain death in *Three*: Senka Veletanlić-Petrović as the young collaborator.

3. 2. 6. *Three* – the Reception

Although Aleksandar Petrović created an alternative vision of World War II in Yugoslavia from the one proselytised by the party, he did not break or alter one of the key directives given by party ideologue Aleksandar Vučo, who said that films on the war should offer viewers "a deeper understanding of the revolutionary struggle".[127] *Three* certainly, in the assessment of Michael Stoil, could be "excluded" from the line of Yugoslav Partisan films,[128] as its representation of the war differs radically from the norm accepted in such work. However, differing from the norm did not cause Petrović to fail in providing "a deeper understanding of the war" – quite the contrary. The fact that he offered a new angle on understanding the war may perhaps be the reason the film was applauded and praised when it premiered in the summer of 1965, at the national film festival in Pula.[129]

The premiere was attended by President Tito, and Petrović and Isaković rushed round after the screening to see his reaction. Tito allegedly said – "A good film, a psychological drama" – to Dejan Obradović, then director of the state film export company, Jugoslavija Film.[130] As by 1965, Tito had accepted further liberalisation of the country and its closer ties with the West, the fact that this film offered a highly individual portrayal of the war fitted into the Yugoslav communists' ideological concept of being different from Soviet communism, where such individualism would probably be questioned. That this was the reason Tito liked the film is highly speculative. Even though the country was on the brink of even further liberalisation at the time of the festival, President Tito, Commander of the Partisans during the war, might simply just have liked the film. Petrović won an award as the best director, and the film won a Golden Arena as the best film of the festival. However, this was probably not due to what President Tito said about the film, but the fact that Petrović had managed to bring his specifically frugal style to perfection; a style that in *Three* Daniel Goulding described as one of "remarkable economy and richness of visual detail."[131] The style was certainly helped by Tomislav Pinter, a cinematographer from Zagreb who had worked with Petrović for the first time.[132] Pinter skilfully reconstructed the visual style Petrović had already established in his previous films and documentaries, specifically: transitions from close-ups to very wide shots investigating a position, or the relation of an individual to its environment; use of frame within a frame technique;[133] and the use of high contrast photography,[134] which was all frequently explored in *Three*. The style became so frugal that every little detail bore a meaning, which thereby enlarged the scope of the story, while at the same time contributing to the main line of the narrative. The critical reception in Yugoslavia, according to Petar Volk, recognised these qualities,[135] and the film was the Yugoslav entry for the then most important East European film festival, Karlovy Vary. In the summer of 1966, according to the Czechoslovak film critic Jan Svoboda, *Three* deservedly won first prize of the festival, together with the Hungarian film *Cold Days* (*Hideg napok*, 1966),[136] directed by András Kovács, which also dealt with the complex and frank portrayal of World War II traumas.[137] This award guaranteed a screening at the New York Film Festival later in the year, after which the film opened in the United States. Finally, the film received an official nomination for the best foreign language film at the Academy Awards in 1967.[138] At that point, *Three* was the most successful feature-length fiction film produced in Yugoslavia, the film that in the early 1980s was assessed by Petar Volk as "probably the best Yugoslav film ever".[139]

The critical reception of *Three* internationally was predominantly positive, and remained so in the subsequent years. The film was praised in the Soviet magazine for film – *Iskusstvo kino* – where Natalia Zelenko stated that in the film "everything is simple, without excess", confirming that it deservedly won the first prize at Karlovy Vary, and adding that "the explorations of the author of the film are interesting and fruitful".[140] Positive reviews from Moscow were followed by ones in the United States, specifically in *The New York Times* and *Variety*, where in the latter Gene Moskowitz's assessment was: "a sharply made film", which has "a knowing pacifistic air though there is no preaching".[141] The success of the film was only the beginning of the rising new wave of Yugoslav film. In 1965, Petrović's peers, Dušan Makavejev and Živojin Pavlović completed their first feature-length films, dealing openly with contemporary themes.[142] Aleksandar Petrović also became a member of the creative board of Avala Film, as a result of *Three*'s achievements, and with the further political changes that were to happen in the country, the door was open for the new cinema to explode, and filmmakers to become even more daring. Concluding on *Three*, Andrew Horton stated that "such a film indicates the high degree of individualism Yugoslav cinema came to allow its filmmakers in treating both the war and filmmaking in general."[143]

Notes

1   See the introduction to the previous chapter.
2   According to John Lampe, by 1961, unemployment in the social sector rose by 6 per cent, whereas: "At the opposite ends of the spectrum, Slovenia's per capita income was three times that of Kosovo in 1950 and five times by 1960." See John Lampe, *Yugoslavia as History: Twice There Was a Country* (Cambridge: Cambridge University Press, 1996) p. 273; 276.
3   On the failure of the Five Year Plan, see John Lampe, *Yugoslavia as History*, p. 278.
4   When Lampe talks about "the second Yugoslavia", he means Socialist Yugoslavia. See John R. Lampe, *Yugoslavia as History*, p. 279.
5   On Tito's "inner circle" see Misha Glenny, *The Balkans 1804–1999: Nationalism, War and the Great Powers* (London: Granta Books, 1999), p. 573.
6   Kardelj created the concept of "self-management" with Milovan Djilas, who later became the first dissident; see the introduction to the previous chapter.
7   See note 2 earlier, and John Lampe, *Yugoslavia as History*, p. 276.
8   See the previous chapter (section 2.4.3); and see John Lampe, *Yugoslavia as History*, p. 278.
9   John Lampe, *Yugoslavia as History*, p. 280.
10   Dejan Jović, *Jugoslavija – Država koja je odumrla: Uspon, kriza i pad Četvrte Jugoslavije* (Beograd: Samizdat B92; Zagreb: Prometej, 2003), p. 145.
11   Dejan Jović, *Jugoslavija*, p. 152.

12 See Daniel Goulding, *Liberated Cinema: The Yugoslav Experience* (Bloomington: Indiana University Press, 1985), p. 70.

13 Lilla Tőke, "Nunta de piatră, Stone Wedding", in *The Cinema of The Balkans*, ed. by Dina Iordanova (London, New York: Wallflower Press, 2006), p. 128.

14 Mira and Antonín Liehm, *The Most Important Art: Soviet and Eastern European Film after 1945* (Berkeley: University of California Press, 1977), p. 356.

15 See the previous chapter (section 2.4.3).

16 Ranko Munitić, *Adio, Jugo-film!* (Beograd: Centar film, Srpski kulturni klub; Kragujevac: Prizma, 2005), p. 124.

17 Boro Drašković, *Roman reditelja*, unpublished manuscript; this information is from an interview with Aleksandar Petrović, 5 March 1987, p. 35.

18 Daniel Goulding, *Liberated Cinema*, p. 96.

19 ibid.

20 On Chetniks see Chapter 1 (section 1.2.2).

21 Daniel Goulding, *Liberated Cinema*, p. 96.

22 Ranko Munitić, *Adio, Jugo-film!*, pp. 136–37.

23 Ranko Munitić, *Adio, Jugo-film!*, p. 137.

24 See: *Filmska enciklopedija 2 (L–Ž)*, ed. by Ante Peterlić (Zagreb: Jugoslavenski Leksikografski Zavod 'Miroslav Krleža', 1990), pp. 316–17.

25 See Petrović's article on the development of the course and his academic contribution, initially published in one of the academy's journals: Aleksandar Petrović, "Školovanje filmskih reditelja", in *Prizor* (annual magazine no 3.), ed. by Snežana Nešković-Simić [articles on Aleksandar Petrović ed. by Radoslav Lazić], (Loznica: Centar za kulturu 'Vuk Karadžić', 2004), pp. 137–40.

26 On the type of formally and thematically experimental short documentary films Vicko Raspor wanted to produce at Dunav Film, see Ranko Munitić, *Adio, Jugo-film!*, pp. 93–108.

27 Aleksandar Petrović, *Sve moje ljubavi/Slepi periskopi* (Novi Sad: Prometej, Tajanstvena Tačka, 1995), p. 60.

28 Aleksandar Petrović, *Sve moje ljubavi*, p. 64.

29 See *Filmografija jugoslovenskog filma 1945–1965*, ed. by Momčilo Ilić (Beograd: Institut za Film, 1970), p. 297, see Filmography.

30 Aleksandar Petrović, *Sve moje ljubavi*, p. 64.

31 As already mentioned, Petrović's inclusion of various marginal characters in his *Days* was severely criticised by the party, and the film was refused permission to be screened at the Melbourne Film Festival in 1963. See the previous chapter (section 2.4.3).

32 Aleksandar Petrović, *Sve moje ljubavi*, p. 60.

33 Aleksandar Petrović, *Sve moje ljubavi*, p. 61.

34 Daniel Goulding, *Liberated Cinema*, p. 71.

35 Herbert Eagle, "Yugoslav Marxist Humanism and the Films of Dušan Makavejev", in *Politics, Art and Commitment in the Eastern European Cinema*, ed. by David W. Paul (London, Basingstoke: The Macmillan Press, 1983), p. 132.

36 Herbert Eagle, "Yugoslav Marxist Humanism", p. 136.

37 See Chapter 1 (section 1.2.3).

38 From an interview with Vladimir Pogačić by Radoslav Lazić, see Radoslav Lazić, *Traktat o filmskoj režiji: U traganju za estetikom režije od Aleksandra Petrovića do Emira Kusturice* (Beograd: Institut za Film, 1989), p. 64.

39 See Paul Hammond, "Lost and Found: Buñuel, *L' Âge d' or* and Surrealism", in *Luis Buñuel: New Readings*, ed. by Peter William Evans and Isabel Santaolalla (London: BFI, 2004), pp. 13–26.

40 Paul Hammond, "Lost and Found", pp. 21–22.

41 Peter William Evans and Isabel Santaolalla, "Introduction: Luis Buñuel – Twenty Years After", in *Luis Buñuel: New Readings*, p. 6.

42 Paul Hammond, "Lost and Found", pp. 22–23.

43 On *Land Without Bread* and changing ideological frameworks, see Mercè Ibarz, "A Serious Experiment: *Land Without Bread*, 1933", in *Luis Buñuel: New Readings*, pp. 27–42.

44 Živojin Pavlović, *Djavolji Film: Ogledi i Razgovori*, 2nd edn (Beograd: Jugoslovenska Kinoteka; Novi Sad: Prometej, 1996), p. 196.

45 Živojin Pavlović, *Djavolji Film*, p. 216.

46 Aleksandar Petrović, "Susret s Lujem Bunjuelom", in *Prizor* (annual magazine no. 2), ed. by Snežana Nešković-Simić [articles on Aleksandar Petrović ed. by Radoslav Lazić], (Loznica: Centar za kulturu "Vuk Karadžić", 2003), pp. 23–25.

47 Aleksandar Petrović, "Susret s Lujem Bunjuelom", p. 23.

48 Aleksandar Petrović, "Susret s Lujem Bunjuelom", p. 25.

49 I translated this from Serbian, where Buñuel's sentences come across as short, sharp and somewhat disjointed, but I decided to leave this appearance in English as well. See Aleksandar Petrović, "Susret s Lujem Bunjuelom", p. 24.

50 Aleksandar Petrović, "Susret s Lujem Bunjuelom", p. 24.

51 See *Filmografija jugoslovenskog filma*, p. 299; see Filmography.

52 For example, Petrović's first three feature films had one-word titles in Serbian: *Dvoje*, *Dani* and *Tri*. Whereas their international titles for distribution varied, scholarly writing translated Petrović's austereness into English, so the above titles were translated as *Two*, *Days* and *Three*, thus even eliminating articles (it would probably be more correct if *Dani* were translated as *The Days*). Consequently, I am translating the titles of these shorts in the same way; the above-mentioned translations of the features were used by Mira and Antonín Liehm, *The Most Important Art*, and were then also used by Daniel Goulding, *Liberated Cinema*.

53 Mercè Ibarz, "A Serious Experiment: *Land Without Bread*, 1933", p. 31.

54 ibid.

55 *Filmografija jugoslovenskog filma*, p. 299.

56 See the previous chapter (section 2.4.1); from an interview with Aleksandar Petrović in Ivo Pondělíček, "Aleksandar Petrovič dokončil svůj nový film", *Film A Doba*, January 1969, p. 43.

57 Personal interview with Nikola Majdak (30 April 2006).

58 In a later interview to Pavel Branko, Petrović explains: "I was born in Paris, however, I moved to Belgrade almost immediately, but with the [rural] environment you are talking about, I got to know it during the filming of documentary films [*Record* and *Assemblies*]".

See Pavel Branko, "Démoni v nás a ve světě, v němž žijeme", *Film A Doba*, December 1969, p. 662.

59 At the same time as *Assemblies*, Dunav Film produced *Sopoćani*, directed by Ratomir Ivković, and filmed by Nikola Majdak, who also filmed *Assemblies*. *Sopoćani* was filmed in the monastery of the same name, but it was only concerned with the historical and cultural value of its architecture and frescoes. However, *Sopoćani* was rarely screened, and was also believed that the film was quietly suppressed. On this film, see *Filmografija jugoslovenskog filma*, p. 299; in addition, this book contains data on many similar films.

60 Dragoslav Adamović, "Prvi padež film", *NIN*, 28 March 1965, p. 10.

61 "Završen festival dokumentarnog i kratkog filma, Bulajić, Škanata i Bourek – prvi", *Politika*, 26 March 1965, p. 11.

62 Adamović states that Dunav Film submitted 31 films for the festival. See Dragoslav Adamović, "Prvi padež film", p. 10.

63 On the Belgrade School of Documentary Film, see Ranko Munitić, *Adio, Jugo-film!*, pp. 93–108.

64 Dragoslav Adamović, "Prvi padež film", p. 10.

65 Ranko Munitić, *Adio, Jugo-film!*, pp. 93–95.

66 Ranko Munitić, *Adio, Jugo-film!*, p. 95.

67 Ranko Munitić, *Adio, Jugo-film!*, pp. 95–96.

68 Mira and Antonín Liehm, *The Most Important Art*, p. 412.

69 Daniel Goulding, *Liberated Cinema*, pp. 59–61.

70 See the previous chapter (section 2.4).

71 That Avala Film wanted to refresh their production was no secret, and by 1966 this was virtually perceived as their official policy. Consequently, while reporting from the Pula Film Festival in 1966, French film critic Gilbert Guez stated: "The recent initiative from Avala Film, the most important production house, to start a policy of favouring debutant directors, enabled the arrival of new talent". See Gilbert Guez, "Pula, 13ᵉ", *Cahiers du Cinéma*, November 1966, p. 17.

72 "Authorial initiatives" means the directors aspiring to be auteurs; see Petar Volk, *Let nad močvarom: Aleksandar Petrović svojim životom, delom, i filmovima* (Beograd: Institut za film; Novi Sad: Prometej, 1999), p. 137.

73 Petar Volk, *Let nad močvarom*, p. 137.

74 Nevena Daković, "Reči, misli i pokretne slike", in *Filma vek 1895–1995*, ed. by Dejan Kosanović (Beograd: Jugoslovenska Kinoteka, SANU, 1995), p. 262.

75 Jasna Dragović-Soso, *"Saviours of the Nation": Serbia's Intellectual Opposition and the Revival of Nationalism* (London: Hurst & Company, 2002), p. 252.

76 On Lazar Stojanović as Petrović's student, see Chapter 6 (section 6.2).

77 Personal interview with Lazar Stojanović (3 January 2006).

78 Jasna Dragović-Soso, *'Saviours of the Nation'*, pp. 23–24.

79 Živojin Pavlović, *Djavolji Film*, pp. 347–48.

80 Živojin Pavlović, *Djavolji Film*, p. 348.

81 The history of East European cinema seemed to have revolved around permissible limits, and if one were to take Soviet filmmakers as an example, then Anna Lawton's assessment

becomes indicative of Eastern Europe as a whole. Lawton claims that Soviet "filmmakers had to test their limits and operate within the realm of the permissible". See Anna Lawton, "Toward a New Openness in Soviet Cinema", in *Post New Wave Cinema in the Soviet Union and Eastern Europe*, ed. by Daniel Goulding (Bloomington: Indiana University Press, 1989), p. 1.

82 See Michael Stoil, *Balkan Cinema: Evolution after the Revolution* (Ann Arbor: UMI Research Press, 1979), p. 5.

83 See the previous chapter (section 2.4.3).

84 Mira and Antonín Liehm, *The Most Important Art*, p. 228.

85 On technical data, cast and crew, see *Filmografija jugoslovenskog igranog filma 1945–1980*, ed. by Branislav Obradović (Beograd: Institut za Film, Časopis Filmograf, 1981), p. 29; see Filmography.

86 See Petar Volk, *Let nad močvarom*, p. 138.

87 Ronald Holloway, "Bulgaria: The Cinema of Poetics", in *Post New Wave Cinema in the Soviet Union and Eastern Europe*, p. 229.

88 Ranko Munitić, *Adio, Jugo-film!*, p. 264.

89 Michael Stoil, *Balkan Cinema*, p. 90.

90 Jasna Dragović-Soso, '*Saviours of the Nation*', p. 100. Daniel Goulding also considers the National War of Liberation as "the central founding myth" of the country; see Daniel Goulding, *Liberated Cinema*, p. 11.

91 Ranković also explains this aesthetically, demonstrating this "specialness" in relation to other art disciplines. See Milan Ranković, *Društvena kritika u savremenom jugoslovenskom igranom filmu* (Beograd: Institut za film, 1970), p. 16.

92 Andrew Horton, "The Rise and Fall of the Yugoslav Partisan Film: Cinematic Perceptions of a National Identity", *Film Criticism*, 12 (Winter 1987–88), p. 19.

93 Vučo quoted in Daniel Goulding, *Liberated Cinema*, p. 9.

94 Mira and Antonín Liehm, *The Most Important Art*, p. 124.

95 Michael Stoil, *Balkan Cinema*, p. 98.

96 Michael Stoil, *Balkan Cinema*, p. 90.

97 ibid.

98 Petar Džadžić, "Proza Antonija Isakovića", the preface for Antonije Isaković, *Paprat i vatra* (Beograd: Nolit, 1967), p. 5.

99 Petar Džadžić, "Proza Antonija Isakovića", p. 8.

100 This film was actually a follow up to another collaboration, and another frank portrayal of the war by Isaković and Stole Janković, *Through the Branches, Sky* (*Kroz granje nebo*, 1958).

101 Daniel Goulding, *Liberated Cinema*, p. 52.

102 See Chapter 1 (section 1.2.2).

103 These four stories are "In the Sign of April" ("U znaku aprila", pp. 19–32), "The Kite" ("Zmaj", pp. 125–38), "The Fern and the Fire" ("Paprat i vatra", pp. 141–54), and "Melons" ("Dinje", pp. 157–86); all in Antonije Isaković, *Paprat i vatra*.

104 From an interview with Aleksandar Petrović by Slobodan Novaković; see Slobodan Novaković, *Vreme otvaranja: Ogledi i zapisi o 'Novom Filmu'* (Novi Sad: Kulturni centar, 1970), p. 113.

105 Petar Volk, *Let nad močvarom*, p. 126.

106 The crowd is unsure whether the stranger simply has a speech impediment, or a foreign accent.

107 See *The BFI Companion to Eastern European and Russian Cinema*, ed. by Richard Taylor et al. (London: British Film Institute, 2000), p. 180. See also the opinion of his peer, Živojin Pavlović, in his autobiography, who claims that with *Three*, Petrović "achieved his authentic expression", in Živojin Pavlović, *Planeta Filma* (Beograd: Zepter Book World, 2002), p. 52.

108 On Petrović's comments on the opening scene, see his interview with Novaković in Slobodan Novaković, *Vreme otvaranja*, p. 112.

109 Petrović explained that he intentionally chose this sound, shown as used to animate an animal to dance, to illustrate the scenes when animalistic feelings are awakened in humans due to extreme circumstances – the war in this instance. Volk quotes Petrović at length on this issue; see Petar Volk, *Let nad močvarom*, pp. 133–34.

110 Andrew Horton, "The Rise and Fall of the Yugoslav Partisan Film", p. 22.

111 Jan Svoboda, "* * * [editorial]", *Film A Doba*, September 1966, p. 452.

112 Michael Stoil, *Balkan Cinema*, p. 98.

113 From an interview with Aleksandar Petrović by Slobodan Novaković; see Slobodan Novaković, *Vreme otvaranja*, p. 113.

114 A brief but accurate description of this actor's career and status can be found in Dina Iordanova, "Crveniot konj, The Red Horse", in *The Cinema of The Balkans*, p. 215.

115 The representation of fearlessness in the Yugoslav Partisan films is described by film historians Mira and Antonín Liehm, who state that these films "saw the past as one great heroic deed". See Mira and Antonín Liehm, *The Most Important Art*, p. 124.

116 Daniel Goulding, *Liberated Cinema*, p. 85.

117 Jan Svoboda, "* * *", p. 452.

118 Andrew Horton, "The Rise and Fall of the Yugoslav Partisan Film", p. 22.

119 That Bojanić is distracted while writing his report, first by the images of married couples on the wall of his room, then as his eyes have met with those of a young woman to be executed and finally with a wedding procession outside, clearly points out that Petrović introduces his favourite theme of, maybe not love but rather, absence of love while death is more than present.

120 Daniel Goulding describes an average representation of the Partisans, as set by an early war film *Slavica*, as "exceptionally brave, fair, enthusiastic, ever-victorious, joining hands and hearts in song and heroic deeds", whereas their commanders are described as "ever-smiling, bold, *compassionate* [my italics]" – see Daniel Goulding, *Liberated Cinema*, p. 17. Evidently, Petrović's protagonist is far from this.

121 Daniel Goulding, *Liberated Cinema*, p. 85.

122 Rada Šešić, "Valter brani Sarajevo, Walter Defends Sarajevo", in *The Cinema of The Balkans*, p. 109.

123 Rada Šešić, "Valter brani Sarajevo, Walter Defends Sarajevo", p. 111. Šešić also designates *Three* as a film that was far away from the usual representation of the war.

124 Andrew Horton, "The Rise and Fall of the Yugoslav Partisan Film", p. 21.

125 Ranković also includes (with *Three*) one film on the war by Živojin Pavlović, three films by Puriša Djordjević, and adds that there are also others. See Milan Ranković, *Društvena kritika u savremenom jugoslovenskom igranom filmu*, p. 7 (note 2).

126 Draško Redjep, *Rapsodija ništavila: Ogledi o Aleksandru Petroviću* (Novi Sad: Prometej, 2001), p. 80.

127 Daniel Goulding, *Liberated Cinema*, p. 9.

128 Michael Stoil, *Balkan Cinema*, p. 98.

129 This was the 12th edition of the festival, held between 26 July and 1 August (usually the last week in July), 1965. See Petar Volk, *Istorija jugoslovenskog filma* (Beograd: Institut za Film, Partizanska knjiga, 1986), p. 520.

130 From an interview with Aleksandar Petrović by Ranko Munitić; see Ranko Munitić, "Smisao filma kao umetnosti", in *Prizor* (annual magazine no 2.), ed. by Snežana Nešković-Simić, p. 102.

131 Daniel Goulding, *Liberated Cinema*, p. 90.

132 Although for his documentaries Petrović always used the same cinematographers, either Nikola Majdak or Jovan Jovanović, depending on who was available, with the only exception being *Record*, which was filmed by Stevo Radović, he kept on changing cinematographers on his feature-length projects – *Two* was filmed by Ivan Marinček, *Days* by Aleksandar Petković and *Three* by Tomislav Pinter.

133 Dušan Stojanović thoroughly analyses Petrović's sets in *Three*, where in key scenes he places characters behind open or closed windows, thus in frames within the film frame. See Dušan Stojanović, *Film kao prevazilaženje jezika* (Beograd: Univerzitet Umetnosti, Institut za Film, 1984), pp. 214–17.

134 See my essay on *Three*: Vlastimir Sudar, "Tri, Three", in *The Cinema of The Balkans*, pp. 49–50.

135 Volk offers a selection of the reviews published in Yugoslavia, including the most prominent film critics like Milutin Čolić and Žika Bogdanović, and the most relevant daily and weekly press, concluding that they were mainly affirmative. See Petar Volk, *Let nad močvarom*, pp. 127–31.

136 Jan Svoboda, "* * *", p. 452.

137 This proves that, contrary to those who claim that Eastern Europe only produced one-dimensional films on the war, complex portrayals of the war experience were a common and praised occurrence in the former Eastern Bloc. On this, see my essay on *Three*: Vlastimir Sudar, "Tri, Three", in *The Cinema of The Balkans*, pp. 47–48.

138 Daniel Goulding, *Liberated Cinema*, p. 90.

139 Petar Volk, *Savremeni jugoslovenski film* (Beograd: Univerzitet Umetnosti, Institut za Film, 1983), p. 215.

140 Natalia Zelenko, "Paporotnik i ogony", *Iskusstvo Kino*, October 1966, p. 89.

141 Gene Moskowitz, "Tri (Three)", *Variety*, 20 July 1966, p. 20.

142 Makavejev directed *Man is Not a Bird* (*Čovek nije tica*), and Pavlović directed *The Enemy* (*Sovražnik/Neprijatelj*).

143 Andrew Horton, "The Rise and Fall of the Yugoslav Partisan Film", p. 22.

Chapter 4

The Artist as a Feather Collector

On 1 July 1966 President Tito opened the Fourth Plenum, a Central Committee meeting, which he convened in order to dismiss his deputy and close collaborator – Aleksandar Ranković.[1] Ranković, a Serbian, was Yugoslavia's vice president and more importantly, the head of its secret police – the SDB (Služba Državne Bezbednosti – Service for State Security) – and wielded what appeared to be unlimited power for running this controversial but highly ranked state service. Nevertheless, Tito turned against his old friend, who had been a member of the Central Committee from before the war as well as a close collaborator during the war. As his place in the new post-war Yugoslavia was as the head of its security force, he was someone who was undoubtedly part of Tito's "inner circle". Historians have most often explained this removal with the claim that Ranković had abused his powers. John Lampe claims that the abuse of power was most in evidence in Ranković's authorisation for the bugging and electronic surveillance of the offices and residences of the highest party officials.[2] It was even alleged that President Tito's bedroom was under close scrutiny by the secret police. Initially unaware of these infringements on the privacy of the party's leaders, including possibly himself, Tito ordered an inquiry and subsequently removed his closest ally from political life for good. However, Ranković was removed not only because of his obsession with spying; Misha Glenny claims "the investigating commission found no evidence that any device had been placed in Tito's house".[3] It was political infighting amongst the high officials of the party, and the struggle to decide the new course for the whole country that perhaps played a more significant role in the demise of this key figure within the country's political elite. Jasna Dragović-Soso claims that Ranković "resisted the economic reform and did what he could to undermine it in his own republic" thus proving his "political conservatism and his centralist tendencies".[4] This in turn helped create a coalition of younger reformist politicians against him, including the pro-market reform supporters in his own republic.[5] Ranković's removal marked the end of the bitter struggle in the innermost circle of the political elite, which culminated between 1963 and 1965, and even caused a temporary "loss of identity" of the elite, exemplified with President Tito's change of mind on the economic reforms.[6] According to Dejan Jović, the conflict lasted for almost ten years, and the winner was Slovenia's Edvard Kardelj, another very close friend of Tito's, who was also an old Central Committee member and Partisan during the war.[7] Kardelj, who was more of an ideologue than Ranković, was the author of all the Yugoslav constitutions after the war. His political position was that Yugoslavia as a state ought to stand on the ideological foundations of *socialism*, rather than archaic and bourgeois concepts of ethnicity, as exemplified in the axiom of *brotherhood and unity*, still favoured by Tito.[8] Although Tito's position was closer to that of

Ranković – the realist – his removal opened the door for Kardelj – the ideologue – to base the country on purely ideological grounds according to Jović. The trope of brotherhood and unity would only survive in Tito's speeches after Kardelj had inaugurated the new constitution in 1974, which would have profound effects on interethnic relations within the country. It is of more significance here that Kardelj supported further market reforms in the economy, whereas Ranković did not, so his removal was "a clear signal in favour of economic reform".[9]

There are many factors behind Ranković's removal, and his conflict with Kardelj. Lampe includes Kardelj's latent disgruntlement when Ranković was designated Tito's potential successor in 1963;[10] Ranković's influence on the early problems in Kosovo was another factor,[11] although these are beyond the scope of this investigation. What is crucial here is that the removal of Ranković, evidently a staunch hardliner, resulted in a liberalisation within the country, bringing what Lampe called "the liberal hour"[12] – an hour that was to last for six years, until 1972 when Tito himself would tighten his grip on power. In 1966, the beginning of the "liberal hour" manifested itself with the proliferation of media,[13] which were, according to Lampe, "significantly less restricted", "published often independent analysis" and were "increasingly informative and reliable", which seemed to be the trend in all parts of Yugoslavia.[14] The film industry benefited from this air of liberalisation as well. Film historians such as Mira and Antonín Liehm also emphasise that Ranković's ("Yugoslavia's 'number 2' man")[15] fall from grace brought further democratisation affecting the film industry, primarily "in the strengthening of creative autonomy" and "in the gradual legalisation of new forms of film production, enabling independent groups of filmmakers to obtain the means to make films outside the framework of existing film enterprises."[16] It is in this kind of political climate that Aleksandar Petrović was to start work on his next film in the autumn of 1966. The expansion of political freedoms, however, was not the only or most important factor that influenced his new production.

4. 1. The New Direction

4. 1. 1. Petrović Focuses on the "Invisible"

Throughout 1966 Aleksandar Petrović's film *Three* continued to draw attention and gain further critical acclaim. The Oscar nomination announced later on in the year was one of the greatest achievements of the Yugoslav film industry to date, and respect for Petrović's work grew steadily.[17] The film would continue to attract favourable reviews internationally in the years to follow, as the screenings in the Market Section of the Cannes Film Festival in 1967 would show;[18] or the belated UK screening, when Mark Powell, commenting on the film, claimed that he had "seen films called masterpieces which are less profound".[19] In such an atmosphere of continuing critical success, it seemed inevitable that Petrović would soon embark on a new project, in conditions more advantageous than his previous ones. Additionally, after *Three*'s successful run in 1965, Petrović was made one of the members of the Avala Film creative board, which helped to consolidate his position within the studio as one of its distinguished members.[20] In the atmosphere of further liberalisation within the country, regardless of the various political, aesthetic, critical and commercial setbacks that had followed Petrović's two early feature films (particularly *Days*), the board of Avala Film was willing to enable Petrović to continue with his work, this time with more financing and independence.

This creative independence was most recognisable in the simple fact that Petrović's new film would be based on his own script and his own ideas. However, this fact not only emphasises the greater degree of authorship on Petrović's part, but it rather illustrates that his success, combined with the liberalisation of the country's policies, enabled him to produce one of the most significant and influential films to come out of Socialist Yugoslavia. As the demise of Ranković had – also in Daniel Goulding's assessment – enabled Yugoslav filmmakers "to widen thematic horizons",[21] Petrović's new project was to examine a theme so far unseen in both Yugoslav and world cinema in general. In the late autumn of 1966, Petrović filmed his fourth feature film *Skupljači perja*, which was distributed internationally as *I Even Met Happy Gypsies*[22] (*Skupljači perja* is literally *Feather Collectors* – I will refer to it as *Happy Gypsies* hereafter in this text), and was released in 1967.[23] It portrayed the life of ethnic Roma, or Gypsies as they are more commonly referred to.[24] The romantic visions of Gypsy life were not an unknown theme in the Yugoslav cinema up to that point: Radoš Novaković's *Sofka* (1948) and Vojislav Nanović's *Ciganka* (*The Gypsy Girl*, 1953) were both films based on the literature of Bora Stanković (1876–1927), a famous Serbian writer from the beginning of the twentieth century.[25] The representation of Gypsies in these films was more reminiscent of the international ones commonly found in arts and literature of that period. Petrović's approach would seriously question these stereotypical representations, opening a new dialogue for examining Roma Gypsies, and in representations of the Other in general. This pertinent thematic concern has helped the film retain its relevance and significance for modern audiences. It is thus worth examining first how and why Petrović decided to make a politically-engaged film about Europe's largest ethnic minority without their own nation state.

It would, naturally, be difficult to lay claim to a knowledge of what exactly was in Petrović's mind in 1966, but familiarity with the available testimonies, both written and verbal,[26] allows for speculation on four key reasons, which brought Petrović's attention to the Roma Gypsies' life at this time. It is difficult to pinpoint these reasons from Petrović's interviews made prior to the film, as they do not reveal a considerable amount of information about the new project. This appears to be more to do with the journalists than Petrović trying to hide anything before the film's completion. They seemed at that time more intrigued with the continuing international interest in *Three* than in Petrović's future plans. It is therefore mainly interviews given after the film's release that give clues to his motivations. Regardless of this, it is important to note that Petrović had emphasised on more than one occasion that his film was about human freedom or free agency per se. What this means generally, and within his oeuvre, will be discussed later, but it is important to underline that freedom is the real subject of *Happy*

Gypsies. In an interview given in May 1969, two years after the film was completed, Petrović underlined this, claiming that the Gypsy story was only a "pretext" to contemplate on the nature of human freedom.[27] As Petrović partly subscribed to the romantic view of Gypsies extant in the European and Yugoslav art and literature traditions, so Gypsy life provided more than a suitable platform for him to meditate on freedom in Socialist Yugoslavia and freedom in general. In his autobiography – *All My Loves* – Petrović starts a chapter entitled *Ljubav prema slobodi* – *Love for Freedom* – with the following sentence: "If the true measure of humaneness is the degree of freedom an individual manages to acquire for him/herself in his/her life, then Gypsies are humans above all."[28] Evidently, Petrović perceived Gypsies as "more free" or inclined to excesses of "euphoric freedom".[29] Therefore it is this belief (although romanticised – which will be addressed later) that can be identified as the first reason Petrović decided to use Roma Gypsies for his film that meditated upon the nature of freedom.

The second reason is related to the fact that, by 1966, Petrović had already developed something that could be considered a cinematic interest in the Roma Gypsy community. As explained in previous chapters, with his second feature film *Days*, Petrović became interested in the social groups that the official Yugoslav media rarely portrayed. Petrović's short documentary *Record* was nothing else but a search for the social strata usually ignored by the media. It was during the filming of this documentary in late 1963 that Petrović came across the Gypsy orchestra of Mikajlo Lakatoš, playing "*Djelem, djelem*", now considered a traditional Gypsy song, that Petrović then recorded for this film.[30] The most common versions of the song mourn the persecution of Gypsies during World War II by the Nazi SS troops, and it was recorded for the first time by Aleksandar Petrović in 1963, whereas the version sung by Olivera Vučo in his *Happy Gypsies* was to make the song world famous. Evidently, Petrović liked the song so much that he used it in *Three* (and in the short *Record*) where he involved the orchestra as well, in a scene portraying Gypsies as a part of Serbian society.[31] It is perhaps in this scene that Petrović considered using Gypsies not only as a part of the bigger picture, but also as a possible focus for a future film. While he was looking at this scene on the editing table, the above-mentioned song influenced his decision to make the latter film, as its full international title – *I Even Met Happy Gypsies* – is a verse lifted directly from the song's lyrics.

In 1966, Petrović travelled to Los Angeles for the first time.[32] In his autobiography he emphasises how shocked he was when he saw the ghettos where African Americans lived, but also how they reminded him of the Gypsies' ghettos in Yugoslavia.[33] As Petrović was a socially engaged artist and filmmaker, he perhaps felt compelled, after his American experience, to address this Yugoslav problem, which also existed in many other European countries at the time. As the third reason for portraying Roma Gypsies, I would suggest Petrović's wish to add a social dimension to his film, which he also elaborated upon in interviews, such as the one given to *Cahiers du Cinéma*, after the film's premiere at the Cannes Film Festival in May 1967.[34]

It is important to add here, in relation to the last argument, that in the mid-1960s, ethnic minority issues across the globe were still taboo, with almost every country, the industrially-developed world included, maintaining a marginalised position for its "underdog" nations.

The Yugoslav version of socialism claimed equal rights for all, but Petrović's film had shown that this was only in theory. As this was one of the earliest works to face this issue so openly, I am tempted to point out the fourth key reason Petrović tackled the difficult social position in which Roma Gypsies found themselves, was because of his genuine humanism.[35] This becomes the most important aspect of the film for this analysis, as the fact that Petrović shows a group, economically and politically deprived in the Yugoslav socialist system, demonstrates that he was continuing to uncover phenomena "invisible" in the society. By continuing his explorations of the marginalised, Petrović continued to examine and criticise the society in which he lived. He was responding critically to the political reality around him, introducing into his narratives his own views on it. If *Three* was Petrović's own vision of the war, distinctly different from the one commonly professed by the state, then *Happy Gypsies* becomes Petrović's own vision of the then contemporary society, specifically focusing on class and ethnic divisions, and portrayed in a way distinct from the official representations. With *Happy Gypsies* Petrović creates another complex dissection of society, one reflective of his own idiosyncratic intellectual and artistic inquiry, rather than a projection of the then officially sought, but unachieved political reality.

The script for *Happy Gypsies* is considered today one of the better examples of scriptwriting in Yugoslav cinema.[36] Petrović was aware that the only complaint from Avala Film regarding his critically acclaimed film *Three* was the fact that it did not attract spectators. Petrović, an outspoken proponent of the theories of authorship and film as art, was known to challenge the idea that a filmmaker should conform to what may be the taste of a general audience. He would add that this should not be understood as disrespect for filmgoers, but rather as a reminder of how complex the work on a film is.[37] Still, as negotiations with Avala Film progressed, Petrović claimed in an interview that he had tried to persuade the studio that this new project would attract large audiences.[38] Although it is of course never possible to foresee such things, Petrović turned out to have been correct, as it was to become the most popular film with the Yugoslav public for decades. Petrović added in the same interview that he had told the producers at Avala Film how the content of the film would refer to universal human problems, and that it would be wider in scope than his previous films, and would thus have the potential to appeal to wider audiences and attract more viewers.[39] Considering the promising script, Avala Film was prepared to offer Petrović better working conditions than before, as well as a larger budget. *Happy Gypsies'* budget was just under 200 million Yugoslav dinars,[40] whereas the cost of *Days* had been approximately 36 million.[41] *Days* had been shot on what was then approximately one-third of the average film budget – this being a sum somewhere between 100 and 150 million dinars. It is thus clear that Petrović's *Happy Gypsies* was produced in a more comfortable atmosphere. In comparison, a large production in Yugoslavia at the time was Veljko Bulajić's *Kozara* (1963)[42] for which the budget was 350 million, almost double that of *Happy Gypsies*.[43]

The extra funds gave the film a new and noticeable dimension in terms of production values. Primarily, the film was shot in colour – as opposed to the previous black-and-white ones – and Petrović employed Tomislav Pinter as the cinematographer again, his collaborator on *Three*. The narrative of *Happy Gypsies* was structured in a way that was reliant on a group of supporting characters, where the earlier films had revolved around one or two main protagonists. The narrative thus became considerably more complex, due to the extra characters, and Petrović opted for a fragmented narration; one that Andrew Horton sees within broader Yugoslav cultural traditions as "non linear".[44] Non-linear narratives were to become more frequently employed over time, but in 1967 their use was still a rare occurrence in cinema. The new film also had a leading female character – Tisa, played by a young non-professional Gordana Jovanović, and her male counterpart Bora, played by a rising film and theatre star Bekim Fehmiu. Jovanović was a Roma Gypsy, untrained in acting like all the other non-professionals cast for the film. She was found in one of the Gypsy ghettos of Serbia and Vojvodina by Petrović and his crew, while they were painstakingly looking for locations, authentic clothes and authentic characters for the film.[45] As already pointed out, apart from the two protagonists, it is the supporting roles that enriched the new project. The

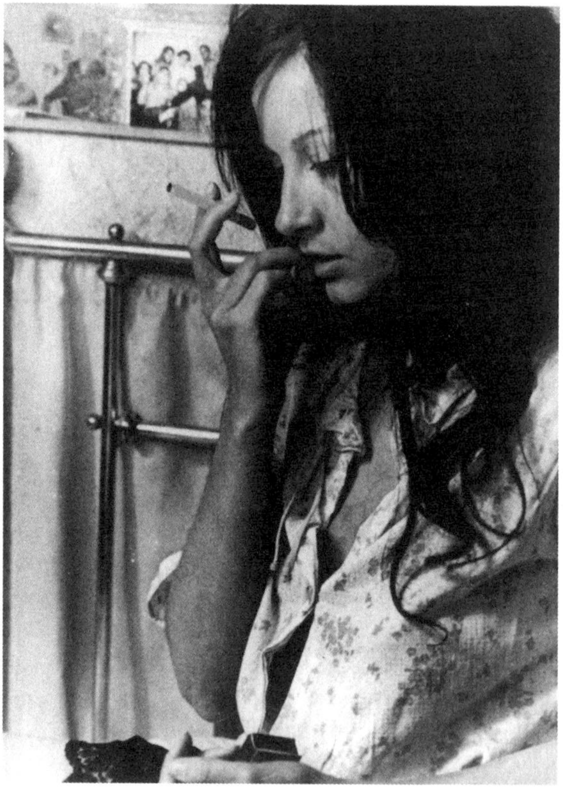

Figure 4.1: Actress Olivera Vučo, later better known as singer Olivera Katarina, in the role of bar chanteuse Lenče.

role of Bora's nemesis Mirta was entrusted to Velimir Bata Živojinović, whom Yamada Koichi characterised as "*l'acteur favori de Petrovic*" in *Cahiers du Cinéma*.[46] The bar singer Lenče was played by another rising acting and singing star, Olivera Vučo,[47] whereas the Priest – Father Pavle – was played by an actor who was a popular comedian at the time, Mija Aleksić.[48] A theatre veteran, Rahela Ferrari, played the Nun, whereas another non-professional, Etelka Filipovska, played Bora's common-law wife. Two other key supporting roles were also entrusted to non-professionals – Milorad Jovanović played Djerdj, Bora's best friend, and an old Gypsy sage, Šandor, was played by Milivoje Djordjević. The orchestra of Mikajlo Lakatoš was brought back to record more music for the film, only this time with Olivera Vučo as a singer. Thus, a larger cast, a more elaborate soundtrack and the use of colour were all new features in Petrović's oeuvre. In a rare interview in which the director actually remarked on the project prior to the start of filming, he described the new film in the following words:

At the beginning of autumn this year, I will start work on my new film. If I tell you that it will be about the beauty of autumn, I guess I will come across as very vague, but to me it seems, at least at the moment, that with this statement any further conversation is already exhausted. In some ways, the film is about the beauty of becoming and regenerating, about that eternal tragic game, about collecting what cannot be collected, about the hypnotic and bitter beauty of death and love. [...] When the film is finished, I hope, it will tell you more than that.[49]

4. 1. 2. *I Even Met Happy Gypsies* or *The Feather Collectors*

Bora Petrović is a Roma Gypsy who lives by buying and reselling feathers. He lives in the Gypsy ghetto of Sombor, a town in the northern Serbian province of Vojvodina, in the 1960s.

Bora's main competitor is Mirta, who has recently bought some feathers from a village that is part of Bora's "territory". Bora confronts Mirta, reminding him that they agreed on the ten villages that only Bora would exploit. Mirta admits that he broke their agreement and "trespassed" on Bora's fiefdom. He compensates Bora with money and offers a partnership. Whereas Bora would acquire feathers from both their territories, Mirta would classify and resell them. Bora accepts. They celebrate the deal in a bar, where they both seem to be infatuated by the singer Lenče, a local *femme fatale*.

Initially Bora's and Mirta's partnership progresses well, but Bora slowly falls for Mirta's beautiful stepdaughter, Tisa. Mirta marries Tisa to a considerably younger man, Pal, which appears to be a custom as Bora is also married to a woman visibly older than himself, Ruža.

However, Tisa soon breaks off the marriage as she considers Pal to be merely a boy, and unfit to be married. Bora invites Mirta for a talk, asking him for Tisa's hand. Mirta refuses angrily, reminding Bora that he is already married, that he is a gambler, an irresponsible and squandering bohemian, and also hinting at the main reason. Mirta too is interested in his stepdaughter, and the marriage to the younger man was a ploy to keep her close to him. Mirta breaks off all relations with Bora.

After a drunken attempt by Mirta to rape Tisa, she leaves home. Bora finds her and convinces her to marry him, and the wedding takes place at night in a church. He takes her home afterwards where he lives with his mother, his common-law wife and their children. As the tension in the house increases with Bora often away, Tisa runs away to Belgrade to pursue a career as a folk singer. Tisa is helped in this by the bar singer Lenče, who Tisa looks up to.

While in Belgrade, Tisa discovers how difficult the life of a Gypsy can be. Mirta finds Bora at a market place in Vojvodina, and tries to kill him with a knife because of his marriage to Tisa, but fails and runs away. In the meantime, Tisa hitchhikes back to Sombor after her unsuccessful sojourn in Belgrade, and is almost raped and then beaten up on the way. She is found in a ditch by an old Gypsy, who helps her back to Mirta's house.

When Bora finds out that Tisa is gone, he goes to look for her. Once he learns that she is back in Mirta's house, he goes there to confront him. They end up fighting with knives, and Bora kills Mirta. Afterwards, Bora leaves his family, giving them a last significant look before he departs. The police search for him soon after, in various Gypsy ghettos, but no one knows where he is, or is willing to reveal this to the authorities.

4. 2. International Recognition

4. 2. 1. While Travelling with the Gypsies

The synopsis of *Happy Gypsies* clearly shows that Petrović has made another film portraying a doomed love affair, very much in the vein of *Two* and *Days*. As in his statement, previously quoted, "hypnotic and bitter beauty of *death* and *love*"[50] remained the theme that Petrović himself maintained was the motif present in his entire oeuvre. To compare these doomed love affairs would demonstrate several interesting developments in relation to Petrović's narratives, but this is not the focus of this investigation. The intention here is to examine what can be discovered about the political and social context by looking at this film. If it is not evident from the synopsis, the social context in *Happy Gypsies* has considerably more weight than it had in either *Two* (where it was very discreet) or *Days* (where it was portrayed more obviously). In this respect, *Happy Gypsies* represents almost a new beginning, or rather a development, in which the context of Petrović's stories grows in importance to almost be on par with the main plot, if not even more important. Certainly, this film is now more often remembered for the social context it portrays, than its passionate love story.[51]

Through his filmmaking practice, Aleksandar Petrović encountered various strata of Yugoslav society that were widely underrepresented. In the early 1960s, many other Yugoslav filmmakers were to expose and examine phenomena or individuals in society that had remained on the margins of social change, and for whom socialism was not a society that had solved their problems. Most prominently, Dušan Makavejev and Živojin Pavlović were to join Petrović in 1965, with their first films *Man Is Not a Bird* (*Čovek nije tica*), and *The Enemy* (*Neprijetelj/Sovražnik*) respectively, both of which were set in Serbian factories, but examined the socialist workplace in a non-orthodox way. Makavejev continued his lucid analysis of society with his *Love Affair, or the Tragedy of a Switchboard Operator* (*Ljubavni slučaj ili tragedija službenice PTT*) in 1967, whereas Pavlović even more robustly portrayed – according to Milan Ranković – "the people rejected from their environment and relegated to the social underground",[52] in his *The Return* (*Povratak*, 1966), and *Awakening of the Rats* (*Budjenje pacova*, 1967). With time, younger filmmakers like Želimir Žilnik were to join the trend, and also expose the Yugoslav underclasses in their films – on which it will be elaborated further in the following chapter. The films of this generation of filmmakers, known as "New Film", became – as Ilja Gregory assesses it – "liberating in [their] revelatory force."[53] Gregory explains that a "distinctly auterist *cinéma engage*"[54] was created, which explored "images of a country ridden with economic and political problems".[55] The increasing focus on such issues was to ignite a conflict between the political establishment of the country and its filmmakers, but the filmmakers seemed compelled, or mesmerised by certain groups that they could not resist showing on the large screen.

Petrović had found various interesting street characters and "drop-outs" for his second Belgrade-based feature film, *Days*. Once he left the big cities and started investigating the Serbian countryside, his revelations of marginal groups exploded as he came across numerous groups that were literally on the margins (sometimes intentionally) because of the socialist project. His two documentaries, *Record* and *Assemblies*, featured many of these groups, and he introduces some of them in *Three* – which was his first feature outside the urban setting. The religious and homeless zealot Zeka, and the small group of Gypsies in *Three* are however still only ornaments within the overall narrative.[56] They are incorporated into a bigger picture of pre-World War II society, where they were also on the margins. With *Happy Gypsies*, Petrović was to "move" these two groups from the margins of society to become the focus of his film.

Petrović focuses primarily on the Roma minority (at the time most often referred to as Gypsies in former Yugoslavia and across Europe) in the film. Although the film is set in Vojvodina, a northern autonomous province of the then Socialist Republic of Serbia, from which he charts a complex and rich ethnic map, his main protagonists are the Gypsies. It is in the relations of the various groups with the Gypsies that this map is drawn. Gypsies were always on the margins of every political and historical system that ruled the area, and this did not change with communism, which was at least in theory supposed to have Gypsies equal with everyone else. In practice, their existence is shown in the graphically naturalist, realist style for which Petrović was to become famous.[57]

Very early on in the film, Beli Bora ("Beli" translates as "white", and refers to the white suit this character often wears), the protagonist, sits at the bar with his partner Djerdj and the two can neither agree on the price of the goods they will sell, nor on how to split the profits. Djerdj invites a policeman, whom he happens to know, and who is sitting at a nearby

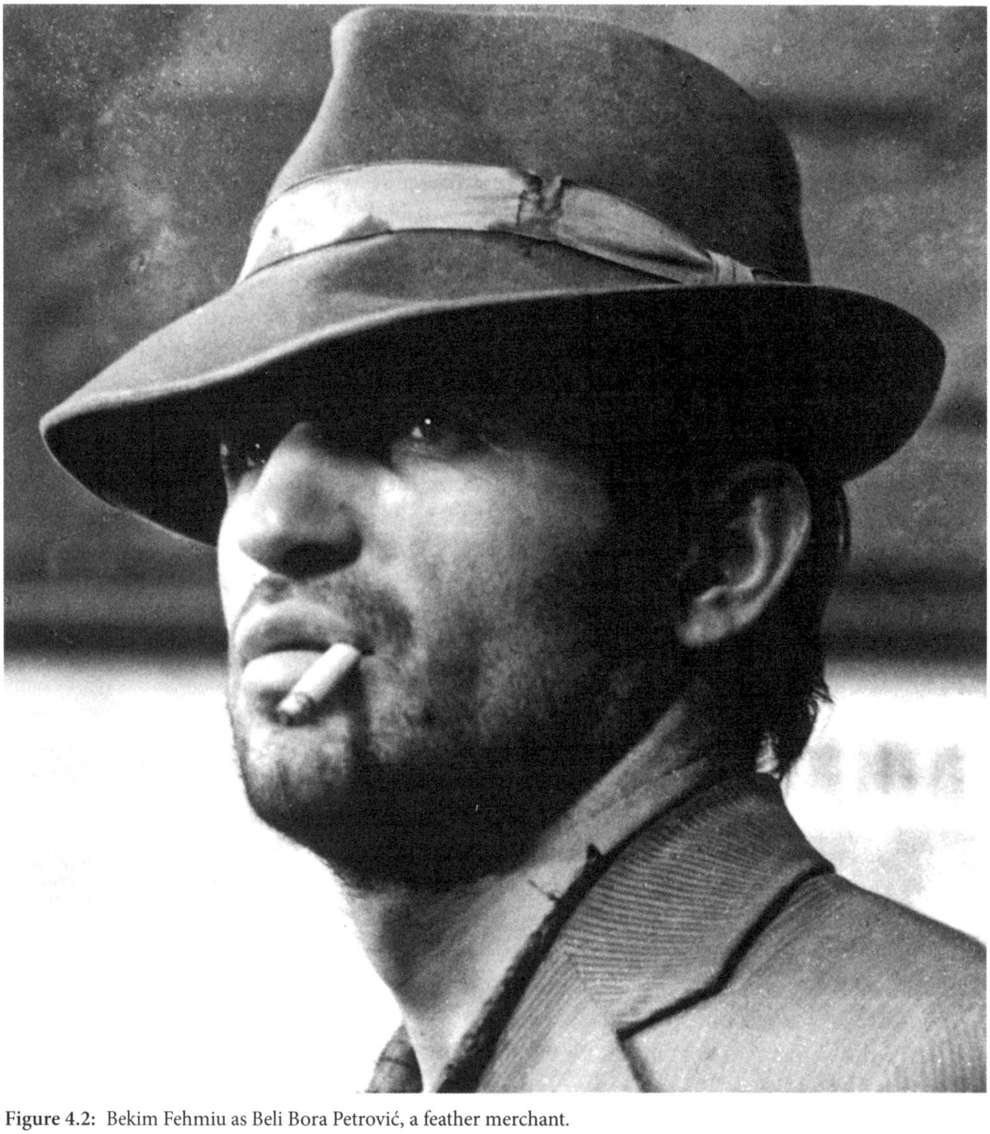

Figure 4.2: Bekim Fehmiu as Beli Bora Petrović, a feather merchant.

table, to join them, and help them resolve their dispute. Bora is not overtly happy with the Policeman joining in, but he continues the conversation. The Policeman jokingly comments that he can either arrest a Gypsy, or sit down and drink with him, but Bora dislikes this joke that reinforces a stereotype. He objects mildly, reminding the Policeman that there is nothing wrong with earning money here and there, as Gypsies, like anyone else, are trying to survive, and there is nothing dishonest about that.[58] As these accusations – or stereotypes – of dishonesty come from a policeman (someone representing the dominant society and its institutions), Petrović is emphasising the fact that Roma Gypsies are alienated from the society, or as Gregory puts it: "They are on the periphery of the system".[59]

This stereotype prevailing in former Yugoslavia (often embraced by the Caucasian population, whether Serbs or Croats), that Gypsies avoid "honest work", is to be reiterated, only a couple of scenes later. As Djerdj, apart from collecting feathers from local villages, also collects antiques, three persons from Belgrade arrive to buy his goods. A woman and a man immediately start asking about old lampshades and furniture, whereas the third person opens a conversation with a similar kind of "joke", reproaching Gypsies for not participating in socialism. The person actually asks Djerdj when the Gypsies are going to join the working-classes, and stop "wheeling and dealing". Djerdj responds swiftly with a sharp and telling pun, often difficult to translate for those unfamiliar with the political climate of the time. He addresses the person with "Mister Comrade", which sets the picture immediately, as post-war communist Yugoslavia agreed to use the term "comrade" for men and women as the formal style of address. Just as the French Republic after the revolution insisted on its subjects addressing each other as "Citizens", socialist countries introduced the term "comrade", as a reminder of everyone's equality. Titles such as "Sir", "Mister" or "Miss", were disqualified as bourgeois and discriminatory. Djerdj, by addressing his customer as "Mister Comrade" uses what may appear to be an oxymoron, although Petrović's use of it here is highly caustic.

The arrival of socialism challenged the class system in name (everyone was to address each other with the same title), but did not change the position of the Gypsies, who were again left on the margins. The work Bora and Djerdj are doing is untaxed, but they cannot claim any social benefits either. They are literally "outside society", not participating equally: this was not of their choice, but it is a reality they cannot easily escape. In such circumstances, people who can be addressed as "Comrades" are lucky, as they are a part of the new system. Gypsies, though, can only see them as privileged, thus their title "Comrade" can be "honoured" with the prefix "Mister". For Djerdj and Bora, mainstream society is too remote even to be desired. After such an address, which hides irony and resentment equally, Djerdj proceeds to say that "wheeling and dealing" anywhere is the same for the ones who have to do it.[60] Therefore, less than 15 minutes into the film, Petrović manages to create a critical picture of Yugoslav society, depicting the specifically awkward position of one of its minorities.[61] In this instance, the minority is also a social class in itself – the class "below" the proletariat.[62] The trio from Belgrade, who arrogantly perceive themselves as the righteous working-classes, and who in pursuit of antiquities arguably display a "petty bourgeois" taste, cynically assume that Gypsies just ought to stop living the way they do and join their society. They are clearly unaware of what such integration might require and are thus representative of Yugoslav society overall, who could have done more to alleviate, if not at least understand, the position of its most impoverished minority. Petrović's picture was and still is accurate, clearly showing the economic position of the Gypsies in order to identify the existence of a class problem in a society, which strived towards classlessness. Early on in *Happy Gypsies*, Petrović thus introduces one of the four political themes that were to permeate his oeuvre, the one that investigates the relationship between the political establishment and non-privileged groups. However, the commentary on the Roma and the Yugoslav state does not stop there. The specific nature of the relationship between the state and the community is elaborated further in the scenes set at the local magistrates' court, where Gypsies are subjected to the rule of law. In two different scenes, one where Bora is being penalised for "causing an obstruction to traffic by throwing feathers on the road", and another when a Gypsy friend of Bora's is bullied into admitting who killed Mirta, Petrović further describes the distance between Gypsies as a group, and the state in which they were living.

Early on in the film, Petrović creates another juxtaposition revealing this side of society hidden in the shadows. One of the first business deals Bora and Djerdj are arranging is with a nun in a monastery of the Serbian Orthodox Church, where they want to buy the feathers from their flock of geese. Serbian Orthodox Christianity was the main religion in that part of the country before the war and revolution, but in the communist era, as elsewhere in the socialist bloc, church and religion were aggressively marginalised and removed from public life.[63] The socialist societies were swiftly moving towards highly secularised states, atheist in principle, where going to church and believing was not necessarily persecuted, but was certainly seen as backward and disadvantageous for individuals aspiring to higher positions in society. The church became the breeding ground for an alternative mode of thinking to that of mainstream society. This was known, and perhaps expected, but rarely addressed by the ruling elites. In later years the Catholic Church took a distinctly more antagonistic role against communism, particularly in Poland, but in the early 1970s also in Croatia. This brewing resentment and opposition is captured by Petrović in the film, mainly in the character of Father Pavle, a Serbian Orthodox priest, who originally befriends Bora in order to sell him feathers.

Father Pavle sells the feathers from the duvets of his fellow priests, who have either died or abandoned the church for domestic life. He thus cannot do anything else but start selling off church property. He adds that it would not be long before he takes off his mantle, and leaves to find work in Germany. Again, this little comment, which caused laughter amongst Yugoslav audiences, was another bitter remark by Petrović, addressing another problem the proletarian state was cultivating. Yugoslavia did not have an aggressively expanding economy, nor were state-run socialist economies intended to be, but this meant it was not able to provide work for its ever-growing population. In the early 1960s, the response to this situation was a tacit arrangement with West Germany, a capitalist state, to satisfy its need for an increased workforce, by allowing Yugoslav workers to take employment there. This caused frequent migrations on a small scale to Germany, where many Yugoslavs looked for work.[64] As he puts it, even an out of work priest would have to go to look for work abroad as communists no longer need "holy things". Father Pavle does not hide his dislike for the authorities; he calls them "antichrists", and foresees their souls burning in hell like "shish kebabs". Moreover, he views them as sinful because they were forcing Gypsies to integrate into society by looking for regular, or conventional, employment.[65] This becomes a crucial comment on the Roma not only as an ethnic community, but on the Gypsy lifestyle as a specific culture, which communists, and many contemporary governments across Europe today, are not willing to understand.[66] Father Pavle, considering that he is a Christian priest, understands the Gypsy desire for freedom from state apparatus and similar constructions as God's will. Consequently, he can have an approving view on the way Bora lives. Socialist ideology however, striving towards a system of all-inclusive social participation and civic responsibility (which concept is also familiar to liberal democracies), could not allow groups happily to wander on its margins, as and if they desired.

Finally, this is the crucial question Petrović poses with his film – one that was not solely addressed to the political mainstream in Yugoslavia: the overall ability of any ideology to create a state, or system, to fit all. Petrović, by questioning the possibility of a "perfect society" as based on a set of ideological schemes, also questions the possibility of, or rather the avenues for, its imposition on the diverse strata of the public. Therefore, Petrović again paints a complex picture of Yugoslav society, investigating and warning about the side effects produced by the socialist edifice. Additionally, Petrović's insistence – as emphasised in his interviews[67] – on the notion of free human agency and individuality, whose expression often does not sit easily with the social or collective, is introduced in the film through the actions and behaviour of Beli Bora, further questioning the validity of any form of total social engineering. Father Pavle openly criticises this "human arrogance" as he talks to Bora who, essentially, only wants to buy feathers. In his struggle to survive, politics is an obsolete concept: it is earning money that enables him to go on.

Bora's relation with the Nun is more representative of the way in which the two marginal groups looked after and helped each other. Bora buys feathers from the Nun and also lends her money that the monastery badly needs. When Djerdj's baby son dies, and his wife does not want to bury him without church rites, Bora goes to see the Nun. She explains that the baby cannot be buried as a Christian as it is not baptised, and it cannot be baptised as it is dead. Again, the Gypsy baby is another metaphor for the position of the largest minority in Europe, one of an infinite limbo. Bora begs the Nun to help, invoking the fact that he has done her favours in the past, and the Nun accepts and baptises the dead child.

It is worth pointing out here that this film, with such an incredibly delicate narrative, has been very difficult to see in the former Yugoslavia or internationally for a considerable period of time. This difficulty has led to numerous – often inaccurate – descriptions of the film.[68] In the scene previously described, the actual process of baptism is not shown, but is metaphorically portrayed using images from frescoes depicting the baptism of Jesus Christ. Petrović adds the Nuns' singing on the soundtrack that usually accompanies baptising, and thus aestheticises what might have been a particularly morbid scene – the baptism of a dead child. In this way, he even departs from being metaphoric, but arguably creates a type of visual "euphemism",[69] which, in return though, allows scope for different interpretations. Ilja Gregory reads the scene differently, claiming that the Nun refused to baptise the child, adding that: "The abbess' [the Nun's] refusal to baptise the baby is ironically juxtaposed with shots of biblical frescoes."[70] The published version of the original script shows that the images of baptising and the Nun's singing are meant to imply that the child is being baptised.[71] Such a reading of the film made Gregory interpret the film in a way that the church, as a marginalised institution, also marginalises the Gypsies.[72] In fact, Petrović's positioning of the Roma community is considerably more complex, thus more reflective of the reality (where marginalised Gypsies were probably closer to the marginalised church, as opposed to mainstream society), rather than just representing Gypsies as a cipher equidistant from all the institutions. This scene, I believe, shows that some form of interaction is, or was, possible. Additionally, through the character of the Nun and particularly Father Pavle, Petrović thoroughly investigates the position of religion in society, which is another of the four politically conscious themes steadily solidifying in his films from this point on.

Petrović thus depicts the position of the Roma community within Yugoslav and Serbian society by juxtaposing the Roma with the latter's institutions. On one side, a policeman, Milanče, and a judge at the magistrate's court represent the mainstream institutions of the society; on the other, Father Pavle and the Nun from the monastery represent a marginalised institution of the dominant ethnic group. In between the two, it is easy to see how and where Roma Gypsies are placed in the society. Although they are not entirely rejected by either, they are certainly not included in the mainstream, whereas the church – also marginalised – becomes a perhaps reluctant partner, but a partner nonetheless. In one carefully framed scene from the film, as Bora argues with another Gypsy, Šandor, while walking through a Gypsy ghetto, the camera reveals an industrial development somewhere in the distance, with factory chimneys puffing away. Clearly, Gypsies are left on the outskirts of the technological progress embraced by socialist society. They are another group excluded from progress, like the one identified in his short film *Assemblies*, the film that clearly served as a sketchbook for this larger and more elaborate work. The main line of inquiry from this previous short documentary remained, and Petrović opens up society for further criticism.

Vojvodina provided a rewarding setting for the film and Petrović did not shy away from engaging with local intricacies as Vojvodina is specifically multi-ethnic; for example, he portrays Slovak and Romanian minorities in the film, who inhabit the region alongside many other ethnic groups. By engaging with the ethnic complexities of Vojvodina, Petrović introduces the third of the four politically conscious themes emerging in his work as a response to Yugoslav politics: the investigation of interethnic relations. Petrović therefore uses the setting to develop and express a particular view on the construction of ethnicity that, if analysed, is universal. His view should not therefore be understood as different from the then mainstream communist one. The latter view is explained in the introduction to this chapter, where Edvard Kardelj considered and criticised the nation state as a bourgeois construction.

When Bora or Mirta enter either Slovakian or Romanian houses, as they converse in Serbian, they are perceived not as Roma, but as Serbs. To another group that has its own way of living, the outsider is just one big "Other" without individual features. This creates another slightly comic situation, as Bora wants a Slovak peasant to describe a guy who bought feathers from him. Bora asks the usual questions – whether the person was a Gypsy, tall, or short – but the Slovak is unsure whether this person can fit any of these descriptions, only mentioning the person by name at the end – Mirta.[73] Bora is enraged, as these inept descriptions were unnecessary; it was the individual name that resolved the problem, and appears to be above a group identity. Petrović's view of the national as a construction, which does not seem to differ from the mainstream socialist view of the time, could perhaps be recognised more clearly in another scene with the same Slovak peasant. National identity in Vojvodina is often linked to a specific religious grouping (such as the Serbs, who would mainly associate themselves with the Serbian Church, Slovaks from Vojvodina often identify with their own Protestant Church). When Mirta goes into the church to negotiate with the Slovak, right in the middle of the sermon as the congregation is singing, the Slovak gives a sign to Mirta to join in the singing. He then shows a perplexed Mirta, who answers that he does not know how to sing, to open his mouth and pretend, as that is what the Slovak is doing as well. The church singing, such as other customs defining a nation, is only a construction we tend to adhere to. The fake singing becomes a comment on the validity of this adherence, the perpetual repetition of customs without questioning their purpose. The repetition yields only an empty and meaningless vessel.[74] In his first open exploration of ideological versus religious construct, Petrović perhaps creates a situation where the viewer could examine when and how an idea becomes empty and dogmatic. Just opening one's mouth instead of singing is the fate that befell communism – we can now conclude with hindsight. Whether the scene in the Slovakian church is a metaphor reaching out to question communism itself remains arguable. What is certain is that Petrović manages to relentlessly question the ideology and the society he belongs to, creating numerous parallels and connections between its various phenomena that he portrays. However graphic it appears in places, Petrović does not lose understanding and empathy in his representations. Consequently, as in *Three*, Petrović offers his own vision of reality, sharply critical but empathic, as he provides a context for his characters' actions, making it difficult to judge them.

The sympathetic view towards his male protagonist, Beli Bora, is perhaps most evident in his full name – Bora Petrović. Giving his main character the same family name as his own, Petrović for the first and only time in his films, deals with his protagonist as an alter ego or surrogate.[75] He wished to be identified with the oppressed minority and even portrayed his own penchant for gambling.[76] Petrović often stood for Gypsy rights, and in his autobiography he mentions that when he officially met President Tito, he asked what could be done to improve their dire position in Yugoslav society. President Tito was unimpressed by such a question from a film director and gloomily ignored it.[77]

Petrović's protagonist, Beli Bora, is almost an archetypal film hero, an uninhibited free agent, whose actions are finally and inevitably doomed. Although his actions are often perceived as unarguably immoral, their background is shown in such a way that we understand them and still empathise with him. His charms probably lie in the fact that he comes across at the same time as irrational but seductively passionate, thus irresistible. The creation of such an ambiguous character is one of the greatest achievements of the film, which Petrović commented on in one of his interviews: "My hero is a criminal, but can we

Figure 4.3: Velimir Bata Živojinović as Bora's nemesis Mirta, with Gordana Jovanović as his stepdaughter Tisa.

judge him?"[78] Bora's female counterpart is Tisa, a young Gypsy girl who wants to become a singer. Similar to Bora, she is a free agent, trying to get in life what she desires, regardless of the consequences. Tisa and Bora are the protagonists of the story, the characters Petrović created to question the relationship of the social and the individual.

The film opens with Bora in a taxi and seeing Tisa walking down the road. He offers her a lift, and in a brief conversation, the forthcoming narrative of the film is mapped out. Tisa is a stepdaughter of Mirta, Bora's rival in the business of feather collecting. Tisa, though, is not interested in the business; she wants to become a singer. Bora, traditionally married to an older woman in what was most likely an arranged marriage, is attracted to Tisa. He tries to kiss her jokingly, and she only hesitantly refuses. Bora's affection towards her would grow to a fully passionate obsession, eventually leading him to murder Mirta, who he feels is in the way of his happiness, as he perceives Tisa as someone who can fulfil his life. Her desire is somewhat different, but equally as unreachable as Bora's; when the film ends she has not become a singer, and as for many archetypal tragic (and romantic) heroes of film and literature, their true happiness is based on transgressions (e.g. Bora is already married, Tisa cannot sing), and is thus unattainable. Bora and Tisa are both tragic in their quest, but they nonetheless pursue it. This is why *Happy Gypsies* is referred to as a film about freedom. In interviews, Petrović described the film as follows:

I made a film about human freedom. I showed that through the life of Gypsies. Not accidentally. Their life points at how tragic human endeavour is to reach self-liberation, and shows the inevitable but beautiful failure that such an endeavour ends with.[79]

Petrović's film hence also becomes a meditation on irrationality, which in the case of his characters is a part of their "tragic human endeavour to reach self-liberation". As mentioned earlier, one of the key scenes exploring the issue of freedom – exercised through irrational (or anti-social) actions – happens at a local magistrate's court. Bora is there because he threw feathers on the road from a moving truck, thus causing an obstruction. After the Judge penalises him and formally closes the case, he proceeds to address him in a friendly manner, and asks him off the record how Bora, a professional feather collector, could just recklessly hurl feathers on the road thus losing them irretrievably. Bora responds in a lacklustre way, explaining this as "Gypsy business", adding that he was drunk, and that the sight of feathers flying off the truck was extraordinarily beautiful, hence he could not stop himself. Petrović has previously created the context for Bora's action: he was feeling melancholic as Mirta had just broken off their partnership, and refused to allow Tisa to marry him. Bora, while drunk, finds solace in this action of feather wasting, which inevitably appears ludicrous to an outsider, particularly a representative of the law. By justifying and humanising this action, and thus creating an empathy with the protagonist's irrational behaviour, Petrović questions the ability of society, its laws and ideology, to fully accommodate or understand the contradictions of human nature. However, in this scene the Judge, often the most common representative of society in arts and literature, sympathises with Bora even though he penalises him for the incident. Petrović does not portray the system as rigidly dogmatic, but with its representatives trying to understand and communicate with its marginal subjects. Such a portrayal of society was to change in his subsequent films, where Petrović's view was not to be as optimistic. However, in 1966, as the liberal hour was in its initial bloom, it could be concluded that Petrović, as exemplified in this scene, still believed that the ideology and its representatives are not too removed from its marginal strata. If they were to leave a dogmatic adherence to the letter of law aside, and open a dialogue with marginalised groups, as the Judge does in this scene, then communication, rapport and inclusion could be possible. Dogmatism rather than understanding is defined as a problem.

It needs to be emphasised though that, regardless of this Petrović's recognition that a possibility of rapport and social integration does actually exist, the film does not end on such an upbeat note. After Bora murders Mirta, we see him at home enjoying – it seems quite genuinely – his family life. Everyone sits in front of the telly while he plays with his youngest child. At one point he gets up and looks at his family for what will probably be the last time before he leaves, but without telling them what is going on. The day after, the police are looking for him in various Gypsy ghettos. Petrović films this scene as if it were a documentary film made by the police or someone working for them. All the characters he films in this scene, including those who acted in the film (Bora's wife, lover Tisa, companion Djerdj) are not professional actors, but are Roma people actually living in these ghettos. All of them refuse to reveal anything about Bora, although it is clear that probably many of them do not actually know where he has gone to hide, either from the law, or possibly revenge.[80] As Petrović films these interviews "to camera", the scene looks like a piece of authentic documentary footage, heightening the sense that we have seen a "real" story. More significantly, Petrović uses this to reiterate his key point. We, as viewers, and he as a filmmaker, are behind the camera with – our – police, whereas the Gypsies are in front, as an object of this cinematic enquiry and, within the fictional world of the film, a police investigation. Petrović here employs what Kristin Thompson and David Bordwell have characterised as his "pseudo-documentary realism",[81] to make it clear that Roma are excluded from society, and exist as its "Other". Integration is thus yet to be achieved, and on this level the film unambiguously criticises Yugoslav socialism.

4. 2. 2. Theorising the Representations of Gypsies

In order to be in a position to conclude on this specific representation of Gypsies as an ethnic minority, I shall indicate several assessments of Petrović's style in this film, some of which have already been summarised. Petrović's passionate love story set amongst Yugoslav Roma Gypsies consisted of "devastatingly real pictorial material" according to Mira and Antonín Liehm.[82] Yugoslav film critic Slobodan Novaković claimed that the film appears as a documentary, as he claimed that the rebirth of Yugoslav film started when filmmakers demonstrated a "tendency to show life truthfully, in an authentic way."[83] Novaković developed such a conclusion while arguing that the *realist* tendency is adopted from the Soviet classic silent films.[84] In a more recent analysis of the film Nevena Daković, without wanting to ignore the specific style of the film, concludes: "Although the whole atmosphere is imbued with magical realism, the film nevertheless manages to be a persuasive social drama; it should also be seen as a documentary with rich ethnological dimensions and implications."[85] As these comments underline, the style of the film resembles a documentary, which without further analysis, is not dissimilar to Petrović's previous films. This was further helped with Tomislav Pinter's camerawork that advances Petrović's obsession with detail, consequently photographed in close-ups. Close-ups dominate the film, and are probably the most salient feature of its style. In several key scenes, as when Bora and Mirta strike their deal in a bar, or when Bora loses his money while gambling in a decrepit bus, Petrović restrains himself from any wide or establishing shots, but leaves the viewers to adopt the space through close-ups of the characters and rare medium shots. He also shows close-ups of other "relevant" details, such as hens on a shelf in a bus, when Bora naively loses his money. The mobile camera between the protagonists, filmed within immediate distance or with telephoto lenses, thus recreates a look of a documentary film, and is reminiscent of the bar scenes already shown in Petrović's *Record*. This documentary style could thus be described as "realist". In addition, it is worth reiterating two other points related to the narrative: Petrović has portrayed the Gypsies as a group, which is first alienated from the institutions, and second, is an economically deprived social class.

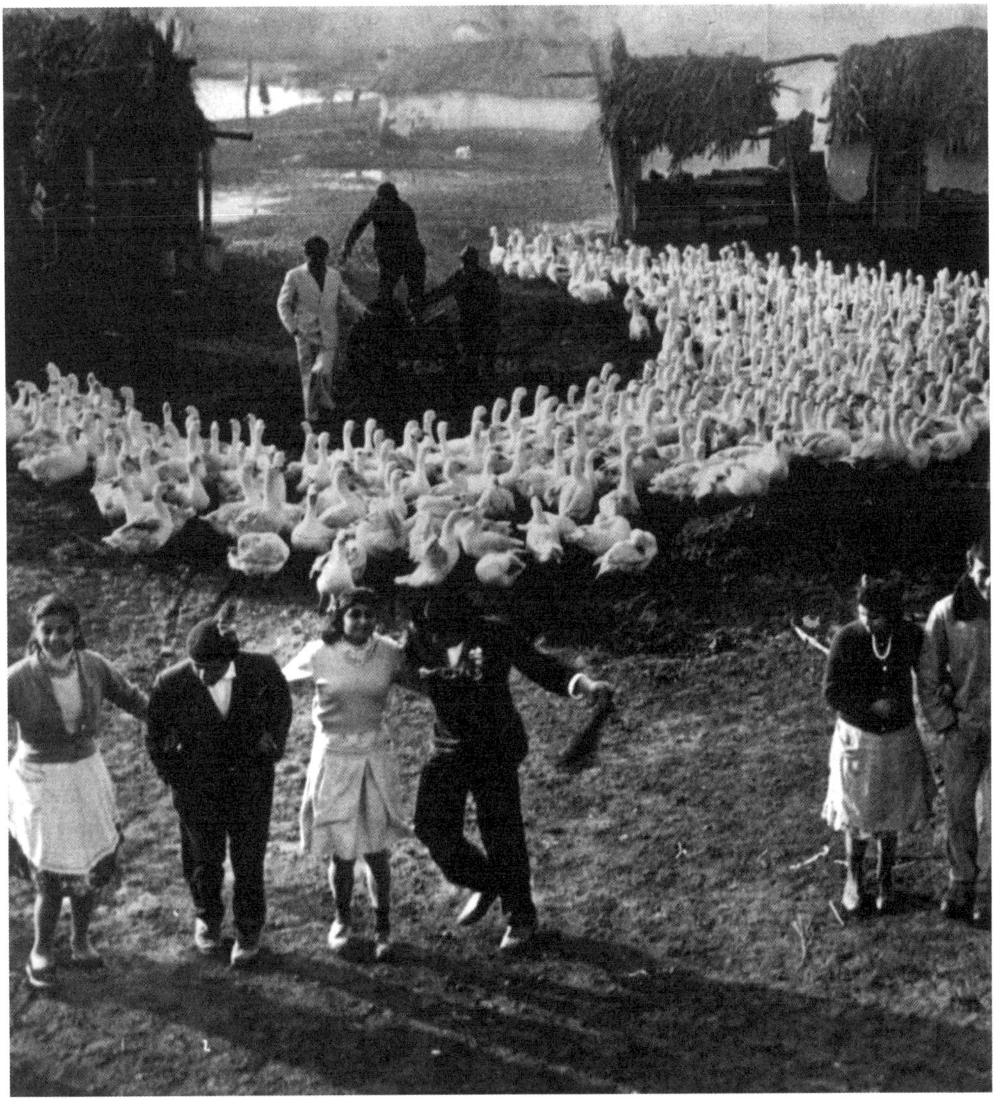

Figure 4.4: *I Even Met Happy Gypsies*: magical scenes set in the context of social critique.

In a seminal work on the history and aesthetics of East European cinema – *Politics, Art and Commitment in the East European Cinema* – editor David Paul emphasised that: "The official ideology of Marxism-Leninism has had a pervasive influence on all aspects of life in socialist Europe, including the arts."[86] Consequently, as an editor of this work, Paul included an essay by Lee Baxandall "Toward an East European Cinemarxism?", in which the author states: "The simple fact that film technology was devised after the deaths of Marx and Engels does not mean that a Marxian aesthetic for the use of this technology may not be extrapolated".[87] Baxandall proceeds to do precisely that, by taking into account views from a very diverse group of devotees to Marxist thought, from Jean-Luc Godard to Andrei Zhdanov, Friedrich Dürrenmatt to Luis Buñuel. What Baxandall articulates from these sources are three theses that could define a Marxist film. In the first thesis, Baxandall claims that "in Marx's opinion" the artwork needs to portray "through vivid characters and events, the implicit trends and developments of class experience and social struggle".[88] In the second thesis, Baxandall underlines realism, which he describes, by quoting Engels, as having: "Besides truth of detail, the truthful reproduction of typical characters under typical circumstances".[89] Finally, the third thesis Baxandall bases on "Marx's principle of *Entfremdung*, alienation, in class divided social life".[90] Baxandall thus creates a theoretical triangle requiring a Marxist film to identify class characterisation and alienation in a realistic manner. If this was to be taken as a valid framework, then Petrović's *Happy Gypsies* could stand as a classic example of a film produced within an East European political and historical time scale, which could be classified as a true Marxist film, because, as outlined, he portrays an alienated and deprived class, or group – Roma Gypsies – in a realistic manner. Baxandall continues to speculate that such films were common in the East and even if "a film such as this [is] antipathetic to Marxism" it is so precisely because of adopting the "elements of Marxian heritage".[91] Although Baxandall explains that such a Marxist critique was initially meant for a bourgeois society, he continues to speculate on its reception in a society that has embraced Marxism. However, these speculations should not be applied to the reception of Petrović's film, as its reception in Yugoslavia was an exceptional case, which will be discussed later. What can be concluded is that Petrović's depiction of Roma Gypsies as an alienated, underprivileged class, which he portrayed in a realistic style, makes him an artist who is "a tribune of the humiliated classes" as defined by Heinrich Heine (who was a friend of the young Karl Marx) in his "humanistic vision", as Baxandall reminds us.[92]

According to this analysis published in 1980 (applied to the film released in 1967), Petrović's vision of the Gypsy world was a Marxist one, thus revolutionary. This is certainly partially true, but the development of theories dealing with the representation of the Other has developed considerably in the meantime, as has film praxis dealing with this notion. Therefore, in her later analysis of the film, published in 2003, Nevena Daković introduced a revisionist theoretical view[93] reminding us of the now "controversial nature of 'Gypsy' films – the fact that the director and actors are not Romanys and do not belong to the ethnic group the film so authentically depicts."[94] Daković also adds that this film broke "new ground and initiated a long line of 'Gypsy' films coming from the wider region", and that "Petrović established the familiar images of 'Balkan exotics', of which Gypsies are an essential part."[95] Although Daković does not suggest that one has to belong to this particular group in order to be able to represent it on-screen, she critically explores the notion of how the portrayal of a class difference and social struggle is enough to create "revolutionary work", and that being "a tribune of the humiliated classes" may not have the same "affirmative" connotations in the postmodern age. As Roma Gypsies have rarely represented themselves in arts, the issue of their exploitation emerged in contemporary theory, critically exploring all the previous work involved with Gypsy themes, revising and revaluing the nature of these representations. This is why Daković perceives such films as having a "controversial nature", and is therefore necessary to explore the debates on representation that surround this "genre".

Svetlana Slapšak, whose view perhaps defines this aspect in the most critical sense, warns that "Roma actually do not exist" as their culture is shaped for them by the "collectives in power".[96] Slapšak thus critically emphasises that all the work in arts (and sciences) representing Roma Gypsies was made by non-Roma. As a consequence, Slapšak reminds us of the still strongly present racism against this minority – across contemporary Europe – to which Europeans are often blind, precisely because of the specific form of this racism. She also reminds us of the inability of Roma to respond to this racism, as the monopoly on their representation is in the hands of outsiders. It may seem that Slapšak has in mind archetypal, but now archaic cultural forms of the representation of Gypsies, exemplified perhaps in Victor Hugo's character Esmeralda (from *Hunchback of Notre Dame*), or Prosper Mérimée's *Carmen*. According to Goran Gocić,[97] the representational rupture with these archaic and romantic forms of representation starts with Petrović's film, followed by the films of Emir Kusturica. Slapšak, however, disagrees and also identifies the films of Emir Kusturica, which stem from the experience of Petrović's films, as perpetrators of the problem. Slapšak concludes that "stereotypes of a different form" were created in some contemporary cinematic representations.[98] Such views are often expressed in film criticism and Vladislav Mijić agrees, stating that Roma are always "exploited" when they become "focal points" of "other" authors' stories.[99] On the same side of the argument is an anthropological study on the cultural relationships between Serbs and Roma Gypsies: *Gypsies, Wars and Other Instances of the Wild* by Mattijs van de Port. Van de Port also claims that Serbian films – Petrović and Kusturica included – fail to accurately portray Roma Gypsy culture.[100] Therefore, these opinions (excluding Gocić) are critical of the representation of Gypsies that has its roots in Petrović's *Happy Gypsies*. What this representation entails, along with its precedents and ramifications, was comparatively examined by Dina Iordanova in her work *Cinema of Flames*. As she focuses precisely on the issue of representation, rather than a more tangential examination (as in many of the above examples), it is worth exploring some of her arguments, with the aim of reaching a conclusion on this complex issue.

In *Cinema of Flames*, Iordanova devotes a chapter to a comparative study of the most important films dealing with the representation of Roma Gypsies.[101] She criticises the obvious notion of exploitation, which is attached to simple romanticising of a truly difficult political and economic position, embedded in the history of European art. This romanticisation, as with Slapšak, is seen in works of art that are evidently not trying to understand Roma or their culture, but reinforce an idealised and romanticised image created by "outsiders'" – ethnic non-Roma. Above all, Iordanova explains several contradictions related to this issue. The representation of Roma Gypsies had to start somewhere and as they are an economically marginal group, this was likely to have been done by an "outsider". The most problematic misconception about Gypsies is that they are "happy" in their poverty, as it keeps them free from the constraints of the state and are thus passionate and life loving. Petrović's film challenges this perception initially with its title – which claims that there may only be *some* happy Gypsies. His film hence undoubtedly portrays Gypsy life as severely economically deprived, without much protection from the state, and if this is the image of "romantic freedom" then it is certainly not an enviable one. Such a break with the idealised view of Gypsy existence is evident and is queried by Petrović; thus from this aspect, he could certainly be absolved of the accusations of exploitation. I would also add that what seems symptomatic is that when Petrović's film is analysed, conclusions are often drawn from only analysing Beli Bora – the protagonist of the film. It is of course important to remember that Bora is not the only representative of Petrović's portrayal of Roma Gypsies, as this image needs to be extrapolated from the representation of all the Gypsy characters in the film. Beli Bora's nemesis, Mirta, whose portrayal Petrović entrusted to one of his favourite actors, is a character counter-distinct to Bora's. Where Bora is careless, Mirta is frugal, where Bora is impulsive, Mirta is calculated, and so on. When Djerdj is added to this equation, a character entirely different from these two, as well as all the other Roma Gypsy characters, I can conclude that Petrović portrays Gypsies as a heterogeneous group, as heterogeneous as any other.

Iordanova points to another phenomenon that also requires scrutiny. This is the idea that certain film directors used Gypsies as a cipher or vehicle, or even a "euphemism" to talk about other Balkan nations, or groups. This phenomenon that Iordanova calls "projective identification" (the concept is also debated by Van de Port)[102] is something that could be applied to Petrović's film. This also implies almost a new dimension to Petrović's work, specifically where he wants to address society. The stereotypes on Gypsies prevalent in Yugoslav society of the time (and probably still today, at least amongst some) enabled Petrović to use Gypsies as a "mouthpiece" in order to say things that were very critical, and thus approached with delicacy. Hypothetically, had Beli Bora not been a Gypsy outsider but rather a Serbian university professor who gambled, drank, constantly pursued impractical plans and finally committed a murder as a result of an uncontrolled passion, the Yugoslav authorities would undoubtedly have been concerned about the "message" of the film. Petrović sets his narrative amongst the Gypsies, who were – sadly – admitted to be outsiders in society, and so he points to society's ills and his authorial critique could go far without offending anyone. If either of the majority groups had been used, they would have undoubtedly been offended, but as their traits were "projected" onto Gypsies, such a harsh critique was safely constructed.[103] Daković also refers to Petrović as specifically cunning with this film, developing "a clever way of bypassing censure and rigid control."[104] This, according to Daković, was about portraying not only Gypsies as an "invisible" group, but others as well: "One should bear in mind that the film was shot at the height of communist rule, at a time when it was quite rare to feature churches and religious rituals so extensively."[105] Of course, as explained at the beginning of this chapter, although this was during the height of communist rule, it was also at the beginning of the "liberal hour", so Petrović had more options for manoeuvre. To conclude, as Petrović used Gypsies to enable himself to criticise the system harder and ultimately, to go back to the earlier hypothesis, with their colourful culture and penchant for music, Gypsies make better film protagonists than university professors, then Petrović was to an extent rightly criticised for exploiting this underrepresented group. This criticism though, in this instance could be problematised. Petrović clearly places his sympathies with the Gypsies, and his main character is his alter ego and is granted his family name – as already discussed. Finally, Petrović questions the fragile construct of ethnicity, as his Gypsies are perceived as Serbs by non-Serbs.

In addition, Iordanova refers to other strategies employed by Petrović to reduce this exploitation.[106] Firstly, all his main protagonists are Gypsies; rather than having the main protagonist a westerner (or any other non-Gypsy) who truly is a hero, while Gypsies become a prop around him/her – a common case in some "Gypsy" films.[107] This is specifically interesting in the case of Tony Gatlif, one of the rare established film directors who is an ethnic Rom. His renowned film *Gadjo dilo*, also known as *The Crazy Stranger* – a French and Romanian co-production released in 1997, exactly 30 years after Petrović's film – could not escape engaging with Roma Gypsy culture through the eyes of a westerner.[108] In contrast, Petrović's protagonists are Roma Gypsies. Finally, where *Happy Gypsies* was truly revolutionary was in the fact that most of the film is spoken in the Romany language, for the first time ever in cinema.[109] Additionally, Petrović found authentic Gypsy music and orchestras to perform the film's score, often from the roadside taverns – *kafana*[110] – as they are called in Serbia. The song "*Djelem, Djelem*" (or "*Gelem, Gelem*" – as it is spelled sometimes), which he had already used in *Three* and *Record*, had become a famous Gypsy song across Europe, and is now recognised as a Roma anthem,[111] thanks to the widespread distribution of this film. The extent to which Petrović was familiar with Roma Gypsy culture was commented on by Daković:

> Even though there are rumours that the director is of Romani origin and even though he displays a detailed knowledge of ethnographic details, Petrović is not of Romani descent but distinctively belongs to the dominant Serbian population.[112]

Consequently, some of the issues debated here will always remain problematic. Petrović was not an ethnic Rom, but with his film he had started a line of films whose representation was not always as well conceived as his. Films by Emir Kusturica in particular have frequently been debated, as he referred to motives portraying Gypsy life more than once in his career, and has thus provoked numerous debates about his intentions.[113] Kusturica has been accused of exploitation mainly for his later films, rather than earlier ones, but this debate is outside the scope of this investigation, as Petrović's work cannot be blamed for what it may or may not have inspired. Nevertheless, *Happy Gypsies* remains, in Daković's words, "one of the finest examples of Eastern European film of the sixties",[114] and an intellectual exploration of Yugoslav society and its complicated ethnic fabric. In this exploration Petrović tackled intricacies of representation, which would always defy an easy standardisation; so these cannot be seen as the film's shortcoming. To sum up, as Gregory correctly states: "At the time of its making, the ethnographic approach of the film to Romanies was pioneering both in the context of Yugoslav cinema and in terms of world cinema,"[115] therefore leaving *Happy Gypsies*, regardless of the notion of exploitation, as a celebration of Gypsy culture.[116]

4. 2. 3. The Reception, Success and Side Effects

The film was premiered at the Cannes Film Festival in 1967. An early review by Gene Moskowitz published in *Variety* before the close of the festival was very positive about the film and predicted: "this entry should be around come prize time at the presently unrolling Cannes Film Festival".[117] This prediction proved correct. The film won the Grand Prix of the festival, which was shared with Joseph Losey's *Accident* (UK, 1967), and at the same time received the International Critics' Prize (FIPRESCI), which is very rarely given to a film that has already received a prize from the jury. This prize was shared with Glauber Rocha's *Anguished Land* (*Terra em Transe*, Brasil, 1967), whereas the coveted Palme d'Or went to Michelangelo Antonioni's *Blow-Up* (UK, 1966). *Happy Gypsies* received an Oscar nomination in the United States in 1968, and a Golden Globe nomination in the same year. In 1968 it also received an award for the best foreign film released in Czechoslovakia. With such distinctions and international recognition, *Happy Gypsies* became the most successful film made in Socialist Yugoslavia for decades to come.

After its success at the Cannes Film Festival, later in the same year, the film received a Golden Arena prize as the best film at the Yugoslav National Film Festival in Pula.[118] Petrović was also awarded a prize for best director. The film opened in Belgrade to unparalleled public success. When its run finished in cinemas, the film had been seen by 400,000 people.[119] The same happened in other parts of Yugoslavia, and in Zagreb, the film was seen by 105,000 viewers in the first three weeks upon its opening.[120] As the population of Zagreb at the time was just under 500,000 inhabitants, this truly was an extraordinary success. *Happy Gypsies* broke all box-office records, and was the most popular domestic and international film that year. In fact, for years to come the film held the record as the most popular film shown in Yugoslavia. The film, according to Goran Gocić, "was subsequently sold in over 100 countries"[121] and film historians unanimously agree that with *Happy Gypsies* Petrović achieved international recognition.[122]

The success of the film was promoted and accepted by the state. This is not only based on the common rumour that President Tito himself loved the film and watched it many times but that Aleksandar Petrović received the award commemorating the 7th of July,[123] the highest honour given by the Socialist Republic of Serbia during communism, which was rarely given to filmmakers. Regardless of the film's bleak portrayal of Yugoslav reality, its success was also celebrated by the regime in power.

In his biography of Petrović, Petar Volk summarises important reviews of the film published in Yugoslavia after its release. Volk shows that Milutin Čolić's review,[124] who wrote for the daily *Politika* and whose reviews were perceived to outline the political elite's opinion of films,[125] and Bogdan Tirnanić's review,[126] who on the contrary was perceived as a supporter of New Film, were both similar and exceedingly positive about the film. Volk also adds reviews of other well-known critics of the time: Bogdan Kalafatović,[127] Mića Milošević[128] and Velimir Stojanović[129] who all praised the film. Dušan Stojanović summarised the most strikingly positive reviews on the film published internationally, and published them in an issue of Yugoslav magazine *Filmske sveske* (*Film Notebooks*).[130] Selections of predominantly French reviews were all very affirmative about the film. The most thorough study of the reception of the film can be found in the work of Svetlana Bezdanov Gostimir, who published a critical history of Yugoslav film criticism. Bezdanov Gostimir reiterates that reviewers were often positive, but also identifies some key objections to the film that appeared in the Yugoslav press. The most prominent objection was that the film was "more commercial, colourful and entertaining"[131] than the previous film *Three*, which is certainly correct. The insistence of some critics on the film's commerciality were evidently proven with its box-office success, but this says more about the critical rigour some of the Yugoslav film critics exercised at the time, than about the film itself. Its commercial accomplishments aside, it is, at least from today's perspective, unusual to stigmatise a film that contains numerous knife stabbings, two rape attempts, a murder and numerous beatings and violence by men against women, set in a dilapidated muddy village and contextualised within a genre of social drama for commercialism. Still, such objections initiated a critical assessment amongst Yugoslav critics, to which Volk also subscribes in his book that with *Happy Gypsies* Petrović broke continuity with his previous work.[132] Petrović himself argued vehemently against such views, as essentially his favourite themes of *love* and *death* were also at the crux of this film. In his interviews he rebuffed claims about discontinuity:

> I don't think that with this film I am interrupting my creative continuity. Essentially, it is the same poetics, atmosphere and spirit. I don't know why some individuals are unhappy that the film talks about Gypsies. They are not something outside our social experience.[133]

What Petrović admitted in another interview is that *Happy Gypsies* does have "wider universal dimensions than [his] other films", and added that this only demonstrates how the film has truly progressed from earlier work, and has opened a new phase in his oeuvre.[134] This appears as a valid explanation, as the fact that Petrović turned to colour and, thanks to bigger budget, introduced more characters into his drama, seems like a natural progression rather than a rupture with his previous work.

The film had a successful run in Paris where it was seen by almost 200,000 viewers,[135] and "opened simultaneously in four Parisian cinemas".[136] As Stojanović's collection of articles demonstrates, the international critical reception was predominantly positive, especially in France where the film was popular. As in Yugoslavia though, some interesting critical observations appeared in the press. *Cahiers du Cinéma* published a review in which Jacques Bontemps reproached the film on the grounds that its "ethnographic flamboyance blinds" the real issue, which is the social one.[137] Robert Benayoun of *Positif* also criticised this image of "*petite Yougoslavie*" wondering why it was favoured at Cannes over other Yugoslav entries like Dušan Makavejev's *The Switchboard Operator* (*Ljubavni slučaj ili tragedija službenice P.T.T.*, 1967) or Zvonimir Berković's *Roundabout* (*Rondo*, 1966).[138] A different type of criticism emerged in English-speaking countries, where the film did not have as enthusiastic a reception as on the continent, and in London the film attracted only "small audiences".[139] More significantly, *The New York Times* reviewer Renata Adler found that "it is nearly impossible to understand the broad outline of the story without programme notes."[140] A similar review was published in London's *The Times*, where John Russell Taylor assessed the story as "difficult to follow".[141] Emir Kusturica's films on Gypsies a few decades later were also unenthusiastically received in the United Kingdom and the United States in comparison to the European continent.[142] However, there were some notable exceptions such as Peter Baker, who in *Films and Filming* reported that he found himself "utterly enchanted by the Yugoslav entry, *I Met Some Happy Gypsies Too*".[143]

In his own recollections of the film's triumph, Aleksandar Petrović refers to a group of negative reactions that such popularity attracts. He was reproached about the party organised for the film's promotion at the Cannes Film Festival as some journalists in Yugoslavia thought it inappropriate that a socialist country spend money on staging such events.[144] Petrović claimed in some of his interviews that he would have been happier if the event did not take place at all.[145] Other allegations proliferated: that the prestigious award at Cannes was a result of Bekim Fehmiu's (the film's male lead) affair with jury member, Shirley MacLaine;[146] complaints by the company in charge of cleaning the Belgrade streets about them being misrepresented in the film; a similar accusation from a Belgrade professor of theology in relation to the church;[147] and then a failed court case of alleged plagiarism.[148] These were all indicators of the public frenzy that followed the opening of the film. Petrović added material to his book, which hints at another interesting campaign that is of more interest in scrutinising the Yugoslav political picture of the period.

Quiet but evident resentment was brewing amongst some sections of the media in neighbouring Croatia. The resentment started before the film received its prize at Cannes. A TV Zagreb programme *Ekran na ekranu* (*Screen on Screen*), which was reporting from Cannes as the festival was running, refused to show a clip of the film and was dismissive.[149] This was addressed and criticised by the press in Belgrade,[150] and was perhaps illustrative of the rivalry that existed between the two largest constituent parts of Yugoslavia. Curiously, the TV show featured two interviewees who had worked on the film. These were Bekim Fehmiu, the actor, who although Belgrade trained and based, was of Albanian ethnic origin from Kosovo, and Tomislav Pinter, the cinematographer, a Croat from Zagreb. Although *Happy Gypsies* is seen as a Serbian film today, at the time when Yugoslavia still existed, it was not difficult to remind oneself how talent from all over the country participated in its making. Instead, the film was implicated in the internecine animosities between the two republics, quietly brewing under the surface notwithstanding state control. This was manifested in the *Screen on Screen* TV show, and these antagonisms continued to grow and became more palpable at the Pula Film Festival in the same year.

After the film started receiving international accolades, it was Zagreb's *Večernji list* that started a long line of articles in sometimes churlish attempts to discredit the film, as when some of the ten critics of *Cahiers du Cinéma* marking films playing at the time in Parisian cinemas gave *Happy Gypsies* bad marks.[151] *Večernji list* immediately ran an article, pleased that they could corroborate their negative views on the film.[152] More significantly, they also found a Croatian film director to express his dismissive remarks about the film. Ante Babaja called *Happy Gypsies* "commercial semi spectacle" and claimed that the film certainly does not belong to "the domain of cinema as an art form".[153] It is interesting to note that Babaja had a new film in the same year entitled *The Birch Tree* (*Breza*, 1967). Babaja's film, like Petrović's, was shot in colour by Tomislav Pinter and was set in a very rustic environment of Zagorje,[154] not much different or far away from Srem and Bačka, where Petrović shot his film. Babaja also had Velimir Živojinović in one of the main roles and the overall look of the film was strikingly similar. The Yugoslav film critic Slobodan Novaković was a rare eyewitness who confirmed that both authors were impressed and influenced by the Soviet director Sergei Paradjanov and his film *Shadows of Forgotten Ancestors* (*Tini zabutykh predkiv*, USSR, 1964).[155] Babaja and Petrović were equally familiar with this Soviet film depicting a rural environment imbued with colourful folklore, which they also depict in their films. Babaja's film shows economic deprivation as well, this time in a Croatian village, and somewhat more cautiously than Petrović, he sets his narrative in the pre-war Kingdom of Yugoslavia. Due to this, his film becomes a historical reconstruction as opposed to Petrović's social critique. It is perhaps on this level that Babaja's film is fairly more predictable than Petrović's. As Babaja sets his narrative during the Kingdom of Yugoslavia, the poverty portrayed only contributes to the justification of the society that took over after the war, and produced his film. Babaja also shows the institutions of society, but the few policemen he shows are schematically cowardly, and are easily ridiculed, implying that the system they represent is equally ridiculous. With such a portrayal of the past, *The Birch Tree* conforms to the then official explanation of history, which is what Petrović daringly challenges in his film, as shown in the earlier analysis.

The study of the similarities and differences between the two films would perhaps be indicative of the two republics' – Serbian and Croatian – competing views on the cultural representation of Yugoslavia, a common entity.[156] Undoubtedly, these differences had started resurfacing with the liberalisation of the country and the fall of Ranković, which many in Croatia perceived as their own political victory.[157] In March 1967 a group of Croatian writers made a "Declaration Concerning the Name and Position of the Croatian Literary Language" that was an open call to an exclusively Croatian national programme.[158] One of the signatories of the declaration was the controversial figure of Miroslav Krleža,[159] who wrote a script for an early Petrović documentary.[160] The tension between Serbian and Croatian filmmakers reflected this and grew, so that at the film festival in Pula enmities were out in the open and mirrored in the behaviour of the audience, which loudly supported some directors and was hostile to others. Petrović claimed this was reminiscent of the bad behaviour of football supporters, who would not hide their national chauvinism when a Belgrade team played one from Zagreb, or vice versa, which is not how films should be "supported".[161] Petrović still won the first prize and Babaja third, but liberalisation had already started to reveal its "other face". Although Petrović succeeded in addressing the country's very sensitive and complex class and ethnic issues with his *Happy Gypsies*, these very ethnic issues started to mutate into ethnic problems, which were to culminate five years later.[162] As early as the mid-1960s, interethnic frictions were felt, and as Dragović-Soso correctly concludes: "As so many times in the past, disputes in the cultural sphere reflected already existing power struggles in Yugoslavia's political leadership."[163]

Notes

1 Misha Glenny, *The Balkans 1804–1999: Nationalism, War, and the Great Powers* (London: Granta Books, 1999), p. 582.

2 John R. Lampe, *Yugoslavia as History: Twice There Was a Country* (Cambridge: Cambridge University Press, 1996), p. 284.

3 Misha Glenny, *The Balkans*, p. 582.

4 Jasna Dragović-Soso, *'Saviours of the Nation': Serbia's Intellectual Opposition and the Revival of Nationalism* (London: Hurst & Company, 2002), p. 30.

5 ibid.

6 See the introduction to Chapter 3, and section 2.4.3 in Chapter 2.

7 Dejan Jović, *Jugoslavija – Država koja je odumrla: Uspon, kriza i pad Četvrte Jugoslavije* (Beograd: Samizdat B92; Zagreb: Prometej, 2003), p. 132.

8 Dejan Jović, *Jugoslavija*, p. 133.

9 Misha Glenny, *The Balkans*, p. 583.

10 John Lampe, *Yugoslavia as History*, p. 284.

11 Jasna Dragović-Soso, *'Saviours of the Nation'*, p. 160.

12 John Lampe, *Yugoslavia as History*, p. 284.

13 On media, Lampe talks about newspapers, magazines and newscasts on radio and television. For example, by 1966 the number of radio stations "jumped to 77, from 21" in 1962. See John Lampe, *Yugoslavia as History*, p. 287.

14 ibid.

15 Mira and Antonín J. Liehm, *The Most Important Art: Soviet and Eastern European Film after 1945* (Berkeley: University of California Press, 1977), p. 416.

16 Mira and Antonín J. Liehm, *The Most Important Art*, pp. 416–17.

17 This only excludes an Oscar for animation that Dušan Vukotić won for his film *Ersatz* in 1961. However, *Three* received one of the first Oscar nominations for a fiction film.

18 See Koichi, Y., "Trois d'Aleksandar Petrovic, Yougoslavie", *Cahiers du Cinéma*, June 1967, pp. 52–53, where the film is characterised as the best surprise of the festival's "Market Section" together with Jerzy Skolimowski's *Le Départ* (Belgium, 1967).

19 Powell, M., "Trio", *Films and Filming*, January 1970, p. 49.

20   Petar Volk, *Let nad močvarom: Aleksandar Petrović svojim životom, delom i filmovima* (Beograd: Institut za Film; Novi Sad: Prometej, 1999), p. 140.

21   Daniel Goulding, *Liberated Cinema: The Yugoslav Experience* (Bloomington: Indiana University Press, 1985) p. 73.

22   There are several international titles that could be found in literature and archives, apart from *I Even Met Happy Gypsies*; it is common to see *I Even Met Some Happy Gypsies*, and in the UK the film was distributed as *Happy Gypsies...!* – where the exclamation mark in the title was questioned by John Russell Taylor, in his review in *The Times*. See John Russell Taylor, "Cameo-Poly: Happy Gypsies. . . !", *The Times*, 15 February 1968, p. 6.

23   For the technical details of the film, cast and crew, see Branislav Obradović (ed.), *Filmografija jugoslovenskog igranog filma 1945–1980* (Beograd: Institut za Film, Časopis Filmograf, 1981), p. 34, or see Filmography.

24   According to *The Oxford Dictionary*, "Rom" is singular, "Roma" is plural, and "Romany" is the language used by ethnic Roma; I will follow these definitions in my work. See *The Concise Oxford Dictionary of Current English*, ed. by Della Thompson, 9th edn (Oxford: Clarendon Press, 1995), p. 1194 ("Rom" and "Roma"), and p. 1195 ("Romany").

25   Film *Sofka* was based on Stanković's novel *Nečista krv* (*Impure Blood*) first published in 1910, whereas *The Gypsy Girl* was based on the popular play *Koštana*, from 1902. Stanković's work was perceived as realist, with psychologically well-defined characters. Most of his work was set in southern Serbia, which remained under the Ottoman rule longer than any other part of Serbia, where Stanković described various conflicts emerging as the result of rapid modernisation following the departure of the colonisers. However, his Gypsy characters were portrayed more or less romantically, as in other European literature of the time. On Stanković's work and biography, see http://www.rastko.org.rs/knjizevnost/umetnicka/proza/bstankovic-krv.html [last accessed 3 September 2012].

26   "Verbal" mainly refers to the personal communication I had with Petrović's colleagues and contemporaries.

27   Lucifero Martini, "Aleksandar Petrović: Snimam što želim", *Novi List*, 29 May 1969, p. 8.

28   Aleksandar Petrović, *Sve moje ljubavi/Slepi periskopi* (Novi Sad: Prometej, 1995), p. 58.

29   ibid.

30   For a detailed account of this event, see Petrović's autobiography: Aleksandar Petrović, *Sve moje ljubavi*, pp. 60–65.

31   See Chapter 3 (sections 3.2.5 and 3.1.2).

32   Aleksandar Petrović, *Sve moje ljubavi*, p. 69.

33   See for example pages 70 and 73 where these points are explicitly made (Aleksandar Petrović, *Sve moje ljubavi*).

34   Bontemps, J. and Yamada, K., "Entretien avec Aleksandar Petrovic: J'ai même rencontré des Tziganes heureux", *Cahiers du Cinéma*, June 1967, p. 42.

35   I also debated this point in a private interview with Aleksandar Petrović's widow Branka Petrović (11 September 2005).

36   For a literary analysis of the script, see the foreword of the published version of the script by Nikola Milošević, in Aleksandar Petrović, *Skupljači perja* (Beograd: Jugoslovenska Kinoteka; Novi Sad: Prometej, 1993), pp. 12–15.

37   An interview with Aleksandar Petrović, see Adamović, D., "Borba za novi filmski izraz i za jeftin film", 11 November 1962, p. 12.

38   An interview with Aleksandar Petrović, see Kostić, A., "Politikantsko prodavanje pravoverja (1)", *Film novosti*, 27 December 1967, p. 3.

39   ibid.

40   An interview with Aleksandar Petrović, see Vukov Čolić, D., "Pojedinci kriju nesposobnost lokalpatriotizmom", *Vjesnik*, 6 August 1967, p. 6.

41   An interview with Aleksandar Petrović, see Adamović, D., "Borba za novi filmski izraz i za jeftin film", p. 12.

42   Aleksandar Petrović, *Novi film 1950–1965* (Beograd: Institut za Film, 1971), p. 175.

43   Petrović's budget was approximately $160,000, but due to a high inflation rate in SFR Yugoslavia over the years, it is difficult to calculate what the budget value meant internationally. Anyhow, this would be beside the point, as these "internal" comparisons clearly show that the first two films were made on very low budgets, whereas *I Even Met Happy Gypsies* was just above the region of an average Yugoslav production. Additionally, translating these values into international currency is also very misleading for another reason. The way films were produced in Socialist Yugoslavia was different from the West, as for example this amount does not include Avala Film staff on regular payroll, who also worked on the film, and various other services film productions received "in kind support and services". A very useful argument on why the correct amounts of money invested in Yugoslav films cannot be shown through the exchange rate of the period can be found in Daniel J. Goulding, *Occupation in 26 Pictures* (Trowbridge: Flicks Books, 1998), pp. 6–7, where Goulding explains this by taking another Yugoslav film as an example, Lordan Zafranović's *Occupation in 26 Pictures* (1978). Comparing the budgets of other Yugoslav productions thus gives a better idea of what these budgets meant.

44   On the non-linear approach in Yugoslav filmmaking, and *Happy Gypsies* as one of its examples, see Andrew Horton, "Filmmaking in the Middle: From Belgrade To Beverly Hills, A Cautionary Tale", in *Before the Wall Came Down: Soviet and East European Filmmakers Working in the West*, ed. by Graham Petrie and Ruth Dwyer (Lanham: University Press of America, 1990), p. 163.

45   Petrović scouted around with a large group of collaborators, which included the main professional actors, the cameraman, set designer, costume designer, Petrović's wife and others. This was confirmed in personal interview with Petrović's widow, Branka Petrović (11 September 2005), and with actor Bekim Fehmiu (3 May 2006). It was not possible to conclude with certainty who actually spotted Gordana Jovanović, as written, and particularly verbal, testimonies do not tally. There were several individuals claiming it was them, but it was certain that this did happen during these location-scouting sessions undertaken by Petrović and his crew.

46   Koichi, Y., "Trois d'Aleksandar Petrovic, Yougoslavie", p. 52.

47   Later better known as Olivera Katarina.

48   On Mija Aleksić, see Chapter 2 (section 2.2.2).

49   An interview with Aleksandar Petrović; see Kostić, A., "Umetnička dela nisu paklene mašine", *Beogradska nedelja*, 1 May 1966, p. 30.

50   ibid (my emphasis).

51   See for example the work of Dutch anthropologist Mattijs van de Port, *Gypsies, Wars and Other Instances of the Wild: Civilisation and Its Discontents in a Serbian Town* (Amsterdam: Amsterdam University Press, 1998) – where he observes Yugoslav Roma Gypsy community, and also uses Petrović's film as research material, see pp. 138–139, 147, 160–161, 165–167, 185 and 202.

52   Milan Ranković, *Društvena kritika u savremenom jugoslovenskom igranom filmu* (Beograd: Institut za film, 1970), p. 71.

53   Ilja Gregory, "Fragments of Nationhood: 'Novi Film' as Seen From the 1990's: Revisioning Yugoslav Social and Political Reality (1947–1972)" (unpublished master's thesis, London: British Film Institute, Birkbeck College, 1995/96), p. 2.

54   Ilja Gregory, "Fragments of Nationhood", p. 11.

55   Ilja Gregory, "Fragments of Nationhood", p. 2.

56   See Chapter 3 (section 3.2.5).

57   See Kristin Thompson and David Bordwell, *Film History: An Introduction* (New York: McGraw Hill, 2003), p. 464, where Petrović's style in this film is characterised as "pseudo-documentary realism".

58   See the published script of the film: Aleksandar Petrović, *Skupljači perja*, p. 30.

59   Ilja Gregory, "Fragments of Nationhood", p. 36.

60   See the published script of the film: Aleksandar Petrović, *Skupljači perja*, pp. 35–36.

61   There were more than 20 ethnic minorities in Vojvodina alone, and consequently more in Socialist Yugoslavia as a whole. In theory, they all had the same rights, but in practice this was probably unmanageable. Additionally, the Italian minority, in Yugoslav Istria, claimed that they were not treated as well as minorities associated with the socialist countries, for example the Romanians living in Yugoslavia, because Italy was a "capitalist enemy" to Socialist Yugoslavia. Therefore, to compare how all the ethnic minorities were treated would be useful, but it is beyond the scope of this investigation.

62   It used to be said in Turkey that there are 72.5 nations living in the country. This "half a nation minority" was in reference to the Roma Gypsies.

63   See the previous chapter (section 3.1.4).

64   On this issue, see Misha Glenny, *The Balkans*, pp. 588–589; and John Lampe, *Yugoslavia as History*, pp. 283–284.

65   See the published script of the film: Aleksandar Petrović, *Skupljači perja*, pp. 69–72.

66   I would be inclined to add here that being Roma means belonging to an ethnic group, with all the attributes that usually entails, primarily speaking the language of the group – Romany – in this instance. However, being Gypsy means living a Gypsy lifestyle, which is sometimes done by members of other ethnic groups (e.g. gypsy travellers), as well as the fact that not all Roma live the Gypsy lifestyle themselves.

67   See Petrović's interview in Lucifero Martini, "Aleksandar Petrović: Snimam što želim", p. 8; or his autobiography, Aleksandar Petrović, *Sve moje ljubavi*, p. 58.

68   Minor inconsistencies exist even in the description of the narrative by Daniel Goulding, who wrongly claims that Beli Bora and Lenče – whom he calls Lenka – do make love at some point, which does not happen nor is it mentioned in the published script.

See Daniel Goulding, *Liberated Cinema*, p. 127. Similar problems exist with another example of a very interesting analysis of the film by James Partridge, but based on the inaccurate retelling of the plot, although the article emphasises that this important film is neglected and not frequently shown. See James Partridge, "Dignity in diversity: Aleksandar Petrović's neglected classic *Skupljači perja*", *Central Europe Review*, 2 (27 November 2000), available on: http://www.ce-review.org/00/41/kinoeye41_partridge.html [last accessed 3 September 2012].

69   This type of "visual euphemism" is arguably different from just a metaphor – in a scene when Mirta attempts to make love, quite forcefully, to Tisa, she defends herself with a knife and runs away. Petrović there edits into an image on the wall, in that room, which shows Jesus holding a wounded heart, or rather a heart with a bleeding cut, implying that Mirta's heart is broken as he was in love with his stepdaughter Tisa. This of course, would provide for a study in itself.

70   Ilja Gregory, "Fragments of Nationhood", p. 38.

71   Aleksandar Petrović, *Skupljači perja*, p. 37.

72   Ilja Gregory, "Fragments of Nationhood", pp. 37–38.

73   The first question Bora asks is whether this person is a Gypsy, and the Slovak answers: "I don't know, he is not a Slovak." See Aleksandar Petrović, *Skupljači perja*, p. 46.

74   It would be interesting to compare Petrović's view from 1966 with some later, scholarly explorations of national constructions, such as Benedict Anderson, *Imagined Communities: Reflections on the Origin and Spread of Nationalism* (London, New York: Verso, 1991). Anderson's view of the nation as a construction, which almost perfectly fits Petrović's depiction of the multi-ethnic interaction in Vojvodina, is best summarised by Andrew Wachtel, who explains this view of a nation as not "a political entity but a state of mind, an 'imagined community' in the lapidary terminology of Benedict Anderson, whose members belong to it not because of any objective identifying criteria such as common language, history, or cultural heritage (although in many particular cases such criteria can be and are adduced) but because they think they do." See Andrew B. Wachtel, *Making a Nation, Breaking a Nation: Literature and Cultural Politics in Yugoslavia* (Stanford: Stanford University Press, 1998), p. 2.

75   In the first scene when Beli Bora's surname is mentioned at the magistrates' court, his surname seems to sound like Pavlović. This, if compared to the published script, is a mistake, as it should be Petrović. See Aleksandar Petrović, *Skupljači perja*, p. 112; later on in the film, the police are looking for Beli Bora Petrović.

76   Petrović's identifying with the oppressed can be seen in a similar way in the opening sequence for *Three*, where he superimposes his name over the image of hanged patriots (see the previous chapter, section 3.2.5). A penchant for gambling is something Petrović talked about in his autobiography, and his character Beli Bora loses all his money on gambling early on in the film. Petrović's explicit statement on gambling is in Aleksandar Petrović, *Sve moje ljubavi*, p. 108.

77   Aleksandar Petrović, *Sve moje ljubavi*, p. 199.

78   An interview with Petrović by Gilles Jacob for *Les nouvelles litteraires*, quoted from Aleksandar Petrović, *Novi film, crni film 1965–1970* (Beograd: Naučna knjiga, 1988),

p. 146; in the same vein see his interview with Bogdan Kalafatović for *Književne novine*, on pages 148 and 149.

79 See an interview with Aleksandar Petrović in Konstantinović, S., "Priznanje se moglo očekivati", *Politika Ekspres*, 21 May 1967, p. 14. Petrović also states in this interview that his film is "some kind of stance of a group of people who are against self-absorption and rigid views prevalent in contemporary art".

80 One character refuses to answer, claiming he does not speak or understand Serbian.

81 Kristin Thompson and David Bordwell, *Film History*, p. 464.

82 Mira and Antonín J. Liehm, *The Most Important Art*, p. 420.

83 Slobodan Novaković, *Vreme otvaranja: Ogledi i zapisi o 'Novom Filmu'* (Novi Sad: Kulturni centar, 1970), p. 69.

84 ibid.

85 Nevena Daković, "Shadows of the Ancestors", *Framework*, 44 (Fall 2003), p. 106.

86 David W. Paul, "Introduction [to Part II: Film, Aesthetics and Ideology]", in *Politics, Art and Commitment in East European Cinema*, ed. by David W. Paul (Basingstoke: The MacMillan Press, 1983), p. 69.

87 Lee Baxandall, "Toward an East European Cinemarxism", in *Politics, Art and Commitment in East European Cinema*, p. 74.

88 Lee Baxandall, "Toward an East European Cinemarxism", p. 79.

89 ibid.

90 Lee Baxandall, "Toward an East European Cinemarxism", p. 81.

91 Lee Baxandall, "Toward an East European Cinemarxism", p. 95.

92 Lee Baxandall, "Toward an East European Cinemarxism", p. 78.

93 I call Daković's theory revisionist, as in her article she debates ideas relating to the notion of "Other" that were more intensely argued and introduced in the theories of postmodernism. The theories of postmodernism, however contradictory, are generally understood as being opposed, or reacting against, the theories of modernism. The fact that Daković uses postmodernism as a platform implies that her analysis departs from modernist theory, and thus re-evaluates and revises previous analyses of the film. In this case, the theory of Lee Baxandall belongs to the domain of modernist thought, thus Daković's views are juxtaposed with it, in order to compare how these two theoretical concepts approach the same film. The interactions of the two theories (modernism and postmodernism) on the issue of "Other" were perhaps best described in brief by David Harvey, who explains: "We thus find Aronowitz arguing in *The Crisis of Historical Materialism* that 'the multiple, local, autonomous struggles for liberation occurring throughout the post-modern world make all incarnations of master discourses absolutely illegitimate.' Aronowitz is here seduced, I suspect, by the most liberative [*sic*] and therefore most appealing aspect of postmodern thought – its concern with 'otherness'. Huyssens particularly castigates the imperialism of an enlightened modernity that presumed to speak for others (colonized peoples, blacks and *minorities, religious groups, women*, the working class) with a unified voice [my emphasis]." Where Petrović's representation would fit in here is I believe evident. For this quote and argument, see David Harvey, *The Condition of Postmodernity: An Enquiry into the Origins of Cultural Change* (Oxford: Basil Blackwell Ltd, 1989), pp. 47–48.

94 Nevena Daković, "Shadows of the Ancestors", p. 105; it is interesting to note that Roma are referred to in this text as Romanys, which according to *Oxford Dictionary* is incorrectly spelled, as it should be Romanies. It is of course significant to note that even the name of the ethnic group is not used as commonly as Gypsies, thus it is often used and spelled in different ways, even in academic work.

95 Nevena Daković, "Shadows of the Ancestors", p. 103.

96 Svetlana Slapšak, *Ženske ikone XX veka* (Beograd: Biblioteka 20 vek, 2001), p. 241.

97 Goran Gocić, *The Cinema of Emir Kusturica: Notes from the Underground* (London, New York: Wallflower Press, 2001), p. 99.

98 Svetlana Slapšak, *Ženske ikone XX veka*, p. 243.

99 Vladislav Mijić, "Witnesses and Commentators: Romani Character in *Ko to tamo peva*", *Framework*, 44 (Fall 2003), p. 114. However, Mijić in this article asserts that the only correct way of representing Gypsies in films made by non-Gypsies is if Gypsies are given supporting roles. This, of course, is a rather reductive prescription, which is simply absurd.

100 Mattijs van de Port, *Gypsies, Wars*, p. 152.

101 Dina Iordanova, *Cinema of Flames: Balkan Film, Culture and the Media* (London: British Film Institute, 2001), pp. 213–232.

102 Mattijs van de Port, *Gypsies, Wars*, p. 154.

103 That this was the case can be corroborated with the fact that Petrović with his following film had shown depravity and social resentment amongst one of the dominant groups in Yugoslavia, and thus caused a serious rift with the authorities; see Chapter 5.

104 Nevena Daković, "Shadows of the Ancestors", p. 106.

105 ibid.

106 Dina Iordanova, *Cinema of Flames*, p. 225.

107 Goran Paskaljević's *Andjeo čuvar* (*Guardian Angel*, SFR Yugoslavia, 1987) is a particularly problematic example, and if one were to follow conscientiously the discourse on exploitation, then its author could be accused of latent racism, even though his narrative seems to advocate the opposite.

108 Dina Iordanova, *Cinema of Flames*, pp. 224–225.

109 Professor Rade Uhlik of the University of Sarajevo, then a rare linguistics expert in the Romany language, was employed by Petrović to teach the professional actors to speak the language; from personal interview with Bekim Fehmiu (3 May 2006). Professor Uhlik is also credited in the film as the translator of the dialogues by Petrović from Serbian to Romany, and vice versa.

110 On *kafana*, see Van de Port, who commits a chapter to this phenomenon; Mattijs van de Port, *Gypsies, Wars*, pp. 177–206.

111 Aleksandar Petrović, *Sve moje ljubavi*, p. 63. See also, http://www.unionromani.org/gelem. htm [last accessed 3 September 2012].

112 Nevena Daković, "Shadows of the Ancestors", p. 105.

113 On Emir Kusturica see: Dina Iordanova *Emir Kusturica* (London: BFI, 2002); and already quoted Goran Gocić, *The Cinema of Emir Kusturica: Notes from the Underground*.

114 Nevena Daković, "Shadows of the Ancestors", p. 103.

115 Ilja Gregory, "Fragments of Nationhood", p. 29.

116 In addition, the then International Roma Association started its world congress that year with the screening of this film as a clear sign that this work was endorsed by Roma community. See an interview with Aleksandar Petrović in Konstantinović, S., "Priznanje se moglo očekivati", p. 14.

117 Moskowitz, G., "Sreo Sam Cak I Srecne Cigane (I Even Met a Happy Gypsie)", *Variety*, 10 May 1967, p. 20.

118 The 14th Yugoslav National Film Festival in Pula was held between 26 July and 1 August 1967. Volk claims that the festival featured a record number of films in competition, with a total of 27. See Petar Volk, *Istorija jugoslovenskog filma* (Belgrade: Institut za film, Partizanska knjiga, 1986), p. 520.

119 An interview with Aleksandar Petrović; see Kostić, A., "Politikantsko prodavanje pravoverja (1)", p. 3.

120 See the report on cultural life in Zagreb, in Stevo Ostojić, "Zagreb: Sezona u zenitu", *Politika*, 9 December 1967, p. 11.

121 Goran Gocić, *The Cinema of Emir Kusturica*, p. 99.

122 See *The BFI Companion to Eastern European and Russian Cinema*, ed. by Richard Taylor et al. (London: British Film Institute, 2000), p. 180.

123 See "Dodeljene Sedmojulske nagrade", *Borba*, 4 July 1967, pages 1 and 7.

124 Petar Volk, *Let nad močvarom*, p. 168.

125 Personal interview with Lazar Stojanović (3 January 2006).

126 Petar Volk, *Let nad močvarom*, p. 172.

127 Petar Volk, *Let nad močvarom*, p. 169.

128 Petar Volk, *Let nad močvarom*, p. 170.

129 Petar Volk, *Let nad močvarom*, p. 171.

130 See *Filmske sveske*, 1 (June–July 1968).

131 Svetlana Bezdanov Gostimir, *Filmom do kritike & vice versa* (Beograd: Institut za film, 1993), p.145.

132 Petar Volk, *Let nad močvarom*, p. 154.

133 An interview with Aleksandar Petrović, see Vukov Čolić, D., "Pojedinci kriju nesposobnost lokalpatriotizmom", p. 6.

134 An interview with Aleksandar Petrović, see Kostić, A., "Politikantsko prodavanje pravoverja (1)", p. 3.

135 An interview with Aleksandar Petrović, see Kostić, A., "Strah od uspeha, Aleksandar Petrović: Politikantsko prodavanje pravoverja (2)", *Film novosti*, 3 January 1968, p. 4.

136 Alistair Whyte, *New Cinema in Eastern Europe* (London: Studio Vista Limited, 1971), p. 130.

137 Bontemps, J., "Skulpjaci perja", *Cahiers du Cinéma*, June 1967, p. 44.

138 Benayoun, R., "Le Cinema Resiste aux Bacilles de Cannes", *Positif*, July 1967, p. 20.

139 An interview with Aleksandar Petrović, in Miodrag Petrović, "Moj film je realan", *Književne novine*, 15 March 1969, p. 16.

140 Adler, R., "Screen: Yugoslavia's 'I Even Met Happy Gypsies': Feather Traders' Lives Limned at Regency", *The New York Times*, 21 March 1968, p. 57.

141 Russell Taylor, J., "Happy Gypsies", *The Times*, 15 February 1968, p. 6.

142 Goran Gocić, *The Cinema of Emir Kusturica*, p. 38.

143 Baker, P., "Cannes", *Films and Filming*, July 1967, p. 6.

144 See Aleksandar Petrović, *Novi film, crni film*, p. 86.

145 An interview with Aleksandar Petrović; see Vukov Čolić, D., "Pojedinci kriju nesposobnost lokalpatriotizmom", p. 6.

146 See the main actor Bekim Fehmiu's account on these events in Konstantinović, S., "(5) Nezaboravna noć sa Širli… [Interview with actor Bekim Fehmiu]", *Politika Ekspres*, 17 May 1967, p. 13.

147 See "Paperjari", *Ekonomska Politika*, 22 July 1967, p. 901.

148 See an unsigned article "Atak na 'Sakupljače perja' sud odbio", *Večernji list*, 13 December 1967, p. 19.

149 Petar Volk, *Let nad močvarom*, p. 178.

150 See for example Pera Psunj, "Po-po-pokislo im perje (Ekran u kratkim pantalonama)", *Politika*, 19 May 1967, p. 22.

151 "Le Conseil des Dix", *Cahiers du Cinéma*, December 1967, p. 6.

152 See Aleksandar Petrović, *Novi film, crni film*, p. 111.

153 An interview with Ante Babaja, see Franjić Z., "Ante Babaja: 'Ukloniti Trabante'", *Večernji list*, 10 August 1967, p. 8. This is not to imply that Babaja himself might have been a Croatian nationalist; quite the opposite as he praises a film by Živojin Pavlović, a film-maker from Serbia in the same interview. This is about how the media interpreted such comments in Croatia, including *Večernji list* that published this interview.

154 Petrović's *Happy Gypsies* and Babaja's *The Birch Tree* were the first two feature films Tomislav Pinter filmed in colour. In a 2004 interview, Pinter explained that there was more preparation work involved during the filming of *Happy Gypsies*, and that the film stocks he used were superior to those used for *The Birch Tree*, implying that he was more satisfied with his work and results in *Happy Gypsies*. See an interview with Tomislav Pinter in Vanja Černul, *Subjektivni kadrovi: Razgovori s filmskim snimateljem Tomislavom Pinterom* (Zagreb: V. B. Z., 2004), p. 23.

155 Slobodan Novaković, *Vreme otvaranja*, p. 74.

156 Further interesting comparisons between Petrović and Babaja can be found in Petar Volk, *Savremeni jugoslovenski film* (Beograd: Univerzitet Umetnosti, Institut za Film, 1983), p. 257, where Volk quotes Novaković, who, as it appears, was fond of exploring these (dis) similarities.

157 Jasna Dragović-Soso, '*Saviours of the Nation*', p. 31.

158 ibid.

159 Misha Glenny, *The Balkans*, p. 585.

160 This was *Petar Dobrović* in 1957; see Chapter 2 (section 2.2.1).

161 An interview with Aleksandar Petrović, see Kostić, A., "Strah od uspeha, Aleksandar Petrović: Politikantsko prodavanje pravoverja (2)", p. 4.

162 I will address this further in Chapter 6.

163 Jasna Dragović-Soso, '*Saviours of the Nation*', p. 137.

Chapter 5

The Artist as an *Agent Provocateur*

After the introduction of the programme for economic reform in 1965, and more importantly, after the fall of the head of the State Security Service, Aleksandar Ranković,[1] the space opened in Socialist Yugoslavia for the consolidation of various critical activities. The cultural historian Jasna Dragović-Soso identifies two key phenomena that established themselves during the 1960s as "the areas of intellectual activity that most seriously challenged the Titoist system."[2] One of the two areas was, according to her, the movement in literature and the visual arts now known as the Black Wave.[3] This is usually referred to as Black Film when the topic of cinema is debated,[4] and is one to which Aleksandar Petrović made a significant contribution, particularly in 1968 as he completed his new project. The other intellectual activity that, according to Dragović-Soso, "led to the development of a multifaceted critique of the unrealised promises of the Yugoslav revolution" was in the domain of philosophy.[5] She identifies this phenomenon as the New Left, and explains that as early as 1960, at the "Conference of the Yugoslav Association for Philosophy and Sociology, a group of Marxist scholars came into open conflict with party ideologues, when they criticised 'dialectical materialism' and argued in favour of a 'creative Marxism' concerned with alienation and humanism."[6] In 1963 the group started an international Marxist summer school on the island of Korčula, and followed this in 1964 with the publication of the journal *Praxis*, in Zagreb. However, it was only in 1966 that the advisory council for the journal was formed, which then included a large group of professors from Belgrade as well.[7] The historian John Lampe explains that from "its first issue in 1964, *Praxis* editors had hammered away at the failings of Yugoslav self-management from the left."[8] This group of philosophers thus pledged their loyalty to "Marxist humanism", according to Lampe.[9] The film historian Daniel Goulding argues that "the basic position of Živojin Pavlović, Aleksandar Petrović, Dušan Makavejev and others [of the Black Film directors] was very close to the philosophical radicalism of the *Praxis* group".[10] Goulding extrapolates parallel positions from the writings of the *Praxis* philosophers and the Black Wave filmmakers' interviews, revolving around the ideas of human beings "who freely and consciously transform their lives" and artists who exercise "complete freedom of artistic expression", consequently forming a notion of "individual engagement".[11] However, in an interview given in 1993, a year before his death, Aleksandar Petrović heavily criticised the *Praxis* intellectuals,[12] implying that there was no direct link between philosophers and filmmakers, thereby reinforcing Dragović-Soso's view that these were two separate phenomena. Goulding is nevertheless correct in his assessment that the phenomena were very similar, both radically criticising society from a humanist and leftist platform.[13]

The proliferation of critical thought, seemingly unrestrained after Ranković's fall in 1966, exploded forcefully in June 1968, when students of Belgrade University started violent demonstrations, clashing with the police. Although Misha Glenny designates a somewhat minor and banal incident as the spark for the students' initial revolt, he explains that the conflict quickly adopted a political tone. The early sloganeering echoed that already seen in the other major student protests happening in Paris, Berlin, Warsaw and Prague.[14] Glenny adds that some specifically East European demands appeared on the students' banners, the ones most illustrative of students' grievances and the situation in the country being "Down with the Red Bourgeoisie" and "There is No Socialism without Freedom, No Freedom without Socialism".[15] Both Glenny and Lampe express the opinion that the New Left, or rather members of the *Praxis* group, heavily influenced the students, and helped them in articulating their political programme, which was profoundly critical of the increasing economic and social injustice in the country.[16] The demonstrators were joined and helped not only by the New Left, but many of the filmmakers of New Film, or the Black Wave to be, were also there. Dušan Makavejev and Želimir Žilnik filmed a considerable amount of documentary footage of the protests,[17] whereas one of the most involving accounts of the event was in a book by Živojin Pavlović, *A Spit Full of Blood* (*Ispljuvak pun krvi*), which he only managed to publish 20 years after the event.[18] The protest started on 2 June and spread quickly: historian Dejan Jović explains that Edvard Kardelj considered it "the greatest potential threat which the Yugoslav regime had to face".[19] Such an assessment coming from Kardelj, who Glenny describes as "the last remaining member of Tito's triumvirate still in power",[20] indicates that the party well understood the threat posed by the protests. In the end, President Tito addressed the nation and the students on television on 9 June,[21] and while displaying "his charisma and political cunning to the full",[22] he "disarmed the rebellious students by backing their main demands".[23] Although this stopped the demonstrations at the time with the students feeling victorious, historians almost unanimously agree that the true winner was Tito, as by "embracing" the students' demands he had consolidated his power at home, and shown that he was still the true "authority", as well as regaining his image as a "liberal" in the West.[24] According to Glenny, "Tito had no intention of carrying out his promises" to the students, but regardless, his public endorsement of their requests was a clear sign, in Dragović-Soso's assessment, of the rapidly increasing levels of the "freedom of expression".[25]

Unlike his peers Makavejev and Pavlović, Aleksandar Petrović did not participate in the student demonstrations in Belgrade. The reason was the fact that he was shooting his new film outside of the city,[26] the film that was to be completed at the end of that famously tumultuous year, 1968. The original Yugoslav title could be translated as *It Will Be the End of the World Soon, So Be It, It Is Not a Great Loss* (*Biće skoro propast sveta, nek' propadne nije šteta*),[27] and although the film was often referred to only as *It Will Be the End of the World Soon*, this rather elongated and awkward title was changed for international distribution to *It Rains in My Village*. As the student protests were truly a significant political moment in the country's history, Petrović included a scene that directly refers to them. *It Rains in My*

Village hence becomes the most openly politically engaged film that Petrović had made, up to that point. This was not a result of the immediate influence of the student demonstrations in Belgrade, as the film was already in production at the time of the protests, but perhaps the film's political radicalism was simply in the spirit of the time.

5. 1. The Benefits of International Recognition

Writing about the 1967 Pula Film Festival, Dušan Stojanović, one of the most significant film theorists in Yugoslavia, passionately praised *I Even Met Happy Gypsies*. He described the film as a "magnificent poetic allegory made out of seemingly documentary 'elements' of life: a revelation of the fantastic in the real; a miraculous symbiosis of traditional and modern approaches to the medium".[28] Stojanović concluded his analysis with the claim that *Happy Gypsies* is an "apotheosis of true art in film."[29] The reception of the film was in fact exceptional. Another Yugoslav art theorist and historian, Milan Ranković, talked about it as an example of work that was liked and praised not only by educated – or informed – critics, but also by wider audiences, both in Yugoslavia and internationally.[30] In January 1968, *Happy Gypsies* was nominated for an Oscar (Foreign Language Film), and perceived as the favourite.[31] The film did not receive the award, but for Petrović this was a second nomination in succession, as *Three* had been a contender in 1967. Petrović's international reputation was therefore consolidated, and the commercial profits made from *Happy Gypsies* in its global distribution were to inaugurate a new chapter in his career – one characterised by international co-productions.

On his way back to Belgrade, following the Oscar ceremony in Los Angeles, Petrović stopped for a dinner party with Ilya Lopert in Paris, who was then head of the European branch of United Artists (registered in France as Les Production Artistes Associés). The new director of Belgrade's Avala Film, Dragiša Djurić, was also at the party. It was during this dinner that Lopert informed Petrović that United Artists, or rather its European branch, was to co-finance his new project.[32] For Petrović this was vital for several reasons, the most obvious being that he was to work on a new project within a very short period of time. In the previous year, Avala Film had faced serious financial difficulties, which mainly manifested in problems with the cash flow available for the ongoing productions. Due to this lack of funds (the so-called cash float), production on *Happy Gypsies* had almost stopped, when at one point money was simply unavailable to pay the extras and other small expenses. Filming was about to be adjourned – although it is notoriously difficult to restart film shoots once they are interrupted (if only for logistical reasons, as exemplified by the availability of crew and locations) – when Petrović decided to put his own money in, until Avala Film resolved its problems. He was helped by many members of the crew, who also chose to fill the financial vacuum: amongst others, the actor Bekim Fehmiu and the cinematographer Tomislav Pinter made their own savings available for the production.[33] This intervention certainly demonstrates the filmmakers' commitment and had probably saved the project, or at least enabled it to be completed on schedule. The departure of Ratko Draževic as director of Avala Film, the person who had been responsible for its rejuvenated film production,[34] may have had something to do with the lack of "petty cash". However, the actual reasons for Serbia's major film studio being short of finances will perhaps be the subject of another study. As a result, Petrovic could only start work on another project immediately if the funds arrived from elsewhere.[35] With principal funding secured from France, Avala Film was still capable of being a co-producer, as, in the words of Lazar Stojanovic, they were the company with "the best equipment and infrastructure" for film production in Serbia.[36] The initial participation from France was $160,000, which, considering the exchange rate and the fact that Avala was to provide equipment and workforce, was a substantial figure for a Yugoslav film project, and was Petrovic's largest budget up to this point.[37]

The introduction of international funding brought new features to this project, features that would persist in Petrovic's subsequent work. Perhaps in order to ease international distribution, Les Artistes Associés offered to pay a French star to act in the film.[38] The choice was Annie Girardot, at the time a very popular French actress, who had built her career by successful appearances in a line of comedies. She was at that point in her career slowly broadening her acting range, so she welcomed this project. To act opposite her, Petrovic invited the Slovak actor Ivan Paluch, a young and handsome rising star from Czechoslovakia. Neither of the two actors who were to play leading roles in the film spoke Serbian, so they were both dubbed during post-production. At the time, this was a common practice in European cinema, and the same "star sharing" system is still in existence. What is perhaps intriguing, and at the same time a familiar occurrence, is how, as films receive larger funding from various sources, principles become compromised. Petrovic was known as someone with a solid theoretical background. He was a cautious filmmaker, particularly in relation to issues of exploitation, as the analysis of *Happy Gypsies* earlier has demonstrated. He was also sensitive to more than just the representation of ethnic issues. Before the release of *It Rains in My Village*, for example, he defiantly stated that "in not a single one of my films, not even in *Happy Gypsies*, have I had naked women, not even loosely dressed",[39] continuing to explain that these were "cheap", tasteless and titillating "tricks" to get the audience to see a film. In the same interview from 1969, he also speaks sceptically about the "star system".[40] However, in his *It Rains in My Village*, Petrovic was to have his first nude love scene, in which he engaged two attractive young stars, one borrowed from the West, and one from the East of the then divided Europe. It could be easy to assume that this was done for the very reasons Petrovic criticised earlier, to facilitate marketing of the film and increase audiences. If this was a compromise Petrovic was prepared to make, it was probably the only one, as *It Rains in My Village* turned out to be one of his strongest and bleakest critiques of Yugoslav socialism. In the assessment of Milan Rankovic, Petrovic had, "in his interest in the rural environment, evolved from the suggestive poetic realism of *Happy Gypsies*, to the shocking naturalism of *It Rains in My Village*".[41]

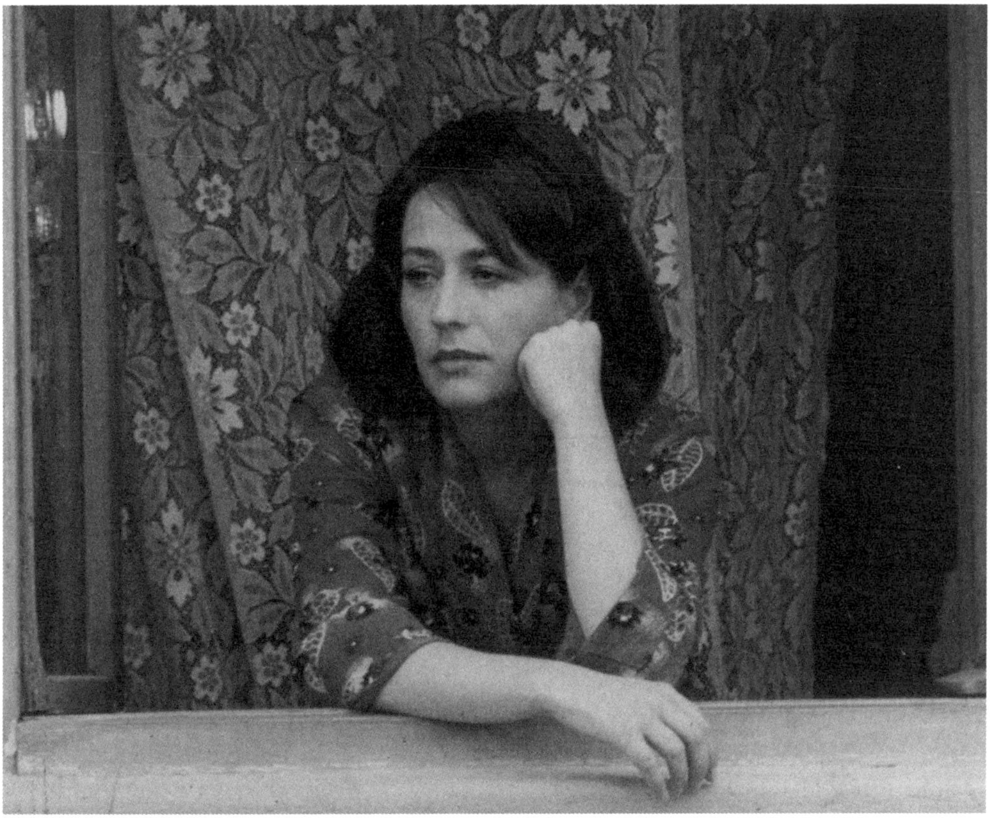

Figure 5.1: French actress Annie Girardot as the Teacher – the star of *It Rains in My Village*.

5. 1. 1. Improvisations and Bertolt Brecht

In a detailed interview given to Bogdan Tirnanić for the Yugoslav film magazine *Sineast* before the film was released, Petrović explained the roots of the project. The initial idea was very simple, and it came from a brief article published in the Belgrade tabloid newspaper, *Politika Ekspres*.[42] The news was about a crime committed in a village in Vojvodina, the same region where *Happy Gypsies* was set, where the father of the culprit assumed the blame, and went to prison instead of his son. Petrović stated that he was inspired by this short report, which he used as a "bare thematic nucleus", and when coupled with "some elements" of Dostoyevsky's *The Devils*,[43] he subsequently "created a synopsis of the film."[44] It is on the basis of this synopsis, and certainly the strength of his previous work, that United Artists decided to finance the project. Considering all his awards, Petrović had no problems in obtaining Avala Film's participation in the project. Although the finished script existed before the shoot, this was Petrović's least-developed project before it went into production.

This could be explained by the fact that Petrović seized the opportunity that came from United Artists and wanted to start work on the new film immediately. The strongest evidence to support such an assumption, however, comes in another component that was a significant novelty of *It Rains in My Village*. Petrović admitted in his interview that some important elements of the film were added during production, claiming:

> When I started the production, some things revealed themselves which absolutely entered the construction of this film, and which are absolutely the product of this moment's political and social situation.[45]

The new component was improvisation, involving more work on the set, with more material filmed than was planned in the script. Petrović shot large amounts of footage according to actress Eva Ras, who played the victim of the murder, a deaf and mute girl called Goca.[46] United Artists' financial support enabled Petrović to film more material than usual, and

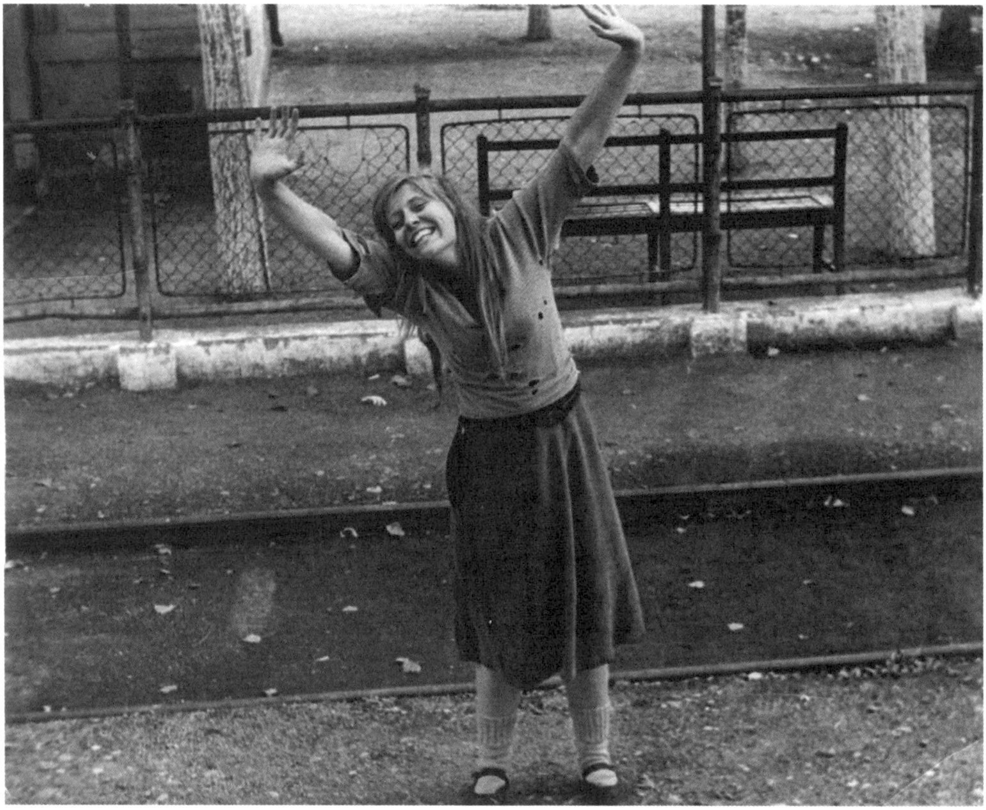

Figure 5.2: One of the Black Wave's favourite actresses, Eva Ras, improvises her role of a deaf and mute girl, Goca.

Ras explains that he exploited this opportunity to the maximum. When she was filmed in a test scene, for example, she sent kisses to the camera while "in character". Petrović liked the footage, re-filmed it, and later included it in the film.

The improvised elements were most obvious and relevant in the scenes that involved what Petrović described as "absolutely the product of this moment's political and social situation."[47] *It Rains in My Village* was filmed during the summer of 1968, when there were two major political events that shook Yugoslavia. As described earlier, the June student protests in Belgrade were characterised by opposition to society from the politically left platform, with students carrying pictures of Che Guevara and Lenin. As Petrović's film was set in a village, he filmed a scene with peasants demonstrating, also carrying pictures of Guevara and Lenin. One character explicitly makes the link with the student protests, thus creating a scene clearly additional to the original script. The second major political event was the Soviet invasion of Czechoslovakia; the event momentous for Yugoslavia, as historian John Lampe explains:

> The Soviet invasion of Czechoslovakia in August 1968 pulled both public and party opinion closer together. If Soviet forces could occupy a fellow bloc member with impunity, did not the old danger of attack against heretic Yugoslavia become real again? In addition, Tito's defiant criticism of the invasion and official refusal to send back any of the thousands of Czechs and Slovaks who had been vacationing on the Adriatic raised Yugoslavia's stock in the West.[48]

Petrović added a scene in which he portrayed a group of Czechoslovak tourists stranded in the village in which the film is set, and unable to go home due to the invasion and the new political disagreement between Yugoslavia and the Soviet Union. This scene was also conceived as political events were unfolding during filming. Petrović had, it can be concluded, intentionally grounded his narrative in the political and historical context of the time. By doing so, his film *It Rains in My Village* openly examines the social and political problems the country faced during the tumultuous period of 1968, the period of further liberalisation of the country.

The political context added during shooting was not the only social concern Petrović introduced into the film. Prior to the start of production, it was clear that, as with *Happy Gypsies*, the new film would be set in the Yugoslav countryside, again exemplified by a village in Vojvodina, Serbia's northern province. The choice of a rural environment was not only linked to the original storyline, adopted from a news article. Historian Misha Glenny emphasises that "by the late 1960s", Yugoslavia had created "the perennially insoluble question of the peasants".[49] The problem was developed as large investments were made in the cities and industrialisation, both of which encouraged what John Lampe calls the "rural exodus".[50] According to Glenny, there was a continually "growing social gap between town and country", causing "mutual antipathy between rural and urban communities" to grow, particularly in the1970s and 1980s.[51] Lampe also agrees that most of the countryside did not benefit from the general economic growth, confirming that this was an evident problem the state was cultivating.[52] Petrović, confirming again that he was a conscientious intellectual, was aware of this, and stated in an interview given prior to the film's release:

> I went to the country with the conviction that the essential social problem of this society is to be found there. More than half of the population of our state lives in the country, and the state of it, frankly, is not how it should be. To be honest, it is actually very bad. By going there I wanted to re-discover this area, so that society can be reminded of it.[53]

It is consequently clear that by setting his narrative in the countryside, Petrović enabled the film to examine a social problem. *It Rains in My Village* was made with a political critique in mind from the onset.

Petrović introduced another structural novelty into the film. Initially, this innovation may appear reminiscent of *Happy Gypsies*, as it also involves a Gypsy orchestra. In *It Rains in My Village*, Petrović makes frequent use of a Gypsy band, performing a special form of folk song, known as *bećarci*.[54] In an interview given to the Czechoslovakian film magazine *Film A Doba*, Petrović explains *bećarci* function as "some kind of chorus which is placed outside the narrative, while their lyrics provide a comment applied in a Brechtian fashion"; thus the film, according to him, becomes a sort of "folk opera".[55] He also explained *bećarci* as songs containing "a specific folk relationship towards all the possible problems life places in front of people, thus the whole film, in fact, is some sort of large *bećarac*."[56] The way these songs are used presents an element unseen in his previous work, and Petrović explained it as "Brechtian composition", in which the "Gypsy orchestra comments on the narrative, integrated in the scene or outside it."[57] With this additional stylistic innovation, Petrović's description of his new project as pertaining to "the problem of the countryside, the news from *Politika Ekspres*, Dostoyevsky, *bećarci*, Che Guevara placards in the village, and the occupation of Czechoslovakia"[58] appears complete. However, he was to meditate on one more social phenomenon, which he identified as the subject of his investigation.

With *It Rains in My Village* Aleksandar Petrović outlines, for the first time unambiguously, what he believes to be the fundamental problem of Yugoslav society, and presents it as such without his usual empathy or what he described as his "polyvalent view".[59] Rather, he identified it as something that needed to be worked on, and this problem would also become the focus of his next film. Petrović felt that the socialist systems had created an ethical crisis. He explained: "We have destroyed conventional morals, but have not created new ones. We are now in a deep moral crisis, in an almost complete ethical vacuum."[60] With growing social and economic inequalities in Yugoslavia at the time, Petrović further adduced an extraordinary "accumulation of destructive tendencies".[61] The global political picture featured ongoing conflicts in Biafra and Vietnam, with students' protests internationally. Petrović felt that the world had entered a period of "crisis of consciousness and morality."[62] As the analysis of his previous work has demonstrated, Petrović had always been a keen social observer, closely scrutinising social problems. However, in the interview he gave prior to the release of *It Rains in My Village*, for the first time Petrović sounds prescriptive, rather than just analytical, explaining that he sees the way of overcoming the problem through "sobering up the consciousness."[63] He adds that the film:

> [...] starts with the presupposition that, if this accumulation of destructive energy is revealed in a committed and engaged way, then *it would engender a need* amongst viewers, to somehow overcome this accumulation, and thereby bring about a new morality[64]

Although Petrović remains adamant that his outlook is "not political, but poetic",[65] *It Rains in My Village* becomes, as will be shown, his most critical analysis of, if not attack on, the socialist regime in Yugoslavia. However, this was in the spirit of the time, as noted earlier. It was a time that was aptly described in an article by a student participant of Belgrade's 1968 demonstrations, an article that Živojin Pavlović included in his book *A Spit Full of Blood*, which was dedicated to this event. In the words of a young protester, one can also trace the thought behind Petrović's film: "The question is in the consciousness that this world is not good for us, and in the readiness to change it."[66]

5. 1. 2. *It Rains in My Village,* or *It Will Be the End of the World Soon*

A Gypsy orchestra arrives in a village in Vojvodina, where they are to start working in a local bar. A young swineherd, Triša, shows them the way.

Joška, the owner of the bar, sees the local village idiot, a young, deaf and mute, but good-looking girl, Goca, making love to a seasonal worker near the train station. Afterwards Joška too tries to make love to her, but she rejects him. At a village wedding, Joška ridicules her cruelly out of spite, but a drunken Triša defends her.

Joška seems insulted by Triša's actions at the wedding, and he and the other local idlers cunningly bully Triša in his bar. This culminates one evening in making the drunken Triša marry Goca for a bet! Initially, Triša is warm to Goca and they have a child, but after a few years Triša refuses to see her. Goca and the child are taken care of by Triša's father, a very religious and pious man, who works hard to rebuild the village church with the local priest.

A young and beautiful teacher[67] arrives in the village. She is a committed communist, pledging herself to emancipate the villagers. One of the local elders employs Triša to help carry the Teacher's canvases on Sundays, as she likes to paint the local fields and landscapes. Young, lonely and bored, she makes love to Triša one day, but makes it very clear that she has no intention of taking the relationship any further.

A plane carrying agricultural supplies crashes in the village, and the Teacher starts an affair with its pilot, which makes Triša jealous. As Triša realises that the Teacher is not interested in him anymore, he murders his wife Goca, whom he blames for being in the way of his new relationship. He does this after arriving home heartbroken and very drunk. Triša's father admits the murder to the police the day after, to protect Triša. Triša becomes an unpopular person in the village, as almost everyone knows that he is the real culprit. In addition, he is always drunk, and still besotted with the Teacher. It soon transpires that the Pilot is married, but during the celebration for his departure, the Teacher starts an affair with a young soldier who helps with the Pilot's plane.

Joška organises demonstrations demanding that the village get its own agricultural aeroplane, but after he sees some Czech tourists camping near the village, unable to go home due to the Soviet invasion, he decides to disband the protest. In the meantime, Triša's father dies in prison, confessing before his death that Triša killed Goca. Later, Joška and his companions ensnare Triša in the ropes attached to the church bells. Enraged peasants, awakened by the noise, find him there, and beat him to death, aware of his guilt and his innocent father's demise.

The day after this, the Teacher is pleased that almost everyone came out to vote in the local elections, and reprimands Triša (in his absence) for not showing up, unaware of what has happened to him. She is next seen standing on the doorstep of the newly rebuilt village church, tempting the Priest from outside with her good looks. A hearse passes nearby carrying a violin case where Triša's coffin should be, and the musicians leave the village.

5. 1. 3. Charting the Decline, Anticipating the Downfall

The narrative of *It Rains in My Village* certainly has many similarities to the narrative of *Happy Gypsies*. The stories of both films are about love and passion, ending with a tragic murder. *Happy Gypsies'* Beli Bora is tragically in love with the young Gypsy girl Tisa, and when this relationship does not work out, he murders her stepfather Mirta, to whom she had returned. In addition, Beli Bora is already married to a woman he does not appear to care for. In *It Rains in My Village*, Triša is also married to a woman he does not care for: the deaf-mute girl, Goca. He is passionately in love with the village's teacher, who does not reciprocate his love. Seeing his wife as an obstacle to his happiness, he murders her when very drunk and heartbroken. It is therefore clear that the motifs of love and death continue to permeate Petrović's work. Of greater interest to this analysis however, is how Petrović treats the social and political context of the film, and as already stated, more openly and critically than in *Happy Gypsies*. As it was argued in the previous chapter, the social context in *Happy Gypsies* is more evident in the subplots, whereas the main plot is a love story. It was in the subplots that Petrović portrayed the relationships of the main characters (who also happened to be from a marginalised ethnic group – Roma), with the institutions of the society and the Serbian Orthodox Church, here representing a somewhat marginalised or "alternative" institution to the socialist state. Petrović also showed shocking economic disparities – although by choosing Roma, an ethnic minority with a very specific culture, as the segment of society living in this deprived and backward world, his revelations of such social conditions was not taken as a direct criticism of the Yugoslav system, and the film was well received.[68] To reiterate, in *Happy Gypsies* Petrović meditated on the social context in the subplots, thus in the background of the film's main storyline. As he showed a marginal group dwelling in economic misery as a metaphor for the poverty in society, Petrović's critique could be seen as oblique and subtle. With *It Rains in My Village*, he abandons obliqueness and subtlety for a more direct approach. He showed deep economic misery again, but not amongst the nomadic Gypsy dwellers, for whom it could almost be "expected" to live in such conditions, but this time the deprivation is in an ordinary Serbian village, with members of the dominant group falling behind economically, and consequently, in other ways. As explained earlier, the rural parts of Yugoslavia were being left behind during this period, and his new film – with the choice of location – thus touched unambiguously on the sensitive areas of the political and social life of the time. As in *Happy Gypsies*, Petrović again portrays the institutions of society, with the addition of the Church as an "alternative" and marginalised, but nonetheless an institution within that social system. Whereas the two types of institutions in *Happy Gypsies* were shown in subplots, and never directly in contact with each other, in *It Rains in My Village* Petrović brings them to the foreground, and also shows their uneasy interaction. He does this by polarising his protagonists, giving them traits that tie them strictly to one group or the other. So whereas the protagonists in *Happy Gypsies* were all Roma, in the new film Triša is an economically deprived peasant without education, who falls for the Teacher, a Communist Party member, thus clearly a representative of the regime. Evidently, the Teacher is educated and considerably more affluent than Triša, and the awkward question of the existence of social classes in socialism arises again, as it did in *Happy Gypsies*. The counterbalance for the character of the Teacher is primarily Triša's old and pious father, as well as the character of the village priest. Throughout the film, the Father, as well as the Priest, project a very different set of values and norms on Triša from the ones the Teacher does. In the moment of Triša's weakness, these values combust tragically, pointing to the complexities of the social interactions in the country. As Petrović moves these issues into the foreground of the story, it could be concluded that *It Rains in My Village* is more openly and directly politically critical than any of his previous films. Such a view is also shared by Milan Ranković, who states that *It Rains in My Village* leaves a "substantially different impression from *Happy Gypsies*", mostly because of "the mode and quality of the critical message: as in the other film [*It Rains*] the critical note is more explicit and emphasised; it encompasses some immediate associations and allusions to current political affairs."[69] Let us now explore these "associations and allusions" with the aim of establishing Petrović's view of Yugoslav socialism in 1968.

In his interview given prior to the release of *It Rains in My Village*, Petrović emphasised that his social criticism observes "the outside" of the mainstream society, exploring phenomena on the margins, such as the Gypsies of the previous film.[70] This obsession, affirmed in the documentaries *Record* and *Assemblies* (as already discussed)[71] continues with his first international co-production. The "invisible" side of society revealed in *It Rains in My Village* becomes the image of country and village life in Yugoslavia that were largely neglected by socialist progress. At the time, modernisation was coming only slowly to the villages, and Petrović exposes the deepening divide between the rural and urban through the relationship of the village youth Triša and the newly arrived teacher. The Teacher is a young and beautiful woman, evidently a stranger to village life. Still, her confidence is striking as she arrives driving her own car, and believes that she can "emancipate" the village. Her first conversation with Triša is more than revealing, after the village elder suggested Triša as her helper when she wanted to go painting the local landscapes. In the field where the Teacher is painting, she asks Triša about his work. He apologises first (as if a serf was allowed to address the lady of the manor!) and then explains that he is a swineherd. He adds that this is the work his forefathers did too. The Teacher offers to teach him to paint, hence broaden his horizons. Triša responds in the plural, as if speaking for the whole village: his answer is negative, and he adds that things are fine just as they are. His village, however, he continues, is dusty, like any other village. Triša does not appear to be willing to change the job he has inherited from the past, however unattractive it may be, nor is he willing to change the "dusty village", although conditions are far from enviable. He is prepared to take things exactly as they are. If Petrović creates the character of the Teacher as the only Communist Party member in the film – as young, beautiful, intelligent, confident, well-spoken and well-dressed – who offers the possibility to Triša of improving village conditions, it is telling that Triša, on behalf of the village, refuses this offer. What this scene implies is that the introduction of progress through modernisation, be it socialist or any other, demands the participation of not only those willing to implement it (in this case, the Teacher), but also of those for whom it is being implemented (the villagers). Petrović is therefore criticising general intellectual laxity and laziness in society, as shown in this traditional rural area, which was obstructing social progress. In an interview with Pavel Branko, Petrović stated that he "really did not want to criticise socialism, but the current situation of mankind".[72] This early scene, however, which may appear to favour a progressive and reforming communist as opposed to a rigid provincial, was to change soon after, and reveal the situation in a more complex way as Petrović had done in his previous work. The characters were to develop further in order to reveal that the initial image of the Teacher may not be deserving of all the positive attributes mentioned earlier; and this would also explain Triša's hesitance and distrust in the face of change.

When the tragic part of the love story starts, certain habits reflective of Yugoslav society surface, indicating somewhat different relations than the ones described above. One Sunday, feeling bored and lonely, the Teacher decides to make love to Triša. Triša, after all, is young and handsome. She then paints his portrait. When Triša meets the Teacher next, she is evidently cold and distant. It is clear that she has no interest in taking the relationship further, and the lovemaking must remain an isolated incident. She adds that it is not her fault Triša is a swineherd, and continues to say that peasants are interesting, but not for long. Petrović thus creates a social comment using the narrative as a pretext. Socialism, as it was built in Yugoslavia, was supposed to be committed to egalitarianism, but in this instance, the Teacher reminds Triša that he is not of her "class". To make this point clear, the Teacher soon falls for a young pilot, whose aeroplane crashes in the village. He stays for a few days and develops a relationship with the Teacher. On the last day, however, he admits to her that he is married, and that he had only been having a good time, thus showing that he is an even bigger "emotional" opportunist than she had been with Triša. In the meantime though, after his "fling" with the Teacher, Triša falls deeply in love with her, while she brutally rebuffs his advances. Feeling increasingly humiliated, and also under pressure from Joška and his idle companions, the drunken Triša commits a gruesome murder. Meanwhile, once she is left by the Pilot, the Teacher quickly falls for a young soldier who arrives to help with the broken aeroplane. Consequently, the Pilot and the Soldier are equal to her, thus she can develop relationships with them, but not with Triša, whom she calls "the director of a herd of swine" in a moment of rage. Her behaviour towards Triša confirms the predictions of Milovan Djilas from the early 1950s, that the majority of the Communist Party members were becoming a "new class", abandoning socialist principles and becoming *petit bourgeois* instead.[73] Djilas was declared a "heretic" and expelled from the party in 1954, but Petrović's film shows this prediction in practice. As a communist, the Teacher ought to be aware that classes of course exist, even in socialism, but perhaps – as a communist – she ought to defy them as well, as communism was supposed to be a classless society. However, what certainly is more commonplace is to refuse the partner she feels is not appropriate for her, even though she had already cynically taken advantage of him. By employing this very human logic, which contradicts the main humanist principles of equality that the communist ideology is supposed to represent, the Teacher betrays her beliefs in practice. Petrović uses this "love incident" as a pretext to reveal the contradiction between human nature and high ideals, and to ask the crucial questions: Is communism in practice possible? Are people who claim that they are communists, true to their beliefs? Or perhaps, is this the time and place to try to implement communism? The answers are certainly not what Petrović has set out to provide, reiterating in his interviews that as an artist he responded to situations and asked questions. Social controversies are not there to be resolved by artists, only to be exposed by them, or as he put it: "Art can sober up humanity, revealing things humanity is unaware of."[74] With this episode, Petrović reveals that the party is not capable of emancipating certain segments of society, and even more so, that the party has become so alienated from these segments, that it is no longer able or even willing to help them. Such a strong political assessment, implying the moral duplicity of some party members, was to stir controversy once the film was released, and will be discussed later in this chapter. To conclude, by openly exposing the development of a new class, Petrović introduced the third of the four political themes that pervade his work, a theme that investigates the relationship between the political establishment (the Teacher, the Pilot) and marginalised groups (Triša, the peasants). It is also interesting that the student protest in Belgrade often addressed the issue of growing inequalities in the country; thus egalitarianism was a political problem of the day, which Petrović tackles in his film.

Petrović introduces social criticism embedded in the love story, which is at the centre of the film's narrative. As already pointed out, Petrović was to include scenes directly referring to two major political events of the time, and also another one depicting a large-scale political event – the local elections. To an extent, Petrović refers to the student protests in an almost satirical fashion, as he films a scene in which the local peasants protest, demanding their own aeroplane to spray the fields with agricultural pesticides. As with the student protests in Belgrade, Petrović's protesters do not want to offend the ruling hierarchies, or to be seen as enemies of the state, so they carry pictures of Tito, as well as of Che and Lenin, at the forefront of their gathering. Whereas the Belgrade students had well-articulated demands, and were protesting about social issues that needed addressing, the peasant protest in Petrović's film is obviously a parody. As this scene was being shot, another crucial historical event happened that Petrović incorporated. The Warsaw Pact army units invaded Czechoslovakia in August 1968, and Soviet tanks rolled into Prague to reverse the country's liberalising political process. In *It Rains in My Village*, Petrović comments on this in the same scene. While the peasants are protesting, Joška, one of their leaders, goes to talk to a group of Czechoslovakian tourists camping in the field. Joška is of course perplexed that these tourists, who would usually just drive through on their way to the Adriatic coast, are now basking in the fields of their remote village. They show him the newspapers, and he realises that the popular dissent in Prague has been crushed by the Soviet tanks. The demonstrations in Belgrade and the unrest in Czechoslovakia were a part of the tainted picture of the contemporary socialist bloc that Petrović integrated into the film.

Finally, Petrović includes a large-scale scene depicting local elections in the village. The scene would later be perceived as one of the more controversial ones in the film.[75] In the socialist doctrine, democracy was seen as a way of making decisions, regardless of the fact that, in practice, all the candidates were from the same political party. Elections were therefore important events, as a society committed to collective decision-making liked to have extensive participation, if only to demonstrate individuals' devotion to the system. In fact, after World War II, it was almost an obligation to vote, although at the time Petrović made the film, public pressure to vote had diminished. Still, in *It Rains in My Village*, the village elections looked like the ones immediately after the war, with youth groups arriving beforehand to agitate, with flags and banners making the atmosphere seem celebratory. The Teacher and the village mayor are in charge of the registry, and the Teacher proudly exclaims that almost everyone voted before 11 o'clock. At that point, an old man is brought in by two younger men, who are helping him to vote as it seems that he is incapable of doing so by himself. The Teacher then realises that Triša is one of the people who did not vote, which makes her angry with him. She is unaware that it is his funeral procession moving outside. The distance between her as a representative of the system, and Triša as a marginal character in the society, is reaffirmed, as she is not even aware of his demise. Petrović recaps the point that the distance between the party and the country is becoming unbridgeable; although the responsibility for this may be mutual, its main weight lies on the party at the end of the film. The Teacher's arrogance and impetuousness with Triša explains to some extent his frustration with her, as well as his frustration with the outside world and the progress she represents. Consequently, Petrović empathises with Triša's feelings

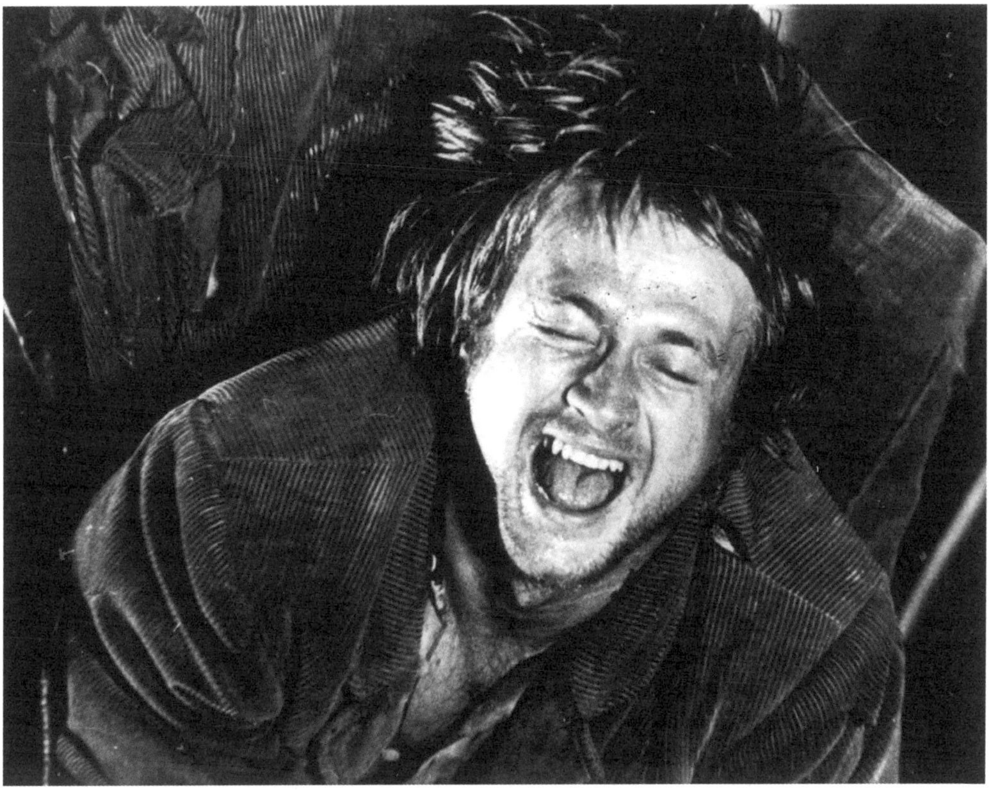

Figure 5.3: Ivan Paluch as naïve swineherd, Triša, facing his gruesome death.

of confusion and humiliation by the outside world, rather than judging him, and thereby humanising the outsider rather than excluding, marginalising or "Other-ising" him.

In the election scene, Petrović employs a considerable number of extras, making it a large-scale scene with young agitators and students arriving in the village across the fields on tractors, waving the Yugoslav and the international communist flags. Filmed from an aerial perspective, the scene betrays the large budget Petrović had at his disposal. In most of the other scenes, however, he remains faithful to his recognisable style, focusing on details, predominantly in close-ups. The scene of the wedding at the beginning illustrates this, in which Triša defends Goca from Joška. The scene is filmed in an enclosed space, without a single establishing shot, the mobile camera following reactions and seeking out relevant details. Although the film was photographed by a new collaborator Alain Levent,[76] a French cinematographer, Petrović continues to favour elements constituting his own style. One of these elements is a frequent, and in this case occasionally extravagant, use of telephoto lenses, although usually for a purpose. The telephoto lens, like a telescope, was made to enable looking at and photographing details placed far away from the camera. It was thus handy for Petrović's semi-documentary style, in which he sought to capture small reactions made by actors while placed far away from the action. In *It Rains in My Village* he uses these lenses unconventionally, and even photographs landscapes and other wide shots with them. According to Lazar Stojanović, an assistant on the set, Petrović used telephoto lenses in the election scene in order to create an effect of the agitators appearing "flattened" to the ground, which would then look as "if the ground below is also going to vote".[77] Petrović maintained his obsession with details, and his tendency to show details from frescoes or "kitchen pictures" to allude to and comment on the action, as exercised in *Happy Gypsies*, continues in *It Rains in My Village*. One significant difference is that in the new film, Petrović used paintings belonging to the folk tradition of the so-called "naïve painting" widespread in the villages of Serbia. These painters were usually uneducated peasants working with local motifs. Petrović frequently uses motifs from these paintings[78] to make visual comments on the narrative in a way reminiscent of his earlier films, particularly *Happy Gypsies* and *Assemblies*. The paintings integrate well as they are present in the diegetic space of the film thanks to the character of the Teacher, who paints as a hobby. With their motifs from the Serbian countryside, Petrović reinforces his stylistic concept of the film being a sort of "folk opera".[79] The same concept is also reinforced by the presence of the Gypsy orchestra. Petrović himself wrote most of the lyrics for the songs – the *bećarci* – played in the film. They therefore comment on the narrative, and he is credited for the music together with Vojislav Voki Kostić.

Another political examination that takes place in the film is one that has already been brought up in previous work, and has been vividly present since he made *Assemblies*. As in *Happy Gypsies*, the uneasy relationship between the state and the Church is a strong current within the narrative. The Priest is again an important character, and his stoical, relentless influence on the believers in the village forms a strong counterpart to the Teacher and Mayor as representatives of the state and the system. This situation of quiet resentment "spills" over at times, as when Triša is shouted at by his father, for "disrespecting the Sunday", as he sees him working for the Teacher. The Teacher asks Triša who is the "cretin who respects Sundays?" Triša admits it is his father. Unabashed by the answer, the Teacher adamantly proceeds to give a "little sermon" to Triša on how detrimental the influence of religion is; thus she comes across as dogmatic, rather than empathic, or sensitive to the situation.

The final, ambivalent scene in the film questions this relationship between religion and socialism. The investigation of this relationship represents the second of the political themes that permeate Petrović's films and reflects on the Yugoslav reality of the time. The village church, destroyed during World War II, is rebuilt and the Priest is delivering his first sermon to a large group of local peasants. As he concludes, "the devil has come to collect his dues" – these being the last words in the film – the Teacher stands in the doorway of the church, not stepping inside, but giving him a tempestuous look from the outside. The Priest, although trying to maintain his composure, cannot resist the beauty and audaciousness of Annie Girardot's seductive but "devilish" eyes, and stutters and struggles to continue his sermon. The political, ideological and religious forces that exist in the country are thus shown as being in a position of permanent standoff, unable to communicate, but threatening each other with quiet antagonism in the hope that this will undermine the other. The existence of such antagonisms was bluntly acknowledged in Petrović's film, and today it transpires that it was historically accurate. According to John Lampe, the rejuvenation of religious life in Socialist Yugoslavia started with the Catholic Church in Croatia being allowed to publish its journal in 1966, and the Serbian Orthodox Church being able to do the same a year later.[80] By looking at the years in which these journals appeared, it seems that this was part of the liberalisation epitomised by the fall of Aleksandar Ranković; however, this was not the case. Lampe explains that the regime waited for the controversial Croatian Catholic Archbishop Alojzije Stepinac to die (which happened in 1960) before any type of rapprochement with any of the religious institutions could start.[81] Archbishop Stepinac had collaborated with the Nazis and the Croatian Ustasha regime. He was perceived to have supported the Catholic clergy who had blessed the concentration camps, and more significantly in the Yugoslav context, blessed the destruction of Orthodox churches, and the persecution and forced conversion of Orthodox Christians.[82] The socialist regime allowed the Serbian Orthodox Church to start rebuilding the destroyed churches in the mid-1960s, and by the end of the decade, according to Lampe, as many as 841 had been restored.[83] The church the peasants are rebuilding in *It Rains in My Village* is one of these churches, demonstrating the degree to which Petrović is responsive to the various developments in the country. By including this detail, Petrović again touches upon a sensitive wound, one that the communists felt awkward in dealing with: not only the existence of the Church as an institution, but the Croatian fascists' genocide during World War II. The genocide could have seriously eclipsed the fragile ethnic relations in the country in the post-war period. Although the party preferred to conceal the issue,[84] precisely for the sake of post-war reconciliation, it is present in Petrović's film, and with historical hindsight it could be suggested that this was indeed an important issue to tackle. Consequently, Petrović here introduced the first of the four political themes, the one that investigates inter-ethnic relationships in society.

The last title credit before the film starts states that, while making the film, Petrović "had in mind" Dostoyevsky's novel *The Devils*. The film is not an adaptation,[85] as it is very different from Dostoyevsky's typically large-scale novel, which would probably be impossible to translate into a two-hour film. Still, to acknowledge the novel as inspiration was indicative of where Petrović's concerns may have lain at the time. Indeed, he seems to have had Dostoyevsky's *Devils* in mind for a while, as the quote from the Bible that opens the novel is also used at the beginning of *Happy Gypsies*. With *It Rains in My Village*, Petrović decided to rethink the motifs from the novel more thoroughly. It is interesting to note that around this time, the same novel provided similar inspiration for other filmmakers. In 1967, Jean-Luc Godard released *La Chinoise*, which was loosely based on the book. As with Petrović's film, this was not immediately evident from following the narrative, but from scrutinising the similarity of their motifs.[86] In 1974 Andrei Tarkovsky's *Mirror* also contained references to the book and its characters, particularly in the printing room scene.[87] Neither of these films tried to adapt Dostoyevsky's ambitious novel for the screen, but their directors clearly wanted to acknowledge the influence of the book on their thinking and work.

The Devils by Fyodor Mihailovich Dostoyevsky is not the most popular or acclaimed of his novels, but it certainly has all the qualities and characteristics of his work. Based on his own experience, the narrative revolves around a group of young aspiring revolutionaries in nineteenth-century Russia, who undertake revolutionary tasks in their provincial town, failing bitterly and mainly causing extraordinary grief to their parents. The key criticism Dostoyevsky provides is that his characters lack the right motives for inciting social change: they are less concerned with social justice than with their own personal rivalries and ambitions. This element of the book was adopted by Godard in his film. Dostoyevsky also skilfully depicts his characters as idle and inconsiderately self-obsessed, which seriously impairs their ability to fulfil themselves emotionally and socially, and hence to reach true happiness. This element is perhaps most explored in Tarkovsky's *Mirror*.[88] Dostoyevsky further shows that the lack of social fulfilment is to do with the protagonists' own personal shortcomings, although as characters they refuse to accept this. They continue to attempt to change the world around them, rather than themselves, which causes yet more problems. Their social objectives get mixed up with their personal desires, and then implode with serious consequences. This is something Petrović exploits in his film, mainly through the character of the Teacher, who zealously pursues and heavy-handedly imposes the values of socialism to all around her, but always fails to establish the personal relationship she yearns for. At the same time, Triša's belief in his own freedom, which would be manipulated by the devilish Joška, who bullies him into marrying Goca – in another event dramatised from the novel – creates something Triša would come to regret with tragic consequences. Petrović, following Dostoyevsky's pattern, asks important questions about the motives behind self-proclaimed perpetrators of social change. As Dostoyevsky charts a myriad of situations depicting misuse of revolutionary ideas to cover up for all sorts of personal ambitions and desires, the question is raised, not about the ideas promoted to improve society, but about the validity and truthfulness of the people promoting them. Petrović too develops this notion from the novel through the character of the Teacher. The misplaced ambitiousness of some of the communist cadres was not a taboo theme to discuss at this time in Yugoslavia. The materialist motives of some of the leading corps were targeted by some of the above-mentioned student protests. *It Rains in My Village* questions the behaviour and analyses the humanness of those claiming to be the minders of the system upon which the country is based. Consequently, Petrović's statement that he was "not criticising socialism, but the contemporary human condition"[89] appears to be correct, as it was not the system that he portrays as incomplete, but some of the party staff in charge of it. The film is thus a social critique, but seen through an existentialist study, which questions the human ability to live up to the political ideals they promote. The fact that Petrović had taken the country's hierarchy and their morals as the subject of his scrutiny would cause an uneasy and prolonged controversy, one that the ruling elite would not get over lightly, if at all.

5. 2. Limelight as Light as Feathers

From the analysis of *It Rains in My Village* it is evident that Aleksandar Petrović had created another political parable examining the social conditions in Yugoslavia in a way that was personal and removed from the official line. This was best illustrated in the fact that he examined the problems of the countryside and the Church; problems that were, at the time, practically taboo. However, it is worth pointing out that a minor but significant change in relation to the rest of Petrović's oeuvre is made with *It Rains in My Village*. I would be inclined to assess that, with this film, as noted earlier, Petrović reduced the element of his "polyvalent view", an important trait of his work. In his theoretical articles, Petrović wrote about the "open metaphor"[90] as something that he saw as an important attribute and a contribution of Yugoslav cinema. In an interview with Pavel Branko, given after the release of *It Rains in My Village*, Petrović explains the "open metaphor" and its "polyvalent" qualities as:

> […] a metaphor which does not have only one meaning, and is thus polyvalent (and its meanings could also be controversial); its final meaning is with the viewer, and considering its polyvalence, this meaning could be different with every viewer.[91]

This polyvalence is often best exemplified in the way Petrović develops his characters, making them fully three-dimensional. Whether they do "bad" or "good" things, Petrović explains their motives, creating the possibility for empathy with their actions, even when these actions are not commendable. As the analyses have shown in previous chapters, there are many examples to illustrate this point and the polyvalence of situations and characters. Petrović gives a multifaceted view of the situation in his first feature film *Two*,[92] where the main character Mirko finally decides that he does not love Jovana and is going to leave her, even though he had made an extraordinary effort to seduce her, and also made her leave her previous partner. In the scene in which Mirko confronts his own decision, he sees it as a result of his own flaws. While showing the details of the build-up to this decision, Petrović is not judgemental, but leaves it to the audience to make their own judgements of the situation and its characters. Beli Bora in *Happy Gypsies* is even more complex[93] than Mirko, but to create a polyvalent view, Petrović's development strategy remains the same. This means that even when Beli Bora's actions are wrong, Petrović provides the context and the motives for his behaviour, enabling the audience to empathise with the character, rather than to be judgemental (although of course this varies with every viewer). That this was Petrović's objective is evident from his statement on this character, admitting that he "is a criminal, but can we judge him?"[94]

With *It Rains in My Village* this strategy remains, to an extent, specifically in relation to the character of Triša, whose condition and background to his crime Petrović describes in great depth and detail, giving his audience the option of a "polyvalent view". For the first time, however, most of the other characters end up with a more brashly polarised view already designed by Petrović. The Teacher's emotional fickleness, her impatience with

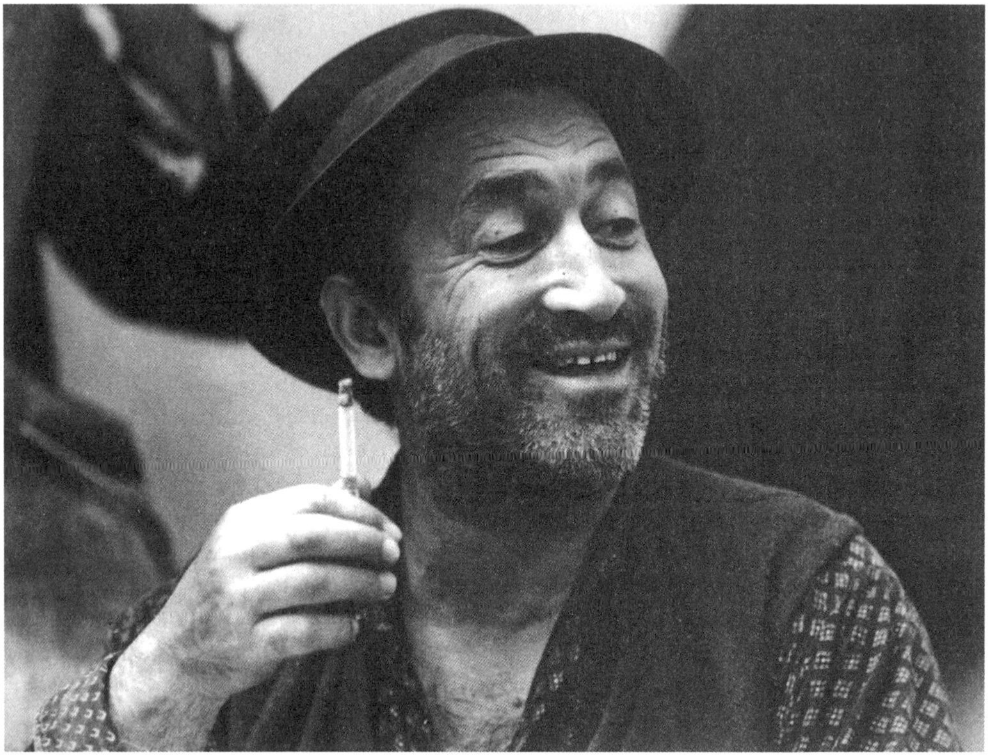

Figure 5.4: Mija Aleksić as the devilish Joška: the face of evil lurking in the village.

the peasants and her overall egotism are never explained, just given. Joška is simply evil incarnate, without any explanation or redeeming features. The Pilot also is an arrogant and rude opportunist, and thus comes across as a very dislikeable character. Overall, the film has a whole string of purely "negative" types, whom Petrović deprives of any sympathetic traits. He explains in an interview: "The only two characters in that village, who have something good in them, are Triša and his father, thus the two of them had to die".[95] If we add Goca as a possible other character who has "something good in her", then all three characters are dead, or more accurately, murdered, by the end, leaving the "bad" characters to survive. Consequently, Petrović's *It Rains in My Village* has a distinctly pessimistic tone, as opposed to his other work, which may be one of the reasons the film did not have such a warm reception as the previous one.

It is important to add that Petrović's unambiguous representation of certain characters as negative certainly had further political connotations. By portraying the Teacher as a character capable of constantly regurgitating communist clichés on progress and emancipation, while at the same time being distant, rude and arrogant to everyone around

178

her, Petrović shows the ruling party as losing its grip on reality. By just rehearsing phrases they are not able to live up to, they are portrayed as people leaving the communist doctrine and socialist principles to slide into meaninglessness: a dogmatic recipe for living, which they are prepared to enforce, but not necessarily to live by themselves. By portraying this as negative, I would therefore conclude that Petrović for the first time formulates an attitude that explicitly speaks, unambiguously and openly, against the dogmatism of the ruling elite. This is slightly different, however, from his previous work, in which his anti-dogmatism could be perceived as the result of a belief in the development of the "open metaphor" and "polyvalent view". As Petrović himself explained:

> In relation to this system of "open" metaphor, I found it very important to point towards some socio-ideological implications of such understanding of film poetry. It is evident that the opinion which starts with the presupposition that a film, as an art work, can have multiple meanings (including even mutually contradictory ones), and which counts on the participation of the audience in the final shaping of its meaning, is in an absolute opposition with any dogmatic or propagandistic understanding of art.[96]

This seems to be true of Petrović's films prior to *It Rains in My Village*, but with this film, Petrović decreases the "openness" and offers a more direct attitude. It is interesting that this attitude is anti-dogmatic, as it is against political dogmatism in Socialist Yugoslavia, but by building it in a way that departs from the concept of the "open metaphor", I would be tempted to conclude that this anti-dogmatic attitude in *It Rains in My Village* is presented somewhat dogmatically. It is important to underline here that in this film Petrović clearly interjects an anti-dogmatic attitude, the attitude that – as ultimately this argument is trying to show – constitutes his authorial persona. In addition, examining the dogmatic understanding of ideologies is the last of the four political themes permeating his work. During 1969, when the film was circulating at festivals and was being shown in cinemas, there were a considerable number of films in Socialist Yugoslavia mercilessly inveighing against the system, and turning this into something of a cinematic trend. This trend, if and when based on a one-dimensional criticism of society, could then also be understood as itself dogmatic. Ultimately, some of these films were reducing social criticism to political provocations; hence the reception of *It Rains in My Village* could not escape being judged against the background of the reaction to other Black Films.

5. 2. 1. The Reception of the *Village*

It Rains in My Village was completed in October 1968,[97] and early exclusive screenings took place at the end of that year. The French director Claude Lelouch, a friend of Aleksandar Petrović's and the distributor of *Happy Gypsies* in France, came to one of these screenings in December 1968.[98] The film finally went on general release in Yugoslavia in March 1969.

Petrović did not wait to open the film in a festival, but opened it for general audience first. Initial reactions to the film were predominantly positive. Milutin Čolić, film critic of the largest national daily, *Politika*, praised the film in general and somewhat expectedly compared it to *Happy Gypsies*. Čolić expressed his preference for *Happy Gypsies*, still adding that "this film [*It Rains*] could be loved less, but who knows whether that gives us the right to appreciate it any less".[99] Considering the deeply political, and as already explained critical, subject matter of the film, it is interesting that this initial Čolić's review is positive. According to the Yugoslav film historian and critic Ranko Munitić, Čolić was "the party's spokesman, who often wrote his reviews in the plural", implying that he was speaking in the name of the party.[100] Nevertheless, his review was affirmative, as were predominantly the other reviews published at the time. Comparisons with the previous film *Happy Gypsies* were common, but that was perhaps inevitable. Dragoslav Adamović, with a critical view not very different to Čolić's, wrote in the weekly magazine, *NIN*: "*Happy Gypsies* is a film which one could love more, but *It Rains in My Village* is a film which one should respect more, and appreciate more".[101] It could be assumed that the early good reception with audiences also rested on the fact that the previous film – *Happy Gypsies* – had been so successful. In its first two days of release in Belgrade, *It Rains in My Village* was seen by 35,000 viewers;[102] by the end of its first week, just over 100,000 people had seen it,[103] which matched the early high attendance of *Happy Gypsies*. *It Rains in My Village* did not fare as well at festivals, however, and the film was not selected for Oscar nominations, as the previous two films had been.[104] This upset some of the tabloid press in Yugoslavia,[105] and although the film was selected for the official competition at the Cannes Film Festival in May 1969,[106] the fact that it won no awards perhaps left it slightly more vulnerable to the string of attacks that were to come. *It Rains in My Village* received a third place award at the Yugoslav National Film Festival at Pula, the Bronze Arena, in the late summer of the same year,[107] whereas international reviews predominantly praised the film. In Czechoslovakia, Ivo Pondělíček called it "a modern film work par excellence", adding that this is because "the narration leaves loose ends, but which allows open space for the film's multiple meanings to be understood emotionally rather than through rational cognition".[108] Pondělíček concluded that Petrović is one of the "ten best directors in the world".[109] Hollywood's *Variety* was not as enthusiastic, but its review was also unambiguously affirmative. Gene Moskowitz stated that although "the story is simple, brash and earthy", it "takes on depths in Petrović's treatment".[110] The most interesting aspect of Moskowitz's review is that he clearly outlines the political core of the film (in line with the previous analysis in this chapter): "It shows that people do not change as quickly as governments and ideologies. While not against socialism, it underlines the crises that can occur when there is a conflict between individual outlooks and theories".[111] Moskowitz's brief but sharp extrapolation of the politically critical tone of the film was not something that was overlooked in Yugoslavia either. After the initial positive reviews, mainly written by film critics, the film came under the scrutiny of journalists more concerned with ideology than with cinema. *It Rains in My Village* was to become an object of investigation that was purely to do with its political connotations, which is of more interest to the analysis pursued in this book than further explorations of the cinematic reception. Therefore, such reactions deserve further attention.

As early as March 1969, the first critical review that seriously questioned Petrović's political intentions with *It Rains in My Village* appeared in the Zagreb weekly magazine, *Vjesnik u srijedu*. Using a somewhat brash and belligerent tone, Neda Krmpotić first expressed her dismay that the film was being screened in two of Belgrade's cinemas that were only 20 yards away from the building where the Ninth Congress of the League of Communists of Yugoslavia was taking place.[112] Krmpotić, a high party official from Croatia and political commentator for this magazine,[113] read the film as the "negation of our struggle for the development of socialism, while wilderness and nihilism are offered as an artistic message."[114] Krmpotić also underlined several events depicted in the film as falsifying the Yugoslav reality. She particularly believed that the scene in which an old and ill man was brought to vote, the scene in which Triša is mob lynched and the scenes portraying the village teacher, who also happens to be a member of the party's secretariat, as a "fickle whore" were impossible in 1969 Socialist Yugoslavia.[115] She was also upset by a scene featuring numerous red flags with hammers and sickles, which, according to Krmpotić, would not be seen as symbols of communism by the international audiences, but as symbols of one superpower and its hegemony (this being the Soviet Union) with which Yugoslavia was "not associated", thus further falsifying reality.[116] Therefore, Krmpotić assessed the film as "a strong artistic work", but in the service of a "reactionary ideology".[117] She concluded her article with a plea to all the relevant state institutions not to ban this film, believing that this "fashionable nihilism" ought to be seen by the working-classes of Yugoslavia, and that they should be the ones to judge it.[118] This article could be seen as one of the first that interpreted Petrović's social criticism as ill intended. Arguably there are two possible aspects that initiated this interpretation. Before they are discussed, it is worth emphasising first that the Yugoslav film historian Petar Volk designated this particular article as "a text that significantly influenced the fate of this film amongst the political functionaries and the social forums of the state".[119] Volk also adds that such an article could not be published as a result of just a single journalist's or editor's opinion. He claims that behind such articles, particularly when aimed at well-known artists such as Petrović, were "the ideologues" of the party.[120] Although Volk does not provide hard evidence for such claims, in this instance it was likely to have been the case as Krmpotić was a member of the Central Committee of the Communist Party of Croatia, and thus an ideologue herself. The fact that the article was published in *Vjesnik u srijedu* is also telling. This is because *Vjesnik u srijedu* continued a sustained campaign to discredit Petrović's film,[121] and according to Volk, they even sent journalists to the Cannes Film Festival to look for information that could support this campaign.[122] As already noted, there are two awkward potential reasons for such actions. The magazine *Vjesnik u srijedu* was published in the Croatian capital, Zagreb. It was also one of the magazines from Zagreb that in the previous year had published articles trying to discredit *Happy Gypsies*, at a time when the issues of "common Yugoslav culture" (specifically common literary language), and consequently representations of this culture abroad, were sensitive issues.[123] In one analysis of these attacks on Petrović (who was a Serbian from Belgrade) by newspapers from Zagreb, Severin Franić in his article *There Was Almost the End of the World* (*Bila je skoro propast sveta*) implies that this could be understood as an expression of Croatian nationalism against a Serbian filmmaker, where issues of ideology are only a pretext.[124] Franić explains that ideologically "orthodox Zagreb" was opposed to "dissident Belgrade",[125] adding that this coincided with their ethnic rivalries. As Franić wrote and published this assessment in Serbia, his view could also be perceived as biased. However, in the late 1960s the so-called Maspok movement, which was generally characterised as a nationalist movement and which will be discussed in more detail in the next chapter, started in Croatia and peaked in 1971. Additionally, when it is taken into account that the Croat politician Miko Tripalo, who had attacked *It Rains in My Village*,[126] was later sacked from his post due to his Croat nationalism in 1972 along with his Central Committee colleague Neda Krmpotić, who had penned the earlier attack, these assumptions on nationalism as a reason for criticising Petrović would be difficult to dispute.[127] It could also be argued that Petrović provoked this attack from Croatia by prodding the most sensitive issues of the Yugoslav conscience – the ethnic conflict and genocide during World War II. As already noted, this issue had been largely ignored during socialism, yet Petrović's character Triša explains in the film that their Serbian church was burned by Croat fascists. Arguably, this could have provoked this first negative and at the same time politically motivated reaction from Croatia. The reaction could be an indication that ethnic animosities and rivalries were still in existence in Yugoslavia, simmering below the surface, to be confirmed by the wars of the country's break-up 20 years later. Although indicative of latent ethnic acrimonies, this aspect is of lesser interest than the other aspect, which initiated this criticism of Petrović and his work. This other aspect is concerned with the ideological issues of Petrović's film, and different understandings of socialism and the role of an artist in it. These attacks, which concerned only the ideological aspect, did not only come from Croatia, but from Serbia as well, and indeed from across Yugoslavia.[128] They were not aimed only at *It Rains in My Village*, but on a string of other films, by that time known as Black Films. These films were part of a wider trend in the arts known as the Black Wave that Jasna Dragović-Soso designated as an "area of intellectual activity that most seriously challenged the Titoist system",[129] as explained in the introduction to this chapter. Further exploration of the reception of Petrović's film will continue in this context.

5. 2. 2. Black Film

Aleksandar Petrović's first film *Two* was one of the films that marked the beginning of the movement known as New Film in 1961. New Film can be broadly defined as the beginning of new formal and thematic concerns in Yugoslav cinema, the concerns that young filmmakers introduced to distance themselves from post-war Yugoslav film. The style of post-war cinema was often described as "nationalist realism", comprising predominantly films that were formally rigid and conservative, and thematically predictable in their treatment of "patriotic war themes" or "enthusiastic construction of a new socialist homeland".[130] Such films neither made any impact abroad nor were they, by the mid-1950s, popular with domestic audiences. Consequently, it was a matter of time before a new generation of filmmakers was to appear, openly breaking with this tradition that Ilja Gregory designates as the Yugoslav version of *cinéma papa*.[131] This comparison is apt, as, in the same way that the French *nouvelle vague* departed from the then traditional tenets of filmmaking in France, Yugoslav New Film did within its own national industry also, both formally and thematically. As it became "easier" to film outside the studio with lighter equipment, the formal style of these films were affected, and they distinguished themselves thematically by observing "contemporary themes" with all their contradictions, rather than the "heroic struggle" of the past.[132] Initially, these films were designated as "intimate films", as for the first time they explored the personal relationships of young people.[133] Apart from Petrović's *Two*, Bošjan Hladnik's *A Dance in the Rain* (*Ples v dežju*), also released in 1961, is another film considered to have spearheaded New Film. As that year saw a dramatic increase in film production, it is often taken as the year that marked the beginning of the new tendencies in Yugoslav cinema.[134] Some film historians such as Ranko Munitić prefer to draw attention to work that precedes New Film, and Munitić favours Vladimir Pogačić as the director whose films, made in the 1950s, already contained major elements to be incorporated later by the directors acknowledged as belonging to New Film.[135] Nevertheless, it was young director–auteurs such as Petrović, who actually worked as an assistant to Pogačić for some time,[136] who were perceived as the harbingers of the new tendencies. The main characteristic of the movement was the adoption of contemporary themes, and their treatment was to develop and become more critical of society with time. The most critical films were to be designated – initially pejoratively by the Yugoslav press and politicians – as Black Film.[137] It is my intention to briefly map out this movement, as further study of the political reception of *It Rains in My Village* can be better understood against this background.

As the blooming of New Film slowed down in 1963, and was then reinvigorated in 1966,[138] some film historians such as Mira and Antonín Liehm talk about a "new generation" (referring only to the first period, 1960–63) and the subsequent "second revolution" (referring to the second period, 1966–72).[139] However, the period between 1961 and 1972 is often perceived as one of unity, which Daniel Goulding calls the Golden Age of Yugoslav cinema.[140] During this time, Yugoslav film production reached its "apogee", in terms of quantity and "the liberalisation of film content and expression," with 1967, 1968 and 1969 being particularly excellent years.[141] Perhaps because the second part of the 1960s saw this increase in production, the tendency to distinguish the films made in that period from the ones made in the early 1960s is commonly found in film studies. This was also due to the fact that the films from the second period did have slightly different aesthetic and thematic concerns, primarily a shift from personal stories to an examination of social problems. They were hence often referred to as Black Films, or Black Wave, although they are also simply described as "radical Yugoslav films of the late 1960s and early 1970s."[142] However, the two terms – New Film and Black Film (or New Wave and Black Wave) – are often confused, or taken as synonymous, and perceived as one phenomenon. This confusion is resolved and clarified in Daniel Goulding's seminal work on the history of Yugoslav film – *Liberated Cinema* – where he explains that by 1972, there was an attack on New Film tendencies, "under the banner of *black film*", meaning "the most radical films of the period".[143] Therefore, Goulding clearly implies that all Black Films were at the same time New Films, but not all New Films were also Black Films. It is worth pointing out that not all the films produced in Yugoslavia during this period were exclusively New or Black Film(s). The film industry still continued to produce light entertainment,[144] and war spectacles redolent of socialist propaganda,[145] which were emblematic of East European film production in general. However, New Film was distinct from these other trends as it resulted from the liberalising political processes in Yugoslavia. It emerged as a film movement in 1961, and continued to grow with varying intensity until 1972, when the liberalising processes were abruptly stopped. It could be thus concluded that New Film, if seen like a tree, grew to have different branches, one of which is now known as Black Film.

The history of Petrović's career provides an apposite case study for elaborating the development of a New Film author into a Black Film one. Petrović's first film *Two* is remembered for its formal experimentation, which radically distanced itself from the aesthetics prevalent in Yugoslav cinema up to that point. Consequently, *Two* could be understood as a classic example of early New Film. With his second film *Days*, Petrović again not only experimented formally, but also involved a wider social context in this film, which still is a good model of early New Film, even if the social context arguably generated some criticism of the society. Petrović's third film *Three* was characterised by formal experimentation skilfully balanced with the narrative, thus I would be tempted to claim that this film is one of the finest examples of Yugoslav New Film. *Three*, which was set in the past, was followed by *Happy Gypsies*, which strongly (re)introduced a contemporary theme. *Happy Gypsies* could thus be perceived as Petrović's work, which moves radically towards being a Black Film, but it is not one entirely. Although it robustly portrays social problems, it also portrays certain social institutions as somewhat, and sometimes, understanding and sympathetic. The Judge, portrayed by Janez Vrhovec, the Slovenian actor who appeared in numerous New and Black films, is one example. Finally, *It Rains in My Village* also vigorously reveals social problems, only this time gloomily portraying the representatives of the state as distant, arrogant and far from the people they claim to represent. Additionally, most of the other characters in the film are represented as venal, idle and without any desire to improve their condition. This general moral decline is firmly grounded in the Yugoslav ideological framework of the period, while portraying the reality as very dark, or "black", and pessimistic. I would thus be inclined to assess *It Rains in My Village* as a Black Film par excellence. Consequently, a Black Film is a New Film, but one with a distinctly pessimistic view on the contemporary Yugoslav reality, and in addition often openly blaming the regime in power for the state of affairs depicted in the film.

The above analysis corresponds to the seminal work by Milan Ranković published in 1970, entitled *Social Critique in the Contemporary Yugoslav Fiction Film* (*Društvena kritika u savremenom jugoslovenskom igranom filmu*). In this work, Ranković charts the development of the social critique in Yugoslav cinema, defining three distinctly different periods: the first one was from 1957 until 1963, in which Yugoslav film started to "move towards contemporary themes as a precondition for the development of socially critical films";[146] the second period is from 1963 until 1967, which Ranković calls the time of "the expansion and strengthening of the socially critical orientation in Yugoslav fiction film";[147] finally, Ranković designates the third period, between 1967 and 1970 (when the book was published) as the "period of development of a distinctly explicit socially critical orientation in Yugoslav cinema".[148] It is the latter films that contain the "distinctly explicit" social criticism, or simply the radically critical films that could be characterised as Black Films. As a result of liberalisation and in the spirit of the time, there was a whole string of films that were often classified as Black Films in the second part of the 1960s.

The increase in production in the mid-1960s required the recruitment of new directors, which in Belgrade happened mainly from the Dunav Film studio, run by an old collaborator of Petrović's, Vicko Raspor. The studio produced short documentary films, often dealing with marginal phenomena in society, just like Petrović's films.[149] When these directors

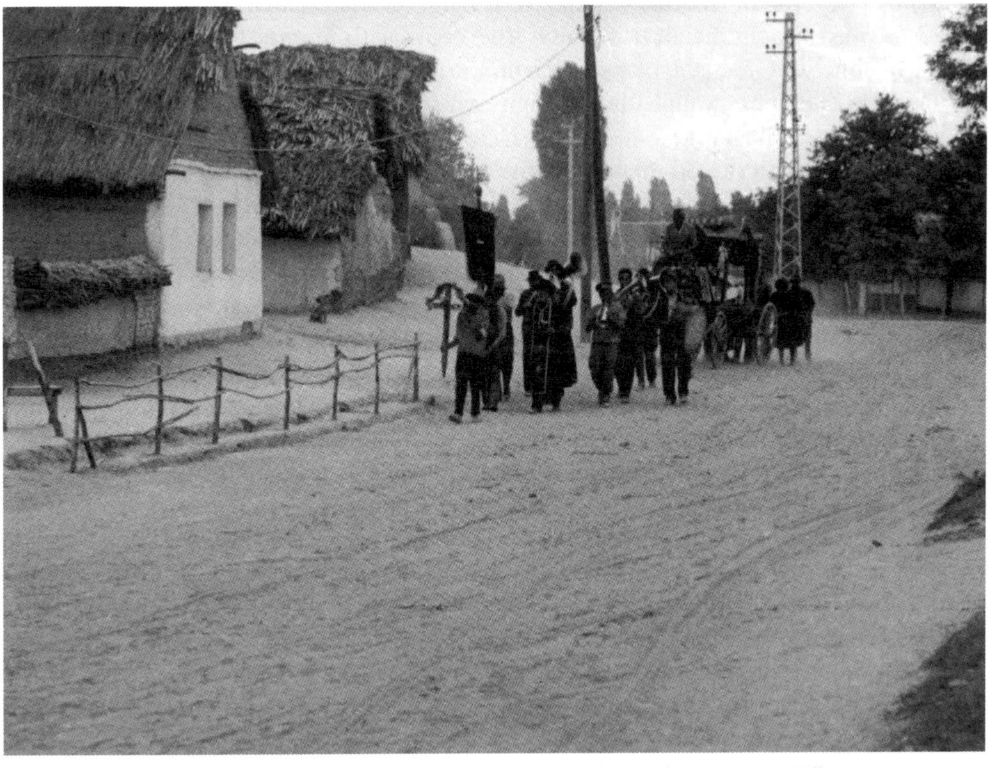

Figure 5.5: Bleak society: the funeral in a dusty and forgotten village – the set of *It Rains in My Village*.

entered the industry to make feature films, according to Ranko Munitić, they brought elements of their documentary styles and subject matters, thus practically propelling Black Films.[150] The other "recruitment centre" was the amateur film club in Belgrade, and Mira and Antonín Liehm underline that from these ranks directors such as Dušan Makavejev and Živojin Pavlović emerged, amongst others, and it was their low-budget aesthetics that created Black Films.[151] According to the Liehms, the first film to illustrate the new aesthetic was *Traitor* (*Izdajnik*), directed by Kokan Rakonjac and produced by Kino Club Belgrade as an independent feature in 1964.[152] However, Daniel Goulding mentions both the documentarists and amateurs as the new names that reinvigorated New Film in the mid-1960s.[153] One of the most distinguished directors to start as an amateur was Živojin Pavlović, whose work has already been mentioned in previous chapters. Pavlović, like Petrović, loved Dostoyevsky, and his first film *The Enemy* (*Neprijetelj/Sovražnik*, 1965) was based on the Russian's classic novel *The Double*. Pavlović was also interested in marginal characters, which occupy his *The Return* (*Povratak*, 1966), *Awakening of the Rats* (*Budjenje pacova*, 1967), and *When I am Dead and Pale* (*Kad budem mrtav i beo*, 1968). Finally, like Petrović, he started to concern himself with the hermeneutics of socialist teachings and the duplicity of communist morals, making his "most controversial" film, according to Goulding, *The Ambush* (*Zaseda*, 1969).[154] The story, set at the end of World War II, was in Pavlović's words "about the ideals of SKOJ [the Yugoslav Communist Youth Organisation], and the realities of OZN [the post-war communist secret police]."[155] So, just like Petrović, Pavlović also examines the high ideals of communism against the reality that can sometimes be disappointingly different.

A similar theme pervaded the first feature film of Dušan Makavejev, who with Pavlović and Petrović was the most significant New and Black Film director. *Man Is Not a Bird* (*Čovek nije tica*, 1965), in a humorous and entertaining way, plays with the idea that for socialism to work, a man must be able to fly, thus to be the bird of the title. Makavejev's film was set in the same factory in Bor, eastern Serbia, where Petrović had shot his very first documentary, *Shoulder to Shoulder*, ten years previously. The two films also share the same image, one that depicts the institutional idea of "bringing culture" to the proletariat by bringing symphonic orchestras to perform Mozart and Beethoven in their factories. Although the youthful zealousness of Petrović seemed to support the idea in his documentary, ten years later Makavejev exposes such practice to sharp scrutiny. While the orchestra is performing, most of the workers are bored. One of them is drunk and wanders around aimlessly, threatening to spoil the programme. The film also shows workers enjoying the bar's – the *kafana* – singers and bands a lot more, perhaps denouncing them as "lumpen proletarians", or perhaps asking the question whether the state and its socialist institutions understand what proletarian culture is? Whatever the answer, it was clear that things had dramatically changed in society between Petrović's *Shoulder to Shoulder* and Makavejev's *Man Is Not a Bird*, not least the artists' relationship to society's representation. Filmmakers were thus eager to look at society considerably more directly and consciously, particularly at its darker, marginalised sides. Makavejev did so with more formal courage than his other two peers, so his following film *Love Affair, or the Tragedy of a Switchboard Operator* (*Ljubavni slučaj, ili tragedija službenice PTT-a*, 1967) introduced a somewhat experimental and fragmented narrative, mixing fiction and documentary footage. This experimentation continued so that Makavejev explained the genre of his next production, *Innocence Unprotected* (*Nevinost bez zaštite*, 1969), as "mysterious, [and] ambiguous: a love – adventure melodrama, actually a film essay, film collage."[156] Apart from these three directors, there were a number of others who also contributed to Black Film. Makavejev's assistant Želimir Žilnik won the Golden Bear in Berlin with his *Early Works* (*Rani Radovi*) in 1969, which then caused a controversy in Yugoslavia.[157] Petrović's student Lazar Stojanović was to make *Plastic Jesus* (*Plastični Isus*, 1971), a film that attempted to address almost every problem Yugoslavia as a country might have had. Bata Čengić, who was Petrović's assistant on *Days*, was one of the few Black Film directors from Bosnia and Herzegovina, with two prominent films, *The Role of My Family in the World Revolution* (*Uloga moje porodice u svetskoj revoluciji*, 1970) and *Scenes from the Life of Shock Workers* (*Slike iz života udarnika*, 1972). In Croatia, Vatroslav Mimica, with his *Prometheus from Vishevica Island* (*Prometej sa otoka Viševice*, 1964), opened his own examination of communist ideals, when an old Partisan fighter returns to his village and grows disillusioned as his dreams of modernisation are met with suspicion. Mimica's most daring film was the formally "abstract"[158] *Kaja, I'll Kill You* (*Kaja, ubit ću te*, 1967) concerned with the emergence of fascism in a small provincial town. International acclaim received for the film *Handcuffs* (*Lisice*, 1969) made Krsto Papić another important representative of Black Film from Croatia. Together with other Croat directors such as Ante Babaja and Zvonimir Berković, including further prominent Serbian ones like Puriša Djordjević, Mića Popović and Dragoslav Lazić, the Black Film movement was considerably enlarged, leaving behind an abundant pool of films highly critical and knowledgeable about the problems of Yugoslav society of the time.[159]

As the movement had grown in size, the initial solidarity that existed between filmmakers in the early 1960s had turned into rivalry by the end of the decade,[160] particularly amongst the three most distinguished directors – Pavlović, Makavejev and Petrović.[161] The rivalry also meant competitiveness; thus, according to Goulding, Pavlović was pleased to be considered as making "the blackest films" of them all.[162] In addition, Ilja Gregory, who agrees with this view, adds that Makavejev's films were then more "playfully ironic", whereas Petrović's were "poetically charged", as overall his "social criticism was allusive rather than explicit."[163] Regardless of the stylistic idiosyncrasies, strong social criticism binds all these films and authors together, which according to film historian Michael Stoil was uniquely a Yugoslav case in the Balkan socialist context, representing "experimentation with the limits of accepted content", which ultimately "led to conflicts between artists and the state".[164] Although all these filmmakers shared a propensity for "experimentation with the limits of what was accepted", they were eventually grouped together by film historians, critics and ultimately Yugoslav politicians, and thus were an artificially created concept, rather than a group with a programme. Consequently, Ranko Munitić compares the protagonists of Yugoslav New Film with the ones of the French *nouvelle vague*, claiming that their common achievements were a result of "independent and individual work", unaffected by the work of their peers.[165]

Writing about Živojin Pavlović's seminal Black Film *When I am Dead and Pale*, Pavle Levi explains that "according to some unfavourable opinions at the time, [Black Wave filmmakers] presented an image of 'the entire country as one big toilet'".[166] Following the attack on *It Rains in My Village* by Neda Krmpotić, and considering the number of films emerging that severely criticised the downsides of Yugoslav socialism, other articles appeared systematically in 1969 questioning the ideological background, not only of this film by Petrović, but other Black Films as well with an exceptional zest and astuteness.[167] The most remarkable resentment expressed against these films came from a meeting of the presidency of the League of Communists of Yugoslavia, and the minutes of this meeting were published in June 1969, in the Belgrade daily *Borba*. At this very high forum of the state, a Croat representative, Miko Tripalo, expressed his anger at "anti-communist and right wing tendencies" found in Yugoslav contemporary art and culture.[168] He was joined by Veljko Vlahović, a federal official at the time, who had attacked Petrović's *Days* in 1963.[169] Vlahović was a poet and a veteran of the Spanish Civil War, where he had fought as a volunteer in the International Brigades. Vlahović, an undoubted authority, fulminated against *It Rains in My Village* and *The Toughs* (*Delije*, 1968) by Mića Popović in particular. He accused Petrović's film of proselytising a philosophy diametrically opposed to the one that the League of Communists stands for, and asked for an adequate answer to these tendencies, "attitudes and ways of thinking".[170] It was this high-level ideological meeting that can be taken as a point from which it was clear that such a liberal and permissive atmosphere to criticism was not to last for long, as the debate on cinema had shifted from journalists and audiences to the politicians and ideologues of the party. The Belgrade daily *Borba* soon after published a long article entitled "The Black Wave in Our Cinema" by Vladimir Jovičić in July of the same year, to coincide with the Pula Film Festival.[171] Perhaps expectedly, by taking a cue from the ideologue Vlahović, Jovičić aggressively criticised Black Film as anti-communist by employing two films as his main case studies: following Vlahović again, one of these films was *It Rains in My Village*.[172] This long and detailed article (eight pages) was, according to Daniel Goulding, to set "the lines of attack" on Black Film, and they were to be "often repeated with varying degrees of emphasis and sophistication."[173] With the framework for the confrontation with Black Film set, on 20 November 1969, an official debate on Yugoslav film production was called by the presidency of the League of Communists of Yugoslavia. The panel had been created by the Commission for Culture of the presidency of the LCY to investigate and report on "the problem".[174] The head of the panel was the famous Yugoslav animator, Dušan Vukotić, who in his opening address explained that the term Black Film is unproductive and misleading, and that they should debate the values of good films as opposed to bad films.[175] The six-hour debate ended up dismissing many attacks on the filmmakers, and, according to one senior official, was "democratic and tolerant".[176] The debate was only the beginning, however, as the issue of Black Film was to precipitate a major conflict between the party and the filmmakers. The initial atmosphere of tolerance soon changed, and became one of repression.

Although the process of liberalisation, begun in 1965 in Yugoslavia, was unprecedented in the socialist world, according to historian John Lampe, President Tito and his close collaborator Edvard Kardelj had no intention of giving away the party's monopoly on power.[177] Liberalisation was taking its toll, however, and its results were an increase in critical thought, which frequently challenged the ability of the communist elite to govern the country. In response to an increasing thrust of criticism, Tito was to reverse the process of liberalisation in the early 1970s, and completely abort the idea of taking the process further. Aleksandar Petrović was to be one victim of this reversal, as well as others. As Dragović-Soso explains, critical thought did not exist only within cinema, but also in the other arts, with writers and painters critically scrutinising society, whereas in the domain of philosophy Yugoslav socialism was questioned from a Marxist platform.[178] Such a broad canvas of critical activities was to be rigorously reduced by Tito and his closest collaborators. Before this happened, Petrović made another film, and *It Rains in My Village* remains as a testament to the challenge to the Yugoslav communist elite, as well as to the rebellious spirit of 1968. Ranko Munitić relates this spirit to Black Film, and in return, calls Black Film a "symbol of 1968, the last collective illusion of freedom and free humanity in the twentieth century."[179]

Notes

1 See the introduction to the previous chapter.

2 Jasna Dragović-Soso, '*Saviours of the Nation*': *Serbia's Intellectual Opposition and the Revival of Nationalism* (London: Hurst & Company, 2002), p. 22.

3 ibid.

4 Black Film as a phenomenon was a continuation of Yugoslav New Film, which will be addressed further, later in this chapter.

5 Jasna Dragović-Soso, '*Saviours of the Nation*', p. 22.

6 Jasna Dragović-Soso, '*Saviours of the Nation*', p. 25.

7 ibid.

8 John R. Lampe, *Yugoslavia as History: Twice There Was a Country* (Cambridge: Cambridge University Press, 1996), p. 295.

9 ibid.

10 Daniel J. Goulding, *Liberated Cinema: The Yugoslav Experience* (Bloomington: Indiana University Press, 1985), p. 81.

11 ibid.

12 An interview with Aleksandar Petrović; see Jovović, J. and Vukotić, V., "Kako frajla otvara kupleraj", *Politika Ekspres*, 3 March 1993, p. 11.

13 On the key ideas of the *Praxis* group, and how they corresponded to the ideas of some of the film directors, see Daniel J. Goulding, *Liberated Cinema*, pp. 81–82.

14 Misha Glenny, *The Balkans 1804–1999: Nationalism, War and the Great Powers* (London: Granta Books, 1999), p. 584.

15 ibid.

16 ibid.; and John R. Lampe, *Yugoslavia as History*, p. 295.

17 Želimir Žilnik edited this material into a documentary film *Lipanjska gibanja*, the title often translated as *June Turmoil*, released in 1969. See *The BFI Companion to Eastern European and Russian Cinema*, ed. by Richard Taylor et al. (London: British Film Institute, 2000), p. 283.

18 The first attempt to publish the book in 1984 failed as the book was banned by a court order; the book was then finally published in 1988. See Živojin Pavlović, *Ispljuvak pun krvi* (Beograd: Dereta, 1990), p. 7.

19 Dejan Jović, *Jugoslavija – Država koja je odumrla: Uspon, kriza i pad Četvrte Jugoslavije* (Beograd: Samizdat B92; Zagreb: Prometej, 2003), p. 168 (note 21).

20 Misha Glenny, *The Balkans*, p. 587.

21 John R. Lampe, *Yugoslavia as History*, p. 296.

22 Misha Glenny, *The Balkans*, p. 584.

23 Misha Glenny, *The Balkans*, p. 585.

24 See Misha Glenny, *The Balkans*, p. 585, and Dejan Jović, *Jugoslavija*, p. 171 (note 27); and for the assessment of Živojin Pavlović, see Živojin Pavlović, *Ispljuvak pun krvi*, pp. 186–87.

25 Jasna Dragović-Soso, '*Saviours of the Nation*', p. 28.

26 Živojin Pavlović also mentions this fact in his book on the demonstrations. See Živojin Pavlović, *Ispljuvak pun krvi*, pp. 67–68.

27 For technical data, cast and crew, see *Filmografija jugoslovenskog igranog filma 1945–1980*, ed. by Branislav Obradović (Beograd: Institut za Film, Časopis Filmograf, 1981), p. 41, and see Filmography.

28 Dušan Stojanović, *Velika avantura filma* (Beograd: Institut za Film; Novi Sad: Prometej, 1998), p. 85.

29 ibid.

30 Milan Ranković, *Društvena kritika u savremenom jugoslovenskom igranom filmu* (Beograd: Institut za film, 1970), p. 19.

31 When the awards were read out, Bob Hope, from an already prepared card, said "the winner is Aleksandar Petrović's film *Closely Observed Trains* [*Ostře sledované vlaky*, Czechoslovakia, 1966]". The mistake was immediately rectified, and the Oscar went to the Czechoslovak director Jiří Menzel. This incident was a sign for the Yugoslav press to start believing that the Oscar should have gone to Petrović, but that the then current political situation in the world made the jury award the film from Czechoslovakia. The American Government supported the political changes that had been embraced by the government in Czechoslovakia, changes that would be crushed by the Soviet invasion within the next six months. As America could not help militarily, support came in the shape of this major film award. Oscar competitions were often seen as deeply politicised, and this interpretation may well be true. Still, *Closely Observed Trains* was, and is today, one of the finest examples of the Czechoslovak New Wave, whereas *Happy Gypsies* is one of the finest examples of the Yugoslav New Wave, thus both films were certainly worthy of the award. The fact that *Happy Gypsies* had already been garlanded with awards from the Cannes Film Festival may have influenced the jury at the American Film Academy, who awarded the well-deserved

prize to the Czech film. See Aleksandar Petrović, *Novi film, crni film 1965-1970* (Beograd: Naučna knjiga, 1988), the pictures of the ceremony are on the unnumbered pages after page 150, at the beginning of the chapter on 1968; see also articles on pp. 154–55.

32   Aleksandar Petrović, *Novi film, crni film*, p. 177, and before the chapter on 1969, amongst the photographs on pages without numbers, there is a photograph of this dinner party with all its relevant participants at the Parisian restaurant L'Étoile de Moscou.

33   This was confirmed in the personal interview with actor Bekim Fehmiu (3 May 2006) and Branka Petrović (11 September 2005).

34   Živojin Pavlović states that it was under Ratko Dražević, in Avala Film, that he and Dušan Makavejev finally had a chance to direct their first feature films. See Živojin Pavlović, *Ispljuvak pun krvi*, p. 53. See also the introduction to section 2.4 in Chapter 2, and specifically Chapter 3 (section 3.2.1).

35   This was to become a curious and controversial element of Petrović's career in Yugoslavia. In an interview given in 1982, he explained: "I will direct, probably, if I get money from abroad. For 15 years now I have been told: 'Get some money from abroad, and you will work in Yugoslavia'. After *Happy Gypsies*, you will not believe me I was in no better position than today. After *Happy Gypsies*, which was very successful, no Yugoslav producer offered me a project. Today I have contracts with foreign producers, but not with ours. This is not something new. This is how it is." See Lela Jovanović, "Verovatno opasan tip", *Reporter*, 2 September 1982, p. 55.

36   Lazar Stojanović was one of the assistants to Petrović during the filming of *It Rains in My Village*; personal interview with Lazar Stojanović (3 January 2006).

37   In the words of Bogdan Tirnanić, the film was three times more expensive than the previous one – *Happy Gypsies*. See Bogdan Tirnanić, "Tiranija zvuka – propast slike", *Odjek*, 1 May 1969, p. 22.

38   Petrović explained in a later interview that the producer paid the star directly in France to act in this Yugoslav film. See Dragan Gajer, "(Za svoj novi projekt 'Majstor i Margareta') Petrović dovodi Romi Šnajder", *Politika Ekspres*, 3 February 1970, p. 10. This arrangement was to be repeated in Petrović's later films.

39   An interview with Aleksandar Petrović; see Petrović, M., "Moj film je realan", *Književne novine*, 15 March 1969, p. 16.

40   ibid.

41   Milan Ranković, *Društvena kritika*, p. 138.

42   An interview with Aleksandar Petrović; see Bogdan Tirnanić, "Aleksandar Petrović, razgovor", *Sineast*, 5 (Autumn 1968), p. 50.

43   In the opening credits to the film, it is stated that Petrović "had in mind Dostoyevsky's *The Devils* while making this film". I will discuss this issue later in this chapter.

44   Bogdan Tirnanić, "Aleksandar Petrović, razgovor", p. 50.

45   Bogdan Tirnanić, "Aleksandar Petrović, razgovor", pp. 50–51.

46   Personal interview with Eva Ras (28 April 2006).

47   Bogdan Tirnanić, "Aleksandar Petrović, razgovor", p. 51.

48   John R. Lampe, *Yugoslavia as History*, p. 294.

49   Misha Glenny, *The Balkans*, p. 587.

50 John R. Lampe, *Yugoslavia as History*, p. 311.

51 Misha Glenny, *The Balkans*, p. 588.

52 John R. Lampe, *Yugoslavia as History*, p. 291.

53 Bogdan Tirnanić, "Aleksandar Petrović, razgovor", p. 51.

54 *Bećarci* is plural, and *bećarac* singular. These are songs with funny, often slightly lewd lyrics, full of puns, which comment on everything from local affairs to global political issues.

55 An interview with Aleksandar Petrović; see Pavel Branko, "Démoni v nás a ve světě, v němž žijeme", *Film A Doba*, December 1969, p. 660.

56 Bogdan Tirnanić, "Aleksandar Petrović, razgovor", p. 52.

57 Aleksandar Petrović, "Razmišljanja o avangardnom u našem filmu, naročito o predigri", in *Prizor* (annual magazine no. 2), ed. by Snežana Nešković-Simić [articles on Aleksandar Petrović ed. by Radoslav Lazić], (Loznica: Centar za kulturu 'Vuk Karadžić', 2003), p. 20.

58 Bogdan Tirnanić, "Aleksandar Petrović, razgovor", p. 52.

59 I will explain this notion of "polyvalent view" later in this chapter.

60 Bogdan Tirnanić, "Aleksandar Petrović, razgovor", p. 52.

61 ibid.

62 Bogdan Tirnanić, "Aleksandar Petrović, razgovor", p. 49.

63 Bogdan Tirnanić, "Aleksandar Petrović, razgovor", p. 53.

64 ibid [the emphasis in the citation is mine].

65 Bogdan Tirnanić, "Aleksandar Petrović, razgovor", p. 52.

66 Simon Simonović, "Od bekstva do akcije", quoted in Živojin Pavlović, *Ispljuvak pun krvi*, p. 207.

67 After carefully viewing the film, it appears that this character is not referred to in any other way than as "the Teacher", and I will consequently refer to this character in the same way. However, in some literature it is emphasised that her name is Reza: see Petar Volk, *Istorija jugoslovenskog filma* (Beograd: Institut za Film, Partizanska knjiga, 1986), p. 191; and see the unnumbered pages with photographs from the film in Aleksandar Petrović, *Novi film, crni film*, after the chapter on 1969, after p. 176.

68 See the previous chapter (particularly sections 4.2.1 and 4.2.2) for all these points.

69 Milan Ranković, *Društvena kritika*, p. 130.

70 Bogdan Tirnanić, "Aleksandar Petrović, razgovor", p. 51.

71 See Chapter 3 (section 3.1).

72 Pavel Branko, "Démoni v nás a ve světě, v němž žijeme", p. 661.

73 Milovan Djilas was arguably the first true political dissident in Socialist Yugoslavia. He was a pre-war communist and a member of the Central Committee, and after the war he was one of Tito's closest collaborators and an ideologue of self-management after Yugoslavia broke its ties with the Soviet Union. On Djilas, see the introduction to Chapter 2, as well as Jasna Dragović-Soso, '*Saviours of the Nation*', pp. 17–22, and one of the first and sharpest critiques of socialism Djilas produced is in Milovan Djilas, *New Class* (New York: Praeger, 1957).

74 Bogdan Tirnanić, "Aleksandar Petrović, razgovor", p. 52.

75 On the film's reception and Black Film, see sections 5.2.1 and 5.2.2.

76 Levent was co-credited with Yugoslav cinematographer Djordje Nikolić; see Filmography.

77 Personal interview with Lazar Stojanović (3 January 2006).

78 Some of the paintings were made specifically for the film, and they were painted by Martin Jonaš, who was credited in the titles as "painter and farmer". I am grateful for the information on this issue to Branka Petrović, from a personal interview (11 September 2005).

79 Pavel Branko, "Démoni v nás a ve světě, v němž žijeme", p. 660.

80 John R. Lampe, *Yugoslavia as History*, p. 288.

81 ibid.

82 Whether Stepinac was really behind this was never proven, but he certainly did not object to these practices either, thus was perceived as a collaborator.

83 John R. Lampe, *Yugoslavia as History*, p. 288.

84 That the party preferred to remain silent on this issue, this Yugoslav's Pandora's box, was reflected in the cinema industry as well, so Yugoslav film historian Ranko Munitić explains that "the central taboo theme of Croatian production was Ustasha's NDH [the Independent State of Croatia] and the mass genocide of Orthodox Christians, Jews and Roma, the motif which the official Yugoslav historiography tried to minimise and marginalise, and Zagreb cineastes used to run away from like vampires from the sun." See Ranko Munitić, *Adio, Jugo-film!* (Beograd: Centar film, Srpski kulturni klub; Kragujevac: Prizma, 2005), pp. 243–44.

85 Petrović explains in an interview to Pavel Branko that the character of "mad" Goca was inspired by a character from Dostoyevsky's novel, and Goca's marriage to Triša is an event taken from *The Devils*. However, according to Petrović, these were the only two things influenced by the book directly, whereas other similarities were "ideological" and the film stems from the "philosophical world of Dostoyevsky". See Pavel Branko, "Démoni v nás a ve světě, v němž žijeme", p. 661.

86 In a recent study of *La Chinoise*, Douglas Morrey writes: "There is, then, an irresistible sense of young people playing at politics and, at times, it is difficult to avoid the impression that Godard is making fun of his young charges", which is precisely what Dostoyevsky does in his novel. See Douglas Morrey, *Jean-Luc Godard* (Manchester, New York: Manchester University Press, 2005), p. 54.

87 That a reference is made to Dostoyevsky's novel in this scene is also argued by Vida Johnson and Graham Petrie in their exhaustive work on Tarkovsky. See Vida Johnson and Graham Petrie, *The Films of Andrei Tarkovsky: A Visual Fugue* (Bloomington: Indiana University Press, 1994), p. 120.

88 In their work on Tarkovsky, Johnson and Petrie emphasise that a supporting character Lisa berates the main protagonist, Masha, "telling her that 'her senseless emancipated ways' are to blame for her marital unhappiness", in the scene in which Lisa compares Masha to a character from *The Devils*. See Vida Johnson and Graham Petrie, *The Films of Andrei Tarkovsky*, pp. 120–21.

89 Pavel Branko, "Démoni v nás a ve světě, v němž žijeme", p. 661.

90 In an interview with Pavel Branko, Petrović explains that the "open metaphor", or "global metaphor" as it was also called is best defined by two other Yugoslav film critics – Slobodan Novaković and Dušan Stojanović. See Pavel Branko, "Démoni v nás a ve světě, v němž žijeme", p. 662.

91 Pavel Branko, "Démoni v nás a ve světě, v němž žijeme", p. 662.
92 On *Two* see Chapter 2 (section 2.4.1).
93 See Chapter 4 (section 4.2.1).
94 See Aleksandar Petrović, *Novi film, crni film*, p. 146.
95 Pavel Branko, "Démoni v nás a ve světě, v němž žijeme", p. 662.
96 ibid.
97 *Filmografija jugoslovenskog igranog filma*, ed. by Branislav Obradović, p. 41; see Filmography.
98 "Najslabša moški in ženska", *Tovariš*, 17 December 1968, p. 56.
99 Milutin Čolić, "Biće skoro propast sveta", *Politika*, 10 March 1969, p. 12.
100 Ranko Munitić, *Adio, Jugo-film!*, p. 100.
101 Dragoslav Adamović, "Hoće li svet propasti?", *NIN*, 16 March 1969, p. 14.
102 See Aleksandar Petrović, *Novi film, crni film*, p. 186.
103 See Dragoslav Adamović, "Hoće li svet propasti?", p. 14.
104 This of course is to be expected if the film was not released in time; nevertheless, some journalists immediately perceived this as a sign of failure, and then they closely followed the selection process for the Cannes Film Festival, see also the following note.
105 See for example the following articles: Dragan Gajer, "Nešto se čudno dešava", *Politika Ekspres*, 17 March 1969, p. 10; and Dragan Gajer, "Petrović optužuje direktora Lebrea", *Politika Ekspres*, 18 March 1969, p. 10.
106 The competitive tone of the tabloid press is well exemplified in the following article, published when the film was accepted for the official selection at Cannes under the title "*It Rains in My Village* in Cannes nonetheless", see V. P., "'Propast sveta' ipak u Kanu", *Politika Ekspres*, 11 April 1969, p. 10.
107 16th Yugoslav Film Festival in Pula was between 26 July and 2 August 1969. See Petar Volk, *Istorija jugoslovenskog filma*, p. 521.
108 Ivo Pondělíček, "Aleksandar Petrovič dokončil svůj nový film", *Film A Doba*, January 1969, p. 43.
109 Ivo Pondělíček, "Aleksandar Petrovič dokončil svůj nový film", p. 44.
110 Gene Moskowitz, "Bice Skoro Propast Sveta (*It Rains In My Village*)", *Variety*, 14 May 1969, p. 34.
111 ibid.
112 Neda Krmpotić, "'Propast svijeta' kongresu iza ugla", *Vjesnik u srijedu*, 19 March 1969, p. 3.
113 Neda Krmpotić was a member of the Central Committee of the Communist Party of Croatia and was thus undoubtedly a high-ranking party member. She was professionally a journalist, and a political commentator of *Vjesnik u srijedu*, and a few other publications from Zagreb. She was a close collaborator of Miko Tripalo and Savka Dabčević-Kučar, the two Croatian party leaders Tito replaced in 1971 under the accusation that they were nationalists. Krmpotić was sacked from the Central Committee with them, and stopped writing regularly for the press afterwards (most likely she was prevented). As they were all sacked as part of the so-called Maspok movement, which was characterised as nationalist, it could be concluded that Krmpotić

was biased while writing the article, as Petrović was Serbian from Belgrade. However, not all the party members during Maspok were Croat nationalists, so this remains in the domain of speculation. For information on Krmpotić I am grateful to historian Dejan Jović from Croatia (personal correspondence January 2007), while Maspok will be further debated in the following chapter.

114 Neda Krmpotić, "'Propast svijeta' kongresu iza ugla", p. 3.
115 ibid.
116 ibid.
117 ibid.
118 ibid.
119 Petar Volk, *Let nad močvarom: Aleksandar Petrović svojim životom, delom i filmovima* (Beograd: Institut za film, 1999), p. 209.
120 Petar Volk, *Let nad močvarom*, p. 210.
121 Aleksandar Petrović himself reprints a large group of these articles in his *Novi film, crni film*, mainly in the chapter on 1969, see pp. 177–303.
122 Petar Volk, *Let nad močvarom*, p. 224.
123 See the previous chapter's last section (4.2.3).
124 Severin Franić, "Bila je skoro propast sveta", *Duga*, 1 October 1988, pp. 54–57.
125 Severin Franić, "Bila je skoro propast sveta", p. 54.
126 Severin Franić, "Bila je skoro propast sveta", pp. 55–56.
127 At a later stage of his career, especially as the relations between Croats and Serbs rapidly deteriorated into ethnic conflict, Petrović himself was convinced that the attacks on his *Happy Gypsies* and *It Rains in My Village* that had come from Croatia were ethnically motivated. In an interview from 1990, he calls his critics from Croatia "chauvinists", which, considering that most of them were removed from power in 1972 as nationalists, is probably correct. See an interview with Aleksandar Petrović in Milojević, M., "Intervju – Saša Petrović", *Pogledi*, 6 December 1990, p. 32.
128 Franić also emphasises that the ideological campaign against the film was not only coming from Croatia nor was it only based on ethnic animosities, but it came from all over Yugoslavia and was deeply concerned with the representation of socialism in the country. See Severin Franić, "Bila je skoro propast sveta", p. 57.
129 Jasna Dragović-Soso, '*Saviours of the Nation*', p. 22.
130 Nationalist Realism was "based on Soviet social realist aesthetic principles, coupled with a strong emphasis on Yugoslav nationalism", as defined by Ilja Gregory. See Ilja Gregory, "Fragments of Nationhood: 'Novi Film' as Seen From the 1990's: Revisioning Yugoslav Social and Political Reality (1947–1972)" (unpublished master's thesis, London: British Film Institute, Birkbeck College, 1995/96), p. 7 (see also note 10 on the same page). See also the introduction to section 1.3 in Chapter 1.
131 Ilja Gregory, "Fragments of Nationhood", p. 9.
132 One of the most detailed discussions of New Film can be found in Daniel Goulding's work, as he explains the importance of "contemporary themes" in these films. "While lacking a specific programme or coherent aesthetic perspective, the advocates of *new film* sought: 1)

to increase the latitude for individual and collective artistic expression […] 2) to promote stylistic experimentation in film form and film language […] 3) to involve film in the expression of *savremene teme* (contemporary themes) […] 4) to do all of these things within the context and premises of a Marxist–socialist state […] [italics in the original text]". See Daniel J. Goulding, *Liberated Cinema*, p. 66.

133 See Chapter 2 (section 2.4). On this first manifestation of New film in the form of "intimate films" see also Daniel J. Goulding, *Liberated Cinema*, pp. 112–25, where Goulding defines this group of films as exploring "failed love relationships, acted out in an alienated urban environment" (p. 112).

134 Film historians largely agree on this. See Mira and Antonín Liehm, *The Most Important Art: Soviet and Eastern European Film after 1945* (Berkeley, Los Angeles: University of California Press, 1977), p. 412; and Daniel J. Goulding, *Liberated Cinema*, p. 67.

135 Ranko Munitić, *Adio, Jugo-film!*, p. 29.

136 Petrović's first job in the film industry was to assist Pogačić on his *Factory Story* (*Priča o fabrici*, 1949); see Chapter 1 (section 1.2.3).

137 Goulding explains that the term "Black Film" was used critically by Vladimir Jovičić in his exhaustively long and critical article published in 1968 in the Belgrade daily *Borba*, an article that will be discussed more in this section. Goulding explains that the term was borrowed from film history (Polish *black series*, Czech *dark wave*, and French films of black pessimism of the 1930s) but whereas Jovičić used it critically, the term Black Film "rhetorically replaced *new film*", and was soon even picked up by the international press and consequently started to dominate. See Daniel J. Goulding, *Liberated Cinema*, p. 79.

138 On this hiatus, see the introduction to Chapter 3, as well as Chapter 2 (section 2.4.3).

139 Mira and Antonín Liehm, *The Most Important Art*, pp. 412–17.

140 Daniel J. Goulding, *Liberated Cinema*, p. 61, and pp. 62–67.

141 Daniel J. Goulding, *Liberated Cinema*, p. 64.

142 *The BFI Companion to Eastern European and Russian Cinema*, p. 265.

143 Daniel J. Goulding, *Liberated Cinema*, pp. 78–79.

144 In the early 1960s, when opportunities were given to new talent, according to Mira and Antonín Liehm, "far greater opportunities [were also given] to less talented people, who proceeded to speculate on the low level of audience taste." See Mira and Antonín Liehm, *The Most Important Art*, p. 417. What this meant according to Goulding was that "New Films also coexisted with a growing number of commercially oriented light-entertainment films, which were often so weak in inventiveness and cinematic style that they failed to reach even the low target of audience taste at which they were aimed." See Daniel J. Goulding, *Liberated Cinema*, p. 77.

145 This light-entertainment and New Film both co-existed with yet another large number of films "which affirmed more orthodox aesthetic values and thematic perspectives." See Daniel J. Goulding, *Liberated Cinema*, p. 77.

146 Milan Ranković, *Društvena kritika*, p. 31.

147 Milan Ranković, *Društvena kritika*, p. 47.

148 Milan Ranković, *Društvena kritika*, p. 85.

149 See Chapter 3 (section 3.1); Petrović directed *Record* and *Assemblies* for Dunav Film.

150 Munitić identifies three important sources: animated films from Zagreb, early Petrović feature films, and the two most prominent directors of documentaries from Dunav Film, Dragoslav Lazić and Dušan Makavejev. See Ranko Munitić, *Adio, Jugo-film!*, p. 149.

151 Mira and Antonín Liehm, *The Most Important Art*, pp. 412–13.

152 Mira and Antonín Liehm, *The Most Important Art*, p. 417.

153 Daniel J. Goulding, *Liberated Cinema*, pp. 59–60, and Goulding defines 1965 as the breakthrough year for New Film, when at Pula Film Festival Petrović's *Three* won the main award, and the first features by Makavejev and Pavlović were shown, see pp. 72–73.

154 Daniel J. Goulding, *Liberated Cinema*, p. 74.

155 Živojin Pavlović, *Djavolji Film: Ogledi i Razgovori*, 2nd edn (Beograd: Jugoslovenska Kinoteka; Novi Sad: Prometej, 1996), p. 227.

156 Dušan Makavejev, "Nevinost bez zaštite", in *Dušan Makavejev: 300 čuda*, ed. by Vladimir Blaževski (Beograd: SKC, 1988), p. 169.

157 On *Early Works* and its controversy, see Branislav Miltojević, *Rani Radovi Želimira Žilnika* (Niš: Sirius, 1992), which contains numerous documents, reviews, scripts, interviews and articles pertaining to this film.

158 Daniel J. Goulding, *Liberated Cinema*, p. 76.

159 On Black Film, see also the study written by Greg DeCuir Jr., focusing on ten selected films, and published in Serbian and English shortly before this book went to press: Greg DeCuir Jr, *Yugoslav Black Wave: Polemical Cinema from 1963–72 in the Socialist Federal Republic of Yugoslavia* (Beograd: Filmski Centar Srbije, 2011).

160 A significant illustration confirming that these directors initially supported each other can be extracted from an incident in 1963, when an early feature project directed by Živojin Pavlović, Kokan Rakonjac and Marko Babac *The City* (*Grad*, 1963) was banned for screening. This provoked Petrović to speak out in defence of the work at that year's Pula Film Festival, stating: "As a result of a lack of comprehension and understanding, one of the best films Yugoslavia has produced was tossed into the wastebasket." See Mira and Antonín Liehm, *The Most Important Art*, p. 416; as well as Chapter 2 (section 2.4.3).

161 This is evident from the interviews given in that period, and this rivalry was to remain until the early 1990s in some instances. In an already quoted interview by Aleksandar Petrović regarding *It Rains in My Village*, he criticises Makavejev without mentioning his name, but it is evident that he is speaking critically about *Man Is Not a Bird*; see Bogdan Tirnanić, "Aleksandar Petrović, razgovor", p. 51. For an example of Živojin Pavlović criticising Petrović and his work, see his interview from 1967 in Živojin Pavlović, *Djavolji Film: Ogledi i Razgovori*, p. 200; and that the rivalry existed and varied in intensity was confirmed in a personal conversation with Dušan Makavejev (7 April 2004).

162 Daniel J. Goulding, *Liberated Cinema*, p. 79.

163 Ilja Gregory, "Fragments of Nationhood", p. 12 (see also footnote 15 on the same page).

164 Michael Stoil, *Balkan Cinema: Evolution after the Revolution* (Ann Arbor, MI: UMI Research Press, 1979), p. 132.

165 Ranko Munitić, *Adio, Jugo-film!*, p. 193.

166 Pavle Levi, "Kad budem mrtav i beo, When I am Dead and Pale", in *The Cinema of The Balkans*, ed. by Dina Iordanova, (London, New York: Wallflower Press, 2006), p. 61.

167 In the following discussion, I will focus on three articles reporting on the three most significant developments in relation to the debate on Black Film. As Krmpotić's article was published in March 1969, the following attack on Black Film happened in late May 1969 at the meeting of Central Committee of the League of Communists of Yugoslavia. This attack was followed by an eight-page supplement to the daily, *Borba*, published in July, where Vladimir Jovičić criticised Black Film. Finally, this resulted in a large meeting between filmmakers and politicians that took place in November, where Black Film was discussed. These articles are listed accordingly in the following notes.

168 See "Delovanje komunista u sadašnjim političkim kretanjima", *Borba*, 2 June 1969, *Borba reflector*: a supplement, p. 22; Tripalo explicitly mentions filmmaking as the practice that reflects "anti-communist and right wing tendencies". It is interesting that, on page 23, Tripalo claims that nationalism as a problem is "overestimated".

169 On Vlahović's attack on New Film tendencies as early as 1963 and Petrović's response to these, see Chapter 2 (section 2.4.3) and Chapter 3 (section 3.1.2). See also Daniel J. Goulding, *Liberated Cinema*, pp. 71–72.

170 "Delovanje komunista u sadašnjim političkim kretanjima", p. 23.

171 Vladimir Jovičić, "'Crni talas' u našem filmu", *Borba*, 3 August 1969, *Borba reflector* [supplement], pp. 21–28.

172 The other film is *Do Not Mention the Cause of Death* (*Uzrok smrti ne pominjati*, 1968), directed by Jovan Živanović, where curiously, the three main characters were played by Bekim Fehmiu, Olivera Vučo and Velimir Bata Živojinović, the same actors who portrayed the main characters in *Happy Gypsies*.

173 Daniel J. Goulding, *Liberated Cinema*, p. 79.

174 Whereas the meeting was organised by the Commission for Culture of the League of Communists, there were around 100 participants at this meeting, including "film directors, film producers, film distributors, representatives of social and political organisations, and various cultural and public workers". The meeting lasted for six hours, and was permeated with a strong but democratic debate; there were no exact conclusions except that all the misunderstandings surrounding Yugoslav cinema cannot be resolved at this one meeting. Petrović was not there. See "O crnom filmu, etiketiranju, kritici", *Borba*, 21 November 1969a, p. 1.

175 Feliks Pašić, "Šta je to 'crni film'?", *Borba*, 21 November 1969b, p. 5.

176 This politician was Avdo Humo, see Feliks Pašić, "Šta je to 'Crni Film'?", p. 5.

177 John R. Lampe, *Yugoslavia as History*, p. 286.

178 See the introduction to this chapter, and Jasna Dragović-Soso, "*Saviours of the Nation*", p. 22.

179 Ranko Munitić, *Adio, Jugo-film!*, p. 228.

Chapter 6

The Artist as Master

The student demonstrations in Belgrade in the summer of 1968 could be understood as marking the highpoint of the liberalising processes Yugoslavia was undergoing during the second part of the decade.[1] The fact that President Tito ostensibly embraced the students' demands was perhaps a clear sign that political discontent could no longer be repressed, but had to be listened to. In the following period, as if in verification of this speculation, numerous other political grievances were expressed across the country. In November 1968, ethnic Albanians demonstrated in Kosovo demanding greater political autonomy.[2] In the summer of the following year, the Communist Party of Slovenia's leadership, backed by the public at home, stood up against a federal decision and asked for a larger share of the loan recently paid by the World Bank for their road building projects.[3] Finally, the most articulate and largest wave of discontent was to take place in Croatia, growing out of events that had already shaken the political leadership in that republic as well as on the federal level.[4]

As mentioned earlier, in 1967, a significant group of Croatia's intellectuals – many of whom were party members – signed a document entitled "A Declaration Concerning the Name and Position of the Croatian Literary Language", demanding that the Croatian language be acknowledged as distinct from Serbian, and taught in Croatian schools as such.[5] This declaration thus implicitly demanded the protection of Croatian national identity, economically and culturally.[6] The first response to the declaration came from Belgrade, where, according to Jasna Dragović-Soso, the Writers' Association of Serbia presented a document entitled "Proposal for Consideration", in which they endorsed Croat suggestions that Serbian and Croatian be considered as two separate languages that would develop with "full independence and equality".[7] Dragović-Soso explains that these two proposals, although their signatories also included some high party officials, were never discussed or acknowledged by the relevant political bodies.[8] In practice, the proposals meant changing the Yugoslav state's constitution, where Serbian and Croatian would be recognised as separate languages, as opposed to the existing, common Serbo-Croat or Croato-Serb (either was officially acceptable). As the two documents also impinged on sensitive national issues, the reaction of the authorities, headed by Tito himself, was to utterly dismiss the proposals and even make reprisals against their instigators in both Croatia and Serbia.[9] Dragović-Soso concludes that "Despite this initial setback, however, the Croatian national revival continued unabated."[10] In January 1970, this "revival" was institutionalised when a conservative member of Croatia's Communist Party, Miloš Žanko, was expelled to open the way for new trends led by the younger Savka Dabčević-Kučar. Her closest associate was Miko Tripalo,[11] who had attacked Black Film the previous year.[12] The leadership by these two younger politicians of the party in Croatia meant that the party now headed the movement known as *Maspok*, a word coined from *masovni pokret*, translating as "mass movement". This period is also known today, particularly after the break-up of Yugoslavia, as the "Croatian Spring". There were several political grievances that this movement wanted to address. According to John Lampe, the grievances were of regional and economic nature, primarily revolving around the distribution of profits from the Croatian tourist industry. They questioned the amount of money Croatia was paying to the federal fund for the underdeveloped republics and autonomous provinces, as well as continuing complaints related to the alleged specific nature of Croats and their culture as distinct from other Yugoslav ethnic groups.[13] In the process of articulating their policies the young Croatian party leadership, according to Misha Glenny, "welcomed the participation of non-communist organisations",[14] which was in the spirit of the general liberalisation in the whole of Yugoslavia at this time. The participation of a large proportion of the Croatian population surprised Miko Tripalo himself,[15] and perhaps due to its broad nature, some of the demands presented during the Croatian Spring went as far, according to Lampe, as to require "a separate [national] bank for Croatia, and what amounted to a separate army and representation in the United Nations as well."[16] During this period, President Tito liked to remind the Croat leaders that he also was a Croat, from Zagorje, Croatia's true heartland.[17] As a Croat, Tito was against unitarism,[18] or centralism, which was often perceived as a cover for Serbian hegemony; thus he at first supported Dabčević-Kučar and Tripalo, and the Croatian Spring.[19] However, as the president of the Yugoslav federation, he found the demands for a virtually independent state of Croatia unacceptable. As Dejan Jović explains "ethnic nationalism remained as the main enemy of the Yugoslav communists",[20] hence "the Croatian Spring (or *Maspok*, the terminology depending on one's point of view) became possibly the biggest challenge to the stability of the Yugoslav state."[21] A veteran Croat communist, Vladimir Bakarić warned Tito that on the Croatian political scene there is an emergence of people "who are not ours [that is, communists]."[22] Tito decided to no longer tolerate the various political "deviations" from the main party line, as he had tolerated the student protests in Belgrade and initially the Croatian Spring. According to Lampe, he had a "programme to re-establish the Party's commanding position."[23] In order to do so, according to Dragović-Soso, Tito had "a new wave of repression prepared".[24]

At the same time in November 1968, Serbia inaugurated two new leaders of their branch of the party: young Marko Nikezić and Latinka Perović, generally identified in history as liberals.[25] They articulated, according to Lampe, five goals for Serbia: "(1) a market economy; (2) a modern Serbia; (3) liberation from the 'ballast' of Serbian Yugoslavism and self-absorption; (4) support for technocrats; and (5) cooperation rather than confrontation with the other republics."[26] In the Yugoslav context of the time, points 3 and 5 were particularly interesting as they implied that if Tito had moved against the Croatian leadership, it would have been difficult for him to count on the Serbian leadership to support him. Serbs now perceived Croatian internal affairs as Croatia's own problems, not Serbia's. Marko Nikezić later explained that they were genuinely tired of Serbia being perceived as Yugoslavia's "guard", and said that "if Yugoslavia is necessary, then it is necessary for all, and not just [for] Serbs."[27] Consequently, Nikezić refused to interfere in the other republics' affairs even when these involved ethnic Serbs.[28] Nikezić had spent his youth in Paris,[29] and gave up the post of Yugoslav foreign minister to become Serbia's party leader. He was considered to be a politician of integrity, and had stood up to Tito in the past, most notably during Israel's attack on Egypt in 1967.[30] Dejan Jović adds that Tito was the subject of criticism in all the republics on different occasions, but "never as frequently and directly as in Serbia."[31] In return, Jović concludes, Tito "removed several generations of leaders [in Serbia] who established independence from" him and his decisions.[32] The same fate was to befall Nikezić and Latinka Perović, as Tito, in Dragović-Soso's assessment, facilitated "the return of a more repressive climate in the 1970s, after two decades of progressive liberalisation".[33]

In December 1971, at a hunting lodge in Vojvodina, which Tito "inherited" from the Serbian royal family (the lodge is called Karadjordjevo, referring to the family name of the dynasty, Karadjordjević), he demanded the resignations of Savka Dabčević-Kučar and Miko Tripalo.[34] After they complied there was "a swift show of force by the police and army in Zagreb which led to hundreds of arrests and the subsequent imprisonment of 'ringleaders'",[35] whereas "over 1000 members were later purged from Croatia's Party apparatus".[36] Somewhat cynically, Glenny adds that "Tito [then] applied his cherished principles of 'brotherhood and unity' elsewhere in Yugoslavia",[37] and in October 1972, he also removed Marko Nikezić, Latinka Perović and all of their allies from the Serbian leadership.[38] Tito proceeded to do the same with the other liberals in the other republics, and by the end of 1972, according to Lampe, liberal coalitions had vanished.[39] Tito's reliance on what Glenny calls the "standard techniques of communist repression"[40] had an impact reaching further than the political arena. According to the film historians Mira and Antonín Liehm, the repression "probably hit film harder than any other sphere of culture."[41] Daniel Goulding explains that Yugoslav filmmakers were to enter a period of "Kafkaesque" repression similar to the one Czechoslovak filmmakers went through in the period of "normalisation" from 1969 to 1973, and that America suffered during "the Hollywood 'blacklisting' which occurred during the McCarthy era."[42] Aleksandar Petrović was to be a victim of this repression, and was to leave the country in February 1973,[43] less than four months after the removal of Serbia's party leadership. How exactly Petrović was persecuted will be addressed later in this chapter, and how severe the consequences for the Yugoslav film industry were is best summed up by Mira and Antonín Liehm, who explain that in 1973, the year Petrović left, Yugoslavia produced a mere 15 feature films, less than half the average annual production of the 1960s.[44] The film that won awards at that year's Pula Film Festival was a three-hour spectacle *Sutjeska* (Stipe Delić, 1973), with Richard Burton as Tito, glorifying his role as a Partisan commander during World War II. According to the Liehms and Goulding, this was the best indication of the direction Yugoslav cinema was to take during the 1970s,[45] or as Yugoslav film historian Ranko Munitić concludes, "Black Wave was replaced with the Red Wave".[46] Before this happened, Petrović completed another film in 1972, which reflected discreetly on the political repressions described earlier.

6. 1. Aleksandar Petrović as the Master

6. 1. 1. Petrović and the Whirlpool of the Decentralisation Debate

During the purges of the Yugoslav republic's senior party officials, Tito found an ally in his regular and long-standing comrade, Edvard Kardelj. Kardelj was the last remaining member of Tito's "inner circle"[47] (which Tito had also purged,[48] although Kardelj had survived), and continued, until his death, to play the role of key advisor on ideological issues. John Lampe claims that even with the beginning of the "liberal hour" in the period 1965–66, Tito and Kardelj had no intention of giving away "the party's monopoly of power".[49] Misha Glenny agrees with this view and explains that "a strong coalition between Serbs and Croats might jeopardise Kardelj's position [he was a Slovenian] as successor to Tito. It might even jeopardise the position of Tito himself."[50] Glenny proceeds to severely criticise Tito and Kardelj for their response to the Croatian Spring and Serbian liberals, calling them "the true villains of the period". He explains that there was a possibility at that moment for the young elites of Serbia and Croatia to resolve their problems without tutelage. But by hampering this process, Tito and Kardelj created a "disaster for Yugoslavia's future".[51] In their quest to retain power, Tito – who was nearly 80 years old at the time – and Kardelj did not "welcome reconciliation between the Serbs and Croats", and to secure their positions, according to Glenny, continued to play them off against each other.[52] Glenny's language may appear brash, but that there was a strongly negative dimension to Tito's and Kardelj's purges of the early 1970s is also deduced by Jasna Dragović-Soso, who concludes:

> The main long-term consequence of the repression of the 1970s was that it dashed any remaining hopes that the Yugoslav system was reformable from within. For both students and professors, writers and filmmakers, the crackdown represented "the moment of truth" which showed the face of autocratic rule for what it was and the impossibility of implementing truly liberal reforms.[53]

Tito, however, believed at the time that he could resolve Yugoslavia's problems with a new constitution, the drafting of which was completed by Edvard Kardelj, the author of all of Socialist Yugoslavia's constitutions. The new constitution was to further develop the concept of decentralisation, or "de-étatization" as Tito and Kardelj would say, initiated in the 1963 constitution.[54] As Lampe explains, decentralisation was to guarantee the "withering away of the State", which was the "original point of distinction in the [ideological] dispute with the Soviet Union."[55] The constitution of 1974, which Glenny describes as "baffling in its complexity",[56] was to further the idea of the decentralisation of the state. Some historians, such as Dejan Jović, explain this radical decentralisation of the state's structure and institutions as the initial framework that actually enabled and guaranteed Yugoslavia to break down as a country in the early 1990s,[57] and this debate could be illustrated with an event taken from the history of Yugoslav film industry. Additionally, it is important to underline that Tito and his elite believed, and had already announced in the early 1970s, that "decentralisation" was to solve the country's problems.

On 20 and 21 March 1971 the final meeting of the Union of Film Workers of Yugoslavia took place in the Slovenian town of Kranj. Aleksandar Petrović was the (last) president of the Union, which at that meeting could not agree on how to transform itself in the spirit of decentralisation. The Union fell apart and never resumed its existence, although the film workers remained members of their particular societies belonging to their respective federal units, these being either republics or autonomous provinces. As a consequence, in April 1971, Petrović became president of the Union of Film Workers of Serbia.[58] Jasna Dragović-Soso claims that these "disputes in the cultural sphere reflected already existing power struggles in Yugoslavia's political leadership."[59] She explains that the break-up of the Yugoslav Writers' Union in the spring of 1989 was "a rehearsal for something much more serious", this being the end of the Yugoslav federation.[60] It is interesting to note that long before the Writers' Union, it was the Union of Film Workers that dissolved. It is also curious that the acronym for the Film Workers' Union was SFRJ, standing for Savez Filmskih Radnika Jugoslavije (the Union of Film Workers of Yugoslavia), which was exactly the same as the acronym for the full name of the country, Socijalistička Federativna Republika Jugoslavija (the Socialist Federal Republic of Yugoslavia). Therefore, Dragović-Soso's claim that the break-up of the Writers' Union precipitated the break-up of the country is right, but it is also tempting to add that the break-up of the Union of Film Workers anticipated this event 20 years earlier.[61]

As president of the Union, Aleksandar Petrović opened the meeting with a speech in which, amongst several other things, he praised Yugoslav New Film and the impact it had had nationally and internationally.[62] The speech was subsequently attacked by the journalist Marko Goluža in the Croatian magazine *Vjesnik u srijedu*,[63] which Misha Glenny praises as one of the more critically liberated publications that emerged as a result of the Croatian Spring.[64] The criticism Goluža makes against Petrović was indicative of the political processes unfolding in the country as a whole. As a result of Tito's decentralising policies, Goluža states:

> The deep changes which our society is experiencing cannot bypass our cinema. In the liquidation of centralised power and beliefs, in the new relations between the Republics, the film workers have also to map out the future framework of their actions and cooperation.[65]

This formulation is interesting, as the film workers had not agreed on the new framework, perhaps illustrating Jović's thesis that too much decentralisation simply dissolved the Yugoslav state and its institutions. The Union was supposed to be replaced with a Conference of Film Workers, but the details on how to vote and operate this new association were never agreed on.[66] As this took place at the height of the Croatian Spring, whereas Petrović concluded his speech by praising Yugoslav culture and Yugoslav cinema,[67] Goluža replied to Petrović that one has to "start with the fact that there is no such thing as one Yugoslav cinema, but national cinemas", implying that the Croatian, Macedonian, Serbian and other cinemas were all different.[68] This view was respected by film critics prior to the intensification of decentralisation as well, reiterating the idea that Yugoslav culture represented a group of mutually distinct cultures, comprising the various nations and nationalities.[69] These debates within the film community, reflecting the fissures appearing in the complex ethnic fabric of Yugoslavia, were augmented by the revival of Croatian nationalism in the early 1970s.

In addition, in his speech to the Union of Film Workers of Yugoslavia, Petrović again clarified his view on those films that are critically engaged in social and political issues. His focus was, evidently, not on ethnic and cultural divisions, but on intellectual and artistic freedom of expression:

> Time has taught us that socially critical films do not talk about societies only through the immediate messages of their contents, but also, and even more so, through the fact that a particular society has evolved to such a level, positively speaking, where such films could be made. In this respect, the new Yugoslav socially critical films are the best ambassadors of our overall social progress.[70]

These words clearly demonstrate how Petrović felt about the society and the industry of which he was a part. In 1971 he was arguably reaching the zenith of his career, just as Yugoslavia was perhaps reaching the zenith of its liberalism and openness. However, as already indicated, the political situation in Yugoslavia was about to change dramatically, with Tito and Kardelj clamping down not only on artists and filmmakers, but also on high party officials. The choice of Petrović's next project anticipated this imminent conflict: a conflict that would end what had been a fruitful period for all the parties involved. While the new film brought to an end one period, it clearly represented a new path in Petrović's development as an artist and filmmaker.

6. 1. 2. Petrović, Literary Adaptations and his New Film

While criticising Petrović's speech at the 7th, and last, Congress of the Union of Film Workers of Yugoslavia, Marko Goluža reproached him for claiming that the financial and logistical situation in the industry had never been as bad.[71] Goluža, in the spirit of the Croatian Spring, added that this may be the case in Serbia, but was certainly not in Croatia, where according to him the situation had never been better.[72] However, production records of the period show that Goluža's statement was unsubstantiated, as Croatia had produced eight films in 1970, but only three in 1971 (with participation in one co-production),[73] when Goluža made this claim. Although he wrote his article early in 1971, it was usually known in advance how many productions would be started in a year, so he is likely to have known the probable production figures.[74] Petrović gave several interviews at the time, primarily as president of – first the Yugoslav and then the Serbian – Union of Film Workers, severely criticising the difficult situation in the industry. In an interview published under the title "There Will Be the End of Cinema Soon", playing on the title of his then latest film, Petrović stated:

> We could freely say that we do not have an organised film industry in Serbia anymore. In fact, we are in the process of its being destroyed. I lost a whole year trying to make a film in this country, and then had to give up.[75]

As the main cause for this difficult situation, Petrović underpinned the continuing decrease in the level of state funding, along with an "irrational" expenditure of these funds within the industry.[76] He added that the level of competence of the governing boards was very low, and concluded that: "It is almost impossible to make films. Artistic and financial results mean nothing anymore. They have created complete chaos."[77] Petrović was specifically upset about the fact that although his *I Even Met Happy Gypsies* had been very successful commercially, he could only make films with the significant participation of foreign finances. In the years to follow, he frequently complained about this.[78] Still, in his interview on "The End of Cinema" given in November 1970, Petrović mentions a project he had been working on for a year. He adds that he had written a script with the French writer Romain Weingarten, and that this script was an adaptation of the then controversial Russian, or rather quintessentially Soviet novel, *The Master and Margarita*, by Mikhail Bulgakov (1891–1940).[79] Although his previous film, *It Rains in My Village* had been inspired by Dostoyevsky, it was not an adaptation. With this new script, bearing the same title as the book, Petrović was to enter a new phase in his career, one characterised by scripts based on literary adaptations, rather than scripts based on his own, original ideas. As the following argument intends to demonstrate, this is only relative, as his adaptations were to emphasise strongly those elements of the adapted novels that were very close to Petrović's own sensibilities.

Petrović announced that he was to film *The Master and Margarita* in February of 1970, in an interview to Belgrade's *Politika Ekspres*.[80] As with *It Rains in My Village*, he had secured finance from France, and similar to the previous film, the French producer was to pay for the participation of well-known French stars in the project, which was to be filmed in Yugoslavia.[81] The French producer was a young member of the Michelin family, the well-known car tyre manufacturers.[82] The role of the Master was to be given to the French star Michel Piccoli, while the role of Margarita was offered to the Austrian-born star of French cinema, Romy Schneider. The two actors were approached and accepted their roles, although the contracts would be signed after the other production formalities had been completed.[83] A major obstacle among the latter was the fact that Petrović was unable to secure a Yugoslav studio, or production house, as a partner in the venture.[84] Considering that a Yugoslav studio would only have to provide the crew, facilities and logistics, whereas the finances and stars were to come from France, it is no wonder that Petrović lambasted the situation in the film industry as chaotic. It is evident from the interview "It Will Be the End of Cinema Soon", published in November 1970, that this situation had not been resolved for almost a year. However, Branka Petrović also adds that the young French producer was getting increasingly nervous and hesitant about the project, due to its ambitious production values.[85] By early 1971 Michelin decided to abandon the production. Petrović's international standing was nevertheless high, and regardless of the fact that *It Rains in My Village* had not received the accolades of *Happy Gypsies*, he was still considered as a major European director. When the deal fell through with Michelin, the Italian maverick producers, Giorgio Papi and Arrigo Colombo, showed an interest in the project.[86] Petrović was soon in Italy where he reworked the script with Barbara Alberti and Amedeo Pagani, essentially making an Italian version with Italian dialogue. As the film was to be a Yugoslav-Italian co-production there would also be a version of the film in Serbo-Croat. The French stars would now be replaced with actors from Italy. Euro International Film from Rome would substitute for Michelin from Paris, while Petrović turned to Vicko Raspor of the documentary studio Dunav Film, his old friend and collaborator, for help in securing a Yugoslav partner.[87] As principal funding was to come from "outside", Raspor agreed that Dunav Film would become a Yugoslav partner and co-producer of *The Master and Margarita*, providing facilities, work force and logistics in Yugoslavia, even though the production was considerably larger than that of their usual output. Raspor was known as a communist of the "Yugoslav type" (as opposed to the Soviet), and according to Nikola Majdak, an old friend of Raspor's and Petrović's, was personally delighted that Petrović was going to film Bulgakov's novel, as the book was so critical of Stalinism.[88]

With finances secured from Italy, and with all the freedom given by his old friend Raspor, Petrović planned to start filming in late 1971. However, he then suffered another setback. The Italian star, Gian Maria Volontè, decided to pull out explaining, while ill and with a high temperature, that he was a communist and would not want to upset the Communist Party of Italy nor its members by appearing in this adaptation of Bulgakov.[89] It is interesting that Lorenzo Codelli, the Italian film critic, indeed assessed the film after its release as offensively "anti-Communist à la [Doctor] Zhivago",[90] confirming Volontè's fears that stalled the production.[91] Volontè was then replaced by Ugo Tognazzi, popular in Italy for his comic roles,[92] whereas Margarita was played by the young American actress Mimsy Farmer, whose first European role was in Barbet Schroeder's *More* (1969). Curiously, Farmer subsequently stayed in Europe, as her pro-communist political convictions of the left alienated her from the United States, at that time engaged in war in Vietnam. She had already started acting in Italian horror – *giallo* – films, and was to achieve fame in this genre. Petrović's film was for her a rare venture outside of this milieu, it could be added with hindsight. The biggest star in the film was to be the French actor, Alain Cuny, who played the diabolical Professor Woland. Petrović completed his adaptation of Bulgakov's novel in 1972, as *Majstor i Margarita* in Yugoslavia, and *Il Maestro e Margherita* in Italy.[93]

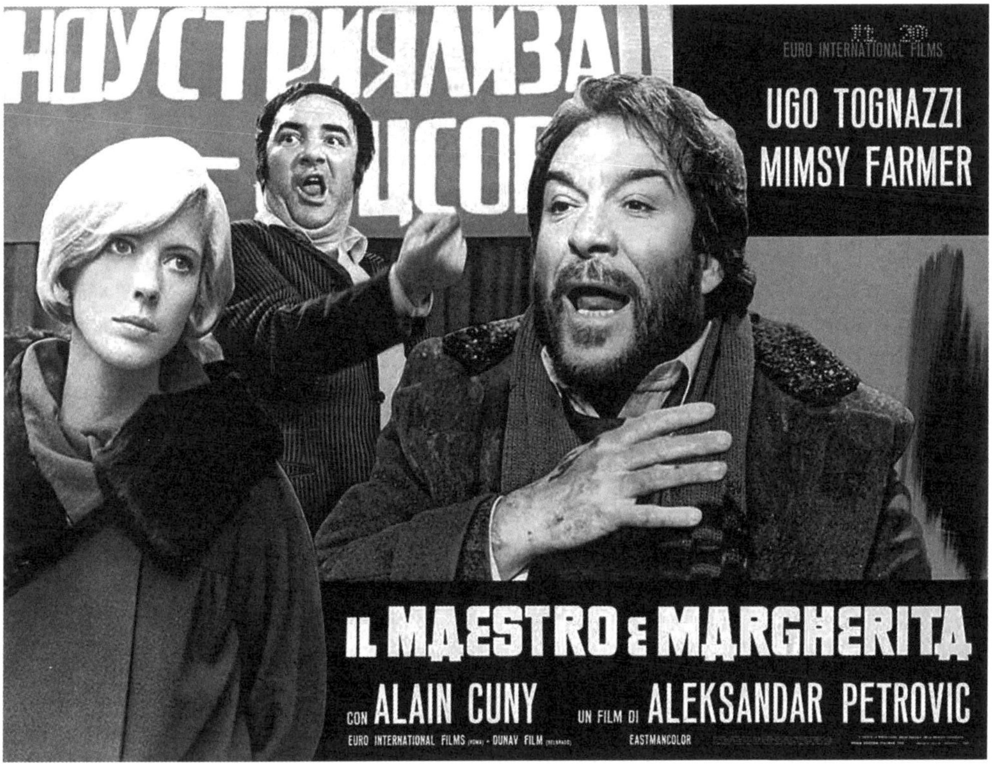

Figure 6.1: Italian poster for *Il Maestro e Margherita* with its international cast: American Mimsy Farmer as Margarita (left), Italian Ugo Tognazzi as the Master (right), and Yugoslav Danilo Bata Stojković (centre) as the venal writer Bobov.

6. 1. 3. Bulgakov and Petrović on Art under Dogmatic Totalitarianism

The period after the release of *It Rains in My Village* appears fraught with contradictions. The processes of liberalisation continued in Yugoslavia until late 1971, but since 1969 there had been signs that the tolerant atmosphere was likely to change. Towards the end of 1969, criticism of the so-called Black Wave was more frequent and more direct, often coming from high party officials, and published in the Belgrade daily *Borba*.[94] One of the party's authorities on questions of culture, Veljko Vlahović, who had initially assailed Petrović's film *Days* in 1963,[95] thereby creating the first real "misunderstanding" Petrović had with the party, began criticising Petrović specifically for *It Rains in My Village* in 1969.[96] To Petrović, this was probably a sign that the success he had achieved in the period between 1963 and 1969 (particularly with *Three* in 1965 and *Happy Gypsies* in 1967), not only for himself but for the country and its film industry, was relative and fragile. This feeling probably became stronger in 1971, when what was to later become one of the best-known Yugoslav films was banned from public distribution. Petrović's peer, another internationally acclaimed director of Yugoslav Black Film, Dušan Makavejev, premiered his *WR: Mysteries of the Organism* (*WR: Misterije organizma*) at the Cannes Film Festival that year,[97] and won the Luis Buñuel award.[98] Makavejev was an internationally respected director, and his film was also a co-production, albeit between Yugoslavia and the Federal Republic of (or, today the former West) Germany. When the film was shown in Yugoslavia it was immediately perceived as ideologically problematic, as the film criticises American capitalist-liberalism and Soviet style communism as equally repressive, as well as criticising Yugoslav self-management socialism, which was seen as squashed between these two superpowers.[99] The fact that Makavejev satirically compared Yugoslav communism with the Soviet variety was, considering Yugoslav ideological disagreements with the Soviets, virtually blasphemous. Bringing American capitalism into the equation, made the Executive Committee of the Regional Cultural Commission of Vojvodina prevent the film from being distributed.[100] Makavejev defended the film and the decision was at first overturned, but after numerous panels and discussions, the film was ultimately stopped from being shown at that year's Pula Film Festival,[101] and was not then seen in Yugoslavia until the late 1980s. As the film had a German co-producer, it was widely shown internationally, although not in the country in which it had been made. This period, at the end of the 1960s and the beginning of the 1970s, was thus controversial and unpredictable for Yugoslav artists and filmmakers. During this time, Aleksandar Petrović would make a film about this phenomenon, perhaps not as "invisible" as the phenomena about which he had made his previous films. However, it was one that was equally complex and troublesome: the one about the relationship between an artist and a socialist state. Petrović, it seems, had sensed the era of liberalism was coming to an end, and that Yugoslavia's *laissez-faire* communism was soon to resemble the oppression of Stalinism.

In order to meditate on the relationship of art and politics in socialism, Petrović chose to adapt the novel *The Master and Margarita*, which examines this relationship in Stalin's Soviet Union of the 1930s. This complex and voluminous novel opens with the meeting of two Soviet artists in a park: the chairman of Moscow's literary association and magazine editor, Berlioz, with his young colleague, the poet Bezdomny. Berlioz "had commissioned the young poet to write a long antireligious poem for the next issue of his journal",[102] and the two are scientifically dismissing religions, claiming that Christ never existed. The conversation is interrupted by a foreigner, Professor Woland, who introduces himself as an expert in black magic, and is actually the Devil himself. Woland contradicts them, claiming that he was there when Pontius Pilate questioned Jesus Christ. While the two Soviet writers assume that the Professor must have lost his mind, Bulgakov uses this as a pretext to retell his own version of this Biblical event in a separate chapter. Bulgakov there makes his own Jesus, Yeshua Ha-Notsri, dispute everything St Matthew, or Levi Matvei (as they are named in the novel), has written down as Jesus' words and teachings.[103] In this way Bulgakov initially questions the idea of "correct" interpretations of teachings and texts, which, in practice, easily ends in dogmatism. Remarkably, he does so by taking as an example the famous Biblical story, while his narrative is set in probably the first modern atheist country, the Soviet Union.

The story proceeds with Woland predicting Berlioz's imminent and ghastly death, which does indeed happen soon afterwards, making the young poet Bezdomny so shocked that he ends up institutionalised. It is in the madhouse that Bezdomny meets another inmate, a writer known simply as the Master. The Master tries to console Bezdomny and believes he has met the Devil. The Master has written a novel on Pontius Pilate, which Bulgakov inserts in his novel, further retelling his own interpretation of the gospels. However, the Master is only introduced as a character in the thirteenth chapter of the book, whereas up to that point the narrative revolves predominantly around Professor Woland. Woland, together with his three assistants, Azazello, Korovyov and a large cat Behemoth, who speaks and behaves like a human, descend upon Moscow confronting its population that denies divine, or diabolic, existence. At the same time, they also confront the population's greed, venality, selfishness and similar sins. This culminates in a theatre show of black magic in which Woland gives away new clothes and cash for free, which all disappear in the following days disgracing the ones who accepted it. Woland then asks for help from the beautiful Margarita, who was the Master's lover before he was locked away. She appears at Woland's ball as his queen, and in return he and his acolytes free the Master from the hospital and bring them back together.[104] Realising that the lovers would probably have a difficult life in Moscow, Woland takes them away to an "eternal refuge", in front of which they meet Pontius Pilate, who is finally given an absolution. The novel ends with an epilogue describing what happened in Moscow after all these supernatural events, and to what extent the people who witnessed them have changed. Bulgakov thus describes his Devil in much the same way as Goethe did his, as "part of the power which forever wills evil and forever works good."[105]

Although this is evidently a fantastic novel, which revolves around the themes of love, morality and religion, it also realistically depicts Moscow under Stalin: the city is not only low on supplies, but people there "disappear" too; the Master himself was informed on by his neighbour, Aloisy Mogarych, to the secret police so that he can move into his flat. Additionally, the Master was labelled as reactionary by the critics and derided for his yet unpublished novel, as its religious theme – Pontius Pilate – is not of interest to the young socialist state. Bulgakov depicts a considerable group of characters, Soviet writers and artists, who are social conformists prepared to suppress talented colleagues that stray from the official dogma. Clearly, Bulgakov knew such types during his lifetime.

Petrović remained faithful to the novel's time frame, and the similarities of the Soviet Union under Stalin in the 1920s and 1930s to Yugoslavia in the early 1970s were not "forced" by Petrović, but came about as a result of Tito's increased repression of artists and intellectuals.[106] Although these parallels will be debated later in the chapter, it is important to highlight here this significant novel's theme of the ill-fated interface between the artist and a dogmatic totalitarian state. Petrović's choice of Bulgakov's work in that respect could not have been more apposite.

In general, Bulgakov was perceived as a writer who was, with his work, continuously repressed under Stalinism. However, in an exhaustive examination of his life and work, Ellendea Proffer demonstrates that Bulgakov's relationship with the system, and particularly

Stalin, was considerably more complex.[107] Bulgakov's biography also has an interesting parallel to Petrović's, in that Bulgakov had a traumatic experience in World War I, which left a strong influence on his *weltanschauung*, just as World War II had on Petrović. Proffer explains that Bulgakov's witnessing of terrible executions during the war "made him rise above his identity as a monarchist White officer and understand that the Civil War was a tragedy for all sides."[108] Similarly, Petrović had witnessed the executions of Yugoslav monarchists as a young "Red" Partisan, also realising and experiencing the detrimental effects of war.[109] The humanist attitude born out of these extraordinarily traumatic experiences brought about a certain empathy in the work of both artists. This resulted in a view, according to Proffer, on Bulgakov (but equally applicable to Petrović) that their "politics resists [simple] interpretations".[110] As shown so far, Petrović's work was highly sensitive to political changes in the country, and he often reflected upon them. Bulgakov too was obsessed with political issues, and in his oeuvre, *The Master and Margarita* included, he continuously examined the relationship between the artist and the powers that be, as it affects hers/his work. Proffer concludes that "[C]onsistently, Bulgakov's artist heroes feel themselves crushed by greater force", the force often represented by tsars, kings, censors or similar – often political – authorities.[111] The novel Petrović adapted was no exception, with the main protagonist – the Master – a writer, ultimately institutionalised due to the fact that he could not deal with the political pressures he faced. This became one of the themes in the novel that Petrović not only carefully transposed to the film, but also amplified, as further analysis will show. As he added elements that make the theme closer to his own experiences and the Yugoslavia of the time, a conclusion could be made that this particular storyline within the novel was a significant factor that drew Petrović to adapt this novel into a film. It was also an important factor as this storyline, or theme rather, corresponds to one of the political themes that had, up to that point, pervaded his work – one that investigates the relationship between the political establishment and the rest of society, particularly its underprivileged groups. Although artists were not necessarily lacking in privileges in socialism, Petrović's new film was to show how the restrictions on their work made them underprivileged in a dogmatic political atmosphere.

In terms of Petrović's inclinations to scrutinise socialist society in his films, there is another key element in *The Master and Margarita* that also drew his attention to this work. This element is, according to Proffer, also dominant in the novel, and to fully understand it, it is important to elaborate further on Bulgakov and the atmosphere in which he worked. Bulgakov's novel was 12 years in the making,[112] and is unique within his oeuvre, as Bulgakov criticises, or rather satirises, certain specific and crudely dogmatic phenomena in the Soviet society of the time. The book was written in the 1930s, but its beginnings could be – according to Proffer – tracked down to a few short stories written in the 1920s, which was a period of "increased anti-religious propaganda".[113] Ellendea Proffer emphasises that Bulgakov was not religious, at least in a classical sense, but his understanding of the divine was rather a peculiar one.[114] Bulgakov was the son of a theologian and the grandson of a priest, but overall, like his father, his interest in theology was "historical, rather than practical".[115] Bulgakov himself was often critical, particularly of the clergy, as they played "very political roles" in the Russian Civil War.[116] However, as a satirist, his main criticism in *The Master and Margarita* is aimed at simplistically vulgar implementations of dialectical materialism in relation to any metaphysical understandings of the divine. His narrative follows the arrival of Satan, or Professor Woland, as he is known in the book, to the Moscow of the 1930s, where he causes havoc and disbelief amongst the non-believers. In a way, Woland could be understood as the main character, as the Master of the title only appears half way through the novel. Consequently, if the Devil is the main character who "tempts" the atheism of Muscovites, then it could be said that the relationship of the metaphysical view of the world as opposed to the dialectical materialist one, or simply, a religious versus communist understanding of the world, is one of the key elements of the novel. Proffer further explains:

> In an early draft of *The Master and Margarita* Bulgakov planned to have a major scholarly character write a work about the "secularization of ethics." This was an essential concern of Bulgakov's generation, including those who were committed Marxists. Bulgakov's much-loved stepfather was an atheist, who demonstrated that such beliefs were not incompatible with the highest ethics. To Bulgakov's mind, however, the Soviet era seemed to abound in disturbing examples of what happens when ethics are divorced from the religious impulse and attached to the vagaries of political expediency.[117]

Bulgakov here also shows that, instead of liberating the society from "the ambiguous role of organized religion", the Soviet Union only "replaces one religion with another".[118] He certainly attacks this new form of religion – atheism – and Proffer correctly concludes: "Bulgakov's entire novel is in a sense a polemic with the dominant force of his time, the belief in enlightened rationalism which in his country ended in a totalitarian structure."[119] In the early 1920s the Soviet authorities were obsessed with this confrontation with the metaphysical understanding of the world; thus they thoroughly supported the psychologist Pavlov and his work, as they perceived in it a scientific method to prove that the "soul" does not exist. In 1926 the Soviet filmmaker Vsevolod Pudovkin was employed to make a film popularising these ideas, and *The Mechanics of the Brain* (*Mekhanikha golovnogo mozga*) was intended to explain these concepts in pictures to the masses.[120] In addition, it is known that Bulgakov used to read the magazine *The Atheist* in the early 1920s, only to scoff at the level of the debates aimed at Jesus Christ (who is also a protagonist in *The Master and Margarita*) and religions in general.[121] It could be then concluded that Bulgakov was not against communism per se, but against, on the one side, the dogmatic and rigid manner – and on the other, the incredible superficiality – with which communist ideas were sometimes proselytised and argued in Soviet society. Taking this into account, it could be concluded that Petrović considered the novel to be an investigation of the dogmatic understanding of ideology, and as this was the fourth political theme also extant in his films, he thus found another significant similarity as a motive to undertake the adaptation.

If Bulgakov was concerned with the "secularisation of ethics", ethics being attached to the "vagaries of political expediency", and finally, atheism being implemented dogmatically, it is interesting that these are all concerns that Petrović already explored in his previous film, *It Rains in My Village*. In an interview given prior to the latter's release, Petrović talked about the crisis of ethics, as one (traditional) set of moral values is abandoned before another is put in its place.[122] In an interview he gave after the film's release, he emphasised that this crisis is particularly felt in the socialist countries.[123] As in his film, the Teacher tends to attack religion impetuously and aggressively, it is evident that Petrović recognised in *The Master and Margarita* the same concerns he was also already exploring. Therefore, another key trait of the novel that attracted Petrović was Bulgakov's examination of the socialist system's relationship to different religions and their metaphysical and non-scientific perceptions of the world, leading to a specific crisis of morality. The investigation of religion within society is, in this instance, the second political theme that pervades Petrović's films, the theme whose presence he recognised in Bulgakov's novel. Consequently, three out of the four political themes usually found in Petrović's films are thoroughly developed in the novel of *The Master and Margarita*, and subsequently in the film, suggesting that they were all reasons behind Petrović's decision to adapt this novel for the screen.

As Proffer claims in her work on Bulgakov, he was not unaware of the numerous shortcomings of the official Russian Orthodox Church, particularly in the years prior to the October Revolution, nor was he sympathetic to the last Russian Tsar Nicholas II, whom he portrays unsympathetically in some of his plays.[124] Bulgakov was a soldier in the so-called White Guard, fighting the Bolsheviks during the Civil War, but who – nevertheless – decided to stay in the Soviet Union and was evidently critical of many practices during the Romanov rule, which ultimately led to the October Revolution. Still, Bulgakov, in a way that has attracted Petrović, was a responsible intellectual, who set out to scrutinise the ills of the new society too. In *The Master and Margarita*, certain moral and intellectual flaws were to be subjected to his harsh humour, irony and cynicism. Bulgakov's idol was Molière, and like him, Bulgakov wanted to be a satirist of his time. However, as his own letters and writings from the time show, the role of a satirist in the Soviet Union "was absolutely unthinkable"[125] and this is what his critics kept on reiterating. Bulgakov believed that they did not understand his irony, which they misinterpreted as "slanders" of the country. This was a misunderstanding between the artist and the official policies of Soviet socialism, similar to the ones Petrović was about to encounter in his own country, where socialism was apparently autonomously Yugoslav. What Petrović could not see, however, was that the consequences of his film would precipitate harsher reprimands for himself than the ones Bulgakov had to face for his novel.

Confirming the earlier assumption on the issues of morality in the novel, Proffer claims that quite a few characters are "only doing what any other person in his position would have done, [they] share one thing: they know that what they are doing is not right, and yet they ignore the voice of conscience".[126] She goes on to conclude that "Bulgakov is a moral absolutist – for him the standards of good and evil remain the same, whether the context is that of the Roman or Soviet empires".[127] This is something Petrović undoubtedly recognised about the author and his book when he decided to work on its adaptation; but as already pointed out, Petrović's loyalty to his own voice of conscience would bring him into real conflict with the official politics of his time.

6. 1. 4. *The Master and Margarita* – The Film

Nikolai Maksudov is a writer living in Moscow, in the 1920s. His new play *Pontius Pilate* is about to open at a theatre. The play investigates the relationship of freedom and power, and Jesus tells Pilate in the play that any form of government is oppressive.

Maksudov's colleagues and the Writers' Union president, Berlioz, are worried about the political content of the play and its possible consequences. They are trying to convince Maksudov to withdraw the play himself, which he refuses to do. Maksudov falls for the beautiful Margarita in the meantime, and their affair becomes central to the story from then on. He is unaware that Satan, who has arrived in Moscow as Professor Woland, is secretly helping him to put his play onstage.

Professor Woland and his retinue rile the citizens of Moscow, trying to shake their rational and anti-superstitious attitudes. Maksudov starts to feel something is "wrong" in Moscow, and tells Margarita that he will write a novel about the Devil.

Berlioz, along with a group of jealous writers and art critics, decides to prevent production of the play by assassinating Maksudov's character at the meeting of the Writers' Union. Maksudov is unyielding, and the play is taken off the programme.

When the reviews are published, regardless of the fact that the play was not performed, Maksudov first confronts his venal and jealous colleagues, and then Berlioz in person. Woland joins the conversation and predicts Berlioz's immediate and gruesome death. As his

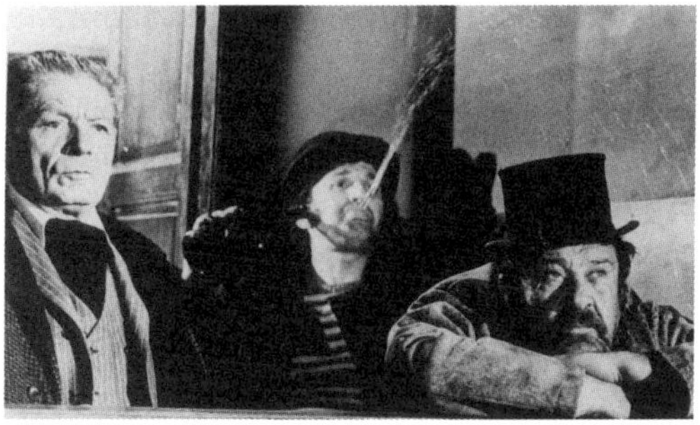

Figure 6.2: The Devil and his acolytes: Alain Cuny as Professor Woland (left), and Velimir Bata Živojinović (middle) and Pavle Vujisić (right) as his assistants.

predictions materialise, Maksudov goes into a state of shock, and goes back to confront his colleagues again, shouting incoherently and accusing them of having "betrayed the revolution". As he is seriously disturbed, he ends up in a mental hospital.

Woland and his entourage, together with Margarita to whom they have promised to return her lover, stage a magic show at the theatre, before Maksudov's *Pontius Pilate* is inexplicably about to premiere on stage. They ridicule the audience and their sceptical view of anything metaphysical, by magically giving the audience clothes and money that later disappears, leaving them naked, disgraced and panicking at the end.

Maksudov is, also magically, released from the hospital, and made to join his lover Margarita at the theatre, where they watch his play together with Woland. Woland grants them peace, but not yet light, and the body of Maksudov is found dead in hospital.

6. 1. 5. Petrović's Margarita and the Master

Apart from the three motifs from *The Master and Margarita* already identified as the reasons for Aleksandar Petrović to adapt this novel, there are other ones that also attracted the filmmaker. As is evident from the synopsis, the narrative of the novel, and consequently the film, revolves around a love story between Margarita and the Master, or Maksudov, as his name is in the film. In both novel and film, the lovers are separated the moment the Master is institutionalised, and it is Margarita who then, with the help of the diabolical Woland, tries to free her lover. However, due to the Master's state, Woland enables them to be together in some kind of limbo, "eternal refuge" after "absolution",[128] as the Master "has not earned light, he has earned peace".[129] In order to reach this "eternal refuge" Margarita and the Master have to die on earth, thus their love is possible only after their physical deaths. Therefore, the novel prominently includes the motifs of love and death, and as Petrović had declared these two motifs present in all his work, as his authorial signature, it is evident that the existence of these motifs in the novel also attracted him to its adaptation. It could be argued that there are many other elements in the novel that were attractive to Petrović besides the ones already identified. The novel is, according to Proffer, "dense with mystery, ambiguity and irony, a subversive work which fits no genre neatly",[130] thus was undoubtedly a multifaceted challenge for adaptation. However, as the aim here is to extrapolate Petrović's social and political views from his films, I will concentrate on the political aspects of the novel that might have inspired Petrović to turn the book into a film. In that respect the motifs initially identified remain the key elements for this investigation, these being the relationship of artists to the regime, the regime's ideology becoming increasingly dogmatic and rigid while eliminating religious morality without putting anything in its place, thereby generating a crisis of morality.[131]

At the time of the film's making, Petrović clearly stated that he was not interested in a faithful adaptation of the novel, but wanted to use it only as a starting point to meditate on his own concerns, concerns parallel to Bulgakov's. Petrović stated:

I do not believe in film adaptations. Bulgakov's work only inspired me. It is a great humanist work, and today very much needed in our socialist world.[132]

That Petrović emphasised the need for this work in the then contemporary socialist world, which had at that point renounced Stalinism,[133] demonstrated that he sensed that Stalinist practices had not been completely abandoned. Whether these practices were not abandoned intentionally by socialist governments is an argument for a different debate, but in any case, Petrović clearly wanted to expose them in his film. They are unambiguously defined as Stalinist, as they are motifs taken from Bulgakov, whose work was satirising precisely this period. To further emphasise the link between Stalinist practices of repression against artists and intellectuals and contemporary Yugoslavia, Petrović had to take liberties in adaptation, and thus gave preference to selected scenes from the novel, sculpting them according to his own experience. In order to do this, Petrović focuses more on the character of the Master in his film, who in the novel was unnamed and only appears halfway through its narrative.[134] Petrović named him in the film as Maksudov, borrowing that name from a character of another Bulgakov's unfinished tale[135] – *Theatrical Novel*.[136] Maksudov is undoubtedly Bulgakov's alter-ego, and this is one of the novels where Bulgakov introduced many of his real-life experiences, making it partly autobiographical. By choosing the name of Maksudov, Petrović demonstrates that he is looking not only at one of Bulgakov's novels in his adaptation, but at his work and life in general. In the years following the film, Petrović would revisit Bulgakov and his work, and write more adaptations of his prose and plays for film and theatre.[137]

By accentuating the story of the writer-artist and eclipsing numerous other strands of the relatively voluminous tome *The Master and Margarita*, Petrović enabled the film to focus on the relationship of a conscientious artist with the institutions of the socialist state. These institutions are represented in the film, as in the book, by other artists, who show traits that are certainly not noble, but are human nonetheless. A combination of their professional jealousy, incompetence and often rigid understanding of the ideology they all embraced brings them into conflict with the artist, who acts upon his own beliefs and merits. This is, obviously, not something only familiar to the socialist countries of the era, but is a universal occurrence, and was something Petrović had frequently encountered in his career, so was willing to address in his work. By focusing his adaptation on this motif, he made the story his own, while at the same time firmly grounding it in the famous novel.

The major "implant" Petrović introduces is a meeting of the Writers' Union, at which Maksudov is publicly criticised and denounced. This denunciation is not directly instigated by someone from the higher ranks of the party or civil service, but is initiated by Maksudov's scheming jealous colleagues. In this part, Petrović also develops more fully the character of Berlioz, who dies in the first chapter of the novel. Petrović uses this character further, making him more rounded and representative of what his experience was likely to be with various institutions, up to that point. Berlioz in the film (as in the book) is an intelligent and educated intellectual, but perhaps a touch too zealous with his commitment to communist beliefs. More precisely, he is dogmatic, and as in the novel, becomes Professor Woland's

(Satan's alias) first victim, as his head is spectacularly severed by a streetcar. In the film we get to know Berlioz better, as a person who fully admires Maksudov's literary talent, but who is wary about the possible political implications and interpretations of his writings. We learn in the film that Maksudov's writings have been understood as provocative before, but that Berlioz had managed to convince him to withdraw these plays himself. The new play Maksudov writes seems evidently heretical within a socialist realist context. The play is entitled *Pontius Pilate* (a novel in the book), and apart from the reworking of the Biblical theme, Petrović focuses on the part where Jesus Christ is at his most revolutionary, denouncing every form of government as repressive and violent. In a brief conversation with Maksudov, Berlioz expresses his unease about such a portrayal of a Biblical story, which emphasises the revolutionary spirit of the Son of God, who condemns all forms of government. It is somehow obvious that such a play would perhaps be inappropriate for a proletarian theatre of any young socialist state. Nevertheless, Maksudov defends his decisions. Ultimately, it is important to add here, Marxism in general affirmed that every state is oppressive, although this was differentiated from the anarchist doctrine that the state must be destroyed. Marx and Engels introduced the notion of a temporary state that exists before society is ready to reach communism, thus the state that "withers away" – thereby making what Maksudov says in his play perfectly acceptable. Regardless, Berlioz, a dogmatist, feels that this is not the most appropriate subject, and suggests that Maksudov should give in. This takes place during a private conversation in a Moscow bar, where we learn that the relation of the two characters is frank and friendly. Berlioz does not deny Maksudov's talent or the literary value of his work, but maintains that he would have to make him withdraw the play. If Maksudov is not prepared to do that discreetly, Berlioz would have to involve the Writers' Union and do this publicly – which in the end, he does.[138]

Perhaps, and as was probably the case in reality, Berlioz is ultimately worried for his own position, and if he were to be accused of encouraging "politically dubious" – not to say "politically incorrect" – art, this would have ended up counting against him and end as his own responsibility. In this respect, Petrović is loyal to the original text, and the main issue becomes the moral dilemma of an individual being loyal to the state, empire or ideology, rather than following, as Proffer puts it, one's "own voice of conscience".[139] Thus Berlioz "betrays" his friend and the latter's work that he believes to be good, in order to prioritise his loyalty to the cause, or even more strangely, to his interpretation of this cause, for which in these works of fiction he is severely punished. As in the novel, Professor Woland, an epitome of evil, appears and joins in the conversation, predicting his death, while the third character present during this event ends up mentally unstable as a result of witnessing the conversation and Berlioz's consequent demise. Whereas in the novel an entirely different character, the poet Bezdomny, is present, in the film it is the Master, or Maksudov, who is there, and who ends up being institutionalised.

Berlioz presides over the meeting of the Writers' Union where he calls on speakers to denounce Maksudov. Here he represents a government apparatchik par excellence, who betrays his friend and conscience in order to maintain the dogmatic outlook in the works

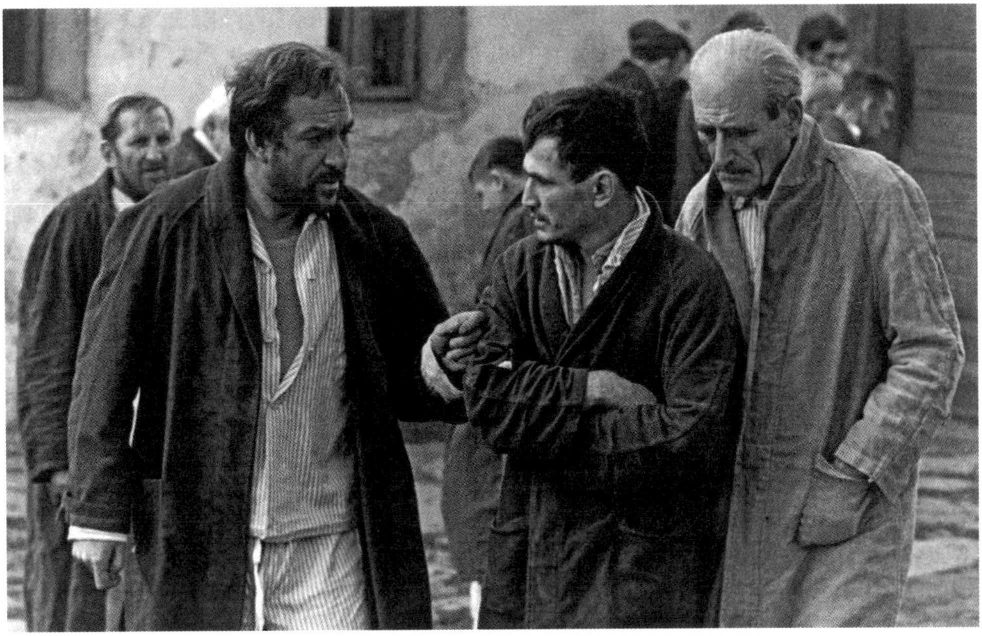

Figure 6.3: For their recalcitrance, artists get institutionalised: Ugo Tognazzi (left) as the Master.

of art produced by the members of his union. Not only does he go against his own personal beliefs, and common sense, but he also orchestrates a tirade against his colleague. The writers he manages to convince to talk against Maksudov – the Master – are venal, petty and simply unhappy individuals. The most outspoken one at the meeting is Bobov, again an amalgamation of several characters from the original novel, who really wants to move into Maksudov's comfortable flat. As he talks he is obviously drunk, and he attracts giggles from his other colleagues. In this atmosphere he comes up with one of the most absurd sentences, in which he objects that whereas Maksudov writes whatever Maksudov wants, he – Bobov – has to toe the "party line". Although this causes laughter amongst his peers, and was probably supposed to amuse the audiences of the time, this is one of the typically acerbic comments Petrović often has in his films. He perhaps had filmmaking colleagues who felt the same about him, as would sadly be seen during the time of *The Master and Margarita*'s release. This scene is also pinpointed by Daniel Goulding in his work on Petrović and Yugoslav cinema, where Maksudov's words "we must be able to write our own thoughts" and "I must say what I believe" are interpreted as a clear sign that Petrović's adaptation of the book draws:

> [...] implicit parallels between the early Stalinist period in the Soviet Union and the ideological campaign then going on in Yugoslavia against non-establishment Marxists, members of the non-Marxist "humanistic intelligentsia", radical student leaders, which reached its great intensity at the time Petrović was making this film.[140]

Another remarkable moment, depicting a distressing phenomenon of the era takes place in the same scene. As the campaign against Maksudov starts, a younger writer, unaware of what is going on, stands up and defends Maksudov, reminding his colleagues that Maksudov is their greatest writer, and that he should not be recklessly attacked by his colleagues. As he sits down, another writer tells him to shut up, and quickly explains that Maksudov's character is about to be "assassinated" at this meeting, and there is no point in going against this. This moment portrays a tragic picture of intellectual complacency and selfishness, and the crisis of moral values, which had sadly rooted itself in those difficult times, which Petrović was to himself experience shortly after the release of the film.

The scene at the Writers' Union does not exist in the original novel, and it is purely Petrović's addition to his adaptation of *The Master and Margarita*. The scene is introduced in order to demonstrate Petrović's criticism of the treatment of artists in socialist states, hinting at what was happening in Yugoslavia. As mentioned earlier, Petrović was president of the Union of Film Workers of Yugoslavia, and had participated in numerous debates reminiscent of the one he fictionalises in the film. Shortly before Petrović made his film, Želimir Žilnik had had to defend his 1969 Berlin Festival winner *Early Works* (*Rani radovi*) in front of similar public and closed meetings in order to gain the right to domestic screenings. As also already emphasised, Dušan Makavejev went through exactly the same process in 1971 in an attempt to have *WR: Mysteries of the Organism* screened. In an interview Petrović gave in 1965, when the processes of liberalisation were beginning, he refused to comment on the absurdity of political censorship by simply saying that he hoped the censorship panels "would soon disappear".[141] However, the tirades against Black Film in the late 1960s, the cases of filmmakers such as Žilnik who had to defend their work, and finally the ban on Makavejev's film in 1971 were a clear sign that the censorship Petrović had hoped would soon disappear did not. He therefore decided to address this phenomenon in the new film, to expose it as a Stalinist practice, and thus unambiguously criticise its existence in Yugoslav society. Through the words of his Master, Petrović clearly states that art and artists must be free. Although the scene was not in the original novel, it evidently demonstrates that Petrović's sentiments are close to Bulgakov's, as they both share the same strong anti-dogmatic feeling towards the state's institutions (both Soviet and Yugoslav respectively) in their dealings with artists and their creativity. Petrović's choice of adapting *The Master and Margarita* thus was not only his homage to a great writer and a great book. His adaptation made sure to emphasise the similarities between the novel's criticism of the 1930s' Soviet Union, and Socialist Yugoslavia of the early 1970s. Petrović introduced his own experiences into the film, just as Bulgakov had introduced his into the book, hence both giving an authentic account of their time and place.

Petrović had made one film inspired by a novel (*It Rains in My Village*, inspired by Dostoyevsky's *The Devils*), and one based on short stories (*Three*, based on the stories of Antonije Isaković) before he turned to his first full adaptation of a novel. As the earlier analysis explains, notwithstanding his use of someone else's work as a basis for the script, Petrović managed to work in elements of the novel close to his own sensibility (love and death), and his concerns, enabling himself to criticise the ills of society (art and state, dogmatism). Consequently, *The Master and Margarita*, in terms of its narrative and thematic concerns, is very much in line with his previous work. While making *Three*, he was able to introduce his own experience into Isaković's stories, thereby strengthening the impact of the film. Petrović succeeds in doing the same with Bulgakov's novel, making the film a new and unique experience although not divorced from the original material. Where *The Master and Margarita* threatened to become very different from Petrović's previous films was in its style, due to two factors. The first is the fact that the film was made with 700 million Yugoslav dinars,[142] and was by far the most expensive of Petrović's films up to that point, with a budget over three times greater than that for his greatest box-office success *Happy Gypsies*.[143] The second factor is that, after making two films set in contemporary Yugoslav urban spaces (*Two* and *Days*), one Partisan war drama (*Three*), and two films set in contemporary Yugoslav rural environments (*Happy Gypsies* and *It Rains in My Village*), Petrović for the first time made a film set in the past, a "costume" or "heritage" film, also set in another country. The larger budget was there to provide for the reconstruction of this "foreign" space – foreign both geographically and historically. However, Petrović retained his directorial approach regardless of the challenges a "costume drama" as a genre may have represented for him. As someone who had entered the industry as a documentary filmmaker, and had continued to maintain some of the documentary film aesthetic in his fiction, he also managed to introduce it into *The Master and Margarita*. Therefore, in the middle of the film, there is an entire vignette of purely documentary material, which was shot in Moscow specifically for the film. Petrović was again courageously innovative in deciding to film the so-called wooden Moscow. At the time Moscow had just won the bid to host the 1980 Olympic Games, and Petrović found out that the city's authorities were to pull down a whole area in the town built entirely out of wood. Although this part of Moscow does not seem, at least from today's perspective, as if it was some kind of squalid "shanty town" (however, it looks tidy and interesting), it obviously did not fit into the image of a Moscow that Soviet officials wanted to project on the international stage. There may have been other reasons for its "replacement", but the fact that its days were numbered encouraged Petrović to arrange for a TV crew to go to Moscow and film this part of the town before it was destroyed forever.[144] Petrović had permission from the Soviet authorities, but the permission was to film for a news bulletin. It was never explained that the footage was intended for a Yugoslav-Italian adaptation of Mikhail Bulgakov's novel, set in the Moscow of the 1920s and 1930s. These images of "wooden" Moscow, shot from a moving car, have a central role in the film, where, like a prototype of a pop-promo, they were edited to a song by the popular Soviet singer-songwriter Bulat Okudzava. The song is about a black cat being a little devil, and it quietly mourns economic depravity – a perfect fit for the film featuring a black cat, who is Lucifer's assistant. To choose Okudzava's music was telling, as this Soviet singer-songwriter knew how to interpolate subtle politically critical comments into his popular songs.[145] He was very much liked by Dušan Makavejev and other Black Wave filmmakers, who also used his songs in their films.

Although documentary footage of Moscow, edited to Okudzava's music, provides an audio-visual interlude – or punctuation mark – at a central point in the film, it is not only this footage that remains from the documentary aesthetic. Petrović retains his propensity for close-ups, often filmed with telephoto lenses, thus discreetly collecting reactions of participants, particularly in numerous crowd scenes.[146] Although directed, due to the lenses employed, these scenes leave a sense of being observed discreetly by an intruder, who in the film is the character of Professor Woland. Extreme close-ups became a tool for Petrović to resolve another element of the novel. Bulgakov wrote a book that has Satan and Jesus Christ as active characters. The book thus has fantastic aspects, and has many scenes where unreal occurrences take place, as when Margarita at one point even flies on a broom like a witch. Petrović downplays these fantastic elements, and the scene with the broom is simply eliminated, whereas he replaced special effects that could not be omitted with more economical cinematic devices. An important assistant of the Devil in the book is a giant cat, which behaves like a human being. Ugo Tognazzi, the male lead, suggested to Petrović that a large mechanical cat should be made for these scenes, which Petrović adamantly refused.[147] Instead, he used frequent extreme close-ups of a real black cat's mouth and teeth, with amplified sounds of her meows, implying that the creature is more sinister than just an ordinary cat. A well-trained cat then performed a few scenes for the film, such as looking into a picture box, and turning the handle with its paw, which conveyed the idea that the creature is part of the diabolical group. In comparison with the novel, Petrović downplayed this extravagantly fantastic character, which has a significantly larger role in the book, albeit difficult to translate on-screen without elaborate technical effects. Having rigorously decreased the fantastic element overall, Petrović decided to rely on it in one scene only – a scene that was designed to be spectacular, with the largest number of extras, when the Devil himself performs sinister magical tricks. This could have also been due to the fact that more effects would have required more finances, but looking at Petrović's productions, he never resorted to spectacular scenes more than was necessary.

The scene at the theatre when the Master's play *Pontius Pilate* is about to be premiered exists in the novel, but in the film it is amalgamated with another scene of Professor Woland's party. In the novel, the actual play is not premiered:[148] it is only Professor Woland's show that goes on stage. In the film, Professor Woland's show of black magic goes on stage prior to the announced premiere of *Pontius Pilate*. It is in this scene that Petrović resorts to special effects. The effects, as seen from a historical perspective, do not appear at all elaborate, and are largely reliant on the animation techniques with which Petrović was familiar from his early career. He employed Dušan Vukotić, an Oscar-winning Yugoslav animator, to take charge of these effects. As Vukotić's special effects cameraman, an old friend and collaborator, Nikola Majdak was employed.[149] The director of photography on the whole project was the Italian Roberto Gerardi.[150] Towards the end of his career Petrović continued to change collaborators for this significant role in the production team. The special effects were employed to show Professor Woland's magic tricks. During his show, the Professor discusses human morals through the example of the Muscovites in the early decades of the

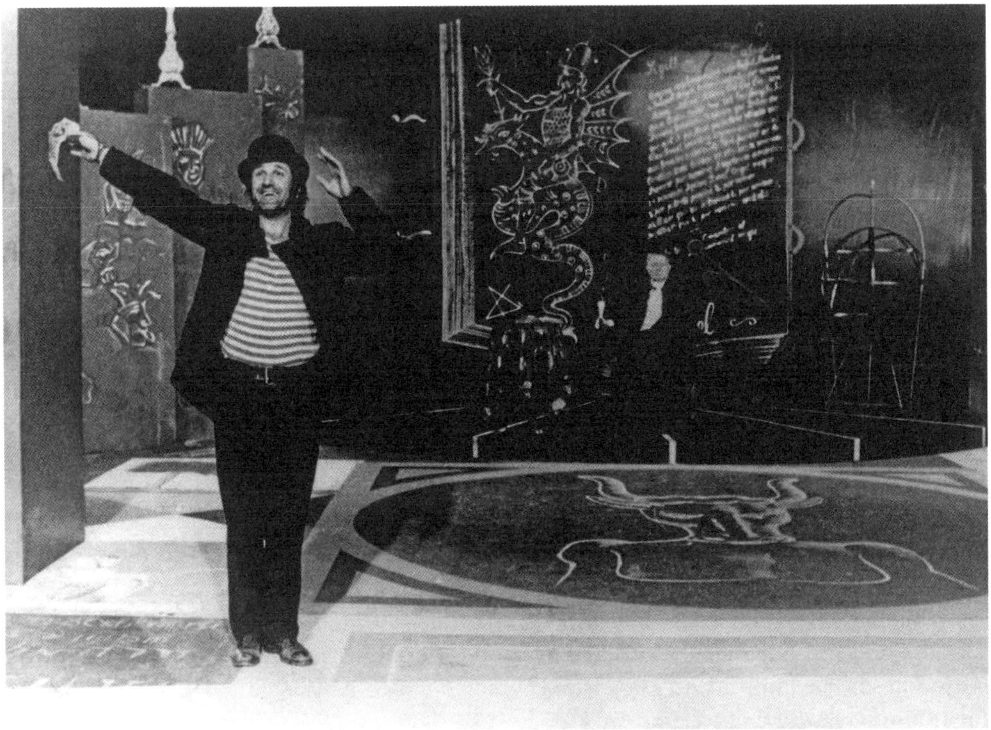

Figure 6.4: The magic tricks show in *The Master and Margarita*: Velimir Bata Živojinović as Professor Woland's assistant (left) and Alain Cuny as Professor Woland (sitting in the back).

new socialist state. He maintains that human nature remains the same, and then proceeds to show its venality, fickleness, opportunism and selfishness in his somewhat brutal magic show. He first offers to the theatre audience to trade in their current clothes for free new clothes and shoes, all of the latest *haute couture*. As everyone is aggressively eager to do this, Professor Woland makes everything fall from the ceiling, causing havoc in the audience. After clothes, he offers the audience money, American dollars, which causes more displays of aggressive instincts amongst the people present. One of the theatre's administrators (another amalgamation of characters from the novel) goes onstage and challenges Woland's tricks, demanding a scientific explanation. Woland responds by ordering one of his assistants to temporarily remove the administrator's head from his shoulders, forcing him to stop prophesising that there is no such thing as magic, God or the Devil. While the bodiless head of the administrator continues to function, however horrified and fearful as to the whereabouts of his body, an older lady in the audience begs for mercy on his behalf, and asks Woland to put the head back on its shoulders. After Woland makes further snide comments on human morality, he orders the head to be reattached to the administrator's body, who, alive and well, although in a state of complete shock, leaves the stage, earning Woland another round of applause from the audience. When the audience leaves the theatre after the show, their new clothes and money disappear, leaving them all disgraced and naked in front of the building, in the most spectacular scene in the film. This is a scene in which, like Bulgakov, Petrović shows that the new society had not managed to change human nature, and that in fact moral behaviour had even further declined, by displaying human venality, selfishness, opportunism and rabid materialism as even more open and aggressive. Despite the socialist tenet of social equality, the fact that materialism and opportunism were on the increase, whereas morality was in crisis, provided Petrović (and Bulgakov) with a sharp criticism of the reality of so-called socialism in power in the countries the two authors inhabited.

As in the previous film, Petrović suggests that human nature may have to change before society can change. In order to reiterate this point, he employed Bulgakov's writing, as he found in it this element of moral decline, as already identified earlier in the chapter. Or, in Petrović's words on why he admired Bulgakov, claiming that this Russian writer:

> [...] noticed one major thing: changing the social system has to be preceded by the transformation of humanity. Substantial changes can occur only if human consciousness is changed first. Bulgakov thus recognised the great moral abyss in which the twentieth century was dwelling.[151]

This opinion was not shared by the Yugoslav authorities, as would become evident within six months of the film's release.

6. 1. 6. The Reception of the Master

In the last week of July 1972, *The Master and Margarita* was premiered at the Yugoslav Film Festival in Pula, where it won the best film award, the Golden Arena.[152] This was Petrović's third film to win this most prestigious award in Yugoslavia, making him one of the most acclaimed directors the country had ever had. In an interview given after the festival, he claimed that he was very pleased with the audience response, which to him was the best sign that his film was not "politically provocative, as some have maliciously claimed", but is in "the great tradition of humanist Russian literature, where a human is in the foreground with universal problems around him".[153] The Italian version of the film was then premiered at the Venice Film Festival in August, where it won an International Award for Promoting Literature through Film.[154] In the autumn the film was shown at the Chicago Film Festival, where it won the Silver Hugo prize. While reporting on the festival for London's *The Times*, John Russell Taylor stated, "there was little doubt" about the film receiving the award, as it was "an intricate ironical drama".[155] Taylor opens another interesting issue, claiming that the film was a "Yugoslav entry", meaning the Yugoslav version of the film was shown, and hinting that it is better than the Italian version.[156] In fact, the two versions were very similar, the key difference being the fact that the main stars, who did not speak Serbo-Croat, are dubbed in the Yugoslav version. However, this should have made the Yugoslav version more awkward, and some journalists pointed to the synchronisation not being perfect.[157] However, there was another significant difference between the two versions. The Italian producers had employed Ennio Morricone, who was already much celebrated, to write the score for the film. Petrović hated the music, and did not use it for the Yugoslav version. Instead, he chose some original Russian music. Morricone's score though remains in the Italian version. Morricone, undoubtedly a great musical talent, may have failed in trying to write a piece of music that was supposed to sound Russian. When *The Master and Margarita* was released in the UK, Derek Elley noted in his review for *Films and Filming*: "Thankfully, it is the Yugoslav print that is being used, rather than the Italian version, which, under the title *Il Maestro e Margherita*, was shown in Italy with a cod-Russian score by Ennio Morricone."[158] It appears then that Petrović may have been vindicated in his choice.

The fact that Petrović's film was a literary adaptation was often the focus of critics' attention. Additionally, politically motivated responses to the film were equally rife, and here worthy of a brief scrutiny. In August 1972, immediately after the Pula Festival, a long and thorough scholarly review by Milivoje Jovanović appeared in the Belgrade magazine *Književne novine* (*Literary News*), severely criticising Petrović's adaptation of Bulgakov's classic.[159] The article meticulously lists the changes Petrović had made to the original text, explaining how each individual change had trivialised and damaged the complexity of Bulgakov's novel. One of the alterations that particularly upset the reviewer was the one identified earlier as representative of Petrović's intention of clarifying his political criticism of contemporary Yugoslav reality, specifically the regime's relationship to the arts. Jovanović claims that, in comparison to Bulgakov, Petrović's representation of "the pressures by untalented artists and political administrators on a suffering artist", an artist who is also "prone to spilling the words of truth in verses", was probably "the worst solution" Petrović could come up with while representing his image of an artist in totalitarianism. The reviewer claimed that with this representation Petrović only engendered a cliché that grossly simplified the fine nuances of the original literary text, where the latter never succumbs to such a trivially romantic view of the arts and artists.[160] In the final paragraph, Jovanović praised several elements of the film, most notably the work of the Yugoslav actors Pavle Vujisić, and Petrović's regular Velimir Bata Živojinović, whose performances as Professor Woland's assistants, he assessed as masterly.[161] Regardless, the overall assessment was that "Petrović's adaptation is a fine example of one of the greatest misfires of cinema in contact with great literature, a misfire that has no excuse."[162] The reviewer admits that the film was successful at festivals and with audiences, but uses that as an argument to claim that this is only a sign of the general "inability to understand real cultural thrusts", and an "impoverished sense of truly great intellectual values."[163] Such a severe criticism was perhaps to be expected from a review coming from a publication on literature. Film reviewers, however, predominantly defended Petrović's streamlining of this complex literary work. Ibrahim Sakić, in Sarajevo's cultural magazine *Odjek* (*Echo*), claimed that in the adaptation "many nuances of Bulgakov's prose are lost, but the engagement certainly gained incredibly", concluding that Petrović

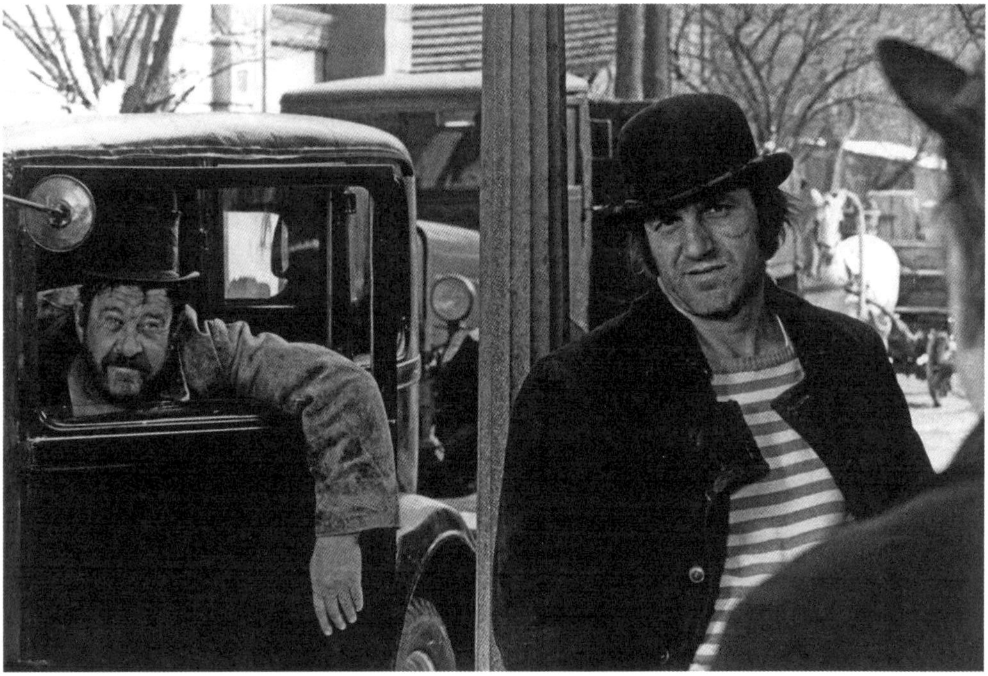

Figure 6.5: Pavle Vujisić (left) and Velimir Bata Živojinović as Professor Woland's assistants.

"successfully amplifies good literature".[164] Sakić claims that Petrović uses "typically filmic tightening" methods, thus praising Petrović for just that which Jovanović criticised in *Literary News*. The ambiguity concerning the value of adapting such literary works is evident in some reviews. Nigel Gearing, in the *Monthly Film Bulletin* for example, states, "perhaps Petrović's course was the only possible one. But unfortunately it tends to polarise what remains of Bulgakov."[165] Even Derek Elley, who wrote an enthusiastically affirmative review, claims: "Petrović's film is a very free version of an almost unfilmable original."[166] Petrović was to continue his career with filming "unfilmable" literary texts, and the criticism of adapting such material was to continue. The question of the adaptations remains ambivalent, perhaps similarly to the theoretical debate on representing "the Other" in the case of *I Even Met Happy Gypsies*.[167]

Whether Petrović has done a service or disservice to Bulgakov's novel also has to be perceived in its historical context. According to Ellendea Proffer, Bulgakov's novel was only printed in the Soviet Union in its entire version in 1973 – a year after the film was made – whereas an edited, hence incomplete, version appeared in 1966.[168] The fact that Petrović, with his film, was drawing attention to a novel still considered controversial in the Soviet Union made some of his colleagues warn the official bodies in Yugoslavia that the film might cause a diplomatic incident.[169] Petrović then took the initiative and organised a screening of the film for the diplomatic core of the Soviet embassy in Belgrade, where unsuspecting diplomats arrived for the film screening with their wives. Before the end of the film, as some of the spouses were crying over the sad destiny of the two lovers, it appeared that there were no international incidents in the making.[170] The stern Soviet zealousness was perhaps exaggerated by Petrović's colleagues, but its myth was not entirely unfounded. The film was thus savaged in the Russian magazine *Sovietsky Ekran* (*Soviet Screen*). While reporting from the Pula Film Festival, D. Pisarevski, in a long and detailed article, appears to be insulted by Petrović's use of the footage of "wooden" Moscow, claiming that Petrović willingly goes for "the exotic à la Russe".[171] Pisarevski lists a long line of complaints against the film, among which he emphasises that Petrović "made a perverted representation of the novel", primarily because he "remained distant from its humanist idea".[172] Pisarevski explains that this is in the spirit of Yugoslav Black Film, which portrays people "as freaks", and usually "focuses on the meaninglessness of human existence".[173] Despite being generally negative about the films shown at the Pula Film Festival in 1972, Pisarevski noted Obrad Gluščević's *Solitary Wolf* (*Vuk samotnjak*, 1972), the only children's film at the festival, as the only film that "actively preaches humanism".[174] Pisarevski concludes:

> One wants to believe that the wind of time will blow away these autumn leaves from the tree of Yugoslav cinema, taking them away. And that this tree will then become green again, and bear fruit nourished by the juices of people's life.[175]

Pisarevski's prediction of a wind blowing the leaves off the tree known as Yugoslav film was indeed prescient.

In the early autumn of 1972, soon after its release in Yugoslavia, while the film was still enjoying a wide distribution internationally, it was discreetly but efficiently withdrawn from cinema theatres throughout the country. Petrović tried to identify why this was the case, but could not find any official explanation.[176] This unofficial ban was in effect for just over ten years, and in 1982 Petrović stated:

> Nobody knows why, or who ordered the film to be banned. I have addressed the relevant institutions with a request that this embargo should finally be lifted. This really is an impossible situation.[177]

This story supports the theory of Michael Stoil, who explained that "the Yugoslav film industry structure is extremely complex and is completely lacking in centralisation and hierarchy",[178] thus was very liberal. Stoil though continued with: "Nevertheless, the regime can intervene decisively through the Film Boards' control of distribution and through the actions of the League of Communists."[179] What exact action was taken to cause *The Master and Margarita* to be withdrawn is still unknown;[180] however, as this was happening in late 1972, when, as already described in the introduction to this chapter, an "avalanche" of repressive measures was to be unleashed by Tito and his party loyalists on various strata in the country, it is easy to assume that the withdrawal of the film was simply part of that process. Petrović soon stopped inquiring about the film's lack of distribution, as he was to have more pressing issues to worry about.

6. 2. The Master and his Student

From the autumn of 1962 Aleksandar Petrović taught film directing at Belgrade's Academy for Film, Theatre, Radio and Television.[181] In that year, the first generation of students to study film directing enrolled, amongst them was Lazar Stojanović, later considered one of the most talented students in the group.[182] Stojanović, born in 1944, had almost completed his degree in psychology at Belgrade University, and was a member of the famous Belgrade's amateur film club (*Kino Klub Beograd*), along with Dušan Makavejev and Živojin Pavlović, when he enrolled in the course. Stojanović was an active young intellectual, who in the years to follow would edit two student magazines, and was to be involved in the student protests of 1968.[183] According to Stojanović, he was due to graduate at the academy with a short film that was supposed to be part of an omnibus feature film, and he submitted the script for this short in 1967.[184] The film was entitled *Travelling in the Same Place* (*Putovanje u mestu*), and it continued to change its shape and potential duration as Stojanović's colleagues, who were supposed to contribute their shorts to this one feature omnibus film, kept on changing their minds. Finally, they all graduated by submitting different projects, hence prolonging the production of this film. Stojanović, with a tacit agreement from Petrović as the main tutor for future film directors, continued to expand his script, leaving the possibility of it being turned into a low-budget feature. Stojanović remembers Petrović as a professor who was far too busy with his own films and had often missed classes, but who knew his students very well personally. Petrović employed them as his assistants on his films, thus giving them a chance to learn through practice, and perhaps compensate for his long absences. Stojanović also adds that Petrović respected his students' political activism, and, although he was away filming *It Rains in My Village* during the student protests of 1968, he told Stojanović and his colleagues that he would, as their professor, support all their demands. Stojanović concludes that Petrović was their true friend. Therefore, in 1969, as Stojanović had not yet graduated, but had produced a script with the potential for becoming a feature length film, relying on a fair amount of found documentary footage, Petrović helped him find a producer. A fairly independent association of film workers entitled the Centre of Film Workers' Associations (Centar Filmskih Radnih Zajednica), which produced many of the Black Films, agreed to co-produce this project with the academy.[185] The film was supposed to be made on a very low budget, between 13 and 14 million Yugoslav dinars, but was still the most ambitious project the academy had undertaken. The dean, film director Radoš Novaković, thus asked a professor of production, Sreten Jovanović, to work as production manager on the project.[186] The agreement of the two institutions came about as a result of Petrović's and Stojanović's negotiations with Centre Film (as this association was usually called) in early 1970, when the production was agreed.[187] Filming then started in April 1970, and was completed later than planned in May, due to an actress's illness. According to Stojanović, there were only 12 days of filming, whereas the most important part of the production was the introduction of the found documentary material, which was inserted in post production.[188] The film was not ready for preview until September 1971.

6. 2. 1. Against the Devil with *Plastic Jesus*

The film entitled *Plastic Jesus* (*Plastični Isus*, 1971) was a feature length collage of a brief narrative story about a young and promiscuous filmmaker, played by Stojanović's colleague from Zagreb, Tomislav Gotovac, interspersed with documentary (archival) footage, primarily filmed during World War II. The film also included short films by Gotovac, and was edited overall in the spirit of the avant-garde films of the 1960s. Stojanović, a self-declared anarchist,[189] edited in his film footage of Nazi soldiers glorifying their might, along with footage of the Ustasha regime in the fascist Independent State of Croatia during the war, adding in footage of Serbian Chetniks loyal to the exiled king, with footage of the communist Partisans, and perhaps more significantly, footage of recent speeches by President Tito on television. Stojanović used a truly broad scope of material, also including footage of the student demonstrations of 1968. However, it was the combination of war footage, where, without a commentary, various political factions appear to be represented in the same way, which was to be understood as controversial. As an anarchist, Stojanović might have wanted to imply a certain criticism of ideologies in general, all with the capacity of committing the same mistakes of violence and repression. He showed the film in October and November 1971 to the panel of professors at the academy and to the Centre Film board.[190] In November, Aleksandar Petrović, as head of the examining panel of the academy gave the highest mark – 10 – to the film, and Stojanović officially graduated. The film was then seen by the Centre Film board together with some professors from the academy, including Sreten Jovanović, and this is where testimonies differ slightly. Stojanović claims that the version of the film he showed them was finished, but that they agreed to consider it as unfinished, and not submit the copy for general release as they all recognised the film could be understood as ideologically problematic. This was in late 1971, when, according to Stojanović (and as the introduction to this chapter shows), it was unclear whether the liberalising processes in the country were to continue accelerating, or end in a less permissive climate instead. They decided to release the film if the liberal atmosphere continued, or, as some evidence indicates, if the liberalising process were reversed, the film would be withheld by Centre Film. Stojanović agreed as he was well aware of the potential consequences of the film's release if the liberalising processes were halted.[191] However, Sreten Jovanović claims that, at the meeting of the Centre Film board, it was agreed that the film was politically provocative, and that Stojanović should change and eliminate certain scenes. He asserts that Stojanović agreed to this, and the film was thus considered unfinished. The footage of President Tito juxtaposed with the footage of his wartime enemies were the images deemed particularly problematic, and according to Jovanović, Petrović also warned the young filmmaker that they could have unpleasant consequences, and should therefore be changed.[192] In both testimonies one thing is certain: the film was filed as unfinished and was never publicly screened, nor was official permission ever requested for distribution. The agreement was that Stojanović was to continue to work on the film once he completed his compulsory national service. In November 1971, immediately after these screenings, he joined the JNA (Jugoslovenska Narodna Armija) – the Yugoslav People's Army.[193] The reels of the film were kept securely at Centre Film, where Jovanović personally put them aside, so that no one could see them even by mistake until Stojanović returned in a year's time.[194] *Plastic Jesus* was thus "left to sleep" in November 1971, one month before Tito moved against the Croatian leadership.

After almost a year in the army, when he was a few weeks away from the end of his national service, Lazar Stojanović, with another soldier, was invited to have a briefing with a young captain, Vuk Obradović,[195] in charge of the soldiers' political education.[196] Captain Obradović invited the two soldiers to talk to him as they were the only two members of the Communist Party in their unit.[197] He wanted to discuss the political changes in the country, specifically Tito's removal of the Serbian political leadership in November 1972, less than a year after removing the Croatian leadership. Tito also sent a letter to all the party's committees asking for, in Stojanović's words, "self-critical examination". Captain Obradović wanted to discuss with his soldiers these changes in the country and the letter addressing all the party members. Stojanović, who was ill all night and had a fever, entered into lengthy discussions with the captain. Stojanović claimed, amongst other things, that the removal of the Serbian leadership was nothing else but Tito's awkward attempt to keep the balance in the country: as he had removed Croatia's leadership, he was almost obliged to remove Serbia's. Stojanović added that he disagreed with Obradović on all the matters they discussed; though he subsequently claimed that he was careful not to "insult directly either Tito, or the party, or the army, its officers, and most of all – not Obradović personally."[198] However, Stojanović told the officer that, if there were other student demonstrations in Belgrade and if the army was used to police the situation, and if they were ordered to shoot at the protesters, he, Stojanović, would refuse to obey such an order. Although this was said hypothetically, this statement was later to be understood as Stojanović claiming that he would refuse to follow orders, which in the military code is an offence. Captain Obradović politely finished the conversation, while Stojanović went to see an army doctor as he was feeling unwell. On 6 November 1972, Lazar Stojanović was arrested under a list of charges by the military police, and detained for further investigation. He was to be charged with "anti-state activities and propaganda" and was to be tried by a military court, which unlike civil courts was not transparent, and the case was thus heard behind "closed doors".[199]

While investigating the case of Lazar Stojanović, the army's prosecutors appeared with a warrant at Centre Film, and confiscated the copies of *Plastic Jesus*.[200] Sreten Jovanović, a professor at the academy who had worked on the film, explained one more significant scene from the film and its impact:

The Military Court watched the film, and I believe that they almost had a heart attack, as amongst other things, they were stunned by the role of the army in the film. There was a scene filmed at the wedding of Ljubiša Ristić [also a director and a friend of Stojanović, who played a minor role in the film] and Višnja Poštić, both of whose fathers were Generals in the army, so you can imagine the kind of guests that were at the wedding. When the top brass of the Yugoslav People's Army, together with one General from its intelligence service, saw themselves in a scene of this anti-state film, one can only imagine the state of panic they were in.[201]

This scene of the private party that Stojanović filmed somewhat secretly at his friend's wedding was taken out of the film, and irretrievably destroyed when the film was "arrested". When Stojanović managed to release the film more than 15 years after this incident, in place of this scene he had a still image stating that "the following scene has gone missing, while the film was 'taken care of' by the state".[202] *Plastic Jesus* thus remained the most severe case of censorship in Yugoslav cinema, and according to Jovanović, "[T]his case is a disgrace for our legal system because it was about an unfinished film, a film that was never publicly shown."[203] Regardless, the military court afterwards passed the case to a civil court, and Stojanović was condemned to a total of three years in prison, for "anti-state propaganda" and the "making of one politically damaging film".[204]

Lazar Stojanović made his film with the help of his professor Aleksandar Petrović, who found a production company to support the project. Petrović was thus credited at the beginning of *Plastic Jesus* as the film's producer. When the military prosecutors found and watched the film, they thought that Petrović should also be held responsible. Or perhaps they finally realised that they had something that could be used against Petrović, whose work was never as politically provoking as that of his peers, most notably Želimir Žilnik and Dušan Makavejev, who at the same time were under pressure due to their latest projects. Petrović, though, appeared unaware of what was going on, even though in 1972 there were serious hints that there were people in the party who did not perceive his films as benevolent criticism, but as something hostile towards the regime.

The hints that Petrović might be perceived as a problem could be best exemplified by the fact that *The Master and Margarita* was mysteriously withdrawn from distribution in autumn 1972, or as Daniel Goulding explains: "In the end, the fate of Petrović's film in Yugoslavia was not far different from that of the Master's play."[205] However, the film had been widely distributed internationally, it had won prestigious awards, including the Golden Arena in Yugoslavia, and most of all, in June 1972, contracts were signed with Neoplanta Film from Novi Sad for Petrović to direct an adaptation of the famous Serbian novel *Migrations* (*Seobe*) by Miloš Crnjanski.[206] Furthermore, in late December 1972, Petrović had a retrospective of his work in Novi Sad, where he gave talks, together with the film theorist Dušan Stojanović, and film critics Slobodan Novaković and Žika Bogdanović.[207] Although *The Master and Margarita* was conspicuously missing from the programme, this retrospective demonstrated the appreciation Petrović's work was enjoying.

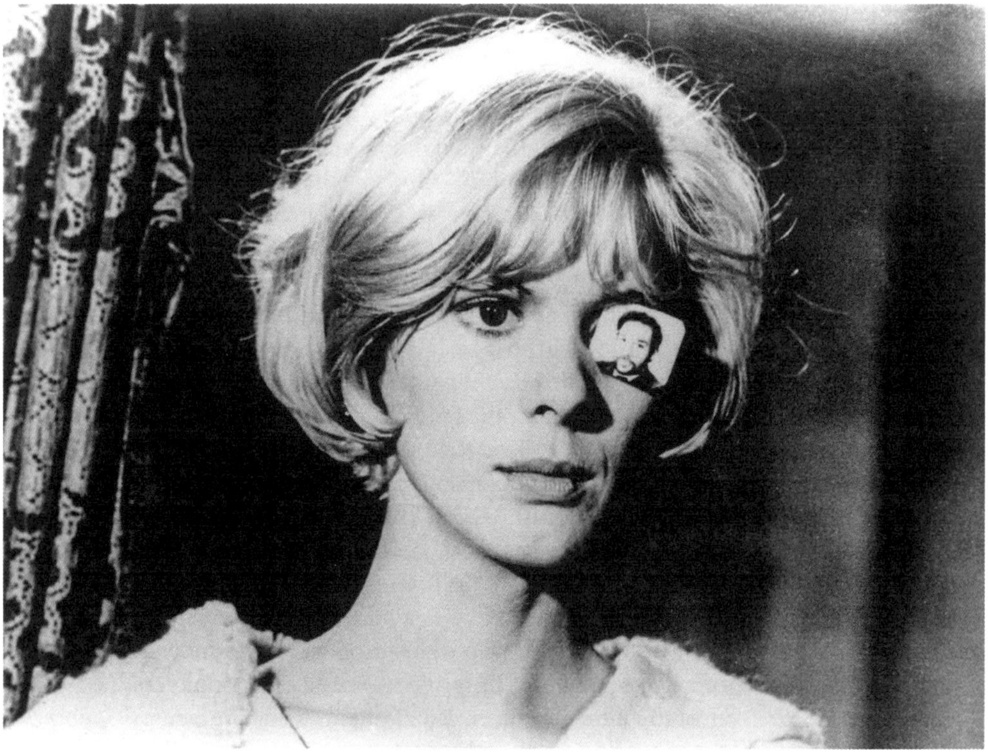

Figure 6.6: Obscured visions: Mimsy Farmer as Margarita.

At the same time, a very different sort of appreciation was in the making. Less than two weeks after this retrospective, at 2 p.m. on 11 January 1973, two policemen came to Petrović's flat and revoked his passport, leaving him a receipt explaining that this was due to the legal chapter 1, paragraph 1, point 6, from the law on travelling documents.[208] After Petrović found out from the legal code that this meant that a passport could be withdrawn "when this is in the interest of the safety of the state, or interests of national defence",[209] he began to understand the gravity of the situation.[210] After realising that he was perceived as a "threat to state security", Petrović learned that on 27 December 1972 the State Security Service (SDB) had sent a report to the magistrates court in Belgrade, with a view to prosecuting him, as he was a "mentor"[211] of Lazar Stojanović and had thus participated in the "realisation and finalisation" of *Plastic Jesus*.[212] Fortunately for Petrović, on 16 and 17 of January 1973, Sreten Jovanović, a professor at the academy who had worked on *Plastic Jesus* and was also under investigation, gave two statements to the police in regard to Petrović's role on the film. In the first statement, Jovanović claimed that work on the film continued after Petrović saw it and marked it, and in the second statement he clarified that Petrović had asked Stojanović to take out all the footage with President Tito and some footage with the Nazi soldiers.[213]

After these two statements, the State Security Service decided not to prosecute Petrović, and his passport was returned in February 1973.[214]

Nevertheless, a disciplinary procedure began at the Academy of Radio, Theatre, Film and Television in order to assess responsibility for allowing *Plastic Jesus* to be made, and clearly, the general atmosphere in Serbia was extremely intimidating. As Jasna Dragović-Soso explains, "in 1973 the criterion of 'moral-political suitability' was introduced as a norm for employment, effectively legalising the discrimination against critical intellectuals and regime opponents"; adding that "Belgrade University was one of the main targets of repression."[215] In effect, all the institutions of "nonconformist" thinking were purged, and most of their members lost their jobs, or were imprisoned.[216] The unorthodox Marxist *Praxis* group, Black Wave artists and filmmakers, and Tito's favourite Partisan war veteran who became a writer, Dobrica Ćosić (at the time the director of the dissident oriented Serbian Literary Cooperative – Srpska književna zadruga), were all severely affected by the purges.[217] Perhaps most dramatically, a professor of law from the University of Belgrade, Mihailo Djurić, who organised a conference on the proposed changes to the constitution, which was to be inaugurated in 1974, and who had thoroughly criticised these changes, was imprisoned and sentenced for two years.[218] In view of the situation, as soon as Petrović received his passport back in mid-February 1973, he left Yugoslavia. In the same year two other prominent Black Film directors, Želimir Žilnik and Dušan Makavejev, did the same. In Petrović's absence, in April 1973, a disciplinary hearing was organised at the academy, and Petrović was expelled as professor due to his "extreme negligence" in his work with the student Stojanović.[219] Petrović was also condemned for being "very irresponsible" by giving the film the highest academic grade, when the film was "deeply politically and morally" problematic, as it "equalises socialism and fascism".[220] Petrović was, according to the article published in *Politika* at the time, in Paris, and he did not respond to the disciplinary panel's invitation to attend the hearing.

6. 2. 2. Without Reconciliation

Aleksandar Petrović was not the only professor at the academy to be reprimanded in the *Plastic Jesus* case. The other members of the panel that awarded the highest mark were also penalised for their "involvement" with the film. Whereas the disciplinary panel decided to expel Petrović from the academy, Professors Marko Babac (also a Black Film director) and Predrag Delibašić received their final formal cautions, and Professor Vladan Slijepčević and assistant Branislav Obradović[221] received formal cautions.[222] Whereas Babac and Delibašić accepted the decision, Slijepčević and Obradović defended themselves. Slijepčević claimed that he watched the film out of personal interest, and was not present as a professor, which was not accepted. Obradović stated that he thought *Plastic Jesus* was not formally and ethically very different from the films shown at the Pula Film Festival in 1970 and 1971, and thus thought it deserved a good grade.[223] Centre Film gave two statements claiming that they assessed the film as unacceptable in May 1972, emphasising that the film was unfinished, and that they never applied for permission to show the film in the country or abroad.[224] *Plastic Jesus* was a liability, so it appears that everyone involved tried to distance themselves from the film. Petrović also made a statement on 22 January 1973, dissociating himself from the film. As this happened in late January, Lazar Stojanović believes that Petrović was intimidated into "renouncing the film" in order to get his passport back.[225] Petrović had a severely disabled 12-year-old son, and had already begun to consider leaving the country, so this scenario may well be possible. However, it would be difficult to find evidence for it as the State Security is unlikely to have documented such threatening and essentially illegal requests – or blackmails rather. Petrović did make a statement to the Belgrade newspaper *Politika Ekspres* stating that the final version of the film, which he had not seen, is "in the domain of political pornography", and that he was "disassociating himself from the political insinuations in the content of the film".[226] This statement, according to Petar Volk, was the key reason many of the Black Film directors and various other political dissidents scorned Petrović for years afterwards.[227] The article left a feeling that Petrović had "betrayed" his student, and had not tried to defend him, although it is unclear what exactly Petrović could have done when Stojanović was already in a military prison. Nevertheless, he continued to suffer such criticism a decade later, when the political repression had safely subsided and when the communist legacy was under revision. Sreten Jovanović, the professor who had also been a producer of the film, criticised Petrović's critics, explaining in 1993, 20 years after the incident, that such reproach from a safe historical distance was unfair:

> Nobody defended me [and Petrović, and Stojanović] when "arms were twisted" because of *Plastic Jesus*. With hindsight today, I absolutely do not recognise any cleverness or courage [from other filmmakers and intellectuals]. I would love to see two sentences that anyone wrote in the defence of Saša Petrović and Lazar Stojanović at the time. As far as I am concerned, my conscience is clear, and I even had the civic courage to write and sign certain statements on Petrović's behalf, which at that moment saved him from going to prison.[228]

As the intimidation and persecution by Tito's party loyalists was extremely harsh, it is clear that few were ready to put themselves in difficult positions by objecting, hence Jovanović is correct in saying that any censure of Petrović, with the advantage of hindsight, could be perceived as unfair. Nevertheless, some international organisations, such as Amnesty International, raised their voice in defence of Stojanović,[229] and *The New York Times* published an article in defence of both him and Petrović at the time.[230] However, the scale of the repression in Yugoslavia was so broad and unrelenting from the previous year that Stojanović and Petrović were just two small pieces in a much larger pattern. Petrović thus went into exile at the first opportunity.

In the 1980s, when both Petrović and Stojanović (who also had left the country in the meantime), were back in Yugoslavia, a bitter exchange between the two started in the press, both accusing the other regarding the *Plastic Jesus* case. Amongst other things, Petrović accused Stojanović of compromising them all (Black Filmmakers), and bringing them into trouble with the law with his tactless film, and for irresponsible remarks made during his military service.[231] Although it is true that *Plastic Jesus* served as a pretext for the party to purge Black Film, considering the historical context of 1972 Yugoslavia, Stojanović's assessment could also be perceived as correct: "Before me, there was a whole series of films, the so called 'Black Wave', and I simply arrived at the end of that series, and served as a reason for its political liquidation."[232] It is also worth adding that this incident with *Plastic Jesus*, considering the Yugoslav Black Wave authors criticised Yugoslav socialism from left-wing political platforms, proves that, in the words of Lazar Stojanović again: "What Lenin meant when he said that film is the most important art, was not understood and interpreted in the same way by socialist politicians, and by socialist filmmakers."[233]

Notes

1 See the previous chapter (particularly its introduction).

2 On this event and its political background and implications, see John R. Lampe, *Yugoslavia as History: Twice There Was a Country* (Cambridge: Cambridge University Press, 1996), pp. 296–98; also Misha Glenny, *The Balkans 1804–1999: Nationalism, War and the Great Powers* (London: Granta Books, 1999), p. 586; and Jasna Dragović-Soso, *'Saviours of the Nation': Serbia's Intellectual Opposition and the Revival of Nationalism* (London: Hurst & Company, 2002), p. 40.

3 On this event, see John R. Lampe, *Yugoslavia as History*, p. 298; and Misha Glenny, *The Balkans*, p. 587.

4 Yugoslavia was a federation consisting of six republics (Bosnia and Herzegovina, Croatia, Macedonia, Montenegro, Serbia and Slovenia) and two autonomous provinces (Kosovo and Vojvodina, both parts of Serbia).

5 See the final paragraph of section 4.2.3 in Chapter 4.

6 On the declaration, see John R. Lampe, *Yugoslavia as History*, p. 299; Misha Glenny, *The Balkans*, p. 585; and Jasna Dragović-Soso, *'Saviours of the Nation'*, pp. 31–32.

7 Jasna Dragović-Soso, *'Saviours of the Nation'*, p. 33.

8 ibid.

9 Jasna Dragović-Soso states that in Croatia nine signatories were expelled from the party, whereas 13 received "final warnings"; in Serbia 42 signatories were made to withdraw their signatures publicly, and they received the party's "warnings". See Jasna Dragović-Soso, *'Saviours of the Nation'*, p. 34; see also Misha Glenny, *The Balkans*, p. 585, on how Tito attempted to make Miroslav Krleža withdraw his signature.

10 Jasna Dragović-Soso, *'Saviours of the Nation'*, p. 34.

11 See Misha Glenny, *The Balkans*, pp. 589–90; and John R. Lampe, *Yugoslavia as History*, p. 301.

12 See the previous chapter (section 5.2.1). The new tendencies were thus not that liberating.

13 John R. Lampe, *Yugoslavia as History*, pp. 300–01.

14 Misha Glenny, *The Balkans*, p. 590.

15 Misha Glenny, *The Balkans*, p. 591.

16 John R. Lampe, *Yugoslavia as History*, pp. 301–02.

17 Dejan Jović, *Jugoslavija – Država koja je odumrla: Uspon, kriza i pad Četvrte Jugoslavije* (Beograd: Samizdat B92; Zagreb: Prometej, 2003), p. 165 (note 17).

18 On Tito identifying "unitarism" as a problem, and his perception of "Croatian cultural nationalism" as an ally in a battle against this problem, see Misha Glenny, *The Balkans*, p. 589.

19 Historians generally agree that Tito was behind the inauguration of Savka Dabčević-Kučar and Miko Tripalo, thus was initially behind the Croatian Spring. See Misha Glenny, *The Balkans*, p. 590. Dejan Jović writes about a warm welcoming speech Savka Dabčević-Kučar prepared for Tito, from which it is easy to extrapolate Tito's connection to the leadership. See Dejan Jović, *Jugoslavija*, p. 164, (especially note 12 on that page).

20 Dejan Jović, *Jugoslavija*, p. 168.

21 Dejan Jović, *Jugoslavija*, p. 156. John Lampe also states, "the maspok's nationalist content still posed the first serious challenge to the communist leadership's political monopoly in post-war Yugoslavia." See John R. Lampe, *Yugoslavia as History*, p. 302.

22 Quoted in John R. Lampe, *Yugoslavia as History*, p. 302.

23 John R. Lampe, *Yugoslavia as History*, p. 304.

24 Jasna Dragović-Soso, 'Saviours of the Nation', p. 46.

25 Misha Glenny, *The Balkans*, p. 592; John R. Lampe, *Yugoslavia as History*, p. 303.

26 John R. Lampe, *Yugoslavia as History*, p. 303.

27 ibid.

28 Misha Glenny, *The Balkans*, p. 592.

29 He was a son of Montenegrin father, who was a merchant, and a French mother. See John R. Lampe, *Yugoslavia as History*, p. 303.

30 With historical hindsight, Nikezić was right in trying to convince Tito that he would lose his good standing in the West if he were to break diplomatic relations with Israel – which Tito did. See John R. Lampe, *Yugoslavia as History*, p. 304.

31 Dejan Jović, *Jugoslavija*, p. 162.

32 Dejan Jović, *Jugoslavija*, p. 170.

33 Jasna Dragović-Soso, 'Saviours of the Nation', p. 17.

34 John R. Lampe, *Yugoslavia as History*, p. 303; and Misha Glenny, *The Balkans*, pp. 592–593.

35 Misha Glenny, *The Balkans*, p. 593.

36 John R. Lampe, *Yugoslavia as History*, p. 303.

37 Misha Glenny, *The Balkans*, p. 593.

38 John R. Lampe, *Yugoslavia as History*, p. 303.

39 John R. Lampe, *Yugoslavia as History*, p. 304.

40 Misha Glenny, *The Balkans*, p. 593.

41 Mira and Antonín Liehm, *The Most Important Art: Soviet and Eastern European Film after 1945* (Berkeley, Los Angeles: University of California Press, 1977), p. 431.

42 Daniel J. Goulding, *Liberated Cinema: The Yugoslav Experience* (Bloomington: Indiana University Press, 1985), p. 83.

43 See the preface to Aleksandar Petrović's script *Emanuela*, written by his wife Branka Petrović; in Aleksandar Petrović, *1973. Godina vampira: Emanuela II, Baron vampir, Džon F. Kenedi* (Beograd: Autorska izdanja, Foto Futura, 2010), pp. 8–12.

44 Mira and Antonín Liehm, *The Most Important Art*, p. 431.

45 Mira and Antonín Liehm, *The Most Important Art*, p. 432; and Daniel J. Goulding, *Liberated Cinema*, p. 83.

46 Munitić numbers a whole list of films made in 1973, 1974 and 1975, all glorifying the Partisan struggle during World War II. See Ranko Munitić, *Adio, Jugo-film!* (Beograd: Centar film, Srpski kulturni klub; Kragujevac: Prizma, 2005), p. 229.

47 On Tito's "inner circle" see Misha Glenny, *The Balkans*, p. 573.

48 As Tito purged Milovan Djilas (see the introduction to Chapter 2), and Aleksandar Ranković (see the introduction to Chapter 4).

49 John R. Lampe, *Yugoslavia as History*, p. 286.

50 Misha Glenny, *The Balkans*, p. 587.

51 Misha Glenny, *The Balkans*, p. 593.

52 ibid.

53 Jasna Dragović-Soso, 'Saviours of the Nation', p. 49.

54 On decentralisation and how the Yugoslav constitution of 1963 supported it, see John R. Lampe, *Yugoslavia as History*, pp. 279–81.

55 John R. Lampe, *Yugoslavia as History*, pp. 280–81.

56 Misha Glenny, *The Balkans*, p. 593.

57 Dejan Jović elaborates this in his book, the title of which could be translated as *Yugoslavia – The State that Withered Away*, alluding to the ideological background extrapolated from Karl Marx. See Dejan Jović, *Jugoslavija – Država koja je odumrla: Uspon, kriza i pad Četvrte Jugoslavije* (Beograd: Samizdat B92; Zagreb: Prometej, 2003).

58 See an interview with Aleksandar Petrović on these issues in Dragan Gajer, "Izbegnut povratak na staro", *Politika Ekspres*, 20 April 1971, p. 10.

59 Jasna Dragović-Soso, 'Saviours of the Nation', p. 137.

60 Jasna Dragović-Soso, 'Saviours of the Nation', pp. 229–31.

61 Jasna Dragović-Soso also provides an interesting assessment of the Croatian Spring, or Maspok, in the light of the later dramatic rise of nationalism in the country, she explains: "For Yugoslavia the most important legacy of the Croatian 'mass movement' was that, for the first time since 1945, 'national homogenisation' had taken place in one republic – bringing together the Party leadership, intellectuals and wider segments of society – around the goal of creating a national state. The Croatian experience thus set a precedent for what was to take place in Serbia and Slovenia in the latter part of the 1980s." See Jasna Dragović-Soso, 'Saviours of the Nation', p. 47.

62 Aleksandar Petrović reprinted this speech in his book; see Aleksandar Petrović, *Novi film, crni film 1965–1970* (Beograd: Naučna knjiga, 1988), pp. 320–25.

63 *Vjesnik u srijedu* could be translated as *The Messenger on Wednesday*, whereas for the article see Marko Goluža, "Kako je pukao jedan stari film", *Vjesnik u srijedu*, 31 March 1971, pp. 30–31.

64 Misha Glenny, *The Balkans*, p. 590.

65 Marko Goluža, "Kako je pukao jedan stari film", p. 30.
66 Goluža discusses this in his article, but for a very different view on this issue see an interview from that period with Aleksandar Petrović; Dragan Gajer, "Izbegnut povratak na staro", *Politika Ekspres*, 20 April 1971, p. 10.
67 Aleksandar Petrović, *Novi film, crni film*, p. 325.
68 Marko Goluža, "Kako je pukao jedan stari film", p. 31.
69 For example, in his book published in 1970, Yugoslav/Serbian film critic and historian Slobodan Novaković explains that "Yugoslav cinema exists as a specific autochthonous entity", but that "contemporary Yugoslav cinema exists *and* as a group of several different national cinemas (Serbian, Croatian, Slovenian, Macedonian and Montenegrin) [my emphasis]". See Slobodan Novaković, *Vreme otvaranja: Ogledi i zapisi o 'Novom Filmu'* (Novi Sad: Kulturni centar, 1970), p. 7. However, when Petrović talked about New Film (Black Film included) he probably thought of it as a Yugoslav phenomenon, in a way in which it is described in the previous chapter, as one movement albeit culturally diverse. This of course was evidently not the way Goluža understood his speech.
70 Aleksandar Petrović, *Novi film, crni film*, p. 322.
71 Marko Goluža, "Kako je pukao jedan stari film", p. 31.
72 ibid.
73 See the production table breakdown at the end of *Filmografija jugoslovenskog igranog filma 1945-1980*, ed. by Branislav Obradović (Beograd: Institut za Film, Časopis Filmograf, 1981).
74 In all fairness, it may be that Goluža had in mind the fact that the largest Croatian studio, Jadran Film in Zagreb, was frequently used by international (most often western) productions at the time, making their own films in this studio – a Croatian equivalent of Avala Film in Belgrade. The foreign productions kept the work force busy, but these films were not Croatian, and were distributed purely as belonging to the "country of origin" of the financial and production companies. In effect, they rarely had anything to do at all with either Croatian or Yugoslav culture. Even the landscapes "stood in" for other locations.
75 An interview with Aleksandar Petrović, see Zoran Predić, "Biće skoro propast filma!", *Radio revija*, 13 November 1970, pp. 22–23; see also another interview on the same subject in Krajčinović, D., "Nije vreme za eksperimente", *Politika Ekspres*, 19 May 1970, p. 10.
76 Zoran Predić, "Biće skoro propast filma!", pp. 22–23.
77 ibid.
78 For example see his interview entitled "Collecting for *Seobe*", mainly revolving around the fact that he had to bring finances from abroad in order to work in Yugoslavia, and was "officially" told that he needed to use his international credentials in order to find co-financiers from outside the country. See Jovo Paripović, "Aleksandar Petrović: Sakupljač za Seobe", *Studio*, 18 September 1987, pp. 10–12.
79 Zoran Predić, "Biće skoro propast filma!", pp. 22–23.
80 An interview with Aleksandar Petrović; see Dragan Gajer, "(Za svoj novi projekt 'Majstor i Margareta') Petrović dovodi Romi Šnajder", *Politika Ekspres*, 3 February 1970), p. 10.
81 Dragan Gajer, "(Za svoj novi projekt 'Majstor i Margareta') Petrović dovodi Romi Šnajder", p. 10.

82　Personal interview with Branka Petrović (11 September 2005); that Michelin was a producer is also mentioned in Dragan Gajer, "(Za svoj novi projekt 'Majstor i Margareta') Petrović dovodi Romi Šnajder", p. 10.

83　Dragan Gajer, "(Za svoj novi projekt 'Majstor i Margareta') Petrović dovodi Romi Šnajder", p. 10.

84　ibid.

85　Personal interview with Branka Petrović (11 September 2005).

86　ibid.

87　See Chapter 2 on Vicko Raspor as a collaborator of Petrović, and Chapter 3 (section 3.1) on Raspor as the artistic director of Dunav Film.

88　Personal interview with Nikola Majdak (30 April 2006). On their friendship, see Chapter 2 (section 2.1).

89　See interview with Branka Petrović in Dajana Djedović, "O reditelju Saši Petroviću i njegovim filmovima", in *Prizor* (annual magazine no 2.), ed. by Snežana Nešković-Simić [articles on Aleksandar Petrović ed. by Radoslav Lazić], (Loznica: Centar za kulturu "Vuk Karadžić", 2003), p. 94.

90　Michel Ciment and Lorenzo Codelli, "Venise crucifiée ou quelques clous ne font pas un festival (la 33e mostra)", *Positif*, November–December 1972, p. 87.

91　See an interview with Aleksandar Petrović explaining that a film star caused the delay with the production, see Zoran Sekulić, "Aleksandar Petrović: Autorski film nije sloboda za diletante", *Student*, 3 December 1971, p. 7.

92　Tognazzi was to later achieve world fame by starring in Edouard Molinaro's *La Cage aux Folles* (Italy, France, 1978).

93　For technical data, cast and crew, see *Filmografija jugoslovenskog filma 1971–1975*, ed. by Momčilo Ilić (Beograd: Institut za Film, 1980), p. 68; or *Filmografija jugoslovenskog igranog filma 1945–1980*, ed. by Branislav Obradović (Beograd: Institut za Film, Časopis Filmograf, 1981), p. 52; also see Filmography.

94　See the previous chapter (sections 5.2.1 and 5.2.2).

95　See Chapter 2 (section 2.4.3) and Chapter 3 (section 3.1.2).

96　See Chapter 5 (section 5.2.2).

97　On *WR: Mysteries of the Organism* and its suppression in Yugoslavia, see Daniel J. Goulding, *Liberated Cinema*, pp. 137–42.

98　Considering how highly esteemed Luis Buñuel was amongst Yugoslav filmmakers (see Chapter 3, section 3.1.3), particularly Black Wave ones, this must have been an especially complimentary award.

99　Daniel Goulding wrote about Makavejev in relation to this film as his having a "unique stance" wishing Makavejev to "continue to celebrate the liberating power of individual creativity (including its quirky, eccentric and bizarrely atypical manifestations) against social conformity, institutional rigidity and the obscenities of repressive power – East or West." See Daniel Goulding, "The Films of Dušan Makavejev: Between East and West", in *Before the Wall Came Down: Soviet and East European Filmmakers Working in the West*, ed. by Graham Petrie and Ruth Dwyer (Lanham, MD: University Press of America, 1990), pp. 155–56.

100 Daniel J. Goulding, *Liberated Cinema*, p. 142.

101 ibid.

102 Mikhail Bulgakov, *The Master and Margarita* (London: Picador, 1997), p. 4.

103 Mikhail Bulgakov, *The Master and Margarita*, p. 16.

104 The novel is also very much about love and the second part opens with the following sentences: "Follow me, reader! Who ever told you there is no such thing in the world as real, true, everlasting love? May the liar have his despicable tongue cut out! Follow me, my reader, and only me, and I'll show you that kind of love!" See Mikhail Bulgakov, *The Master and Margarita*, p. 185.

105 Bulgakov opens his novel with this quote from Goethe's *Faust*. See Mikhail Bulgakov, *The Master and Margarita*, p. 1.

106 It is important to add here that at the time, for some critics – mainly Soviet ones – the issue of time frame was problematic. The novel is set in the 1930s, when Stalinist rule had degenerated into the paranoid regime of purges and gulags – something that even Soviet critics of the 1970s would admit. Petrović, though, sets the story of his film apparently in the 1920s, when the regime was not as hard on its opponents, and when Stalin listened to his peers, according to these same critics. This is why they found Petrović's mixing of the two decades historically inaccurate. However, this is not of key significance for the following analysis.

107 See Ellendea Proffer, *Bulgakov: Life and Work* (Ann Arbor, MI: Ardis, 1984).

108 Ellendea Proffer, "Afterword: Bulgakov the Magician", in Mikhail Bulgakov, *The Master and Margarita*, p. 364.

109 See Chapter 1 (section 1.2.2); Petrović describes this event in his autobiography; see Aleksandar Petrović, *Sve moje ljubavi/Slepi periskopi* (Novi Sad: Prometej, Tajanstvena Tačka, 1995), pp. 211–14.

110 Ellendea Proffer, *Bulgakov*, p. 104.

111 Ellendea Proffer, "Afterword: Bulgakov the Magician", p. 360.

112 Ellendea Proffer, *Bulgakov*, p. 525.

113 Ellendea Proffer, *Bulgakov*, p. 255.

114 Proffer demonstrates this by analysing another of Bulgakov's novel – *White Guard*. See Ellendea Proffer, *Bulgakov*, p. 150.

115 Ellendea Proffer, *Bulgakov*, p. 2.

116 Ellendea Proffer, *Bulgakov*, p. 579.

117 Ellendea Proffer, "Afterword: Bulgakov the Magician", p. 363.

118 Ellendea Proffer, *Bulgakov*, p. 540.

119 Ellendea Proffer, "Afterword: Bulgakov the Magician", p. 363.

120 On this film and the Soviet policies behind it, see Amy Sargeant, *Vsevolod Pudovkin: Classic Films of the Soviet Avant-Garde* (London, New York: I.B. Tauris, 2000), who quotes Pudovkin as stating in 1925: "It is clear to everyone, how important it is to propagate this idea, corroborated by the materialist world view, that for the present time the notion of the 'Soul' is conclusively extinguished." See p. 49, p. 54 (note 92).

121 Ellendea Proffer, "Afterword: Bulgakov the Magician", p. 367.

122 See the previous chapter. For this interview and this particular opinion, see an interview with Aleksandar Petrović in Bogdan Tirnanić, "Aleksandar Petrović, razgovor", *Sineast*, 5, 1968, p. 52.

123 Ivo Pondělíček, "Aleksandar Petrovič dokončil svůj nový film", *Film A Doba*, January 1969, p. 45.

124 Ellendea Proffer, *Bulgakov*, p. 521.

125 Ellendea Proffer, *Bulgakov*, p. 319.

126 Ellendea Proffer, *Bulgakov*, p. 532.

127 ibid.

128 Mikhail Bulgakov, *The Master and Margarita*, pp. 321–25.

129 Mikhail Bulgakov, *The Master and Margarita*, p. 305.

130 Ellendea Proffer, "Afterword: Bulgakov the Magician", p. 357.

131 It is interesting to note that with *The Master and Margarita*, in contrast to Petrović's previous work, two of the four political themes are often intertwined: one on the investigation of religion in society and another investigating the dogmatic understanding of ideology. The dogmatic understanding of ideology could be, as this chapter will demonstrate, also extrapolated from the relationship of the establishment and the artist, so that the delineation of these themes is not always straightforward. However, *The Master and Margarita* is the only mature Petrović's film where the first of his four political themes – the one exploring interethnic relationships – is not present at all. Or only in a very rudimentary way, as Professor Woland is perceived as a "foreigner" in Moscow; but this aspect of the story is not developed sufficiently in the film, as it is in the book. Thus the debate on how Muscovites in the film perceive this diabolical group as "the Other" could not be built on the base of the narrative as it is. However, some hints do exist.

132 An interview with Aleksandar Petrović; see Kuzmanovski, R., "Ne veruvam vo filmski adaptacii", *Nova Makedonija*, 4 August 1972 (in the clipping file on Aleksandar Petrović, Belgrade: Jugoslovenska Kinoteka Library).

133 With a few exceptions – at that time, most notably China and Albania.

134 That the Master "gave up" his name; see Mikhail Bulgakov, *The Master and Margarita*, p. 114.

135 According to Proffer, Bulgakov "dropped *Theatrical Novel*" in 1937 in order to concentrate on finishing *The Master and Margarita*. However, when he died in 1940, "he had finished the writing of *The Master and Margarita*, although not the final editing, which he worked on up to months before his death." See Ellendea Proffer, "Afterword: Biographical Note", in Mikhail Bulgakov, *The Master and Margarita*, p. 356.

136 This unfinished novel, originally entitled *Notes of the Deceased*, was a satire on life in a Soviet theatre, and through that, the theatre scene in general. See Ellendea Proffer, *Bulgakov*, p. 461.

137 See Chapter 8 (section 8.1.1).

138 This episode is reminiscent of a real-life event, although it would be difficult to prove any real connection. However, Dušan Makavejev liked to tell a story about a very influential, and I would be tempted to add controversial, communist intellectual and writer Miroslav

Krleža, who was also a high official of the party (on Krleža, see Chapter 2, section 2.2). When Krleža saw a short documentary film by Dragoslav Lazić, *Zadušnice*, he wept, calling it an ingenious piece of work, which depicts the hard life of poor Serbian peasants in a very touching and poignant way. Yet, due to its real, well-crafted and touching representation, it cannot be shown publicly and has to be banned. See an interview with Dušan Makavejev in Zdenka Aćin, "Zašto smo srećni", in *Dušan Makavejev: 300 čuda*, ed. by Vladimir Blaževski, (Beograd: SKC, 1988), p. 37.

139 Ellendea Proffer, *Bulgakov*, p. 532.

140 Daniel J. Goulding, *Liberated Cinema*, p. 135.

141 An interview with Aleksandar Petrović, see Miodrag Petrović, "Umetnik mora da voli ono što otkriva", *Književne Novine*, 28 May 1966, p. 12.

142 An interview with Aleksandar Petrović, see Milomir Marić, "Vreme relaksacije", *Duga*, 6 January 1979, p. 20.

143 The budget for *Happy Gypsies* budget was under 200 million dinars – see Chapter 4 (section 4.1.1).

144 This information came from a personal interview with Branka Petrović (11 September 2005).

145 Without wanting to make any crude comparisons, or be unfair to any of the artists mentioned, it could be said that Bulat Okudzava was Soviet Union's Leonard Cohen, or Bob Dylan from his politically more radical phase.

146 The key crowd scenes would be the meeting at the Writers' Union, the Master in the Writers' Union bar twice, and the theatre scene with Professor Woland's show. Large groups of extras were also used in all the street scenes, Berlioz's funeral and others overall – considerably more frequently than in any previous film by Petrović.

147 An interview with Branka Petrović in Dajana Djedović, "O reditelju Saši Petroviću i njegovim filmovima", pp. 94–95.

148 In the novel, the Master writes a novel about Pontius Pilate, whose parts are then "interpolated" into Bulgakov's novel, thus it has the structure of a novel within a novel. Petrović turns this "other novel" into a theatre play, thus justifying the fact that he kept parts of that material. He shows them in the film as a theatre play, through the structure of a play within a film. In one scene, during the rehearsals, the Master shouts at the director of the play complaining about a detail happening on the stage. Off-screen, it is Petrović's voice that responds: "You are the writer of this play, but please leave directing to me", which clearly underlines Petrović's views on adaptations.

149 Nikola Majdak filmed some of Petrović's early documentaries, described in Chapter 2 and one of them in Chapter 3 (*Assemblies*). Majdak then committed himself to filming more animation rather than live action or documentary films from the mid-1960s: personal interview with Nikola Majdak (30 April 2006).

150 According to Branka Petrović, the Italian producers did not mind Petrović employing a Yugoslav cinematographer of his choice for the project, but the Italian laws on co-productions involved quotas on how many Italian staff had to be employed, so Petrović had to choose someone from Italy: personal interview with Branka Petrović (11 September 2005).

151 An interview with Aleksandar Petrović given in Yugoslavia ten years after the film, as the new air of liberalisation had been breezing through. See Lela Jovanović, "Verovatno opasan tip", *Reporter*, 2 September 1982, p. 55.

152 19th Yugoslav Film Festival in Pula was between 26 July and 2 August 1972. See Petar Volk, *Istorija jugoslovenskog filma* (Beograd: Institut za Film, Partizanska knjiga, 1986), p. 522.

153 An interview with Aleksandar Petrović in Mirko Urošević, "Više je zbrke oko političkih nego oko estetskih motiva", *Vjesnik*, 6 August 1972, p. 6.

154 See "Nakon nagrade u Veneciji: Saši Petroviću pozivi za nove festivale", *Novi list*, 6 September 1972, p. 10.

155 John Russell Taylor, "Strange Films from Unlikely Places", *The Times*, 28 November 1972, p. 10.

156 Taylor adds that the Italian star, Ugo Tognazzi, had by that point already "disowned his role in the film", but as Taylor appears to be very positive about the film, he hints that this may be due to the fact that the Italian version is inferior. See John Russell Taylor, "Strange Films from Unlikely Places", p. 10.

157 See the review by Ibrahim Sakić, "Snaga simbola", *Odjek*, 15 January 1973, pp. 18–19.

158 Derek Elley, "The Master and Margarita", *Films & Filming*, April 1975, p. 46.

159 Milivoje Jovanović, "'Finski nož' za Mihaila Bulgakova", *Književne novine*, 16 November 1972, p. 5.

160 ibid.

161 ibid.

162 ibid.

163 ibid.

164 Ibrahim Sakić, "Snaga simbola", pp. 18–19.

165 Nigel Gearing, "Maestro i Margarita (The Master and Margarita)", *Monthly Film Bulletin*, March 1975, p. 59.

166 Derek Elley, "The Master and Margarita", p. 47.

167 See Chapter 4 (section 4.2.2).

168 Ellendea Proffer, *Bulgakov*, p. 530.

169 See an interview with Branka Petrović where she names Puriša Djordjević, a film director, as one of those colleagues, in Dajana Djedović, "O reditelju Saši Petroviću i njegovim filmovima", p. 93.

170 See an interview with Branka Petrović, in Dajana Djedović, "O reditelju Saši Petroviću i njegovim filmovima", p. 94.

171 Pisarevski, D., "Pula – 72: Temi sovremennosti", *Sovietsky Ekran*, October 1972, p. 18.

172 ibid.

173 ibid.

174 Pisarevski, D., "Pula – 72: Temi sovremennosti", p. 16.

175 Pisarevski, D., "Pula – 72: Temi sovremennosti", p. 18.

176 Daniel Goulding provides some interesting material on this case, although it is inconclusive. See Daniel J. Goulding, *Liberated Cinema*, p. 136.

177 An interview with Aleksandar Petrović, see Milomir Marić, "Vreme relaksacije", p. 20.

178 Michael J. Stoil, *Balkan Cinema: Evolution after the Revolution* (Ann Arbor, MI: UMI Research Press, 1979), p. 55.

179 ibid.

180 On the obscure and "roundabout" ways in which films, particularly Black Wave ones, were withheld from distribution in Yugoslavia, thus effectively banned, see an unpublished master's thesis by Vanja Valtrović, "BW – Mystery of the Suppression or Pessimism in an Optimistic Society" (unpublished master's thesis, University of Amsterdam, 1999).

181 See the introduction to section 3.1 in Chapter 3.

182 See for example Svetlana Slapšak, "Splav meduze, The Raft of Medusa", in *The Cinema of The Balkans*, ed. by Dina Iordanova (London, New York: Wallflower Press, 2006), p. 154.

183 On Lazar Stojanović in his own words see Lazar Stojanović, "Ko behu disidenti", *Republika*, 16 February 1998, available: http://www.yurope.com/zines/republika/arhiva/98/182/182_11. HTM [last accessed 3 September 2012], and an interview with Lazar Stojanović in Aleksandar Milosavljević, "Pobednici u izgubljenom ratu", *Dnevnik*, 4 March 1990, pp. 18–19.

184 Personal interview with Lazar Stojanović (3 January 2006).

185 All the information described comes from a personal interview with Lazar Stojanović (3 January 2006).

186 An interview with Sreten Jovanović, see "NESTAŠNI STUDENTI, ili ko je bio plastični Juda III", in Milan Nikodijević, *Zabranjeni bez zabrane: Zona sumraka jugoslovenskog filma* (Beograd: Jugoslovenska kinoteka, 1995), pp. 93–94.

187 Personal interview with Lazar Stojanović (3 January 2006).

188 ibid.

189 Stojanović still maintains this political attitude, and elaborated it eloquently (personal interview with Lazar Stojanović [3 January 2006]).

190 ibid.

191 ibid.

192 An interview with Sreten Jovanović, see "NESTAŠNI STUDENTI, ili ko je bio Plastični Juda III", p. 94.

193 Personal interview with Lazar Stojanović (3 January 2006).

194 An interview with Sreten Jovanović, see "NESTAŠNI STUDENTI, ili ko je bio Plastični Juda III", p. 94.

195 At the time when Yugoslavia started breaking up in the early 1990s, Vuk Obradović was a general, and was a spokesman for the Yugoslav People's Army.

196 All the information in this paragraph comes from a personal interview with Lazar Stojanović (3 January 2006), although Stojanović also writes in great depth and detail about these events in Lazar Stojanović, "Ko behu disidenti".

197 When asked how he, as a self-declared anarchist, was at the same time a member of the Communist Party, Stojanović explained that he joined the party believing that this was the only way for him to influence society; from a personal interview with Lazar Stojanović (3 January 2006). It was common in one-party political systems to join the party in order to be able to either influence the system, as Stojanović explained, or to simply have a career. Yugoslav socialism was no different.

198 Lazar Stojanović, "Ko behu disidenti".

199 Personal interview with Lazar Stojanović (3 January 2006); also see Lazar Stojanović, "Ko behu disidenti".

200 An interview with Sreten Jovanović; see "NESTAŠNI STUDENTI, ili ko je bio Plastični Juda III", p. 94. It is also worth adding that while *Plastic Jesus* was in production, some basic advertising of the film was introduced, so it was known that the film was being made. This resulted in several international film festivals, including Cannes, showing an interest in previewing the film for their events once it was finished. Subsequently, the film was never shown, but its existence was not a secret; from personal interview with Lazar Stojanović (3 January 2006).

201 An interview with Sreten Jovanović, see "NESTAŠNI STUDENTI, ili ko je bio Plastični Juda III", pp. 94–95.

202 See *Plastic Jesus*, directed by Lazar Stojanović.

203 An interview with Sreten Jovanović, see "NESTAŠNI STUDENTI, ili ko je bio Plastični Juda III", p. 95.

204 ibid.

205 Daniel J. Goulding, *Liberated Cinema*, p. 136.

206 Draško Redjep, then director of Neoplanta Film, talks about this in his book on Petrović, with whom he became a close friend over the years. He mentions that the contract was first signed with the writer, Miloš Crnjanski, who then kept on reminding them that the film had to be directed by Petrović. See Draško Redjep, *Rapsodija ništavila: Ogledi o Aleksandru Petroviću* (Novi Sad: Prometej, 2001), p. 15 and p. 17. Petrović confirmed in one interview given in late August of the same year that the contracts had been signed; see an interview with Aleksandar Petrović in Dj. M., "Izgleda da sam isključen …", *Večernji list*, 29 August 1972, p. 11.

207 D. R., "Filmsko delo", *Dnevnik*, 25 December 1972, p. 8.

208 This information is from a personal interview with Branka Petrović (11 September 2005), but is also available from her preface to Aleksandar Petrović's script *Emanuela*; in Aleksandar Petrović, *1973. Godina vampira*, pp. 8–9.

209 Copies of these original documents exist in the clipping file on Aleksandar Petrović in the library of Jugoslovenska Kinoteka in Belgrade; also see the preface to Aleksandar Petrović's script *Emanuela*, written by his wife Branka Petrović; in Aleksandar Petrović, *1973. Godina vampira*, p. 9.

210 Jasna Dragović-Soso explains that the withdrawal of passports was a repressive measure Tito's regime often used when it wanted to silence intellectuals. Consequently, in December 1976, a group of human rights activists signed a petition, led by lawyer Srdja Popović, who had defended in court many Black Wave artists and *Praxis* professors a few years previously, demanding the abolition of this practice and a guarantee for the "freedom of movement". They also complained against "moral–political suitability" as a criterion for employment in 1978. See Jasna Dragović-Soso, '*Saviours of the Nation*', p. 50.

211 It is often mentioned in some of the literature on this incident that Petrović was Stojanović's "mentor". Stojanović was an undergraduate student, so he did not have a mentor or supervisor. Petrović was rather his professor, or tutor, but not his mentor as the State Security Service accusations claimed.

212 See Branka Petrović's preface to Aleksandar Petrović's *Emanuela*; in Aleksandar Petrović, *1973. Godina vampira*, p. 10.

213 These two statements are available in the library of Jugoslovenska Kinoteka in Belgrade, in the clipping file on Aleksandar Petrović; see also an interview with Sreten Jovanović in "Nestašni studenti ili ko je bio Plastični Juda III", pp. 93–94.

214 See Branka Petrović's preface to Aleksandar Petrović's *Emanuela*; in Aleksandar Petrović, *1973. Godina vampira*, p. 11.

215 Jasna Dragović-Soso, *'Saviours of the Nation'*, p. 48.

216 Jasna Dragović-Soso explains: "Since the vast majority of intellectuals depended on the state for both employment and access to the public sphere, the regime could effectively use threats of dismissal from work and censorship to silence criticism." See Jasna Dragović-Soso, *'Saviours of the Nation'*, p. 16; and see pp. 16–17 for the articles of the Yugoslav Criminal Code usually used against critical intelligentsia.

217 Jasna Dragović-Soso, *'Saviours of the Nation'*, pp. 47–49.

218 Jasna Dragović-Soso, *'Saviours of the Nation'*, p. 47.

219 See Sretić, M., "Disciplinska komisija odlučila da A. Petrović bude isključen sa Akademije", *Politika*, 10 April 1973, p. 6.

220 ibid.

221 Not to be confused with Captain Vuk Obradović, who had a conversation with Stojanović.

222 See Sretić, M., "Disciplinska komisija odlučila da A. Petrović bude isključen sa Akademije", *Politika*, 10 April 1973, p. 6; "Potvrdjena kazna Aleksandru Petroviću o isključenju iz radne organizacije", *Politika*, 11 April 1973a, p. 6; "Zbor radnih ljudi usvojio predlog disciplinske komisije", *Borba*, 11 April 1973b, p. 5; D. G., "Predlog da se Petrović isključi sa akademije", *Politika Ekspres*, 10 April 1973, p. 2; "Spriječen put na ekran", *Večernje novine*, 22 January 1973, p. 4.

223 D. G., "Predlog da se Petrović isključi sa akademije", *Politika Ekspres*, 10 April 1973, p. 2.

224 "Negativna ocena još u maju", *Nedeljne novosti*, 21 January 1973 (in the clipping file on Aleksandar Petrović, Belgrade: Jugoslovenska Kinoteka Library).

225 Personal interview with Lazar Stojanović (3 January 2006).

226 Aleksandar Petrović, "*Plastični Isus* je politička pornografija", *Politika Ekspres*, 22 January 1973, p. 12.

227 Petar Volk, *Let nad močvarom: Aleksandar Petrović svojim životom, delom i filmovima* (Beograd: Institut za film; Novi Sad: Prometej, 1999), p. 267.

228 An interview with Sreten Jovanović, see "NESTAŠNI STUDENTI, ili ko je bio Plastični Juda III", p. 99.

229 Personal interview with Lazar Stojanović (3 January 2006).

230 Raymond H. Anderson, "Yugoslav Student's Film Stirs Demands Teacher Be Punished", *The New York Times*, 26 January 1973, p. 5.

231 An interview with Aleksandar Petrović in "Aleksandar Saša Petrović, PROFESOR, ili ko je bio Plastični Juda I", in Milan Nikodijević, *Zabranjeni bez zabrane*, pp. 62–63.

232 An interview with Lazar Stojanović in "Lazar Stojanović, DJAK, ili Ko je bio Plastični Juda II", in Milan Nikodijević, *Zabranjeni bez zabrane*, p. 78.

233 Personal interview with Lazar Stojanović (3 January 2006).

Chapter 7

The Artist in Exile

According to Dejan Jović, Socialist Yugoslavia was "an ideocratic state: its official identity was (even when that was contrary to the real feelings of the majority of its citizens) based on ideology".[1] Jović further explains that "Yugoslav socialism was a project run by the elite", as is the case in countries with politically ideocratic systems.[2] This elite was epitomised by the League of Communists of Yugoslavia, which was "conceived as an historical, intellectual and political avant-garde".[3] Jović reminds us that, as Karl Marx's famous thesis stated, philosophers interpreted the world differently, "while now (in socialism) the point is to change it, but in order to change it, it has first to be interpreted".[4] Jović states that the "interpretation of reality and even more, envisioning the future was the main task of the conscious forces [i.e. the elite]," and concludes that "the main political conflicts in socialism were conflicts between various interpretations of reality and visions of the future".[5] Within this framework, the political situation in Yugoslavia in the early 1970s therefore embodies a moment of accumulated and sometimes conflicting interpretations of the future within the elite itself. Serbian "liberals" had one vision, Croatian "nationalists" another, while Edvard Kardelj's and Josip Broz Tito's shared visions were very different from the first two. This situation was best exemplified by Marko Nikezić, the then leader of the Serbian communists, who stated: "the question is not socialism or not, but what kind of socialism".[6] However, as Jović also suggests,[7] in ideocratic societies, "more than in others, unity is grounded in the unity of discourse".[8]

It might appear as if the brutality with which Tito and Kardelj reasserted "the unity of discourse", or rather, reimposed their own vision of the future by stifling and purging all others in 1971 and 1972, was done for the good of the country and socialism.[9] Tito's adherence to Kardelj's concept of decentralisation, which distinguished Yugoslav socialism from the highly centralised Soviet version (after the initial distancing of the two countries in 1948), was still strong in the early 1970s. This concept prevailed throughout this period, and was further legitimised in the constitution of 1974, which marked the full "emergence of Kardelj's interpretation of Marxism".[10] According to John Lampe, Kardelj's constitution was "the world's longest with 406 articles, surpassing that of India," and had "the most complicated electoral system seen anywhere during the twentieth century. Few Yugoslavs ever understood it fully".[11] Regardless, Tito and Kardelj jealously guarded their own vision of the future, and Misha Glenny states that "the mechanisms of the 1974 Constitution were little more than window dressing",[12] as "policy was made by the two elderly leaders".[13] Lampe adds that Tito also purged the Central Committee in 1974, bringing in a large number of army officers, who were all "seen primarily as Tito's men".[14] That Tito and Kardelj were prepared to continue to jealously guard their own vision of socialism was clear from the fact that repression continued into the mid-1970s. Jasna Dragović-Soso adds that "the law governing state-university relations was changed in 1975, allowing the state's direct interference in university affairs", due to "the considerable resistance in Belgrade University".[15] When Lazar Stojanović, Aleksandar Petrović's student and director of *Plastic Jesus*,[16] was released from prison in November 1975 after serving a three-year sentence, he stated that "the atmosphere in the country resembled the late 1950s more than the relatively liberal period that had preceded [my] arrest".[17] Tito's and Kardelj's vehement reassertion of their own vision of socialism brought, in Dragović-Soso's assessment, "the return of dogmatism in the 1970s".[18]

In 1973, Tito and Kardelj brought to an end the brief flowering of liberal tendencies and diverse interpretations of socialism, as well as the introduction of other political leanings in Yugoslavia. They did so by forcibly reasserting their own vision of socialism, engendering this vision as a dogmatic view from which there should be no deviation. This return of dogmatism, as described in the previous chapter, had a detrimental effect on all the non-conformist thinkers, including filmmakers such as Aleksandar Petrović, who went into exile in February 1973. The consequences for the film industry were also striking, confirming Michael Stoil's assessment that "experimentation with the limits of accepted content led to conflicts between artists and the state."[19] This dogmatism meant an end to experimentation and a reduction of production in general. Daniel Goulding thus explains: "The period from 1973 to 1977 marked Yugoslavia's lowest ebb of domestic feature film production since the beginning of the sixties".[20] Although Goulding also blames the drop in production on "television's rapid advancement" in that period, he still adds political reasons for "the low and flat profile of film production", that was "matched by a general lack of thematic boldness and cinematic experimentation."[21] If filmmakers such as Aleksandar Petrović wanted to continue their intellectual inquiries, as well as experimenting with cinematic language, they could do so only if they left Yugoslavia. In fact, this repressive atmosphere did not last for long: it subsided significantly in the late 1970s, a period marked by the deaths of both the octogenarian Yugoslav leaders. In the meantime, however, Petrović continued his career in exile.

7. 1. Exile

After Aleksandar Petrović's passport was taken away by the police on 11 January 1973, he was visited by the French consul to Belgrade, who offered him assistance.[22] In the autumn of 1969, on behalf of the French government, Petrović had been awarded the medal of Chevalier des Arts et des Lettres, one of the highest state honours in France given to artists.[23] The medal was awarded by the French embassy in Belgrade, thus Petrović was plainly well known to its senior staff. It is perhaps worth underlining that in an official explanation of the award, in addition to being given for Petrović's films, it was also given for his "exceptional contribution to the development of relations in culture and co-operation between Yugoslavia and France."[24] Petrović, had also been born in Paris,[25] and according to the citizenship laws of the time, could have applied for French citizenship, and thus acquired another – or rather a different – passport. Such discreet support for Petrović from the French government could also be perceived within the larger picture of Cold War politics, where the western states sought to benefit from supporting persecuted artists and intellectuals in socialist countries. In fact, Petrović's Yugoslav passport was soon returned, in February 1973, following statements made by Professor Sreten Jovanović. The statements led to Yugoslav State Security dropping their charges against Petrović; however, he decided to leave the country with his family anyway.[26]

In February 1973 Aleksandar Petrović, with his wife Branislava, Branka, and their 12-year-old son Dragomir, Dragan, went to Budapest, Hungary.[27] Although Budapest is the closest European capital to Belgrade, Petrović's choice may appear unexpected as Hungary was also a socialist country. However, Hungary was part of the Eastern Bloc, and Yugoslavia – strictly speaking – was not, thus relations between the two countries were often "cold", following the Yugoslav-Soviet lead. Just as pro-Soviet Yugoslav communists tended to defect via Hungary, Hungarian dissidents used to cross over to Yugoslavia to find a refuge when they needed one. Petrović was not in Hungary to express political grievances against Yugoslavia though, nor were there any indications that he had intended to. He was in Hungary for a different reason, and had actually been planning this move for some time, while the political pressures in Yugoslavia only accelerated the process.[28]

Petrović's only child, Dragomir, suffered from cerebral palsy and Budapest had one of the world's leading medical centres specialising in treating this condition – the Professor Pëto Institute. Petrović had been making arrangements to move to Budapest for some time so that his son could receive therapy and treatment there. Somewhat fortunately for Petrović and his family, all the arrangements for their move had been made before his prosecution started, and they already had the necessary visas and permission from the Hungarian Ministry of Health for their son to be treated at the Institute.[29] As Petrović was one of the most acclaimed European film directors of the time, who regularly visited festivals and also represented Yugoslavia as president of its Union of Film Workers, he had many friends, acquaintances and colleagues in the international filmmaking community. One of these was István Dosai, the head of Hungarofilm, the major Hungarian film company, and who now sought to assist him. Dosai helped the Petrovićs settle in Hungary,[30] and deal with the notoriously complicated immigration issues.[31] Once the family had taken up residence in Budapest, they made another trip, this time to Paris. As Aleksandar Petrović was born there, the first reason for this visit was that he, and consequently his family, could become French citizens.[32] By having dual citizenship, Petrović would then be protected if a situation similar to his recent problems were to arise again. As a result of this infamous repressive incident, Petrović had found another homeland – France.

After acquiring French citizenship, Branislava and Dragomir returned to Budapest, while Aleksandar Petrović started sharing his life between Paris and Budapest.[33] The second, probably more significant reason, for the Petrovićs' visit to Paris was, according to Branislava, so that her husband could look for work in order to be able to continue to support them.[34] As indicated above, Petrović was an internationally-acclaimed director, and Paris was – as it still is – the European filmmaking capital. In addition, Petrović had a working relationship with the European branch of United Artists, which was based in Paris and which had co-produced his *It Rains in My Village*.[35] He also had close personal friends in the French film industry, such as the French director Claude Lelouch, whose company had distributed *I Even Met Happy Gypsies* in France.[36] Petrović thus set out to try his luck as a European director, outside of his own country in which his career had started.

In the 1970s, Petrović was not the only East European director seeking work in the West, and it is interesting to observe how his work developed in the countries of "free thought", as well as the "free market". Petrović had perhaps few misconceptions of what his new environment might bring, just as he had few misconceptions about the state of affairs in his own country, which he had just left. By acquiring French citizenship for himself and his family, he had become immune to the type of political intimidation to which he had been recently exposed to in Yugoslavia. However, he was to become vulnerable to a different kind of pressure. Working as a film director in the West was to prove as confining as at home, although the constraints proved to be of an economic, rather than a political nature.

7. 1. 1. Pornography, or Living as an Artist in the West

According to Branislava Petrović, once the family moved to Hungary, their financial situation worsened rapidly.[37] The cost of living in Hungary and France was much higher than in Belgrade. Aleksandar Petrović was under pressure to find work urgently, thus he started considering offers that were not directly linked to the projects in which he was interested, as they were in Yugoslavia. One of the most significant of these offers came from the French producer Yves Rousset-Rouard.[38] Rousset-Rouard had just completed *Emmanuelle* (1974), and was expecting large profits in return. Like every "great" producer, Rousset-Rouard was precocious with his investments and made great returns through creating this first example of "family porn". *Emmanuelle* is understood today as an erotic classic, but at the time its success was due to the fact that the film was made for general release rather than for "adult" cinemas, in which such films were ordinarily exclusively distributed.[39] Following the sexual revolution of the 1960s, Rousset-Rouard shrewdly anticipated the profits such a film could generate, and immediately began preparing a sequel. He was a producer who liked Petrović's films and he invited the latter to write *Emmanuelle 2* (1975).[40] The script was thus commissioned, with a promise of substantial financial returns. Although Branka Petrović claims that her husband[41] had nothing against "this kind of cinema",[42] the contract included a clause that Petrović's name would not appear in the credits.[43] His hiding behind *nom de plume* was not an unusual practice as many filmmakers did the same at the time.[44] Erotic and soft porn films were then still seen as "marginal", although films such as the *Emmanuelle* franchise helped to broach the taboo, and started changing the accepted "seedy image" of erotica for good. The director of the second *Emmanuelle*, Francis Giacobetti, signed up for the project proudly, as someone who sought to bestow, with his photographic work, artistic credibility on what was then a marginalised practice.[45]

Looking more closely at *Emmanuelle 2*, it would be interesting to try to identify recognisable traces of Petrović's work. One such trace might be Sylvia Kristel's Emmanuelle watching animated erotic pictures in an antiquated viewer, reminiscent of Margarita doing the same in *The Master and Margarita*. However, as numerous changes have been made to the original script, and more significantly, the film was not directed by Petrović, it would be difficult to ascertain clearly what Petrović's thematic contributions to this project were. In addition, this was a commissioned work that Petrović accepted in order to resolve his financial problems and not to continue with his own intellectual investigations. Fortunately for the exiled director, *Emmanuelle 2* was a financial success, and Petrović wrote another two synopses for the same producer, and the same company, Trinacra Films.[46] One outline was for a fiction film entitled *Banker – Vampire* (an interesting title for a filmmaker coming from a socialist country), and the other for a documentary film on John Fitzgerald Kennedy.[47] According to Branka Petrović, her husband was also paid for these, and along with his work for *Emmanuelle 2*, their livelihoods were now more secure, and her husband could try to develop projects closer to his own interests.[48]

It is worth noting here that once in the West, Petrović, like many other filmmakers coming from socialist countries, found that economic pressures formed a new type of limiting environment for their creativity, as much, if not even more limiting, than the political censorship they had faced at home. These contrasts have been the subject of numerous studies. Graham Petrie explains that during the period of "early cinema", European directors going to Hollywood faced similar problems to those East Europeans who went to the West during the Cold War:

> Many filmmakers had to cope with the paradox that American producers [and ones in the West in general], distributors and audiences were rarely interested in the kind of serious intellectual debate that they were accustomed to conducting by means of film in their homeland, and that the requirement to produce acceptable commercial entertainment was, in the long run, just as confining and soul-destroying.[49]

It is illustrative that Petrović, after making the type of films in Yugoslavia described in previous chapters, was involved in writing erotica and soft porn once in the West – films of a very different genre. It is also indicative of Petrie's point that this was often the fate of film directors arriving from socialist countries. Roman Polański's first contract once in the West was with a company specialising in "soft porn."[50] However, individual cases were different, and their comparison to Petrović would require another study. What is important is that Petrović earned his living by working in the film industry, and after writing *Emmanuelle 2* and other projects for Trinacra Films, he found time to pursue projects closer to the interests he had been cultivating back in Yugoslavia.

Apart from Trinacra Films that offered paid commissioned work, Petrović also established a working relationship with the Sofracima production company, which was interested in producing work closer perhaps to that which Petrović had made in Yugoslavia. On the basis of his previous film, *The Master and Margarita*, Petrović started writing an adaptation of an earlier novel by Mikhail Bulgakov, *Heart of a Dog*, for Sofracima. In 1974, however, it was announced that the Italian director Alberto Lattuada had already started making a film based on the same literary text,[51] so Sofracima decided to abandon the project.[52] It could have been ideal for Petrović had his first film outside Yugoslavia also been based on Bulgakov – as his latest film produced in Yugoslavia had been – but this was not to happen. The fates of the two artists, however, continued to be strangely intertwined. Bulgakov wisely never attempted to publish *The Master and Margarita* during his lifetime, and contrary to general belief, as Ellendea Proffer's biography demonstrates, he was not a victim of Stalinism, nor was he ever significantly persecuted. Quite the opposite: Stalin saw Bulgakov's play *The Days of the Turbins* many times,[53] and personally intervened on Bulgakov's behalf in order to get him a job in a respected theatre.[54] Responding to Bulgakov's letter, Stalin even telephoned him, and offered him the chance to emigrate if he so wished, but Bulgakov decided to stay in Russia.[55] In contrast, Petrović released his film of *The Master and Margarita* in Yugoslavia, attempting to make a satirical parallel with it between early Stalinism and Titoism. As result, the film was withdrawn and he had to leave the country.

After work on adapting *Heart of a Dog* was abandoned, Petrović started writing another adaptation for Sofracima. He again turned to Russian literature, this time a collection of short stories called *Odessa* by Isaac Babel (1894–1941).[56] Petrović completed the script under the title *Benjie the King*. The script was acquired by Sofracima, but the film was never made.[57] Another more feasible project emerged as an idea in early 1975. According to Branislava Petrović, it was Ginette Billard, wife of *Le Point*'s editor Pierre Billard, who suggested that Petrović think about adapting the German Nobel Prize winner Heinrich Böll's latest novel *Group Portrait with Lady* (*Gruppenbild mit Dame*, 1971).[58] The novel had been well received and Ronald Holloway assumes that it "played a large role in winning the author"[59] this most respected literary prize in 1972. However, there was another crucial reason why Ginette Billard drew Petrović's attention to this German novel. As early as 1972, Petrović had made a provisional agreement with ZDF, the German national television station, to direct a project for them.[60] Since it seemed at the time that he would continue working in Yugoslavia, and he had signed a contract for *Migrations* that year,[61] the work for German television had been put on hold. However, after two years in exile, Petrović decided to reactivate his contacts in Germany, and Böll's book could have provided a sound basis for collaboration.

Petrović first decided to meet Heinrich Böll in Cologne, where the director showed him *The Master and Margarita*, at the writer's request. They then discussed the adaptation of *Group Portrait with Lady*.[62] Böll agreed to work with Petrović after seeing the film, and it is then that Petrović contacted the German producer, Dieter Geisler Filmproduktion, whom he "knew would put the new project together."[63] Petrović thus started work on his first and only entirely non-Yugoslav film. It was also his most expensive and complex project to date, at least in production terms. Petrović also helped to raise funding for the film, which in the end totalled 12 million French francs.[64] According to Petrović, the film was conceived

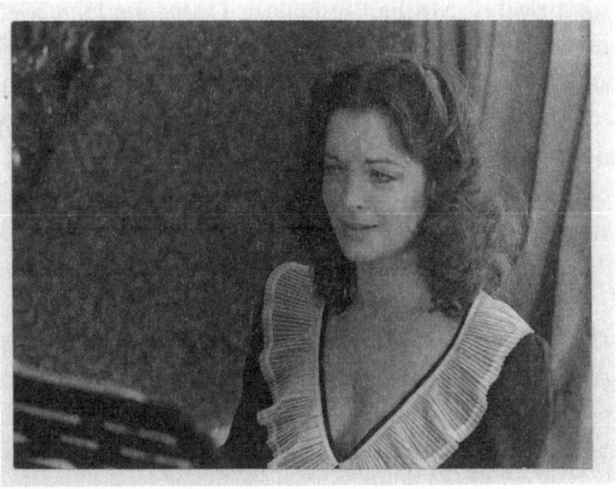

Figure 7.1: *Group Portrait with Lady:* Romy Schneider as Leni Gruyten.

as a German and French co-production, in which finance from Germany amounted to 7 million francs, contributed by ZDF, Stella Film and Cinema 77 from Munich, while 3 million francs came from United Artists – or Les Artistes Associés rather, its European arm in France – with which the latter acquired the international distribution rights.[65] Petrović added that the remaining finance would come from private sources.[66] In April 1976, *Variety* announced that filming would start in August 1976 and that the main star in the film would be the Austrian born – but French domiciled – actress, Romy Schneider.[67] Filming actually started later in autumn 1976,[68] and the film was not completed until 1977. It is known as *Gruppenbild mit Dame* in Germany, *Portrait de groupe avec dame* in France, while, for the sake of brevity, it will be referred to as *Group Portrait* hereafter in this text.

7. 1. 2. Petrović and Heinrich Böll

Heinrich Böll was already an intellectual giant in Germany at the time Aleksandar Petrović met him. Discussing Böll and his work in the early 1970s, James Reid defined the most salient feature of Böll's work as his love for freedom, and the understanding of an artist and intellectual as someone who always questions and redefines this notion. Böll was so committed to this exercise that he often scandalised his compatriots, particularly the more conservative ones. Reid explains that Böll would cause outrage with his speeches, demanding "that art should always 'go too far' in order to test the extent of its so-called freedom; freedom, says Böll, is meaningless unless it is always exploited to its limits."[69] These calls to test the limits of freedom made Böll into something of an outsider in Germany, which became clear when his Nobel Prize award was viewed with suspicion by some sections of the German press.[70] Reid explains this by Böll's major conflict with the German mainstream media, which arose as a result of his demands for a fair trial for the radically left Baader-Meinhof terrorist group.[71] While Böll was concerned with the possible rise of "lynch-justice", by pleading "for understanding," he exposed himself to attacks from the tabloid press, which claimed he was a terrorist sympathiser.[72] Böll, it seems, was only doing what a responsible intellectual or citizen should have done: he promoted a reasonable, sober and humane approach to the grave internal crisis that Germany faced. Moreover, Böll was known as someone who despised bureaucracy of any kind, along with the rigid forms through which state apparatuses usually operate. Reid quotes him as stating:

> Bureaucrats, whether Catholic or Communist, are of necessity cushioned against life, estranged from the world of ordinary people, concerned merely with preserving the status quo which they are paid to administer.[73]

Böll evidently had intricate political views, although he was not committed to any particular political party.[74] According to Reid, Böll's role as writer and intellectual was closer to what German writers cultivated in the 1950s, which Reid describes as follows:

> In the 1950s writers were the conscience of the nation, reminding their readers of the atrocities of the immediate past and protesting against a contemporary pursuit of purely material wealth regardless of the values of justice and humanity.[75]

It would be easy to assume that this description of Böll's artistic prerogatives is reminiscent of Petrović's: Petrović depicted the love of freedom in his *I Even Met Happy Gypsies*, while at the same time meditating on its limits.[76] His exploration of, and support for, marginal groups is also visible in that film, as well as in his documentaries *Record* and *Assemblies*,[77] and in *It Rains in My Village*.[78] Finally, the exploration of state repression through its bureaucratic apparatus and the corrupting influence of materialism were subjects of Petrović's *The Master and Margarita*.[79] Petrović, like Böll, was a responsible intellectual scrutinising society in order to see how it could be improved. Petrović stated in an interview upon the film's subsequent release that he had been pleased to work on the novel as Böll's "conception of the world, and his vision of humankind and life, are very close to mine."[80] In addition, there is a description of Böll in Reid's book which could equally well be applied to Petrović:

> Böll's political standpoint has from the earliest times been formed not by theory, reading political writers, but by experience. His "socialism", if it may be called that, is emotional rather than political.[81]

Consequently, as with Bulgakov, Petrović chose to adapt a work by a writer with whom he shared similar experiences, which – while they were drawn from similar backgrounds – were from different cultures. The novel Petrović adapted together with Böll – *Group Portrait with Lady* – proved to be an interesting and challenging task.

Gruppenbild mit Dame had been published in Germany in 1971 to mixed critical reaction.[82] Although Böll introduced various new elements in his writing, the most important themes of the novel were very much his usual ones, among them, according to Reid, "anti-militarism", and more significantly here "anti-clericalism".[83] These two themes were also interesting and familiar to Petrović, specifically the latter one, leading to another concern he shared with Böll, as well as Bulgakov, and that is a complex relationship to religion.[84] The religious motif here operates on several levels, and it is not only against the Church hierarchy, but is also partially metaphorical. The most prominent characters in the book behave as if they had withdrawn from the system in which they live, the system being that of Nazi Germany. Reid claims that: "The withdrawal of Böll's protagonists is related to the situation of the early Christians in a hostile world".[85] Böll develops this analogy further to examine German post-war society, developing his criticism so far as to show that "the contemporary German administration is by analogy fascist."[86] Böll's inclination to strongly criticise social structures in his country, comparing them to its darkest past, was similar in its method to Petrović's, who has just criticised his own society comparing it to the "darkest" parts of socialist history: the Stalinist purges and repression.

Böll's detailed, multifaceted novel, following the life of a German woman, Leni Gruyten – from her childhood in pre-war Germany, through extraordinary events during the war, and her life twenty years after – had many segments that Petrović could exploit. As he himself had had unforgettable wartime experience, working on this film became another opportunity to revisit them. The fact that this time the story is not a "victorious" Yugoslav one, but a "defeated" German one, left significant space for Petrović to explore his recognised stance on the tragedy of war, and how the pain, suffering and humiliation affect the winners as much as the losers. Petrović emphasised that this dimension of the novel attracted him, as it gave:

> […] the possibility of having another look at Germany; not as one of the executioners with whom we were all too familiar, but from the perspective of a country which had suffered, been wounded and made sacrifices.[87]

Considering the extent of Serbia's and Yugoslavia's traumatic experiences under Nazi occupation,[88] it might have seemed extraordinary that Petrović would have wanted to accept work on such a story, but as Branislava Petrović comments:

> Saša [Petrović] read the novel very carefully, and thought that it offered an opportunity to make a film about "another" Germany. Saša was prone to reconciliation. The real kind of reconciliation, not the one that is born out of fear or calculation, but the one born out of goodness, and the desire for people to live together. That was Saša's nature.[89]

Petrović worked on the script with Böll himself, and the final film reveals thoughts that come out of both of these authors' experiences. However, the film indisputably evokes themes which result from Petrović's life and career up to that point, which will be analysed further below. Perhaps, it is actually easier to detect such elements in this particular film, as it was made entirely outside Yugoslavia and the socialist system. It is clear that he sought to criticise not just a single social structure, but to analyse a more universal concept: one that is destructive in any time or space. If this film is sometimes misunderstood as another project Petrović just worked on while in exile (in order to survive in the West), the words he says in an interview to a German TV channel after its release, defy such views: "I just want to say that I really wanted to make this film."[90]

7. 1. 3. *Group Portrait with Lady* – The Film

In a catholic monastery in 1930s' Germany, Sister Rahel is interrogated about her teaching methods. She is accused of "mystical materialism", and is told that "God should not be looked for, but believed in." She is also asked about her Jewish background, while her young student, Leni Gruyten, is refused communion.

Thirty years later, roses grow on Sister Rahel's grave in December. The nuns are concerned about the phenomenon, and they suspect that Leni Gruyten may be behind it. Sister Clementine is sent to investigate, and she hears Leni playing a piano in her flat, and this moment is used for the narrative to go back in time.

In the same room, during the war, Leni plays the piano to Erhart, her boyfriend, and his younger brother, Heinrich. They are both officers in the German army, but they do not hide their contempt for the war and the Nazis.

Leni's father is an industrialist making bunkers for the army, and is well connected. He helps the brothers get transferred to Denmark, where it is safe. Leni goes to visit them, but they tell her they will desert to Sweden. However, they are both killed in the attempt.

Leni's father is discovered to be a conscientious saboteur of the Third Reich, and is sent to a concentration camp. Leni faces financial ruin, so she finds a job with a local florist, who makes wreaths for dead German soldiers.

A young Soviet prisoner of war – Boris – well-educated and fluent in German, is brought to help at the florist's. Leni sympathises with him at first, and eventually they start an affair.

The war is at an end and Leni is in love with Boris. She organises a fake army document for him, and he assumes the identity of Alfred Bullhorst, a German soldier. Her father comes back alive from the camps, and starts a business with Pelzer, the florist. Boris works with them too, but he gets arrested as Alfred – a German – by the American troops.

Before Leni and Pelzer can help him, he is transferred to a camp in France, where he dies in an accident. Shortly after, Leni's father too, dies in an accident.

Back in the present time of the film, Leni serves tea and biscuits in her flat to all the people she knew during the war, but they are only an apparition. Sister Clementine is there, and she starts dancing with a young gentleman.

7. 1. 4. Petrović's Portrait of Germany

The story of *Group Portrait* is of Leni Gruyten and her love for two men: first a German soldier, and later a Russian prisoner of war, both of whom get tragically killed. The novel therefore, includes the motifs of love and death, so far vividly present in all of Petrović's films. This may perhaps go some way towards explaining the initial affection he had for the project when he decided to make this adaptation for the screen. Petrović and Böll worked on adapting the novel in 1975. Petrović produced the first version on his own, although Böll subsequently convinced him to try again.[91] As *Group Portrait* is a rather voluminous novel, covering thirty years of German history – beginning in the early 1930s with the rise of Nazism, and ending in the mid-1960s with the German economic boom – it had to be radically shortened for the film. Aleksandar Petrović explained: "I made the new version with him [Böll], and I think that this version gave what a film can deliver; because we still had 500 pages of the novel left."[92] To incorporate the narrative of the book into the film, a severe reduction of events and characters had to happen, just as with *The Master and Margarita*. Many significant characters needed to be lost, or amalgamated with others. Böll seems to have understood this as inevitable, and was very fair considering that his novel was being severely abridged for the screen. With a heavy heart, he accepted that one vital character had to go, that of Margret Schlömer,[93] Leni's best friend:

> I understood that there was no space for both characters; purely technically, because film has its own limitations, which we had to respect. I was not too concerned about the elimination of other characters because what the film lost in relationship to the novel, was then shown in another place with different features.[94]

Böll also recognised that the production was slowed down with various other problems, mainly financial ones, which frequently contribute to the frustrations of film production. Böll concluded the collaboration by calling Petrović stubborn, but explained himself:

> When I talk about stubbornness, I talk about stubbornness in the most positive sense. He [Petrović] remained faithful to the structure of the novel, theme, characters, and did so for years. There were many difficulties, questions and financing, borrowings and other problems. But Mister Petrović prevailed.[95]

Where Petrović prevailed in the most constructive way is in the selection of events, from this long and eventful book, in a manner which, as Böll agrees, preserves its principle motifs. Two of these mentioned above are love and death. However, it is precisely in this his only non-Yugoslav film, that it is interesting to focus on the motifs and events that express Petrović's political views of the time. These views are carefully interpolated into the film, and it can be argued that they comment on the political changes he had witnessed in Yugoslavia just before his departure. However, it can equally be argued that they are shown as ills existing in other societies, subscribing to other ideologies, and this is where this film may be read as Petrović's work. It is pertinent to note that Petrović opens the film with an interrogation of a nun in a catholic monastery in 1930s Germany. Sister Rahel is accused of non-orthodox practices, and is judged by a panel of her peers. While her practices may not appear exceptional to us, she still has to answer for those actions that do not strictly follow the canon. Most importantly, she is reminded that "God should not be looked for, but believed in." It is often pointed out that Böll hated bureaucracy, and believed in the appeal to common sense. This first scene exposes something of Böll's beliefs, and experiences as a Catholic. However, it is also clear that this first scene carries something which is very much related to Petrović's experience. As a filmmaker in Yugoslavia, particularly before his departure, he often sat in front of similar panels where his work was criticised by his peers, who were somehow seen as more "faithful" than himself.[96] Thus, to question a given dogma, primarily with common sense, is something that crystallises itself in Petrović's films as a central motif, now also born out of his own recent experiences.[97] While Maksudov, the Master from the previous film, answered to a panel of communist writers who were his colleagues, Sister Rahel is questioned by a group of Catholic nuns, her peers. To make her more of a Petrović character, Rahel is also a social outsider, a Jew in Nazi Germany. Sister Rahel's answers are genuine and she admits her Jewish origins, but reasserts that she is a Christian. However, her practice is not to be condoned. Just as the Master had departed from the dialectical materialist dogma in *The Master and Margarita*, Sister Rahel has strayed from the Catholic dogma. Both of these stories are fully reminiscent of Petrović's experiences, as well as of those of many similar intellectuals in Yugoslavia, who strayed from Tito's and Kardelj's path during the early 1970s.[98] The two leaders used force to keep everyone on this path, while intellectuals, such as Petrović, were also indirectly told to believe in rather than to search for. Consequently, by opening the film with an event and character that are only introduced in the second chapter of the novel, Petrović rearranges the events so that his own immediate experience can be brought to the fore, and which then sets the tone for the whole film. The opening scene of the film shows dogmatism as repressive, represented here by the Catholic hierarchy, although as Böll famously wrote: "bureaucrats, catholic or communist, are alike." Petrović, along with Böll, does not criticise ideological content, but the means by which it is imposed, particularly when these are dogmatic, and contrary to reason and common sense. By showing this idea through a dispute in the teaching methods of a Catholic monastery, Petrović explores the notion of religious teaching as ideology. Exploring religion in society is the second of his four political themes and now forms also a section of this film. Religious teaching in this film, however, is not perceived as marginalised in the way that it was in *The Master and Margarita*, which was set in the Soviet Union. Here, Petrović is concerned with what happens with such teachings when they are imposed dogmatically.

To reiterate his anti-dogmatic point, Petrović returns to the motive of such dogmatic rigidity within the next few scenes, elaborating further his and Böll's corresponding view. When, thirty years after the interrogation, roses start to grow on Sister Rahel's grave in December, to evade requests for the sanctification of this intentionally marginalised colleague,[99] the nuns order an investigation to pre-empt the possible claims of a miracle. The investigation is entrusted to the young and assertive Sister Clementine, who invites Walter Pelzer, Leni's former employer at the florist's, for an interview. As Pelzer arrives in the reception room and starts to speak, he politely asks whether he may smoke. It is clear that Sister Clementine is uneasy about this, as the ascetic monastic life should not permit indulgence in such ephemeral earthly pleasures. Still, to please her guest, from whom she needs information, she allows him to do so. Politely, Pelzer offers Clementine a cigarette, as is customary. Clementine, not surprisingly, refuses. Then, in a long moment of silence, she changes her mind, accepts a cigarette, lights it and astutely comments on the superiority of Virginia tobacco. She adds that her smoking should not be mentioned to her peers, as it is evidently "against the rules". Therefore, within the first ten minutes of the film, Petrović makes another comment on the futility of dogmatic beliefs, adhered to against one's own nature. This is exemplified with Sister Clementine's passion for smoking that is in opposition to the uniform she wears. Such criticism was usually aimed at the duplicity of communist morals in Petrović's previous work, but has here found an equivalent target, now that he found himself in the West. History had so far, perhaps, shown that the western liberal-capitalist model was more vital and sustainable than the state organised socialist one.[100] Petrović, as an artist who questioned the very foundations of socialism, relentlessly poking at its inconsistencies, had now decided to do the same in the West, similarly exposing its ideological foundations to scrutiny.[101] The liberal capitalist countries still based their morals on Christianity, as opposed to the rationality of Marxist dialectical materialism in the (former) East. It is the flaws within this western ideological – essentially religious – structure that Petrović was

Figure 7.2: Yugoslav actress Milena Dravić as Sister Clementine and French actor Michel Galabru as Walter Pelzer, wartime owner of the florist.

prepared to uncover, and it was precisely these parts of Böll's novel that Petrović reorganised for the screen.

That examination of dogmatism is of crucial importance to Petrović is clear as he persistently returns to this question within the narrative, although later he shifts it away from the Catholic nuns and religion. As soon as Erhart and Heinrich Schweigert are introduced in the storyline – two out of the three active German soldiers that Petrović fully develops as characters in the film – it is immediately clear that another dogma is to be probed. In the first scene in which the brothers are introduced, Heinrich has his army jacket unbuttoned, and his feet on the coffee table. When he is reproached by his older brother for this, he jumps up, shouting phrases from a German army manual, repeating the stereotypes about German "innate inclination towards discipline". He then sits back angrily, histrionics amplified, his jacket still dishevelled, and puts his feet on the table again. He thus becomes a living image of a German who is deliberately different from the image created and imposed – through army manuals and their infamous brutality – by the German Nazis. It is this playful meditation on images that is a key strategy employed by Petrović from his earlier work. It is exemplified here with the juxtaposition of a German created by an ideology that was notoriously and self-destructively dogmatic, with that of a young German who refuses to conform to this ideology. Petrović employed this strategy consistently ever since his documentary *Assemblies*, where the images from the medieval frescoes were juxtaposed with similar images in a contemporary world.[102] In *Group Portrait*, Petrović plays with the image of German soldiers held by most "outsiders" to the country at that time, probably including himself, as opposed to the images and self-perceptions that the same characters had of themselves. In the scenes that follow (conclusively, with their tragic attempt to desert to Sweden), the two brothers have nothing but profound contempt for the life that the Nazis had conceived for Germany. They thus have nothing to do with the stereotypical image of German soldiers in World War II as senseless and belligerent killing machines.[103] When later, Boris' guard Boldig is introduced in the narrative, another active German soldier, the image of a German everyman is not very different from that of the two brothers. This character is again far from the robotically committed soldier that Hitler wanted his "warriors" to be. The character of Boldig is, as in the novel, just trying to survive.[104] He is venal but good spirited, willing to help indiscriminately and clearly has nothing against Boris simply because Boris is Russian. To emphasise the humanity of these characters representing the foot soldiers of the German army, Petrović briefly introduces the character of Simon, a German soldier who is a victim of Nazi indoctrination. Simon was to kill Boldig in the film, by simply "following orders". He hence stands for someone who has intentionally suspended common sense and "the universal sense of moral" (as Ellendea Proffer defines the ideologically deluded characters in Bulgakov's novel, but applicable here as well),[105] in order to adhere to a given set of rules. However, Simon is only a boy, a minor drafted into the German army in 1945 (when it was facing a crushing defeat), thus his susceptibility to Nazi dogma is unsurprising. Not that Petrović claims that teenagers were the only ones seduced by Nazism: he develops numerous other characters who also come close to "evil" in times of hardship. While Petrović exposes the human shortcomings that bring them to such a position, he does not justify them, but seeks instead to explain their actions. Similarly to the characters in *Three*, his other war film set in a very different environment, these characters struggle and often fail to remain morally sound under pressure, while the audience is left to meditate upon these nadirs of human misjudgement without guidance or didacticism.[106] Petrović's construction of such subtly nuanced contradictory traits of his characters also comes to the fore in this film.

Perhaps the most complex figure in *Group Portrait* is Walter Pelzer, the owner of the florist's which, as it was wartime, was busy making floral wreaths for dead German soldiers. Pelzer initially comes across as opportunistic and venal, and he is even seen stealing a wreath from a grave so that it can be quickly overhauled and sold again. His employees perceive him as shifty, but Petrović also reveals a different side to this character: the stolen wreath becomes a prelude to two conversations on the state of the Third Reich. Pelzer has the first conversation with the Russian prisoner Boris and his guard Boldig, while the second unfolds in the florist's with all the workers present. Pelzer reminds them that the

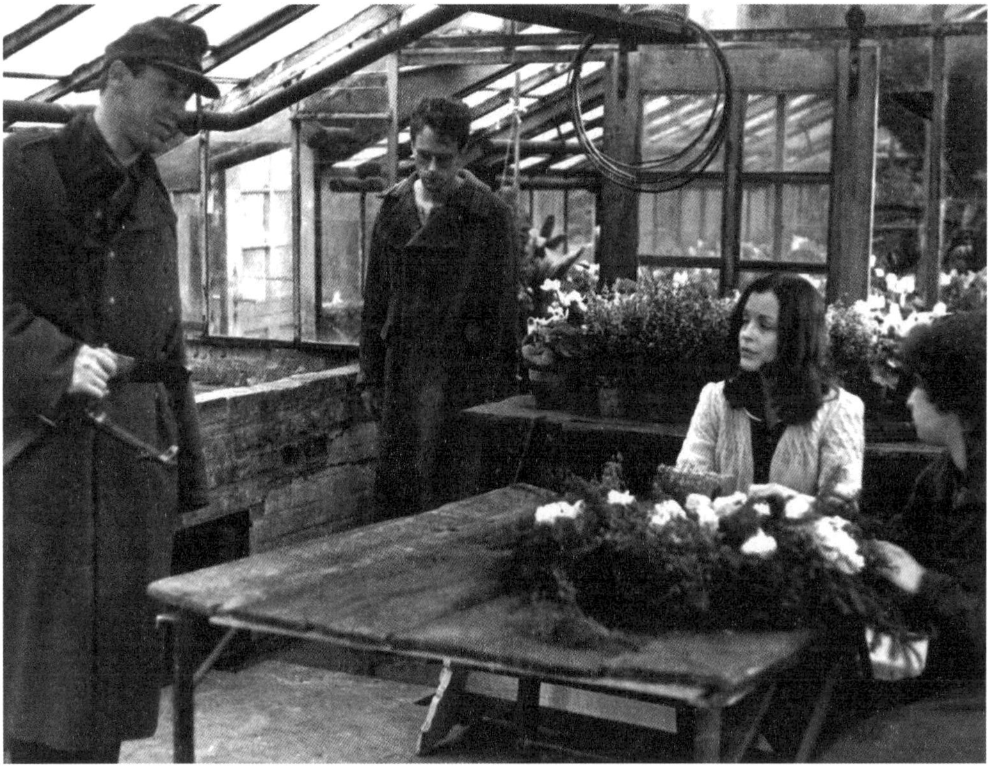

Figure 7.3: At the florist: German actor Rüdiger Vogler as Boldig (left), American Brad Dourif as Boris, and Austrian and French Romy Schneider as Leni.

work they do is of primary national importance, as each hero fallen on the front for the German fatherland deserves a wreath of his own. However, Pelzer adds, considering the numbers of young men dying, particularly on the Eastern Front, his small shop simply cannot handle the demand. Therefore, the wreaths are frequently "recycled", and they now have to make sure not to put the family names on them, just the first names of the dead. So the same wreath with common German names such as Hans or Otto does not even have to be changed: all they have to do is to wait for another of these namesakes to die, whereupon the wreaths can be reused. Pelzer also reminds his staff that the corpses of most of these young men are lying somewhere on the battlefields of the Eastern Front. The bodies will never be recovered, but regardless, an open grave and a wreath for these fallen soldiers exists in their hometowns in Germany. It is difficult to take Pelzer's diatribe entirely seriously, but it would also be difficult to claim that he is just mischievously cynical. In any case, his defence of the business – and his business savvy methods – as being of national importance, clearly remind us that Adolf Hitler had turned Germany into one large open grave, continually expecting more devastation.

To make the overall situation more complex, and consequently more appropriate for a Petrović film, the Russian prisoner of war, Boris, is brought to the shop to help out, as his work duty, unpaid, of course. One of the employees in the shop, Krempf, is an evidently disgruntled and spiteful German ex-soldier, who has lost his leg on the Eastern Front. As he is now incapable of fighting, he works in the shop and, apart from the boss Pelzer, is the only man amongst the many women working there. As soon as Boris is brought in, Krempf openly shows his dislike for him, exclaiming that he only likes seeing dead Russians. This prompts Boldig to harshly remind him that he is responsible for Boris, and that as his guard, he has to bring him to the shop every morning alive, and also take him back alive to the prisoner of war camp in the evening. Boldig, a disciplined German soldier, reminds another German soldier that here, duty comes first. In addition, quite brutally, Boldig tells Krempf that if he really wants to kill Russians, he can go back to the front, jumping there on his one leg. After this insult, Boldig smiles and lifts his left arm to wave at him with an empty coat sleeve, as he has lost his arm on that same front in Russia. If Pelzer's character was used to remind us that Hitler brought Germany only death and misery, then the characters of Boldig and Krempf are used to remind us that he has also scarred and crippled those who survived. As in his Yugoslav set war drama *Three*, Petrović's stance could not be more unambiguously against the war. However, this position is not presented as a simplistic pacifist eulogy – which was quite common in similar films of the period – but its austere restraint and dark humour convey this anti-war feeling in a specifically mordant way, as demonstrated in this scene between the two German soldiers.

The introduction of Boris as a character, a Russian prisoner in Germany, enables Petrović to introduce the first of his four political themes, that of interethnic relationships. While this is the only theme that had been neglected in his previous film, *The Master and Margarita*,[107] here it is given almost central importance. Although the character of Professor Woland in the previous film was perceived as a foreigner in Moscow, Petrović, whilst juggling numerous other strands in this complex novel's adaptation, had to drop this one, and did not develop it into a fully coherent theme. In *Group Portrait*, on the other hand, the love of the German woman, Leni, for the Russian soldier Boris during the war, and the process of learning to know and accept the "Other", on and from both sides, becomes the backbone of the whole film. Petrović returns fully to his examination of the nature of ethnic identity and belonging. When Boris is brought to the florist's, jaws literally drop at the sight of him, since, as we soon find out, most of the employees there have never seen a Russian in their life. The only one who has is Krempf, who lost his leg to them on the front line. His somewhat extreme view – that the Russians he wants to see are dead ones – may therefore come as no surprise. However, Boris, deftly played by the American actor Brad Dourif, is, again in a very Petrović way, in stark contrast to how the Russian Red Army soldiers were portrayed to Germans through their own war propaganda. Boris, who is more fey than bear-like and boorish, is thin, shy and bespectacled. Above all, he speaks excellent German. As a trained engineer, he contributes good ideas for improving the performance of the shop's production, which also perhaps explains how as a prisoner he has earned such a privileged job.[108] Slowly, he wins almost everyone over. Boris is also familiar with German poetry, and loudly recites verses by Georg Trakl,[109] thereby attracting more than just the attention of Leni Gruyten. More importantly for Petrović, it is Boris' relationship with Krempf that cannot be changed, as the latter continues to despise him. Krempf has never heard of Georg Trakl, and he reports Boris to the Gestapo for singing Russian songs. The question Petrović indirectly raises is who is more of a German here: the Russian Boris, operating as some repository of German culture that he evidently knows and admires, or Krempf, who only knows that he is German as he fought against its "Other", the Russians. Rather, Petrović again raises the question of the relativity of ethnic belonging and identity in general. As he did in *I Even Met Happy Gypsies* in the Yugoslav context,[110] here he does the same in a wider European context. It is emphasised in the film that Leni, in her old age, cried on the grave of one Alfred Bullhorst, a German soldier, in whose grave Boris is buried. In order to help Boris, Leni buys a fake German identity card for him in the name of Alfred Bullhorst. However, Boris is then arrested as Alfred, a German soldier, by the incoming American troops. Before his real identity is revealed to the Americans, he has already died in a prisoner of war camp in France, this time among Germans, as "one of them". That a Russian lies in a German grave is a typical Petrović comment, pointing to the futility of war and of hatred towards the "Other". In actual fact, the scene toward the end of the film, when Boris has now left his unguarded prisoner of war camp to look for Leni with another Russian inmate, emphasises this thought again. While they are cooking a stew from whatever they could find on the heap of rubble into which frequent bombardments had turned this German town, Boldig accidentally meets them. As these three "century old enemies" eat and chat on the mountain of debris – all that remains of their cities – one has no doubt of what Petrović thinks about war, and in particular this grand war of the mid-twentieth century. He successfully demonstrates how futile and destructive it was, to the level where the film could be used to illustrate the ideological roots of the European Union, based on the mutual promise between France and Germany: Never again![111]

In this complex weaving of storylines, Petrović does not forget his "polyvalent" view.[112] It may appear, for example, that Krempf comes across as a dim and spiteful character, regardless of Petrović's explanation of his history. But in his economical fashion, Petrović uses Krempf to reveal another nuance of the then ideologically divided Europe. When the employees at the florist's have a coffee break, Krempf barks that no coffee should be given to Boris, as he gets his ration of coffee in the camp. Leni gives him a cup anyway, and Krempf aggressively pushes it off the table with his crutch. Leni, always a rebel, then goes and makes Boris a special cup of coffee, from high quality beans which she has bought on the black market, and which she usually keeps only for herself. Disgruntled, Krempf complains about wasting high quality coffee on "a Bolshevik".[113] Here, indirectly of course, one is reminded that communist ideology emphasised ideas of equality to such a degree that industrial production forfeited high quality products, which by their nature are produced in smaller quantities, in favour of the mass production of "simpler" goods, but available to all. Krempf's comment shows that he is not dim, but in his own way too conscientious about why he thinks his enemy does not deserve a good cup of coffee. As mentioned above, such careful shading of Petrović's characters is most in evidence in that of Pelzer, the florist shop's boss, and the film is actually his recollection to Sister Clementine of all these stories. With the introduction of a Gestapo officer, for two scenes only, with Pelzer in both, Petrović introduces the third of his four political themes – that of the relationship of privileged to underprivileged groups: in this case, between the members of the Nazi party and those who are not. The Gestapo Officer arrives at the shop to investigate whether Boris was actually singing Russian songs, which is, of course, forbidden. Pelzer defends Boris and dismisses such a report as ridiculous. He also explains that Boris speaks German just like a German, and that the song he sang was a German song. Even though Pelzer convinces the Officer to leave them all in peace, the Officer is coldly arrogant, emanating that air of superiority for which the Nazis were notorious. The Officer actually only gives in when Pelzer reminds him that he too is a member of the party, thus "one of them". As the vagaries of politics are unpredictable, we later see the Gestapo Officer in civilian clothes, his stern superiority replaced with a meek sense of loss, as he desperately tries to escape from the advancing Americans. He has come to plead with Pelzer to give him his motorcycle, which the latter refuses. When the Officer reminds him that they are both party members, Pelzer tells him that he returned his card a week ago, by recorded delivery so he has a receipt, and that he has nothing to do with him or his clique anymore. The notion of political privilege, as well as of class and ethnicity, are all fragile human constructions in Petrović's films.

Petrović, regardless of the various strands within this story, makes sure he shows Germany under Nazism as very different from that which the Nazis intended. Again, Petrović's concern, as in his Yugoslav films, is to confront an ideological image with one that is probably closer to "the real". In all these films, a discrepancy emerges in such a portrayal; a discrepancy which Petrović offers as proof of the pitfalls of dogmatism and the political desires of the powers that be. With *Group Portrait*, he carries his experience from the system in which he lived to that of another, filtering out what was important in this experience, so as to make it universal. It is dogmatism that destroys societies and states, as it alienates its subjects from the system. The case study in this Petrović's film is Nazi Germany, while in Heinrich Böll's source novel, certain phenomena of post-war Germany, such as its economic boom, were compared to fascism, also including motifs of the passive inhumanness of the Church. In conjunction with Petrović's body of work which tackled dogmatism in socialism, the overall picture of the film is dominated by this very broad stroke portraying dogma as a societal evil which is no longer time or space specific, but is exposed as a universal problem corroding all societies present and future. Petrović's protagonists struggle to resist the stereotypes and expectations dogmatically imposed and enforced by social structures, which deny the protagonists their right to question or criticise. It is clear that Petrović focuses strongly on the examination of dogmatism in this film, which is the fourth and ultimate political theme pervading his work. It is the theme on which he focused significantly in *It Rains in My Village* and *The Master and Margarita*, so it can be concluded that with *Group Portrait* this motif strongly establishes itself as a crucial component of Petrović's work.

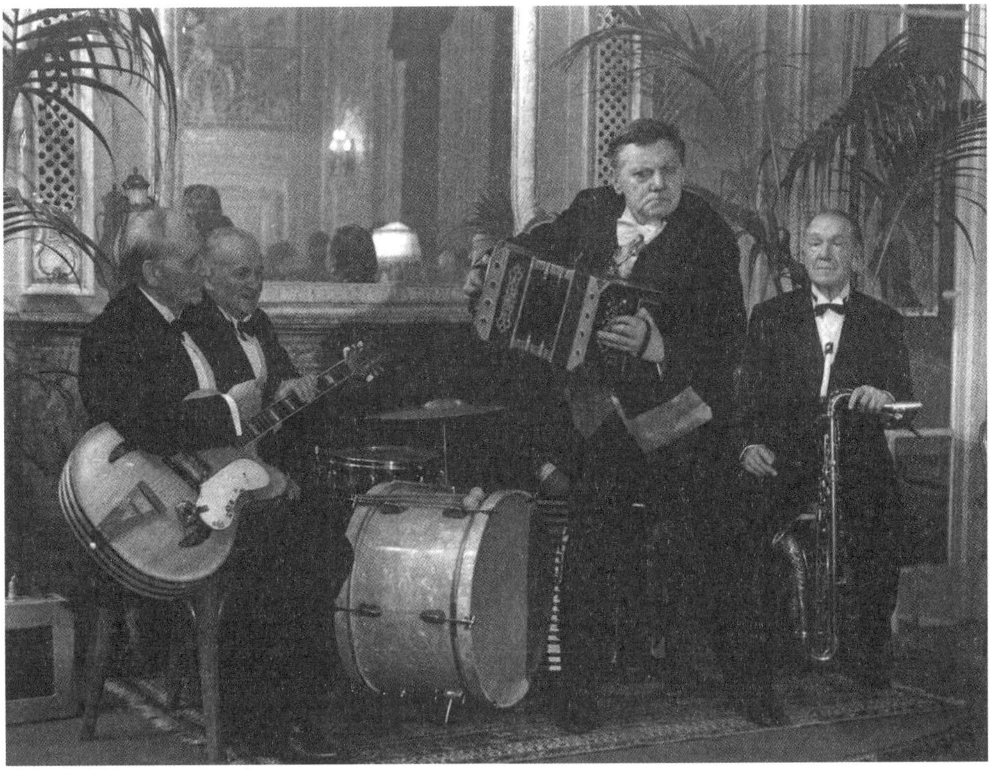

Figure 7.4: *Group Portrait:* as the Reich is falling apart, the band plays on.

7. 1. 5. Style and Reception of the *Portrait*

Petrović premiered *Group Portrait with Lady* at the Cannes Film Festival in 1977 and the film was Germany's official entry for that year. Consequently, the German version of the film was screened with a German soundtrack. There was also another version of the film with French dialogue. The film was a German and French co-production, in the same way that *The Master and Margarita* had been a Yugoslav and Italian co-production. The latter was also released in two versions – one spoken in Italian, the other in Serbo-Croat. The German and French versions of *Group Portrait* were initially pretty much the same,[114] the difference being the dubbing of the actors into different languages. The star of the film, Romy Schneider, who played Leni Gruyten, proved to be an ideal choice as an Austrian-born French actress. She spoke her German lines in the film for the German version, and then dubbed herself into French for the French version. However, the rest of the cast was truly international,[115] and Petrović resorted to an interesting, if unusual, strategy by which everyone spoke their lines in their own language. Afterwards, the French actor Michel Galabru's lines in French were kept in the French version of the film, while he was dubbed into German for the German version. In the same way, German actors in the film, such as Rüdiger Vogler (Wim Wenders' favourite at the time), Richard Münch, Rudolph Schündler, and others were dubbed in French, while their German was kept in the German version. Petrović also invited actors from Yugoslavia, most notably Black Film regulars Eva Ras, who played Sister Rahel, and Milena Dravić, who played Sister Clementine. Petrović's regular, Velimir Bata Živojinović, played a Russian prisoner of war, while Mija Aleksić and Dragomir Gidra Bojanić had smaller parts. The main male protagonist, Russian prisoner of war Boris, was played by the American actor Brad Dourif. Petrović had these actors speak their lines in their own languages, in order to be able to support their performances, and they were then dubbed into French and German. This created an interesting situation with actors speaking to each other in different languages in the same scene. Michel Galabru praised this strategy, taking as an example the scene in which he addresses Milena Dravić's Clementine in French, while she responds in Serbian.[116] Galabru stated that using this strategy, the dialogues were turned into music, to which he as an actor responded: different languages enabled a "reinvention of dialogue."[117] Film critics, however, particularly the German ones, did not share this opinion. As the dubbing of actors in different languages created an inconsistency between their lip movements and the words spoken, Hellmuth Karasek in *Der Spiegel* stated that in the film "the lips don't know what the mouth says."[118] This discrepancy was emphasised by the fact that Petrović remained faithful to his favourite stylistic device – the frequent use of close-ups – which exacerbated the synchronisation issue. The use of close-ups was savaged by the German critics, with Hans Blumenberg of *Die Zeit* denouncing them as television aesthetic.[119] Karasek similarly took every opportunity to criticise the use of close-ups, explaining that all they allow viewers to do is to "count each pore and every stubble in this face parade."[120] However, Petrović had a propensity for using close-ups in all his films, even the ones made prior to television taking over, and he maintained this in *Group Portrait*, where for the first and only time, he worked with the acclaimed French cinematographer, Pierre William Glenn. Petrović was aware that close-ups suit television aesthetics, and when, in 1970, his films were shown on Yugoslav television, he stated: "I would think that my film aesthetic is close to that of television's, which is because I give special attention to the frequent use of close-ups."[121] In this respect, the criticism that Petrović succumbed to television aesthetics was incorrect, as he was faithful to his own style. Nevertheless, the close-ups exacerbated the problem of dubbing and synchronising actors, which in Germany in particular justified a specific critical trend.

After its premiere at the Cannes Film Festival, the German press was heavily, negatively critical towards the film. At the time, *Die Zeit* reported that the film was "idiotic",[122] that it "went catastrophically wrong",[123] and was "an illiterate, painful rendering of Böll's novel," where it is "sheer coincidence what it achieves."[124] Karasek of *Der Spiegel* was similarly unambiguously negative, stating that the film "excretes the cinematic sweat of strenuousness."[125] It is easy though, to notice one major problem the German press had with the production: *Group Portrait* was a quintessentially German novel, dealing with an exceptionally sensitive part of German history. That the novel was made into a film by, as Karasek puts it, "a Yugoslav director with a French cameraman, as a German-French co-production for an American renting agency [he is referring here, somewhat pejoratively, to United Artists, the distributor], with Yugoslav actresses as German nuns, and an American as a Russian,"[126] was perceived by *Die Zeit* as a "hit below the belt against German cinema."[127] *Die Zeit* also went so far as to develop a "cinematic" conspiracy theory that Maurice Bessy, the then director of the Cannes Festival, had chosen this film for competition deliberately to show German cinema as "rubbish [*müll*],"[128] while there were considerably better German films, such as those by Niklaus Schilling (*Vertreibung aus dem Paradies*) and Werner Herzog (*Stroszek*).[129] That the German press was outraged by Germany being represented through this "international" film could be concluded by Karasek's remark that *Group Portrait* was a "homeless film about the homeland [*heimatloseren Heimatfilm*]."[130] Despite these vicious attacks on the film, in 1977 Romy Schneider received the Federal Republic of (former West) Germany Film Prize for her role in the film. The film was also awarded this state funded prize as the Best Film made in Germany that year.[131] American *Variety* was also exceedingly positive about the film, in which Ronald Holloway explained that: "Emotional changes of expression on the screen are Petrović's unique trademark," concluding that "United Artists may have a critical winner at Cannes."[132]

However, the film received no awards at Cannes, while its reception in France was mixed. Although the film was not seen through the German concept of *heimat* in France, other issues surfaced in its critical reception. As with *The Master and Margarita*, these issues were to do with the film being based on a famous novel, one complex to adapt to another medium. Michel Sineux, writing in *Positif*, assessed the adaptation as a "rubbish cinematic transposition," thus the film should not be seen, but "the book should be read."[133] His overtly negative review ends by admitting that he was "appalled" by *I Even Met Happy Gypsies*, as well as *The Master and Margarita*, concluding that he did not like Petrović's work at all.[134] Philippe Carcassonne, on the other hand, was positive about the film, finding fault only with

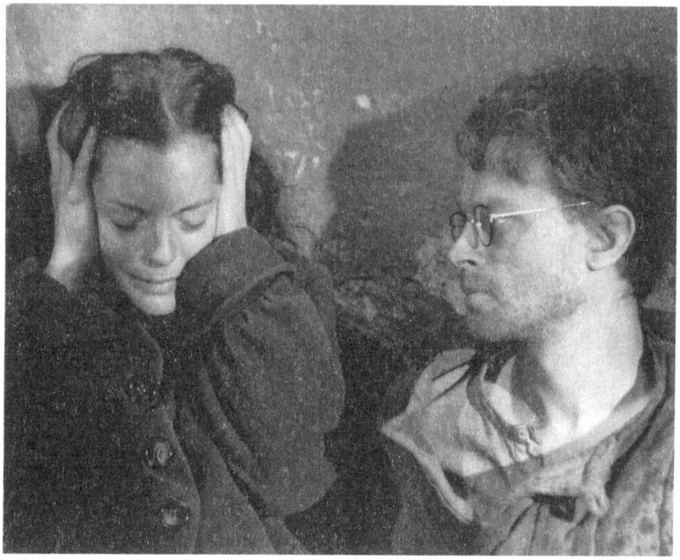

Figure 7.5: Breakdown under frequent bombardments in close-up: Romy Schneider and Brad Dourif as Leni and Boris.

the adaptation, although he explained: "I am not reproaching Petrović for his infidelity to Böll's book, but quite the contrary, for his scrupulous respect for the text."[135] Carcassonne praised the film for being "more suggestive than enunciated," and "forming a network of ideas and feelings," putting them forward "without didacticism."[136] It is interesting that a similar understanding of the film could be found in the German press, although this was not published until years after the dust of Cannes had settled, when the film was shown on German television. Clara Menck claimed that Zero Hour,[137] as depicted in the film, presents a "convincing picture", further explaining that:

> There is an unforgettable image of people who one after the other walk into the wreckage of a city in a suddenly deadly silent break of dawn; there are images of the same flowers which lay on two very different graves and tell more about the mischief of dying than many words would; and there are many minor characters who impressively illustrate how individuals relent under the pressure of circumstances.[138]

What Menck and Carcassonne recognised and praised was Petrović's aim or objective, an objective best described in an earlier interview in which he stated: "I am not explaining ideas, I dramatise psychological and emotional states, and not action."[139] Petrović was thus interested in "internal life."[140] This explains why some critics, such as Karasek, have found the film demanding or "strained", since Petrović (as with his Yugoslav films) was not interested in action, but in emotions. This obviously failed some critical expectations in the

West, particularly considering the subject matter and the novel's acclaim. Regardless, it can be concluded that *Group Portrait* can be perceived as very much a Petrović film, both stylistically and in terms of its narrative.

Notes

1 Dejan Jović, *Jugoslavija – Država koja je odumrla: Uspon, kriza i pad Četvrte Jugoslavije* (Beograd: Samizdat B92; Zagreb: Prometej, 2003), p. 18.
2 Dejan Jović, *Jugoslavija*, p. 155.
3 Dejan Jović, *Jugoslavija*, p. 452.
4 Dejan Jović, *Jugoslavija*, pp. 102–03.
5 Dejan Jović, *Jugoslavija*, p. 103.
6 Quoted in Dejan Jović, *Jugoslavija*, p. 195.
7 I would be tempted to disagree on theoretical grounds with this suggestion by Jović; however, as Jović talks about the experience extrapolated from the former socialist countries of Eastern Europe, specifically taking Yugoslavia as his case study, with historical hindsight it would be very difficult not to agree with his assumption in this instance.
8 Dejan Jović, *Jugoslavija*, p. 396.
9 See the previous chapter (particularly its opening).
10 Dejan Jović, *Jugoslavija*, p. 8.
11 John R. Lampe, *Yugoslavia as History: Twice There Was a Country* (Cambridge: Cambridge University Press, 1996), p. 306.
12 I would disagree with Glenny that the constitution was "mere window dressing". However, I think that Glenny probably uses this here as a figure of speech only, to emphasise his conclusion that Tito and Kardelj were the true power holders in the country – a conclusion with which it is difficult to disagree. Later in the chapter, he discusses the legacy of the constitution, himself showing that it meant more than "window dressing".
13 Misha Glenny, *The Balkans 1804–1999: Nationalism, War and the Great Powers* (London: Granta Books, 1999), p. 623.
14 John R. Lampe, *Yugoslavia as History*, p. 308.
15 Jasna Dragović-Soso, *'Saviours of the Nation': Serbia's Intellectual Opposition and the Revival of Nationalism* (London: Hurst & Company, 2002), p. 49.
16 See Chapter 6 (section 6.2).
17 Quoted in Jasna Dragović-Soso, *'Saviours of the Nation'*, p. 49.
18 Jasna Dragović-Soso, *'Saviours of the Nation'*, p. 104.
19 Michael J. Stoil, *Balkan Cinema: Evolution After The Revolution* (Ann Arbor, MI: UMI Research Press, 1979), p. 132.
20 Daniel J. Goulding, *Liberated Cinema: The Yugoslav Experience* (Bloomington: Indiana University Press, 1985), p. 143; Goulding states that there were 19 films completed in 1973, 17 in 1974, 18 in 1975, 16 in 1976 and 18 in 1977.
21 Daniel J. Goulding, *Liberated Cinema*, p. 143.
22 Personal interview with Branka Petrović (11 September 2005).

23 See an unsigned article: "Petrović Vitez lepih umetnosti", *Mladina*, 3 November 1969.

24 From an unsigned article: "Vitez lepih umetnosti", *Radio revija*, 8 October 1971.

25 See Chapter 1 (section 1.2.1).

26 See the previous chapter (section 6.2.1).

27 See the preface to Aleksandar Petrović's script *Emanuela*, written by his wife Branka Petrović; in Aleksandar Petrović, *1973. Godina vampira: Emanuela II, Baron vampir, Džon F. Kenedi* (Beograd: Autorska izdanja, Foto Futura, 2010), p. 11.

28 Personal interview with Branka Petrović (11 September 2005).

29 See the preface to Aleksandar Petrović's script *Emanuela*, written by his wife Branka Petrović; in Aleksandar Petrović, *1973. Godina vampira*, p. 11; and from a personal interview with Branka Petrović (11 September 2005).

30 It is interesting to note that István Dosai, who generously helped Petrović during his move, was considerably more cautious when it came to Hungary's internal affairs and filmmakers. The Hungarian director Károly Makk remembers that Dosai personally made a report to the Hungarian Minister of Culture, which stalled his production of the film *Love* (*Szerelem*, 1970) based on a text by the "dissident" Tibor Déry; see an interview with Károly Makk in David Robinson, "Szerelem, Love", in *The Cinema of Central Europe*, ed. by Peter Hames, (London, New York: Wallflower Press, 2004), p. 176.

31 Personal interview with Branka Petrović (11 September 2005).

32 ibid.

33 See the preface to Aleksandar Petrović's script *Emanuela*, written by his wife Branka Petrović; in Aleksandar Petrović, *1973. Godina vampira*, pp. 11–12.

34 ibid.

35 See Chapter 5 (particularly the introduction to section 5.1).

36 On when Lelouch was Petrović's guest in Belgrade see an unsigned article "Najslabša moški in ženska…", *Tovariš*, 17 December 1968, p. 56.

37 An interview with Branka Petrović, see Dajana Djedović, "O reditelju Saši Petroviću i njegovim filmovima", in *Prizor*, (annual magazine), issue no 2., ed. by Snežana Nešković-Simić (articles on Aleksandar Petrović ed. by Radoslav Lazić), (Loznica: Centar za kulturu 'Vuk Karadžić', 2003), p. 92.

38 ibid.

39 With Paul Thomas Anderson's *Boogie Nights* (USA, 1997), soft porn became part of Hollywood and very much part of the mainstream; however *Emmanuelle* was made more than 20 years previously. In addition, it could be argued that *Sex and the City* from the late 1990s further affirmed this trend.

40 An interview with Branka Petrović, see Dajana Djedović, "O reditelju Saši Petroviću i njegovim filmovima", p. 92.

41 It is worth remembering here that Petrović boasted how he would not use sexual exploitation in his own films (see Chapter 5 – introduction to section 5.1). However, *Emmanuelle* was a film of a different genre, entirely based on this kind of exploitation.

42 Branka Petrović published her husband's script *Emmanuelle 2* as *Emanuela* – in Serbian – in 2010. Branka Petrović also wrote a preface for this edition, which describes their

situation in Yugoslavia, and the *Plastic Jesus* case and their persecution, in great depth and detail.

43　An interview with Branka Petrović, see Dajana Djedović, "O reditelju Saši Petroviću i njegovim filmovima", p. 92.

44　To anyone with a basic understanding of colloquial English it may appear that the name of *Emmanuelle*'s first director – Just Jaeckin – is most likely invented. However, it is not, and the director later made his name famous, directing similar types of films. There is an interesting debate on this issue of using *nom de plume* in another mainstream, albeit European film, *The Pornographer* (*Le Pornographe*, France, 2001) by Bertrand Bonello.

45　Francis Giacobetti, the famous French photographer, was well known for his photographs of Cuba and its revolutionaries, the artist Francis Bacon, as well as some much stylised nudes. He is unusual as a photographer in that he photographed Pirelli's calendar twice, and is known as the person who revolutionised the calendar's image in the early 1970s. He later said of his photographs that whatever they are about, "the human factor always stands at the centre." This humanism could be related to Petrović's, although this would perhaps be stretching the argument too far. However, what could be said for certain is that the producer, Rousset-Rouard, chose his team with great care.

46　See the preface to Aleksandar Petrović's script *Emanuela*, written by his wife Branka Petrović; in Aleksandar Petrović, *1973. Godina vampira*, p. 12.

47　These two scripts are available in Aleksandar Petrović, *1973. Godina vampira: Emanuela II, Baron vampir, Džon F. Kenedi* (Beograd: Autorska izdanja, Foto Futura, 2010).

48　See the preface to Aleksandar Petrović's script *Emanuela*, written by his wife Branka Petrović; in Aleksandar Petrović, *1973. Godina vampira*, p. 12.

49　Graham Petrie, "Introduction", in *Before the Wall Came Down: Soviet and East European Filmmakers Working in the West*, ed. by Graham Petrie and Ruth Dwyer, (Lanham, MD: University Press of America, 1990), p. 13 (note 3); see the whole essay on the issue of migrating filmmakers.

50　See Herbert Eagle, "Polanski" in *Five Filmmakers: Tarkovsky, Forman, Polanski, Szabó, Makavejev*, ed. by Daniel Goulding, (Bloomington, Indianapolis: Indiana University Press, 1994), p. 115.

51　Lattuada completed and released the film in 1975 as *Cuore di cane*, or *Dog's Heart* for international release, with the well-known Swedish actor Max Von Sydow in the main role.

52　See Milica Zdražilová, "Gladiátor z arény zvané jugoslávská kinematografie", *Film A Doba*, January, 1989, p. 49.

53　Ellendea Proffer, *Bulgakov: Life and Work* (Ann Arbor, Michigan: Ardis, 1984), p. 230.

54　Ellendea Proffer, *Bulgakov*, p. 324.

55　Ellendea Proffer, *Bulgakov*, p. 322.

56　An interview with Aleksandar Petrović, see Guy Braucourt, "Sur les plateaux – Petrovic: Des acteurs de tous pays", *Le Film Français*, 6 May 1977, p. 16.

57　This script was published in Serbia in 1998 as *Benja Kralj*, explaining that the production rights were jointly owned by Sofracima Paris, and Warner Bros Inc., USA. Supposedly, it is one of many projects that were acquired, although the moment never came for it to go into production; see Aleksandar Petrović, *Benja Kralj* (Beograd, Novi Sad: Jugoslovenska Kinoteka, Prometej, 1998).

58 An interview with Branka Petrović, Dajana Djedović, "O reditelju Saši Petroviću i njegovim filmovima", pp. 92–93.

59 Ronald Holloway, "Gruppenbild Mit Dame (Group Portrait with Lady)", *Variety*, 18 May 1977, p. 21.

60 Petrović mentions this in numerous interviews given at the time, see for example: Dj. M., "Izgleda da sam isključen…", *Večernji list*, 29 August, 1972; and an unsigned article "Više je zbrke oko političkih nego oko estetskih motiva", *Vjesnik*, 6 August, 1972.

61 See the previous chapter (section 6.2.1).

62 An interview with Branka Petrović, Dajana Djedović, "O reditelju Saši Petroviću i njegovim filmovima", p. 93.

63 An interview with Aleksandar Petrović, see Guy Braucourt, "Sur les plateaux – Petrovic: Des acteurs de tous pays", p. 14.

64 This amounted to approximately £1.2 million, although due to the inflation rate over the decades, this amount would be considerably larger today; the initial figure is taken from an interview with Aleksandar Petrović, see Guy Braucourt, "Sur les plateaux – Petrovic: Des acteurs de tous pays", p. 14.

65 An interview with Aleksandar Petrović, see Guy Braucourt, "Sur les plateaux – Petrovic: Des acteurs de tous pays", p. 14.

66 ibid.

67 Filming did not start until the autumn, and *Variety* also reported that Schneider was to be paid US $400,000 for her role; see an unsigned article "Berlin (News)", *Variety*, 7 April 1976, p. 44.

68 See an article by Petrović's assistant director Stevan Petrović, "Moja sećanja: Srbin i mala Austrijanka", *Politika*, 31 August 1996.

69 James H. Reid, *Heinrich Böll Withdrawal and Re-emergence* (London: Oswald Wolff, 1973), p. 21.

70 James H. Reid, *Withdrawal and Re-emergence*, p. 9.

71 James H. Reid, *Withdrawal and Re-emergence*, p. 10.

72 ibid.

73 James H. Reid, *Withdrawal and Re-emergence*, p. 19.

74 James H. Reid, *Withdrawal and Re-emergence*, p. 13.

75 James H. Reid, *Withdrawal and Re-emergence*, pp. 10–11.

76 See Chapter 4 (sections 4.2.1 and 4.2.2).

77 See Chapter 3 (section 3.1).

78 See Chapter 5 (section 5.1.3).

79 See Chapter 6 (section 6.1.5).

80 An interview with Aleksandar Petrović, see Guy Braucourt, "Sur les plateaux – Petrovic: Des acteurs de tous pays", p. 16.

81 James H. Reid, *Withdrawal and Re-emergence*, p. 12.

82 James H. Reid, *Withdrawal and Re-emergence*, p. 69.

83   James H. Reid, *Withdrawal and Re-emergence*, p. 70.

84   James H. Reid, *Withdrawal and Re-emergence*, pp. 18–19.

85   James H. Reid, *Withdrawal and Re-emergence*, p. 75.

86   ibid.

87   An interview with Aleksandar Petrović, see Guy Braucourt, "Sur les plateaux – Petrovic: Des acteurs de tous pays", p. 16.

88   See Chapter 1 (section 1.2.2).

89   An interview with Branka Petrović, Dajana Djedović, "O reditelju Saši Petroviću i njegovim filmovima", p. 93.

90   An interview with Aleksandar Petrović and Heinrich Böll, "Grupni portrets damom (1977): Intervju sa Hajnrihom Belom i Aleksandrom Petrovićem za ZDF (drugi program nemačke televizije) 1977.", in *Prizor* (annual magazine), issue no 2, p. 28.

91   An interview with Aleksandar Petrović and Heinrich Böll, "Grupni portrets damom (1977)", p. 26.

92   ibid.

93   Indeed, Margret Schlömer is an important character – practically the second protagonist in the novel; see her description and introduction to the narrative in Böll's novel, Heinrich Böll, *Group Portrait with Lady* (London: Secker & Warburg, 1973), pp. 6–7.

94   An interview with Aleksandar Petrović and Heinrich Böll, "Grupni portrets damom (1977)", p. 27.

95   An interview with Aleksandar Petrović and Heinrich Böll, "Grupni portrets damom (1977)", p. 26.

96   See the previous chapter (section 6.1.5 – specifically on the scene at the Writers' Union, which does not exist in the original novel, and is purely Petrović's addition to his adaptation of *The Master and Margarita*).

97   On Petrović's persecution, see the previous chapter (particularly section 6.2).

98   See the introduction to this and the previous chapter.

99   How familiar all this sounds when one compares it to artists and intellectuals in the Eastern Bloc, who were also vilified and then rehabilitated, including Petrović himself, following the vagaries of political fashion – a subject ideal for Petrović after *The Master and Margarita*.

100 Considering the environmental crisis, and particularly the economic one faced at the end of the first decade of the twenty-first century, this of course is a highly questionable asseveration.

101 Petrović's other Black Wave colleagues – Želimir Žilnik and Dušan Makavejev – also have done the same once in the West, as they have also exposed various problematic political practices there, in the same way they used to do in Yugoslavia. It is interesting that they then had problems with censorship, and that Žilnik's projects were stopped in Germany. One of his films had as its subject matter conflicts between immigrants of different ethnic backgrounds, while another dealt with the controversial Baader-Meinhof group, and according to Marina Gržinić, "Žilnik soon realised that in Germany he was subjected to similar levels of censorship and scrutiny as at home." See Marina Gržinić, "Rani Radovi, Early Works", in *The Cinema of The Balkans*, ed. by Dina Iordanova, (London, New York: Wallflower Press, 2006), p. 69.

102   See Chapter 3 (section 3.1.4).

103   It is worth bearing in mind that this film was made in 1977, when most films about World War II, wherever they were made, reiterated these stereotypes about German soldiers.

104   Heinrich Böll, *Group Portrait with Lady*, p. 195 – Boldig's description; and p. 196 – his famous catchphrase, "Enjoy the war, bud, peace is going to be terrible", which is frequently used in the film.

105   See the previous chapter (specifically the end of section 6.1.3).

106   See Chapter 3 (section 3.2.5).

107   See the previous chapter (specifically note 131).

108   We are also shown that Boris has secret protectors amongst German high officers, once friends of his diplomat father.

109   Georg Trakl was actually an Austrian poet, who, naturally enough, wrote in German. He committed suicide in 1914, unable to accept the atrocities he had witnessed on the Eastern Front at the beginning of War World I.

110   See Chapter 4 (section 4.2.1).

111   It is interesting to be reminded here that the film was a German and French co-production.

112   See Chapter 5 (particularly the introduction to section 5.2).

113   This is the only time in the film that Boris is referred to as a "Bolshevik".

114   Although I have seen both versions of the film, at the time of writing neither was generally available. According to Branka Petrović, her husband was dissatisfied with the version of the film made for distribution in Germany, after the Cannes Film Festival premiere. It is thus the French version with which Petrović was more satisfied, as it was closer to his original edit premiered at Cannes. From a personal interview with Branka Petrović (11 September 2005).

115   For the cast and crew and technical data see the review in *Variety*, in Ronald Holloway, "Gruppenbild Mit Dame (Group Portrait with Lady)", *Variety*, 18 May 1977, p. 21; also see Filmography.

116   See Michel Galabru's statement in Philippe Carcassonne, "Aleksandar Petrovic", *Cinématographe*, June 1977, p. 20.

117   ibid.

118   Hellmuth Karasek, "Im Rasierspiegel", *Der Spiegel*, 6 June 1977, p. 198.

119   Hans Blumenberg, "Hinrichtung eines Böll-Romans", *Die Zeit*, 27 May 1977, p. 52.

120   Hellmuth Karasek, "Im Rasierspiegel", p. 198.

121   An interview with Aleksandar Petrović, see Zoran Predić, "Biće skoro propast filma!", *Radio revija*, 13 November 1970.

122   Hans Blumenberg, "Die Angst des Kinos vor dem Kino", *Die Zeit*, 3 June 1977, p. 35.

123   "Gruppenbild mit Dolchstoss-Legende", *Die Zeit*, 3 June 1977, p. 34.

124   Hans Blumenberg, "Hinrichtung eines Böll-Romans", p. 52.

125   Hellmuth Karasek, "Im Rasierspiegel", p. 198.

126   ibid.

127   Hans Blumenberg, "Hinrichtung eines Böll-Romans", p. 52.

128   "Gruppenbild mit Dolchstoss-Legende", p. 34.

129   Hans Blumenberg, "Hinrichtung eines Böll-Romans", p. 52.

130 "*Heimatfilm*" is also a film genre within Germany (similar perhaps to Ealing comedy in Britain), and those films have very much a German "flavour"; this quote is from Hellmuth Karasek, "Im Rasierspiegel", p. 198.

131 Ronald Holloway, "Gruppenbild Mit Dame (Group Portrait with Lady)", p. 21; and Stevan Petrović, "Moja sećanja: Srbin i mala Austrijanka".

132 Ronald Holloway, "Gruppenbild Mit Dame (Group Portrait with Lady)", p. 21.

133 Michel Sineux, "Portrait de groupe avec dame", *Positif*, July/August 1977, p. 123.

134 Michel Sineux, "Portrait de groupe avec dame", p. 124.

135 Philippe Carcassonne, "Portrait de groupe avec dame", p. 21.

136 ibid.

137 "Zero Hour" refers to the period in German history just after the capitulation in World War II.

138 Clara Menck, "Stunde Null im Weitwinkel", *Frankfurter Allgemeine Zeitung*, 21 May 1980, p. 24.

139 An interview with Aleksandar Petrović, see Ivo Pondělíček, "Aleksandar Petrovič dokončil svůj nový film", *Film A Doba*, January 1969, p. 42.

140 ibid.

Chapter 8

The Artist, *Migrations*, and the Last Days

With the benefit of hindsight, it seems easy to see where Tito and the last comrade from his inner circle, Edvard Kardelj, went wrong in building Yugoslavia as a state, and socialism as its ideological support system. Their reassertion of power in 1972, the elimination of any opposition,[1] and the introduction of the new constitution in 1974,[2] which according to Misha Glenny was nothing but a guarantee that all the threads of power were firmly in their hands,[3] inevitably tied the fate of the country and its political system to that of its autocratic rulers.[4] Edvard Kardelj died in 1979 and Josip Broz Tito in May 1980.[5] Twelve years later, Yugoslavia was officially no more. However, there is no intention here to reduce all the reasons for the country's demise to the fact that Tito held the reigns too firmly. There were, of course, numerous other factors that contributed to the process. The American historian John Lampe explains that: "The political crisis that Yugoslavia's émigré detractors had predicted the moment Tito died in 1980 did not come into the open for another eight years."[6] Then again, the root of the problem was certainly in the authoritarian mode of power, which was never supplanted by a self-sustaining, functional system. Lampe thus equally underlines:

> [Tito's] longevity had allowed Edvard Kardelj to continue elaborating an incomprehensible electoral framework that made sense only as a device to prevent the organization of any rival to Communist power on the local, republic, or federal level. Then Kardelj died in 1979, the year before Tito, and in little more than a decade, so did the Yugoslav experiment that took a modern European country down with it.[7]

In order to acquire a clearer perception of Yugoslavia's final decade, it is worth dividing the process of its demise into three distinct periods. Although the beginning of the first period is usually heralded by Tito's death, it may be argued that it started slightly earlier. In relation to the tight grip on power that Tito and Kardelj held up to 1975, this period is signified by a mild process of "thaw" – if nothing else – as the two leaders were by then both very ill and very old. Their deaths did not signal an immediate or radical change, however. Jasna Dragović-Soso describes the situation as follows:

> Tito's death in May 1980 changed very little for Yugoslavia on the surface. The transition of power to the collective presidency was smooth, the agreed strategy of the leadership was continuity "along Tito's path" and the lavish state funeral of Yugoslavia's late leader

symbolised the commitment of his successors to maintaining the status quo. Appearances hid underlying tensions, however.[8]

This status quo could not last for long, and the underlying tensions that Dragović-Soso discusses would inevitably resurface. Again, the reasons are numerous, but the one often singled out was the grave economic crisis of 1979. This crisis was in fact a global phenomenon,[9] and it significantly affected Yugoslavia, causing unpleasant ripples through all economic strata. Lampe assessed it as "a demoralizing economic decline" which "deepened too relentlessly over the next five years", and was according to him, begging for "the anticipated domestic reforms".[10] These were not forthcoming, as the sobering up following the mourning of Tito's death needed to arrive in stages. Therefore, 1983 could be identified as the year that marked the end of this first stage, and the beginning of the next. The historian Dejan Jović explained that "in 1983 it became clear to most that the Yugoslav problem could not be resolved purely through economic stabilisation or through measures of repression".[11]

The most outstanding characteristic of this second stage was the "the outburst of history", in the words of the Belgrade weekly *NIN*, and according to Dragović-Soso, this marked the process of confrontation with the official historiography of Socialist Yugoslavia.[12] Dragović-Soso explains this in the words of Jovan Mirić, a professor at the University of Zagreb, who was invited to analyse the crisis, which was at that point recognised by everyone. In his book published in 1984, Mirić wrote: "When a society is confronted with a crisis, it usually turns to its foundations; it examines and reconsiders its basic principles."[13] Mirić proceeded to do so, in search of the key to unlocking the Yugoslav problems. He subsequently became a political historian, one amongst the many, who identified the constitution of 1974 as the root of the problem, assessing it as something that had legally incapacitated the country and its institutions. According to Dragović-Soso, however, the most revealing of the new investigations into recent history – and one that examined a specific taboo – was Vladimir Dedijer's biography of Tito.[14] Dragović-Soso explains that Dedijer was "the official chronicler of the Partisan struggle" as well as "Tito's hand-picked biographer."[15] However, his *New Contributions to the Biography of Josip Broz Tito* (*Novi prilozi za biografiju Josipa Broza Tita*) opened "the floodgates of historical revisionism", and Dragović-Soso concludes that: "[Dedijer's] disclosures made it impossible to defend the infallibility both of the revolution and its leader and it gave rise to a full scale reinterpretation of [Yugoslav] history".[16] This reinterpretation of history allowed for numerous reassessments of past decisions and persecutions, and by 1987, which arguably can be perceived as the cathartic year in this second post-Tito period, the system had begun rehabilitating many previously persecuted artists and intellectuals, including Aleksandar Petrović. The process of the questioning and reconstruction of recent history opened doors for the third and final stage in Yugoslavia's demise, which lasted up to the country's dissolution. It can be argued that the final stage began in 1988 and culminated in 1991 with the first war of secession, which started in Slovenia. The third stage ultimately ended in 1992 with the recognition of Slovenia and Croatia as independent successor states. The first country on the international scene to recognise them was, intriguingly but not unsurprisingly, the then recently reunified Germany, thereby reaffirming the close ties it has long had with this part of Europe.

John Lampe also designates 1988 as the landmark year, considering that "the League of Communists' federal prime minister and his cabinet were forced to take the previously unthinkable step of resigning."[17] It is worth adding that in 1988, Yugoslavia truly found itself on the cusp of breaking up.[18] However, as always in history, it is difficult to draw clear lines of separation amongst the many crucial factors that bring about such major events. Lampe explains, for example, that it was actually in 1986 that one of the key changes took place, since at that moment Yugoslavia lacked as common a leader as Tito was. Instead, the "power vacuum" was filled separately in two of Yugoslavia's republics: "in 1986 two younger men seized this chance – Milan Kučan of Slovenia and Slobodan Milošević of Serbia."[19] The ideas that the two new leaders had on the much needed restructuring of Yugoslavia proved to be irreconcilable. With the free democratic elections organised in 1990, these two still "communist" options pursued in the respective republics "interacted" with the new political options stemming from the other Yugoslav republics, and Yugoslavia broke apart within two subsequent years.[20] What is more germane to this investigation is that in 1988, Aleksandar Petrović was supposed to complete what turned out to be his final film. In order to understand how it was made, the wheel of history needs to be turned back to 1978.

As noted above, Tito's and Kardelj's firm grip on power started to gently loosen after 1975. Kardelj had already been diagnosed as terminally ill, so it was apparent that time would inevitably take its toll. Whether due to the two men's frailty, or simply that they had asserted their power long enough, a process of unofficial "thaw" started in the late 1970s. As opposed to political and general historians, who see the leaders' deaths as emblematic of this process, film historians tend to emphasise that the process began somewhat earlier. For example, the Yugoslav film historian Ranko Munitić claims that this process of "thawing" started in 1978.[21] Daniel Goulding agrees that 1978 heralded a positive change, and corroborates this view with the fact that film production jumped to over twenty films per year, at which level it stayed into the 1980s.[22] This new air of liberalisation, gently breezing through the country at the end of 1970s, also enabled Aleksandar Petrović to return to Yugoslavia.

8. 1. The Return

After leaving the country in February 1973, Petrović and his family did not return to Yugoslavia until the summer of 1977.[23] This was the summer after *Group Portrait with Lady* was completed and premiered in Cannes, and the family decided, under relentless pressure from their son Dragan, to go for a holiday in Yugoslavia. Dragan loved the little town Rovinj on the Istrian coast, which was a popular resort, particularly amongst people from Belgrade. It was so popular that Petrović, accidentally but not unexpectedly, met Sava Lazarević there, who was then head of Nolit, the largest publishing house in Belgrade.[24] At that time, Nolit published the work of Miloš Crnjanski (1893–1977), one of the greatest Serbian writers of the twentieth century. Before going into exile in the summer of 1972, Petrović had signed a contract with Neoplanta Film of Novi Sad,[25] to make an adaptation and direct a film of Crnjanski's acclaimed novel, *Migrations* (*Seobe*, 1929).[26] According to his widow Branka, Petrović learned, while chatting to Lazarević, that there was still interest in filming *Migrations*. Perhaps more importantly, he also learnt that the political oppression towards intellectuals of 1972 and 1973 was, by this time, dissipating.[27] In the small seaside resort, Petrović "tested the water" and sensed that the time might be right for him and his family to return to Yugoslavia.

In a personal interview, Branka Petrović stated that the strongest motive for her husband's return to Yugoslavia was the possibility of restarting his work on Crnjanski's *Migrations*.[28] This could be understood as Petrović's longest cherished project, since he had talked about adapting the novel for the screen as early as 1957. As a budding filmmaker back then, he had written to Crnjanski in London where he lived in exile, asking him for permission to write a script based on the book.[29] Crnjanski wrote back and promised the novel to the young director, based on the latter's early short film *Flight over the Swamp*.[30] Crnjanski was persuaded that Petrović would be able to adapt his novel, perhaps because parts of the book's narrative take place in the marshlands near the Danube, which Petrović used as locations for his documentary. Since that time, Petrović had often mentioned that, sooner or later, he would turn *Migrations* into a film. After the release of his first feature, *Two* in 1961, Petrović had given an interview in which he insisted on modern cinema abandoning traditional narrative structures in order to open more space for the development of cinematic language. The interviewer went on to ask him why he wanted to adapt *Migrations*, which was after all a literary work, for the screen then? Petrović responded that Crnjanski's novel would be easy to adapt, using a "true" film language – "the camera's stream of thoughts."[31] The idea persisted, and almost materialised in 1972, when Crnjanski officially signed the rights to the novel to Neoplanta Film.[32] Soon afterwards, however, Petrović went into exile and the project was postponed indefinitely. In 1977 though, working on the novel appeared as if it might be possible again. In the summer of that year, Petrović gave an interview to Belgrade's magazine *Duga*, under the title "Why is he not making films in his own country?" The journalist Žika Lazić wrote in the most complimentary way about Petrović, the international release of his *Group Portrait*, and the benefits for Yugoslav culture of Petrović's possible return.[33] Petrović mentioned in the interview that he would love to direct *Migrations* if he was to come back to Yugoslavia,[34] and it appeared clear that he would do so.

Late in 1977, Petrović made several trips to Belgrade. On one of them, in the autumn, he met Sava Lazarević again, and they went to see Miloš Crnjanski together. The author died a few weeks later, on 30 November 1977.[35] While Petrović's resolve to return to Yugoslavia was growing, his profile in the country was increasing. In September of the same year, a group of film critics declared Petrović's film *Three* to be the best Yugoslav film on the "War and the Revolution". Mira Boglić seized the opportunity to write an article on Petrović in Zagreb's daily *Vjesnik*, a newspaper that had often criticised him and his work.[36] In her article, Boglić asserts that Petrović in his oeuvre had:

[...] made some truly significant films, although he also had failures due to his misunderstandings and disagreements with our social reality. As a result, and following criticism of the so called "Black" film, he has been alienated for some time from Yugoslav cinema.[37]

Boglić emphasised that one of these failures was *It Rains in My Village*, while she also observed *The Master and Margarita* was not well received by domestic audiences, although she praised *Three* and *Happy Gypsies*.[38] I would be tempted to view Boglić's article, albeit somewhat speculatively, as a letter to Petrović from the Yugoslav authorities. It was as if the regime wanted to let him know that he might return, although if he was to work, he should remember what was permitted and what not. The Yugoslav film historian Petar Volk comments:

It was easy to observe that the ideological campaigns in cultural life were usually short-lived and self-defeating; they managed to fracture existing relations, but without establishing anything in their place. They were usually soon forgotten.[39]

Therefore, according to Volk, once the processes of unifying the country's political discourse in 1972 and 1973 were over, and then as good as forgotten by 1977, the various conflicts, such as the one with Petrović, could also lapse. Consequently, in the summer of 1978, Petrović resettled in Belgrade with his family. This was preceded by another symbolic, but significant event: in January 1978, *Group Portrait* was screened at Belgrade's International Film Festival – FEST, the festival Petrović had helped set up seven years previously. The film was acquired for distribution in Yugoslavia, and it went out to cinemas in 1979.[40] Aleksandar Petrović was back home again, and so was his filmmaking.

8. 1. 1. Screenplays and the Theatre

In the abovementioned interview with Žika Lazić, apart from *Migrations*, Petrović also mentioned his project of turning the Serbian epic folk song "*Banović Strahinja*" into a script, which he entitled *The Hawk* (*Soko*).[41] He stated that he would like to direct both these projects in Yugoslavia. He also confirmed that his script *Benjie the King*, based on Isaac Babel's short stories,[42] had been acquired by a French production company, with interest from financiers in Hollywood.[43] Petrović went on to add that interest in his adaptation of Bulgakov's *Heart of a Dog* had been rejuvenated in France, as the Italian film based on the same text (as a result of which, work on Petrović's project had ceased) had only been released in Italy.[44] At the time of this interview, Petrović still lived between Paris and Budapest, but it was clear that, even if he did return to Yugoslavia, his career was now international.

After his return in late 1978, Petrović started reworking his adaptation of Bulgakov's *Heart of a Dog* from a film script into a theatre play, as he had been offered an opportunity

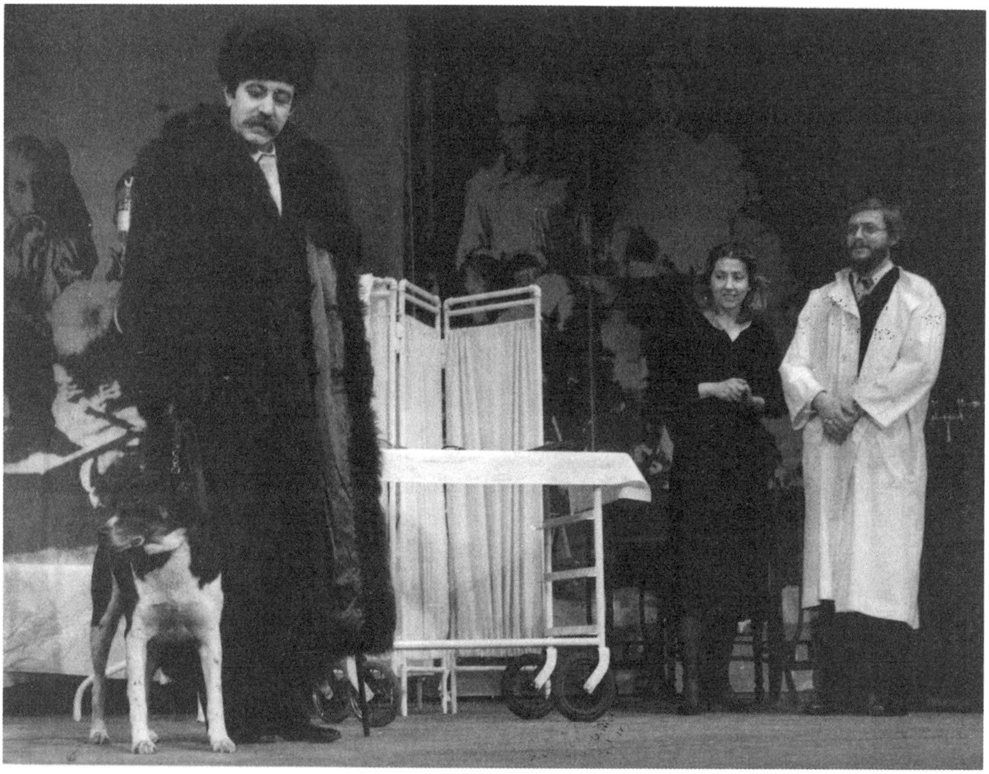

Figure 8.1: Petrović's adaptation of Bulgakov's *Heart of a Dog* at Belgrade's theatre Atelje 212.

to put it on the stage of Belgrade's Atelje 212 theatre.[45] The play opened in February 1979 to a very warm reception from audiences, according to Petar Volk, which led to another offer to direct in the theatre.[46] This opportunity was more flattering, and in April 1982, Petrović's adaptation of *The Master and Margarita* opened as a theatre play at the main stage of the National Theatre in Belgrade.[47] Petrović evidently admired Bulgakov and his work very much, but his adaptation of *The Master and Margarita* for the stage had additional connotations.[48] Petrović was upset that as a result of his film being "quietly" withdrawn from distribution in 1972, it had remained largely unseen in Yugoslavia.[49] With the theatre performance, in which he incorporated projections of certain scenes from the film, Petrović was openly, according to his interviews, trying to rehabilitate his film of *The Master and Margarita*.[50]

In 1982, Petrović expressed his concern that there still existed a subtle – but not ineffective – repression of certain artists and their arts. At that particular moment, Petrović had a personal reason for being perplexed by his own situation in the country. His adaptation of the epic folk song "*Banović Strahinja*" into the film script *The Hawk* had been acquired by his old producers, Avala Film. Avala Film then found co-producers in Jadran Film, Zagreb's major studio, and German Television Company, ZDF. Together, in 1981, they turned the script into a large scale historical film, which starred the Italian Franco Nero and reinstated the original title *Banović Strahinja*. Although Petrović was credited as a scriptwriter, he had assumed that he would be offered the script to direct, since he had written it. Avala Film never informed him of its production however, nor that they had employed as director Vatroslav Mimica, a Croatian director and Petrović's friend and colleague.

In later years, Petrović claimed that he had not been allowed to direct the project due to interference by party officials, who still saw him as politically and intellectually hostile to Yugoslav socialism.[51] Petrović thus had personal reasons for believing that various forms of repression against artists were still operating "behind the curtain" in the cultural life of the country. As this happened two years after Tito's death, in the period designated above as the first stage in Yugoslavia's demise, it is clear that the processes of liberalisation unfolded slowly at first. In addition, according to John Lampe, as Tito's funeral in May 1980 was attended by the representatives of 122 states, "such international respect also seemed to sanction the existing political system".[52] Dejan Jović concludes that "public discourse insisted that after Tito's death there would be no major changes, and his policies would continue."[53] As described above, in the period immediately after Petrović's return, the overall situation in Yugoslavia was somewhat better than it had been in 1973, but was not significantly different. The party still had all power, and was continuing with its political culture of dogmatism. It would take several more years before Petrović would be rehabilitated.

There is one other visible detail characterising Petrović's return to public life in the Yugoslavia of the early 1980s, although it is one which has no political value. Petrović, and his Black Film peers such as Živojin Pavlović and Dušan Makavejev, were often referred to by journalists in this period as the "old guard".[54] This was due to the fact that in the late 1970s a new generation of filmmakers had appeared on the scene in Yugoslavia – a generation which by the early 1980s had established themselves with a body of work that drew public attention at home, as well as critical acclaim abroad. Curiously, this was a generation of filmmakers who had studied outside of Yugoslavia in the early and mid-1970s, when Tito and Kardelj were purging the party and persecuting intellectuals at home. As this generation of filmmakers had all trained at the eminent Prague film school FAMU, the same one that Petrović had attended for a year between 1947 and 1948,[55] they were known as the Prague School.[56] They included, amongst others, Srdjan Karanović, Goran Marković and Goran Paskaljević in Serbia, Rajko Grlić and Lordan Zafranović in Croatia, and Emir Kusturica in Bosnia, and were thus a Yugoslav-wide phenomenon. Petrović stated in an interview that there was no conflict between the "old guard" and the "Czech school", as Petrović saw in the latter a logical development of Yugoslav cinema, from the Black Film of the 1960s and early 1970s, to the wave of films produced by this new generation.[57] Petrović now had this generation of the "young Turks" of Yugoslav cinema to compete with, and perhaps there were politicians active in Yugoslavia who observed his return with distrust. Regardless, Petrović was to spend the 1980s energetically fighting to turn into a film his adaptation of Miloš Crnjanski's novel *Migrations*, which was to be his last project.

8. 2. *Migrations* and the Slow Processes of Rehabilitation

8. 2. 1. Petrović and Miloš Crnjanski

The long and arduous path of the production of *Migrations* officially started on 28 June 1972, when the writer, Miloš Crnjanski, signed the film rights of the novel to Neoplanta Film of Novi Sad.[58] Draško Redjep, then the director of Neoplanta Film, explained that Crnjanski told them, whilst signing the contract, that he had promised the adaptation of *Migrations* to Aleksandar Petrović, and that Petrović should direct the film.[59] In his book on Petrović, Redjep reprints Crnjanski's letter from as early as January 1963, in which Crnjanski designated Petrović as *Migrations*' director.[60] Crnjanski most likely felt this way as he had liked Petrović's short film *Flight over the Swamp*, and the writer was quoted as saying: "Only Aleksandar Petrović can evoke those swamps and mist, which permeate the novel like doom."[61]

Miloš Crnjanski was one of the most controversial writers in Yugoslav and Serbian history. Born in 1893, in the then Austro-Hungarian Empire, he studied arts and philosophy in Vienna. He was drafted into the army during World War I where, particularly as an ethnic Serb, he suffered immensely, fighting for Austria. An outbreak of cholera saved him from being sent to fight against the Serbian army immediately in 1914.[62] In his seminal work on Crnjanski, David A. Norris explains: "As a Serb in the Hapsburg Empire he soon learned of the ways in which the lives of individuals are affected by historical events beyond their control."[63] Evidently, by the time Petrović started pre-production on the film, he was himself very much aware of the same phenomenon. Living in exile, he had many similar experiences to Crnjanski, and had found his life to have been overshadowed by political events beyond his control. After World War I, Crnjanski published his first novel *The Diary About Čarnojević* (*Dnevnik o Čarnojeviću*, 1921). This was very much a modernist novel, and described his experience of the war. The diarist of the novel is a Serb who has to fight for the Austrian army, sometimes against his own compatriots. He is thus a victim of the policies of colonialism, which are by their nature inherently brutal. This theme reappeared as an important motif in his second major novel, *Migrations* (*Seobe*), although here the narrative takes place in the eighteenth century.

Crnjanski was known as an exceptionally awkward character, and during his life made a sharp political shift from left to right. Norris explains that in the same decade Crnjanski was initially a socialist, then an anarchist, and finally, by the end of 1920s, a forthright fascist.[64] Norris goes on to add that although the writer was outspoken about these ideas, he was never really committed to them, and he had admitted this in his later interviews. Crnjanski's primary aim was "to shock complacent bourgeois society,"[65] whilst his political prevarications tell more about his whimsical nature and flippant temperament, rather than truly describing his political character. The Yugoslav literary critic and historian, Petar Džadžić agrees with this view and explains that Crnjanski was "more a person of moods, than of convictions" so it was not easy to "identify his political character" which shifted frequently.[66] These shifts however, made him quite unpopular in his day and, like the two previous writers Petrović had adapted for the screen, it can be argued that Crnjanski's politics also "resisted easy classifications".

Crnjanski had been a Yugoslav diplomat before and throughout World War II, and he ended up in London during the war, together with the rest of the Kingdom of Yugoslavia's government.[67] Since he had been in London with the king's cabinet, the Yugoslav communists started a vicious campaign against him immediately after the end of the war, which peaked in 1954, mainly trying to discredit him as a political rightist and a fascist.[68] The most intriguing aspect of the campaign was that it was led by his fellow writers. One of them was his once close friend, the well-known poet, Marko Ristić. The two fell out as early as 1932, when Ristić became close to the surrealist movement, and started criticising Crnjanski's modernism as archaic in Belgrade's literary press.[69] The conflict between the two former friends alas, had a political undertone. As mentioned earlier, the surrealists internationally had dallied with communist ideas.[70] In contrast, Crnjanski had already made his shift to the political right, and in 1934 had begun publishing a proto-fascist magazine *Ideas* (*Ideje*). Like the archetypal writer, or poet rather, Crnjanski was not only incredibly difficult on a personal level, he also appeared ill at ease with his environment, unlike Bulgakov and Böll. Following his conflict with Ristić, within months he had publicly broken off relationships with pretty much everyone in the Yugoslav literary community.[71] It is also worth adding here that most of this community were sympathetic to socialist and communist ideas. His friend Ristić, although from an economically privileged background, was a high official of the Communist Party after the war. Perhaps he never forgave Crnjanski for criticising Belgrade's "bourgeois children" – including himself – for "play-acting" communists.[72] After the war, he declared Crnjanski a "dead poet", although Crnjanski was still alive and well, albeit in exile. As in numerous similar situations already described, Crnjanski's literary "assassination" was not due to his work, but to his politics. While his politics, as also explained, were never easily characterised, he soon fell out even with the Serbian émigré community in London, who were loyal to the king's regime and decidedly conservative.[73] His status as an incorrigible outsider was thus confirmed. At the same time, he was discredited in Yugoslavia and was not allowed to return until 1965, although informally, he had been invited to come back before.[74] Crnjanski waited and felt quite paranoid at the time, according to his biographer Radovan Popović.[75] Only when he felt safe, and once various amnesty laws had been passed in relation to those individuals who had spent the war years abroad, did he return to Yugoslavia. Therefore, the contract to film *Migrations* was signed only after the writer's full rehabilitation had taken place and he was back living in Belgrade.

The one thing the Yugoslav post-war regime was not able to discredit was Crnjanski's literary talent. Whilst the campaign against him initiated by the literary establishment was raging, the writer still had supporters in Belgrade. His place in the history of Yugoslav literature was defended and soon undisputed. His texts were republished and his plays performed on theatre stages during the 1950s and 1960s, while he was still living in political exile.[76] The swathe of scholarly reappraisals appeared after his full political rehabilitation.

According to the Belgrade scholar Nikola Milošević, Crnjanski was an undeniable modernist genius of international significance, whose rich and particular formal style is unique in world literature.[77] Milošević also adds that his style manages to be melodic, while full of often philosophical content.[78] Norris agrees with this view, as does Džadžić, summarising an overall assessment that Crnjaski was an "outstanding lyricist" and that "his work [is] that of a poet rather than a novelist".[79] He also quotes Crnjanski who explained his projects "as the search for the 'unstable rhythm of mood' and the 'rhythm of each mood'".[80] Consequently, his work is extremely difficult to translate into other languages, as well as other media. The view that Crnjanski is a genuine master of the written word is often reiterated by other scholars familiar with his work,[81] which meant that the adaptation of his prose to film would present Aleksandar Petrović with his most difficult task to date. Initially, Petrović had in mind what became known as the "First Book" of *Migrations*, which was published in 1929. In 1962 however, Crnjanski published the "Second Book" of *Migrations* (he planned more but they never materialised) in two large volumes.[82] Petrović decided to include these later volumes of the novel in his adaptation.

As a novel, *Migrations* seemed to be able to provide Petrović with suitable material, content and characters that were close to his own work and interests. Petrović decided to adapt the first book of *Migrations* into a feature film, while he proposed to turn the two recent volumes of the Second Book into a TV series. The feature film was completed, yet the TV series was not, and it was only in 2002 that Branka, Petrović's widow, assembled a "rough cut" of the material for the series, in a two-and- a-half hour long programme. Although this is an unfinished edit, a work in progress and not meant for release, it still provides an insight into Petrović's vision of the series. The decision to use two different forms for the adaptation – film and a TV series – is not so surprising when one is familiar with the novel. As Nikola Milošević explains, the first part is formally very different from the second,[83] which again is not surprising, as it was written almost twenty-five years later. The use of different visual formats to accommodate Crnjanski's unique prose is therefore easily justified.

Migrations may be classified as a historical novel, and in it Crnjanski fictionalises the hard life of the Serbs who escaped the Ottoman Empire in the eighteenth century, and populated the territory of what is today the province of Vojvodina. At that time, parts of Vojvodina operated as a sort of no man's land between the Ottoman and Austrian Empires, which both empires used as a playing field on which to fight each other. The Serbs who arrived in Vojvodina formed army regiments to fight against the Ottomans, but under the Austrian command. Although they had escaped the Ottoman persecution, they found themselves unwelcome in the Austrian Empire where they remained outsiders. Or rather, they were welcome but only once they had lost their lives as soldiers for that empire's interests. Aware of their unenviable position, they started dreaming of emigrating to Russia, an empire they saw as their own. This was following the testament of the Russian Tsar, Peter the Great, who stated that Russia needed to take care of its Slavic "brothers and sisters" suffering under the Ottoman yoke. Crnjanski clearly had his own experiences invested in the book, as he too had fought unwillingly in Austrian uniform. According to Petar Džadžić, Crnjanski's literature was very much informed by his own experiences,[84] and Džadžić concludes about the novel: "Is it not a paradox that the heroes of the most poetic novel in our language are soldiers!"[85]

The main protagonist of the novel is a soldier, an officer, Vuk Isaković, but his character is juxtaposed with its opposite, that of his brother, the merchant, Arandjel Isaković.[86] The dynamic between these two reflects the symbolic duality of the one nation, yet with well rounded characters "who are not made of the same stock, and within whom a struggle rages between different, often diametrically opposed tendencies."[87] The third character is Vuk's wife, Dafina, whom he leaves to go to war. She stays with her brother-in-law, who falls in love with her. Politics, love and death, war, and the deep tragedy of existence are the themes imbuing this novel, and the themes that permeate Petrović's cinematic oeuvre. There is little doubt of Petrović's reasons for wanting to adapt it for the screen, as it seemed to be pre-designed for him.

8. 2. 2. Rehabilitation without Reconciliation

In 1979, soon after he was back in Yugoslavia, Petrović announced that the filming of *Migrations* would start in 1980, as a co-production between Neoplanta Film in Novi Sad and Avala Film in Belgrade.[88] He went on claiming that two films would be made, one for each book of *Migrations*,[89] and that he would cast predominantly the Yugoslav actors with whom he had worked before: Bekim Fehmiu and Olivera Vučo (*Happy Gypsies*), Pavle Vujisić (*The Master and Margarita*), Milena Dravić (*Group Portrait*), and his regular Eva Ras.[90] However, filming was quickly cancelled due to the fact that he could not raise the funds for such an ambitious project. In 1980, Avala Film was already working on a large-scale historical production – *Banović Strahinja* – which although it had been written by Petrović, was not directed by him, as discussed above.[91] As also recounted earlier, Yugoslavia had other more pressing concerns during this first period after Tito's death. Jasna Dragović-Soso explains that "Tito's death coincided with the onset of a grave economic crises,"[92] which further explains why it was so difficult for Petrović to find funding for his long cherished, and very ambitious, project. It was as if a further political shift in the country had to take place before Petrović could rework his strategy and finally bring *Migrations* to life.

Petrović relaunched the project in 1983, which also happened to be a landmark year for political life in the country. He submitted the project to Television Belgrade and Television Novi Sad, who were to co-produce the project.[93] He provided one script for a film, as an adaptation of the First Book, and a second script for a TV series, as an adaptation of the Second Book of *Migrations*. According to Petrović, the two Serbian television companies informed him that the project was too expensive, and that they would undertake it only if there were other sources of finance on board, preferably from abroad.[94] Petrović realised that he would have to find at least part of the funding himself, probably from a number of different sources, as he had done with his previous production *Group Portrait*. The breakthrough came at the beginning of 1986, when the French Ministry of Culture decided to grant two million French francs to the project. After this substantial grant, two French production companies decided to participate, Mediteranea and Adrianeé, along with Yvone Obadia, a private financier from Switzerland. As a result, in May 1986, Petrović signed a contract with Television Belgrade and Television Novi Sad to start production of both the film and the TV series of *Migrations*. The participation of French production companies, as with his previous films, entailed the participation of French stars and a version of the film in French. Jacques Doniol-Valcroze, of *Cahiers du Cinéma* fame, worked on the French draft of the script. The French actress Isabelle Huppert was to star as Dafina Isaković in the female lead role. Another French actor, Richard Berry, was to play Arandjel Isaković, her lover, while Bernard Blier had a smaller role as a French priest. The internationally acclaimed Swedish actor Erland Josephson would play a bishop of the Serbian Church, while the male protagonist, Dafina's husband Vuk Isaković, was to be played by Avtandil Makharadze, the Soviet actor from Georgia. Makharadze's involvement may be explained by the fact that Soviet State Television was supposed to co-produce, as was Czechoslovakian Television, but both these organisations left the project during pre-production. *Migrations* was the most complex production Petrović ever undertook, so to identify how, why, and at what point the

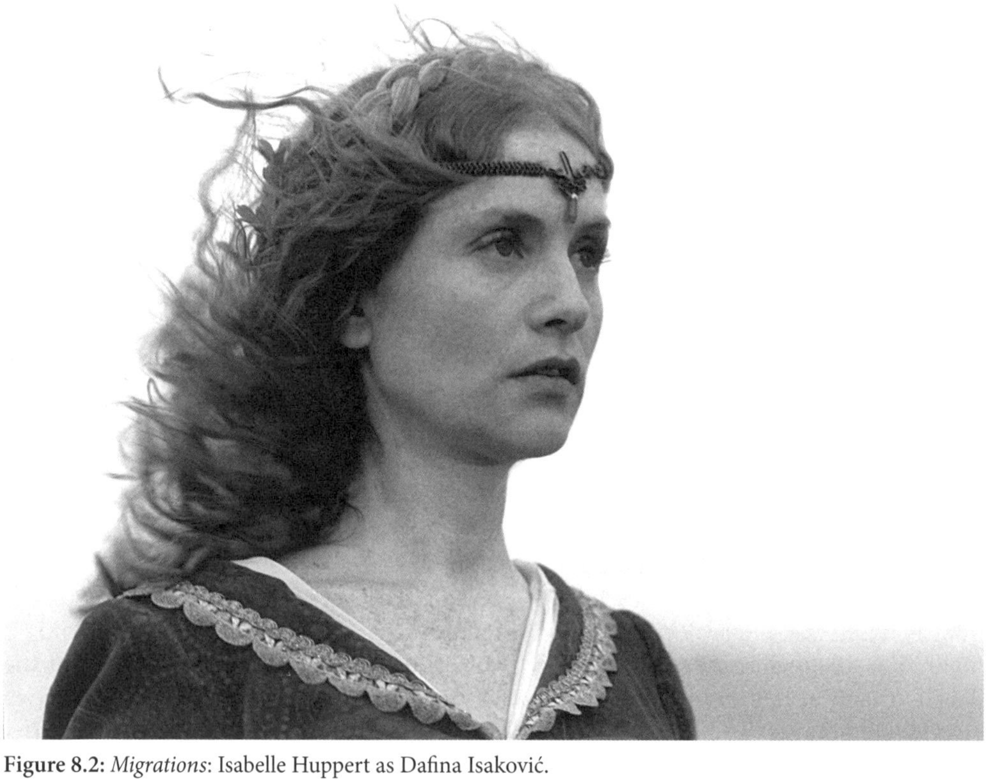

Figure 8.2: *Migrations*: Isabelle Huppert as Dafina Isaković.

various co-producers changed would require a separate study. The budget for the project however, was 12 million US dollars, and filming started in August 1987.[95]

The struggle to assemble the finances for the film started in 1983, and continued solidly for two years.[96] As explained in the introduction to this chapter, the process of confrontation with Yugoslavia's official history also began in 1983, a process which Dragović-Soso characterised "as that of 'the outburst of history'".[97] This more open and critical re-evaluation of the country's socialist past, and particularly Tito's role, led to a re-examination of the status of many persecuted, or simply marginalised, artist and intellectuals. Many of the alleged "enemies" of the state were rehabilitated, and this process accelerated in subsequent years. Petrović, as ever, was busy with his work, and to some extent oblivious of the rapid political changes thrust upon Yugoslavia, but the fact that the pre-production of *Migrations* was gaining ground was indicative. The state did not forget its most awarded filmmaker on the national level, and in December of 1987, Aleksandar Petrović received the highest state award in Yugoslavia[98] – the AVNOJ.[99] Although this took place only a few years before the system itself collapsed, the award could be understood not only as a sign of Petrović's full rehabilitation, but also of his appreciation in the country. He received it just after he started filming his final project, *Migrations*.

The award was supposed to, if not erase, then at least alleviate the injustices Petrović had suffered in 1973. He was not fully satisfied, however, as another shadow from that period remained hanging over his career. Many still thought that he should have behaved differently during the *Plastic Jesus* affair, although discussion of this issue was mainly restricted to art scene gossip. More significantly, Petrović was not offered his previous post at the Faculty of Dramatic Arts which he had lost in 1973 due to the *Plastic Jesus* incident.[100] Understandably, he raised this issue on many occasions, but received no official response.[101] One reason for this may be that Dejan Kosanović, a Yugoslav film historian, who presided over the disciplinary panel investigating the *Plastic Jesus* case, was still a senior at the faculty. Petrović himself considered him to be one of the people responsible for his persecution.[102] While the faculty long evaded the issue,[103] Petrović was finally reinstated in October 1991, by which point, however, the system that had persecuted him no longer existed. Such rehabilitation thus had only nominal value.[104] A very different set of woes had by that time befallen the remnants of Yugoslavia – Serbia included – and Petrović himself had other issues to worry about, which will be addressed later in this chapter. What did matter in the early autumn of 1987, was that the new project was underway, and that Petrović was to direct his new film.

8. 2. 3. *Seobe* or *Migrations* – The Film

Major Vuk Isaković, commander of a Serbian regiment, takes his troops to fight in the Austrian army against France, in the war of 1744. He leaves his wife, Dafina, and their two little children, to stay with his bachelor brother, the rich merchant, Arandjel. Dafina, upset and worried, tells Vuk to take care of himself.

The Austrian officers suggest to Vuk that he should convert to Catholicism, as this would help him to be promoted. If he was to "Germanise" himself and his soldiers, they would be treated better in the Austrian Empire. Vuk is offended by this, and talks about Russia and the beauty of Orthodox Christianity.

Once at the battlefield, the Serbs are continually sent to the front lines first. An Austrian aristocrat hints that they are expendable. Vuk feels that they are treated badly and starts telling his soldiers that they should all emigrate to Russia. The Austrians ordered Vuk to take no prisoners amongst the French.

At the same time Dafina is getting restless in Zemun,[105] in the house of her brother-in-law. She and Arandjel grow closer together.

A French officer spares Vuk's life, while Vuk is pinned down by his horse. The Officer claims that they never shoot at people who cannot defend themselves. The luck of war soon changes and the French Officer is subsequently captured by Vuk. Vuk decides not to kill him, despite his orders.

Dafina is seduced by Arandjel, but soon she falls ill. Feverish, she seems confused and regrets her adultery. Nevertheless, she demands that Arandjel ask the church for a divorce from Vuk, so that she can marry his brother.

Vuk grows more despondent and angry as he realises how hypocritically the Austrians treat him and his men. They see them as mercenaries at best, and he realises that he will never be promoted. Secretly, he lets the French Officer go free. When the French Officer comes upon a group of French soldiers, he waves at them, but thinking him to be a deserter, they shoot him dead.

The bishops of the Serbian Church refuse to marry Arandjel and Dafina, reminding them that she is Vuk's wife. Arandjel, annoyed with them, criticises as idealists those Serbs who are soldiers and officers. He says that they are destroying the nation, while merchants are not respected, even though they are the real defenders of the nation's well-being. Dafina, ill and sorrowful, dies. Arandjel throws golden coins from his carriage in despair.

Vuk is arrested for disobeying orders, as he had liberated the French Officer. He is executed in prison.

As the first soldier comes back to the village from the war, an apparition of Dafina comes out of the house to greet an apparition of Vuk, coming back on his horse.

8. 2. 4. Petrović's *Migrations*

As explained above, the atmosphere in Yugoslavia changed drastically between 1987 and 1989, the period that Petrović was filming *Migrations*. Most specifically, the feeling that socialism as a political project was coming to an end was omnipresent and more openly discussed as time passed. Mikhail Gorbachev, the leader of the Soviet Union, introduced radical reforms to the principle country of the Eastern Bloc in 1985. This restructuring had accelerated considerably by 1987, and ended in 1989 with the collapse of the socialist system.

In 1987 it was becoming increasingly clear that so-called "real socialism" was ill, hence would have to be severely modified, or perhaps even replaced with a liberal-capitalist democracy. As these thoughts were more openly expressed, certainly in Yugoslavia, the intellectuals started looking to the pre-socialist past, trying to find clues as to where to go next. This recovery of the pre-communist past started first in the arts. Dragović-Soso singles out Slobodan Selenić's[106] novel *Fathers and Forefathers* (*Očevi i oci*) published in 1985 as "[T]he novel [which] represented a rehabilitation of the old Serbian bourgeoisie with its liberal democratic values."[107]

This process also affected cinema production, and films appeared in distribution romanticising the pre-war bourgeoisie, which had been brutally marginalised by the communists and their sympathisers immediately after World War II. Films such as *Hey Babu Riba* (*Bal na vodi*, 1986) by Jovan Aćin, and *Deja Vu* (*Već vidjeno*, 1987) by Goran Marković,[108] represented the pre-war bourgeois class as educated, polite and wise, while communists were shown as upstarts, uneducated brutes, who abused Marxism to forcefully repossess what did not belong to them. Although the stories of these films were far from unfounded, the portrayal seen in them is crudely simplified. This fitted the political atmosphere of the late 1980s, which started an uncritical glorification of everything pre-communist to the point of a mystical adoration of the innocence lost with communism.

Petrović's interest in Crnjanski's *Migrations* could also be perceived as fitting this trend. Crnjanski was certainly bourgeois, unashamedly so, until his death. He was ostracised by the communists after the war, and remained in exile for twenty years. His novel *Migrations* could be understood as an ontological study of the Serbian national being, before it was modified by modernism or communism. However, Crnjanski was a complex writer, and it is this very complexity that Petrović tried to transpose to the screen. In contrast to the abovementioned films of the 1980s, there is no clear polarisation of "good" and "bad" in *Migrations*. On the contrary, the film's main characters, with whom audiences might be expected to sympathise, display a wide range of character traits vulnerable to moral temptations. *Migrations*, the novel and the film, are more concerned with questioning, rather than reasserting political or historical points.

Crnjanski was accused of Serbian nationalism at various points in his career, and with *Migrations* he was accused of "creating a nationalist mythology."[109] Nikola Milošević, a scholar on Crnjanski, deconstructs this accusation, and demonstrates, amongst other things, how the novel portrays a character who initially sees his nation as privileged, but then learns that not all his countrymen are good; characters of other ethnic groups are given sympathetic traits; and various other examples that prove how "the writer consistently overcomes the potential limitations of the 'nationally' biased theme."[110] Petrović's characters, based on Crnjanski's, are not models one should look up to, but representations of human beings under pressure, from whose moral dilemmas we can learn and draw our own conclusions, as in Petrović's previous films. These characters have, according to Petar Džadžić, "an increased desire for freedom, purity and harmony, as a response to an increasingly repressive social and historical reality."[111] Crnjanski's

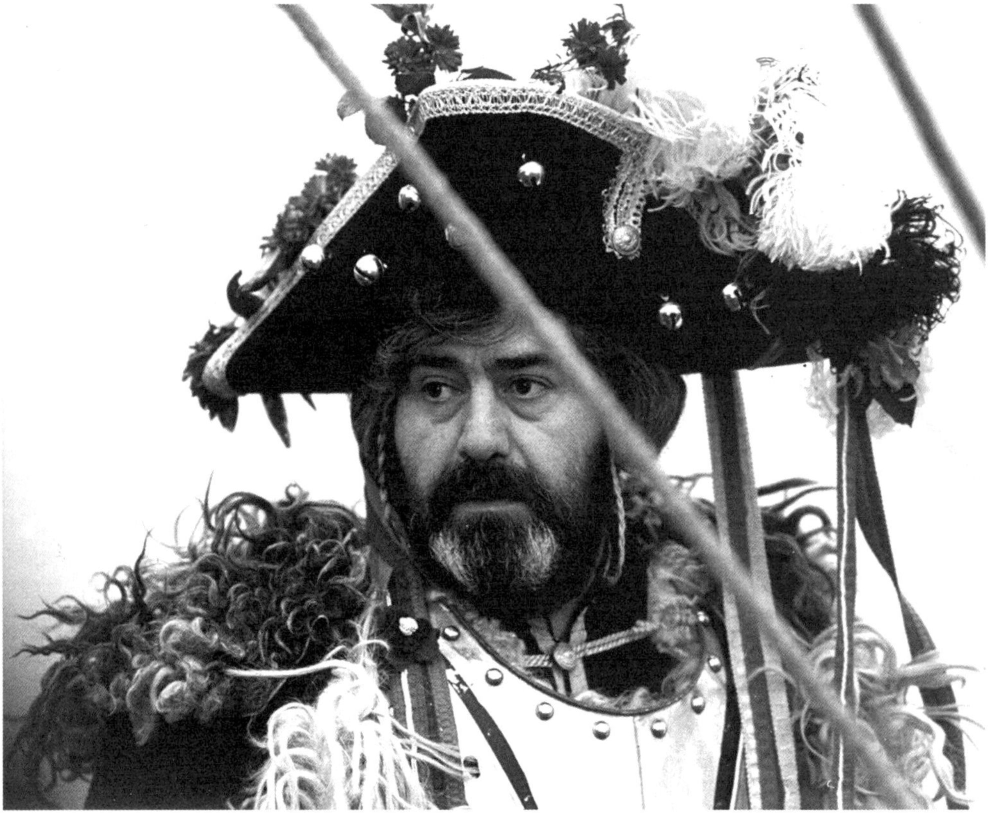

Figure 8.3: Georgian actor Avtandil Makharadze as the soldier, Major Vuk Isaković.

characters therefore became ideal protagonists for a Petrović film, fitting easily into the "family" of characters from his other work. Petrović's "upper-class" Serbs would grow to face themselves and their illusions through the course of the film, and by realising their mistakes, pay a price for this knowledge at the end. There is thus no idealisation of their social class in the film, as there was in the work of Marković and Aćin, for example. Nor is the nation idealised, as was the case with another major historical film that Television Belgrade made at the time, Zdravko Šotra's *The Battle of Kosovo* (*Boj na Kosovu*, 1989). Until the end, Petrović remained a responsible intellectual who questioned, rather than promoted, social ideas and ideologies. He did so in his work during the communist period, in his work in the West, and finally, in his work at the time of this early social and political transition, into which Serbia and the other Yugoslav republics entered at the end of the 1980s.

Petrović's protagonists in *Migrations* all give in to their desires and end up being consumed by them, as they fail to recognise their desires as destructive. Vuk Isaković goes to war on

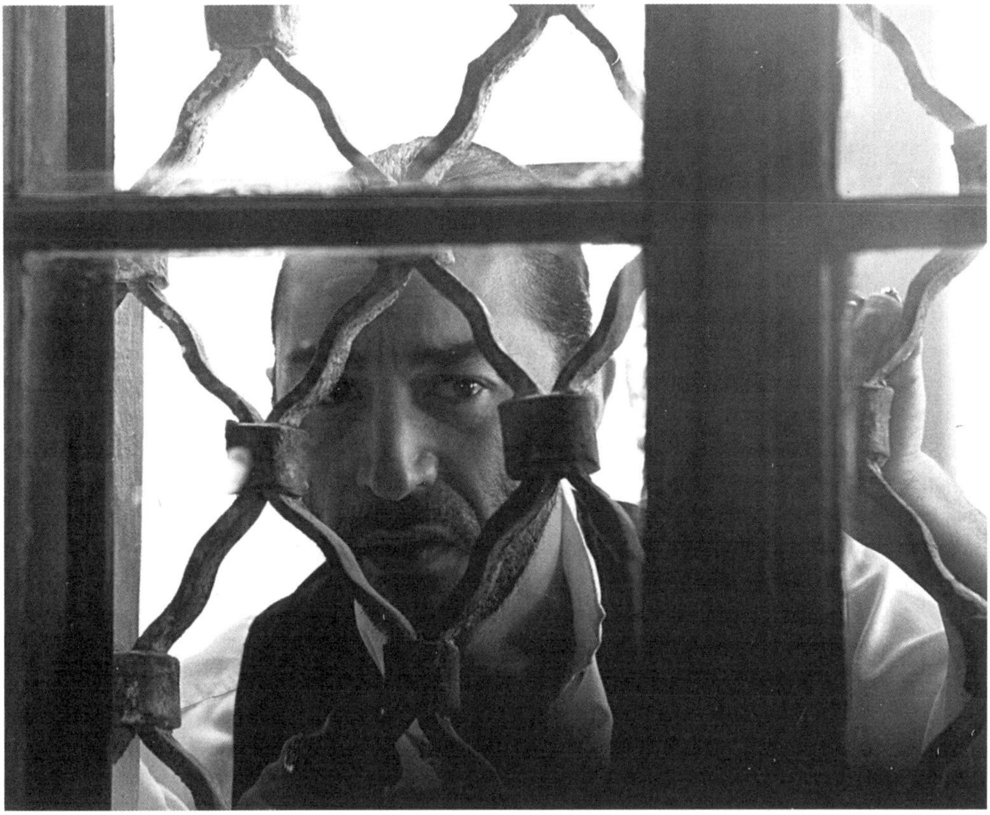

Figure 8.4: French actor Richard Berry as Vuk's brother, Arandjel Isaković, the merchant.

behalf of Austria, hoping for financial rewards and a higher rank in the army. However, as fort after fort is conquered, he sees his countrymen dying in considerable numbers, killed not only by the enemy, but also by the duplicitous Austrian ruling classes, and he realises how wrong and costly his ambition has been. When he confronts the Austrian field marshal about this, it is too late. It is also misplaced, as one of his officers points out: the Serbs made a mistake by going to Austria in the first place. Vuk's "sin" is punished by death at the hands of the Austrians for whom he has just been fighting. In the novel, Vuk comes back from the war, whereas this episode in the film is entirely Petrović's, to emphasise the shortcomings of Vuk's character.

Vuk's brother Arandjel in the film, on the other hand, has very different beliefs to Vuk's. He believes in the power of commerce, and has made himself very rich. At the same time, he frowns upon the popularity of his brother as a war hero, believing that wars and soldiers are "mad", and that the future and existence of the Serbian nation is in commerce, and not in dying for the conquest of territory. Arandjel too, however, takes his position too literally, for he discovers, at the end, that wealth cannot buy him happiness. Nor can he save Dafina's life, for the doctors' claim that there is no hope, notwithstanding his promises of extravagant rewards, nor can he "buy" her a divorce from the church so that she can die content next to her "new" husband. Realising that he cannot buy everything, certainly not happiness, Arandjel casts his gold coins upon the road, the road that takes him back home to the dead Dafina.

Dafina also pays a heavy price for not accepting her fate in Petrović's film. She is annoyed with her husband, and rightly so, as he frequently leaves her and their children to go off to wars from which she never knows whether or not he will return. She starts to wonder whether she should leave him for a more loving and responsible spouse. Her temptation manifests in her brother-in-law, Arandjel, a professional trader who returns home at the end of each day, and who believes in having a family home. Unlike her husband Vuk, a mercenary, here is a man who could be there for her. Dafina initially seems to have accepted the nature of her husband's profession, but she is perturbed when she realises that he has not gone to war against the Ottomans. War with the Ottomans was equally frightening for her, as with any other, but it was a war she could understand on an ideological level. The Ottomans have occupied Serbia, and have made their life there unbearable, if not impossible. Thus, fighting against them makes sense. On this occasion, when Vuk has gone to fight against a country she has never heard of, she starts to doubt her marriage. Before she succumbs to Arandjel's charms, she meditates on how hard a soldier's life is, and how the life of a soldier's wife is even harder. Dafina falls for Arandjel, but finds no happiness with him, as she loves Vuk. It is this desire for an ideal life that leads them all to make their mistakes, and she fails to replace her husband with a better one. Dafina's life ends tragically, not only with her dying, but like her husband, realising her mistake before her death. Petrović has clearly taken literary material in which his favourite theme of love and death can again be expressed.

Ultimately, in *Migrations*, it is the main characters who have to face themselves, and their personal failings arising from their dogmas. The trader Arandjel may be right in criticising his soldier compatriots as idealists that literally drive themselves to death. He is eloquent in explaining that only successful commerce can maintain the nation and its cultural heritage. Nevertheless, he too ends up disillusioned, throwing golden coins on the road. Money, ultimately, cannot give him what he needs. A radically more severe comeuppance awaited his brother Vuk. Unwilling to take a more "ordinary" job, once they moved to Austria, such as Arandjel had, he remained a professional soldier, and moreover, a wildly ambitious one. He quickly learns that his desired promotion to colonel, and his brave command of a Serbian regiment, primarily adds up to his soldiers' body count. Vuk starts to wonder whether his promotion is nearly as important as seeing his young men die in considerable numbers, let alone as important as leaving his beloved wife and children behind. Although he realises his mistake, he does so too late, and turning against his Austrian commander proves to be fatal. Vuk is hanged in prison, fully aware of how futile his life has been. The military career, in which he took such pride, has not brought the rewards and life for which he had hoped. His wife Dafina is also portrayed as a complex character. She is fully aware of the shamelessly dire position of women in the mid-eighteenth century, and Crnjanski thoroughly develops this aspect in his novel.[112] Following this lead, Petrović's Dafina explains the abovementioned adage on a soldier's sad fate, and the even sadder fate of his wife. Examining her situation while in the family home of her brother-in-law, she decides to take charge of her life. However, simply replacing one husband with another does not change things for the better. She too dies, realising her mistake. The fact that all three characters' beliefs are turned upside down in the end, takes the idea of questioning dogmatism to another level, in contrast with Petrović's earlier work. This questioning in *Migrations* actually brings it back closer to *Two*, Petrović's first film, in which the main protagonist Mirko questions himself and his actions.[113] Petrović hence does not question the dogmatism of the so called "grand narratives" – religions or ideologies – but emphasises the struggles that individuals have with their passionate attachments to their own, private beliefs. If these are taken too far, against the facts as well as against reason, just as with adherence to grand narratives, they easily end in tragedy. For Petrović, questioning dogmatism remains a key theme of his work – the fourth of his four political themes – and in his final film he adds this other aspect to the overall picture. By looking at the whole body of his work, it is noticeable that he elaborates his anti-dogmatic stance as a complex notion, operating on various levels, be they social or personal.

If the notion of anti-dogmatism may be understood as complex after looking at Petrović's films as a whole, the same could be said of his relationship to the church, or rather religion in general. If the second political theme that he develops in his films is an examination of religion in society, then this theme is also vividly present in *Migrations*. Petrović portrayed religion in communist society in a rather convoluted position in *Happy Gypsies*. His view of its multifarious – if awkward – position in socialism was perhaps more sympathetic in *It Rains in my Village*, and certainly more so in *The Master and Margarita*. However, in *Group Portrait* he confronted the dogmatism of the church itself, and his portrayal was more critical. In *Migrations*, he gives arguably his most nuanced view. Petrović first introduces a Catholic priest, who is brought in by the Austrian aristocrats to convince Major Vuk Isaković that he and his soldiers ought to convert to Catholicism. They want to impress him by showing him how luxurious Catholic churches are, and they do not hide the connections between Catholicism and the Austrian throne. Maria Theresa, the Austrian empress, was known to be a devout Catholic, merciless towards any attempt at reformation or other schisms in her domain. As a result, the Austrian aristocrats would like to see the Serbian newcomers conform to their beliefs, as the Serbs were all Orthodox Christians. Here, Petrović portrays religion as a mere instrument of power, used as an aid by kings and queens to keep their subjects in order. On the other hand, he portrays the Serbian Orthodox Church in a light visibly different to Catholicism. The independence of Serbian Orthodoxy from Constantinople in the thirteenth century could be explained as motivated by the Serbian kings in order to maintain their own spiritual powers over their subjects.[114] In conjunction with translating the Bible into Serbian (or old Slavic, at that time), this has ultimately left the Serbian Orthodox Church positioned on an equal footing to that of Catholicism in Austria during the Hapsburgs. However, with the fall of the Serbian kingdom to the Ottomans, the position of the Serbian Orthodox Church changed dramatically, and it is this subsequent position that is relevant both to the novel and the film. The Church became marginalised, and the priests and clergy in the film are also shown as refugees. Furthermore, to the Serbs their Church remained as the last institution of their lost kingdom – a sort of repository for their culture and identity. Both brothers are shown in the film as well known patrons of the Church, but who also, if need be, asked for things in return. Arandjel, once he decided to marry his sister-in-law, first has to secure her divorce by the Church. He arranges a meeting with one of the Church's archbishops, and introduces himself as a successful merchant, who has already given generously, but will give incomparably more to the Church, providing he can marry Dafina. That in the eighteenth century redemption could be purchased from the Church, is now well known. However, Arandjel forgets who is he up against, for his older brother – Vuk – is considered a war hero, and has also generously supported the Church. Dafina is refused a divorce, and the two cannot be married. This prompts Arandjel to speak out against the Church, his nation and his brother, for whom he says that he never knew the treasure he had – a wife like Dafina. Arandjel tries to talk to the archbishop again, but to no avail. He then talks to another bishop, Nenadović, who helps Arandjel accept the Church's decision.

At the entrance to the monastery, Arandjel encounters a monk who has been tortured by the Ottoman soldiers in Serbia, which prompted him to escape to Austria. Nenadović tells Arandjel that "We devour each other, while the Lord is in our hearts." He tries to remind Arandjel how everything around them is simply wrong, and that does not only include the brutality of the Ottomans towards the Serbs, but equally the fact that his brother is a mercenary fighting for the Austrians, and that he desires his brother's wife. The Bishop further reminds him of the emptiness of existence, especially when one is on the wrong path. Nenadović is charismatically played by the Swede, Erland Josephson, and this scene provides a different image of the Orthodox Church to the one of the Catholic Church given earlier in the film. The Orthodox Church becomes a moral parameter, helping the protagonists deal with the angst of their existence. If Petrović's relation to the Church were to be extracted from this portrayal of both Christian denominations, it could be concluded that his relationship was and remained complex. Petrović does not offer answers or attitudes, but engages with the multifaceted roles that the Church and religious beliefs play in different times and places.

The important subplot from the novel, carefully developed in the film, is the relationship between the Austrian aristocrats commanding the army, and the Serbian soldiers, who for them are strangers and renegades, even refugees, from the Ottoman Empire. This awkward relationship between them enables Petrović to develop his third political theme – the link between those who are privileged and those who are not. It very quickly becomes clear that this link is an uncomfortable marriage of convenience, in which each side quickly becomes distrustful of the other. Again, the overall picture is not easily polarised. An Austrian aristocrat initially explains to Vuk that he needs to get promoted, and that due to his skills he should not have a problem with that. To do so, however, he and his soldiers need to fully "embrace" the Austrian empress, and become subjects of the empire. The way to do this is through converting to Catholicism. For the Serbs, who believed that they maintained their national identity under the Ottomans by not accepting the occupier's official religion of Islam, and who stayed Orthodox Christians, this is taken as an insult. For Vuk, promotion means acceptance, but he wants to be accepted on his own terms and has no intention of converting. At this point, he starts talking about the need for all the Serbs who have left Serbia under the Ottomans to emigrate to Russia and find their home there. However cumbersome the Austrian aristocrat's offer of assimilation, he did indeed made the offer. As in the novel, the Serbian soldiers are portrayed as uncouth and unruly bunch. They have seen atrocities in their conflicts with the Ottomans, and now, as refugees, they have nothing left to lose. The Austrians decide to push them to the front lines first, and Vuk gets the impression that his men are fighting the French, while the Austrian soldiers follow behind, keeping a check on them. Vuk is provoked by the fact that his soldiers are frequently arrested and punished, and loses his temper when he finds out that a group of them has been arrested for stealing cabbages in a French village. He turns angrily to the Austrian guards, stating that his Serbs bleed for Austria on the battlefield, and should not be penalised for the sake of a few cabbages. When the Austrian high commander, Karl von Lothringen, takes an interest in Vuk, asking why the Serbs are always so angry, it is already too late. The years of strife and bloody conflicts have perhaps made them difficult to understand for the well-cushioned Austrian aristocracy. Communication breaks down completely when another commander, Leopold von Berenklau, decides to arrest Vuk for letting a French officer free. He is not only reprimanding Vuk for disobeying orders and letting prisoners go, but he insults Vuk by hinting that the Officer was a nobleman, whereas Vuk is not. Vuk realises that he has only been taunted with the prospect of promotion by the Austrians, as he ultimately will never receive it: the Austrian Empire would never accept them for who they are. To emphasise this point is interesting in the context of the novel, and the subsequent history of the Austrian-Hapsburg Empire. Miloš Crnjanski fought as a soldier for the Empire in their ultimate war, War World I. By that point, numerous ethnic groups living in the empire had grown to despise it, and were unwilling to fight for its interests. Above all, the crude authoritarian rule of the last Emperor, Franz Joseph, who was unwilling to modernise or moderate its system, only secured its collapse. This collapse came in 1918, four years after the declaration of war on Serbia. The lesson to be drawn from this theme is that the dismissal of social groups, class, ethnic, or otherwise, in contrast to their integration, leads to the polarisation of society, which then often leads to conflict. These questions were worthy of consideration for those who had inherited Tito's Yugoslavia, a country born out of the ashes of the Austro-Hungarian Empire. However, Petrović's *Migrations* arrived too late to provide them with such a lesson.

The more intriguing political theme, the first of the four political themes that Petrović developed in his work, is that concerning the nature of ethnicity, and interethnic relationships. As noted above, this theme is very much present in this film, and is especially relevant considering the political situation in Yugoslavia at the time. In order to see how Petrović

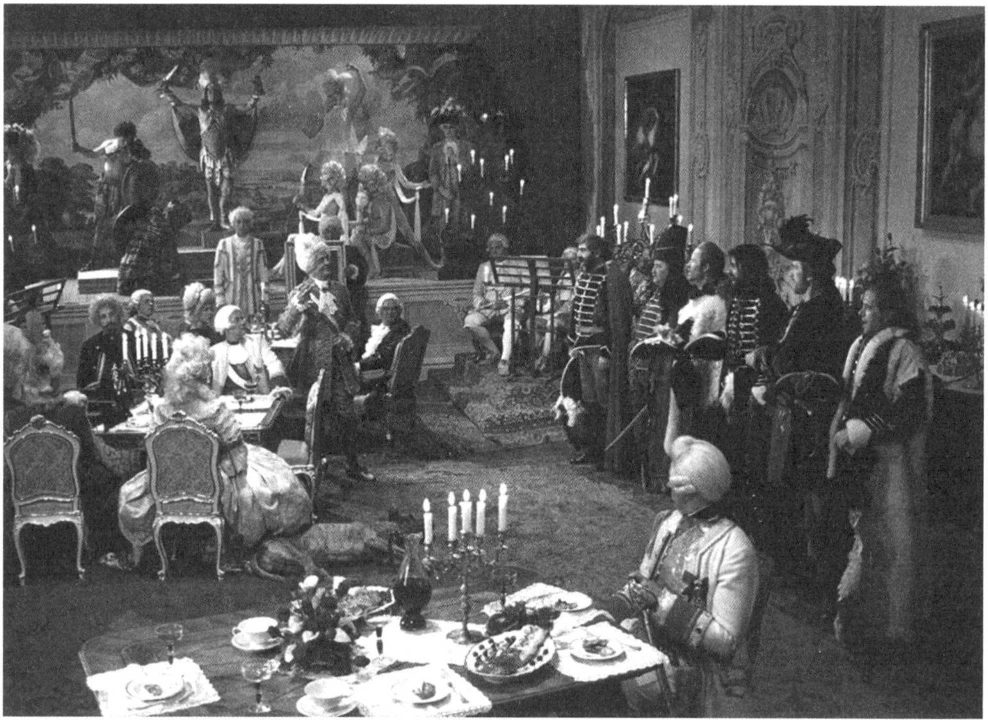

Figure 8.5: Serbs at the luxurious reception hosted by the Austrian aristocrats…

perceived this issue, it is worth unearthing its various aspects within *Migrations*. Initially, the story is inhabited by characters of diverse nationalities, as in most of Petrović's films. Petrović was much concerned with these issues, and treated them carefully. In *Migrations* an almost schematically correct approach to the topic may thus be extracted. The most sympathetic character is the main protagonist's enemy, the French Officer that Vuk arrests in battle. Although Vuk does not send his prisoner to death, as he was ordered to do, it is not Vuk who ends up appearing gallant in this affair. Vuk saves his prisoner's life, as the French Officer has previously forgiven him his. Vuk asks him why he did this, and the French Officer states that the French do not kill those who cannot defend themselves. Vuk responds that the Frenchman is wrong, as Vuk's soldiers always kill their enemy, providing they have a chance. The Serbs are thereby shown as savage, hardened soldiers, while the French appear as if they are trying to be humane, even in war. Again, Petrović ensures that this representation is not over-simplified. The French army, however humane, is also shown as compulsively killing their deserters.

Above all, Petrović's portrayal of the aristocracy is very critical. A French aristocrat is described as being of German birth, but is oblivious to anything but the struggle to maintain his privileges within the French army and court. This means fighting against Germans

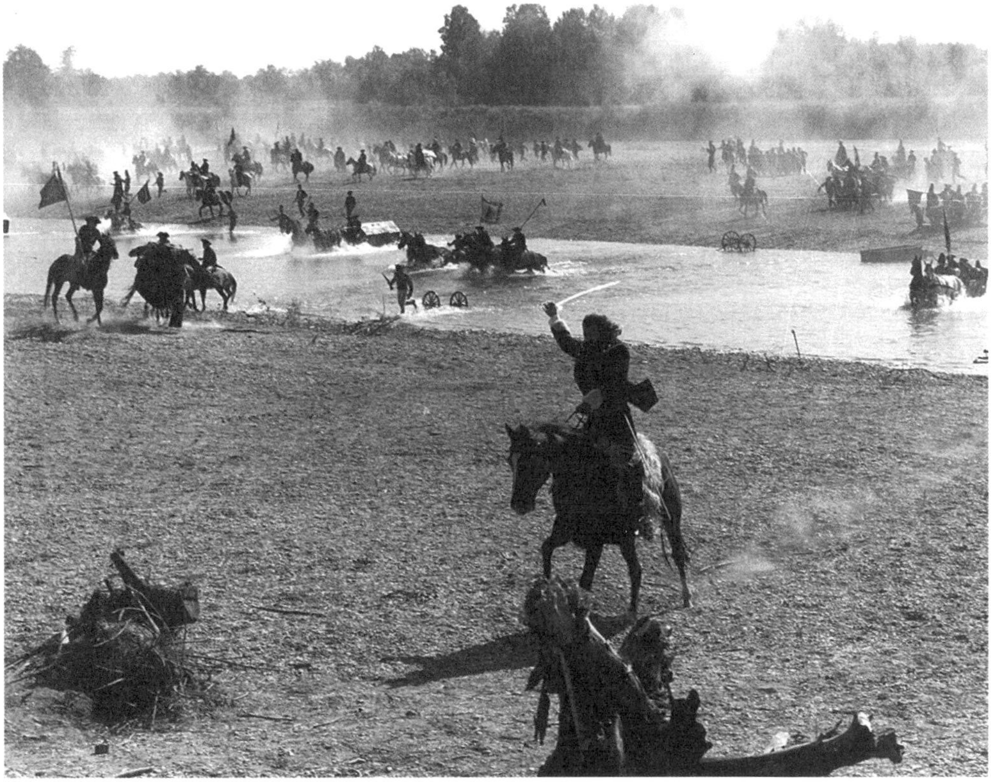

Figure 8.6: ... and the Serbs facing the horrors of the battlefield.

too. Petrović's saves his most scathing portrayal for that of the Austrian aristocracy and commanders. On the one hand, they are shown as cultured and polite, and even willing to engage with the Serbs. On the other though, they are viciously ambitious, and thirsty for conflicts that will enlarge their empire, as well as entertain them. Thus, Karl von Lothringen observes a pitiless battle with binoculars from a safe distance. Sheltered under a plush canopy, with food and drink in front of him, he is entertained by a chamber orchestra and opera singer to one side. In this atmosphere, Lothringen explains how after winning the war with the French, he plans a war with Prussia. The Austrian aristocrats in the film come across as haughty, duplicitous and difficult to sympathise with. This certainly has its roots in the novel, as Crnjanski had personal experience of the last generation of this aristocracy, before the Hapsburg Empire collapsed. Intriguingly, although the Ottoman Turks are badly spoken of in the film, the only Turkish character is a doctor whom Arandjel employs to cure Dafina. He comes across as wise and trustworthy, and a very kind character. It is clear that Petrović's portrayal is almost schematically correct, making sure that any nation mentioned in the film is portrayed in a three-dimensional way, being neither beatified nor demonised.

Petrović's focus in *Migrations* is on the Serbs, however, and their portrayal needs to be examined more closely. To start with, there is nothing intrinsically different in the way the Serbs are portrayed compared to those of any other nationality. Nevertheless, as the Serbs are the main protagonists of the film, their portrayal unambiguously reveals the nature of nationhood for Petrović. As noted above, the two protagonists, the brothers Vuk and Arandjel, are very different, both physically and psychologically. More importantly, they articulate this difference eloquently. One is a proud soldier, who dreams of emigrating to the new homeland – Russia. The other is a merchant, who claims that his homeland is where his business is, and openly shows his disagreements with his brother. Dafina is torn between the two: rationally, she wants the merchant, whereas emotionally she connects with the soldier. The members of the Serbian Church, even though uniformed clergy, are very diverse too. While the archbishop does not even want to address Arandjel directly, Bishop Nenadović takes time and sympathises with the sinner. Overall, just as with his Roma-Gypsies in *Happy Gypsies*, or the Germans in *Group Portrait*, Petrović's Serbs are portrayed as a heterogeneous group. In the late 1980s, in Yugoslavia, this perspective had significant meaning: as the common country – Yugoslavia – was disintegrating, its constitutive elements started re-grouping along ethnic lines, Serbs included. This re-grouping often involved the reiteration of ethnic stereotypes, as well as finding comfort in the rediscovery – and re-building – of national mythologies. For Petrović to show that there is no such thing as a coherent image of a nation, but that a nation is, by its very nature, heterogeneous, and has to be understood and accepted as such, was another pithy political comment on the current situation in Yugoslavia. As a Serbian himself, he showed this by portraying Serbs at a time of historical and political hardship: his engagement with this sensitive issue was responsible as well as timely.

Petrović's Serbs in *Migrations* are a wandering nation. Like his Germans in *Group Portrait with Lady*, they are trying to compensate for historical and social pressures by developing abstract concepts through which to look for redemption. These concepts for Serbs or Germans, as with any nation, end tragically, as such idealised solutions are bound to fall short of people's expectations. Whilst Dafina is dying, Arandjel, in his thoughts, berates Vuk and his officers for developing their myth of Russia, in which the entire nation's problems would be solved. Instead, Arandjel claims that they are not aware of what they have already got when they leave their families and homes to go off to fight futile wars. However, Arandjel also realises that his commerce is not enough to find happiness. All the characters end up discovering that the higher concepts they looked up to were not what life was about. Their zealous – or dogmatic – pursuit of these concepts brought no reward in the end. Finally, in relation to Crnjanski's characters in the novel, Petrović slightly amplifies this point, but only slightly, as David Norris concludes: "Salvation for Crnjanski's characters remain limited, tenuous, and only ever potential."[115]

In this respect, Crnjanski's *Migrations* does tackle an important political and historical myth in Serbia: that which promises the Serbs another motherland in Russia, where their problems and misfortunes will cease to exist. In his novel, Crnjanski – albeit artistically – deconstructs and undercuts this "Russophile myth". It should be added here that, in his other major work, *A Novel About London* (*Roman o Londonu*, 1971), he deals with the other – perhaps opposite – myth nurtured in Serbian history. This myth seeks salvation in Europe, where a "Europhile myth" is artistically summed up as an "Anglophile myth". Crnjanski shows in both novels that these myths are just myths. As is seen in Petrović's earlier work, myths and idealism, whether political or historical, particularly if followed zealously or dogmatically, bring individuals and even nations to tragedy. At the end of the war in which Vuk Isaković served, it is clear that he should not have gone to war, and that his people died for nothing. Before *Migrations* was finally screened in Yugoslavia in the early 1990s, the nation was already engaged in a bloody civil conflict. Art, it can be argued, cannot change the world – but it can serve as a warning. Petrović's *Migrations* was a compelling warning, but it was a warning that arrived too late.

8. 3. The Lessons of *Migrations* and the Last Days

8. 3. 1. A Few Notes on Petrović's Adaptations

In a brief review of Petrović's *The Master and Margarita*, written in the early twenty-first century, Clarke Fountain of the *All Movie Guide* qualified the film as "a brave attempt to film the unfilmable".[116] This assessment could easily apply to all three of these adaptations. The three novels he chose to turn into films could hardly be more elaborate and difficult to bring to the screen. If compared to his adaptation of Isaković's stories for *Three*, or taking Dostoyevsky's motifs for *It Rains in my Village*, these three novels represent a much more ambitious encounter with literature.

All three of *The Master and Margarita*, *Group Portrait with Lady* and *Migrations* are considerably lengthy, and if all the events depicted in them were included, the resulting films would have lasted at least three or four times longer than an average feature film. To deal with this problem, Petrović resorted to two main methods when turning the books into film scripts. One was a thorough reduction of events and characters, while the other was an amalgamation of the same elements. Particularly with *The Master and Margarita* and *Migrations*, Petrović also added whole episodes that did not exist in the original texts. These episodes were needed to translate into images certain motifs from the novels that were too literary, as well as to allow Petrović to elucidate his own view on the issues in question. Two obvious examples are the scene at the Writers Union in *The Master and Margarita*,[117] and the abovementioned episodes with the captured French Officer in *Migrations*. Evidently, Petrović had to alter the original novels considerably in order to make the "unfilmable" filmable. Nevertheless, as may have been expected, these attempts to "lens" such acclaimed texts caused avalanches of criticism. Petrović's adaptation of *Migrations* was qualified as "cold" by his friend and collaborator Draško Redjep,[118] while Jean-Michel Frodon assessed it as "too academic" in *Le Monde*.[119] This again, could have been anticipated considering the expectations the public had for the adaptation of one of the major novels written in the Serbian language. The same happened with *The Master and Margarita*, where literary critics in Yugoslavia and Russia split hairs over various alterations of the novel.[120] In this respect, there is no need to add that the reception of the film of Böll's novel in Germany was similar.[121] In the decades since their initial release, these three major films have not been as readily available as one might have expected them to be,[122] and they were simply not nearly as popular with international audiences as *I Even Met Happy Gypsies* had been. The three films were often critically dismissed on the premise that the literary texts on which they were based, considering their unique literary forms, were not suitable for cinematic adaptation.

After carefully scrutinising Petrović's adaptations, it could be easily argued that the films are in fact well thought out and very thoroughly executed. This applies to the scripts, as well as the films. Even where Petrović has radically altered the novels, he found elements in the texts from which to develop his "implanted" episodes.[123] What may have been a more crucial reason for these films' lack of success is to be found on a different level. The three films were all international co-productions, and were all made in two different versions: *The Master and Margarita* exists in Italian and Yugoslav versions; *Group Portrait with Lady* in German and French versions; and *Migrations* in French and Yugoslav. This meant that the actors would speak for themselves in the language of one version only, and in the other version they would be dubbed – their voices synchronised by another actor. Furthermore, as the cast was international on all three productions, for each film there were at least a few actors who were dubbed in both versions. This had an inhibiting effect on the actors' performances in an attempt to ensure that they could be easily dubbed as necessary – which in turn inevitably impaired the acting. The original novels were long and complex: long episodes with nuanced emotional feelings had to be shown in short scenes on film, which thus required the actors to deliver ever more intricate emotional portraits of their characters. The actors found themselves on the verge of an impossible task, as they had to deliver highly nuanced performances without speaking the necessary, or indeed any, language. This "mouth opening", which was not followed by the right emotional response, produced characters who often ended up looking stilted. This was a significant setback for these films, as the acting was incongruous in these otherwise lavish productions. Examples of this are the scene in which Avtandil Makharadze, as Vuk Isaković – an actor who spoke neither Serbian nor French – had to deliver a subtle speech on why he would not accept Catholicism; or where Ugo Tognazzi as the Master declares, somewhat abruptly, his love to Margarita; or the scene where Isabelle Huppert as Dafina questions her fidelity to Vuk. All of these scenes fail to convey the emotional subtleties that were expected and needed. As the sub-chapters on the reception of these films have shown, such use of synchronisation or dubbing was criticised in all three films, and the acting itself criticised as a consequence. Although such criticism could be understood as fair, it is also important to note that the practice of dubbing actors into foreign languages was and still is very common. However, the synchronisation of the added voice-track, regardless of technological advances, is still not easy to match perfectly. On the contrary, even with Luchino Visconti's 1963 classic *Il Gattopardo*, although discretely mitigated through framing, it was noticeable that Burt Lancaster, the American actor, did not speak his lines in Italian. Regardless, the film is now perceived as one of the masterpieces of world cinema. In another example, made decades after *Il Gattopardo*, it is also clear that the German actor Bruno Ganz does not speak his lines in Greek in *Eternity and a Day* by Theo Angelopoulos, and this did not prevent the film from winning the coveted Palme d'Or at the Cannes Film Festival in 1998.[124] The practice of dubbing certainly deserves the criticism it receives, although the nature of these international co-productions necessitated Petrović working with international casts – which meant the actors had to be dubbed. The only way the indispensable finances could be raised was by employing "stars" – but this concept proved to be a double-edged sword. Petrović was a director who had managed to successfully direct actors who did not speak Romany, although they spoke their lines in that language in *I Even Met Happy Gypsies* – and made them believable.[125] This worked in that particular film since Romany is not perhaps as well-known a language as German, Italian or French, and more crucially, since it was spoken and not dubbed. The same strategy could not always be applied with the same results, however.

Overall, these adaptations were very ambitious, and there are numerous other smaller or larger elements that undermine them as a whole. They certainly deserve another, more detailed, separate study, which could not be pursued here. As the above analyses have shown, however, Petrović's intellectual and artistic intentions were well conceived and well thought out. Well conceived and well thought out plans do not guarantee successful results, particularly in arts, and this seems to have been the fate of his last three films. If his work warned about the discrepancy between wishes and outcomes, the reception of this impressive large-scale production, his final film, provided an ironic twist.

8. 3. 2. *Migrations* Thus Far

There are four different years which are often claimed as the year in which *Migrations* was released. These are 1988, 1989, 1993 and 1994. None of them is quite correct, but considering what happened to the project, none of them is entirely false either. The first version of the film was completed in 1988, and was supposed to be screened in 1989. It was this supposed premiere in 1989, when the film was to open the Cannes Film Festival, that makes this year the most common one for the year of production. The screening did not happen due to a legal dispute between the French producers in Paris. The first unofficial premiere took place in the small French seaside town of Saint Malo, in 1993, and there was an unofficial screening of the film at the Cannes Film Festival in the same year. Notwithstanding continuing difficulties, Petrović finished the Serbian version of the film in time to be shown at the Sava Centre in Belgrade on 28 April 1994. All four years may therefore qualify as the year of release.

Migrations ended up as a very "unlucky" project, and to list all the setbacks that hamstrung the production would form a tragic novel in itself. Petrović almost abandoned the production in the early stages of filming, as his only son, Dragan, died on 9 November 1987. He returned to the set, but while he was filming in Yugoslavia, he found out that the negatives were being legally "blocked" in France, where the laboratories were processing the film stock. This was due to the fact that, according to *Le Figaro*, the French production companies changed owners in problematic ways.[126] Petrović had to start a legal battle in France, and he finally reclaimed the film from the courts only in time for the screening at a smaller festival in Saint Malo. In the meantime, the war in Yugoslavia was at its most vicious, and across Western Europe and North America, the Serbs were being blamed as the instigators. The Republic of Serbia, then part of the newly formed Federal Republic of Yugoslavia,[127] was under international economic and cultural sanctions. Petrović had difficulty finding a distributor in France, according to Petar Volk, as some distributors wanted to see all the legal disputes with previous producers resolved, while others were politically minded, and refused to take the film because of the war in Yugoslavia.[128] The fact that this film has an obvious anti-war stance appeared to be irrelevant. Petrović continued to work on the Serbian language version, and tried to arrange a screening in his war-torn country.

Along with the death of his son, all the legal battles he had to fight in relation to *Migrations*, and at the same time, with the political situation in his country rapidly eroding, Petrović's health started to decline.[129] Early in 1994 he was diagnosed with a brain tumour in Belgrade. Petrović returned to Paris, this time to be operated on.[130] At the time of *Migrations*' premiere in Belgrade, his health was failing. He died in the Salpêtrière hospital in Paris, on the 20 August 1994.

After the premiere in Belgrade, there were a few other screenings of the film in Yugoslavia, mainly at local festivals, but as the country was falling apart physically and economically, with the highest inflation rate ever, the film was not subsequently distributed. *Migrations*, in this respect, remains an "unseen" film, as it was never properly distributed, neither in Serbia, nor Yugoslavia, nor internationally. The film thus still awaits judgement by audiences, if or when it gets into distribution. Petrović's death in 1994 and continuing problems in what was once Yugoslavia have so far thwarted all efforts to show the film. It remains, however, as a significant legacy of a country and system, which are now no more. *Migrations*, the film, has disappeared for the time being, just like Yugoslavia, the country in which it was made.

8. 3. 3. Last Days

After Tito's death in 1980, the death of Yugoslavia followed soon after. As explained in the introduction to this chapter, this happened in three short stages, the last of which started in 1988. In January 1990, the League of Communists of Yugoslavia fell apart at its 14th Interim Congress without ever delivering the much needed constitutional change. The representatives passed that responsibility to those who would take over power after the already imminent open democratic elections. These elections took place not on the federal level, but on the level of individual Republics, and the Republics inevitably went their separate ways. The speed with which the country and its political system disintegrated was extraordinary. As noted above, the blaze of disintegration was ignited by the Republics' irreconcilable policies on federal restructuring. These were first signalled by the new leaders in Slovenia and Serbia. In particular, the rise to power of Slobodan Milošević in Serbia, in September 1987, was of momentous significance for the future development of the country.

Slobodan Milošević is widely perceived as one of the key culprits in the violent break-up of Yugoslavia, although his rise to power in Serbia was controversial. As Jasna Dragović-Soso explains in her seminal work on Yugoslav dissident culture during communism, Milošević was initially perceived as a liberal reformer. After taking office, he rehabilitated many who had been persecuted for decades, most importantly Milovan Djilas,[131] the true heretic of Yugoslav communism.[132] The all-pervasive atmosphere of increased tolerance in 1987 and 1988 has confused many intellectuals in Belgrade. This included Vesna Pešić, the academic with a longstanding career in the struggle for freedom of speech during communism, who explained "how indeterminate the atmosphere in 1988 was", and how difficult it was to judge "which way things would go – towards genuine democratic change or greater intolerance and fear."[133] This was particularly interesting in Belgrade, where there was a long intellectual tradition of struggle for democratic reforms and free speech. It was when Milošević proposed constitutional changes before the free democratic elections that numerous intellectuals started rallying against him. As a former communist leader, who reformed the Serbian branch of the party into the Socialist Party of Serbia, it was his flirtation with nationalism that has perplexed many. By 1989, countless dissidents against Tito's communism now regrouped against Milošević.[134]

This process of rehabilitating dissidents, as already noted, had an effect on Aleksandar Petrović, who received the largest state prize in 1987. However, as also pointed out, this reappraisal was tenuous, and it could be argued, lacking in an element of true reconciliation. The first reason was Petrović's pursuit of a response or explanation for not being immediately reinstated as professor at the Faculty of Dramatic Arts.[135] As this did not happen until 25 October 1991, when the system that had persecuted him was no more, the amends were not made in time.[136] More importantly, with the situation in both Serbia and Yugoslavia becoming increasingly chaotic at the tail end of communist rule, and with the first free elections announced, Petrović decided to enter politics. He had never been a member of the Communist Party,[137] and in the late 1980s, he began a political career, although it did not last long, due to his untimely death. He joined the Liberal Party, which was very critical of Milošević's policies.[138] As a candidate for parliament in the first democratic elections, he stood against Velimir Bata Živojinović, the famous actor whom he had cast in five out of eight of his feature films – and who was the candidate of Milošević's Socialist Party of Serbia.[139] Needless to add, the actor won the seat in these elections, presumably as actors' faces are much better known to the public than those of film directors. Petrović's resentment of the political system grew, both the former of Tito and the latter of Milošević, in particular after his son's death. In 1990, Petrović returned all the state awards he had ever received, including

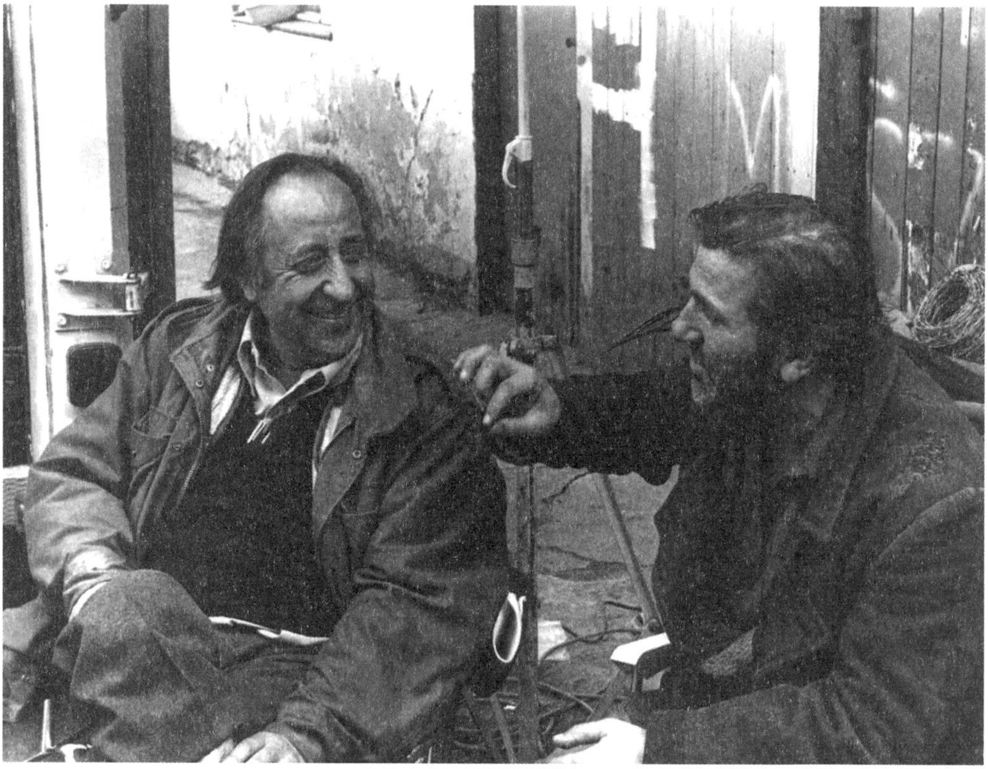

Figure 8.7: Aleksandar Petrović (left) with one of his favourite actors, Velimir Bata Živojinović, on the set of *Group Portrait with Lady*.

the financial rewards attached to them.[140] The system and one of its most distinguished filmmakers were never reconciled.

It is also important to remember that in that turbulent period – 1987 and 1988 – Petrović was filming *Migrations*. The legal problems which affected the film in France in 1989 obstructed its completion and distribution. Once these problems were finally resolved, albeit only partially, Yugoslavia was already engaged in a bloody civil conflict. The West's insistence on Milošević's exclusive culpability for the situation in Yugoslavia saw Serbia under international sanctions from 1992 until 1996.[141] Boro Drašković, the Yugoslav film director and colleague of Petrović, explains how they organised a well attended Central European film festival in Belgrade in 1991.[142] Due to the international sanctions, however, similar cultural activities, including this one, had to come to a halt. Petrović, who was still well respected internationally, together with other Serbian filmmaking colleagues, lobbied for the sanctions on culture and film to be lifted.[143] Most of the filmmakers and intellectuals were known to be opposed to Milošević's policies, and sanctioning everyone was to have potentially grave consequences. The opposition's room for manoeuvre against the regime was thus also restricted, and Drašković commented: "what film has achieved, politics ruined."[144]

Throughout these events, Petrović fought to release *Migrations*. As the situation in Yugoslavia became progressively worse, he tried to rescue the film as a French co-production. Ultimately, he was a Frenchman too.[145] He was also in conflict with Milošević's regime in Serbia, frequently blaming it for instructing Television Belgrade to stop production of the TV series.[146] However, it was also difficult to release the film in France. As noted above, some producers wanted to see the legal disputes resolved in their entirety, which was difficult due to the situation in now former-Yugoslavia. Others were concerned with the political sanctions imposed on Serbia. The news in France was dominated with images of the war in Bosnia and Herzegovina, with the Serbs blamed as perpetrators. Although the previous analysis of *Migrations* has demonstrated that this was clearly an anti-war film, with a very complex portrayal of a nation, this nation was – nonetheless – the Serbian nation. Additionally, at a brief glance, it could be argued that the Serbian Church comes across rather better than the Catholic one in the film, and more importantly, that the Serbian soldiers are shown to be victims of the duplicitous policies of the European superpowers. David Norris, while writing on the source novel explains: "The political intrigues and military contests between the European powers determine the fate of the Serbs with no regards for the Serbs themselves."[147] The film did focus on that part of history in which the Serbs were persecuted and struggling for their survival, which perhaps goes some way towards explaining their distrust of the great powers. In the early 1990s, however, while in France and the West in general, the Serbs were perceived as the architects of the Yugoslav conflict, no one could perhaps be persuaded that distributing a film on the history of Serbian suffering was a viable commercial proposition. Had *Migrations* been released in 1989, it would have been a timely film, but in 1993, the time it seems was no longer right.

Together with the death of his only child in 1987, Petrović had the death of his country to mourn from 1991, which he did publicly in *Cahiers du Cinéma*.[148] The production of *Migrations* had been beset with continuing problems, and he was still struggling to obtain the release of the negative when, in 1993, he fell ill. He died on the operating table in the summer of 1994, at the age of 65, in France, far away from the country in which he had made the majority of his work. In the obituaries published internationally it was often emphasised that he was a Serbian director, but that he was politically opposed to Milošević's regime.[149] Even the French communist newspaper *L'Humanite* emphasised this fact.[150] In fact, his opposition to Milošević often eclipsed the mention of his films in the obituaries, demonstrating that even in death, politics continued to cast a dark shadow over his career and work.

Migrations did not get a cinematic release during Petrović's lifetime. His country fell apart, as well as the political system that had supported it. *Migrations* itself could also be read as a film about things falling apart: the two brothers wrong each other, and the wife abandons her husband. In the last scene, however, a ghostly Dafina leaves her house to greet the ghost of her husband Vuk on his horse, coming back from the war. This is accompanied by Aleksandar Petrović speaking in the voice-over, explaining that it is only an apparition in front of our eyes. Film, as a medium, works as an apparition, a shadow play in time unfolding in front of one's eyes. In films everything is possible, and the reconciliation of these characters, which did not take place during their lives, took place after them, in death. Or rather, in an imagined time and space that perhaps these characters inhabited in the afterlife. As such a scene ends Petrović's final film, I would be tempted to read it as his call for reconciliation – a reconciliation that he felt he might not, and indeed did not, find during his lifetime. However, it is a reconciliation that he still hoped would eventually materialise on the territory of the country once known as Yugoslavia.

Notes

1   See the introduction to Chapter 6.
2   See the introduction to Chapter 7.
3   Misha Glenny stated that "the mechanisms of the 1974 Constitution were little more than window dressing", as "policy was made by the two elderly leaders"; see Misha Glenny, *The Balkans 1804–1999: Nationalism, War and the Great Powers* (London: Granta Books, 1999), p. 623.
4   Tito was declared President for Life of Yugoslavia in 1974.
5   On their deaths, particularly Tito's, see Misha Glenny, *The Balkans*, pp. 622–23.
6   John R. Lampe, *Yugoslavia as History: Twice There Was a Country* (Cambridge: Cambridge University Press, 1996), p. 293.
7   John R. Lampe, *Yugoslavia as History*, pp. 293–94.
8   Jasna Dragović-Soso, *'Saviours of the Nation': Serbia's Intellectual Opposition and the Revival of Nationalism* (London: Hurst & Company, 2002), p. 64.
9   For example, this crisis had a severe impact on the economic, political, and above all, social life in the United Kingdom, and enabled the rise to power of Margaret Thatcher.
10   John R. Lampe, *Yugoslavia as History*, p. 293.
11   Dejan Jović, *Jugoslavija – Država koja je odumrla: Uspon, kriza i pad Četvrte Jugoslavije* (Beograd: Samizdat B92; Zagreb: Prometej, 2003), p. 308.
12   Jasna Dragović-Soso, *'Saviours of the Nation'*, p. 77.
13   Mirić quoted in Jasna Dragović-Soso, *'Saviours of the Nation'*, p. 77. Mirić's book was entitled *The System and the Crisis (Sistem i kriza)*.
14   Jasna Dragović-Soso, *'Saviours of the Nation'*, p. 78.
15   ibid.
16   Dedijer's book was published as early as 1981. See Jasna Dragović-Soso, *'Saviours of the Nation'*, p. 78.
17   John R. Lampe, *Yugoslavia as History*, p. 293.
18   On the significance of this year it is worth closely scrutinising the work of all the historians frequently quoted in this book, namely Dragović-Soso, Glenny, Jović and Lampe.
19   John R. Lampe, *Yugoslavia as History*, p. 325.

20 See John R. Lampe, *Yugoslavia as History*, p. 325; as well as all of his Chapter 11: "Ethnic politics and the end of Yugoslavia".

21 Ranko Munitić, *Adio, Jugo-film!* (Beograd, Kragujevac: Srpski kulturni klub, Centar film, Prizma, 2005), p. 16.

22 Daniel J. Goulding, *Liberated Cinema: The Yugoslav Experience* (Bloomington: Indiana University Press, 1985), p. 143.

23 See the preface to Aleksandar Petrović's script *Emanuela*, written by his wife Branka Petrović; in Aleksandar Petrović, *1973. Godina vampira: Emanuela II, Baron vampir, Džon F. Kenedi* (Beograd: Autorska izdanja, Foto Futura, 2010), p. 12.

24 Personal interview with Branka Petrović (11 September 2005).

25 See Chapter 6 (section 6.2.1).

26 David A. Norris, the British scholar on Crnjanski, suggests that the title of the novel ought to be translated as *Emigrations* (see David A. Norris, *The Novels of Miloš Crnjanski: An Approach through Time* [Nottingham: Astra Press, 1990], p. vii). However, I opted for *Migrations* in order to be consistent with the original French title of the film.

27 Personal interview with Branka Petrović (11 September 2005).

28 ibid.

29 Petrović used to describe these events frequently, particularly in his interviews from the period; see Milomir Marić, "Vreme relaksacije", *Duga*, 6 January 1979, p. 20; R. Popović, "Ima seoba – smrti nema", *Politika*, 19 August 1978; and Žika Lazić, "Zašto ne snima u našoj zemlji", *Duga*, 23 July 1977, p. 21. This correspondence is also mentioned in the biography of Miloš Crnjanski, and his letter to Petrović, dated 9 September 1959, has been reprinted; see Radovan Popović, *Život Miloša Crnjanskog* (Beograd: Prosveta, 1980), pp. 221–22.

30 On this short film, see Chapter 2 (section 2.1.2).

31 An interview with Aleksandar Petrović, quoted from Aleksandar Petrović, *Novi Film 1950–1965* (Beograd: Institut za Film, 1971), p. 79.

32 This is also mentioned in Miloš Crnjanski's biography, where it is stated that when the contract was signed, a verbal agreement was made that the film would be directed by Aleksandar Petrović; see Radovan Popović, *Život Miloša Crnjanskog*, p. 243.

33 Žika Lazić, "Zašto ne snima u našoj zemlji", pp. 20–21.

34 Žika Lazić, "Zašto ne snima u našoj zemlji", p. 21.

35 Aleksandar Petrović describes this meeting in his autobiography; see Aleksandar Petrović, *Sve Moje Ljubavi/Slepi periskopi* (Novi Sad: Prometej, Tajanstvena Tačka, 1995), pp. 223–25.

36 Mira Boglić, "Film 'Tri' i njegov autor", *Vjesnik*, 19 August 1977, p. 13.

37 ibid.

38 ibid.

39 Petar Volk, *Let nad močvarom: Aleksandar Petrović svojim životom, delom i filmovima* (Beograd: Institut za film, 1999), p. 299.

40 An interview with Aleksandar Petrović; see Milomir Marić, "Vreme relaksacije", *Duga*, 6 January 1979, p. 20.

41 Žika Lazić, "Zašto ne snima u našoj zemlji", p. 21.

42 On this project see Chapter 7 (section 7.1.1).

43 Žika Lazić, "Zašto ne snima u našoj zemlji", p. 21.

44 This was Alberto Lattuada's *Cuore di cane*; see Chapter 7 (section 7.1.1).

45 Milomir Marić, "Vreme relaksacije", p. 19.

46 Petar Volk, *Let nad močvarom*, pp. 303–05.

47 Petar Volk, *Let nad močvarom*, p. 305.

48 Petrović's adaptations of Bulgakov are published in Serbia; see Aleksandar Petrović, *Pseće srce, Majstor i Margarita, dramatizacije; Purpurno ostrvo, adaptacija; Po delima Mihajla Afanasijeviča Bulgakova* (Beograd: Paideia, 2007).

49 See Chapter 6 (section 6.1.6).

50 On this issue specifically, see the interview with Aleksandar Petrović, Lela Jovanović, "Verovatno opasan tip", *Reporter*, 2 September 1982, p. 54.

51 In an interview given in December 1992, Petrović even named various party officials whom he believed were responsible for preventing him directing *Banović Strahinja*; see an interview with Aleksandar Petrović: "Aleksandar Saša Petrović: PROFESOR, ili ko je bio Plastični Juda I", in Milan Nikodijević, *Zabranjeni bez zabrane: Zona sumraka jugoslovenskog filma*, (Beograd: Jugoslovenska Kinoteka, 1995), p. 61.

52 John R. Lampe, *Yugoslavia as History*, p. 318.

53 Dejan Jović, *Jugoslavija*, p. 262.

54 See for example Milomir Marić, "Vreme relaksacije", pp. 19–21.

55 See Chapter 1 (section 1.2.3).

56 On the Yugoslav Prague School filmmakers see "Yugoslav Prague Group", in *The BFI Companion to Eastern European and Russian Cinema*, ed. by Richard Taylor et al., (London: British Film Institute, 2000), p. 266; and Jasmina Papa, *The Prague Group: Film as Cultural Non-Nationalism in 1980s Yugoslavia* (Budapest: Central European University, 1999), unpublished master's thesis.

57 An interview with Aleksandar Petrović, Milomir Marić, "Vreme relaksacije", p. 20.

58 The contract was signed in Belgrade in the offices of the publishing house Nolit; see Draško Redjep, *Rapsodija ništavila: Ogledi o Aleksandru Petroviću* (Novi Sad: Prometej, 2001), p. 15.

59 Draško Redjep, *Rapsodija ništavila*, p. 17.

60 Draško Redjep, *Rapsodija ništavila*, p. 44.

61 Crnjanski quoted in R. Popović, "Ima seoba – smrti nema", *Politika*, 19 August 1978.

62 See the biography of Miloš Crnjanski: Radovan Popović, *Život Miloša Crnjanskog*, p. 17.

63 David A. Norris, *The Novels of Miloš Crnjanski*, p. 17.

64 David A. Norris, *The Novels of Miloš Crnjanski*, pp. 17–18.

65 David A. Norris, *The Novels of Miloš Crnjanski*, p. 18.

66 Petar Džadžić, *Povlašćeni prostori Miloša Crnjanskog* (Beograd: Zavod za udžbenike i nastavna sredstva, 1995), p.13.

67 See the biography of Miloš Crnjanski: Radovan Popović, *Život Miloša Crnjanskog*, p. 206.

68 This campaign was often led by Marko Ristić; see David A. Norris, *The Novels of Miloš Crnjanski*, p. 21.

69 See the biography of Miloš Crnjanski: Radovan Popović, *Život Miloša Crnjanskog*, p. 155.

70 See Chapter 3 (section 3.1.3).

71 See the biography of Miloš Crnjanski: Radovan Popović, *Život Miloša Crnjanskog*, p. 158.

72 See Chapter 1 (section 1.2.2).

73 See the biography of Miloš Crnjanski: Radovan Popović, *Život Miloša Crnjanskog*, p. 207.

74 In March 1957, Moša Pijade, then president of the Yugoslav parliament, asked Crnjanski in London why he did not simply return home; see the biography of Miloš Crnjanski: Radovan Popović, *Život Miloša Crnjanskog*, p. 216.

75 See the biography of Miloš Crnjanski: Radovan Popović, *Život Miloša Crnjanskog*, pp. 231–32.

76 His early novels, the first book of *Migrations* included, were republished as early as 1956; see David A. Norris, *The Novels of Miloš Crnjanski*, p. 22.

77 Nikola Milošević, *Roman Miloša Crnjanskog* (Beograd: Srpska književna zadruga, 1970), p. 247.

78 Nikola Milošević, *Roman Miloša Crnjanskog*, p. 250.

79 David A. Norris, *The Novels of Miloš Crnjanski*, p. 1.

80 Crnjanski quoted in David A. Norris, *The Novels of Miloš Crnjanski*, p. 171.

81 Petar Džadžić draws very similar conclusions; see Petar Džadžić, *Povlašćeni prostori Miloša Crnjanskog*, p. 216.

82 Crnjanski planned six volumes, or parts, but never managed to write them all; see David A. Norris, *The Novels of Miloš Crnjanski*, p. 26.

83 Nikola Milošević, *Roman Miloša Crnjanskog*, p. 150, and then the same point is elaborated on pages 156, 161 and 244.

84 Petar Džadžić, *Povlašćeni prostori Miloša Crnjanskog*, p. 119.

85 Petar Džadžić, *Povlašćeni prostori Miloša Crnjanskog*, p. 69.

86 Nikola Milošević, *Roman Miloša Crnjanskog*, p. 131.

87 Nikola Milošević, *Roman Miloša Crnjanskog*, p. 135.

88 See Petrović's statements in R. Popović, "Ima seoba – smrti nema", and his interview in Milomir Marić, "Vreme relaksacije", p. 20.

89 An interview with Aleksandar Petrović, see Milomir Marić, "Vreme relaksacije", p. 20.

90 See Petrović's statements in R. Popović, "Ima seoba – smrti nema".

91 Vatroslav Mimica, who directed the film, was Petrović's friend, and there was apparently no bad feeling between the two as a result of this project (personal interview with Branka Petrović [11 September 2005]). Petrović was more concerned with the possible political ramifications underlying the decision that he should not direct it.

92 Jasna Dragović-Soso, '*Saviours of the Nation*', p. 65.

93 An interview with Aleksandar Petrović, see Jovo Paripović, "Aleksandar Petrović: Sakupljač za Seobe", *Studio*, 18 September 1987, p. 11.

94 ibid.

95 On the production history, see an interview with Aleksandar Petrović in D. BT. "Reditelj Aleksandar Petrović: 'Seobe' čekaju uslove", *TV Novosti*, 19 October 1989; Petar Volk also gives a detailed account in his book, see Petar Volk, *Let nad močvarom*, p. 316, with all the dates quoted in the paragraph.

96 An interview with Aleksandar Petrović, see Jovo Paripović, "Aleksandar Petrović: Sakupljač za Seobe", p. 12.

97   Jasna Dragović-Soso, '*Saviours of the Nation*', p. 77.

98   The speech delivered by Milo Kralj when Aleksandar Petrović received the AVNOJ Award, on 15 December 1987, is one of the most concise and accurate summaries of Petrović's career and work, clearly defining his theoretical, thematic and stylistic concerns. See Milo Kralj, "Aleksandar Petrović", unpublished (in the clipping file on Aleksandar Petrović, Belgrade: Jugoslovenska Kinoteka Library).

99   AVNOJ stands for *Antifašističko vijeće narodnog oslobodjenja Jugoslavije*, which translates as the Antifascist Council of the People's Liberation of Yugoslavia. The award commemorated the meeting of this council in 1943 at which a Socialist Yugoslavia was proposed – if not yet formed.

100   On *Plastic Jesus* see Chapter 6 (section 6.2).

101   Petrović even wrote a letter to the 14th Interim Congress of the League of Communists of Yugoslavia, asking for his full rehabilitation, and hence his return to the faculty. However, this was the last Congress of the Party, or rather the League of Communists, and at it, the party infamously fell apart. A copy of this letter is kept in the archives of the Yugoslav Cinematheque. See Aleksandar Petrović, "Četrnaestom kongresu SKJ", March 1990, (in the clipping file on Aleksandar Petrović, Belgrade: Jugoslovenska Kinoteka Library).

102   Petrović's widow Branislava maintained this stance long after this case was "closed"; see her preface to Aleksandar Petrović's script *Emanuela*, in Aleksandar Petrović, *1973. Godina vampira*, p. 11.

103   Petrović did not mention Kosanović by name, although he did emphasise that the dean of the faculty was responsible – who was Dejan Kosanović; see interview with Aleksandar Petrović in Miodrag Milojević, "Intervju – Saša Petrović", *Pogledi*, 6 December 1990, pp.31–33, and specifically page 32.

104   On Petrović finally being reinstated at the faculty, see J. Jovović, "Gorko sećanje na pogrom", *Politika Ekspres*, 9 November 1991, p. 17.

105   Zemun is now part of Belgrade. However, it is situated on the north bank of the River Sava, while the main, original, part of Belgrade is on the south bank. For two centuries, the Sava formed the border between Austrian and Ottoman Empires, which meant that Zemun was in the former and Belgrade in the latter.

106   On Slobodan Selenić see section 3.2.1 in Chapter 3.

107   Jasna Dragović-Soso, '*Saviours of the Nation*', p. 96; See also Dragović-Soso's argument on how certain novels during the 1980s in Serbia offered an alternative history to the pre-communist past from the one established during communist rule. Dragović-Soso explains how these novels were important in shaping public opinion in the last years of communism, and apart from Selenić's novel, she also emphasises the significance of Dobrica Ćosić's *A Time of Death* (*Vreme smrti*, 1987) and Danko Popović's *The Book About Milutin* (*Knjiga o Milutinu*, 1985), but other novels as well; see her chapter "'De-Titoisation' and the revision of history in Serbia: Yugoslavia reconsidered", in Jasna Dragović-Soso, '*Saviours of the Nation*', pp. 77–100.

108   I chose these two films for their popularity and critical acclaim when released, but there were others at the time too.

109   Nikola Milošević, *Roman Miloša Crnjanskog*, p. 232.

110 Nikola Milošević, *Roman Miloša Crnjanskog*, p. 232. Milošević reiterates this point when he talks about another Crnjanski's novel – *Dnevnik o Čarnojeviću* – on page 88. David A. Norris agrees with this view and explains that even when Crnjanski embraced fascism, this was "not synonymous with support for fascist ideology, and [Crnjanski] did not translate his nationalist feelings into naked chauvinism." See David A. Norris, *The Novels of Miloš Crnjanski*, p. 19.

111 Petar Džadžić, *Povlašćeni prostori Miloša Crnjanskog*, p. 240.

112 David Norris briefly comments on, and analyses this aspect of the novel; see David A. Norris, *The Novels of Miloš Crnjanski*, p. 77 and p. 150.

113 See Chapter 2 (section 2.4.1).

114 This could be perceived as analogous to Henry VIII's behaviour towards Rome, and the establishment of the Church of England.

115 David A. Norris, *The Novels of Miloš Crnjanski*, p. 140.

116 Clarke Fountain, "The Master and Margarita", *All Movie Guide*, available: http://www. allrovi.com/movies/movie/the-master-and-margaret-v126415 [last accessed 3 September 2012].

117 See Chapter 6 (specifically section 6.1.5).

118 Draško Redjep, *Rapsodija ništavila*, p. 167.

119 Jean-Michel Frodon, "La mort d'Alexandre Petrovic, le dernier cinéaste yougoslave", *Le Monde*, 23 August 1994, p. 13.

120 On the reception of this film, see Chapter 6 (section 6.1.6).

121 The reception in Germany was exceptionally hostile; see the previous chapter (section 7.1.5) for details of the reception of *Group Portrait*.

122 This was still the case at the time of writing. Indeed, one of the reasons why I have written this book is to help these films become available again.

123 In *Migrations* for example, Petar Isaković was eliminated as a character in the film and TV series, although in the novel it is reiterated that this character was famous for capturing high enemy officers alive. This clearly gave Petrović the opportunity to "(re) invent" the episode with the captured enemy officer.

124 See *Eternity and a Day* (*Mia aiwniothta kai mia mera*, Greece, France, Italy, 1998).

125 The actors were trained before filming, by a Romany language expert; see Chapter 4 (section 4.2.2).

126 In November 1989, Georges Suffert explained that the film is blocked due to the "obscure conflicts amongst producers and financiers, and discreetly delaying manoeuvres of the Yugoslav administration." See Georges Suffert, "Qui libérera 'Migration'?", *Le Figaro*, 16 November 1989, p. 41.

127 The Federal Republic of Yugoslavia consisted of Serbia and Montenegro only, and it aspired to legally inherit the former Socialist Federal Republic of Yugoslavia that consisted of six republics. This Yugoslavia was dissolved soon after Slobodan Milošević lost power in 2000.

128 Petar Volk, *Let nad močvarom*, p. 334.

129 A detailed document on the production of *Migrations*, including lengthy interviews with Petrović, as well as interviews with actors, editor, two cameramen, costume designers, etc,

can be found in the book by Boro Drašković, another well-known Yugoslav/Serbian film director; see Boro Drašković, *Film o filmu* (Novi Sad: Prometej, 2010).

130 Petar Volk, *Let nad močvarom*, pp. 337–38.

131 On Milovan Djilas see the introduction to Chapter 2.

132 Jasna Dragović-Soso, *'Saviours of the Nation'*, p. 211.

133 Vesna Pešić quoted in Jasna Dragović-Soso, *'Saviours of the Nation'*, p. 214.

134 See Jasna Dragović-Soso, *'Saviours of the Nation'*, pp. 206–20.

135 See, for example, the following articles from as late as 1991: Verica Petkovska, "Bunkerisana Pravda", *Borba*, 18 January 1991; D. Lakić, "Odlučiće pravnici", *Politika*, 4 April 1991, p. 21. It is noteworthy that it does appear as if there was a resistance at the faculty to Petrović being re-instated; whether the background was political, or otherwise, deserves another study.

136 Petrović's statement after the event can be found in J. Jovović, "Gorko sećanje na pogrom", *Politika Ekspres*, 9 November 1991, p. 17.

137 On his brief membership of the Union of Young Communists of Yugoslavia (SKOJ), see Chapter 1 (section 1.2.2).

138 On his participation in the Liberal Party as a party against the regime, see the obituary by his friend and president of the party, Nikola Milošević (no relation to Slobodan Milošević – although it is the same Nikola Milošević who was quoted above as a Crnjanski scholar): Nikola Milošević, "Slučaj komedijant", *NIN*, 26 August 1994, p. 42.

139 Velimir Bata Živojinović describes this election campaign in one of his later interviews; see Dušan Bulić, "Velimir Bata Živojinović (an interview with)", *Maxim* [Serbia and Montenegro edition], January 2006, p. 122.

140 Petrović returned all his state awards in 1990; see an unsigned article "Aleksandar Petrović vraća nagrade za umetnički rad", *Politika*, 30 May 1990, p. 11.

141 Serbia was also under international sanctions from 1998 until Milošević was deposed in 2000.

142 Boro Drašković, *Film o filmu*, pp. 239–41.

143 See K. R., "Saša Petrović u Evropskoj akademiji za film i TV", *Borba*, 9 March 1993 (the clipping file).

144 Boro Drašković, *Film o filmu*, p. 241.

145 See the introduction to section 7.1 in the previous chapter.

146 See the following interview with Petrović: Miodrag Milojević, "Intervju – Saša Petrović", pp. 31–33.

147 David A. Norris, *The Novels of Miloš Crnjanski*, p. 155.

148 Petrovic, S., "Ceux qui filment… Sacha Petrovic", *Cahiers du Cinéma*, March 1994, p. 112.

149 The most obvious examples would be the two obituaries from German film magazines: Brandlmeier, T., "Aleksandar Petrović 14.1929 – 20.8.1994", *EPD Film*, October 1994, p. 14; and FD., "Aleksandar Petrovic", *Film-dienst*, 30 August 1994, p. 39. This fact was an important feature of most of the other obituaries; see for example Jean-Michel Frodon, "La mort d'Alexandre Petrovic, le dernier cinéaste yougoslave", *Le Monde*, 23 August 1994, p. 13.

150 See Patrick Apel-Muller, "Ecartelé entre mémoire et creation", *L'Humanite*, 22 August 1994, p. 15.

Conclusion

What did it avail to pray when he knew that his soul lusted after its own destruction?

James Joyce[1]

A leksandar Saša Petrović is a filmmaker whose career left a significant mark on the three golden decades of European cinema: the 1960s, 1970s and 1980s. During this period, he was the most awarded filmmaker in his home country – Yugoslavia – and received major awards at renowned film festivals globally, including Cannes, Chicago, Karlovy Vary and Venice. His *I Even Met Happy Gypsies* was a major box office success in Yugoslavia, as well as internationally, and had 200,000 admissions in Paris alone. Thanks to the success of this film, he is mentioned in all major film histories, and is considered a classic director of so-called European "art house" cinema. During his career, he worked with some of the greatest European actresses and actors of the time, as well as producers, cinematographers and editors. More significantly, he adapted for the screen some of the most famous novels of the twentieth century.

Petrović's career reflects the classical experience of a filmmaker of his time. He was an itinerant director, who made films as large co-productions outside his home country. He was a director who also filmed projects as large international co-productions in his own country, as well as low budget features in which he had to work very economically. He cut his teeth making short films, and received awards for his documentaries. This aspect of his career, the career slowly built step-by-step, certainly deserves to be studied in depth, as it is a path travelled by many filmmakers. Petrović was also an artist who knew how to translate philosophical, literary and painterly influences in his work. These influences ranged from Dostoyevsky, via Brecht, to Šumanović and Buñuel. Further study of his work within the context of such artistic authorities should certainly prove rewarding for a deeper understanding of his career. Above all else, a thorough study of his literary adaptations would probably be most informative in relation to this most widespread marriage in arts, of literature and cinema. These themes have not been fully explored in this study, as the focus here was the link between Petrović and the political context in which he worked.

Considering the attention Petrović and his work received during his lifetime, it was surprising how quickly he disappeared from critical and public view after his death in 1994. This study has tried to argue that the reason for this was lined to the destruction of his country Yugoslavia, and the consequent disappearance of its common culture. As a result, the approach used in this study has been to analyse the influence politics had on Petrović's life and career. As his career coincided with the life of his country, and as he himself often commented how much politics interfered in his work, unravelling this specific relationship imposed itself as an approach worth prioritising – at least at this time. It needs to be emphasised that this is only for the present, as any debate relating to phenomena stemming from the Yugoslav experience is still prejudiced by the country's bloody demise. Within such a framework, this study has thus prioritised politics over numerous other possibilities to study Petrović's work. As this is the first study committed to his work outside the former Yugoslavia, it is written in the hope that others will follow, exploring the abovementioned aspects of Petrović's work and career, as well as the many others for which his films provide an adequate context. In time, the Yugoslav conflicts and their politics will cease to be the only approach to understanding the country's legacy. It is then that the rich body of his work and career will be open to exploration, as a pool of ideas outside and beyond politics.

The situation just described was not, however, the only reason why politics was taken as the key to analyse Petrović's films. The film industry in Yugoslavia was developed under the ideological tenets of socialism and communism, which Tito's Partisans established as their ideological framework for developing Yugoslav society. Although he came from an upper middle-class background, young Aleksandar Petrović had been familiar with communist ideas in his youth, and undoubtedly sympathised with them. In addition, he briefly studied filmmaking in Prague, Czechoslovakia, which was then another young socialist state similar to Yugoslavia. He was taught by various Marxist thinkers in Prague, including Béla Balázs, before being forced to return to continue his education at the university in Belgrade. In both instances, Petrović was brought up within socialist structures and had a Marxist education. His career thus provided an exceptionally apt case study to observe the creative and intellectual development of a filmmaker in the context of the growth of this modernist political and ideological system, which is now – at

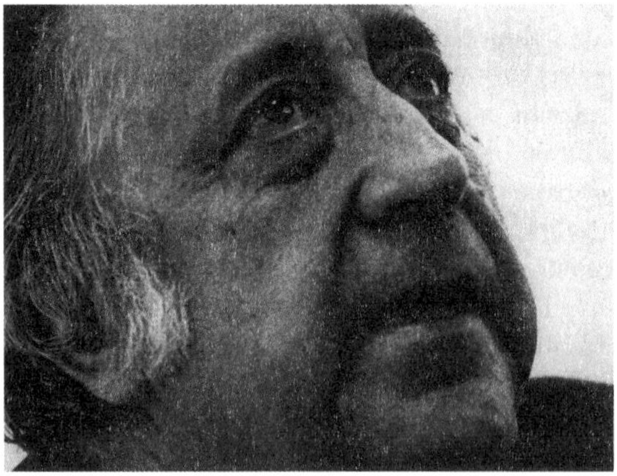

Figure 9.1: Aleksandar Saša Petrović

least at present – no more. Petrović's trajectory, as observed in this study, was from that of a Marxist educated artist to the one who questioned the tenets of socialism. The fact that Petrović could be perceived as a mainstream film director within the country's film industry has turned his career and work into an even more intriguing subject for the exploration of the interface of an artist, and the political framework in which she or he operates.

This enquiry was intended to focus primarily on Aleksandar Petrović's films, and attempt to draw its conclusions on both the filmmaker and the system in which he functioned by analysing his work. The films, indeed, provide a detailed picture of a time and place, as well as indicating the composite thematic fabric from which Petrović produced his work.

The methods and theories commonly used in film studies were primarily employed in this analysis, as Petrović's films were its main focus. Petrović was of the generation of filmmakers who inaugurated the New Wave in the 1960s, and he shared that movement's concern with cinematic authorship and artistry – as epitomised in François Truffaut's famous phrase "*la politique des auteurs*". These ideas concerned with cinematic authorship were used to discuss his work. However, bearing in mind the inherent shortcomings of the auteur theory, the theory also had to be modified in order to accommodate an investigation in precisely those elements of Petrović's composite thematic fabric that responded to the political situation around him: the elements that provided a visceral commentary on the nature of the situation. I have argued that in his mature work Petrović developed four political themes that grappled with the issues he recognised as significant in everyday social intercourse. The first one concerned interethnic relationships, which with hindsight proved to be of an incommensurable cultural and political significance for the now former Yugoslavia, as well as the Balkans in general. The second theme had to do with the position of religion in society. This explored religion, not only as an institution, but also the significance of religious beliefs as enduring and essential elements of culture. As in his investigation on interethnic relationships, Petrović examined the positions of ethnic minorities, and thus observed the interaction of those in positions of power with those on the margins of society. This theme of the interplay between the privileged and the disenfranchised, on many social, class and ethnic levels, is the third theme to be extrapolated from his work. These three themes often supported the fourth, which was concerned with the issues that emerged as a result of the dogmatic attachment to principles, religions or ideologies. Petrović exposed how detrimental the effects of dogmatism can be, constructing a specific anti-dogmatic approach of his own, which visibly characterises his films.

While auteur theory ideally leads to studies being grounded in empirical research and argument, it is regrettably still most commonly used to praise, even fetishise individuals – auteurs – as romantic artists and heroes, thereby elevating their style and themes to products of a single creative genius. The analysis in this book has sought to somewhat displace such notions. My focus has been on those themes that have arisen as a result of social pressure. The auteur is not seen here as a lone genius, but as someone continually struggling and interacting with her or his environment in order to produce their work. Nowhere perhaps is this concept as intriguing as in cinema, as films are ineluctably expensive, and almost always the product of collective endeavour. To look at the work of a socialist filmmaker, where the state has financed production, moved the focus from the purely personal to the interaction of personal and social, and the impact that this had on the films themselves. That four themes can be extracted as a result of this interaction shows that the auteur theory can be stretched further. It also shows that film studies could examine these sorts of relationships more frequently. As Paul Willemen emphasises, there are no creative decisions in filmmaking not influenced by the economics behind the production. The current study has tried to move towards unravelling these significant connections.

As Petrović was a mainstream filmmaker, his work has already being seen through the lens of auteur theory, and the themes of love and death have been highlighted as the most outstanding signifiers of his work. It is true that each of his films involves a passionate love story, sometimes interpreted by film stars such as Isabelle Huppert or Romy Schneider. Partly because of the tragic destruction of his country, this study has sought to examine his relationship with its political and social system, and also learn something about the latter from his films. I have viewed Petrović's films as an historical resource, exposing views on the politics of the time and space in which they were made. This is why auteur theory has been modified into what I have called "the theory of the political auteur", and hopefully set an example of how such a study may be performed. Such analyses could easily be pursued within film studies and would serve to reveal these less glamorous, but potentially more complex and pertinent aspects of filmmaking, as both creative and economic endeavour.

This study has demonstrated that filmmakers from Socialist Yugoslavia engaged openly and deftly with the political and social problems their country faced. Of course, this is something that Daniel Goulding's seminal history of Yugoslav cinema has already amply demonstrated. However, the focus here has been on a specific filmmaker, and on the outcomes of a specific engagement. As pointed out, it was Petrović's engagement with the nature of ethnicity as well as interethnic issues that was prescient in the Yugoslav context. More intriguingly, Petrović perceived the ethnic as a fragile construct, in the same way that sociological and historical scholarship has described it in the decades after *I Even Met Happy Gypsies* was released. On the other hand, Petrović recognised and empathised with the need to "belong" to these constructs, even when this belonging works against those who seek adherence. It is one thing to deny the existence of ethnicity, but this factor has returned as being of very real significance throughout the twentieth century, particularly in War World II, which has marked Petrović's life so vividly. Equally, this study has shown that the Yugoslav communists in power questioned these constructs too, as much as Petrović did but without the same empathy; and it is these very ethnic constructs that came to haunt the country in the early 1990s, tearing its fabric apart.

Equally thorough and perspicacious was Petrović's engagement with religious teachings and institutions. Just as with interethnic relationships, this study has shown that he provided a multifaceted portrait of the phenomenon. He portrayed religious institutions as instruments of power, although he also depicted them as a soothing moral refuge against the anxieties of everyday existence. Petrović hence presented religious views as either comfortingly amorphous and supportive (*It Rains in My Village*), or menacingly dogmatic and coercive (*Group Portrait*). Although this book has been concerned with mapping political themes, it could not exhaustively explore all their facets. The question of Petrović's political relationship to the Divine, as well as with the elusive institutions that seek to represent it, could provide for a far more detailed study. Equally, this applies to the three other political themes identified in this work.

The third of these themes touched on a sensitive point of the socialist system. Yugoslav society, although committed to equality, was also conceived of as being led by an elite – that of the Communist Party. Petrović thus started questioning the relationship of the elite to that of the mass, from those with power to the disempowered. Once again, he foreshadowed problems that were nascent in Yugoslav society. Any political culture that excludes social groups on any level is likely to lead itself into conflicts with these groups, sooner or later. That such a situation caused grave frictions in Yugoslavia in the 1990s is now well-known. That Petrović and other Yugoslav intellectuals were openly warning about this problem in the 1960s points to a different conclusion. Certainly, the political atmosphere in Socialist Yugoslavia was on one level open and exceedingly lively. What this work has been unable to resolve, although it may have contributed somewhat to its understanding, was the contradiction that, on the one hand, production of such highly critical work was enabled and encouraged in socialism, while on the other, the same work was persecuted and silenced once it entered the political and social arenas. What remains as a hypothesis is that it was precisely this inability of the system to listen to criticism – which instead it harshly suppressed in order to stick rigidly to its own preconceived notions of how to proceed – led, ultimately, to its complete collapse. Dogmatism, instead of dialogue, was socialism's downfall.[2]

Wrestling with dogmatism, therefore, becomes the fourth political theme Petrović incorporated into his work. Again, the notion as represented is composed of a diverse material, and is observed on personal, social, ideological and religious levels. Petrović was at his least ambiguous in dealing with dogmatism, as in his films it is shown as leading only to bitter failure. Whether his characters zealously adhered to political concepts, or to some personal principles that they were afraid ever to question, Petrović criticises the possibility of any prescription for living which is carved in stone. Unsurprisingly, this led him into conflict with assorted communist ideologues of his time. Still, the significance of his anti-dogmatism could be read as twofold: as personal and as social. Petrović talked about his passion for gambling in his youth, and how this gambling nature helped him survive the war. An understanding of life as permanently unpredictable was what also brought him to the literature of Miloš Crnjanski,[3] and other authors who opened this debate in the second half of the twentieth century. Petrović's thinking in this area was in the spirit of the locus of much philosophical thought of the time. It was in the later part of his own career that Jean Baudrillard wrote about the "aleatory nature" of everything. It is precisely this aspect of nature that Petrović reminds us of in his work, an aspect which affects the life of every individual.

As Petrović's anti-dogmatic attitude was very much present in the only film he made outside of Socialist Yugoslavia, it is also clear that he did not confine the corrosive properties of dogmatism to socialism alone. What stands as a warning extracted from his work is that adhering blindly to abstract sets of rules and laws in any political structure leads only to disaster. The fact that Petrović predominantly showed this in communism points towards an additional conclusion. His cinema was a cinema of self-reflection, and again in the spirit of time, he inevitably had to confront the failures of modernism – the same modernism he had embraced as a young man. Here he may be perceived as an example of, perhaps, an East European post-modernist. Yet, although he was a post-modernist who did not disregard the achievements of modernism, he did not flinch at examining the "moral abyss" – as he had called it – to which assorted aspects of modernism were leading to either. Again, with hindsight, Petrović had recognised another key issue: this moral abyss led Yugoslavia to its vicious conflicts of the 1990s. Nevertheless, for him, the key problem remained the dogmatism with which these modernist ideas were enforced. The way to live cannot be prescribed but – in Michel Foucault's words – is more accommodating if negotiated. Petrović's fiction unambiguously conveys this thought.

Through the work of Aleksandar Petrović, it is therefore easy to show how rich and sophisticated cultural production was in Socialist Yugoslavia. This analysis of his work is intended to contribute to the field of film studies by expanding on the existing knowledge of Yugoslav and Balkan cinema. In order to construct this argument, this study has had to rely on numerous historical works on the country and its politics. However, in terms of contributing to the discourse of Yugoslav history, my scope has been intentionally limited. At most a modest contribution may have been made to this discourse, on a level that separates history from the overwhelmingly emotional reception of the events of the 1990s. The "Yugoslav problem" has often been perceived through the framework of these events, or even based on "snapshots" of what was going on in the 1990s, thus confusing causes and effects. As most historians have continued to remind their readers, political decision-makers included, the conflicts that emerged in Yugoslavia each had their own background and genealogy, the understanding of which was key to resolving the problem. This was often forgotten under the barrage of media conditioned images of the 1990s, to which, admittedly, the author of this book also tended to surrender. However, as pointed out in the introductions to the history books cited in this work, the conflicts in Yugoslavia all had identifiable causes, often – but not exclusively – revolving around unresolved interethnic conflicts from World War II: the war which made an enormous impact on the young Aleksandar Petrović, and the war which he depicted in two of his films, from both Yugoslav and German perspectives.

This work has been based on scholarly history, and has sought to distance its analysis from the mediated, popular view of the conflict in Yugoslavia, which crudely simplified its representation.

Ultimately, the career of Aleksandar Petrović and particularly his films have proven to be a unique resource easily worthy of continued exploration and revisiting. I trust that this study amply demonstrates that further studies of this filmmaker, as well as the context in which he worked, would be more than welcome.

Notes

1 James Joyce, *A Portrait of the Artist as a Young Man* (London: Penguin, 2000), p. 111.
2 This is not to say that dogmatism was the sole reason for the downfall of socialism, but that, certainly following an analysis of Petrović's oeuvre, it may be seen as one of the key components contributing to it.
3 Crnjanski regularly talked about those accidents, not necessarily negative ones, which happen in one's life and completely change its course. These accidents he called the greatest of life's comedians.

Filmography

A ll the data on the films is taken either from *Filmografija jugoslovenskog filma 1945–1965*, ed. by Momčilo Ilić (Beograd: Institut za Film, 1970), or from *Filmografija jugoslovenskog igranog filma 1945–1980*, ed. by Branislav Obradović (Beograd: Institut za Film, Časopis Filmograf, 1981), unless otherwise indicated.

Films co-directed by Aleksandar Petrović and Vicko Raspor

Short documentaries

Uz druga je drug (Shoulder to Shoulder)
Production company: Umetnički studio
Scriptwriters: Nusret Seferović, Vicko Raspor
Directors: Vicko Raspor, Aleksandar Petrović
Cinematographer: Nikola Majdak
Composer: Aleksandar Obradović
Editor: Milada Rajšić-Levi
Length: 1,124 metres (39 minutes approx.)
Type: 35mm, black-and-white, standard – documentary
Date: 28 December 1955
(Ilić, p. 98)

Petar Dobrović
Production company: Zagreb Film
Scriptwriter: Miroslav Krleža
Directors: Aleksandar Petrović, Vicko Raspor
Cinematographers: Nikola Majdak, Jovan Jovanović
Music: [archival]
Editor: Kleopatra Harisijades
Length: 412 metres (14 minutes approx.)
Type: 35mm, colour, standard – documentary
Date: 30 December 1957
(Ilić, p. 132)

Features

Jedini izlaz (The Only Exit)
Production company: Zastava Film, Belgrade
Scriptwriters: Antonije Isaković, Stjepan Zaninović
Directors: Vicko Raspor, Aleksandar Petrović
Cinematographer: Jovan Jovanović
Composer: Ivo Tijardović
Set designer: Nikola Radanović, Miodrag Kostić
Editor: Kleopatra Harisijades
Cast: Mija Aleksić, Zlatko Madunić, Borislav Radović, Stane Potokar, Fahro Konjhodžić
Length: 2,330 metres (80 minutes approx.)
Type: 35mm, colour, standard
Date: 25 July 1958
(Obradović, pp. 14–15)

Films directed by Aleksandar Petrović

Short documentaries

Let nad močvarom (Flight over the Swamp)
Production company: Slavija Film
Scriptwriters: Aleksandar Petrović, Vicko Raspor (text [in voice-over])
Director: Aleksandar Petrović
Cinematographer: Jovan Jovanović, Sekula Banović
Music: [archival]
Editor: Kleopatra Harisijades
Length: 445 metres (15 minutes approx.)
Type: 35mm, black-and-white, standard – documentary
Date: 18 January 1957
(Ilić, p. 114)

Putevi (The Roads)
Production company: Avala Film
Scriptwriter: Aleksandar Petrović
Director: Aleksandar Petrović
Cinematographer: Nikola Majdak
Music: [archival]
Editor: Neva Paskulović Habić

Length: 485 metres (18 minutes approx.)
Type: 35mm, colour, standard – documentary, a film about art
Date: 27 December 1958
(Ilić, p. 154)

Rat Ratu (The War on War)
Production company: Avala Film
Scriptwriter: Aleksandar Petrović
Director: Aleksandar Petrović
Cinematographer: Jovan Jovanović
Music: [archival]
Editor: Stanka Komar
Length: 612 metres (19 minutes approx.)
Type: 35mm, colour, standard – documentary
Date: 28 December 1960.
(Ilić, p. 195)

Zapisnik (Record)
Production company: Dunav Film
Scriptwriter: Aleksandar Petrović
Director: Aleksandar Petrović
Cinematographer: Stevo Radović
Music: [archival]
Editor: Aleksandar Ilić
Length: 442 metres (15 minutes approx.)
Type: 35mm, black-and-white, standard – documentary
Date: 29 December 1964
(Ilić, p. 297)

Sabori (Assemblies)
Production company: Dunav Film
Scriptwriter: Aleksandar Petrović
Director: Aleksandar Petrović
Cinematographer: Nikola Majdak
Music: [archival]
Editor: Aleksandar Ilić
Length: 350 metres (11 minutes approx.)
Type: 35mm, black-and-white, standard – documentary
Date: 1 March 1965
(Ilić, p. 299)

Features

Dvoje (Two)
Production company: Avala Film, Belgrade
Scriptwriter: Aleksandar Petrović
Director: Aleksandar Petrović
Cinematographer: Ivan Marinček
Music: [archival, chosen by: Aleksandar Petrović]
Set designer: Zoran Zorčić
Editor: Mirjana Mitić
Cast: Miha Baloh, Desanka Beba Lončar, Miloš Žutić, Borislav Radović
Length: 2,400 metres (80 minutes approx.)
Type: 35mm, black-and-white, widescreen
Date: 31 July 1961
(Obradović, p. 21)

Dani (Days)
Production company: Avala Film, Belgrade
Scriptwriter: Aleksandar Petrović
Director: Aleksandar Petrović
Cinematographer: Aleksandar Petković
Composer: Vasilije Belošević
Set designerer: Nikola Rajić
Editor: Mirjana Mitić
Cast: Olga Vujadinović, Ljubiša Samardžić, Mila Dimitrijević, Tatjana Lukijanova
Length: 2,150 metres (77 minutes approx.)
Type: 35mm, black-and-white, widescreen
Date: 29 April 1963
(Obradović, p. 25)

Tri (Three)
Production company: Avala Film, Belgrade
Scriptwriters: Aleksandar Petrović, Antonije Isaković , based on his short stories *Paprat i vatra* (*The Fern and Fire*)
Director: Aleksandar Petrović
Cinematographer: Tomislav Pinter
Music: [archival]
Set designers: Vladislav Lašić, Nikola Rajić
Editors: Mirjana Mitić
Cast: Velimir Bata Živojinović, Senka Veletanlić-Petrović, Voja Mirić, Ali Raner, Slobodan Perović, Mića Tomić

Length: 2,200 metres (80 minutes approx.)
Type: 35mm, black-and-white, widescreen
Date: 17 May 1965
(Obradović, p. 29)

Skupljači perja (*I Even Met Happy Gypsies*)
Production company: Avala Film, Belgrade
Scriptwriter: Aleksandar Petrović
Director: Aleksandar Petrović
Cinematographer: Tomislav Pinter
Music: [authentic folk and archival]
Set designer: Veljko Despotović
Editor: Mirjana Mitić
Cast: Bekim Fehmiu, Velimir Bata Živojinović, Olivera Vučo, Gordana Jovanović, Mija Aleksić, Rahela Ferari
Length: 2,565 metres (84 minutes approx.)
Type: 35mm, colour, widescreen
Date: 27 March 1967
(Obradović, p. 34)

Biće skoro propast sveta – Il pleut dans mon village (*It Rains in My Village*)
Production companies: Avala Film, Belgrade, and Les Production artistes associés S.A., Paris
Scriptwriter: Aleksandar Petrović
Director: Aleksandar Petrović
Cinematographer: Djordje Nikolić and Alain Levent
Music: [authentic folk]
Set designer: Veljko Despotović
Editor: Katarina Stojanović
Cast: Annie Girardot, Ivan Paluch, Mija Aleksić, Dragomir Bojanić, Eva Ras
Length: 2,280 metres (80 minutes approx.)
Type: 35mm, colour, widescreen
Date: 30 October 1968
(Obradović, p. 41)

Majstor i Margarita – Il Maestro e Margherita (*The Master and Margarita*)
Production companies: Dunav Film, Beograd, and Euro International Film S.P.A., Rome
Scriptwriters: Aleksandar Petrović with assistance of Amadeo and Barbara Pagani, based on the motifs of the novel of the same title by Mikhail Bulgakov
Director: Aleksandar Petrović
Cinematographer: Roberto Gerardi
Music: [archival]

Set designer: Vlastimir Gavrik
Editor: Mihailo Ilić
Cast: Ugo Tognazzi, Mimsy Farmer, Alain Cuny, Velimir Bata Živojinović, Pavle Vuisić, Ljuba Tadić, Eva Ras, Fabijan Šovagović, Taško Načić, Danilo Stojković, Zlatko Madunić, Fahro Konjhodžić, Janez Vrhovec, Radomir Reljić
Length: 2,600 metres (91 minute approx.)
Type: 35mm, colour, widescreen
Date: 15 July 1972
(Obradović, p. 52)

Gruppenbild Mit Dame – Portrait de Groupe avec Dame (**Group Portrait with Lady**)
Production companies: Les Artistes Associés, Paris and Stella Film/Cinema 77, Munich
Distributor: United Artists
Producer: Martin Hellstern
Scriptwriter: Aleksandar Petrović, based on the novel of the same title by Heinrich Böll
Director: Aleksandar Petrović
Cinematographer: Pierre William Glenn
Composers: Mozart, Schubert, Russian folk songs
Set designers: Reinhard Sigmund, Vlastimir Gavrik
Sound editor: Gerhard Birkholz
Assistant directors: Wigbert Wicker, Stevan Petrović, Milan Dor
Editors: Agape Dorstewitz, Marika Radvanyi
Cast: Romy Schneider, Michel Galabru, Brad Dourif, Richard Münch, Vadim Glowna, Milena Dravić, Rüdiger Vogler, Velimir Bata Živojinović
Length: 2,803 metres (100 minutes approx.)
Type: 35mm, Eastmancolor, standard
Date: 14 April 1977
(Ronald Holloway, 'Gruppenbild Mit Dame', *Variety*, 18 May 1977, p. 21)

Seobe (**Migrations**)
Production companies: Radio Television of Serbia, Economic Trade Milan Pejić, Belgrade
Executive producer: 'Tri' Belgrade (French and Yugoslav co-production)
Scriptwriters: Aleksandar Petrović, based on the novel of the same title by Miloš Crnjanski
Script collaboration: Jacques Doniol Valcroze
Director: Aleksandar Petrović
Cinematographers: Igor Luther, Witold Dabal
Music: [archival, chosen by Branka Petrović]
Set designers: Milenko Jeremić, Boris Moravec
Costume designers: Divna Jovanović, Jacques Fonteray
Editor: Vuksan Lukovac

Cast: Avtandil Makharadze, Isabelle Huppert, Richard Berry, Bernard Blier, Erland Josephson, Dragan Nikolić, Predrag Miki Manojlović, Rade Marković, Petar Božović, Ljubomir Ćipranić, Jelica Sretenović, Dobrica Jovanović, Jovan Janićijević, Ružica Sokić, Aljoša Vučković, Stojan Arandjelović, Ivica Pajer, Mladen Krstevski, Martin Oberning, Dragana Jugović, Branislav Jerinić
Length: 3,228 metres (111 minutes approx.)
Type: 35mm, colour, widescreen
Date: 20 March 1994
(Petar Volk, *Let nad močvarom: Aleksandar Petrović svojim životom, delom i filmovima* [Belgrade: Institut za film; Novi Sad: Prometej, 1999], p. 358)

Bibliography

Books by Aleksandar Petrović

– published in Serbia and Yugoslavia

Petrović, Aleksandar, *Novi film 1950–1965* (Beograd: Institut za Film, 1971).

———, *Novi film, crni film 1965--1970* (Beograd: Naučna Knjiga, 1988).

———, *Skupljači perja* (Beograd: Jugoslovenska Kinoteka; Novi Sad: Prometej, 1993).

———, *Sve moje ljubavi/Slepi periskopi* (Novi Sad: Prometej, Tajanstvena Tačka, 1995).

———, *Benja Kralj* (Beograd: Jugoslovenska Kinoteka; Novi Sad: Prometej, 1998).

———, *Pseće srce, Majstor i Margarita, dramatizacije; Purpurno ostrvo, adaptacija; Po delima Mihajla Afanasijeviča Bulgakova* (Beograd: Paideia, 2007).

———, *1973. Godina vampira: Emanuela II, Baron vampir, Džon F. Kenedi* [with preface by Branka Petrović] (Beograd: Autorska izdanja, Foto Futura, 2010).

———, *Soko* (Zrenjanin: Agora, 2011).

Interviews with, and articles by, Aleksandar Petrović

– published in Serbia and Yugoslavia

Adamović, D., "Borba za novi filmski izraz i za jeftin film", *NIN*, 11 November 1962, p. 12.

———, "Film, jedinstvena poetska celina", *Politika*, 21 May 1967, p. 17.

D. BT., "Reditelj Aleksandar Petrović: 'Seobe' čekaju uslove", *Večernje novosti*, 19 October 1989, (in the clipping file on Aleksandar Petrović, Belgrade: Jugoslovenska Kinoteka Library ["the clipping file", hereafter]).

———, "Slučaj komedijant", *Večernje novosti*, 20 April 1994, (the clipping file).

Dautović, S., "Vatra i ništa", *NIN*, 18 June 1993, pp. 40–42.

Dj. M., "Izgleda da sam isključen…", *Večernji list*, 29 August 1972, p. 11.

Gajer, D., "Nešto se čudno dešava", *Politika Ekspres*, 17 March 1969, p. 10.

———, "Petrović optužuje direktora Lebrea", *Politika Ekspres*, 18 March 1969, p. 10.

———, "Izbegnut povratak na staro", *Politika Ekspres*, 20 April 1971, p. 10.

Jovanović, L., "Verovatno opasan tip", *Reporter*, 2 September 1982, pp. 53–55.

Jovović, J. and Vukotić, V., "Kako frajla otvara kupleraj", *Politika Ekspres*, 3 March 1993, p. 11.

Konstantinović, Sl., "Priznanje se moglo očekivati", *Politika Ekspres* [Sunday review], 21 May 1967, p. 14.

Kosanović, J., "Seoba ima – smrti nema", *Oslobodjenje*, 3 July 1988, p. 12.

Kostić, A., "'Umetnička dela nisu paklene mašine'", *Beogradska nedelja*, 1 May 1966, p. 30.

Kostić, A., "Aleksandar Petrović: Politikantsko prodavanje pravoverja (1)", *Film novosti*, 27 December 1967, pp. 2–3.

———, "Strah od uspeha, Aleksandar Petrović: Politikantsko prodavanje pravoverja (2)", *Film novosti*, 3 January 1968, p. 4.

Kuzmanovski, R., "Ne veruvam vo filmski adaptacii", *Nova Makedonija*, 4 August 1972, (the clipping file).

Lakićević, O., "Poezija je instrument ljudske spoznaje" *Telegram*, 9 June 1967, pp. 6–7.

Lazić, R., "Režija – jedinstvena umetnost, razgovor s Aleksandrom Petrovićem", *Sineast*, 1986, pp. 160–65.

Lazić, Ž., "Zašto ne snima u našoj zemlji", *Duga*, 23 July 1977, pp. 20–21.

Ležaja, M., "(Ne)povjerenje inkvizitoru srpskog filma", *Vjesnik*, 6 May 1989, (the clipping file).

Marić, M., "Vreme relaksacije", *Duga*, 6 January 1979, pp. 19–21.

Martini, L., "Aleksandar Petrović: Snimam što želim", *Novi List*, 29 May 1969, p. 8.

Milojević, M., "Intervju – Saša Petrović, *Pogledi*, 6 December 1990, pp. 31–33.

Paripović, J., "Aleksandar Petrović: Sakupljač za Seobe", *Studio*, 18 September 1987, pp. 10–12.

Petrović, A., "'Plastični Isus' je politička pornografija", *Politika Ekspres*, 22 January 1973, p. 12.

———, "Ne volim festivale", *Duga*, 4 February 1978, p. 34.

———, "Zmijsko jaje sa dva reptila", *Duga*, 4 March 1978, pp. 34–35.

———, "Nisam bio 'mentor'", *Večernje novosti*, 11 January 1990, (the clipping file).

———, "Četrnaestom kongresu SKJ", March 1990, (the clipping file).

Petrović, M., "Umetnik mora da voli ono što otkriva", *Književne Novine*, 28 May 1966, p. 12.

———, "Moj film je relan", *Književne novine*, 15 March 1969, p. 16.

Popović, R., "Ima seoba – smrti nema", *Politika*, 19 August 1978, p. 11.

Predić, Z., "Biće skoro propast filma!", *Radio revija*, 13 November 1970, pp. 22–23.

Savković, D., "Dan kada je letelo perje", *Auto svet*, October 1982, pp. 42–45.

Sekulić, Z., "Aleksandar Petrović: Autorski film nije sloboda za diletante", *Student*, 3 December 1971, p. 7.

Tirnanić, B., "Aleksandar Petrović, razgovor", *Sineast*, 1968, pp. 46–53.

Urošević, M., "Više je zbrke oko političkih nego oko estetskih motiva", *Vjesnik*, 6 August 1972, p. 6.

Vukov Čolić, D., "Pojedinci kriju nesposobnost lokalpatriotizmom", *Vjesnik*, 6 August 1967, p. 6.

– published internationally

Bontemps, J. and Yamada, K., "Entretien avec Aleksandar Petrovic: J'ai même rencontré des Tziganes heureux", *Cahiers du Cinéma*, June 1967, pp. 42–43.

Branko, P., "Démoni v nás a ve světě, v němž žijeme", *Film A Doba*, December 1969, pp. 660–62.

Braucourt, G., "Sur les plateaux – Petrovic: Des acteurs de tous pays", *Le Film Français*, 6 May 1977, pp 14–16.

Frodon, J.M., "Comment y croire encore?", *Le Monde*, 8 August 1991, p. 10.

Langlois, G., "Alexandar Petrovitch, réalisateur de la nouvelle vague Yougoslave, une interview de G.L.", *Art et Essai*, November 1965, pp. 17–19.

Marcel, J., "Les années de plomb – Entretien avec Alexandre Petrovic", *24 Images*, Summer 1991, pp. 56–57.

Montaigne, P., "'Migrations': les Serbes en quête de bonheur", *Le Figaro*, 29 April 1987, p. 40.

O. M., "Letní interview", *Film A Doba*, February 1966, pp. 66–78.

Petrović, A., "Situace jugoslávského moderního filmu", *Film A Doba*, February 1966, pp. 66–81.

Petrovic, S., "Ceux qui filment... Sacha Petrovic", *Cahiers du Cinéma*, March 1994, p. 112.

Pondělíček, I., "Aleksandar Petrovič dokončil svůj nový film", *Film A Doba*, January 1969, pp. 42–45.

Secondary sources

– published in Serbia and Yugoslavia

Bezdanov Gostimir, Svetlana, *Filmom do kritike & vice versa* (Beograd: Institut za film, 1993).

Blaževski, Vladimir (ed.), *Dušan Makavejev: 300 čuda* (Beograd: SKC, 1988).

Bulgakov, Mihail, *Dnevnik Majstora* (Beograd: Izdavačko preduzeće 'Rad', 2004).

Crnjanski, Miloš, *Dnevnik o Čarnojeviću* (Beograd: Nolit, 1978a).

———, *Roman o Londonu* (Beograd: Nolit, 1978b).

———, *Seobe*, 3 vols (Beograd: Nolit, 1978c).

Černjul, Vanja, *Subjektivni kadrovi: Razgovori s filmskim snimateljem Tomislavom Pinterom* (Zagreb: V.B.Z., 2004).

Čolić, Milutin, *Jugoslovenski ratni film*, 2 vols (Beograd: Institut za Film; Titovo Užice: Vesti, 1984).

———, *Filmski portreti: Od Manakija do Makavejeva* (Beograd: Prosveta, 2007).

DeCuir, Greg Jr., *Yugoslav Black Wave: Polemical Cinema from 1963–72 in the Socialist Federal Republic of Yugoslavia* [English and Serbian text in the same edition] (Beograd: Filmski centar Srbije, 2011).

Dragović-Soso, Jasna, *"Spasioci nacije": Intelektualna opozicija Srbije i oživljavanje nacionalizma* (Beograd: Fabrika knjiga, 2004).

Drašković, Boro, *Roman reditelja: Razgovori sa Aleksandrom Petrovićem* (unpublished, 1987).

———, *Film o filmu* (Novi Sad: Prometej, 2010).

Džadžić, Petar, *Povlašćeni prostori Miloša Crnjanskog* (Beograd: Zavod za udžbenike i nastavna sredstva, 1995).

Fehmiu, Bekim, *Blistavo i strašno* (Beograd: B92, 2002).

Ilić, Momčilo (ed.), *Filmografija jugoslovenskog filma 1945–1965* (Beograd: Institut za Film, 1970).

——— (ed.), *Filmografija jugoslovenskog filma 1966–1970* (Beograd: Institut za Film, 1974).

——— (ed.), *Filmografija jugoslovenskog filma 1971–1975* (Beograd: Institut za Film, 1980).

Isaković, Antonije, *Paprat i vatra* (Beograd: Nolit, 1967).

Jović, Dejan, *Jugoslavija – Država koja je odumrla: Uspon, kriza i pad Četvrte Jugoslavije* (Beograd: Samizdat B92; Zagreb: Prometej, 2003).

Kalafatović, Bogdan, *Znaci sa ekrana* (Beograd: Institut za film, 1985).

Katarina, Olivera, *Aristokratsko stopalo* (Beograd: Prosveta, Drugo dopunjeno izdanje, 2006).

Kosanović, Dejan, *20 Godina jugoslovenskog filma, 1945–1965* (Beograd: Savez Filmskih Radnika Jugoslavije, 1965).

———, *Uvod u proučavanje istorije jugoslovenskog filma* (Beograd: Univerzitet Umetnosti, 1976).

——— (ed.), *Filma vek 1895–1995* (Beograd: Jugoslovenska Kinoteka, SANU, 1995).

Lazić, Radoslav, *Traktat o filmskoj režiji: U traganju za estetikom režije od Aleksandra Petrovića do Emira Kusturice* (Beograd: Institut za Film, 1989).

Mihajlov, Mihajlo, "Disidentstvo – stvarnost i legende", *Republika*, 181 (1 February 1998), http://www.yurope.com/zines/republika/arhiva/98/181/181_19.HTM.

Milošević, Nikola, *Roman Miloša Crnjanskog* (Beograd: Srpska književna zadruga, 1970).

Miltojević, Branislav, *Rani Radovi Želimira Žilnika* (Niš: Sirius, 1992).

Munitić, Ranko, *Kino klub Beograd: Trojanski konj jugoslovenskog modernog filma* (Beograd: Centar Film; Kragujevac: Prizma, 2003).

———, *Adio, Jugo-film!* (Beograd: Centar film, Srpski kulturni klub; Kragujevac: Prizma, 2005).

———, *Filmski prijatelji: Autobiografski putopis* (Beograd: Jugoslovenska Kinoteka; Novi Sad: Prometej, 2007).

Nešković-Simić, Snežana (ed.), *Prizor*, 2 [articles on Aleksandar Petrović edited by Radoslav Lazić], (Loznica: Centar za kulturu 'Vuk Karadžić', 2003).

——— (ed.), *Prizor*, 3 [articles on Aleksandar Petrović edited by Radoslav Lazić], (Loznica: Centar za kulturu 'Vuk Karadžić', 2004).

——— (ed.), *Prizor*, 4 [articles on Aleksandar Petrović edited by Radoslav Lazić], (Loznica: Centar za kulturu 'Vuk Karadžić', 2005).

——— (ed.), *Prizor*, 5 [articles on Aleksandar Petrović edited by Radoslav Lazić], (Loznica: Centar za kulturu 'Vuk Karadžić', 2006).

——— (ed.), *Prizor*, 6 [articles on Aleksandar Petrović edited by Radoslav Lazić], (Loznica: Centar za kulturu 'Vuk Karadžić', 2007).

——— (ed.), *Prizor*, 7 [articles on Aleksandar Petrović edited by Radoslav Lazić], (Loznica: Centar za kulturu 'Vuk Karadžić', 2008).

——— (ed.), *Prizor*, 8 [articles on Aleksandar Petrović edited by Radoslav Lazić], (Loznica: Centar za kulturu 'Vuk Karadžić', 2009).

——— (ed.), *Prizor*, 9 [articles on Aleksandar Petrović edited by Radoslav Lazić], (Loznica: Centar za kulturu 'Vuk Karadžić', 2010).

——— (ed.), *Prizor*, 10 [articles on Aleksandar Petrović edited by Radoslav Lazić], (Loznica: Centar za kulturu 'Vuk Karadžić', 2011).

——— ed., *Prizor*, annual magazine no. 11 [articles on Aleksandar Petrović edited by Radoslav Lazić], (Loznica: Centar za kulturu 'Vuk Karadžić', 2012).

Nikodijević, Milan, *Zabranjeni bez zabrane: Zona sumraka jugoslovenskog filma* (Beograd: Jugoslovenska Kinoteka, 1995).

Novaković, Slobodan, *Vreme otvaranja: Ogledi i zapisi o "Novom Filmu"* (Novi Sad: Kulturni centar, 1970).

Obradović, Branislav (ed.), *Filmografija jugoslovenskog igranog filma 1945–1980* (Beograd: Institut za Film, Časopis Filmograf, 1981).

Pavlović, Živojin, *Zadah tela* (Beograd: Prosveta, 1982).

——, *Belina sutra* (Beograd: Prosveta, 1983).

——, *Ispljuvak pun krvi* (Beograd: Grafički Atelje Dereta, 1990).

——, *Djavolji film: Ogledi i razgovori*, 2nd edn (Beograd: Jugoslovenska Kinoteka; Novi Sad: Prometej, 1996).

——, *Davne godine (1954–1963)* (Beograd: Institut za Film; Novi Sad: Prometej, 1997).

——, *Planeta filma* (Beograd: Zepter Book World, 2002).

Peterlić, Ante (ed.), *Filmska enciklopedija 1 (A–K)* (Zagreb: Jugoslavenski Leksikografski Zavod 'Miroslav Krleža', 1986).

—— (ed.), *Filmska enciklopedija 2 (L–Ž)* (Zagreb: Jugoslavenski Leksikografski Zavod 'Miroslav Krleža', 1990).

Popović, Radovan, *Život Miloša Crnjanskog* (Beograd: Prosveta, 1980).

Radović, Borislav, Munitić, Ranko and Pavlović, Živojin, *Živojin Pavlović* (Beograd: Centar Film, RTS; Kragujevac: Prizma, 1997 [supported by the 38th International Thessaloniki Film Festival]).

Ranković, Milan, *Društvena kritika u savremenom jugoslovenskom igranom filmu* (Beograd: Institut za film, 1970).

Redjep, Draško, *Rapsodija ništavila: Ogledi o Aleksandru Petroviću* (Novi Sad: Prometej, 2001).

Slapšak, Svetlana, *Ženske ikone XX veka* (Beograd: Biblioteka XX vek, 2001).

Stojanović, Dušan, *Film kao prevazilaženje jezika* (Beograd: Institut za Film, Univerzitet Umetnosti, 1984).

——, *Velika avantura filma* (Beograd: Institut za Film; Novi Sad: Prometej, 1997).

Stojanović, Lazar, 'Ko behu disidenti', *Republika*, 182 (16 February 1998), http://www.yurope.com/zines/republika/arhiva/98/182/182_11.HTM.

Tirnanić, Bogdan, *Crni talas* (Beograd: Filmski centar Srbije, 2008).

Volk, Petar, *Svedočenje: Hronika jugoslovenskog filma 1896–1945, I deo* (Beograd: Slobodan Mašić, Petar Volk, 1973).

——, *Svedočenje: Hronika Jugoslovenskog Filma 1945–1970, II deo* (Beograd: Slobodan Mašić, Petar Volk, 1975).

——, *Savremeni jugoslovenski film* (Beograd: Univerzitet Umetnosti, Institut za Film, 1983).

——, *Istorija jugoslovenskog filma* (Beograd: Institut za Film, Partizanska knjiga, 1986).

——, *Let nad močvarom: Aleksandar Petrović svojim životom, delom i filmovima.* (Beograd: Institut za film; Novi Sad: Prometej, 1999).

Vučković, Miroljub (ed.), *Kad budem mrtav i beo, film Živojina Pavlovića* (Beograd: Institut za Film, 1997).

– published internationally

a) on cinema

Allinson, Mark, *A Spanish Labyrinth: The Films of Pedro Almodovar* (London, New York: I.B. Tauris, 2000).

Andrew, Dudley, *Concepts in Film Theory* (Oxford, New York: Oxford University Press, 1984).

Bazin, André, *What is Cinema? Vol.1*, ed. by Hugh Gray (Berkeley, Los Angeles: University of California Press, 1967).

Bordwell, David, *Narration in the Fiction Film* (London: Methuen, 1985).

Bordwell, David and Thompson, Kristin, *Film Art: An Introduction* (New York: McGraw Hill, 1993).

———, *Film History: An Introduction* (New York: McGraw Hill, 2003).

Burch, Noël, *Life to those Shadows* (Berkley, Los Angeles: University of California Press, 1990).

Buscombe, Edward, "Ideas of Authorship", *Screen*, 14–3 (Autumn 1973), pp. 75–85.

Caughie, John (ed.), *Theories of Authorship: A Reader* (London, New York: Routledge, 1981).

Carroll, Noel, *Mystifying Movies* (New York: Columbia University Press, 1988).

Cook, David A., *A History of Narrative Film* (New York: Norton & Company, 1990).

Daković, Nevena, *Cinematic Balkans/Balkan Genre* (NEXUS Research Project, 2002–03).

———, "Shadows of the Ancestors", *Framework*, 44–2 (Fall 2003), pp. 103–07.

Durgnat, Raymond, *WR – Mysteries of the Organism* (London: BFI, 1999).

Elsaesser, Thomas, "Vincent Minnelli", in *Genre: The Musical: A Reader*, ed. by Rick Altman (London: Routledge & Kegan Paul, 1981).

Evans, Peter William and Santaolalla, Isabel (eds), *Luis Buñuel: New Readings* (London: British Film Institute, 2004).

Filipović, Stevan and Milivojević, Marko, *Yugoslav Cinema Between Two Wars, 1945–1995* (Bradford: Bradford Studies on South Eastern Europe [3], 1997).

Gerstner, David A. and Staiger, Janet (eds), *Authorship and Film* (London, New York: Routledge, 2003).

Goulding, Daniel J. (ed.), *Liberated Cinema: The Yugoslav Experience* (Bloomington: Indiana University Press, 1985).

———, (ed.), *Post New Wave Cinema in the Soviet Union and Eastern Europe* (Bloomington: Indiana University Press, 1989).

———, (ed.), *Five Filmmakers: Tarkovsky, Forman, Polanski, Szabó, Makavejev* (Bloomington: Indiana University Press, 1994).

———, *Occupation in 26 Pictures* (Trowbridge: Flicks Books, 1998).

———, *Liberated Cinema: The Yugoslav Experience, 1945–2001*, 2nd edn (Bloomington: Indiana University Press, 2002).

Gocić, Goran, *The Cinema of Emir Kusturica: Notes from the Underground* (London: Wallflower Press, 2001).

Gregory, Ilja, "Fragments of Nationhood: 'Novi Film' as seen from the 1990s: Revisioning Yugoslav Social and Political Reality (1947–1972)" (unpublished master's thesis, London: British Film Institute, Birkbeck College, 1995/96).

Hames, Peter (ed.), *The Cinema of Central Europe* (London, New York: Wallflower Press, 2004).

Hibbin, Nina, *Eastern Europe: An Illustrated Guide*, Screen Series (London: A. Zwemmer Ltd; New York: A. S. Barnes & Co., 1969).

Horton, Andrew, "The Rise and Fall of the Yugoslav Partisan Film: Cinematic Perceptions of a National Identity", *Film Criticism*, 12–2 (Winter 1987–88), pp. 18–27.

———, (ed.), *Comedy, Cinema, Theory* (Berkeley: University of California Press, 1991).

———, *The Films of Theo Angelopoulos: A Cinema of Contemplation* (New Jersey: Princeton University Press, 1997).

Imre, Anikó (ed.), *East European Cinemas* (London, New York: Routledge, 2005).

Iordanova, Dina, *Cinema of Flames: Balkan Film, Culture and the Media* (London: BFI, 2001).

———, *Emir Kusturica* (London: BFI, 2002).

———, (ed.), *The Cinema of The Balkans* (London, New York: Wallflower Press, 2006).

Johnson, Vida and Petrie, Graham, *The Films of Andrei Tarkovsky: A Visual Fugue* (Bloomington: Indiana University Press, 1994).

Liehm, Mira and Liehm, Antonín J., *The Most Important Art: Soviet and Eastern European Film after 1945* (Berkeley, Los Angeles: University of California Press, 1977).

MacCabe, Colin, *Godard: A Portrait of the Artist at Seventy* (London: Bloomsbury, 2003).

Mijić, Vladislav, "Witnesses and commentators: Romani Character in *Ko to tamo peva*", *Framework*, 44–2 (Fall 2003).

Morrey, Douglas, *Jean-Luc Godard* (Manchester, New York: Manchester University Press, 2005).

Nemes, Karoly, *Films of Commitment: Socialist Cinema in Eastern Europe* (Budapest: Corvina, 1985).

Nichols, Bill (ed.), *Movies and Methods*, vol. 1 (Berkley: University of California Press, 1976).

Nowell-Smith, Geoffrey, *Luchino Visconti* (London: Secker and Warburg, 1967).

———, "Six Authors in Pursuit of *The Searchers*", *Screen*, 17–1 (Spring 1976), pp. 26–33.

———, (ed.), *The Oxford History of World Cinema* (Oxford: University Press, 1996).

Papa, Jasmina, "The Prague Group: Film as Cultural Non-Nationalism in 1980s Yugoslavia" (unpublished master's thesis, Budapest: Central European University, 1999).

Partridge, James, "Dignity in diversity: Aleksandar Petrović's neglected classic *Skupljači perja*", *Central Europe Review*, 2 (27 November 2000), http://www.ce-review.org/00/41/kinoeye41_partridge.html.

Paul, David W. (ed.), *Politics, Art and Commitment in the Eastern European Cinema* (London, Basingstoke: The Macmillan Press, 1983).

Petrie, Graham and Dwyer, Ruth (ed.), *Before the Wall Came Down: Soviet and East European Filmmakers Working in the West* (Lanham, MD: University Press of America, 1990).

Powrie, Phil, *Jean-Jacques Beineix* (Manchester, New York: Manchester University Press, 2001).

Romney, Jonathan, *Atom Egoyan* (London: BFI, 2003).

Sadoul, Georges, *Dictionary of Films*, ed. by Peter Morris (Berkeley, Los Angeles: University of California Press, 1972).

Sargeant, Amy, *Vsevolod Pudovkin: Classic Films of the Soviet Avant-Garde* (London, New York: I.B. Tauris, 2000).

Schroeder, Paul A., *Tomas Gutierrez Alea: The Dialectics of a Filmmaker* (New York, London: Routledge, 2002).

Sklar, Robert and Musser, Charles, *Resisting Images: Essays on Cinema and History* (Philadelphia: Temple University Press, 1990).

Stoil, Michael J., *Balkan Cinema: Evolution after the Revolution* (Ann Arbor, MI: UMI Research Press, 1979).

Tarkovsky, Andrei, *Sculpting in Time* (Austin, TX: University of Texas Press, 1984).

Tasić, Zoran and Passek, Jean-Loup (eds), *Le Cinema Yougoslave* (Paris: Centre Georges Pompidou, 1986).

Taylor, Richard et al. (eds), *The BFI Companion to Eastern European and Russian Cinema* (London: British Film Institute, 2000).

Valtrović, Vanja, "BW – Mystery of the Suppression or Pessimism in an Optimistic Society" (unpublished master's thesis, University of Amsterdam, 1999).

Vitali, Valentina and Willemen, Paul (eds), *Theorising National Cinema* (London: BFI, 2006).

Whyte, Alistair, *New Cinema in Eastern Europe* (London: Studio Vista Limited, 1971).

Willemen, Paul, *Looks and Frictions: Essays in Cultural Studies and Film Theory* (Bloomington: Indiana University Press; London: BFI, 1994).

Wollen, Peter, *Signs and Meaning in the Cinema* (Bloomington: Indiana University Press, 1972).

b) history and general

Anderson, Benedict, *Imagined Communities: Reflections on the Origin and Spread of Nationalism* (London, New York: Verso, 1991).

Appleby, Joyce et al. (eds), *Knowledge and Postmodernism in Historical Perspective* (London, New York: Routledge, 1996).

Babel, Isaac, *Benia Krik: A Film-Novel* (London: Collet's, 1935).

Badiou, Alan, *Ethics: An Essay on the Understanding of Evil* (London, New York: Verso 2001).

Bakić-Hayden, Milica, "Nesting Orientalisms: The Case of Former Yugoslavia", *Slavic Review*, 54–4 (1995), pp. 917–32.

Barthes, Roland, *Image-Music-Text* (London: Fontana, 1977).

Baudrillard, Jean, *Simulacra and Simulation*, trans. by Sheila Faria Glaser (Ann Arbor, MI: University of Michigan Press, 1994).

Beckett, Samuel, *Company, Ill Seen Ill Said, Worstward Ho, Stirring Still*, ed. by Dirk van Hulle (London: Faber & Faber, 2009).

Böll, Heinrich, *Group Portrait with Lady* (London: Secker & Warburg, 1973).

Bulgakov, Mikhail, *The Master and Margarita*, trans. by Diana Burgin and Katherine Tiernan O'Connor (London: Picador, 1997).

Chatman, Seymour, *Story and Discourse: Narrative Structure in Fiction and Film* (Ithaca, New York: Cornell University Press, 1978).

Čolović, Ivan, *The Politics of Symbol in Serbia*, trans. by Celia Hawkesworth (London: C. Hurst & Co, 2002).

Djilas, Milovan, *New Class* (New York: Praeger, 1957).

Dostoyevsky, Fyodor Mikhailovich, *The Devils*, trans. by David Magarshack (Harmondsworth: Penguin, 1953).

Dragović-Soso, Jasna, *'Saviours of the Nation': Serbia's Intellectual Opposition and the Revival of Nationalism* (London: Hurst & Company, 2002).

Erlich, Victor, *Russian Formalism: History Doctrine* (The Hague: Mouton, 1965).

Feagin, Susan and Maynard, Patrick (eds), *Aesthetics* (Oxford: Oxford University Press, 1997).

Fernie, Eric (ed.), *Art History and its Methods: A Critical Anthology* (London, New York: Phaidon Press, 1995).

Foucault, Michel, *Power: Essential Works of Foucault 1954–1984 Vol. 3*, ed. James D. Faubion (London: Penguin, 2002).

Glenny, Misha, *The Rebirth of History: Eastern Europe in the Age of Democracy* (London: Penguin, 1990).

———, *The Balkans 1804–1999: Nationalism, War and the Great Powers* (London: Granta Books, 1999).

Harvey, David, *The Condition of Postmodernity: An Enquiry into the Origins of Cultural Change* (Oxford: Basil Blackwell Ltd, 1989).

Joyce, James, *A Portrait of the Artist as a Young Man* (London: Penguin, 2000).

Judah, Tim, *The Serbs: History, Myth and the Destruction of Yugoslavia* (New Haven, CT, London: Yale University Press, 1997).

Lampe, John R., *Yugoslavia as History: Twice There was a Country* (Cambridge: Cambridge University Press, 1996).

Levinson, Jerrold (ed.), *Aesthetics and Ethics: Essays at the Intersection* (Cambridge: Cambridge University Press, 1998).

Lummis, Trevor, *Listening to History: The Authenticity of Oral Evidence* (Totowa, NJ: Barnes & Noble Books, 1988).

Nichols, Bill, *Blurred Boundaries: Questions of Meaning in Contemporary Culture* (Berkeley, Los Angeles: University of California Press, 1995).

Norris, David A., *The Novels of Miloš Crnjanski: An Approach through Time* (Nottingham: Astra Press, 1990).

———, *In the Wake of the Balkan Myth: Questions of Identity and Modernity* (New York: St. Martin's Press, 1999).

Poster, Mark (ed.), *Jean Baudrillard: Selected Writings (Second Edition)* (Cambridge: Polity Press; Oxford: Blackwell Publishers Ltd, 2001).

Proffer, Ellendea, *Bulgakov: Life and Work* (Ann Arbor, MI: Ardis, 1984).

Reid, James Henderson, *Heinrich Böll: Withdrawal and Re-Emergence* (London: Oswald Wolff, 1973).

Said, Edward W., *Orientalism* (New York: Vintage Books, 1978).

Rusinow, Dennison, *The Yugoslav Experiment, 1948–1974* (London: Hurst, 1977).

Todorova, Maria, *Imagining the Balkans* (Oxford, New York: Oxford University Press, 1997).

———, (ed.), *Balkan Identities: Nation and Memory* (London: C. Hurst & Co., 2004).

Wachtel, Andrew B., *Making a Nation, Breaking a Nation: Literature and Cultural Politics in Yugoslavia* (Stanford, CA: Stanford University Press, 1998).

Wallis, Brian (ed.), *Art After Modernism: Rethinking Representation* (New York: The New Museum of Modern Art, 1984).

White, Hayden, *The Content of The Form: Narrative Discourse and Historical Representation* (Baltimore: Johns Hopkins University Press, 1987).

———, *Tropics of Discourse: Essays on Cultural Criticism* (Baltimore: Johns Hopkins University Press, 1986).

Press articles, news, reviews, obituaries, and related interviews

– published in Serbia and Yugoslavia

Adamović, D., "Festivalsko pismo iz Kana, Ko od četvorice?", *NIN*, 17 May 1957, p. 18.

———, "Prvi padež film", *NIN*, 28 March 1965, p. 10.

———, "Hoće li svet propasti?", *NIN*, 16 March 1969, p. 14.

Aleksić, M., 'Zaštitnik glumaca', *Večernje novosti*, 22 August 1994, (the clipping file).

Anon, "Nagrade za ostvarenja našeg kulturnog stvaralaštva", *Politika*, 3 July 1959, p. 8.

———, "Nagradu za režiju dobio Jože Babič za film tri četvrtine sunca", *Borba*, 7 August 1959a, pp. 1 & 6.

———, "Prva nagrada za režiju kratkometražnog filma pripala je Aleksandru Petroviću", *Politika*, 7 August 1959b, p. 8.

———, "(Završen festival dokumentarnog i kratkog filma) Bulajić, Škanata i Bourek – prvi", *Politika*, 26 March 1965, p. 11.

———, "Čije je perje letelo", *Ekonomska Politika*, 13 May 1967, p. 588.

———, "Komercijalni uspeh 'Skupljača perja'", *Politika*, 26 May 1967, p. 11.

———, "Dodeljene Sedmojulske nagrade", *Borba*, 4 July 1967, pp. 1 & 7.

———, "Paperjari", *Ekonomska Politika*, 22 July 1967, p. 901.

———, "Atak na 'Sakupljače perja' sud odbio", *Večernji list*, 13 December 1967, p. 19.

———, "Aleksandar Petrović", *Filmske Sveske*, 6, 1968, pp. 378–406.

———, "Francuzi odlikovali Petrovića", *Politika Ekspres*, 3 March 1969, p. 9.

———, "Delovanje komunista u sadašnjim političkim kretanjima", *Borba* [section *Borba reflektor*], 2 June 1969, pp. 17–24.

———, "Slobode ima na pretek", *Borba*, 5 August 1969, p. 8.

———, "Francuski ambasador u Beogradu predao Aleksandru Petroviću orden 'Vitez lepih umetnosti'", *Borba*, 9 October 1969, p. 10.

———, "Petrović Vitez lepih umetnosti", *Mladina*, 3 November 1969, p. 6.

———, "Vitez lepih umetnosti", *Radio revija*, 8 October 1971, p. 12.

———, "(Nakon nagrade u Veneciji) Saši Petroviću pozivi za nove festivale", *Novi list*, 6 September 1972, p. 10.

———, "Falsifikati i uvrede", *Oslobodjenje*, 20 January 1973, p. 4.

———, "Negativna ocena još u maju", *Nedeljne novosti*, 21 January 1973, (the clipping file).

———, "Spriječen put na ekran", *Večernje novine*, 22 January 1973, p. 4.

———, "Potvrdjena kazna Aleksandru Petroviću o isključenju iz radne organizacije", *Politika*, 11 April 1973a, p. 6.

———, "Zbor radnih ljudi usvojio predlog disciplinske komisije", *Borba*, 11 April 1973b, p. 5.

———, "Živojin Pavlović nepodoban kao professor Akademije", *Politika*, 24 June 1973, p. 8.

———, "Mojster in Margareta in Kmalu bo konec sveta", *Ekran*, 1983, pp. 90–95.

———, "Aleksandar Petrović vraća nagrade za umetnički rad", *Politika*, 30 May 1990, p. 11.

———, "Ima seoba, smrti nema", *Politika Ekspres*, 21 August 1994, (the clipping file).

———, "Na kraju – roman", *Večernje novosti*, 22 August 1994a, (the clipping file).

———, "Oproštaj od Petrovića", *Večernje novosti*, 22 August 1994b, (the clipping file).

———, "Veliki rapsod ništavila", Borba, 22 August 1994c, p. 17.

———, "Lider novog talasa", *Borba*, 24 August 1994, (the clipping file).

———, "Danas sahrana", *Borba*, 25 August 1994a, (the clipping file).

———, "Danas sahrana Aleksandra Petrovića", *Politika*, 25 August 1994b, (the clipping file).

———, "'Izabel' – Sašin epilog", *Borba*, 25 August 1994c, (the clipping file).

Belan, B., "O crnom filmu u – mraku", *Borba*, 26 October 1969, p. 13.

Blečić, P., "Za filmom o Karadjordju Kinoteka tragala više od šest decenija", *Blic Online*, 31 July 2011, http://www.blic.rs/Vesti/Reportaza/268857/Za-filmom-o-Karadjordju-Kinoteka-tragala-vise-od-sest-decenija.

Bogdanović, Ž., "Ni vizija, ni iluzija", *NIN*, 22 April 1994, pp 36–37.

———, "Usud na velikana", *Borba*, 22 August 1994, p. 17.

Boglić, M., "Film 'Tri' i njegov autor", *Vjesnik*, 19 August 1977, (the clipping file).

Bulić, D., "Velimir Bata Živojinović", *Maxim* [Serbia and Montenegro edition], January 2006, pp. 122–23.

Cvetićanin, R., "Rasplet na akademiji", *NIN*, 15 April 1973, p. 44.

Čolić, M., "Brazilci – iznenadjenje", *Politika*, 21 May 1962, p. 9.

———, "Biće skoro propast sveta", *Politika*, 10 March 1969, p. 12.

———, "(Filmovi koje gledamo) 'Jedini izlaz'", *Politika*, 16 April 1959, p. 10.

———, "(Šesti filmski festival u Puli) U Areni i dalje razočaranja", *Politika*, 29 July 1959, p. 8.

———, "(Šesti festival jugoslovenskog filma) Arena aplaudira Čapu!", *Politika*, 30 July 1959, p. 9.

D. BT., "'Perje' u Francuskoj", *Večernje novosti*, 6 May 1993, (the clipping file).

D. G., "Predlog da se Petrović isključi sa akademije", *Politika Ekspres*, 10 April 1973, p. 2.

D. R., "Filmsko delo", *Dnevnik*, 25 December 1972, p. 8.

D. S., "Najbolji filmovi Evrope", *Večernje novosti*, 23 April 1991, (the clipping file).

Dautović, S., "I seobe, i smrti", *NIN*, 22 April 1994, p. 36.

Drašković, B., "Začetnik novog", *Večernje novosti*, 22 August 1994, (the clipping file).

———, "Ja sam ekran", *Politika* [section *Kultura, umetnost, nauka*], 15 August 2009, p. 5.

Drljača, D., "Zapažen uspeh jugoslovenskih filmova", *Politika*, 5 September 1966, p. 10.

Djordjević, A., "Mnogo poštovan", *Večernje novosti*, 22 August 1994, (the clipping file).

Franić, S., "Bila je skoro propast sveta", *Duga*, 1 October 1988, pp. 54–57.

Franjić, Z., "Ukloniti trabante [an interview with Ante Babaja]", *Večernji list*, 10 August 1967, p. 8.

Gajer, D., "Gorko i sočno", *Politika Ekspres*, 10 March 1969, p. 9.

———, "Imamo snažne ličnosti", *Politika Ekspres*, 5 August 1969, p. 10.

———, "(Za svoj novi projekt 'Majstor i Margareta') Petrović dovodi Romi Šnajder", *Politika Ekspres*, 3 February 1970, p. 10.

Gajić V. P., "Film koji se pamti", *Borba*, 30 April 1994, p. 10.

Gligorijević, M., "Proizvodnja neprijatelja", *NIN*, 26 August 1994, pp. 52–54.

Goluža, M., "Kako je pukao jedan stari film", *Vjesnik u srijedu*, 31 March 1971, pp. 30–31.

Guberinić, S., "Maestro i Margareta Aleksandra Petrovića", *Sineast*, 19, 1972–73, pp. 107–11.

Isaković, A., "Za istoriju", *Borba*, 22 August 1994, p. 17.

J.S., "Dug velikom majstoru", *Politika*, 25 August 1994, (the clipping file).

Jovanović, M., "'Finski nož' za Mihaila Bulgakova", *Književne novine*, 16 November 1972, p. 5.

Jovičić, V., "'Crni talas' u našem filmu", *Borba* [section *Borba reflektor*], 3 August 1969, pp. 21–28.

Jovović, J., "Gorko sećanje na pogrom", *Politika Ekspres*, 9 November 1991, p. 17.

K. K., "Film Aleksandra Petrovića pozvan u Kan", *Politika*, 17 April 1969, p. 10.

K. R., "Komemoracije Saši Petroviću", *Borba*, 23 August 1994, (the clipping file).

K. R., "Saša Petrović u Evropskoj akademiji za film i TV", *Borba*, 9 March 1993, (the clipping file).

Kodemo, M., "Vitez našeg filma", *Večernje novosti*, 21 August 1994, (the clipping file).

Konstantinović, S., "(1) Istina o Širli Meklejn [interview with actor Bekim Fehmiu]", *Politika Ekspres*, 13 May 1967, p. 13.

———, "(2) Prvi festivalski dan… [interview with actor Bekim Fehmiu]", *Politika Ekspres* [Sunday review section], 14 May 1967, p. 20.

———, "(3) Aplauz i ponuda od 160 000 dolara [interview with actor Bekim Fehmiu]", *Politika Ekspres*, 15 May 1967, p. 8.

———, "(4) Susret sa Širli Meklejn… [interview with actor Bekim Fehmiu]", *Politika Ekspres*, 16 May 1967, p. 13.

———, "(5) Nezaboravna noć sa Širli… [interview with actor Bekim Fehmiu]", *Politika Ekspres*, 17 May 1967, p. 13.

———, "(6) Širli ima kartu više [interview with actor Bekim Fehmiu]", *Politika Ekspres*, 18 May 1967, p. 13.

———, "(7) 'Beli Bora' i kraljica šarma… [interview with actor Bekim Fehmiu]", *Politika Ekspres*, 19 May 1967, p. 8.

Kostić, S., "Tragovi bolje prošlosti", *Vreme*, 29 December 2005, pp. 56–61.

Krajčinović, D., "Nije vreme za eksperimente", *Politika Ekspres*, 19 May 1970, p. 10.

Krmpotić, N., "'Propast svijeta' kongresu iza ugla", *Vjesnik u srijedu*, 19 March 1969, p. 3.

Lakić, D., "Odlučiće pravnici", *Politika*, 4 April 1991, p. 21.

Lazarević, V., "Filmski poeta", *Politika Ekspres*, 22 August 1994, (the clipping file).

M. M., "'Let nad močvarom' odličan domaći dokumentarni film", *Politika*, 28 January 1957, p. 10.

Makavejev, D., "Srećna šetnja", *Politika*, 22 March 1959, p. 18.

Marković, G., "Zašto nam treba Avala film", *Vreme*, 29 December 2005, pp. 58–59.

Milosavljević, A., "Pobednici u izgubljenom ratu [interview with Lazar Stojanović]", *Dnevnik*, 4 March 1990, pp. 18–19.

Milošević, M., "Zanosi i zablude borbe za novi film", *Borba*, 20 November 1971, p. 9.

Milošević, N., "Za sledeći vek", *Borba*, 22 August 1994, p. 17.

———, "Slučaj komedijant", *NIN*, 26 August 1994, p. 42.

Ostojić, S., "Krug se proširio", *Politika*, 18 February 1958, p. 8.

———, "(Drugi 'Gran Premio Bergamo') Uspeh bez pogovora", *Politika*, 14 September 1959, p. 7.

———, "Zagreb: Sezona u zenitu", *Politika*, 9 December 1967, p. 11.

Pašić, F., "Početak dijaloga o filmu", *Borba*, 15 November 1969, p. 10.

———, "O crnom filmu, etiketiranju, kritici", *Borba*, 21 November 1969a, p. 1.

———, "Šta je to 'crni film'?", *Borba*, 21 November 1969b, p. 5.

Petkovska, V., "Bunkerisana Pravda", *Borba*, 18 January 1991, (the clipping file).

Petrović, S. Dj., "Moja sećanja: Srbin i mala Austrijanka", *Politika*, 31 August 1996, (the clipping file).

Redjep, D., "Sveta reč sloboda", *Borba*, 22 August 1994, p. 17.

S. K., "Teret zle sudbine", *Borba*, 25 August 1994, p. 17.

Sakić, I., "Snaga simbola", *Odjek*, 15 January 1973, pp. 18–19.

Sretić, M., "Disciplinska komisija odlučila da A. Petrović bude isključen sa Akademije", *Politika*, 10 April 1973, p. 6.

Tadić, Lj., "Za sledeći vek", *Borba*, 22 August 1994, p. 17.

Tirnanić, B., "Tiranija zvuka – propast slike", *Odjek*, 1 May 1969, p. 22.

Tucaković, D., "'Seobe' kao sudbina", *Borba*, 22 August 1994, p. 17.

V. P., "'Propast sveta' ipak u Kanu", *Politika Ekspres*, 11 April 1969, p. 10.

V. P., "'Propast sveta' čeka zvanični stav", *Politika Ekspres*, 12 April 1969, p. 10.

V. P. G., "I na kraju – spektakl", *Borba*, 28 April 1994, p. 17.

Vitezica, V., "Ljubavne i svetske krize", *Večernje novosti*, 10 March 1969, p. 8.

Vlajčić, M., "Utemeljivač našeg modernog filma", *Politika*, 21 August 1994, (the clipping file).

Vučinić, S., "Večne nesanice Pontija Pilata", *Politika* [cultural supplement], 26 April 2008, p. 12.

Ž. J., "Film – esej", *Borba*, 25 August 1994, p. 17.

– published internationally

Adler, R., "Screen: Yugoslavia's 'I Even Met Happy Gypsies': Feather Traders' Lives Limned at Regency", *The New York Times*, 21 March 1968, p. 57.

Anderson, R. H., "Yugoslav Student's Film Stirs Demands Teacher Be Punished", *The New York Times*, 26 January 1973, p. 5.

Anon, "Three Pictures Lead Oscar Nominees", *The New York Times*, 21 February 1967, p. 55.

———, "J'ai même rencontré des Tziganes heureux", *Art et Essai*, 16 November 1967, pp. 3–6.

———, "Le conseil des dix", *Cahiers du Cinéma*, December 1967, p. 6.

———, "Berlin [News]", *Variety*, 7 April 1976, p. 44.

———, "Gruppenbild mit Dolchstoss-Legende", *Die Zeit*, 3 June 1977, p. 34.

———, "Obituaries", *Screen International*, 2–8 September 1994, p. 44.

Apel-Muller, P., "Ecartelé entre mémoire et création", *L'Humanite*, 22 August 1994, p. 15.

Baker, B., "Obituaries 1994", *Sight & Sound*, 5: 3, March 1995, pp. 28–30.

Baker, P., "Cannes", *Films & Filming*, July 1967, pp. 4–8.

Benayoun, R., "Le cinema resiste aux bacilles de Cannes", *Positif*, July 1967, p. 20.

Blumenberg, H. C., "'Hinrichtung eines Böll-Romans'", *Die Zeit*, 27 May 1977, p. 52.

———, "Die Angst des Kinos vor dem Kino", *Die Zeit*, 3 June 1977, p. 35.

Boisset, Y., "Lettre de Belgrade", *Cinéma 64*, May 1964, pp. 81–84.

Bontemps, J., "Commentaires – Skulpjaci Perja", *Cahiers du Cinéma*, June 1967, p. 44.

Brandlmeier, T., "Aleksandar Petrović 14.1.1929 – 20.8.1994", *EPD Film*, October 1994, p. 14.

Carcassonne, P., "Aleksandar Petrovic, Portrait de groupe avec dame", *Cinématographe*, June 1977, pp. 20–21.

Cervoni, A., "Porretta Terme", *Cahiers du Cinéma*, August 1966, pp. 10–11.

———, "Une illustration soignée: 'Le Maître et Marguerite' d'Alexandar Petrovic", *L'Humanite*, 27 October 1973, p. 12.

Ciment, M., "La Yougoslavie à Pula", *Positif*, November 1968, pp. 1–11.

Ciment, M. and Codelli, L., "Venise crucifiée ou quelques clous ne font pas un festival (la 33ᵉ mostra)", *Positif*, November–December 1972, pp. 79–94.

Crowther, B., "(Movie Also Opening at the Little Carnegie) 'Three' and 'Roundup'", *The New York Times*, 19 September 1966, p. 57.

Czarnecki, S., "Czy rzeczywiście przeglad?", *Ekran*, October 1961, pp. 8–9.

Elley, D., "The Master and Margarita", *Films & Filming*, April 1975, pp. 46–47.

FD., "Aleksandar Petrovic", *Film-dienst*, 30 August 1994, p. 39.

Fiala, M., "'Cross Country' jugoslávského filmu", *Film A Doba*, October 1969, pp. 531–41.

Fountain, C., "The Master and Margarita", *Rovi*, http://www.allrovi.com/movies/movie/the-master-and-margaret-v126415.

Frodon, J. M., "La mort d'Alexandre Petrovic, le dernier cinéaste yougoslave", *Le Monde*, 23 August 1994, p. 13.

G.A.H., "Skulpjaci perja (Happy Gipsies…!)", *Monthly Film Bulletin*, April 1968, pp. 55–56.

Gearing, N., "Maestro i Margarita (The Master and Margarita)", *Monthly Film Bulletin*, March 1975, p. 59.

Grcar, M., "Jeune Cinéma, Yougoslavie", *Cinéma 66*, July–August 1966, pp. 58–64.

Guez, G., "Post-scriptum Yougoslave", *Cinéma 64*, June 1964, pp. 27–29.

———, "Pula, 13ᵉ", *Cahiers du Cinéma*, November 1966, pp. 16–17.

Holloway, R., "Gruppenbild Mit Dame (Group Portrait with Lady)", *Variety*, 18 May 1977, p. 21.

J.-P.B., "Aleksandar Petrovic", *Le Film Français*, 2 September 1994, p. 32.

Karasek, H., "Im Rasierspiegel", *Der Spiegel*, 6 June 1977, p. 198.

Lane, J.F., "Cannes", *Films and Filming*, July 1962, pp. 17–18 & 46–47.

Laurent., "IVe Festival international de cinéma libre de Porretta Terme (24–29 June 1966)", *Cinema International*, 1966, p. 523.

Lefevre, R., "Venise", *Cinéma 72*, November 1972, pp. 22–26.

Martin, M., "Karlovy Vary, au moins un dialogue", *Cinéma 66*, November 1966, pp. 98–100.

———, "Venise", *Ecran*, November 1972, pp. 50–52.

———, "Pula", *Ecran*, December 1972, pp. 34–35.

Menck, C., "Stunde Null im Weitwinkel", *Frankfurter Allgemeine Zeitung*, 21 May 1980, p. 24.

Moskowitz, G., "Sreo Sam Cak i Srecne Cigane (I Even Met a Happy Gypsy)", *Variety*, 10 May 1967, p. 20.

———, "Tri (Three)", *Variety*, 20 July 1966, p. 20.

———, "Bice Skoro Propast Sveta (It Rains In My Village)", *Variety*, 14 May 1969, p. 34.

M. S., "Portrait de groupe avec dame", *Positif*, July–August 1977, pp. 123–24.

Pisarevski, D., "Pula – 72: Temi sovremennosti", *Sovietsky Ekran*, October 1972, pp.16–18.

Powell, M., "Trio", *Films & Filming*, January 1970, pp. 44 & 49.

Roud, R., "Festivals 67, Cannes", *Sight and Sound*, Summer 1967, pp.122 & 157.

Roulet, S., "Skulpajaci Perja (J'ai même rencontré des Tziganes heureux)", *Cahiers du Cinéma*, December 1967, p. 74.

Russell Taylor, J., "Cameo-Poly: Happy Gypsies. . . !", *The Times*, 15 February 1968, p. 6.

————, "Strange films from unlikely places", *The Times*, 28 November 1972, p. 10.

Seguin, L., "Le Festival de Cannes", *Positif*, July 1962, pp. 64–68.

Stein, E., "Karlovy Vary", *Sight and Sound*, Autumn 1966, pp. 171–72.

Stojadinovic, M-J., "Alexander Petrovic (1929–1994)", *Balkan Media*, 3, 1994, p. 11.

Suffert, G., "Qui libérera 'Migration'?", *Le Figaro*, 16 November 1989, p. 41.

Svoboda, J., "* * * [editorial]", *Film A Doba*, September 1966, pp. 452–53.

Zdražilová, M., "Gladiátor z arény zvané jugoslávská kinematografie", *Film A Doba*, January 1989, pp. 48–49.

Zelenko, N., "Paporotnik i ogony", *Iskusstvo Kino*, October 1966, pp. 88–89.

Documents

(All in the clipping file on Aleksandar Petrović, Belgrade: Jugoslovenska Kinoteka Library)

Receipt from a police station in Belgrade dated 11 January 1973 that Petrović's passport had been withdrawn.

Two statements by Sreten Jovanović, dated 16 and 17 January 1973, claiming that after Petrović saw *Plastic Jesus*, the film had still to be worked on, and that Petrović had pointed out how certain scenes were problematic.

Kralj, M., "Aleksandar Petrović" – unpublished, the full text of the speech delivered when Aleksandar Petrović received the AVNOJ Award, the highest state award of SFR Yugoslavia, 15 December 1987.

Petrović, A., "Četrnaestom kongresu SKJ", a copy of the original letter sent to the 14th Congress of the League of Communists of Yugoslavia (March 1990).

————, "'Fatamorgane' Aleksandra Petrovića – odgovor Lazaru Stojanoviću", a copy of the original letter sent to *Duga* magazine on 3 May 1990.

List of interviews

Bekim Fehmiu, 3 May 2006.

Radoslav Lazić, 12 September 2005.

Nikola Majdak, 30 April 2006.

Dušan Makavejev, 7 April 2004.

Branka Petrović, 11 September 2005.

Eva Ras, 28 April 2006.

Lazar Stojanović, 3 January 2006.

Želimir Žilnik, 11 April 2004.

Velimir Bata Živojinović, 8 January 2009.

Index